SOUTH-WESTERN SERIES IN
HUMAN RESOURCES MANAGEMENT

COMPENSATION, ORGANIZATIONAL STRATEGY, AND FIRM PERFORMANCE

Luis R. Gomez-Mejia
Professor, Department of
Management
Arizona State University

David B. Balkin
Associate Professor of
Management
University of Colorado

COLLEGE DIVISION South-Western Publishing Co.

Cincinnati Ohio

Publisher: Roger L. Ross

Production Editor: Sue Ellen Brown

Production House: CompuText Productions

Cover and Interior Designer: Joseph M. Devine

Marketing Manager: Tania Hindersman

GJ63AA
Copyright © 1992
by SOUTH-WESTERN PUBLISHING CO.
Cincinnati, Ohio

ALL RIGHTS RESERVED

The text of this publication, or any part thereof, may not be reproduced or transmitted in any form or by any means, electronic or mechanical, including photocopying, recording, storage in an information retrieval system, or otherwise, without the prior written permission of the publisher.

Library of Congress Cataloging-in-Publication Data

Gomez-Mejia, Luis R.
    Compensation, organizational strategy, and firm performance / Luis
  R. Gomez-Mejia, David B. Balkin. –1st ed.
        p.   cm.
    Includes bibliographical references and index.
    ISBN 0-538-80269-3
    1. Compensation management–United States.   I. Bakin, David B.,
  1948–   .   II. Title.
  HF5549.5.C67G66 1992
  658.3' 22 - - dc20   91-28393
                                                                CIP

1 2 3 4 5 6 MT 7 6 5 4 3 2

Printed in the United States of America

To my wife, Diane Gomez and my children, Vince and Alex
—Luis R. Gomez-Mejia

To my parents, Daniel and Jeanne Balkin
—David B. Balkin

EDITORS' INTRODUCTION
TO THE HUMAN RESOURCES
MANAGEMENT SERIES

The effective management of human resources has been of interest to organizational scientists and administrators for quite some time. But, perhaps due to productivity concerns and the contemporary quality of work life focus, human resources management issues have never been more prominent. As a result of this renewed interest, there is a greater need and demand for educating people about human resources management in organizations, which has manifested itself as expanded curriculum in this area in business schools and labor institutes, as well as in management education and development programs.

The South-Western Series in Human Resources Management is designed to provide substantive knowledge and information on important topics in the field to researchers, students, and practicing professionals who wish to more fully understand the the implications of theory and research for the management of human resources. The topics for books in this series are carefully selected with a concern for traditionally important issues, new topics in the field, and new, innovative treatments of traditional topics. Thus, the series is open-ended with regard to both content and size, with no contraints on the number of volumes that will be included. The volumes in the series are all written by notable scholars, recognized throughout the field of human resources management.

Gerald R. Ferris
Kendrith M. Rowland
Series Consulting Editors

PREFACE

This is a research oriented book concerned with the impact of the compensation system on firm performance. It is an eclectic, interdisciplinary volume drawing extensively from many disciplines outside the traditional human resource management (HRM) domain, including accounting, finance, economics, sociology, political science, and strategic management. It has been primarily written for an academic rather than a practitioner audience, but much of the material is accessible to advanced undergraduate and graduate students as well as sophisticated practitioners. More specifically, Chapters 1-2 (which provide an overview of the entire book) and Chapters 6-11 (dealing with strategic employee groups and the HRM subsystem) would be particularly attractive to advanced undergraduate students, students in MBA programs, practitioners and scholars. Chapters 3-5 deal with the linkages among the compensation system, organizational strategies, and firm performance and are more likely to be of interest to those engaged in scholarly research such as doctoral students and faculty.

This book may be used as a supplement to a regular compensation text or as a stand-alone text in courses that follow a seminar format. The content, tone, and scope of the book should have wide appeal to a variety of research oriented faculty and students, particularly those interested in macro HRM issues and strategic management. It can also be used as a valuable resource by people who do compensation research and by practitioners or consultants who design and administer reward systems in industry.

We feel that the broader macro treatment of compensation issues advanced in this book will provide a better understanding of the role that could be served by the compensation system as part of the firm's overall business strategy. It is our hope that this volume will provide added impetus for continuing research about theory and practice in compensation from an interdisciplinary perspective.

We would like to acknowledge the contributions of Professor George T. Milkovich from Cornell University whose valuable comments made this a much better book. We would also like to acknowledge the inputs of Gerald Ferris and Ken Rowland whose reactions to an earlier draft of the manuscript were very helpful to us in enhancing the overall quality of the book. We also appreciate the hard work and support of the editorial and production staff at South-Western Publishing Co., in particular Roger Ross and Sue Ellen Brown.

Luis R. Gomez-Mejia
Arizona State University

David B. Balkin
University of Colorado-Boulder

CONTENTS

Part 1
General System

COMPENSATION: BREAKING FROM THE PAST AND SEARCHING FOR NEW DIRECTIONS

OLD CONCEPTUAL ROOTS
  Equity Theory
  Neoclassical Labor Market Theory

THE TRADITIONAL COMPENSATION TOOLS
  Job Evaluation and Internal Pay Structures
  Market Surveys
  Individual Pay Assignments

BREAKING FROM THE TRADITIONAL MODELS
  The Deterministic Nature of Traditional Models
  Inapplicability to Executive, Managerial, and Professional Ranks
  Lack of Flexibility
  Socially Induced Inequities
  Questioning the Market
  Obstacle to Professionalization

EMERGENCE OF THE STRATEGY PARADIGM IN COMPENSATION

ALTERNATIVE FRAMEWORKS TO STUDY COMPENSATION ISSUES
  The Agency Perspective
  The Behavioral Perspective of the Firm
    Access to Dominant Coalitions
    Role of Dominant Coalitions in Formulating Compensation
      Strategies
    Locus of Control as Determinant of Compensation Structure
    Role of Subunit Power in Job Evaluation
    Role of Institutional Power within Internal Labor Market
  The Resource Dependence Perspective
    Shifting Criteria of Worth
    Boundary Spaning and Job Evaluation
    Environmental Interface and Strategic Employee Groups
  Constituency Perspective
  Competitive Strategy Perspective
    Developing an Adaptive Compensation System
    Finding an Ecological Niche
    Capitalizing on the Firm's Distinctive Competence

Erecting Barriers to Entry
Engaging in Proactive Moves

PLAN FOR THIS BOOK AND OVERALL MODEL

As a field of study, compensation is undergoing a radical transformation as we move into the twenty-first century. The old ways of examining pay issues in personnel management—a very micro, mechanistic orientation—are giving way to a new, more macro perspective of how pay should be allocated in organizations. While still the heart of most compensation texts, the traditional paradigms of equity theory and neoclassical labor economics are no longer as unquestioned as they once were. The emerging paradigm of the field is based on a strategic orientation where issues of "internal equity" and "external equity" are viewed as secondary to the firm's need to use pay as an essential integrating and signaling mechanism to achieve overarching business objectives.

The human resource management (HRM) function has been historically characterized as "reactive; an appendage to mainstream functions of finance, production, or marketing; a dumping ground for obsolete executives; and more interested in its own technologies than in serving the needs of its clients" (Tsui and Gomez-Mejia, 1988, p. 188). Over the past two decades, a large number of practitioners and academics have attempted to change this unflattering image and have advocated a strategic orientation to the field. (See reviews by Dyer and Holder, 1988; and Butler, Ferris, and Napier, 1991.) People espousing a strategic orientation believe this perspective makes the HRM field more businesslike and less confined to its traditional role of handling bureaucratic minutiae and "touchy feel" stereotypes.

With a few notable exceptions (e.g., Debejar and Milkovich, 1986; Gupta and Govindarajan, 1984; Guthrie and Olian, 1991), the literature on HRM strategy has been prescriptive in nature. This is particularly true in compensation because very limited research has been conducted on the linkage between pay strategies and firm performance. Perhaps the lack of empirical work is due in large measure to the difficulties encountered to publish HRM strategy type research (which, by its very nature, tends to be risky because of its general systems approach) in more prestigious HRM outlets accustomed to the rigor of testing carefully stated hypotheses on micro HRM phenomena (e.g., the impact of different performance appraisal formats on rater accuracy). Indeed, most HRM strategy writings appear in specialized journals that typically do not publish empirical research. Likewise, mainline strategy journals tend to shun HRM work because it is viewed as "too functional."

Fortunately, a discernible trend in the recent past bridges the fields of strategy and human resource management, and places firm performance as the central focus. Several papers on HRM strategy and its relationship to firm performance have appeared in the leading scholarly strategy journal (*Strategic Management Journal*) since the late 1980s. Many well-known strategy researchers are abandoning the deeply rooted notion that strategy is the province of top management (and, therefore, outside the scope of functional areas such as HRM). This opens the door for HRM investigators to study HRM-related strategic issues at multiple organizational levels. For instance, Burgelman (1983) depicts strategy formulation and implementation as a product of autonomous behaviors initiated outside top management. Mintzberg and Waters (1985) argue that strategy results from a combination of deliberate planning by senior executives and emergent decisions at different levels in the organization. In a follow-up paper, Mintzberg (1990) severely criticizes the entrenched view in strategic management that top executives are responsible for strategic decisions and relegate other members of the organization to subordinate implementation roles. Wooldridge and Floyd (1990) argue for the necessity to study the role of middle management and nonmanagement employees in strategy formulation. They conclude that "future research should recognize the possibility of a broad scope of strategic involvement well beyond the managerial ranks" (p. 240). Likewise, Hambrick, Black, and Frederickson (1992) and Keeley and Roure (1993) suggest that active involvement of technical professionals in both strategy formulation and implementation has a significant positive impact on the performance of high technology firms. More to the point in terms of the subject of this book, a survey by consultants Booz, Allen, and Hamilton (1990) reports "Only 37 percent of the senior officials think other key managers completely understand business goals. Only 4 percent of the top bosses think middle managers totally understand . . . not surprisingly, compliance drops with understanding, to the point where nearly half the top executives believe that middle managers go along with new strategies at best partially or not at all. The top bosses believe pay policies at their companies may be working against the strategy changes they try to push. Half say performance rewards actually encourage counterproductive or narrowly focused behavior" (reported in *The Wall Street Journal*, May 1, 1990, p. 1. Reprinted by permission of *The Wall Street Journal*, © 1990 Dow Jones & Company, Inc. All Rights Reserved Worldwide).

Similarly, many micro HRM scholars recognize the need for linking HRM policies and practices to organizational strategy and study HRM issues in light of their relationship to firm performance. (For recent reviews of this literature, see Butler, Ferris, and Napier, 1991; Martell, Carroll and Gupta, 1992; Dobbins, Cardy, and Carson, 1991; Lawler, 1990; Tsui and Gomez-Mejia, 1988). A symposia of distinguished industrial psychologists (sponsored by the Fifth Annual Conference of the Society for Industrial and Organizational Psychology, 1990) advanced the notion that one of the most significant trends for the 1990s and beyond is to incorporate contextual factors when examining the impact of personnel practices, such as "business strategies, organization's history, firm size and structure, economic and legal conditions, and host country" (conference program, p. 8). A similar theme runs through a symposia of well-known management scholars (R. Cardy, W. Cascio, G. Dobbins, G. Ferris, C. Manz, R. Schuler, and H. Sims) held at the 51st Annual Meeting of the Academy of Management in 1991 (Cardy, 1991).

No other HRM subfunction has been as guilty of myopic focus as compensation, with its well-known predilection for tools and techniques. Perhaps this may be attributed to the fact "it has been the practitioners and not the scholars who have made the greatest contributions to the compensation field" (Rock, 1991, p. 10). Ironically, of all the traditional HRM areas (e.g., selection and placement, training and development, performance appraisal), compensation offers the greatest potential from a strategic perspective in terms of theoretical development, empirical research, and application. There are several reasons for this:

1. Compensation's central variable of interest—money—represents the most generalized medium of exchange known to humankind. This means it is an integral part of practically all transactions occurring within and across organizational boundaries.

2. Money is the quintessence of all business language, and top decision makers readily understand its significance. For example, designing staffing and training programs to select and develop employees to fit strategy (e.g., Rothwell and Kazanas, 1988, 1989) may be more appealing to personnel specialists than they are compelling concerns to upper management.

3. Compensation dollars have a direct impact (and in most firms, the most important one) on the cost side of all financial statements. Not only does this make compensation

a very crucial tangible resource to management, but also how it is allocated becomes a de facto component of the firm performance calculus. While procedures have been developed in HRM (e.g., human resource accounting, utility analysis) to estimate the cost-benefit sensitivity of intangible factors such as improving employee attitudes, honing employee skills through training programs, increasing the validity of selection methods and appraisal programs, etc. (Boudreau, 1988; Cascio, 1987; Kleiman and Faley, 1992; Ledvinka, Archer, and Ladd, 1990), most managers outside personnel know little about and are less easily convinced by such data. Many personnel managers and academics alike believe mathematical estimates of the value of HRM programs are abstruse and a bit confabulated.

4. Of all the variables typically associated with the HRM field, compensation can be most easily manipulated and directly controlled by management. Thus, it has a great deal of inherent strategic flexibility. For example, it is much easier (although by no means easy) to change the pay mix or pay system design than it is to replace employees and keep attuned to changing environmental conditions and strategic objectives. Variables such as employee characteristics, skills levels, attitudes, etc., are difficult to mold in order to meet varying organizational contingencies—at least in the near term. The organization also faces significant ethical and legal constraints in trying to manipulate most other HRM subsystems to match its business strategies.

5. Unlike most HRM variables, compensation links directly to the conceptual frameworks of other mainline business fields (such as finance and accounting). Thus, one is able to draw upon a wealth of theoretical work and empirical research from those disciplines. Building on this literature, one can develop models and make predictions about the relationship between compensation strategies and firm performance.

This chapter provides an overview of compensation management from this new strategic vantage point. First, the traditional, conceptual roots of the compensation field and administrative procedures developed to operationalize them are briefly examined. This discussion provides a context to understand better the alternative approaches to the study of compensation. We also use this discussion as a base to explore why the traditional apparatus is no longer universally accepted. (*Note:* Because top executives are treated as one of a kind individuals who are seldom covered under standard compensation plans, Chapters 6 and 7 are exclusively devoted to that group. Therefore, many controversial issues surrounding executive pay are avoided altogether in this chapter but are discussed in depth later in the book). Second, the essential tenets of the new strategic orientation in the compensation field and major models used to examine pay from a business policy perspective are discussed. Finally, we present a model that ties together the entire book and a schematic summary of all subsequent chapters.

OLD CONCEPTUAL ROOTS

The traditional underpinnings of compensation as an academic subfield are found in both social psychology (motivation theories) and labor economics (labor markets), although scientific management has also played a role in their development. Because the traditional foundations of the field are covered at length in most textbooks (e.g., Hills, 1987; Milkovich and Newman, 1990) and reviewed in other integrative works (e.g., Rock and Berger, 1991; Gerhart and Milkovich, 1993), we only address the most important points.

Equity Theory

The centrality of equity in compensation is reflected in the following statement by Wallace and Fay (1983, p. 69): "The critical theme that exists at the center of *all* compensation theory and practice [is] equity." Indeed, a large academic and practitioner literature in compensation has focused on this construct under the general rubric of equity theory. Its underpinnings consist of exchange theory (Gouldner, 1960) and cognitive dissonance theory (Festinger, 1957), which originated in social psychology.

According to the equity paradigm, each employee in an organization exchanges a set of inputs or contributions (e.g., education, effort, long-term commitment) for a set of outcomes or inducements (e.g., pay, promotion, prestige). This exchange process takes place within a social setting, not in isolation. Individuals are constantly comparing their input relative to their outcomes vis-a-vis other employees (called *referent others*) inside and outside the firm. In what is perhaps the best-known version of equity theory, Adams (1965) argues that "distributive justice" is achieved when the proportionate relation between contributions and inducements is equal for all employees. Thus, distributive justice *as perceived* by all parties defines equity according to the following ratio:

$$\frac{O_p}{I_p} = \frac{O_o}{I_o}$$

where O_p = Employment outcomes of a given individual

I_p = Inputs of a given individual

O_o = Employment outcomes received by referent others

I_o = Inputs offered by "referent other"

The word "perceived" is crucial to most equity theorists. Employees do not assess the inducement contribution ratio in a rational, calculated manner but through a subjective determination of how the individual's ratio fares against those of other people chosen for comparison. In common parlance, equity theory holds that "truth is in the eyes of the beholder." If an unbalance is perceived, the employee will experience "cognitive dissonance" and try to correct this imbalance in a number of ways such as reducing inputs (e.g., not taking work home), attempting to increase outcomes by voicing complaints to the supervisor, or joining in concerted action with other disgruntled employees to extract concessions from management. As an ultimate recourse, the individual is likely to leave the firm.

Although nonpecuniary outcomes may be important to employees (Adams, 1991), pay is the outcome of central concern to most equity theory formulations. According to Milkovich and Newman (1990, p. 215): "Money is one of many outcomes that is evaluated in the exchange relationship. But since money is one of the most visible components . . . it becomes extremely important."

Because individuals are likely to compare their pay/contribution ratio with other employees in the organization, as well as with employees in other firms, the key task of the compensation system from an equity perspective is to ensure that distributive justice is accomplished vis-a-vis the referent or relevant other. If wage rates for jobs within the company are set so that employees perceive a fair input/outcome balance relative to referents within the organization (internal equity) as well as a market referent (external equity), then equity is achieved. The importance of *external equity* is given added impetus in the work of Jaques (1961) who suggests the relevant standard in determining equity is intrinsic to the individual. This individual sense of equity depends on the employee's past wage experiences, which are used to judge appropriate levels of current pay. This means the compensation system must be perceived as equitable relative to pay standards of other firms (Jaques, 1979).

Achieving internal and external equity becomes paramount in the traditional compensation systems because it affects two critical employee behaviors: the individual's decisions to join and stay with the organization. In the words of Hills (1987, p. 33): "The individual must first feel that a potential employment exchange with the organization is equitable, and then, once the individual is a member of the organization, must perceive that the employment exchange contract remains equitable. These are minimum requirements to attract and retain people, yet they are fundamental in that if the organization is unable to attract and retain people, all other human resource activities are meaningless."

In short, equity theory is concerned with notions of fairness and deservedness, which depend on a social comparison process within and outside the firm. From a traditional perspective and to the extent that equity can be achieved by matching rewards to perceived contributions for each employee in relationship to referent others, the pay system accomplishes its primary mission. These notions are reinforced by the neoclassical labor market models to be discussed next.

Neoclassical Labor Market Theory

The second underpinning of traditional compensation thinking and practice is found in neoclassical labor economics. The dependent variables in these models are the wage rate and employment level that are determined through the interaction of supply and demand for labor. As every undergraduate student taking an introductory economics course knows, *ceteris paribus* (e.g., perfect information and mobility), the wage rate of a given occupation is set at a point where the labor supply and labor demand curves cross. So from this perspective, external equity is achieved if a firm pays the "going rate" in the market place for each job. These rates in turn reflect the relative strengths of supply and demand for different types of labor. Other things equal, the less employers are willing to pay (i.e., low demand) and the less pay workers are willing to accept (i.e., high supply) for a given job, the lower its wage rate.

Demand for labor is derived from the market demand for the firm's product or service, which slopes downward. The lower the price of a product, the more units will be sold. To the extent that demand shifts to the right, consumers are willing to purchase more units at any given price. This causes a shift to the right of the labor demand curve. When this happens, employers are willing to pay more for any given number of employees hired. Labor demand is also a function of the marginal product of labor. Labor competes with other factors of production such as capital and will be utilized up to the point where labor can be substituted for other production factors (i.e., capital) more efficiently. The supply of labor, on the other hand, is said to depend on the availability of skills required to perform the job, training costs, and task desirability (Marshall, Briggs, and King, 1984; Reynolds, 1951).

Labor demand is aggregated across all employers, and labor supply is aggregated across millions of workers. Thus, the firm is depicted as a "price taker" that cannot influence market wages and must pay the prevailing rate in order to attract and retain employees (Bronfenbrenner, 1956; Cartter, 1959; Ehrenberg and Smith, 1988). (However, in the case of a monopsonist company that is the sole employer in an area, this is not true.)

The neoclassical economic model has two main implications for compensation practice and research. First, to attract and retain a qualified work force, the firm must identify what the prevailing wage is for each of its jobs. Second, and related to the first point, the "going rate" in the labor market becomes the key factor for ascertaining job value or worth and, hence, external equity. In the words of Wallace and Fay (1983, p. 41): "Indeed, external equity is defined as the exchange rate for labor on a job clearing in the external labor market."

Of course, compensation scholars have always realized the labor market is not perfect. Poor information, variations among workers in what they seek in a job (e.g., compatible co-workers vs. a larger paycheck, willingness to accept risks vs. more job security), transaction costs in changing jobs (e.g., loss of pension benefits, moving expenses), dual-career problems, and discrimination, among others, affect employment decisions. But even if one were to relax the stringent assumptions of perfect competition, a firm cannot stray too far from the competitive wage. If it does, the firm soon finds itself unable to hire workers or unable to compete effectively in the product market because its labor costs are too high.

THE TRADITIONAL COMPENSATION TOOLS

The equity paradigm from social psychology and the labor market model from economics have had a profound effect on the field of compensation. In fact, all compensation textbooks rely on these models to justify in part the widespread use of job evaluation and salary surveys (to be discussed later). Whether these compensation practices, emerging through years of experimentation and in response to administrative demands, led academics to search for theories to justify them or whether the conceptual apparatus led to the development of operational systems to implement them is not clear. Most likely, it is an interaction of these two forces: Administrative procedures are developed to rationalize pay structures, and the equity/labor market models offer a conceptual framework to support their use. Textbook writers, however, generally treat job evaluation and salary surveys as attempts to operationalize the constructs of equity and labor market rate. These procedures (graphically summarized in Figure 1.1) are briefly discussed next. (Note: Given space limitations, only a superficial treatment of these operational systems is possible here. For a more detailed description turn to Belcher and Atchison, 1987; Milkovich and Newman, 1990.)

Job Evaluation and Internal Pay Structures

Job evaluation is perhaps the best-known and most commonly used procedure in compensation. In fact, the typical compensation text devotes over half of its chapters to the various steps involved in this process. *Job evaluation* is generally defined as a formalized system for ascertaining the relative value or contribution of different jobs (*not* individual employees) in an organization (e.g., Kanin-Lovers, 1991; Lange, 1991; Gerhart and Milkovich, 1993). It is intended to provide a rational, orderly, and systematic hierarchy of jobs, based on their worth to the firm. Executives and managers are at the top of the hierarchy, while unskilled hourly workers are assigned to the bottom of the structure. In a large organization, hundreds or perhaps thousands of other jobs (e.g., administrative assistants, machinists, sales reps, computer operators) fall somewhere in between.

To separate individuals' characteristics from the actual value of their contributions, the job is used as the unit of analysis. The job, independent of the incumbent, is evaluated as a group of positions that are similar in terms of skills, efforts, responsibilities, and working conditions. The higher the job in the evaluation hierarchy, the more pay its incumbents receive because the nature of their work is judged to be more valuable to the organization.

By design, most traditional job evaluation approaches draw a clear demarcation between the incumbent's performance and individual traits from the job itself. The upper and lower value limits of each job are established by assessing a job's worth relative to other jobs, and incumbents' earnings should not fall outside those perimeters, regardless of how well assigned tasks are performed or how impressive personal traits are. So the question of interest from a job evaluation perspective is "Tell me what you do?" rather than "How well do you do it?" The latter question is relegated to performance appraisal as a distinct and separate procedure. For example, the best assembler in a factory may have a Ph.D. in electrical engineering, but because the job is ranked at the lowest level in the evaluation hierarchy, the worker's pay should fall somewhere between the minimum and maximum pay range established for assemblers, in spite of the impressive credentials.

While job evaluation systems preceded explicit formulations of equity theory (e.g., see earlier work by institutional economists such as Livernash [1957] and industrial psychologists such as Viteles [1941]), the key objectives of job evaluation revolve around judgments of equity. The first judgment is to attain internal consistency in pay relationships. This can be accomplished through the development of a definite plan in which differences in pay are based on variations in job requirements and content, *not* people. This process, by focusing on the job and not individuals, is easier to explain to employees and enjoys wider acceptability. The second judgment, to provide the firm with a step-by-step procedure to document how pay decisions are made, is important from a governance and legal perspective. To achieve a common understanding as to the basis for pay allocation in large, complex organizations is the third judgment. It, therefore, forces management to systematically identify factors that will be used to distribute rewards. Finally, as discussed in the next section, job evaluation allows the firm to link internal pay relationships to the labor market in order to achieve both internal and external equity.

Figure 1-1 outlines the steps that are followed in a typical job evaluation procedure. Most textbooks describe each of the components in painstaking detail (e.g., Hills, 1987; Milkovich and Newman, 1990). The first step consists of job analysis, or gathering information about "what, how, why" of various tasks comprising the job. Numerous procedures have been developed to conduct job analysis over the years (e.g., Fine, 1973; Lange, 1991; McCormick, 1979; U.S. Civil Service Commission, 1973). The input from job analysis is used to identify similarities and differences in job content, either subjectively or through the use of computer-based algorithms (e.g., Ash, Levine, and Sistrunk, 1983; Downs, 1991; Gomez-Mejia, Page, and Tornow, 1979, 1982, 1987; Gordon, 1991; Thompson and Thompson, 1982). This information is generally reduced to a written document that identifies, defines, and describes all jobs in terms of duties, responsibilities, working conditions, and requirements. This is commonly known as a *job description*.

Standard format job descriptions are then used to rate all jobs using a predetermined system. Several well-known job evaluation procedures have evolved over the years to do this. Among them are: ranking (ordering of job descriptions from highest to lowest based on relative assessed value), factor comparison (a variant of the ranking method), point plan (points are assigned to different aspects of the jobs being rated and added to create an evaluation composite), and policy capturing (use of regression equations to estimate the relative value of each job based on the firm's past practices). Almost all plans utilize a set of "compensable factors" or evaluative

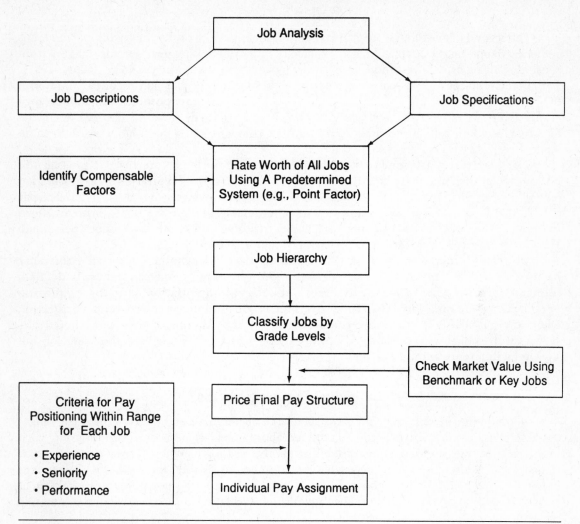

FIGURE 1-1 Traditional Compensation Model

criteria to rate jobs. The Hay System, for example, uses three compensable factors: know-how, problem solving, and accountability. It is perhaps the most widely used system. More than 5,000 employers around the world are subscribers, including 25 percent of the largest U.S. corporations (Milkovich and Newman, 1990).

The rating process then leads to a hierarchy of jobs in terms of assessed worth. For the sake of simplicity, most large organizations classify jobs into grades. In Control Data Corporation, for instance, thousands of jobs were grouped into less than twenty grade levels (Gomez-Mejia, Page, and Tornow, 1982). All jobs in a given grade are judged to be essentially the same in terms of worth. The last step in the process consists of linking the job evaluation results (reflecting internal equity based on the employer's assessment of the job's worth) to the labor market. This leads us to the next section.

Market Surveys

The second administrative mechanism most frequently used under the traditional models is gathering labor market data. This is done either by purchasing market information from consulting firms or, less common, by conducting in-house salary surveys (e.g., Lichty, 1991). The ultimate objective is to learn the market values of different jobs and reconcile them with the results of internal job evaluation procedures. Because most positions are unique to a given employer, only *key* or *benchmark jobs* are used in market surveys. *Key jobs* are those for which accurate matches to similar jobs in other companies in a given labor market can be made.

The salary survey data for each key job within a given grade level is then used to price all jobs previously classified into that grade. It is also possible to use regression procedures to link market data with job evaluation scores (e.g., Roy, 1991). The organization has the choice to develop pay policies that lead, match, or lag the market rate. Presumably, to the extent that a firm can afford it, paying above market should improve its ability to attract and retain high-caliber personnel. More is discussed on these three pay policies in Chapter 10.

Ultimately, market surveys are designed to ascertain whether external equity has been achieved. In the words of Fay (1989, p. 73): "External equity, as generally defined, refers to the range of wages and other monetary compensation paid by employing organizations in some labor market for a similar job. From an employee's perspective, external equity exists if his or her compensation package is equivalent to one offered employees with similar qualifications (e.g., education, experience) who hold the same job but work for a different organization."

Individual Pay Assignments

In traditional models, once the pay structure has been finalized by determining pay ranges for each job (following the procedures outlined above), the last step consists of assigning each individual a pay rate within the range established for his or her job. Where a given employee's pay is positioned within the range depends on a number of factors, most commonly previous experience, company tenure, and assessed job performance. Some people refer to this as *individual equity* as opposed to internal equity (via job evaluation) or external equity (via market surveys).

BREAKING FROM THE TRADITIONAL MODELS

The equity paradigm and the neoclassical labor market models, operationalized through the use of job evaluation and salary survey procedures, have clearly dominated the field of compensation for the past fifty years. These perspectives have provided valuable insights in the past, and the administrative process to implement them have been of much practical use to employers. However, they are being increasingly questioned. Disenchantment with these models became pronounced in the late 1970s (e.g., Walker, 1978) and have taken greater impetus in the 1980s and 1990s (e.g., Berger, 1991; Hambrick and Snow, 1989; Lawler, 1986, 1990; Masters, Tokesky, Brown, Atkin and Schoenfeld, 1992; Smith, 1990). Several reasons account for rising dissatisfaction with traditional thinking in compensation, and the search for new paradigms to study pay issues is underway. These are discussed next.

The Deterministic Nature of Traditional Models

Both equity and labor market models and their operationalization (namely job evaluation and market surveys) have a largely deterministic view of the world. In essence, internal equity can be achieved if organizational rewards are distributed in proportion to job value (as per job evaluation), and external equity can be accomplished by pegging the organization's pay to that of the market (or at least within a narrow band around the going rate as determined through market surveys). This deterministic view has been questioned in a number of related ways.

First, most organizations have considerable discretion in terms of pay allocation, basis for pay decisions, and administrative procedures. In other words, organizations are confronted with a wide range of pay policy alternatives, and dramatic differences in the choices made are evident across firms (Milkovich, 1988; Milkovich and Broderick, 1991). Second, compensation problems and challenges in each firm are typically unique and less structured than the traditional models would lead one to believe. Considerable creativity is required to synthesize large amounts of external and internal information and to develop a plan outlining the direction of a firm's future pay policy. Heavy reliance on "off-the-shelf" job evaluation procedures and surveys (typically conducted by consultants) emphasize a universal perspective that may not be relevant and perhaps even detrimental to the firm. Such prescriptive approaches ignore the environmental forces and business context that confront and impact the firm (Balkin and Gomez-Mejia, 1987, 1990). Finally, due to the rapid increase in mergers and acquisitions as well as internal diversification, most organizations are complex, and varied compensation systems may be more appropriate for different parts of the organization. Traditional pay systems with their emphasis on consistency neglect the particular contingencies confronting diverse organizational units (Carroll, 1987, 1988; Martell et al., 1992; Salscheider, 1981).

Inapplicability to Executive, Managerial, and Professional Ranks

Another problem with traditional pay systems is that their basic assumptions are largely inappropriate to higher occupational groups. At these levels, it is nearly impossible to separate individual contributions from the job itself. In other words, the incumbent helps define and mold the job. Forcing managerial and professional employees into grade levels can be counterproductive because their contributions are less a function of tasks performed than they are personal characteristics. Given a more sophisticated work force and the increase of professional and managerial ranks as the economy becomes more service-oriented, jobs are becoming more and more broadly defined. Job descriptions often become meaningless generalities. Therefore, to the extent that job analysis and job descriptions produce ambiguous data, the rest of the system on which they are based has little validity either.

Forcing a mechanistic pay system can backfire in some situations. For example, in the high technology industry, scientists and engineers (S & Es) often contribute more to the organization than top executives. (See Adler and Ferdows, 1992; Kanzanjian, 1993.) Yet application of traditional evaluation procedures designed for a manufacturing environment are often used with disastrous consequences (Gomez-Mejia, Balkin, and Milkovich, 1990). By establishing an elaborate hierarchy of grade levels for scientists and engineers and making rewards contingent on fine distinctions in the nature of the task being accomplished, many high tech firms foster competition, artificial barriers among people, fragmentation, and an individualistic climate in the work force. The behaviors and culture fostered by traditional job evaluation procedures in this situation run counter to what it takes to succeed in a R & D environment, namely, intense team effort, integration of activities among many individuals, fluid tasks, exchange of knowledge, and minimal status barriers to facilitate interaction among multi-disciplinary S & Es working on common problems. (See Stephens and Tripoli, 1992.)

Lack of Flexibility

The traditional, lockstep compensation system based on job evaluation gives a high priority to pay relationships within the firm. These systems work reasonably well for firms faced with stable markets and high continuity in their socio-technical system. Such was the case, for example, of the automobile industry in the United States for several decades (McNichols, 1983). However, these systems cannot be easily adapted to rapidly changing economic environments. (See Emerson, 1991.) Once a job evaluation program is in place, it is difficult to change.

Because it relies on fixed salary and benefits associated with each level in the hierarchy (as set through job evaluation and market surveys), American industry's primary mechanism to cope with economic downturns is to lay off employees to reduce costs. The Japanese, on the other hand, often provide 20-30 percent of an employee's pay on a variable basis and use this as a cushion to absorb the ups and downs in the firm's economic health. According to the Department of Commerce, almost five million long-term workers (those who had been on a job for three years or more) had been terminated for business reasons between 1983-1989, a period of relative prosperity (U.S. Commerce Department, 1989). A third of those had to accept jobs that paid at least 20 percent less than their previous positions, and 25 percent were still looking for employment.

The difficulty U.S. employers have in adjusting salary levels to the business cycle is likely to have a negative impact on the morale of U.S. workers. The unwanted side effect, unemployment, may be impossible to avoid. A poll conducted by Yankelovich, Clary, and Shulman in late 1989 shows a dramatic decline in the extent employees and managers feel loyal to the firm. Almost two-thirds report lack of trust in their company. And there was a widespread expectation of future employer changes (Yankelovich, Clary, and Shulman, 1989). This suggests the net result of inflexible job evaluation systems that allow little variability in the pay mix (and, therefore, limited maneuverability to control the cost structure other than through employee dismissals) is a decline in employee commitment. A depressing portrayal of this process is captured in the following excerpt from a lead story in *Time* magazine for labor day, 1989 (September 11, 1989: 53): "Company loyalty is dying. Even as American business seeks to inculcate a new corporate credo of worker participation and involvement, it is confronting a shell shocked, apathetic, and risk adverse labor force. The cost cutting may depress corporate creativity and competitiveness for years to come." In that same lead story, Madelyn Jennings, senior vice president of Gannet Co., is quoted as saying: "Employees are running so scared that there is a whole culture that says don't make waves, don't take risks—just at a time when we need innovation."

Socially Induced Inequities

The women's movement has also had a negative effect on the perceptions of fairness of both job evaluation and market surveys which are suspect in terms of contributing to the continued low earnings of females. (See review by Judd and Gomez-Mejia, 1987.) Although empirical attempts to test the presumed gender bias in job evaluation have generally failed to support some of the worst fears of its foes (e.g., Doverspike and Barrett, 1984; Grams & Schwab, 1985; Rynes, Weber, and Milkovich, 1989; Schwab and Grams, 1984) and comparable worth has had limited legal success in the U.S., many people are still convinced women get the short end of the stick in the job evaluation process. (See Herzlinger, 1988; "U.S. News & World Report," 1986; *Work in America Institute*, 1990.) The essence of their criticism, much of which is political rather than technical in nature, is that job evaluation is intrinsically biased against those occupations traditionally filled with women such as clerical, teaching, nursing, and the like. A common statistic used is that among the top 25 percent highest earning occupations, women represent a pitiful proportion or less than 2 percent of the total (Fogel, 1979; Judd and Gomez-Mejia, 1987). Logical paradoxes are frequently used by critics (such as garbage collectors evaluated higher than teachers) to demonstrate vividly how "women's jobs" are systematically kept at the lowest levels in the pay hierarchy in ways that are difficult to justify on a rational basis (Viera, 1985).

According to critics, biases may creep in at different points in the job evaluation process. (See review by Arvey, 1987.) At the job analysis stage, women's jobs may be understated in terms of skill requirements and task complexity. The compensable factors used may have a distinct masculine rather than feminine orientation (e.g., working conditions and effort). The subjective process used to evaluate jobs, coupled with compensation committees consisting mostly of males, may present subtle cognitive discriminatory biases against women. Finally, a self-fulfilling prophecy may be perpetuated in the job evaluation process. That is, knowledge of the previous status of a job is likely to influence how the compensation committee will assess it in the future. In other words, job evaluation does not take place in a vacuum. Customary practices (e.g., clerical jobs expected to be evaluated at low levels) may contribute to depressed earnings among women.

In short, while the tough indictment against job evaluation from feminist groups may be exaggerated in light of empirical findings to date, the comparable worth movement and the widespread press it has received have served to raise some serious doubts about the purported objectivity and fairness of traditional compensation methods.

Questioning the Market

The traditional compensation models assume that pay norms exist among firms in a given market and that going rates for particular jobs can be identified. As noted earlier, wage surveys have been used for many years to operationalize the concepts of *competitive pay* or *equitable market pay*.

In recent years, however, the use of wage surveys has also come under fire, fueled in part by the comparable worth movement during the 1980s. Early criticisms of the market rate can be traced to Dunlop (1957) who argued that it may be an illusionary concept. He found that workers performing almost identical work, that required the same skills, and organized by the same union and in the same geographical area (Boston) were receiving a rate of pay markedly different among different employers with 60 percent differences not uncommon. About 25 years later, Treiman and Hartmann (1981) reported a huge variance in the pay of identical jobs in the Newark area with a ratio of almost 3 to 1 between highest and lowest paying employers. Foster (1985) found that after controlling for job content, company size, and company performance, differences between 35 to 54 percent in pay for identical jobs within the same industry are not uncommon. Foster (1985, p. 70) concludes "Clearly, the pay practices of firms in the same industry are often widely divergent . . . No doubt, this means that employers, on the basis of carefully selected survey samples, can justify widely divergent pay practices (a point frequently ignored when competitive pay is analyzed and discussed)." More recent data (1990) shows that even within a relatively small and isolated county away from any large metropolitan area (such as Alachua county in Northern Florida), a large range in weekly pay for the identical occupational title is common. (See Table 1-1.)

Rynes and Milkovich (1986) in a review paper entitled "Market Surveys: Dispelling Some Myths About the Market Wage," argue that both the construct and measurement of the market wage have not been sufficiently examined by either academics or the courts. Some of the problems with the market wage concept and its operationalization and salary surveys include (as per Rynes and Milkovich, 1986): widely divergent criteria as to how the "appropriate market" is defined, existence of multiple wage levels for the same job in a given market, differences in sampling methodologies and statistical analysis, mismatching of jobs among organizations with identical titles, and difficulties in estimating total pay (salary plus benefits and incentives).

This suggests that a fundamental assumption of the traditional compensation models—that the relevant market can be measured and used as a frame of comparison to adjust the internal job evaluation hierarchy—is no longer accepted at face value. There is an increasing awareness that firms have wide discretion in establishing wage levels and how the market rates are determined. (Note: For a more extensive discussion on these issues, see Gerhart and Milkovich, 1993.)

TABLE 1-1
Example of Intera-occupational Pay Dispersion:
Weekly Earnings for Workers in Alachua County, Northern Florida (1990)

Occupation	Average	Range
Accountants and Auditors	$496.92	$209.50-$865.38
Administrative Services Managers	487.23	190.00-1548.08
Civil Engineers	700.73	365.60-1049.20
Computer Programmers	549.60	160.00-1025.00
Construction Managers	525.08	390.00- 700.00
Drivers/Sale Workers	210.09	140.00- 550.00
Financial Managers	799.75	230.79-1466.00
First Line Supervisors—Clerical	393.06	138.40- 800.00
First Line Supervisors—Production	717.14	280.00-1000.00
Food Service and Lodging Managers	362.36	185.00- 702.00
Industrial Engineers	803.10	484.00-1080.00
Industrial Production Managers	855.86	290.00-1310.00
Personnel Relations Managers	555.97	220.00-1325.00
Purchasing Agents	461.23	170.00- 703.20
Purchasing Managers	563.15	184.80- 991.00
Systems Analysts	1,411.98	576.92-2950.00
Wholesale Retail Buyers	476.43	300.00- 923.79

Source: Florida Department of Labor and Employment Security

Obstacle to Professionalization

As noted earlier, human resource practitioners and academics alike realize HRM needs to shed its old image of being a low-level administrative function relegated to record keeping and paper shuffling, engaged in what seems like an endless creation of new forms and administrative procedures, and responsible for the enforcement of petty rules despised by line managers. In part, the contemporary use of the term "human resources" rather than "personnel" is indicative of an attempt to dispel past stereotypes of a function pejoratively depicted as run by "glorified secretaries" and a depository of managers who had failed elsewhere in the corporation (Tsui and Gomez-Mejia, 1988).

Unfortunately, compensation specialists and consultants selling their wares (e.g., various point methods, universal "guide charts," and standardized market surveys) have been among the worst culprits in reinforcing a negative image of the HRM profession. In the words of Tomasko (1982, p. 90): "The problem is that pay systems have become the province of staff people, who are fascinated with the technical details of how compensation programs work, and have ceased to be a tool for line managers. The result is an elaborate pay system that encourages rigid behaviors when attitudes should be more flexible." A similar theme runs through the work of such influential writers as Devanna, Fombrum, and Tichy (1981); Kanter, (1983); Lawler, (1990, 1991); and Tichy (1983).

Most compensation textbooks still contain page after page of instruments, techniques, forms, and the like. However, many realize a more professional image of the field can only be created if compensation becomes more of a business discipline rather than a personnel tool kit. This calls for a broader perspective capable of analyzing internal and external forces impacting the organization and the ability to devise pay systems to cope with them. In this context, the mechanics of the pay system are a means to achieving business objectives rather than an end in itself.

By assisting top management and key stockholders in finding solutions to pressing organizational problems via the reward system, compensation develops a business rather than a parochial function specific focus. For example, in an era of intense foreign competition and continuing decline in international market share for most U.S. corporations, incentive systems can be effectively used to induce top-level managers and decision makers to engage the firm in exporting activities and reverse the declining trend in foreign sales (Gomez-Mejia, 1988). In terms of academic research, this business perspective calls for more organization-wide conceptualizing and empirical work that is several steps removed from the traditional emphasis on procedural issues and micro focus.

EMERGENCE OF THE STRATEGY PARADIGM IN COMPENSATION

The traditional compensation systems reviewed earlier are giving way to a new strategic perspective on pay issues. This emergent paradigm is not unique to compensation, however, and sweeps across all business fields. A strategic orientation involves developing a long-term vision and multifunctional programmatic steps to cope with the unique contingencies affecting the organization. The term, derived from Greek, comes from the military and is loosely translated as "art of the general." This means concern for the big picture rather than tactical considerations. The term *strategy* is used in such diverse areas as "financial strategy," "production strategy," "R & D strategy," and "marketing strategy." According to Pascale (1982, p. 115): "Our strategy fetish has become a cultural peculiarity. We get off on strategy like the French get off on good food and romance." Compensation is perhaps one of the last remaining bastions to move in this direction. While some writers began to apply strategy to compensation as early as 1973 (Salter, 1973)—almost exclusively in the area of executive pay—it wasn't until the mid to late 1980s when the strategic movement began to gain a foothold in the field.

Dissatisfaction with traditional compensation thinking, along with keen competitive pressures on a global basis, are energizing this change process in the field. While some of the strategy trappings may be faddish, rapid changes in technology, increasing complexity of markets, the growth in mergers and acquisitions, deregulation, and the globalization of business are here to stay and, if anything, are likely to increase in the future. All these factors give a greater sense of urgency to strategic positioning to achieve a sustained competitive advantage. In 1950, the majority of the Fortune 500 companies were single-product firms. Forty years later, very few large companies are, and approximately one third of the Fortune 500 firms consist of huge conglomerates (Weitz and Wensley, 1988). A truly global economy has greatly complicated doing business as compared to even a decade ago. A few statistics illustrate how dramatic this trend is. Investments overseas by U.S. multinational corporations (MNCs) increased more than ten fold during the 1980s. During this same period, foreign firms increased ownership of domestic (U.S.) companies by more than 300 percent (Gomez-Mejia and Welbourne, 1991). In 1988 alone, American companies built nearly 150 factories in Asia and Europe in an attempt to position production facilities strategically (Gomez-Mejia and Welbourne, 1991). Likewise, the Japanese are heavily investing in U.S. operations, and employed approximately 350 thousand U.S. citizens in the late 1980s. This number is projected to increase to one million by the turn of the century (Beatty, McCune, and Beatty, 1988).

In short, the formulation of appropriate strategic responses is essential to companies' survival and growth in the rapidly changing business environment as the twenty-first century approaches. Economic, social, governmental, and technological shifts provide an opportunity for those companies able to plan ahead and make strategic moves that capitalize on these forces.

Because compensation typically represents 10-50 percent of total operating costs and as much as 90 percent in service or knowledge intensive organizations, firms cannot ignore the strategic importance of that resource (Gerhart and Milkovich, 1993). This calls for customizing the reward system to withstand jolts coming from rapid shifts within and outside the firm. This means that in order to maintain or increase a differential advantage over other firms, compensation professionals can no longer rely on "cookie cutters" or "off the shelf" systems to make pay decisions.

Compensation must be viewed as a pivotal control and incentive mechanism that can be flexibly used by management to achieve business objectives. This requires a departure from some of the simplistic notions embedded in the traditional compensation paradigms and administrative procedures. In the words of Milkovich and Newman (1987, p. 11), most compensation research emphasizes techniques "where the mechanics become the focus, ends in themselves . . . the purposes of the pay system are often forgotten . . . to date we really do not know enough to recommend [pay] policies under different conditions." A few years later, these same authors remarked (Milkovich and Newman, 1990, p. 13) "Examining and dissecting techniques is so seductive that . . . doing so become the focus, the ends in themselves for some compensation specialists. All too often, traditional pay systems seem to have been designed in response to some historical but long-forgotten situation or purpose. Questions such as 'So what does this technique do for (to) us?' 'How does this help achieve pay objectives?' and 'Why bother with this technique?' are not asked." This situation obviously has to change. Fortunately, we have seen a frenzy of activity since the mid 1980s among compensation managers, consultants, and academics to bring some fresh air into the field. A few extremists would argue that internal equity is no longer relevant or that the labor market model is moot. However, there seems to be a general realization that it is time to search for new ways of analyzing compensation phenomena by linking pay to business objectives and major contingencies facing the firm. We have kept our noses too close to the ground, and we need to develop a long-term, broader perspective of the field.

According to McCann (1987, p. 358):

> Strategic planning has such fundamental implications for the way an organization functions that many entrenched rewards and incentives will also require major change... rewards and incentives should shift over time with development toward more proactive, comprehensive, and influential strategic planning processes ... this demands more creative thinking, innovative action, and cooperative behaviors ... [but] a major barrier to improved linkages between strategic planning and rewards is the historically fragmented way management researchers have studied organizations. The split between more "micro" aspects of the organization at individual and group levels of analysis, such as compensation and personnel, and more "macro" aspects at division, total organization, and industry levels of analysis has been seriously dysfunctional.

As noted in the above quotation by McCann (1987), while the dichotomy between macro strategic processes and micro human resource activities (including compensation) is still deeply grounded in the mind of many academics and practitioners, it is ultimately misleading. It discounts the necessity for strategic thinking at the behavioral level in general and the compensation function in particular. An alternative perspective, a strategic role to compensation, holds that:

1. The pay system must operate within the organizational context of strategic decisions and be an integral part of strategy formulation.
2. Compensation plays a major role, either explicitly or by default, in strategic decision-making processes, including formal systems for planning, implementation, and controlling.
3. The specific pay policies of the firm must reflect the wishes of its major constituencies and stakeholders.

The next section of this chapter examines some of the new theoretical frameworks—other than equity theory and labor market models—that are currently being used to study compensation issues from a macro strategic perspective.

ALTERNATIVE FRAMEWORKS TO STUDY COMPENSATION ISSUES

There are several concerns about the challenges to the traditional compensation paradigm discussed earlier. The implications of these themes can be understood through a new set of emerging concepts that have growing theoretical support and also address directly the role of the compensation system in the strategy formulation process. There is a loose consensus in this new perspective about the desired nature of the compensation system in general and the compensation function in particular. Namely, they should:

1. Initiate.
2. Negotiate.
3. Manage the implementation of pay schemes with key internal groups or constituencies.
4. Search for sustainable, long-term competitive advantages.
5. Respond in a flexible and customized manner to the specific needs of the total organization and its subunits on the basis of internal and external contingency factors that mediate the success of particular compensation strategies.
6. Be leery of generalized prescriptions for the pay system based on uniform mechanistic approaches that have deflected compensation's attention from the critical issue of using pay in a discretionary manner as a source of competitive advantage.
7. Place firm performance as the ultimate criterion of success for strategic pay decisions and operational compensation programs.

Several major theoretical frameworks spanning a variety of disciplines (e.g., finance, managerial economics, organization theory, and business policy) provide insights to the strategic role of compensation in organizations. It should be noted, however, that much of this is still unexplored territory as far as compensation is concerned. Indeed, only a handful of conceptual and even fewer empirical papers are found that directly link these theories to compensation phenomena, particularly below the top executive level. Moreover, contemporary compensation texts devote little space to the subject. Typically, a brief mention is made in introductory chapters about the importance of linking organizational goals and strategies to compensation, but further development of the topic is seldom found. There is rarely any discussion of how compensation interacts with other organizational subsystems or how the compensation function may participate in the strategy formulation process. The discipline, however, is beginning to appreciate fully the explanatory power and practical value of a broader, more strategic perspective. (See Gomez-Mejia and Welbourne, 1991.)

Productive research and theory development in compensation may be enhanced in the future by greater cross-fertilization with other disciplines. This will allow compensation to transcend the traditional paradigms grounded in industrial/social psychology and labor economics to incorporate such notions as the development of systems for monitoring and incentive alignment, negotiating exchanges with internal and external coalitions, coping with environmental uncertainty, and balancing the needs and demands of multiple constituencies.

In the following section, several broad theoretical frameworks that may be and/or are currently being used to study a variety of compensation phenomena at a macro level of analysis are reviewed. Most of these will be covered in subsequent chapters as they are applied to specific areas such as executive compensation and sales compensation.

The models to be reviewed next provide a point of departure toward the formulation of a theoretical framework that would help predict the antecedents and consequences of strategic compensation choices. They were not selected because they can all be subsumed under a coherent strategic model or paradigm. Indeed, we are a long ways from reaching this stage! However, because they are relevant to compensation from a nonfunctional perspective, they hold promise for analyzing compensation issues in terms of the larger picture. They are also concerned with the interaction between lower and upper echelons within the firm, and they emphasize dynamic relationships between the firm and the external environment. They also affirm overall organizational performance implications that may be attributed at least in part to strategic compensation choices.

The Agency Perspective

The central concept of the agency perspective is that firm owners can utilize monitoring and incentive alignment mechanisms to induce managers (and their subordinates) to engage in those behaviors that will improve shareholder wealth. In a corporation improving shareholders' wealth is equivalent to increases in the price of the firm's stock. (See Copeland and Weston, 1979; Fama and Jensen, 1983; Fama and Miller, 1972.) Agency theory treats all managerial decisions as an investment. Thus, the decision to open a new plant, merge with another firm, diversify into unrelated product areas, or to adopt a new compensation plan should be assessed on the basis of its risk-adjusted net present value. Unlike the firm's economic theories, in which profit maximization is the ultimate objective, the market value rule allows for the consideration of relative risk differences among alternative managerial decisions (e.g., expanding an existing plant vis-a-vis purchasing another firm).

Because most modern corporations separate owners (in the hands of dispersed stockholders) and managers (hired to maximize shareholder wealth), an agency relationship exists. The *agency relationship* is defined by Jensen and Meckling (1976, p. 308) as a "contract under which one or more persons (the principal(s)) engage another person (the agent) to perform some service on their behalf which involves delegating some decision-making authority to the agent." In any relationship where the owner is not present "to mind the store," the agent is in a position to engage in self-serving behaviors and pursue short-run rather than long-term goals. Unconstrained discretion, potential conflict of interest, asymmetrical information between owners and managers, and the ability to shift risks into the future when present management is likely to have moved on to other firms have implications for managerial behavior that are at odds with traditional economic models. Management could actually invest in suboptimal projects at the expense of long-term profits.

As discussed in the executive compensation chapters (Chapters 6 and 7), the pay system can be deliberately used to redirect managers' and subordinates' decisions to the benefit of shareholders. In other words, compensation may become a powerful mechanism to align the interest of the agents (managers and subordinates) to those of shareholders. While owners can closely monitor managers through a board of directors and prevent managers from abusing their privileged position, a fail-proof monitoring system can never be implemented. As shown in Chapter 6, a more practical alternative from an agency perspective is to structure the managerial pay package so that managers are rewarded for maximizing the firm's present value. This is a crucial issue at the top executive level because these individuals are responsible for strategy formulation affecting the entire firm.

The Behavioral Perspective of the Firm

The behavioral theory of the firm can be traced to the early writings of Cyert and March (1963), March and Simon (1958), and Simon (1955, 1959, 1964). The *behavioral theory* views the organization as a coalition of individuals who are, in turn, members of subcoalitions. The coalition members may include managers, workers, suppliers, customers, tax collectors, regulatory agencies, stockholders, etc. As in agency theory, there is no guarantee profit maximization will occur. Dominant coalitions compromise on firm goals and are more likely to satisfice than maximize.

A quasi-resolution of conflict is used to determine the goals of the organization and the relative priority of those goals. It is entirely possible that contradictory goals are pursued by various coalitions. Thus, organizational subunits and functions typically rely on "local rationality." They deal with a limited number of goals, and there is no guarantee that consistent objectives will be pursued in different parts of the firm. In this perspective, jobs emerge as "independent constraints imposed on the organization through a process of bargaining among potential coalition members." (Cyert and March, 1963, p. 3). These objectives, and the implementation strategies to achieve them, are internally inconsistent and are subject to change over time as changes occur in the coalition structure.

As discussed in Chapter 5, the behavioral model of the firm has some important implications for compensation. Unlike the traditional compensation models reviewed earlier, this perspective suggests that organization-wide rationality, when trying to determine the contribution of various jobs to the firm, may be an elusive goal in complex organizations. Lack of perfect information, power imbalances and shifting alliances among coalitions, and the difficulties of coordinating local decisions made by decentralized departments and divisions with their own agendas will get in the way of achieving overall rationality in the pay system. *Rationality* is defined as providing monetary rewards proportionate to input (i.e. value or worth) of each job in the firm. This raises a number of crucial issues for compensation research and practice, and they are discussed next.

Access to Dominant Coalitions. The compensation function is seldom part of the dominant coalition in organizations (Cook, 1981). Therefore, it tends to have very limited influence in establishing pay policies for the firm and is often relegated to low-level administrative tasks. In many cases, it may not even have enough muscle to enforce existing rules and procedures uniformly across organizational subunits. In the words of Henderson and Risher (1987, p. 332):

> Although it would be comforting to think that compensation professionals currently provide useful and valuable insights into the strategic planning process, these opportunities are available to very few. Managers are implored to look ahead, to anticipate the future, to take action now that will soften the impact of "worst possible scenarios," to look at current practices and operations and then think "what if." ... [unfortunately] compensation is, most often, a reactive, short-run, decision-making process, and compensation strategic considerations are, most often, found only in textbooks ... just as personnel-related decisions frequently have an extremely low priority in planning for the long-term survival and health of the organization, compensation decisions have had an equally low priority within the personnel and human resources field. This means, if we are to move from a strictly tactical, support-staff mode to a strategic-oriented mode, then compensation professionals must find a way to become part of the dominant managerial coalition responsible for charting the strategic direction of the enterprise.

Role of Dominant Coalitions in Formulating Compensation Strategies. Various coalitions within the firm are likely to have different ideas as to how the compensation system should operate, and the dominant coalition will probably exert much influence on the features characterizing the compensation system at a particular point in time. For example, the dominant coalition may believe that the organization should be held together not by a system of labor contracts but by a set of common values and beliefs with an intensive socialization in them. A unitary language, shared goals, internal commitment, corporate citizenship, personal development, and adherence to norms may be viewed as essential (Kerr and Slocum, 1987; Ouchi, 1980). Hambrick and Snow (1989) cite IBM, Hewlett-Packard, J.C. Penney, and Johnson and Johnson as corporations fitting that mold. According to Kerr and Slocum (1987), the reward system associated with those firms, labeled as "clans" by Ouchi (1980), is characterized by:

1. Status differentials reinforced through an intricate system of perquisites.
2. Modest bonuses and generous offerings of stock to inculcate a sense of corporate-wide membership and fate.
3. A centrally administered reward system that uses pay as a powerful instrument of socialization and development.
4. Intensive concern for internal equity and predictability.

In contrast, the dominant coalition may believe self-interest and utilitarianism must be fostered as the key to organizational success where superiors are placed in the role of negotiators and resource allocators rather than mentors. An implicit assumption is made that the relationship between employees and the firm is purely calculative, so that either party may terminate the relationship with little remorse if a better alternative exists.

According to Hambrick and Snow (1989), this set of beliefs is prevalent in ITT, Textron, North American Phillips, and Gulf and Western. Kerr and Slocum (1987) and Hambrick and Snow (1989) argue that in this type of firm rewards are very utilitarian and self-serving, focus is placed on financial aspects, and perquisites and tenure-related entitlements are deemphasized. Bonuses, consisting mostly of cash, play a major role in line with the parties' arm's length sentiment toward each other. Stock-based programs are less prevalent because dominant coalitions do not perceive a need to foster a long-term, strong commitment to the firm. Because money is viewed as the overriding force keeping the firm and employee together, the compensation system is "explicit, unambiguous, and essentially formula based" (Hambrick and Snow, 1989, p. 36).

Locus of Control as Determinant of Compensation Structure. Influence patterns and power structure within the firm have a major impact on pay mix for managers. The greater the amount of power and leverage exercised by major stockholders vis-a-vis top executives, the more variability, downside risk, and long-term orientation of bonuses and long-term income (Tosi and Gomez-Mejia, 1989). When stock ownership is widely dispersed and an effective coalition of stockholders cannot be easily accomplished, the top executive group can influence the designers of the compensation package (consultants, board of directors, compensation officers) to minimize executive pay risk by creating pay structures that mask the relationship between pay and performance and, by inference, to the detriment of owners (McEachern, 1975). One way to restore managerial control without increasing the number of large equity holders in a firm is to reduce the involvement of management in the election of directors. Thus, the board would be independently elected and not as responsible to top-executive coalitions as they seem to be when stockholders are widely dispersed. (See Chapter 7.)

Role of Subunit Power in Job Evaluation. The results of job evaluation and future decisions made under the system may not be as impersonal and objective. The more powerful departments and units are likely to exert influence to have their jobs evaluated at a higher level (Welbourne and Gomez-Mejia, 1992). This can be done in a number of related ways such as changing job titles and inflating job descriptions, allowing incumbents to earn above the maximum range established for their present positions, or, more directly, reclassifing jobs with minimal "fuzz" from the personnel department. A strong director or department manager, historical factors, networking, and the like can make a difference in how much the unit "can get away with."

Role of Institutional Power Within Internal Labor Market. The traditional labor market models do not deal with the process by which wages are determined. For the most part, that process is assumed to be one of competitive labor market behavior. However, institutional power within the "internal labor market" of the firm can produce high occupational earnings for certain groups. Through control of entry, an increase of job specifications and required credentials, the presence of influential individuals from that group (e. g., a CEO who came from a particular functional area), and powerful unions, institutional power is gained (Fogel, 1979). Foster (1985) found that when controlling for industry, job content, company size, and performance, there is a wide variation in the pay scales for identical job families among different companies. He concludes (p. 71): "[A] question our research brings up is why companies tend to pay some job families more favorably than others. Answers are rarely documented. Experience tells us that differences can sometimes be attributed to historical internal relationships, a dominant or weak function head . . . or long-standing organizational bases. Whatever the reason, many companies clearly fall short of achieving the across-the-board competitive pay equity that their policy statements promise." In a similar vein, Hambrick and Mason (1984) present an "upper echelon" perspective of organizations. They argue that characteristics of the top management team in terms of age, functional track, career experiences, heterogeneity of group, etc., have a great effect on the design of compensation programs (e.g., complexity of incentive compensation schemes and eligibility criteria), and the pay distribution resulting among occupational groups.

The Resource Dependence Perspective

The resource dependence model takes the coalitional nature of firms as given. Pfeffer and Salancik (1978) portray organizations as fluid coalitions of interests where purpose and direction may be altered in response to changes taking place in the coalitional structure. These authors distinguish between common interest groups functioning within the firm and external coalitions. For example, a common interest group would be department heads with a similar orientation aligned with a powerful CEO. Diverse stakeholder groups such as shareholders, regulatory agencies, suppliers, and pressure groups are among external coalitions. Pfeffer and Salanick's primary focus is on the latter. Organizations are not only political systems, but they are also open systems dependent on exchanges with their environment. Pfeffer and Salancik (1978, p. 24) argue "to describe adequately the behavior of organizations requires attending to the coalitional nature of organizations and the manner in which organizations respond to pressures from the environment." The underlying rationale for their environmental emphasis is the ability of an organization to obtain resources and support from its external coalitions greatly determines its relative success or even survival. To accomplish this, the firm exchanges various inducements for contribution of resources and support from outside coalitions (Barnard, 1938; Simon, 1964). However, what various external interests may have to offer the firm are not equally valued. Thus, coalitions that offer "behaviors, resources, and capabilities that are most needed or desired by other organizational participants come to have more influence and control over the organization." (Pfeffer and Salancik, 1978, p. 27). By the same token, the more a given organizational subunit can deal with critical contingencies related to coalitional contributions, the more power and influence it will have on the organization (Crozier, 1964; Perrow, 1970). In other words, the most important subunits are those that deal with uncertainty and ensure the continued supply of valued resources, while assisting the organization to adapt readily to environmental contingencies. These issues are discussed in greater depth in Chapter 8.

In short, the resource dependence model depicts organizations as "structures of coordinated behaviors" aimed at garnering the required environmental support for survival. As in the behavioral perspective, goals and objectives still emerge by exchanges and negotiation among various internal coalitions. As next discussed, the resource dependence perspective has a number of implications for compensation theory and research.

Shifting Criteria of Worth. Valued activities and the factors used to judge their relative worth will vary among different parts of the organization. Research addressing this issue is perhaps most commonly associated with Mintzberg (1980), who developed a taxonomy of managerial roles broken down along interpersonal, informational, and decisional dimensions. Expanding on Mintzberg's work, investigators have discovered differences in managerial roles by level or function (Alexander, 1979; Kurke and Aldrich, 1979; Whitely, 1978) and by skills, knowledge, and abilities (Dreyfus and Bird, 1992; Pavett and Lau, 1983).

Gomez-Mejia, McCann, and Page (1985) found a clear specialization of managerial activities by function. Controlling and coordinating resource flows, core technology-related units (engineering, materials, production, etc.) focus on the organization's products and services and direct supervision. Other units, like product sales and marketing, play boundary roles by interacting with customers. Accounting, with its controllership function, and administration are deeply engaged in monitoring and planning. Most importantly, Gomez-Mejia, et al. also showed different managerial activities exhibit widely varied relationships with pay grades, ranging from a low negative correlation (-.21) for supervising to high positive correlations for monitoring business indicators (.74) and long-range planning (.89). This suggests that managerial activities such as planning, supervising, and coordinating are engaged in by most units, but the intensity of these and how they relate to the reward structure vary among units and organizations. Gomez-Mejia, et al. (1985) conclude: ". . . The extent and pattern of task specialization across functional units should reflect more than the task characteristics imposed by the organization's core technology. The emphasis upon specific activities within specific functional units discloses management's choices about how the organization chooses to confront environmental contingencies through its alignment of activities and deployment of resources and rewards."

Boundary Spanning and Job Evaluation. The resource dependence perspective suggests employees in boundary spanning functions and whose activities are linked to environmental factors strategically important to the organization cannot easily fit into standard job evaluation plans without negative consequences. At the least, they must be treated as special groups for pay purposes. The primary reason for this, according to Newman (1988, p. 203), "centers on the shortcomings of current job evaluation systems in identifying and attaching sufficient weight to tasks involving environmental interaction . . . compensable factors appropriate for a mature organization that has successfully shielded itself from the external environment may not be appropriate for firms dependent upon environmental decline for survival." Because it is safe to say that fewer and fewer organizations fit the classical-stable mode (even textbook examples such as AT&T and utility companies are now passe for the most part), more units are exposed to environmental turbulence than ever before. Thus, greater adaptability is required from the compensation system. (See also Montanari and Lockwood, 1992; Newman and Huselid 1992.)

Environmental Interface and Strategic Employee Groups. As an extension of the previous point, individuals who cope with environmental requirements should be viewed by management as a key strategic employee group. (See Hambrick, 1981; Roberts, 1992; Prescott and Allenby, 1993) In the high technology industry, for example, scientists and engineers are responsible for new product development and capitalizization on environmental opportunities (Wiersema and Page, 1992). These firms have developed an array of creative compensation programs for this employee group. Working with hundreds of high technology firms, Gomez-Mejia and Balkin (1985) found the typical compensation package for R & D workers is characterized by shared ownership, use of customized pay plans, and avoidance of mechanistic pay approaches (e.g., job evaluation). Also typical of these packages are few written policies or procedures as tools to control behavior, aggregate rewards to promote cooperation and team cohesiveness, and rewards to promote entrepreneurship (e.g., availability of company funds to start new projects or ventures with compensation linked to their eventual outcome). Long-term incentives to tie employees to the firm, front-end hiring bonuses, key contributor awards, frequent external equity adjustments, and professional perks (e.g., paid sabbaticals) are also included.

Ironically, these same firms have neglected the boundary spanning activities of production and marketing employees in the design of compensation programs. While the United States is a world leader in R & D, the U.S. trade deficit in high technology products has been escalating faster than in most other areas. The main reason, according to Hill, Hitt, and Hoskisson (1988), is that foreign countries focus their R & D expenditures on marketable innovations and improvements in production processes. This suggests that U.S. high technology firms should devote more attention to pay policy decisions in the production and marketing functions, which tend to be framed, often with little thought, within the traditional job evaluation system (Coombs and Gomez-Mejia, 1991).

Constituency Perspective

The constituency perspective views the major functional areas as specialists responsible for providing particular resources to the organization (Connolly, Conlon, and Deutsch, 1980). In other words, the primary objective of each function consists of ensuring an uninterrupted flow of valued resources from the environment and working with line managers to effectively allocate them. As functional areas become more specialized, they view key organization coalitions as constituencies to be both served and managed. From this vantage point, the chief responsibility of the compensation function is to satisfy the long-term needs of key coalitions.

In trying to achieve its own objectives, each functional area is constrained by the self-interest and agendas of other departments. In attempting to assume maximum satisfaction from key coalitions, the compensation function is constrained by the demands of other functional areas. For example, increasing the pay of R & D employees may reduce the financial resources necessary to maintain the support of suppliers, creditors, and perhaps some top management groups. In the constituency framework, functions jockey with each other for power and influence. The introduction of new pay plans may be interpreted by other functional areas as taking place at the expense of their own programs. Those areas that can generate crucial resources (as perceived by key coalitions) are likely to have greater power.

Tsui (1984, 1990) developed an effectiveness model that shows the HRM function, including compensation, is confronted with preferences and expectations from multiple constituencies. These may include employees, operating managers, functional or line executives, the government, the professional community, and unions. In Tsui's words (1984, p. 1988): "Each constituency has its own set of expectations regarding the personnel department's activities; each holds its own standards for effective performance; each applies its own criteria for assessing the extent to which the department's activities meets its expectations; and each attempts to prescribe preferred goals for the subunit or presents constraints to its sphere of discretion. Multiple constituencies often compete directly or indirectly for the attention and priority of the personnel department."

Because effectiveness in this view is more a political rather than a rational, scientific construct, the reputation of the HRM departments in meeting the demands of the coalitions becomes the criteria of effectiveness. This, in turn, determines its relative power and influence in the organization. Extending this line of reasoning to pay in particular, as discussed in Chapters 9 and 10, and from a constituency based perspective, the role of the compensation function reduces to two major activities. First, compensation must identify the optimal pay policy choices that will assure "client satisfaction" and support of important groups in the organization. According to Henderson and Risher (1987, p. 334): "Looking at the hundreds of compensation components available, it becomes readily apparent that the problem for the compensation manager is probably not the amount of compensation available to offer employees but rather the design of a compensation package that fits the unique demands of each employee group and individual member." Second, compensation professionals must "earn" a good reputation with top executives and managers of other functional areas before their recommendations are implemented and they can successfully compete for resources. Furthermore, the constituency perspective suggests compensation must take an active role in promoting its strategic value to the company. Demonstrating how pay programs can assist dominant coalitions in achieving their long-term goals is one strategy.   This is not an easy task, however, for the typical compensation director under the traditional functional structure because it requires an intimate knowledge of the interests, viewpoints, and desires of these groups.

Competitive Strategy Perspective

The competitive strategy perspective is most commonly associated with the work of Porter (1980, 1985, 1990). It holds that in order to survive and prosper, all organizations must cope with external competitors. The essential task of strategy formulation is to develop approaches that allow the firm to use its resources (including compensation) in such a way that it can develop and maintain a differential advantage over other firms. This differential advantage may result from knowledge base, geographical location, timing of product introduction, etc. From a compensation viewpoint, a differential advantage may be achieved if the firm can design a pay system capable of attracting and retaining a superior work force and inducing their employees to perform at their maximum capacity as compared to competitors. In the traditional systems, "ability to pay" is hypothesized to be the main predictor of wage levels, and these, in turn, determine attraction and retention of high-quality employees (Reynolds, 1951). While this is generally true, other factors are also important, according to the competitive strategy perspective. Alternative approaches to achieving a sustainable competitive advantage via the compensation system are discussed next. These issues are covered in greater depth in Chapters 4 and 5.

Developing an Adaptive Compensation System. From a competitive perspective, the pay system may be used to attain a differential advantage. Deemphasizing standardized formats for handling pay issues, viewing the world as relative and contextual rather than universal and absolute, being willing to experiment with alternative pay approaches, and promoting a futuristic rather than a tactical orientation are among the ways to attain that differential.

Operationally, adaptive thinking in compensation may be fostered in a number of ways. First, as noted earlier, payment can be molded to meet the special needs of strategic employee groups. For example, high technology firms may offer lower salaries to R & D workers in exchange for the potential to become rich in the future through equity based compensation (Gomez-Mejia and Balkin, 1985). This allows many start-up high tech firms to attract and retain younger, risk-taking employees (Gomez-Mejia and Welbourne, 1990). Likewise, the firm may develop differential pay policies that are appealing to diverse employee populations (e.g., team-based incentives for scientists and engineers versus "fast track" promotional ladders for midlevel managers).

Second, decentralized pay policies for large, diversified firms may allow each unit flexibility to compete in a particular labor market. Third, the compensation program should take into account contingency factors that may moderate its effectiveness. For example, if the nature of work requires strong cooperation (such as groups of engineers working on common projects), introduction of competitive rewards based on individual performance may prove to be highly counterproductive. Likewise, as seen in Chapter 8, if customer service is crucial to the firm's image, paying its sales force on strict commission could prove disastrous.

Finding an Ecological Niche. According to Porter (1990), firms may achieve a differential advantage by moving into areas where there are fewer competitors. This typically occurs when a firm specializes in a narrow section of the market. For example, Cray corporation specializes in supercomputers, and Coca-Cola and Pepsi-Cola are the undisputed kings in the cola market. In the case of compensation, while all firms compete in the general labor market, a company may be able to tap a labor force that is generally "left alone" by other firms and may be hired at low cost. For example, McDonalds has been very successful in hiring senior citizens to staff many of its stores. Likewise, some firms rely heavily on spouses at home to perform paperwork via computer modums. Under the maquiladora program, some American firms utilize lower paid Mexican labor in border towns for assembly work, and others hire computer programmers in India to write software. These are also examples of developing ecological niches that may give a firm a competitive advantage. (See Gomez-Mejia, Domicone, and Headrix, 1991.)

Capitalizing on the Firm's Distinctive Competence. A competitive advantage may be achieved by reinforcing the firm's idiosyncratic strengths. For example, Radio Shack and Computer-Land compete in retailing computers; Compaq and IBM produce microcomputers that offer portability capabilities. Because of the time it takes to "learn" a given industry or product market area, a firm may be able to outperform competitors by building on its current area of expertise. In the case of compensation, a firm may be able to identify a core number of employees who are crucial to maintaining its distinctive competence and target its compensation system to lead the market in that area. For example, business schools are seldom able to excel in all areas (finance, management, marketing, etc.), given the high cost of recruiting business faculty and limited university budgets. Even the wealthiest schools would have a difficult time developing a reputation for excellence across the board. A common strategy is to target certain departments to become the "flagship" of the college. With its compensation system playing a major role, the university can attract well-known academics from other universities into those departments by offering large salaries, reduced course loads, secretarial support, etc. to these individuals and by hiring the most promising assistant professors by paying above market.

Erecting Barriers to Entry. A basic tenet of industrial and organizational economics is: in the long run, competitive advantages may be temporary because other firms will try to move in and imitate the success of existing firms. Perhaps one of the best examples of this is the invasion of hundreds of small personal computer manufacturers into a market formerly controlled by IBM. However, a firm can develop strategies to discourage imitators. (See Lapides and Ottensmeyer, 1983.) Among them are: erecting barriers to entry through economies of scale; brand identification; need to invest large financial resources in unrecoverable expenditures in up-front advertising and R & D; and access to distribution channels.

Compensation can play a major role in erecting barriers to entry. This is particularly true in the knowledge intensive industries where top-level scientists and engineers may leave corporate research labs to start their own companies. Armed with venture capital and lured by the success stories of people such as Edson de Castro (who left Digital to start Data General) or Robert Noyce (former Fairchild engineer who founded Intel), they can be successful. If successful, they could become major competitors and eat away their previous employer's market share. If they fail, the firm still suffers from the loss of its most valuable human capital and could pay a heavy price in lower rates of innovation and major interruptions in the commercialization of new products. With a payout formula based on both employee longevity and firm performance, the pay system can be quite effective in preventing this from happening. To this end, an employee ownership plan that ties a portion of the individual's earnings to the firm's stock value is most frequently used. Leaving prior to a stipulated length of time (e.g., let's say four years) implies forfeiting the financial reward. This may allow the firm to hold onto scarce personnel needed to maintain a differential advantage.

While equity based compensation has been used mainly among executive ranks, a growing number of firms are extending this approach to broader layers of key employee groups where attrition may have serious implications for the firm. Science Applications International Corporation (SAIC) provides a good example of a company that relies on equity compensation to minimize the attrition of R & D employees (Gomez-Mejia, Balkin, and Milkovich, 1990). SAIC is a 20-year-old high technology firm with 200 offices and 9,000 employees throughout the United States. This company, which is one of the most profitable firms in the instrumentation and electronics industry, has been providing an extensive offering of employee stock ownership plans (ESOP) to its R & D employees during the past two decades. It also has an S & E turnover rate well below industry standards. Some of the plans R & D employees can choose from include: (a) acquiring company stock by devoting up to 10 percent of their salary, which is matched by SAIC dollar-for-dollar, (b) offerings of company stock to select R & D teams based on their contribution, and (c) allocating division managers with a pool of stock that can be distributed to individual R & D employees or teams who are deemed exceptional performers.

In short, the compensation system may be used to increase the transaction costs of an employee if he or she were to change employers, and it effectively shields the firm from pirating of its human capital by other organizations. This, in turn, represents a barrier to entry because important inputs to success in a given industry (scarce labor) are less available to potential competitors. These issues are covered in greater detail in Chapter 5.

Engaging in Proactive Moves. Successful firms need to anticipate shifts in the factors underlying competitive forces and "respond to them, with the hope of exploiting change by choosing a strategy appropriate for the very competitive balance before opponents recognize it" (Porter, 1979, p. 97). This means, successful strategies are anticipatory, not static, and always responsive to competitor's moves and future environmental changes. Some of the trends affecting compensation are examined in Chapter 10. The implication for compensation professionals is that they need to plan ahead. Environmental trends will impact the company, and they need to develop pay contingencies to help the firm cope with them. For example, in the not too near future, white males will be in the minority in the United States' labor force. Firms that can most effectively utilize the labor pool of women and minorities are likely to gain a competitive edge in the market place. Provision of such benefits as day care, maternity leave, flexible work hours, training internships, co-op programs with colleges and universities, etc. can all contribute toward this goal.

In short, compensation professionals can assist the firm to achieve and sustain a competitive advantage by:

1. Preventing future problems (e.g., loss of key personnel) by neutralizing threatening forces beforehand (e.g., brain drain to competitors).
2. Advising top-level managers and working closely with other functional heads so that strategic pay decisions reflect the best available alternatives (e.g., group based vs. individual based incentives).
3. Reducing resistance to change by instilling a strategic pay mentality among line managers (e.g., willingness to give up merit-pay prerogatives in lieu of team-based rewards).
4. Helping the organization make adjustments in its pay system in response to anticipated environmental jolts (e.g., increase variable pay to provide a financial cushion to the firm if profits decline, instead of cutting costs by laying off employees) rather than be forced to make radical changes in a reactive fashion.

PLAN FOR THIS BOOK AND OVERALL MODEL

This is not a book about compensation administration. There are no detailed discussions of the psychological and economic basis of pay as a tool to "attract, retain, and motivate" employees; the pros and cons of different techniques to achieve equity at the individual and organizational level; and the administrative operations of compensation as a subfunction within the general personnel umbrella. The reader who expects a traditional approach to the subject will be disappointed. Important as these issues may be, they are only incidental to this volume. Readers interested in pay administration concerns will find about two dozen books published since the late 1980s focusing primarily on compensation management issues (e.g., Balkin and Gomez-Mejia, 1987; Belcher and Atchison, 1987; Burgess, 1989; Gomez-Mejia, 1989; Henderson, 1989; Hills, 1987; Milkovich and Newman, 1990; Plachy, 1991; Rock and Berger, 1991; Sibson, 1991; Wallace and Fay, 1988).

This book deals with theoretical and empirical questions at a macro level of analysis concerning the interface between compensation systems, organizational strategies, and environmental forces and how their interaction affects firm performance. It draws from many disciplines, most notably accounting, finance, economics, organizational theory, and strategic management. Readers interested in a more applied treatment of compensation strategy issues with an emphasis on alternative reward approaches will find excellent sources in Lawler (1990) and Wallace (1990, 1991).

The overall conceptual model for the book is graphically summarized in Figure 1.2. As shown in the figure, the central variable of concern is firm performance, and this drives all the

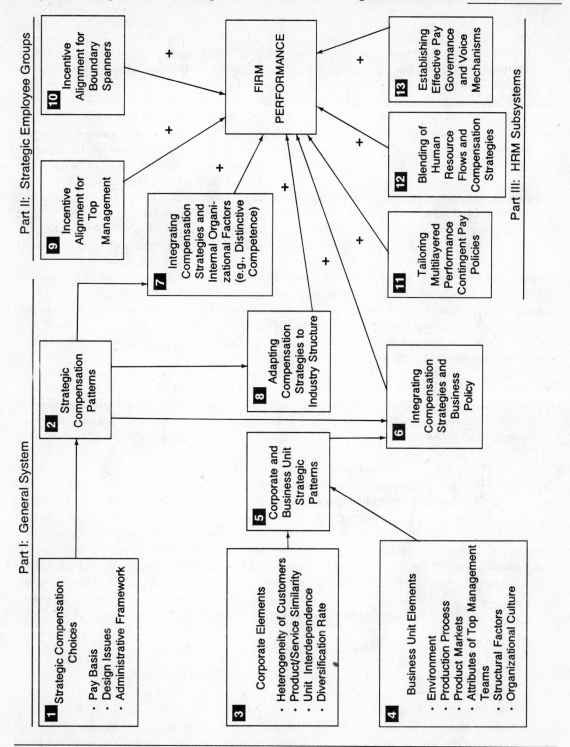

FIGURE 1-2   Overall Model Depicting Relationship Between Compensation Strategies and Firm Performance

components in the model. In other words, firm performance serves as the ultimate criterion of success for the pay system within the strategic perspective advanced here.

This book is divided into three parts, each of which deals with a separate portion of the model in Figure 1.2. The first part, which includes Chapters 2-5, develops a broad framework to explicate why firm performance is a positive function of the integration among compensation strategies, business strategies, internal organizational factors, and industry structure.

The unit of analysis in Part 1 is the firm as a holistic entity. Components 1 through 6 in this general system (see Figure 1.2) are concerned with the linkage between corporate and business unit strategies and pay strategies and their interactive impact on firm performance. Based on an extensive literature review, Chapter 2 ascertains the key strategic compensation choices facing organizations. Seventeen such choices are identified, and their contingency factors and policy implications are discussed. (See Component 1.) Chapter 3 examines the strategic pay choices introduced in Chapter 2 at a higher level of aggregation. It develops a set of composite strategic compensation patterns that tend to "hang together" (Component 2). It also discusses the key elements that underlie variations in corporate (Component 3) and business unit (Component 4) strategies and describes several well-known taxonomies used to study organizational strategies at both of those levels (Component 5). The materials in Chapter 3 serve as a conduit to examine how strategic compensation patterns relate to corporate and business unit strategies in Chapter 4 (Component 6). The central thesis of Chapter 4 is that compensation strategies (in terms of pay basis, pay package design, and administration) should be formulated and implemented in a gestalt fashion, where each substrategy (e.g., job vs. skills; short- vs. long-term orientation) represents an indivisible part of a larger comprehensive system.

Chapter 5 provides a capstone for Part 1, examining how the interactive relations of compensation strategies and organizational strategies (Component 6), the synchronization of compensation strategies and internal organizational factors (such as firm characteristics, values of dominant coalitions, distinctive competence, transaction costs, and resource availability; see Component 7), and the adaptation of compensation strategies to industry structure (Component 8) all affect firm performance.

Part 2 of the book (see Components 9 and 10 in Figure 1.2) is concerned with the role compensation strategies play in aligning the interests of strategic employee groups with those of the firm and the effect this has on firm performance. Chapters 6 and 7 (See Component 9) focus on top management groups who are seldom part of the administrative apparatus used to compensate the majority of employees and who enjoy an unprecedented amount of discretionary power to make decisions that may have major repercussions for the firm's future performance or even survival. Chapter 6 examines the theoretical and empirical foundations on the predictors and correlates of executive pay and how the incentive system for executives affects firm performance. Chapter 7 builds upon the materials presented in Chapter 6 and discusses the policy choices and implementation issues that should be considered in the strategic design of executive compensation programs. About half of the strategic compensation choices discussed in Chapter 2 are germane to top management groups (e.g., short- vs. long-term orientation) and these are covered again from an upper-echelon perspective.

Part 2 is also concerned with strategic employee groups, other than executives, who are responsible for boundary spanning activities and whose compensation program is treated as a special case distinct from that of the general work force. (See Component 10 in Figure 1.2.) Because sales personnel play a crucial and almost universal boundary spanning role in private sector organizations (being responsible for the disposal of firm output and the acquisition of financial resources), Chapter 8 devotes special attention to this group. Similar to the executive pay chapters (i.e., Chapters 6 and 7), strategic compensation choices discussed in Chapter 2 that are relevant to sales compensation (e.g, incentives vs. fixed pay) are covered within this specific context.

Part 3 of this book examines compensation strategies from a human resource management perspective. Three important areas are covered. The first (see Component 11 in Figure 1.2) concerns alternative performance contingent pay policies at different levels of analysis (i.e., individual, team, business unit, and corporate) and factors mediating their relative impact on firm performance. This is the subject of Chapter 9.

Chapter 10 in Part 3 examines those compensation strategies that are most important relative to the flow of human resources into, through, and out of the firm. These are pay level vs. market, fixed pay vs. variable pay, and job-based vs. skill-based pay. The central thesis of Chapter 10 is that strategic compensation choices made are more likely to have a positive effect on firm performance if they support the functional strategies of the HRM unit with respect to its planned flows of human resources. (See Component 12 in Figure 1.2.)

The last component (No. 13) in Figure 1.2 focuses on issues of governance and voice mechanisms related to compensation, including compliance with the external regulatory system. Chapter 11 deals with these issues at three different levels: relationship between management and individual employees, bargaining between management and organized labor, and interface between the firm and the legal framework. The primary argument in Chapter 11 is that the existence of effective governance and voice mechanisms for the compensation system may have a positive effect on firm performance by facilitating the implementation phase of pay policy decisions, reducing the possibility of concerted actions, and protecting the firm from unwanted litigation.

A total of 116 research propositions are submitted in the book. These propositions are interspaced throughout those chapters where the body of theory enables statement of explicit hypotheses. If the empirical literature has advanced to the point where some of these propositions have been tested (e.g., in the executive compensation area), the extent of support is discussed.

CHAPTER 2

STRATEGIC CHOICES IN COMPENSATION

BASIS FOR PAY
    Job vs. Skills
    Performance vs. Membership
    Individual vs. Aggregate Performance
    Short- vs. Long-Term Orientation
    Risk Aversion vs. Risk Taking
    Corporate vs. Division Performance
    External vs. Internal Equity
    Hierarchial vs. Egalitarian
    Qualitative vs. Quantitative Performance Measures

DESIGN ISSUES
    Compensation Level vs. Market
    Fixed Pay vs. Incentives
    Frequency of Rewards
    Monetary vs. Nonmonetary Rewards

ADMINISTRATIVE FRAMEWORK
    Centralization vs. Decentralization
    Open vs. Secret Pay
    Employee Participation vs. Nonparticipation
    Bureaucratic vs. Flexible Pay Policies

AGGREGATING COMPENSATION CHOICES BY BUSINESS STRATEGY:
SOME KEY ASSUMPTIONS

SUMMARY

As noted in Chapter 1, the strategic perspective on compensation is based on two underlying assumptions. First, the pay system cannot be analyzed in isolation because its effectiveness depends upon how responsive it is to internal and external forces impacting the organization and the firm's structural configuration. If the pay system is not attuned to the macro organizational context within which it operates, then, at best, important opportunities are being missed and, at worst, pay policies are counterproductive or act as an impediment to the firm's overall strategic thrust.

Second, the organization has discretion to choose among a large variety of pay policies and procedures, and each of these may have strategic implications. Even if the focus is on a narrow program such as gainsharing, there are "literally thousands of different ways to implement and structure a gainsharing plan" (Bullock and Lawler, 1984, p. 34). Each of these—e.g., participative vs. nonparticipative plans—may be appropriate for a particular situation. Bullock and Lawler (1984), Welbourne and Gomez-Mejia (1988, 1991) describe multiple contingencies affecting the relative success or failure of various gainsharing plans.

A general definition of the term compensation strategy, which flows from the above two assumptions, can be advanced. *Compensation strategy* is the deliberate utilization of the pay system as an essential integrating mechanism through which the efforts of various subunits and individuals are directed toward the achievement of an organization's strategic objectives, subject to internal and external constraints. When properly designed, contingent upon the organization's strategic objectives and constraints, it can be an important contributor to firm performance.

Consistent with this definition, each firm faces a repertoire of pay choices. The degree of success associated with each of these depends on two factors. The first is how well the alternative(s) selected enable the organization to cope better with contingencies affecting it at a given point in time. The second is the extent to which the pay choices made are synchronized with the firm's overall strategic direction.

The purpose of this chapter is to map the domain of strategic compensation decisions. Seventeen *strategic pay choices* (see Figure 2-1) are distilled from the extant literature and discussed. In turn, this material provides the foundation for much of the remainder of this book. Chapter 3 examines how these 17 strategic pay choices "hang together" in a predictable pattern. Chapter 4 analyzes the determinants of the observed compensation pattern, while Chapter 5 deals with the *so what* question in terms of firm performance implications.

While Chapters 3-5 provide a global treatment of compensation strategies at a high level of abstraction, with the entire work force and the firm as units of analysis, Chapters 6-11 are more focal in nature. Chapters 6-8 examine specific compensation choices that are pivotal to strategic employee groups whose idiosyncratic pay programs set them aside from the rest of the work force, namely executives and sales personnel. The last three chapters (9-11) zero in the HRM subsystem and the special role played by select strategic compensation choices. In other words, Chapters 3-5 are concerned with the large picture, approaching the 17 strategic compensation choices in Figure 2-1 as an interlaced tapestry of internally consistent pay decisions. Chapters 6-11 turn on the power microscope to study the antecedents and consequences of particular compensation strategies that are most important within crucial yet narrower domains.

Two points need to be addressed before the actual compensation choices are discussed. First, much of this research is unfolding and remains at a relatively early and, in some cases, speculative stage of inquiry. A skeptic may ask the question, "How do we know that these 17 pay choices are really strategic?" In truth, there is no definite answer to that question because they are not empirically derived or drawn from a tight and well-developed theoretical framework. We are simply not there yet. However, there are sufficient grounds to believe that these dimensions are useful in understanding and analyzing compensation phenomena from a strategic perspective. These 17 choices have been isolated from an extensive review of the literature on compensation strategy across a variety of related fields.

As seen in Chapter 3, these 17 choices form meaningful patterns, suggesting there is some empirical evidence of construct validity. As discussed in Chapters 4 and 5, these patterns are related in an expected manner to organizational strategies, and greater integration between the two is associated with firm performance. This provides indirect support

FIGURE 2-1   Strategic Compensation Dimensions Most Frequently Used in Literature*

	Balkin & Gomez-Mejia	Balkin & Gomez-Mejia	Berg	Broderick	Carroll	Ehrenberg & Milkovich	Gomez-Mejia & Balkin	Gerhart & Milkovich	Gomez-Mejia	Hambrick & Snow
Year	1990	1987	1973	1986	1987	1987	1989	1990	1992	1987
Type of Paper	Empirical	Empirical	Conceptual	Empirical	Conceptual	Empirical	Empirical	Empirical	Empirical	Conceptual
STRATEGIC COMPENSATION DIMENSIONS										
Basis for Pay										
Job vs. Skills	X			X					X	
Performance vs. Membership	X			X					X	X
Individual vs. Aggregate Performance	X		X		X		X		X	X
Short- vs. Long-Term Orientation	X				X	X	X	X	X	X
Risk Aversion vs. Risk Taking	X						X		X	
Corporate vs. Division Performance			X	X					X	X
Internal vs. External Equity	X				X	X			X	X
Hierarchical vs. Egalitarian	X					X			X	X
Qualitative vs. Quantitative Performance Measures			X	X	X	X	X		X	X
Design Issues										
Pay Level vs. Market	X	X	X	X	X	X	X	X	X	X
Fixed Pay vs. Incentives	X	X	X	X	X	X	X	X	X	X
Frequency of Rewards		X			X		X	X	X	X
Monetary vs. Nonmonetary Rewards									X	X
Administrative Framework										
Centralization vs. Decentralization	X		X	X		X			X	X
Open vs. Secret Pay	X			X		X			X	
Participation vs. Nonparticipation	X			X		X			X	
Bureaucratic vs. Flexible Pay Policies	X			X		X			X	X

* Updated version of a similar chart appearing in L. R. Gomez-Mejia and T. Welbourne, "Compensation Strategy: An Overview and Future Steps," *Human Resource Planning*, 3 (November 1988), 175.

FIGURE 2-1 (continued)   Strategic Compensation Dimensions Most Frequently Used in Literature

Author	Kerr	Kerr	Lawler	Lorsch & Allen	Miles & Snow	Milkovich	Murthy	Napier & Smith	Pitts	Rappaport
Year	1985	1982	1983	1973	1984	1988	1977	1987	1974	1978
Type of Paper	Empirical	Conceptual	Conceptual & Case Studies	Empirical	Case Studies	Conceptual	Empirical	Empirical	Empirical	Conceptual
STRATEGIC COMPENSATION DIMENSIONS										
Basis for Pay										
Job vs. Skills	X		X							
Performance vs. Membership	X		X			X				
Individual vs. Aggregate Performance	X	X	X							
Short- vs. Long-Term Orientation	X	X	X			X				X
Risk Aversion vs. Risk Taking			X			X				
Corporate vs. Division Performance	X	X	X	X	X	X		X		
Internal vs. External Equity			X		X	X	X			
Hierarchical vs. Egalitarian	X		X		X	X				
Qualitative vs. Quantitative Performance Measures	X	X	X	X			X	X	X	X
Design Issues										
Pay Level vs. Market			X			X				
Fixed Pay vs. Incentives	X	X	X	X	X	X	X	X	X	
Frequency of Rewards		X	X			X				X
Monetary vs. Nonmonetary Rewards			X							
Administrative Framework										
Centralization vs. Decentralization			X	X	X	X		X		
Open vs. Secret Pay			X			X				
Participation vs. Nonparticipation			X			X				
Bureaucratic vs. Flexible Pay Policies								X		

FIGURE 2-1 (continued)   Strategic Compensation Dimensions Most Frequently Used in Literature

Author	Salscheider	Salter	Schuler	Steers & Ungson	Stonich	Tichy, Fombrun, & Devanna	Tosi & Gomez-Mejia	Weber & Rynes
Year	1981	1973	1987	1984	1981	1982	1989	1991
Type of Paper	Case Studies	Case Studies	Conceptual	Conceptual	Conceptual	Case Studies	Empirical	Empirical
STRATEGIC COMPENSATION DIMENSIONS								
Basis for Pay								
Job vs. Skills								
Performance vs. Membership								
Individual vs. Aggregate Performance						X		
Short- vs. Long-Term Orientation	X	X	X	X	X		X	
Risk Aversion vs. Risk Taking		X					X	
Corporate vs. Division Performance		X						
Internal vs. External Equity			X	X				X
Hierarchical vs. Egalitarian			X					
Qualitative vs. Quantitative Performance Measures		X		X	X	X	X	
Design Issues								
Pay Level vs. Market	X		X					
Fixed Pay vs. Incentives	X	X	X	X		X	X	X
Frequency of Rewards		X		X	X			
Monetary vs. Nonmonetary Rewards				X				
Administrative Framework								
Centralization vs. Decentralization		X					X	
Open vs. Secret Pay								
Participation vs. Nonparticipation			X					
Bureaucratic vs. Flexible Pay Policies			X					

to the predictive validity of these choices. So, while some healthy skepticism is in order, these 17 dimensions are the basic analytical tools to conduct additional research on compensation strategies and to interpret much of the existing literature.

Second, each of the 17 strategic compensation choices listed in Figure 2-1 and discussed below represent two opposite poles on a continuum. In reality, as seen in Chapter 3, most firms fall somewhere between these two poles, and very few are designated as a pure type. For instance, a firm may rely on fixed pay much more than the typical firm, even though it offers some incentive compensation. None of these choices should be conceptualized and measured as mutually exclusive categories such as A vs. B. They should, however, be viewed as relative gradings. Some organizations will be closer to A; some, closer to B; others, in the middle; and a handful, at the extremes. In other words, the labels should be seen as heuristic guideposts. An organization's choice for each dimension should be interpreted as a relative positioning on the scale or the extent to which it is more similar to one end than the other. In accordance with our definition of compensation strategy, an organization has much discretion to decide deliberately where it wishes to be in terms of this continuum for each strategic compensation choice.

The 17 strategic pay choices (see Figure 2-1) are broken down into three broad categories reflecting the common themes underlying each set of choices: basis for pay, design of pay system, and administrative framework. Each of these is discussed next.

BASIS FOR PAY

The strategic pay choices listed under this category are concerned with the most salient factors or criteria used to distribute rewards. These include the following.

Job vs. Skills

Job-based pay is the approach used in traditional compensation methods where the job, rather than individual characteristics, is the unit of analysis to ascertain value to the firm. Because workers are paid depending on where their jobs fall in the structure, the wage rate generally changes only when the employee changes jobs. In skill-based pay (also known as knowledge-based pay), on the other hand, employees are paid based on the jobs they can do. That is, the abilities they have can be successfully applied to a variety of tasks and situations. The more "hats an individual can wear," the higher his or her pay. Thus, skill-based pay rewards for versatility, rather than for actual tasks performed. In the words of Tosi and Tosi (1986, p. 34), "This is a very different philosophy from the conventional approach to worker compensation . . . the worker starts out at a flat hourly rate and then receives pay increases as he or she learns how to perform a certain job better or how to perform other jobs within the plant or department. The worker gets that hourly rate regardless of his or her job assignment."

Ledford (1991), Tosi and Tosi (1986), and Wallace (1991) suggest that job-based pay works best in situations where

1. Technology is stable.
2. Jobs don't change often.
3. Employee exchanges are minimal.

4. The entire human resources philosophy stresses a hierarchical controlling orientation and longevity within the firm.

Skill-based pay, on the other hand, works best if the following conditions exist:

1. A supportive HRM philosophy characterized by mutual trust and a conviction that employees have both the ability and willingness to perform is in operation.
2. An entire array of HRM programs such as Scanlon plans, participative management, and job enrichment are in place to go along with skill-based pay. The latter has little chance to succeed as a free-standing compensation approach.
3. Technology and organizational structure experience frequent changes.
4. Employee exchanges are common.
5. Opportunities to learn new skills are present.
6. Employee turnover is relatively high.
7. Worker values are consistent with teamwork and participation. Other dimensions of skill-based pay are examined in Chapter 10.

Performance vs. Membership

When performance is used as a basis to distribute rewards, payment is provided for an individual's or group's contribution to the firm. Strict *performance-contingent compensation* delivers payment for output or outcome and most closely resembles the operation of traditional piece-rate plans or sales commissions. Because strict performance-contingent compensation is feasible and desirable only in a very limited number of situations (when meaningful output measures are readily available, when these can be unambiguously attributed to specific individuals or groups, and when interdependencies are low), modified performance-contingent plans are more practical in most cases (Mahoney, 1989). These plans include awards for cost-saving suggestions, bonuses based on behavioral performance measures (such as perfect attendance), and merit pay based on supervisory appraisals.

Membership contingent compensation, on the other hand, provides the employee a paycheck and benefits for logging a prescribed number of hours of work. This assumes at least satisfactory performance is achieved to justify keeping the person on board. This operates like a qualifying step function, with unsatisfactory employees being terminated and those who are deemed satisfactory in a given job receiving the same or a similar wage. Typically, salary progression takes place by moving up through the grades based on length of time on the job, even when "there is either no association or a negative association between experience and relative rated performance" (Medoff and Abraham, 1980, p. 703). Furthermore, different performance appraisal systems appear to have little effect on this process (Gomez-Mejia, 1988).

While most firms publicly embrace a pay-for-performance credo, sometimes with much fanfare, in practice a majority of companies primarily reward for seniority (Gomez-Mejia 1989b, 1990b; Gomez-Mejia, Page, and Tornow, 1985). For instance, a survey conducted by the Hay Group Inc. in 1986 found merit budgets for exempt employees hovered around the 6 percent mark, with the most typical spread between highest and lowest performers in the 5 to 7 percent range (Greeley and Ochsner, 1986). These investigators concluded "with only a 2 percentage point difference treatment between highly rated performers and their lower rated counterparts, it is very difficult to make a strong case for pay for performance in today's administration of pay programs" (p. 15). A similar view, expressed several years later by Jesse M. Smith (1990), president of the American Compensation Association, argued that merit pay has become an entitlement without any effective differentiation. In Smith's words, "Everyone gets it, regardless of performance" (1990, p. B8).

In general, an emphasis on performance to distribute rewards is most appropriate when the organization's culture is performance driven (Kerr, 1985), competition among individuals and groups is encouraged (Pearce, 1987), the firm is experiencing rapid growth (Balkin and Gomez-Mejia, 1987a), and relevant performance indicators are available (Mahoney, 1989). Perhaps because these conditions are not easily met, performance-contingent compensation is not always feasible. As an alternative, firms rely on job-contingent and tenure-based pay, "with a job description serving as the best available indicator of desired performance" (Mahoney, 1989, p. 10). Performance-contingent compensation policies are examined in greater detail in Chapter 9.

Individual vs. Aggregate Performance

Individual contingent rewards (e.g., merit pay) are offered based on the notion that reinforcing desired employee behaviors is important for motivational reasons. The closer the linkage between desired behaviors and rewards, the more likely the employee is to engage in those behaviors in the future (Hinkin, Podsakoff, and Schriesheim, 1987). Reinforcement theory (Cherrington, Reitz, and Scott, 1971) and expectancy theory (Graen, 1969) are most often used to justify the value of individual contingent rewards. These plans are also deeply rooted in the cultural myth that people who work harder and perform better should get more pay than those who are lazier and contribute less. They are intended to communicate clear performance expectations to each individual and give employees the opportunity to earn additional income through their own efforts. Merit pay, individual bonuses, special awards, etc., are commonly used programs designed to identify and recognize the unique contributions of each employee. (See Gerhart and Milkovich, 1993, for additional discussion of these issues.)

Aggregate pay-for-performance systems, on the other hand, use group contribution as a basis to distribute rewards. Thus, the pay off an individual receives depends on his or her and coworkers' performance. Different levels of aggregation may be used to determine how performance is to be measured. These may include team performance (e.g., project bonuses), business-unit performance (e.g., gainsharing), and corporate-wide performance (e.g., profit sharing).

Reliance on individual contingent rewards has met considerable negative reactions from both management and employees (Campbell and Barron, 1982; Lazer and Wikstrom, 1977; Pearce, 1987; Peck, 1984). To a large extent, failures in individual based pay-for-performance systems may be traced to the fact that these can work in a limited number of situations only. One or more insurmountable obstacles are often present. "Performance may prove too difficult to define or measure; desired performance may vary over time; and performance may depend on factors outside the worker's control" (Mahoney, 1989, p. 10). In general, individual based plans are more likely to be effective when performance contributions can be attributed to specific employees, competition between employees is a desired outcome, there are few interdependencies, and the plan is framed in the context of a larger set of HRM programs (e.g., supervisory training, developmental activities, work planning, etc.) (Mount, 1987; Gomez-Mejia, Page, and Tornow, 1985).

Aggregate based pay-for-performance plans are most effective under the following conditions. (See review by Gomez-Mejia and Balkin, 1989.)

1. When the socio-technical system within the firm fosters a cooperative structure. In the words of Pearce (1987, p. 187), "Aggregate incentive plans are based on the assumption that the greater the uncertainty, interdependence, and complexity of organizational work, the greater the cooperation among employees required for successful performance and that individual performance-based pay can provide powerful disincentives for cooperation."

2. When the nature of the tasks per se does not allow clear identification of individual contributions. Aggregate incentive plans are easier to implement because individual contributions do not have to be singled. They do not require unrealistic distinctions among employees.

3. When greater flexibility is desired. Typically, aggregate incentive systems offer greater flexibility in closely timing the reward to actual task accomplishment or in making pay contingent on specific targets or jobs. Unlike the most commonly used individual contingent reward (i.e., merit pay), aggregate incentives are not limited to a fixed fiscal budget and are given on a one-time only basis to reward specific achievements.

4. When the task is difficult or unique and the employees are intrinsically motivated. Free-riding is less likely to occur under these circumstances. Otherwise, (because aggregate plans provide financial rewards to multiple contributors based on the achievement of common goals), group incentives may be vitiated by free riders or individuals who provide low work inputs and receive the same reward as other group members.

Short- vs. Long-Term Orientation

Short- vs. long-term orientation strategic pay choice has fueled much controversy and is discussed at length in Chapters 6 and 7 on executive compensation. The central issue is the time horizon used to measure performance and distribute rewards. Reinforcement theory and operant conditioning suggest that the closer the reward is provided to actual behavior, the greater its motivational impact (Hammer, 1974). For most people, delayed rewards are less powerful in energizing behavior than is more immediate reinforcement. On the other hand, an organization's success depends more heavily on what happens in the long run than in the near term. This would call for a reward system based on an extended time horizon.

The dilemma noted in the previous paragraph would not be problematic if the long-term success of the firm is the simple composite of short-term successes. Unfortunately, what may improve the bottom line in the short run (e.g., laying off employees as a cost-cutting measure) may prove to be highly detrimental in the long run (e.g., reduced employee loyalty). So, organizations face an important strategic choice as to the length of time used to measure performance for pay purposes, which could range from daily (as in some piece-rate systems) to yearly (as in the case of merit pay and cash bonuses) to periods extending five years or more as in some equity-based plans. This decision may have some serious implications as to what employees, particularly executives in powerful positions, will maximize.

One of the major challenges when making strategic compensation choices is to develop effective means of leading the charge toward a long-term perspective. Because of U.S. cultural forces that emphasize a short-term orientation and interfirm mobility, it has been difficult in the past to reorient employees and managers toward rewards contingent on long-term performance (Fombrun, 1984; Gomez-Mejia and Welbourne, 1991). In addition, short-term performance is easier to quantify, and executives are often reluctant to commit to long-term goals because they appear risky and rather nebulous (Gomez-Mejia and Welbourne, 1988). A survey conducted by Spencer and Associates in December, 1989, found that twice as many companies have short-term incentive plans as compared to long-term incentives plans (reported in *CompFlash*, 1989). Furthermore, this same survey reports that the emphasis on short-term incentives among all management levels appears to be growing.

Carroll (1987) and others argue that firms with business strategies designed to maintain existing market share are more likely to have objective data that can be readily used to reward short-term performance at different levels in the organizational hierarchy. Firms that are undergoing fast growth and aggressively expanding their market share often do not have reliable objective performance data on hand. Thus, they emphasize long-term performance based on subjective assessments.

Risk Aversion vs. Risk Taking

An important strategic pay choice is whether to reward or punish employees' risk-taking behavior. Stonich (1981) suggests that Japanese workers are more willing to make risky decisions and engage in innovative, entrepreneurial endeavors *within* their firms because they are less concerned with the potential negative effect of these activities on job security. Greater job security allows managers to take calculated risks without worrying about the consequences of their business decisions on continued employment and income. Some U.S. firms allow individuals to undertake risky projects and ensure them a job. 3M, for instance, is a "no-layoff" company that has special funds to encourage new ventures and links rewards to the eventual outcome of such projects. (Gomez-Mejia, Balkin, and Milkovich, 1990.) However, this is the exception.

In general, high growth U.S. companies reward risk taking (although job security is seldom the norm), while established firms with a stable market share encourage risk aversion (Gomez-Mejia and Welbourne, 1988). Younger, risk-taking employees gravitate toward high growth companies with greater opportunities for career advancement and financial gains. This, in turn, supports the entrepreneurial climate desired by these firms. Mature firms, on the other hand, are content with their current technology and products and are likely to discourage behaviors that deviate from standard operating procedures. Unlike growing firms, however, they provide more job security.

Corporate vs. Division Performance

As discussed in future chapters, one of the main concerns in the empirical research on compensation strategy is the level of aggregation used to measure firm performance. This is particularly important when designing pay packages for top-level executives, but it is also a crucial issue in such aggregate incentive systems as gainsharing and profit sharing.

The highest level of aggregation is *corporate performance*, which refers to the entire organization regardless of the number of industries in which it competes or its size. For instance, a conglomerate may be operating in such diverse areas as tourism, manufacturing, and retailing. Thus, corporate level performance would correspond to the performance indicators for the whole complex firm as a single entity. *Business unit* or *division performance*, on the other hand, refers to "that level in an organization at which responsibility for the formulation of a multifunctional strategy for a single industry or product market area is determined. . . . Thus, for a multiindustry company, the business level normally would correspond to the divisional level" (Hofer, 1975, p. 124). In a single-product line company, the business and corporate level would be the same.

The level of aggregation used to measure firm performance for pay purposes has strategic relevance in a number of ways:

1. The larger and more diverse the company, the more difficult it is for top executives to evaluate the performance of various business units. This may prompt the firm to rely exclusively on objective performance indicators for each unit (e.g., return on assets). This may have some serious drawbacks as will be discussed later.

2. The longer the distance between individual inputs and the level at which performance is assessed, the more tenuous the perceived effect of employees' personal contributions on aggregate performance and rewards based upon it. Thus, the motivational effect of an incentive system tends to be diluted as the performance level becomes more aggregate.

3. The more interdependent the various units of the firm are, the more difficult it is to identify the contributions of a given unit. For instance, it would be demoralizing to workers and managers if their unit's performance is low, thereby affecting their pay. However, this may be attributed to other units that "did not come through" (e.g., suppliers, sales).

4. When utilizing only division performance as a measuring rod to distribute rewards, the corporation loses synergy. It may have less influence over its business units than desired and looses control as to how pay should be allocated. At the other extreme, relying strictly on corporate performance allows some divisional managers and employees to receive undeserved rewards.

5. It may be important for a corporation to use the headquarter's staff as an integrative force involved in decisions affecting corporate performance. Costs can be reduced by centralizing functions under one umbrella. In these conditions, division performance is not totally under the control of divisional managers since it reflects the contributions of corporate involvement.

6. Because product knowledge of employees is unique at each location, the corporation may be unable to transfer employees between headquarters and the division.

Firms that have narrow and relatively stable product market domains and are vertically integrated base pay on corporate performance (Gomez-Mejia and Welbourne, 1988). Because corporate staff is involved in decisions impacting division performance, performance assessment among all divisions should reflect the effectiveness of corporate role. In other words, financial indicators of performance for each unit partly reflect headquarter's contributions. Because division performance is only partially the responsibility of divisional managers, it should not be used exclusively to distribute rewards among them.

According to Kerr (1985), Leontiades (1980), and others, division performance is the appropriate unit of analysis for pay purposes among firms that expand through acquisitions. Acquired firms remain relatively independent of the acquirer, and division performance is a more meaningful indicator of unique contributions to overall corporate wealth. Reliance on division performance also enhances an entrepreneurial climate within each unit and prevents managers accustomed to autonomy from moving into other firms when a takeover occurs.   Another reason for using division performance for these firms is that the product knowledge of employees is unique at each location.   Therefore, the corporation is not concerned with transferring employees between headquarters and the division.

External vs. Internal Equity

This compensation strategy dimension concerns the extent to which the organization places more emphasis on meeting market prices for labor, *external equity*, than maintaining consistency in the pay structure, *internal equity*. Quite often these two objectives are at odds with each other.   For example, internal equity dictates that assistant professors in business administration be paid less than associate or full professors who have a longer publication record and more seniority.   However, because salaries of assistant professors have skyrocketed during the past ten years, many business schools have opted for matching or exceeding market rates when recruiting at this level.   However, the pay of senior faculty already on board has increased at a modest pace.   The end result of this policy is *pay compression* and in many instances *pay inversion*.   Since the late 1970s, the pay ratio between assistant and associate ranks has narrowed by over 60 percent and between untenured and tenured faculty by more than 31 percent (Gomez-Mejia and Balkin, 1988).

During the period 1982-1989, the mean salary offered to new doctorates in business exceeded that of practicing assistant professors by five percent and narrowly missed the average for associate professors.   In accounting and finance, new doctorates earned five percent more on average than associate professors during 1989-1990.   During the same academic year (1989-1990), salaries offered to new doctorates increased 25 percent faster than the average increase for present business faculty.   (See *AACSB Newsline*, 1990.)   In newly emerging research schools in the West and South, freshly degreed business PhDs earn more than senior professors who have been in the system for ten years or more (Gomez-Mejia and Balkin, 1992).   Similar inequities may be found in engineering and technical professions (Cascio, 1990; Kail, 1987).

The issue of external vs. internal equity has strategic relevance for a number of reasons.   First, employers must balance the desire to be fair to current employees with the need to cope with going rates in the labor market to recruit high-quality employees (Bergmann and Hills, 1987).   Also, the employer may make a "triage" decision.   That is, it must decide which employee group's pay will be adjusted upward to keep up with external rates and which one will be allowed to lag the market based on its relative importance to the firm (Newman, 1988).   Ideally, of course, all jobs should be paid at or above market, but this is seldom feasible given cost constraints.   Second, as discussed in Chapter 10, the traditional, lockstep compensation system based on job evaluation gives a high priority to pay relationships within the firm.   Unfortunately, these systems often have difficulty adjusting to a rapidly changing economic environment.

Thus, firms often find themselves caught in a dilemma.   They either emphasize consistency and predictability, using job evaluation at the expense of maneuverability, or utilize a flexible-adaptive approach that provides managers with the ability to respond to market jolts yet face the risk of an anarchical pay structure that leads to increased costs and lower employee loyalty (Carroll, 1988).   In this regard, it is interesting to note the empirical findings of Weber and Rynes (1991).   While firms that emphasize internal equity place less weight on market survey data than those that emphasize external equity,

The former did not place more emphasis on job evaluation. Put another way, internally oriented respondents were distinguished more by their reluctance to act on market data...than by any tendency to place greater emphasis on job evaluation per se. The reluctance of internally oriented managers to cut pay when market rates were lower than their firm's current rates resulted in their paying more on the average than externally oriented managers. This result suggests that having an internal orientation may be an expensive proposition if it prevents a firm from taking advantage of lower competitive rates in an external market (1991, p. 107).

The extent to which divisions are autonomous or dependent may make a difference on the relative emphasis placed on external vs. internal equity. If autonomous, external equity is the main concern. The opposite would be true for dependent divisions (Gomez-Mejia and Welbourne, 1988). The more linkages, interactions, and interdependencies exist among various units, the more important it is to maintain internal pay consistency. Employees' frame of reference transcends the boundaries of any particular unit. If there is minimal interface among various units, then each is less restricted by a concern for consistency and more free to pursue its own market policy.

Hierarchical vs. Egalitarian

The hierarchical vs. egalitarian strategic pay dimension concerns the extent to which the firm allows a wide cross-section of the work force to partake in the same reward system or if a differential reward structure is established by organizational level and/or employee group. For example, the number of management levels eligible to receive bonuses or long-term income may range from the CEO exclusively in some firms down to line supervisors in other companies. Some firms develop elaborate pay incentives for specific employee groups (such as R & D), while others make these accessible to all employees.

The strategic importance of this issue is attributed to a number of factors. First, if pay and perquisites are closely linked to upward mobility, this tends to produce a traditional organizational hierarchy based on a pecking order. Employees develop a corresponding expectation as to what it takes to succeed in the organization. While performance may play a role in this process, time on the job is frequently the main predictor of upward mobility (Lawler, 1989; Medoff and Abraham, 1980; Ronan and Organt, 1973). If the firm instead deemphasizes the traditional differentials between job grades, allows individuals to increase earnings without moving into management, and minimizes status-related perquisites, an egalitarian atmosphere is more likely to emerge. This, in turn, can influence the organization's culture. According to Hambrick and Snow (1989) and Kerr and Slocum (1987, p. 10), the hierarchical pay structure engenders a "clan" type culture. "An organization is held together not so much by a system of labor contracts as by a set of common values and beliefs and intense socialization into those values and beliefs." An *egalitarian pay system*, on the other hand, produces more of a "market" type culture. The relationship between firm and individual is strictly contractual, and there is less expectation of a long-term commitment. A second strategic implication of this pay policy choice is that use of an egalitarian approach may allow companies to deploy the work force into new areas, projects, or positions without changes in formal grade levels. However, this may be done at the expense of a stable work force (Milkovich, 1988).

A *hierarchical pay structure* is more prevalent among mature firms that focus efforts on harvesting current market share and are satisfied with their existing profit levels (Gomez-Mejia and Welbourne, 1988). At the opposite end, companies that aggressively try to expand their market share, are willing to take risks, and heavily invest in new ventures and product areas are more likely to follow a more egalitarian pay pattern.

Qualitative vs. Quantitative Performance Measures

As seen in Figure 2-1, next to the short/long-term issue, the qualitative vs. quantitative strategic pay choice receives the most attention. The central concern here is the extent to which criteria used to reward employees, particularly executives, is derived from an objective, outcome-oriented, formula-based process or, alternatively, is based on subjective assessments, inferential judgments, or other qualitative strategic, political, and organizational factors.

A relatively large body of literature has evolved around the question of how much influence the degree of corporate diversification has on the use of quantitative vs. qualitative measures of performance. It pertains mostly to managerial pay. (This literature is reviewed in greater detail in Chapters 4 and 5.) The purported relationship is: As the corporate portfolio expands, the more dissimilar the business units become. Corporate executives are less able to control effectively diverse business units because they can't understand and accurately interpret idiosyncratic data unique to each unit. As a result, highly diversified companies rely on objective, formula-based, quantitative indicators of performance (such as market share and return on investment) for pay purposes. Requiring very little subjective judgment or interpretation on corporate executives' part, pay is comparable among subunits. Low diversity is associated with superior knowledge of business units' operation. Corporate management is, thus, more likely to make judgment decisions and formulate performance expectations based on many factors (e.g., changes in environmental conditions, product characteristics) as opposed to relying exclusively on quantitative formulas. In the words of Frederickson, Hambrick, and Baumrin (1988, p. 257), the performance judgment for each business unit of a less diversified firm may be shaped by "beliefs about what constitutes good performance, an awareness of other firm's performance levels, beliefs about the severity of particular organizational problems or symptoms, and attributions regarding top management's ability to alter the firm's performance."

As empirical evidence strongly suggests, more diversified firms do generally rely on output controls, while less diversified companies rely on behavioral and process controls. Berg (1969, 1973) reported that in conglomerates, corporate control was carried out by linking rewards of division managers to quantitative financial measures of their units. Very little discretion was exercised by corporate executives in passing judgments as to how well the individual was actually managing the division. Apart from whether corporate executives could make meaningful judgments about businesses of which they may know little, Berg reported another rationale for relying on quantitative results. By not making executives of acquired divisions dependent on corporate headquarters, independence and entrepreneurship are fostered. Berg also implied this serves to retain managers, who are used to high autonomy, in the acquired businesses.

Lorsch and Allen (1973) examined compensation practices of two conglomerates and one vertically integrated firm. They noted several important differences. Conglomerates relied almost exclusively on financial results and formula-based approaches to distribute rewards among division managers. Vertically integrated firms, on the other hand, associated a division manager's compensation with the performance of the entire corporation and used the superiors' subjective evaluation process to arrive at bonus amounts. Bonuses involved inferential assessments and judgment calls not tied to predetermined indices.

Pitts (1974, 1976) found similar results to those of Lorsch and Allen. Firms that had grown through aggressive acquisition of unrelated businesses were more likely to rely on objective, formula-based approaches to reward division managers. He contrasted these to firms that had diversified slowly through internal expansion. Among the latter group, the corporation's performance was also considered when calculating the division manager's bonus. The process was largely subjective and involved significant interaction between the division manager and corporate executives.

A more recent sample of 22 firms by Kerr (1985) indicates diversification also plays a major role in whether a firm uses objective vs. subjective procedures to determine pay. Firms that grow by increased penetration of existing markets or by diversifying into closely related markets rely on subjective evaluations. Top executives have had a chance to absorb changes slowly and learn the way different units operate. A benefit of this approach, according to Kerr (1985, p. 251), is that "the practice of cross-fertilization and the emphasis on corporate rather than individual performance promotes a systemic perspective in managers ... requiring careful consideration of interdependencies and system-wide consequences of decisions."

In short, the above studies suggest that as diversification increases

1. Quantitative indices are used to appraise managerial performance.
2. Objective formulas are used to determine pay allocation to various units.
3. Performance measures are more likely based on subunit performance rather than on corporate results. Furthermore, the process of diversification also has an effect on how much a firm relies on subjective vs. objective formulas.

Napier and Smith (1987) reported some data that disagreed with those of other researchers. This data showed that less diversified firms use more objective pay criteria for payment of managers. According to Milkovich, (1988), the discrepancy may be explained by the fact that earlier studies focused on business unit general managers only, whereas Napier and Smith (1987) focused on a more heterogeneous group of corporate level managers. In any case, the preponderance of evidence to date suggests that diversification and the use of objective data go hand in hand. Apparently, this is not always true.

At the business unit level, firms that are aggressive in exploring new market opportunities and those at an early developmental stage should rely on subjective performance measures. Firms not sharing those characteristics should emphasize objective performance criteria to distribute rewards (Carroll, 1987; Kerr, 1982). Two reasons are given for this recommendation. First, a subjective assessment process of performance is more appropriate when managers are expected to act as entrepreneurs. Quantifiable performance measures are difficult to find for this group, are very gross, such as "meeting business plan on schedule," and generally not very meaningful. Therefore, subjective judgments are more appropriate. Second, for mature firms trying to maintain secure positions in relatively stable product or service areas, objective data is more readily available, particularly for publicly traded companies where stock price may be used as a barometer of market performance (Fama and Jensen, 1983). In addition, the performance of these firms is less susceptible to dramatic fluctuations, and more predictable formula-based compensation packages may be implemented.

DESIGN ISSUES

The next subset of compensation strategy dimensions concerns the design choices facing the firm when assembling the compensation package. Choices of market positioning, pay mix, reinforcement schedules, and the relative emphasis placed on monetary vs. nonmonetary rewards are each discussed.

Compensation Level vs. Market

The compensation level vs. market dimension refers to the extent to which the firm's total compensation package, including salary, incentives, and benefits, exceeds that of its competition. This is a critical strategic pay choice for many reasons.

First, compensation level is by far the main determinant of pay satisfaction, which is, in turn, one of the best predictors of employee attrition (Lawler, 1981; Gomez-Mejia, 1985; Gomez-Mejia and Balkin, 1984; Ronan and Organt, 1973; Weiner, 1980). Likewise, pay level is one of the most important factors potential recruits consider when selecting alternative employment opportunities (Rynes, 1987). Thus, the amount of total compensation received by employees relative to other opportunities they may have has a clear effect on attraction and retention.

Second, a firm may choose to lead the market across the board or for highly targeted employee groups only. The former is likely to enhance a firm's ability to recruit new hires and to reduce attrition throughout the entire organization. It can also create a climate where employees feel part of an elite group. "Blue chip" companies such as 3M, IBM, and Procter & Gamble are well-known for following this strategy. On the other hand, the organization may deliberately decide to be clearly ahead of the competition in total pay for some employee groups and be at or below market for others. This is an important strategic decision that explicitly recognizes the importance of certain groups, even if it discriminates against others.

For example, smaller, high technology organizations heavily channel their pay dollars toward R & D employees and drain resources from other employee groups such as production and marketing (Coombs and Gomez-Mejia, 1991). Likewise, as noted earlier, some universities may decide to pay substantially above market for certain faculty groups, while barely meeting the minimum pay requirements to attract and retain mediocre faculty in other areas. So, presumably those employee groups that can make a greater contribution to the organization's "core technology" or mission may be singled for favorable treatment under this policy. Pay level and its relationship to human resource inflows is examined in greater detail in Chapter 10.

Third, and related to the previous issue, organizations entering periods of decline are obviously concerned with labor costs. In this situation, organizations usually slow down the rate of pay increases or, worse, seek pay concessions. This may work in the short run as a cost-saving device for "internal employees that are partially sheltered from the vagaries of the external market ... this may be tolerated if for no other reason than ignorance of the market rate" (Newman, 1988, p. 199). According to Newman (1988), declining organizations must place an extreme value upon high-quality monitoring of the environment. "Consequently, reward systems designed for these groups must be particularly attuned to, and competitive with, external market wages" (Newman, 1988, p. 205).

Fourth, pay level should be associated with the level of risk, although two contending forces may be at work here. The more aggressive firms, those which continually search new product and market opportunities, require employees to take more risks. Therefore, high base pay relative to competitors should be offered those employees to compensate for the higher risks incurred (Carroll, 1987). On the other hand, growing firms making riskier business decisions may offer a lower base salary relative to the market and (as will be discussed below) offer greater incentives in pay mix to minimize fixed costs incurred at this stage (Balkin and Gomez-Mejia, 1987a, 1990).

Fixed Pay vs. Incentives

Fixed pay vs. incentives is another compensation strategy dimension that has recently received much attention in the literature. Organizations face a choice between paying employees the same amount on a predictable basis (e.g., monthly paycheck) or providing a substantial portion of an employee's income on a variable basis. The latter choice is pegged to ups and downs of preestablished performance criteria. Variable compensation comes in a wide variety of forms such as individual bonuses, team bonuses, gainsharing, profit sharing, and literally hundreds of stock ownership programs. Based on a sample of 16,000 managers across 200 firms, Gerhart and Milkovich (1990, p. 664) report that "organizations tend to distinguish themselves through decisions about pay contingency or variability rather than through decisions about the level of base pay."

As will be seen in Chapter 6, much of this concern is in the area of executive compensation. At the top executive rank, providing only half of the individual's compensation on a salary basis is not unusual. The remainder usually comes in the form of bonuses and long-term income intended to tie the executive's personal fortune to that of stockholders. Likewise, as discussed in Chapter 8, heavy reliance on variable pay is common in sales jobs where commissions are used in lieu of direct supervision. In recent years, however, risk sharing has been extended to a broader set of employee groups, particularly when the payoff of their work to the firm is uncertain, direct supervision is ineffective, and work outcomes are long-term. Reliance on variable compensation for R & D employees, for example, serves to key their attention on the development of commercial applications rather than pure research per se, and used to strengthen R & D team cooperation through the generous dispensing of team-based bonuses (Welbourne and Gomez-Mejia, 1991). Tenure-related, long-term incentives are also heavily utilized in the high technology industry to bond valuable scientists and engineers to the firm (Gomez-Mejia, Balkin, and Milkovich, 1990; Milkovich, Gerhart, and Hannon 1991). In Chapter 9, the major types of performance-contingent pay policies are reviewed and critiqued.

The risk sharing concept in compensation has also been applied organization-wide and not simply to targeted groups such as sales and executives. This is a function of the firm's life cycle and strategies. Firms facing financial constraints, such as companies supported by venture capital, try to improve their position in the relevant labor market by influencing employees' perception of *future* income stream (Gomez-Mejia, Balkin, and Welbourne, 1990). If successful in creating those *anticipatory* feelings on employees' part, the company may recruit and retain high-talent employees without tying up the firm's scarce cash (Gomez-Mejia and Balkin, 1985). For instance, employees may be willing to work for a fledgling firm at very low wages because they have faith that if the business succeeds, they could become millionaires. Business failures far outstrip successes, but such optimism may be enough, particularly among younger employees, to delay immediate gratification in hopes of high long-term returns.

In other words, firms that are hungry for cash while expanding their market share prefer to offer low salaries but add to the incentive component of the pay mix. This gives them more flexibility to shift resources into growth areas and keep the lid on fixed expenses. In turn, employees are willing to accept higher risks if these are perceived to be associated with opportunities for larger incomes. Stable firms operating in a mature market offer employees more security and a higher salary plus benefits but lower probabilities of earning large incentives via bonuses or equity sharing (Balkin and Gomez-Mejia, 1984, 1986, 1990; Salscheider, 1981).

Frequency of Rewards

This pay strategy dimension refers to the reinforcement schedule used by organizations to distribute rewards. Each firm faces a choice as to how often rewards should be distributed and how chronologically close they should be to desired behaviors (e.g., meeting agreed-upon deadlines). The choices derive from the traditional reinforcement perspective. To promote desired behaviors, rewards should be closely tied to actual accomplishments. Further, the schedule of reinforcement has a profound effect on how long a newly learned behavior persists before it regresses to former behavior patterns during periods when rewards are unavailable (such as when budgets are cut).

At an individual level, the frequency and magnitude of reinforcement and whether it is variable or continuous is less important from a motivational standpoint than rewards contingent on the achievement of specific goals (Frisch and Dickinson, 1990; Latham and Dossett, 1978). This literature suggests that noncontingent rewards have little effect on an individual's behavior. The drawback inherent with contingent rewards, however, is that individuals may be tempted to maximize goals that will trigger the rewards but ignore other important aspects of the job (Mahoney, 1989).

At a more macro level, use of continuous, interval reinforcement schedules such as Christmas bonuses and merit pay raises encourage a short-term perspective, while a variable, interval reinforcement schedule based on deferred compensation may foster a long-term orientation (Carroll, 1987; Kerr, 1982). Whether this is good or bad may depend on the firm's strategy. There is disagreement as to whether continuous reinforcement schedules should be used by firms with a high need for cost efficiency and a number of unstable tasks (Gomez-Mejia and Welbourne, 1988). This confusion reflects different opinions about whether short- or long-term goals are most relevant for each of these types of firms (Note: Empirical research here is almost nil.)

Monetary vs. Nonmonetary Rewards

There is a large volume of research dating back to the 1800s as to whether monetary or nonmonetary rewards are more important to employees. (See review by Opsahl and

Dunnette, 1966.) As its name implies, *monetary rewards* involve a tangible cash or benefit payment to employees such as merit pay adjustments, annual bonuses, employee stock ownership plans, etc. *Nonmonetary rewards* are of an intangible nature such as employment security, recognition, employee involvement in decision making, increased responsibility, etc.

Typically, employees do not rate pay as one of the most important aspects of their jobs. For two primary reasons, there has never been a clear understanding as to what this means to organizations. First, because avarice is a social taboo, there is a social desirability bias in employee responses to pay issues. Therefore, according to Seidman and Skancke (1989, p. 10), "Many employee surveys seem to indicate that money alone is not the best motivator, but it may rank higher than people care to admit to others—or to themselves. In practice, it appears that good old-fashioned cash is as effective as any reward that has yet been invented."

Second, since Biblical times, much debate has taken place about the role of money as a motivator. Most HRM practitioners and scholars alike agree that the way pay dollars are allocated sends a powerful message to all organizational members as to what the firm deems important and the types of activities it encourages. Furthermore, people do those things they perceive will lead to a valued reward. This is just as true for the top executive as it is for the lowest paid worker. Thus, the distinction between monetary and nonmonetary rewards, while obvious at face value, may not hold under close scrutiny. Pay has a deep psychological and symbolic meaning that goes well beyond its purely materialistic value.

Yet, even with the above caveats in mind, most organizations do have some choices as to how much emphasis is placed on purely calculative, utilitarian rewards versus a work environment that is interesting, challenging, developmental, and conducive to a moral commitment to the firm. For example, Amway is well-known for its heavy reliance on monetary incentives while Xerox and Texas Instruments have a long-standing reputation for providing intrinsic rewards through employee participation programs and job enrichment (even though they also use performance-based pay incentives). Lawler (1983) argues that a firm can acquire a competitive edge if it can provide both financial and intrinsic (e.g., achievement, recognition) rewards to employees. Gomez-Mejia and Balkin (1985) and Balkin and Gomez-Mejia (1985) admit pride in one's work, career advancement, and self-actualization are important rewards. However, "the pot at the end of the rainbow" is a very powerful lure to attract quality employees and keep them highly committed to a particular company. This is particularly true in tight labor markets such as those faced by high technology firms (Masters et al., 1992; Milkovich, Gerhart and Hannon, 1991).

Hambrick and Snow (1989) argue that the relative emphasis on monetary vs. nonmonetary rewards should depend on certain organizational characteristics. According to them, firms that seldom make major adjustments in their technology, structure, or methods of operation should make a concerted attempt to infuse intrinsic rewards whenever possible. The rationale given is that achievement-oriented employees demand excitement, recognition, and responsibility in their jobs. However, there is little glamour associated with this type of firm. Organizations undergoing frequent changes and expansion, researching product and market innovation, and utilizing multiple technologies generally provide those intrinsic rewards because of the very nature of the business. This means, according to Hambrick and Snow, that those firms do not have to devote as much attention to work designs that offer intrinsic rewards to attract and retain achievement-oriented employees.

ADMINISTRATIVE FRAMEWORK

The last set of compensation strategy dimensions concerns the organization's policies and procedures that govern the pay system. The administrative apparatus is strategically important for two major reasons. First, it provides the context within which compensation decisions are made. If the mechanisms used to distribute rewards conflict with the criteria used for payment or the design of the compensation package, then the effectiveness of the pay system suffers. For example, egalitarian rewards may be more effective in a more decentralized, open, participative system than it is in a highly centralized, secretive, nonparticipative system.

Second, and building on the previous point, the administrative framework does not exist in isolation from the organization's strategy or environmental forces impacting the firm. The delivery mechanism for the reward system must be designed to facilitate the implementation of a firm's strategy. It must also assist the firm to cope with forces in its external environment. Third, how the pay system is administered plays a major role in the level of pay satisfaction, and this, in turn, directly affects employee turnover. For example, Dyer and Theriault (1976) found that inclusion of administration variables in a regression equation more than doubled the explained variance of pay satisfaction over the variance explained by including a large number of factors such as salary level, job inputs, and perceived job difficulty. Similar results were reported by Weiner (1980). Administrative variables most relevant to compensation strategy are discussed next. These issues are covered again in greater depth in Chapters 4 and 5.

Centralization vs. Decentralization

Centralization vs. decentralization refers to the degree to which pay decisions and approval procedures are tightly controlled by corporate headquarters or delegated to various plants, divisions, and other subunits within the firm. Lawler (1983) argues that when headquarters can provide expertise not available to subunits and when internal equity is an important organizational goal, centralized pay makes the most sense. Miles and Snow (1984) make a similar argument and suggest that centralized pay should be implemented under two conditions.

First, if substantial savings and economies of scale can be realized, pay decisions should be centralized. For example, corporate headquarters can hire a full-fledged compensation department with specialists in job evaluation, salary survey, and benefits. Duplicating these services in various subunits would be prohibitive and inefficient. Second, when the organization is in a sensitive position regarding legislative requirements, administration demands a highly centralized compensation function. This may happen, for example, if an increased number of suits are being brought against the company under Title VII. Also, in situations such as in Ontario, Canada, employers must comply with very restrictive rules demanding much paperwork under a sweeping comparable worth legislation passed by the province (Pay Equity Commission, 1988).

Carroll (1987) and Balkin and Gomez-Mejia, (1990) note some additional conditions under which centralized pay may be more appropriate. One condition is firms attempting to protect their market share and business units and trying to retain their market position while minimizing costs. Companies following these objectives create a greater bureaucracy as part of their control function, particularly for compensation, which represents on average more than fifty percent of total costs.

On the other hand, decentralized pay works better under some conditions (Gomez-Mejia and Welbourne, 1988). First are large conglomerates where strategic business units (SBUs) are very heterogeneous in terms of their mission, products, work force, life cycle, and markets. Because of limited knowledge of local conditions, corporate headquarters cannot make good decisions about pay decisions. As an extreme example, California's college system established a fixed pay scale for faculty by rank during the 1970s and 1980s. While this did not have much effect on the low market areas (e.g., the liberal arts), it became a major problem for the high market areas (e.g., business administration) characterized by high demand and a national shortage of qualified faculty. California colleges resorted to strange practices such as granting full professor status to freshly degreed PhDs in business to recruit new faculty (Gomez-Mejia and Balkin, 1987).

One model that has worked reasonably well in many organizations is a local operating compensation function. It assists unit managers in making pay decisions and program implementation, and the compensation staff at corporate headquarters act as consultants to all the business units. The local unit compensation managers have access to headquarters' expertise, yet they retain the autonomy to make decisions suitable to local conditions.

A second condition favoring decentralized pay consists of entrepreneurial, single-product firms that invest in risky ventures. These firms are characterized by informal pay policies, and many compensation contracts are one of a kind deals with individual employees (Gomez-Mejia, Balkin, and Welbourne, 1990).

Open vs. Secret Pay

There is a relatively large literature, most of it appearing in the late 1960s and early 1970s, revolving around the question of how much pay information should be divulged to employees. Some of this research is reviewed in Chapter 11 within the context of pay system governance.

Clearly, organizations vary significantly on how much employees know about co-workers' pay. At one extreme, some firms require all employees to sign an oath, under penalty of termination, that they will not divulge their pay to other employees. At the other extreme, as the case of most public universities, some organizations make pay information widely available and even publish individual pay data in employee newspapers. The best-known advocate of open pay systems is Edward Lawler (1965, 1983, 1990) who for years has been arguing for greater emloyee access to compensation information. His rationale is that, number one, keeping pay a secret does the organization no good. Employees overestimate the pay of co-workers and superiors, and this leads to greater pay dissatisfaction. Number two, he argues, pay secrecy engenders low trust and more dependent employees. According to Lawler, when pay is made public, greater pressure is on management to administer the compensation system more fairly and effectively because its flaws cannot be hidden under a shroud of secrecy.

Limited empirical evidence to date suggests that Lawler's assertions may be true in some situations. However, open pay is not for everyone. Balkin and Gomez-Mejia (1990) report that, based on a survey of a large sample of compensation managers, open pay systems function better in organizations with a culture that emphasizes employee participation and involvement, trust, strong employee commitment, and egalitarianism. The rationale for these findings is that open pay can only lead to constructive dialogue and mutual respect if the organizational context is supportive of and breeds a nurturing, caring employee relations climate. Otherwise, open pay can actually exacerbate hostilities and conflicts and add fuel to an already volatile situation.

Participation vs. Nonparticipation

Much has been said about the value of employee participation in organizations, and compensation is no exception. Firms have a great deal of discretion as to how much participation employees are allowed in setting pay policies and distributing rewards. This topic is discussed at length in Chapter 11. So, only the essential issues are covered here.

Several compensation programs are based on the assumption that getting employees involved and rewarding employee suggestions that may improve current methods of operation ultimately enhances firm performance. Most gainsharing programs, for example, are centered on employee participation and make extensive use of employee committees to generate ideas and suggestions (Welbourne and Gomez-Mejia, 1988). Some team-based incentive systems and profit-sharing plans also rely heavily on inputs from employee committees to distribute rewards (Gomez-Mejia and Balkin, 1989; Welbourne and Gomez-Mejia, 1991).

Despite much lip service paid to the value of employee participation among academics and practitioners alike, a "top down" approach to pay administration is quite typical. This is particularly true among the vast majority of firms that rely on traditional job evaluation procedures. Management chooses the specific job evaluation system (usually with the help of an external consultant), the compensable factors, methods to link job evaluation results to market data, pay policies, etc. Likewise, most compensation and pay grievance committees are normally appointed by management.

Gomez-Mejia (1992) found that (as reported by compensation managers) greater employee input is more common in:

1. Entrepreneurial firms.
2. Companies with a large proportion of highly educated professional employees.
3. Companies that have faced sudden environmental jolts. For example, some computer firms have lost substantial market share in a short time period.
4. Firms that offer a large proportion of an employee's pay on a variable basis.
5. Companies that are willing to implement innovative reward schemes.

Low employee participation, on the other hand, fits the traditional bureaucratic compensation approach used by most mature firms.

Bureaucratic vs. Flexible Pay Policies

Bureaucratic vs. flexible pay is a crucial strategic decision when designing the administrative apparatus of any pay system. It reflects how tolerant administration is of alternative approaches, the amount of discretion it allows to create exceptions, and the ability it has to make unique judgments depending on the idiosyncrasies of the situation.

Organizations vary widely on this dimension. For example, Gomez-Mejia, Balkin, and Welbourne (1990) found that in many start-up firms, the pay package of managers and other professionals is often decided by entrepreneurs and venture capitalists while they socialize at informal settings and react to their "instincts" or "gut feelings." At the other extreme, in many civil-service jurisdictions, an employee's pay is based strictly on job grade, and promotional decisions through the grade hierarchy are made based on scores in a written test and seniority (Gomez-Mejia, 1978). Similarly, some labor contracts are highly regimented, and time on the job is the main determinant of career progression within the firm.

In some cases, managers have a great deal of flexibility in making some pay decisions but very little in others. This creates an interesting dynamics. For example, college deans have much freedom in deciding how much to offer outside applicants. However, deans have very limited discretion in allocating pay among existing faculty. This generally contributes to a severe pay compression problem and attrition of superior faculty. The primary way for a faculty member to improve substantially his or her pay is to move onto other institutions. In fact, Gomez-Mejia and Balkin (1992) found that on average, over a 20-year-period, the "future value" of each move to an individual faculty member exceeded $40,000. This is far superior to any merit pay adjustments received during this same period by the faculty member if he or she were to stay at the same institution.

Bureaucratic pay systems have met severe criticism in recent years. They prevent managers from making decisions that are most appropriate in a given situation, and they do not allow the organization to adapt the compensation system as the firm's strategic orientation changes (Lawler, 1986, 1990). Balkin and Gomez-Mejia (1990) found that this criticism is clearly justified for entrepreneurial and rapidly growing firms. However, the situation is not as clear-cut in more established organizations. As firms get larger, more mature and complex, and more entrenched in a given market niche, their natural tendency is to "rationalize" pay decisions by developing procedural mechanisms to systematize pay allocations. For these firms, too much flexibility, ad hoc decisions, and frequent modifications to the pay system can result in a lack of coherent policies. Also, because organizations have long memories, it is difficult to make those changes smoothly without the system itself loosing continuity and credibility (Hambrick and Snow, 1989). The challenge for these firms is to develop systems that are formalized yet flexible enough to allow modifications when necessary.

AGGREGATING COMPENSATION CHOICES BY BUSINESS STRATEGY: SOME KEY ASSUMPTIONS

The most common approach in the compensation literature is to adopt one of the taxonomies from strategic management and then attempt to delineate a compensation strategy profile that seems to characterize firms within each of the organizational strategy categories. Authors generally provide a list of pay choices representing an "ideal" compensation type for each strategic grouping (e.g., Broderick, 1986; Fay, 1987). There are several important assumptions implicit in most of this work that should be pointed out before moving on to Chapter 3 (which describes several typologies relevant to strategic compensation choices).

First, it is generally assumed that organizational strategies are causal antecedents to compensation strategies. Thus, the latter, along with other functional strategies, should flow directly from the firm's overall strategy. In the words of Fay (1987, pp. 119-1201), "Strategic compensation planning is a derived process, in that its starting point is based on overall organizational goals and objectives. . . . this is because compensation is a tool, and tools rarely are ends in themselves." A similar view is advanced by Milkovich and Newman (1990) and Milkovich and Broderick (1991). Second, as noted earlier, it is possible to find meaningful patterns in a stream of compensation decisions, even if these emerged over time through trial and error.

Third, the observed pay patterns that may have evolved historically are not necessarily the most appropriate ones given the organization's overall strategies. Current ways of allocating pay and existing compensation policies may be well entrenched, yet these could still be separated from organizational strategies. For example, as noted by Gomez-Mejia, Balkin, and Milkovich (1990), many firms rely on job evaluation procedures for R&D workers, even though "this may foster competition, artificial barriers among people, fragmentation, and an individualistic climate in the work force. These behaviors and culture often run counter to successful R&D environments. A successful R&D operation often requires intense team effort, integration of activities across many individuals, fluid tasks, exchange of knowledge, and minimal status barriers to facilitate interaction among multidisciplinary scientists and engineers working on common problems."

A common reason for separation has been alluded to earlier. Compensation professionals are seldom in the strategy making group of the organization and are not often regarded as fully participating members of the executive team. Compensation practices are often based on custom, imitation from other firms, administrative convenience, and ad hoc programs developed through narrow functional lenses (Coombs and Rosse, 1992). As a result, the firm may not fully adapt its compensation strategies to organizational strategies, and there may be a tendency to maintain the status quo in the pay system despite significant changes in business strategy and environmental conditions.

Fourth, as discussed in Chapter 5, a notion borrowed from organization theory and the strategy literature is that the effectiveness of the pay system and its contributions to firm performance depend on the cohesion between organizational and compensation strategies. Several normative terms are frequently used interchangeably in the literature to denote the degree of alignment between the two. These terms include "congruency," "consistency," "match," "fit," and the like (e.g., Berger, 1991; Burack, 1988; Devanna, Fombrum and Tichy, 1981; Rothwell and Kazanas, 1989; Schuler, 1987; Tichy, 1983). In the words of Milkovich (1988), "The degree of fit between compensation strategy and organization strategy contributes to firm performance by signaling and rewarding those behaviors that are consistent with the organization's objectives." This goodness of fit premise, derived from contingency approaches to the study of organizations, means that "there is no best way to organize" (Tosi, Rizzo, and Carroll, 1990, p. 15) and "effectiveness at realizing intended strategies depends significantly on the existence of a match between strategies and organization" (Gupta and Govindarajan, 1984, p. 27).

SUMMARY

This chapter has examined the 17 strategic pay choices that have received the most attention in the literature. The choices made for each of these should be attuned to the organization's overall strategic objectives and contingencies affecting the firm. Another central theme throughout this chapter is that each of these dimensions cannot be studied in isolation. They must be viewed in the context of a larger framework where different strategic pay choices interact with each other as well as with organizational and environmental forces. While each of the strategic pay choices has been introduced individually in this chapter for the sake of clarity in presentation, these rarely occur as independent entities but form strategic groupings or patterns. These composite pay patterns, in turn, are related to organizational strategies that are themselves aggregations of many complex, interactive, individual strategic decisions. The following chapter examines the composite strategic pay patterns emerging from dimensions discussed here and the taxonomies of corporate and business unit strategies most frequently used to study an organization's strategic orientation. Chapter 4, in turn, shows how the strategic pay patterns relate to the corporate and business unit strategic groupings. Chapter 5 explores the consequences of these linkages for subsequent firm performance. Lastly, Chapters 6-11 discuss those strategic pay choices that are most important to strategic employee groups and HRM subsystems.

Note that in future chapters, mostly in the second half of the book dealing with more focused issues, the term "pay policy" or "pay policy choice" is sometimes used. This term is meant to denote a concrete, operational version of the more abstract notion of strategic compensation choice or dimension. For instance, merit pay vs. individual bonuses is a pay policy choice; the emphasis on performance vs. seniority represents a strategic compensation choice. Thus, the pay policy decisions discussed in this book come under the aegis of one or more of the 17 broader strategic compensation dimensions introduced in this chapter.

PATTERNS OF COMPENSATION AND ORGANIZATIONAL STRATEGIES

                Growth Stage
                Mature Stage

SUMMARY

APPENDIX

The previous chapter examined the key strategic pay choices organizations can choose, as well as the contingency factors and policy implications of those choices. The central thesis of this chapter is that firms seldom make these choices one at a time. Pay choices are an interrelated set of decisions evolving into common patterns or themes. Likewise, the organizational strategies driving these pay choices also form strategic groupings.

Creating and using generic compensation and organizational strategies in both research and practice take several related forms. First, generic strategies capture the essential commonalities of individual, situation-specific strategies and enhance our understanding of broader strategic patterns. Second, they provide a basis for making systemic decisions that are internally consistent yet comprehensive in nature. They may be used to allocate resources and formulate pay policies among diverse subsidiaries and divisions in complex organizations, as well as within a given business unit. Third, taxonomic efforts may be of value to practitioners by reducing a large number of variables to a manageable model of the situation, which reduces any unwarranted variability of strategic actions. Fourth, in addition to simplifying the vast array of variables a researcher must consider, a typology has the advantage of providing gestalt. That is, each type within a taxonomy reflects a holistic combination of interacting attributes.

Following this vein of thought, this chapter examines strategic pay choices and organizational strategies at a higher level of aggregation. First, the overall strategic compensation patterns resulting from the intercorrelation of the pay choices presented in Chapter 2 are discussed. Next, the major taxonomies used to classify firms into strategic groupings are described. This material provides a foundation to examine how the strategic pay patterns described here vary as a function of firms' strategic groupings (Chapter 4) and how their interaction, in turn, affects firm performance (Chapter 5).

STRATEGIC COMPENSATION PATTERNS

Strategic pay choices seldom occur in isolation; rather, they tend to form meaningful clusters or patterns. This means firms choose multiple pay strategies that are internally consistent. Two separate analyses, one heuristic (Gomez-Mejia and Welbourne, 1988) and one empirical (Gomez-Mejia, 1992), strongly suggest that pay choices evolve into two distinct patterns. Furthermore, firms that adopt a particular compensation strategy within each of these patterns also make other related pay choices germane to that pattern.

The first study, Gomez-Mejia and Welbourne (1988), reviewed 18 different papers during a 15-year period (1973-1988) on compensation strategy issues. By subjectively recording and sorting compensation strategy dimensions postulated by various authors, they were able to extract two underlying patterns. The first one, labeled "mechanistic," "reflects formalized rules and procedures that routinize pay decisions and are applied uniformly across the entire organization" (p. 181). The second pattern, labeled "organic," consists of "pay practices that are more responsive to varying conditions, contingencies, and individual situations" (p. 183).

A more powerful statistical study by Gomez-Mejia (1992) used actual data from 243 firms on their pay choices, which were based on managerial responses to a battery of 48 items.   (Note: See Appendix 3A following this chapter for additional information on measures and sample used. This study will be reviewed again in Chapters 4 and 5.)   A factor analysis of that data again suggested that two major strategic compensation patterns emerged. These two patterns, labeled "experiential" and "algorithmic," are profiled in Table 3-1. Table 3-2 shows the subscales defining each of the compensation strategy dimensions and the factors on which they correlate.

TABLE 3-1
Summary Profile of Experiential and Algorithmic Compensation Patterns

Basis for Pay	Compensation Strategy*	
	Algorithmic	**Experiential**
Unit of analysis	Job	Skills
Criteria for pay increases	Tenure	Performance
Level of performance measurement	Individual	Individual and aggregate
Time orientation	Short-term	Long-term
Risk sharing	Low	High
Strategic focus	Corporate	Division and business unit
Equity concern	Internal consistency	Market driven
Reward distribution	Hierarchical	Egalitarian
Type of control	Monitor of behaviors	Monitor of outcomes
Design Issues		
Salary market policy	Above market pay	Below market pay
Benefits market policy	Above market benefits	Below market benefits
Incentives in pay mix	Low	High
Total compensation	Low future potential with higher immediate payoffs	High future potential with lower immediate payoff
Reinforcement schedule	Fewer rewards with low frequency	Multiple rewards with high frequency
Reward emphasis	Nonmonetary	Pecuniary
Administrative Framework		
Decision making	Centralized pay	Decentralized pay
Pay disclosure	Low	High
Governance structure	Authoritarian	Participative
Nature of pay policies	Bureaucratic	Flexible
Superior dependency	High	Low

*Based on the research of Gomez-Mejia (1992).

TABLE 3-2
Compensation Elements Associated with the Algorithmic and Experiential Pay Patterns*

Basis for Pay	Strategic Compensation Pattern
Jobs vs. Skills	
Firm uses a job-based pay system. That is, factors within the job are key determinants of the amount of pay.	Algorithmic
Company relies on a skill-based pay system. That is, individuals are rewarded in part on their mastery of job skills.	Experiential
The job is a more important factor than an incumbent's ability or performance in the determination of pay rates. Heavy emphasis is placed on job evaluation procedures to determine pay levels.	Algorithmic
Performance Emphasis	
Firm has a strong commitment to distribute rewards based upon contributions to organization.	Experiential
There is a large pay spread between low performers and high performers in a given job.	Experiential
An employee's seniority plays an important role in pay decisions.	Algorithmic
Individual vs. Aggregate Performance	
Individual appraisals are used almost exclusively with little variance in performance ratings.	Algorithmic
Interdependencies are seldom taken into account when making decisions about an individual's pay.	Algorithmic
Short- vs. Long-Term Orientation	
The pay system has a futuristic orientation. It focuses employee's attention on long-term (two or more years) goals.	Experiential
The pay system rewards employees for short-term accomplishments during a fixed time period.	Algorithmic
Risk Sharing	
A portion of an employee's earnings is contingent on achievement of group or organization performance goals.	Experiential
Compensation system is designed so that a significant proportion of total labor costs is variable in nature.	Experiential
Firm strongly believes that employees should be risk takers with some of their pay.	Experiential
Corporate vs. Business Unit Performance	
Corporate performance is used as criteria for pay decisions concerning top management and aggregate incentive programs (e.g. gainsharing, profit sharing) for employees.	Algorithmic
Division or business unit performance is used as criterion to reward executives and determine aggregate incentive dollars for employers.	Experiential

*Based on the research of Gomez-Mejia (1992).

TABLE 3-2 (Continued)
Compensation Elements Associated with the
Algorithmic and Experiential Pay Patterns

Internal Consistency in Pay Relationships vs. Market Forces

Internal pay equity is an important goal of the pay system.	Algorithmic
The firm tries hard to achieve comparable pay relationships across different parts of the organization.	Algorithmic
The firm gives a higher priority to internal pay equity than to external market factors.	Algorithmic

Emphasis on Hierarchy and Status Differentials

The compensation system reflects a low degree of hierarchy. In other words, firm offers a minimum of perks (reserved parking spots, first-class air travel, etc.) to top executives.	Experiential
Firm offers special pay packages and privileges as status symbols to the higher echelons in the organization.	Algorithmic
Firm tries to make pay system as egalitarian as possible. There are very few special rewards available to any "elite" groups of employees.	Experiential

Quantitative vs. Qualitative Performance Resources

Firm relies heavily on objective performance measures (e.g. earnings per share, return on investment) as a basis for top executive pay and aggregate incentive programs (e.g. gainsharing, profit sharing).	Experiential
Firm relies on subjective evaluations to monitor subordinates.	Experiential

Design Issues

Pay Policy Relative to Market

Preferred position of organization's salary levels with respect to competitors is clearly above market.	Algorithmic
Preferred position of organization's benefits level with respect to competitors is clearly above market.	Algorithmic

Role of Salary and Benefits in Total Pay Mix

Base salary is an important part of the total compensation package.	Algorithmic
Base salary is high relative to other forms of pay that an employee may receive in the organization.	Algorithmic
Benefits are an important part of total package.	Algorithmic
Employees' benefits package is very generous compared to what it could be.	Algorithmic

Role of Pay Incentives in Total Pay Mix

Pay incentives such as a bonus or profit sharing are an important part of the compensation strategy in this organization.	Experiential
Pay incentives are designed to provide a significant amount of an employee's total earnings in this organization.	Experiential

TABLE 3-2 (Continued)
Compensation Elements Associated with the
Algorithmic and Experiential Pay Patterns

Design Issues	Strategic Compensation Pattern

Frequency of Rewards

Bonuses are provided often; frequency of bonuses is viewed at least as important as their magnitude.	Experiential
Organization provides a variety of deferred compensation plans in addition to bonuses.	Experiential
Firm relies on annual pay raises, which may include both a merit and a cost-of-living component.	Algorithmic

Reliance on Pecuniary vs. NonMonetary Rewards

Firm tries hard to meet the psychological needs of employees by offering intrinsic rewards through such means as job enrichment and quality of work life programs. Monetary rewards are underemphasized.	Algorithmic
While intrinsic aspects of the job are not ignored, firm clearly uses pecuniary rewards as a crucial part of its human rewards strategy.	Experiential

Administrative Framework

Autonomy vs. Centralization

Pay policy is applied uniformly across all organizational units.	Algorithmic
The personnel staff in each business unit has freedom to develop its own compensation programs.	Experiential
There is a minimum of interference from corporate headquarters with respect to pay decisions made by line managers.	Experiential

Pay Disclosure vs. Secrecy

Firm keeps pay information secret from employees.	Algorithmic
Firm has formal policies that discourage employees from divulging their pay to co-workers.	Algorithmic
Firm does not openly disclose the administrative procedures on how pay levels and pay raises are established.	Algorithmic

Participative vs. Authoritarian Pay System Design

Employees' feelings and preferences for various pay forms (e.g. bonus vs. profit sharing) are taken very seriously by top management.	Experiential
Many different kinds of employees (individual contributors, managers, personnel staff, executives) have a say in pay policies.	Experiential
Pay decisions are made on an autocratic basis. Firms tend to "follow the book" very closely. Very few employees have any input to pay decisions.	Algorithmic

TABLE 3-2 (Continued)
Compensation Elements Associated with the
Algorithmic and Experiential Pay Patterns

Administrative Framework	Strategic Compensation Pattern
Bureaucratic vs. Flexible Policies	
Pay system is highly regimented with procedures carefully defined.	Algorithmic
Compensation structure is very complex yet changes very slowly.	Algorithmic
While general rules exist, many pay decisions are one of a kind with considerable discretion on a case by case basis.	Experiential

Algorithmic Pay Pattern

The first pattern in Table 3-1 is designated "algorithmic" because the main emphasis is on the use of predetermined, standardized, repetitive procedures that can be used to process pay decisions with minimal attention to mitigating circumstances, exceptions to the rule, and external contingency factors. The key distinguishing features of the algorithmic pay pattern are:

1. Heavy reliance on traditional job evaluation procedures.
2. Seniority as an important criterion in pay adjustments.
3. A short-term performance orientation with appraisals conducted at the individual, rather than group, level.
4. Minimal risk sharing between employees and the firm.
5. A corporate strategic focus with an emphasis on internal equity and hierarchical position as the basis to distribute rewards.
6. Monitoring of behaviors rather than outcomes.
7. Heavy reliance on base salary and benefits in the pay mix with minimal variable compensation.
8. Above market pay with high job security.
9. More bureaucratic, formalized pay policies.

Several corollaries revolve around the characteristics listed above. The *algorithmic pay pattern* is associated with low emphasis on deferred income with the pay of top executives linked to corporate performance indicators. Because of a "lead market" salary policy and tenure-related compensation, employees find it difficult to obtain a comparable pay package elsewhere and spend many years with the firm. Upward mobility through a narrowly defined grade structure is encouraged as a means for employees to increase their income within the "internal labor market." This creates an organizational climate that promotes commitment and discourages employee attrition. Relative position in the vertical structure is the best predictor of an employee's pay, and the immediate supervisor serves as a gatekeeper in promotion decisions through the annual appraisal reviews. Because behaviors, rather that outcomes, are measured in the appraisal process, superiors exercise much judgment and subjectivity in assessing the performance of subordinates. This means that the reward system encourages high dependence on superiors with a top-down decision-making structure. Paradoxically, even though subordinates' performance is frequently measured by supervisors and the variance in performance ratings is quite low, tenure, along with its associated income and perquisites, is nonetheless the main factor explaining position in the hierarchy. The administrative framework is highly centralized, pay secrecy is enforced, employee participation is not encouraged, and compensation policies and procedures are carefully defined.

Experiential Pay Pattern

The second pattern empirically derived in the Gomez-Mejia (1992) study, and profiled in Table 3-1, may be designated "experiential" because the firm's compensation strategies are flexible and adaptive. Thus, these strategies can be molded to respond to changing circumstances, factors mediating their effectiveness, sudden environmental shifts, and idiosyncratic situations.

The algorithmic and experiential compensation patterns have opposite orientations. The experiential pattern emphasizes:

1. Skills and personal attributes, rather than job evaluation procedures focusing on work tasks, as a basis for pay determination.
2. Demonstrated performance, rather than tenure, as a basis for pay progression.
3. Performance assessments at multiple levels, including individual, team, business unit, and corporate levels.
4. Multiyear considerations in the distribution of rewards, particularly for top-level managers.
5. Extensive risk sharing between employees and the firm.
6. A greater emphasis on assessing division performance, rather than overall corporate performance, for firms with several business units.
7. More sensitivity to the market, rather than internal equity concerns, in setting pay levels.
8. Deemphasis of hierarchical structures in favor of more egalitarian pay schemes.
9. Greater reliance on outcomes, rather than supervisory judgments, of performance for divisional managers, resulting in less dependence on corporate superiors.
10. Lower pay relative to the market ("follow market" policy) yet offers an attractive pay package. The package incorporates substantial incentives and premiums on top of fixed salary and benefits and makes greater use of deferred income, in addition to cash incentives for a broad cross-section of employees.
11. Multiple rewards given on a frequent and sometimes unpredictable intervals. Money is used explicitly as a mechanism to influence employees' behavior and creates a calculative, utilitarian employment relationship.

The administrative framework of the *experiential pay pattern* is decentralized, and lower organizational levels and local units have much discretion in allocating compensation dollars. There is little trepidation about making pay open and sometimes using these public displays to motivate other individuals in the organization to work harder toward the achievement of strategic goals. There is greater solicitation of employee inputs, and pay policies are flexible and can change, depending on situational factors rather than simply following rules of the book.

Relative Measure of Pay Patterns

The algorithmic and experiential pay patterns described above are two poles on a continuum, and most organizations fall somewhere between them. The factor analytic technique used by Gomez-Mejia (1992) to identify these two major patterns also allowed a calculation of the extent to which a particular firm is more or less algorithmic or experiential *relative* to other firms. An *interval*, rather than a categorical, *measure of compensation patterns* was calculated by Gomez-Mejia (1992).

First, by adding the scores of all items defining that dimension, a composite score was created for each of the strategic pay choice dimensions. The dimensions and items are

TABLE 3-3
Correlation (Positive or Negative) Between Each Strategic Pay Choice and Overall Compensation Strategy Factor*

	Correlation (Loading) with Overall Compensation Strategy Factor**
Basis for Pay	
Job, rather than skill emphasis	–
Performance, rather than tenure, emphasis	+
Individual and aggregate incentives	+
Long-term orientation	+
Risk sharing	+
Emphasis on corporate performance	–
Emphasis on internal consistency	–
Emphasis on hierarchy	–
Monitor of behaviors, rather than outcomes	–
Design Issues	
Above market pay	–
Above market benefits	–
Emphasis on incentives, rather than fixed pay	+
High frequency of rewards	+
Reliance on pecuniary, rather than nonmonetary, rewards	+
Administrative Framework	
High autonomy	+
High pay openness	+
Emphasis on participation	+
Bureaucratic pay policies	–
Superior dependence	–

* Based on the research of Gomez-Mejia (1992).
** Negative signs correspond to an algorithmic orientation; positive signs, to an experiential orientation.

listed in Table 3-2. For example, the "Pay Policy Relative to Market" dimension is calculated by adding the responses to the following two items: "Preferred position of
organization's salary levels with respect to competition is clearly above market" and "Preferred position of organization's benefits level with respect to competitors is clearly above
market." Second, the composite scores of all the strategic pay choice dimensions were factor analyzed, and one statistically significant factor emerged. Some of the strategic pay choice
dimensions showed a high positive correlation (technically referred to as *factor loading*) with
that one factor, while others showed a high negative correlation with that same factor. Those
dimensions with positive correlations (i.e., positive loadings) are characteristic of the experiential pattern (e.g., performance emphasis, risk sharing, pay incentives), while those dimensions with negative correlations (i.e., negative loadings) correspond to the algorithmic pattern (e.g., above market pay policy, high salary and benefits in total pay mix, an emphasis
on job rather than skills). Table 3-3 shows the direction of the loadings (positive or negative) for each strategic pay choice on the overall compensation strategy factor. Third, by
multiplying the standardized value of each strategic pay choice score by its respective loading, either positive or negative, on the factor and summing across all the multiplicative terms,
a total factor score was calculated for each firm. Mathematically, this is represented as follows:

Overall Compensation Strategy = (Strategic Pay Choice 1 X Loading)

+ (Strategic Pay Choice 2 X Loading) . . . +

(Strategic Pay Choice *n* X Loading)

The end result of the above calculations is that each firm obtains a total compensation strategy score. The firm's total score is the sum of each of the pay choice dimensions
multiplied by its respective factor loading. The higher the total score, the more experiential the firm's pay policies are relative to other firms. Vice versa, the lower the total score,
the more algorithmic the firm's pay policies are relative to other companies.

Table 3-4 shows the resulting distribution of 243 firms in Gomez-Mejia's (1992) sample.
This is based on the total compensation strategy score, which was calculated according to
the procedures described above. The results reported in Table 3-4 indicate that firms can
fall somewhere between the two poles in their compensation strategies with many different
gradients in between. Some firms are closer to the algorithmic end of the continuum (those
with low scores); others, near the experiential end (those with high scores). As seen in the
next chapter, a firm's relative standing on that continuum depends in part on its business
strategies.

While, in general, the strategic pay choices made by a firm are consistent or hung
together, this is not always the case. In some situations, this may be deliberate. Specific
conditions affecting the firm may call for algorithmic strategies in some cases; experiential
strategies, in others. For instance, a high technology firm may use an experiential pay pattern for its R&D work force yet adopt a highly algorithmic pay strategy for manufacturing
workers (Coombs and Gomez-Mejia, 1991). As seen in Chapter 5, however, the failure of a
firm's compensation strategies can often be attributed to the fact that its strategic pay choices
work at cross-purposes, which neutralize their overall effectiveness. For example, a firm may
be trying to foster a long-term orientation, an egalitarian climate, and risk taking among
R&D workers through the development of an aggregate incentive system. But if this is done

TABLE 3-4
Distribution of Firms Along the Algorithmic-
Experiential Compensation Strategy Continua*

Score Ranges (z scores)	Number of Firms	Percent
-1.65 to -1.34	14	6.3
-1.35 to -1.05	25	11.0
-1.04 to - .74	8	3.6
- .73 to - .43	11	5.0
- .42 to - .13	57	25.8
- .12 to + .18	32	14.5
+ .19 to + .49	11	5.0
+ .50 to + .80	5	2.3
+ .81 to +1.11	22	9.1
+1.12 to +1.42	26	11.8
+1.43 to +1.73	10	4.5

*Based on the research of Gomez-Mejia (1992). These ranges are in the form of standardized (z) scores. The more negative the score, the more algorithmic the compensation strategy, and vice versa, the more positive the score, the more experiential the compensation strategy. Not all firms in the sample are shown because of missing data.

side by side with an elaborate job evaluation plan that rewards R&D employees according to position in the grade structure, the end results are likely to be disappointing (Gomez-Mejia, Balkin, and Milkovich, 1990).

ORGANIZATIONAL STRATEGIES

Early theorists portrayed strategy as a situational art in which top executives would develop a comprehensive plan of action idiosyncratic to the organization. Much of the development was presumed to be done through "gut feeling." That is, consideration would be given to the types of activities appropriate to environmental opportunities and threats, internal strengths and weaknesses of the firm, and managerial values (Andrews, 1971; Chandler, 1962). The "old" field of business policy relied heavily on case studies. It assumed that each situation is different and that detailed scenario descriptions would help students arrive at a gestalt feel of the situation and develop their own unique approaches to the problem. Firm strategy was primarily viewed as an adaptation mechanism, cogently discussed only relative to competitors' strategies and myriads of characteristics and nuances unique to the organization.

The modern view of strategy began to emerge in the 1970s as an attempt to develop normative models and theories that could generalize across broad classes of situations and, therefore, serve to guide future research. This new approach began to question early assumptions that firm strategies were so unique to a given situation that no general models or propositions could be developed. Typical of the emergence of other scientific fields, strategic management (which by most accounts is less than 30 years old) has placed a great emphasis on the development of typologies or taxonomies to classify organizational strategies. Typologies are then used to examine how environmental factors, internal organizational features, and managerial values relate to these strategic classifications. Literally, dozens of strategy typologies have been developed since the 70s, although they tend to overlap (e.g., Hambrick, 1984; Segev, 1989). In this book, the focus is on those firm strategy groupings that are most useful for analyzing compensation related strategies.

Organizational strategy typologies have been developed at two different levels of analysis: corporate (in what business should the organization be?) and business unit (how does the firm compete in a given business?). The main strategy taxonomies and their underlying dimensions at each of these levels are reviewed next, and the attention is on those most valuable in understanding compensation phenomena. Chapter 4, in turn, examines how the strategic compensation patterns discussed earlier in this chapter relate to the organizational strategies to be discussed next.

Corporate Level Strategies

As noted earlier, corporate strategies refer to the top level of the entire organization, regardless of the number of different industries in which it competes or how many divisions or business units it has. The main strategic concern at this level is the mix of businesses the corporation should hold and the flow of resources between the businesses. Thus, top corporate executives handle this portfolio in a manner similar to how a mutual fund manager administers a portfolio of stocks. The corporate portfolio consists of an array of strategic business units (SBUs) that may be very similar to or completely different from each other. Some units can share little in common. At the corporate level, the main strategic decisions concern acquisition, divestment, diversification, and flow of funds. A great number of "portfolio" models have been developed to study corporate level strategy (e.g., Boston Consulting Matrix, General Electric Grid, Shell Planning Grid), and their primary concern is on how resources should be moved across business units depending on their relative market share and rate of growth. However, the taxonomies most pertinent to compensation strategies are those concerned with extent of diversification and process of diversification.

A review of the literature reveals a great deal of variation in the way both extent and process of diversification are conceptualized, defined, and measured. (See Ramanujam and Varadarajan, 1989, for an extensive discussion of these issues.) However, there are five key elements that underlie most of this work and have implications for compensation strategies and their contribution to firm performance (as seen in Chapters 4 and 5).

1. *Heterogeneity of customers.* Heterogeneity of customers refers to the number of markets, industries, and constituencies served by the corporation.
2. *Product/service similarity.* Similarity refers to the degree to which the corporation's products or services are related or unrelated to each other.
3. *Unit interdependence.* Following earlier theoretical work by Thompson (1967), unit interdependence concerns the extent to which different business units are autonomous or share many resources in common.

4. *Diversification mode.* Diversification mode refers to the degree to which a corporation relies on internal business development vis-a-vis acquisitions as a means of entering new markets.

5. *Diversification rate.* Diversification rate pertains to how fast the corporation is growing by adding new businesses into its portfolio.

At least 60 different taxonomies have been developed to classify corporations according to extent and process of diversification (Ramanujam and Varadarajan, 1989). In this book, attention is devoted to those taxonomies that have been most commonly used in previous research in the strategy field and that are useful in conceptualizing and studying compensation phenomena. Table 3-5 summarizes how the selected taxonomies (to be described below) capture the five elements discussed above.

Type of Diversification. The best known typology, particularly in its compensation applications, is that developed by Rumelt (1974, 1977). In the Rumelt framework, extent of diversification is defined according to a fourfold taxonomy based on percent of revenue derived from various products.

Single-Product Firms. Single-product firms obtain 95 percent or more of their revenue from a single-product domain. These firms are characterized by homogeneous customers and a high degree of product similarity.

Dominant-Product Firms. Dominant-product firms derive between 70 and 94 percent of their revenues from a single-product domain. These firms are characterized by low customer heterogeneity, medium product similarity, high unit interdependence, an internal diversification mode, and a slow pace of diversification.

Related-Product Firms. Related-product firms derive less that 70 percent of their revenues from a single-product domain, and the remainder of their revenues is from a related-product domain. These firms are characterized by medium heterogeneity of customers, some product similarity, medium unit interdependence, both internal and acquisitive diversification modes, and a moderate rate of diversification growth.

Unrelated-Product Firms. Unrelated-product firms receive less than 70 percent of their revenues from a single-product domain, and the reminder of its revenues is from an unrelated-product domain. These companies are characterized by high heterogeneity of customers, little or no product similarities, low unit interdependence, an acquisitive diversification mode, and a fast rate of diversification growth.

Patterns of Linkage. Furthermore, Rumelt (1974) identifies several patterns of linkage between business units.

Vertical. Vertical linkage refers to a vertically integrated business such as an automobile manufacturer owning an aluminum firm that produces inputs necessary in the production of cars. These firms are characterized by homogeneous customers, high degrees of product similarity and unit interdependence, and an internal diversification mode.

Constrained. In constrained linkage, a single core strength or characteristic permeates all the businesses owned by the firm. For example, in the hospitality industry, a hotel chain may own a restaurant chain. These firms are characterized by some customer heterogene-

TABLE 3-5
Key Dimensions Underlying Corporate Diversification Taxonomies

Dimensions	Extent of Diversification				Type of Diversification / Patterns of Linkage					Diversification Process	
	Single-Product	Dominant-Product	Related-Product	Unrelated-Product	Vertical	Constrained	Linked	Multi-business	Conglomerate	Evolutionary	Steady State
Heterogeneity of Customers	Minimal	Low	Medium	High	Minimal	Low	Medium	High	Very High	Very High	Low
Degree of Product Similarity	High	Medium	Low	Minimal	Very High	High	Medium	Low	Minimal	Minimal	High
Unit Interdependence	—	High	Medium	Low	High	High	Medium	Low	Minimal	Minimal	High
Diversification Mode	—	Internal	Mixed	Acquisitive	Internal	Internal	Mixed	Mixed	Acquisitive	Acquisitive	Internal
Diversification Rate	—	Slow	Medium	Fast	—	Slow	Medium	Medium	Fast	Very Fast	Slow

ity, medium product similarity, high unit interdependence, an internal diversification mode, and a slow rate of diversification growth.

Linked. If business units are linked, then each firm in the portfolio relates to one other firm but not necessarily more than one. These firms are characterized by medium heterogeneity of customers, medium product similarity, medium unit interdependence, both internal and acquisitive modes of diversification, and a medium rate of diversification growth.

Multibusiness. Multibusiness linkage refers to a corporation comprised of a relatively small number (two to four) of unrelated businesses. These firms are characterized by high customer heterogeneity, low product similarity, low unit interdependence, both internal and acquisitive modes of diversification, and a medium rate of diversification growth.

Conglomerate. Many different businesses are owned by the corporation, and little attempt is made to link them together. These firms are characterized by very high customer heterogeneity, minimal product similarity and unit interdependence, acquisitive diversification, and a fast rate of diversification growth.

Process of Diversification. The Rumelt framework portrays a static view of diversification where firms are classified into a predetermined taxonomy. In an attempt to examine how firms diversify, Pitts (1974), and later extensions by Leontiades (1980), and Kerr (1985), developed a dichotomous taxonomy resting on differences in the process of diversification.

Evolutionary Firms. Evolutionary firms grow by aggressively acquiring diverse firms into their portfolio. These firms are willing to change industries by purchasing or divesting businesses. Actively searching for opportunities in diverse markets and industries, these companies have a distinct external orientation and are eager to engage in acquisitions, mergers, and joint ventures. They are characterized by very high heterogeneity of customers, minimal product similarity and unit interdependence, and a very fast rate of diversification growth.

Steady State Firms. Steady state firms choose to compete within their respective industry or industries and to expand either by greater penetration of present markets (nondiversified growth) or by investment in internally generated diversification (internal growth). Because of their inward focus, these companies "are concerned with the internal development of new products and technologies and with coordination across business units." (Kerr, 1985, p. 159). These firms are also characterized by low heterogeneity of customers, high degrees of product similarity and unit interdependence, and a slow pace of diversification growth.

Business Unit Strategies

Strategic decisions at the business unit level primarily reside on the formulation of a multifunctional strategy for corporate subunits that operate in a single industry or product market area. While this definition appears simple at first glance, the business unit concept is not always clear-cut. If a company operates in diverse industries, business unit level would normally correspond to the division. In single-product firms, the business and corporate level would be identical. For related-product firms, however, the way a business unit is defined may be an arbitrary decision, depending on how much resource sharing and interdependencies exist across various segments of the corporation.

Corporations display much variability in how much autonomy is allowed to various divisions and how closely they are linked to each other (Kerr, 1985; Leontiades, 1980; Rumelt, 1974). Some corporations, particularly those practicing acquisitive growth, provide a great deal of autonomy to their divisions so that each may be considered a business unit in its own right with much discretion to develop its own strategies. Corporations that grow slowly through internal resources, the steady state firms, concentrate most strategic decisions at the corporate level and emphasize resource sharing and coordination. In this situation, business units are not treated as separate entities vis-a-vis corporate headquarters and each other.

At least 20 typologies appear in the literature designed to classify business units responsible for their own strategy formulation into a parsimonious set of strategic groupings. (See reviews by Hambrick, 1983; Herbert and Deresky, 1987; Segev, 1989.) (Note: Over 80 classification labels with such exotic titles as "explosion," "domain offence," "multiplication," "slip," "niche," "climber," "stuck in the middle," "cash cows," "dogs," and the like are used.) Despite this bewildering diversity of proposed taxonomies and varying labels to denote each category, several recurrent themes are predominant in this literature.

Dimensions of Taxonomies. The key dimensions that underlie these typological schemes, most of which have compensation implications as seen in Chapters 4 and 5, are briefly described in the following discussion.

Environmental Dimensions. The first set of dimensions concerns the environment facing the business unit. The environment can be depicted in terms of four crucial factors:

1. *Degree of uncertainty.* The degree of uncertainty refers to how much accurate information is available to top management. Information is needed to predict environmental changes so that appropriate responses can be devised.
2. *Volatility.* Volatility is the rate of change in the firm's relevant environment (e.g., shifts in product demands, changes in technology, changes in legislation).
3. *Magnitude of change.* The magnitude of change refers to the amount of discontinuous change in the firm's relevant environment. (For instance, in the medical field, appearance of the ultrasonic imaging instruments in the early 1970s made the electrodiagnostic instruments obsolete almost overnight. Many other similar examples of discontinuous change in that industry are provided by Mitchell, 1989.)
4. *Complexity.* Complexity pertains to the number and heterogeneity of external elements that may impact the organization either singly or in an interactive fashion.

Production Process Dimensions. The second set of dimensions underlying most SBU taxonomies concerns the production process used by the firm. The four key factors under this rubric include:

1. *Innovation requirements.* Innovation requirements refer to the novelty of the production process used to transform inputs into services and products. For instance, a firm specializing in custom design of airplanes or a biotechnology company would be high on this dimension.
2. *Degree of standardization.* The degree of standardization is the extent to which the production process is routine and relatively stable with few exceptions to established procedures. For example, the manufacturing process of pencils has not changed much over the past 100 years and is very routine in nature.

3. *Fixed investments.* Fixed investments are the amount of resources irrevocably sunk into the firm's core technology. For example, investments in production equipment and facilities are much greater on a per capita basis in a steel mill or an automobile assembly line than in an advertising firm or a management consulting company.

4. *Technological diversity.* Diversity is the extent to which the technology used in the production process is dissimilar or homogeneous. For instance, successful production of a lunar landing module by NASA involved the utilization of multiple technologies spanning several fields. The typical lumber company, on the other hand, utilizes a very homogenous technology to cut down trees, namely manual labor and chain saws.

Market Dimensions. The third set of dimensions interwoven across most SBU typologies concerns the firm's market interface and behaviors. Three factors play a major role here:

1. *Rate of growth.* As the term implies, rate of growth refers to sales expansion with respect to industry norms and previous sales volume.

2. *Product innovation.* Product innovation relates to the number and novelty of new products/services launched by the firm. Volkswagen, for instance, did not change it basic car model for over 40 years, while General Motors has changed its car design every year since its inception.

3. *Product market domain focus.* Product market domain focus refers to whether a firm chooses a narrowly defined market niche (e.g., computer programs for medical applications) or casts a wider product net (e.g., software for statistical analysis, inventory, and home entertainment).

Managerial Dimensions. The fourth set of dimensions defining SBU taxonomies concerns the attributes of top management teams. Four factors frequently come into play here:

1. *Risk taking.* Risk taking is the degree to which top management teams are willing to make commitments that require substantial resources and to invest in projects with a low probability of success but high potential returns.

2. *Degree of control.* Degree of control is the extent to which management develops elaborate procedures to standardize behavior and monitor employees' activities to insure compliance.

3. *Hierarchical emphasis.* Hierarchical emphasis refers to how many levels in the organization are involved in making important decisions and the extent to which power, prestige, and influence are related to positioning in the "pecking order."

4. *Environmental proactiveness.* Proactiveness is the degree to which top management teams attempt to shape environmental forces and events, as opposed to taking a reactive posture to external threats and opportunities.

Organizational Structure Dimensions. The fifth set of dimensions underlying most SBU taxonomies refers to structural factors in the organization. The following three structural elements are commonly cited:

1. *Centralization.* Centralization is the extent to which decision-making authority is empowered at the top level, usually in a single location.

2. *Modus operandi.* When the internal organization is known for its formalized rules, procedures, and clearly defined roles, it is generally labeled "mechanistic." At the opposite end, an "organic" firm is characterized by flexible and adaptive rules and procedures, free-flowing and loose methods for accomplishing tasks, and wide discretion given to employees to define their jobs.

3. *Focal unit.* This refers to the unit of analysis used to organize the firm's operations. The two most common ones include the traditional functional breakdown (e.g., marketing, finance, production, personnel) and a product-based approach (i.e., by product line).

Cultural Dimensions. The sixth and last set of dimensions distinguishing different SBU strategic groups is not as commonly mentioned as the first five. Yet it implicitly or explicitly plays an important role in most SBU taxonomies. It is the organization's culture. The two most important cultural factors are:

1. *Cultural climate.* Cultural climate refers to whether a firm has an entrepreneurial climate (one that encourages individualism, risk taking, flexibility, creation of new ideas, willingness to experiment, and tolerance for mistakes) or a regimented climate (with tight controls, emphasizing compliance, risk avoidance, strict adherence to norms, "business as usual," and low tolerance for mistakes).

2. *Type of commitment.* Commitment refers to the nature of employees' involvement with the firm. Two major concepts in this regard have a long tradition in the sociological literature. (For a review, see Penley and Gould, 1988.) The first one has been coined "moral commitment," to denote identification with organizational goals. This orientation emphasizes internalizing organizational norms, long-term attachment to the firm, loyalty, and a base of attitudes, habits, and values that foster strong emotional allegiance to the employer. The second orientation, labeled "calculative," represents an instrumental, utilitarian, hedonistic view in which employees are depicted as exchanging their contributions for the inducements provided by the organization. Employees and/or the organization are both free to break this bond whenever the exchange is not of mutual benefit. Thus, calculative commitment is the opposite of moral commitment and involves little affective organizational attachment. Empirical evidence strongly supports the notion that these two types of employee involvement are distinct and independent and that firms vary on the extent to which they rely on one type versus the other.

In this book, those SBU taxonomies that have gained wide acceptance in the strategy field and that are useful for analyzing compensation strategy items are discussed. These taxonomies can be divided into those concerned with recurring viable strategic patterns and those focusing on structural features based on life cycle concepts. Table 3-6 summarizes how each of the dimensions discussed above relate to each of the SBU typologies used in this book (to be described next).

Strategic Business Unit (SBU) Patterns. Perhaps the best known and most widely used SBU typology was developed by Miles and Snow (1978). The Miles and Snow typology has proven to be very robust and adaptable as evidenced by its successful application to the study of a wide variety of strategic issues. It has been used to examine changes in R&D intensity (Hambrick, MacMillan, and

TABLE 3-6
Key Dimensions Underlying Strategic Business Unit Taxonomies

| | Strategic Patterns | | | | | Structural Features | |
| | Miles and Snow | | | Gerstein and Reisman | | Life Cycle | |
Dimensions	Defenders	Prospectors	Analyzers	Dynamic Growth	Rationalization/ Maintenance	Growth Stage	Mature Stage
Environmental							
Uncertainty	Low	High	Middle	High	Low	High	Low
Volatility	Low	High	Middle	High	Low	High	Low
Magnitude of Change	Low	High	Middle	High	Low	High	Low
Complexity	Low	High	Middle	High	Low	High	Low
Production Process							
Innovation Requirements	Low	High	Middle	High	Low	High	Low
Degree of Standardization	High	Low	Middle	Low	High	Low	High
Fixed Investments	High	Low	Middle	Low	High	Low	High
Technological Diversity	Low	High	Middle	High	Low	High	Low
Market							
Rate of Growth	Low	High	Middle	High	Low	High	Low
Product Innovation	Low	High	Middle	High	Low	High	Low
Product Market Domain Focus	Narrow	Broad	Middle	Broad	Narrow	Broad	Narrow
Managerial							
Risk Taking	Low	High	Middle	High	Low	High	Low
Degree of Control	High	Low	Middle	Low	High	Low	High
Hierarchical Emphasis	High	Low	Middle	Low	High	Low	High
Environmental Proactiveness	Low	High	Middle	High	Low	High	Low
Organizational Structure							
Centralization	High	Low	Middle	Low	High	Low	High
Modus Operandi	Mechanistic	Organic	Mixed	Organic	Mechanistic	Organic	Mechanistic
Focal Unit	Functional	Product	Mixed	Product	Functional	Product	Functional
Cultural							
Cultural Climate	Regimented	Entrepreneurial	Mixed	Entrepreneurial	Regimented	Entrepreneurial	Regimented
Commitment	Moral	Calculative	Mixed	Calculative	Moral	Calculative	Moral

Barbarosa, 1983), distinctive competence and performance (Snow and Hrebiniak, 1980); manufacturing and service strategies (Adam, 1983); strategic awareness (Hambrick, 1981); environmental scanning (Hambrick, 1982); strategic choice (Burgelman, 1983; Segev, 1989); and, most important to this book, compensation strategies (Broderick, 1986; Gomez-Mejia, 1992). Empirical results also provide strong support for its reliability and validity (Shortell and Zajac, 1990).

Based on three studies in four industries (college textbook publishers, electronics, food processors, and health care), Miles and Snow (1978) concluded that viable SBU strategies can be categorized into three basic types:

Defenders. Defenders are business units that prefer to maintain a secure position in a relatively stable product or service area. Rather than emphasizing new product development, they emphasize protecting the market share. Key features of defenders include (see Tables 3-6 and 3-7):

1. Stable forms of organization.
2. A narrow and relatively immutable product domain with competition primarily on the basis of quality, price, delivery, or customer service.

TABLE 3-7
Miles and Snow Scales for Measuring SBU Strategy Types*

Defenders

A defender organization attempts to locate and maintain a secure niche in a relatively stable product or service area. The organization offers a more limited range of products or services than its competitors, and it tries to protect its domain by offering higher quality, superior service, lower prices, and so forth. Often, this type of organization is not at the forefront of developments in the industry. It ignores industry changes that have no direct influence on current areas of operation and concentrates instead on doing the best job possible in a limited area.

Prospectors

A prospector organization typically operates within a broad product-market domain that undergoes periodic redefinition. The organization values being "first in" in new product and market areas even if not all of these efforts prove to be highly profitable. The organization responds rapidly to early signals concerning areas of opportunity, and these responses often lead to a new round of competitive actions. However, this type of organization may not maintain market strength in all of the areas it enters.

Analyzers

An analyzer organization attempts to maintain a stable, limited line of products or services, while at the same time moves out quickly to follow a carefully selected set of the more promising new developments in the industry. The organization is seldom "first in" with new products or services. However, by carefully monitoring the actions of major competitors in areas compatible with its stable product-market base, the organization can frequently be "second in" with a more cost-efficient product or service.

*Reprinted from "Strategy, Distinctive Competence, and Organizational Performance" by Charles C. Snow and Lawrence G. Hrebiniak. Published in *Administrative Science Quarterly*, Volume 25, #2, June, 1980, by permission of Administrative Science Quarterly.

3. Infrequent adjustments in technology structure or methods of operation.
4. A single, capital-intensive technology.
5. Functional structure characterized by an emphasis on efficiency, extensive division of labor, hierarchical communication channels, and centralized control.
6. A regimented organizational culture with an emphasis on moral commitment.

Prospectors. The strategic patterns of prospectors is opposite to that of defenders. "Unlike the defender, whose success comes primarily from efficiently serving a stable domain, the prospector's prime capability is that of finding and exploiting new product and market opportunities" (Miles, Snow, Meyer, and Coleman, 1978, p. 548). Even in the face of repeated failures, prospectors are willing to enter risky and unexplored product and market areas. Key characteristics of prospectors include (see Tables 3-6 and 3-7):

1. A strong concern for product and market innovation.
2. A diverse product line.
3. A product or divisionalized structure.
4. A great deal of flexibility in its technology and administrative style.
5. A management system that is decentralized, emphasizing loose planning, low degree of formalization, and lateral as well as vertical communication.
6. An entrepreneurial organizational culture with a calculative commitment.

Analyzers. Analyzer's strategies fall between those of prospectors and defenders. These SBUs are seldom first in new product or market areas, but they are often fast followers by imitating successful product or market innovations of prospectors. Analyzers attempt to exploit market opportunities in a more cautious way than prospectors, while akin to the defender, they try to retain simultaneously a firm core of traditional products and customers. Key features of analyzers include (see Tables 3-6 and 3-7):

1. A balance between conflicting demands for technological and organizational flexibility, on the one hand, and technological and organizational stability on the other.
2. A dual "technological core," one stable bearing a strong resemblance to that of defenders (with high levels of standardization, routinization, and mechanization) and one flexible resembling that of prospectors (unstandardized, nonroutine, and organic).
3. An administrative structure and processes that try to accommodate both stable and flexible areas of operation, usually via a matrix organizational structure.

A second typology found useful in studying human resource and compensation issues is that of Gerstein and Reisman (1983). Its central concepts greatly overlap those of Miles and Snow's taxonomy, but it has one advantage. It is relatively free of academic jargon and is intuitively meaningful and more appealing to practicing managers (Balkin and Gomez-Mejia, 1990). This is an important attribute when conducting field research in compensation. While the Gerstein and Reisman (1983) typology has six separate categories, only the two most commonly used groups in compensation research are discussed in this book. These are (see Table 3-6):

Dynamic Growth. Although the business unit is past the entrepreneurial stage, projects with significant financial risks are undertaken frequently. Market share expansion is of highest priority. A conflict may be felt between resource allocation to carry out existing activities and building support for the future. SBU is in the early stages of developing policies and procedures to provide a framework of control and structure for future expansion. Dynamic growth is roughly equivalent to that of prospectors in the Miles and Snow (1978) taxonomy.

Rationalization/Maintenance. The business unit is interested in retaining its position in the market while at the same time minimizing costs. The primary goal is to maintain existing profit levels rather than additional growth. Some layoffs and other cost-cutting activities may be occurring. An extensive set of policies/procedures are in place as part of the organization's control system. This SBU strategy greatly overlaps with the defender category in Miles and Snow's (1978) typology.

Organizational Life Cycle. The organizational life cycle is perhaps the most widely known structural variable used to describe a business unit strategy. Its central concept is that each business unit follows a cycle in the sale of its primary product. The business cycle is akin to the biological cycle of an individual who goes through a number of stages such as infancy, adolescence, adulthood, and old age. These stages are purported to occur sequentially, in a hierarchical progression, and are triggered by both internal pressures (e.g., transition from entrepreneurial to administrative leadership; increasing age, size, and complexity) and external pressures (e.g., maturation of technology in industry; market saturation) (Adizes, 1979; Downs, 1967; Gray and Ariss, 1985; Greiner, 1972; Kazanjian, 1988; Kimberly and Miles, 1980; Lippitt and Schmidt, 1967; Mintzberg, 1984; Quinn and Cameron, 1983; Walsh and Dewar, 1987). Its origin can be traced to the "production learning curve." Sales increase fast at first as cost-per-unit drops because of "organizational learning," improvements in technology and production processes, and greater economies of scale. Then sales reach a point where volume flattens out and finally begin to decrease as the market is saturated (Day and Montgomery, 1983).

The beauty of the life cycle concept lies in its simplicity and the facts that "the most fundamental variable in determining an appropriate business strategy is the stage of the product life cycle" (Hofer, 1975, p. 788) and that "empirical investigation has demonstrated that production processes normally move by a process life cycle that parallels the product life cycle" (Neidell, 1983, p. 32). Expanding on this theme, a number of authors have argued that HRM and compensation strategies vary according to the phase in which the firm's main product finds itself (Ellig, 1981).

However, life cycle models have been criticized in many fields, including marketing (Day and Montgomery, 1983), production (Dhalla and Yuspeh, 1976), entrepreneurship (Sexton, 1990), human resource management (Kerr, 1982), and strategy (Wiersema and Page, 1992). Major criticisms across these fields include:

1. Extending a biological analogy to organizations is questionable because they do not face stages with fixed chronological delimiters as living organisms do.
2. Different sets of policies may be appropriate for each stage. Therefore, it may be deceptive to offer universal prescriptions for any given organizational cycle.
3. The beginning and end of any given phase are difficult to measure reliably.
4. A business unit may have several products at different stages of the life cycle.

5. Many products enjoy a long maturity stage.
6. Life cycle curves do not always follow the traditional shape.
7. Life cycle theory does not account for radical innovations.
8. Authors often apply the term "life cycle" in a sloppy fashion to describe organization, corporate business unit, industry, or even functional strategies.

It would be beyond the scope of this book to delve into this controversy regarding the validity of life cycle models. Our position is that the life cycle concept, just like any simple model, can be criticized for being too naive. However, it is still a very useful heuristic device for understanding organizational processes and seems to be implicit in most business unit typologies such as those of Miles and Snow (1978) and Gerstein and Reisman (1983) reviewed earlier. For example, defender strategies refer to more "mature" business units and prospector strategies refer to "growing" business units. Similar overlaps may be found with other business unit typologies. In fact, Gomez-Mejia (1992) found that the way managers rate their business unit in terms of life cycle vis-a-vis other typological strategies are highly correlated. This suggests that there is a common underlying dimension, at least perceptually. This is consistent with the earlier conclusions of Hofer (1975) and a comparative study of SBU generic strategies by Herbert and Deresky (1987). A sensible interpretation of life cycle research is advanced by Neidell (1983, p. 33), who suggested that "the [life cycle] concept, by itself and in concert with other empirical findings and theoretical constructs, can be a valuable tool for the analysis and development of competitive strategies."

While several phases have been identified by various authors, the following categories are typical of life cycle stages used in previous compensation related research. (See Balkin and Gomez-Mejia, 1984, 1987, 1990; Gomez-Mejia, 1992.)

Growth Stage. In the growth stage, sales grow at 20 percent or more annually in real terms. Technology and competitive structure are still changing. These firms are characterized by a more entrepreneurial culture. (Note: See Table 3-6 for other key features of firms at the growth stage.)

Mature Stage. In the mature stage, an organization's products or services are familiar to a vast majority of prospective users. Technology and competitive structure are reasonably stable. These firms are characterized by a more regimented culture. (Note: See Table 3-6 for other key features of firms at the mature stage.)

SUMMARY

In this chapter, several frameworks used to classify firms in terms of their compensation strategies and corporate and business unit strategies are reviewed. The central notion behind the taxonomic models discussed here is that both pay and organizational strategies consist of multiple elements that can be clustered into meaningful subgroups, and these, in turn, may be used to study a firm's relative standing along a number of key strategic dimensions. The models presented in this chapter are recalled in the next two chapters as the linkages between the algorithmic-experiential compensation patterns and organizational strategies (Chapter 4) and how the alignment between the two affects firm performance (Chapter 5) are discussed.

APPENDIX 3A

METHODOLOGICAL NOTE ON GOMEZ-MEJIA'S (1992) STUDY

The most senior compensation director in corporate headquarters was asked to complete a survey that included questions pertaining to the firm's compensation and organizational strategies. The response format for all pay choice items consisted of a one (1) to five (5) Likert scale ranging from "strongly agree" to "strongly disagree." Directors were asked to describe the corporation's diversification strategies in terms of extent and process. In the subsample (N=112) where the business unit and the corporation may be treated as a singular entity, they were asked to describe their business strategies using the Miles and Snow's (1980) typology.

Because the primary intent of the study was to examine the interactive effect of the relationship "organizational strategy x compensation strategy" on firm performance as the dependent variable, firms were deliberately sampled from Compustat that were in the top, second, third, and fourth quartile based on a five-year average of several accounting and stock related performance measures (earning per share, return on equity, common stock return, and market value change).

There are a number of methodological limitations that should be taken into consideration when interpreting the results reported here. Most of these are inherent problems in field research and are difficult to avoid. First, there is no guarantee that the sample is representative of U.S. firms (these were all manufacturing firms) and potential sample biases may influence the results. Second, method variance is always a danger in field research when data is obtained concurrently from the same respondents. For instance, greater intercorrelation among the pay choice dimensions may be obtained via a survey approach than there is in the real world due to perceptual cognitions on the respondent's part. This, however, is not a problem for the performance measure because it was obtained independently from a separate source (i.e., Compustat). Third, only one respondent (i.e., the Compensation Director) answered the survey from each firm. It may be that, in fact, different perspectives would come to light if multiple respondents were obtained from each firm (e.g., Chief Executive Officer, division managers). Costs and time constraints prevented us from doing that. Fourth, there is the potential problem that exogenous factors not included (such as other HRM policies) may confound the observed findings. Finally, the results are not cross-validated on a separate sample. Ideally, a separate sample should be used to cross-validate the results. Again, cost and time constraints became major obstacles to doing this.

OVERARCHING STRATEGIC COMPENSATION PATTERNS AND BUSINESS STRATEGIES

This chapter discusses the corporate and business unit (SBUs) strategies that are purported to be affiliated with the algorithmic or experiential compensation strategies and builds on the material presented in the previous two chapters. This paves the way to the following chapter, which focuses on the extent to which alignment between organizational and compensation strategies impacts the overall effectiveness of the pay system and firm performance. First, pay strategy issues at the corporate level are examined. Next, the determinants of compensation strategies for SBUs are given attention.

<h1 style="text-align:center">RELATIONSHIP BETWEEN CORPORATE AND
COMPENSATION STRATEGIES</h1>

The upper portion of Table 4-1 shows the most prevalent compensation patterns (algorithmic or experiential) associated with various corporate strategies. Figure 4-1 presents a model that summarizes much of the conceptual and empirical research on the underlying predictors of strategic compensation patterns at the corporate level. According to that model, an experiential compensation pattern (see Appendix 4A for a detailed listing of strategic pay choices associated with various corporate strategies) is inversely related to knowledge of organizational transformations on the part of corporate managers, the degree to which pooled interdependence is prevalent among SBUs, corporate growth that is internally generated, commitment to a narrow product line/market niche, organizational complexity, and the need for a unitary corporate-wide ethos. On the other hand, an experiential compensation pattern is a positive function of the rate of new business acquisitions under the same corporate umbrella, the need to encourage independent thinking and entrepreneurial activities on the part of divisional managers, cash flow constraints, and the heterogeneity of SBUs. A review of the supporting literature follows.

Corporate Structure and Strategic Pay Patterns

Berg (1969, 1973) noted that large diversified firms, roughly equivalent to the "unrelated products" or conglomerate group in Rumelt's taxonomy, attempt to maintain an entrepreneurial atmosphere. They accomplish this by providing variable bonuses, high risk sharing, rewards based on business unit performance, and low dependence on superiors. These pay characteristics are associated with the experiential compensation strategies discussed in Chapter 3.

Encouraging an entrepreneurial culture in conglomerates makes sense because each business unit is independent and shares few resources in common. Furthermore, corporate level managers are unlikely to have significant experience in more than a few of the firm's businesses. Each business unit enjoys substantial freedom, and the pay system encourages SBU managers to experiment by making the magnitude of potential rewards for top management proportionate to level of risk assumed. According to Berg, attempts to administer a compensation system centrally under such conditions and to base a SBU manager's pay on the judgment of "naive" top executives in corporate headquarters is likely to demoralize divisional managers and dampen creativity and local initiatives.

Along a similar vein, Lorsch and Allen (1973) noted that vertically integrated firms, roughly corresponding to related- and dominant- product classifications in the Rumelt typology, have the opposite compensation strategies of conglomerates.   That is, the evaluation of each division manager is based on the performance of the corporation as a whole, high dependence on superior's feedback, and relatively low "at risk" pay.

Two reasons were advanced by Lorsch and Allen for this observed pattern.   First, top executives in vertically integrated firms know a great deal about each of the businesses.   Second, all units in these corporations are highly interdependent and share many common resources.   Therefore, it is difficult to make unambiguous performance

TABLE 4-1
A Summary of Strategic Compensation Patterns Associated with Various Corporate and Business Unit Strategies

Corporate Strategy	Strategic Compensation Pattern
Extent of Diversification	
Single-Product	Experiential
Dominant-Product	Mixed
Related-Product	Algorithmic
Unrelated-Product	Experiential
Patterns of Linkages	
Vertical	Algorithmic
Constrained	Algorithmic
Linked	Mixed
Multibusiness	Experiential
Conglomerate	Experiential
Process of Diversification	
Evolutionary Firms	Experiential
Steady State Firms	Algorithmic

Business Unit Strategy	
Strategic Patterns	
Defenders	Algorithmic
Prospectors	Experiential
Analyzers	Mixed
Dynamic Growth	Experiential
Rationalization/Maintenance	Algorithmic
Life Cycle	
Start-up Stage	Experiential
Growth Stage	Experiential
Mature Stage	Algorithmic
Decline Stage	Algorithmic

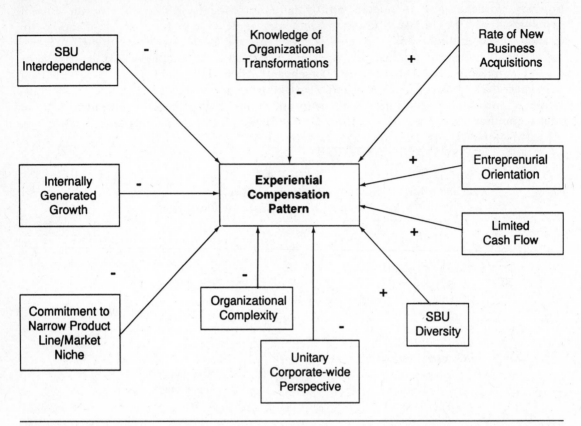

FIGURE 4-1 Key Factors Underlying Observed Variations in Compensation Strategies at the Corporate Level

attributions to any one unit. Likewise, Salter (1973) made a cogent argument that corporate-division and interdivision relations play a major role in reward system design for top management. As diversification increases, the interdependence between divisions and the corporation and among divisions declines. As each division or business unit becomes a unique entity, the reward system acquires more of the characteristics of the experiential reward pattern, with a tendency to define managerial rewards in terms of results of operating units, rather than the corporation as a whole. This would be particularly true of conglomerates where interdivisional sharing of resources tends to be nil.

More recently, Balkin and Gomez-Mejia (1990) report that single-product firms (in which the corporation and business unit are one and the same) are associated with lower pay levels relative to the market, high emphasis on incentives in the compensation mix, reliance on long-term income, and flexible pay policies. All of these reflect an experiential pay pattern. Several related reasons may account for this.

First, single-product firms do not need a compensation system with elaborate rules to govern pay decisions. Less complexity in the organization demands fewer detailed policies and procedures to cover multiple contingencies. Second, top management in single-product firms is more likely to foster an entrepreneurial climate, with many decisions made on an ad hoc basis as unique situations arise. The HRM function is less formalized, with extensive prerogatives given to line managers in making personnel-related decisions. Third, a long-term orientation becomes important in single-product organizations that are interested in "nurturing" a particular product and market, particularly those that are at the initial stages of growth where they are preparing for rapid expansion along a narrow product line. A more flexible, organic compensation system with generous long-term pay offerings is more suitable to these conditions. Fourth, heavy reliance on incentive pay by single-product firms may be a useful strategy to attract and retain employees, while at the same time underemphasizing expensive fixed pay components (salary and benefits) relative to more established, mature firms. Such a compensation strategy would free scarce dollars in the short run and allow more investment to finance continued expansion. Although pay level may be below market for these firms, employees may choose to work there in exchange for greater potential returns in the future. Gomez-Mejia and Balkin (1985) found that to be the case among smaller, high technology firms in the New England area that provide up to 70 percent of an employee's pay on a variable basis. Similar results were reported several years later on a much larger sample of high technology firms by Milkovich, Gerhart, and Hannon (1991).

Balkin and Gomez-Mejia (1990) also report that as corporate strategy shifts from a low to a higher level of diversification (but still remains in the related business category with substantial interdependence among units), the compensation system becomes more bureaucratic and inflexible, exhibiting many of the traits associated with the algorithmic compensation pattern. These more highly diversified firms are characterized by an above market or going rate pay level, greater emphasis on salary and benefits vis-a-vis incentives, less long-term pay, more pay secrecy, pay centralization, job-based pay, a weaker pay for performance linkage, and a less egalitarian, more autocratic administration of the compensation system. As additional business units are added to the corporate structure, pay comparisons across business units are made by corporate management. Pay policies that ensure fair, consistent treatment of employees in different business units are developed at the corporate level. Internal pay equity, operationalized through job evaluation procedures, becomes increasingly important as diversification increases.

Two primary reasons account for the algorithmic compensation strategies observed among related-product firms. First, diversified companies with interdependent business units do not wish to provide much autonomy to divisional managers or to design pay packages that encourage entrepreneurial behaviors among SBUs whose activities and goals are deeply intertwined. The main task of the pay system is viewed as one of control. Thus, compensation policies and procedures are designed to link SBUs to corporate headquarters, foster dependence on superiors, and reduce risk taking at the local level. Second, related business companies are keenly interested in creating a systemic, rather than a fractionalized, view of the total organization. Uniform, standardized pay policies and procedures across SBUs reinforce a unitary corporate perspective. This means managing the potential conflict in the pay system between the desire for fairness and equity, on the one hand, and the need for adaptiveness and differentiation on the other hand, becomes a major challenge for related-product corporations.

Balkin and Gomez-Mejia (1990), however, warn that the findings discussed above are only applicable to corporate diversifiers where corporate management possesses a core of management expertise that relates to the different businesses in the corporation. Their sample did not include conglomerates, where the business units are heterogenous and highly independent.

In a separate study including a large sample of conglomerates, Gomez-Mejia (1992) found that as firms diversify by acquiring SBUs that share little in common, the overall compensation strategy shifts to a more experiential style, similar to that of single-product firms. As can be seen in Figure 4-2, he reports that the average scores on the algorithmic-experiential continuum (where higher scores indicate a more experiential orientation) were .74, .40, .45, and .51 for single-product, dominant-product, related-product, and unrelated-product firms, respectively. These findings are consistent with those reported earlier by Berg (1973) and Lorsch and Allen (1973). So it appears that the relationship between degree of diversification and the extent to which a firm relies on a more experiential compensation pattern is *U* shaped, rather than linear, with single- and unrelated-product firms relying on more experiential compensation strategies and dominant- and related-product firms utilizing a more algorithmic approach.

As noted in Chapter 3, Rumelt (1974) describes corporate strategy not only in terms of extent of diversification but also according to patterns of linkages across business units. The underlying concept behind his five types of linkages (vertical, constrained, linked, multibusiness, and unrelated business) is the degree to which divisions share common resources and are subject to pooled interdependencies. No empirical research examining how reward systems vary according to each of these configurations exists. However, the same logic used for diversification extent should apply here. One would expect vertical (i.e., an integrated chain of businesses) and constrained (i.e., all business units related to a single core or characteristic) patterns of linkages to rely on more algorithmic pay strategies because of greater interdependencies across units. One would also expect that firms consisting of unrelated businesses would lean toward experiential pay strategies. Linked firms, where some of the business units are related, would more likely fall somewhere in between the algorithmic and experiential pay patterns.

Process of Diversification and Strategic Pay Patterns

The research reviewed above relies primarily on Rumelt's framework and takes a largely static view of diversification strategy. Outlining the compensation strategies associated with each category, this research provides important insights. However, a number of investigators argue that it is not enough to stop at the "extent" or patterns of linkages. There is also a need to examine how compensation strategies vary according to the process by which diversification takes place. Pitts (1976) reports that "acquisitive diversifiers," or firms that diversify by purchasing existing businesses, pay managers based on the performance of their unit, with little dependence on superiors to make a judgment of performance. Firms that diversify in this manner provide division managers with more autonomy, and a more experiential compensation

PAY— Motivation, & Control

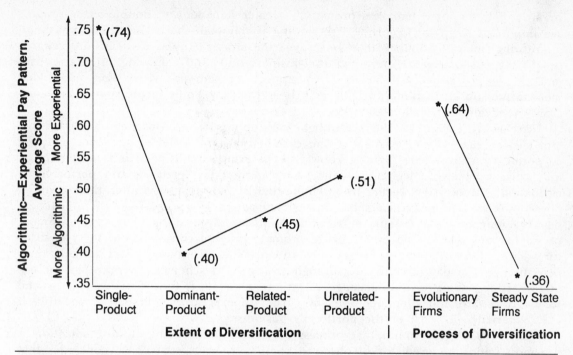

FIGURE 4-2   Graph Showing Extent to Which a Given Corporate Strategy Exhibits an Experiential (High End of Scale) or an Algorithmic (Low End of Scale) Compensation Pattern*

* Based on the research of Gomez-Mejia (1992).

strategy appears to be most appropriate.   The opposite is true for firms that have grown through internal expansion (what Pitts calls "internal diversifiers"), where there is a greater degree of interdependence and interaction between managers of various divisions.

Reaching essentially the same conclusions, Leontiades (1980) and Kerr (1985) expand upon Pitts' earlier work.   According to Leontiades, steady state firms, which have a clear commitment to existing product/market areas and exhibit a strong reluctance to engage in mergers and acquisitions, are associated with a more intimate form of control by top management, inculcation of organizational values for junior managers, consistency in procedures, long careers with the company, and a system-wide perspective because of extensive interdependencies across organizational subunits.   Evolutionary firms, on the other hand, aggressively engage in mergers, acquisitions, joint ventures, etc., even in unfamiliar areas.   Among evolutionary firms, the management of change becomes crucial to survival.   Entrepreneurship is encouraged; control is deemphasized to promote innovation; shorter tenure with the firm is the norm as the employment relationship is based on a calculative commitment; and a systemic perspective is discouraged because problems facing each business unit are unique.

Kerr (1985) found that compensation strategies vary according to these two diversification processes.   Among steady state firms, the reward system falls closer to the algorithmic pattern because superiors exercise a great deal of direct control on the rewards of lower level managers promoting greater dependence; nonmonetary rewards are important (e.g., job security); risk sharing is minimal; there is more emphasis on monitoring behaviors, rather than outcomes; the strategic focus to distribute rewards lies in the corporation, rather than the business unit; and achieving internal consistency in the pay structure is necessary to support a system-wide view. Kerr found that mechanistic job evaluation procedures such as the Hay Point factor system are commonly used among steady state firms.

According to Kerr's (1985) findings, evolutionary state firms have a reward system sharing many characteristics of the experiential compensation pattern. Because corporate executives have limited knowledge of acquired business units that may be quite diverse, there is less dependence on superiors for feedback and performance evaluation. Monitoring occurs by linking rewards to outcomes, rather than through observation and judgment of subordinates' behaviors. The low level of interdependence among divisions lessens the need for centralized control and the establishment of mechanisms such as job evaluation to promote internal consistency in the pay structure across different business units. Evolutionary state firms emphasize variable compensation in the pay mix (mostly through equity-based schemes) to promote a sense of ownership among division managers. At the same time, they circumvent the need to justify reward allocation decisions by corporate executives who may have little, if any, experience in each of the portfolio's businesses.

Kerr (1985) also found that process of, rather than extent of, diversification is the most important predictor of observed compensation patterns. He concludes that "the extent to which a firm derived revenue from a more or less narrow set of activities did not adequately explain the composition of the [compensation strategies] clusters ... these results suggest that, in itself, a firm's level of diversification does not represent a primary influence on the design of its reward system." (p. 170).

Some caution should be used in interpreting Kerr's (1985) findings. These are based on interviews with a small sample of 20 firms, relying on a heuristic approach to make sense of his data. More recently and using the composite compensation strategy measure described in Chapter 3, Gomez-Mejia (1992) found that in a sample of 243 firms, pay strategies do vary by diversification process in a manner similar to that proposed by Kerr (1985). As can be seen in Figure 4.2, the average standardized compensation strategy score for evolutionary state firms was almost twice as high (.64) than that of steady state firms (.36), indicating a more experiential pay pattern. Unlike Kerr, however, Gomez-Mejia (1992) found that *both* extent and process of diversification are important predictors of compensation strategy. Firms that are both highly diversified and evolutionary in nature are more experiential in their compensation strategies than firms that are less diversified and steady state in nature.

In summary, the above findings suggest that while extent of diversification and patterns of linkages among business units have a bearing on pay strategies, the process of corporate diversification can also affect where a corporation lies on the algorithmic-experiential compensation strategy continua. The algorithmic pay pattern is more prevalent among dominant- or related-product firms with vertical or constrained patterns of linkages that follow a steady state diversification strategy. The experiential pay pattern, on the other hand, is more common among single-product or unrelated-product firms with a multibusiness or conglomerate patterns of linkages following an evolutionary diversification strategy.

RELATIONSHIP BETWEEN BUSINESS UNIT AND COMPENSATION STRATEGIES

The lower portion of Table 4-1 shows the most prevalent compensation pattern (algorithmic or experiential) associated with various SBU strategies. Figure 4-3 presents a model that depicts the underlying predictors of strategic compensation patterns at the SBU level. This model, based on the literature to be reviewed shortly, indicates that an experiential compensation pattern at the SBU level is a positive function of an organizational culture that encourages utilitarian values and calculative commitment, an early growth stage in the SBU's product life cycle, a willingness to capitalize on environmental opportunities, a rapidly changing and unstable environment, and heavy reliance on innovation as a means to achieve competitive advantage. On the other hand, an experiential compensation pattern at the SBU level is negatively related to the presence of high entry barriers in the industry, a strong control orientation, and a mechanistic organizational structure.

Next reviewed is the supporting literature from which the general model shown in Figure 4-3 was derived. As discussed in Chapter 3, the SBU typology developed by Miles and Snow (1978) and, to a lesser extent, Gerstein and Reisman (1983) have often been used in conceptualizing business unit strategies, particularly when examining compensation issues. In terms of structural characteristics at the business unit

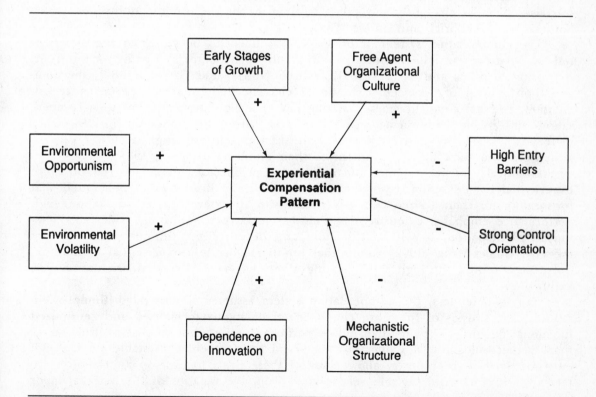

FIGURE 4-3 Underlying Factors Affecting Compensation Strategies at the Business Unit Level

level, the life cycle concept has also played a pivotal role in the compensation strategy literature. The following discussion revolves around these typologies, focusing on the key elements responsible for a more experiential (or less algorithmic) strategic compensation pattern. (*Note:* Appendix 4B shows a detailed chart of how different compensation strategy dimensions vary as a function of SBU strategies and life cycle stages.)

SBU Strategic Patterns: Miles and Snow Typology

Hambrick and Snow (1989), Miles and Snow (1984), Carroll (1987), and Wallace (1987) have all argued that the compensation strategy of a business unit depends on the extent to which it follows a prospector, defender, or analyzer strategy. As noted in Chapter 3, prospectors emphasize growth and capitalization of environmental opportunities through innovation, development of new products, and willingness to be first movers in new product or market areas, even if some of these efforts fail. This prospector strategy "is best implemented through an organic or loose, nonformalized organization that emphasizes decentralization of decision making and lateral communication" (Carroll, 1987, p. 345). Thus, a prospector strategy is associated with organic structures, fluid and complex tasks, and unstable environments with a rapid rate of change. This means that "there is less formalization and centralization—managers are freer to develop policies fitting their unique situations" (Wallace, 1987, p. 176). Furthermore, a *free agent relationship* between employee and firm is the norm. This means there is no expectation of a long-term commitment, and the employment contract is subject to change at any point in time, depending on the utility derived by both parties (Hambrick and Snow, 1989).

The compensation system of prospectors is likely to be closer to the experiential pay pattern, which is more suited to the prospector's organic orientation. According to Miles and Snow (1984), Wallace (1987), and Carroll (1987), the compensation strategy of prospectors should be characterized by a high performance orientation, external competitiveness, variable pay as a high proportion of total compensation, and an emphasis on aggregate incentives. Ironically, long-term incentives are generously given in an attempt to diminish a potentially high attrition rate of employees who show little attachment to their employer (Carroll, 1987).

Empirical evidence supports the notion that prospectors do indeed rely on more experiential compensation strategies. A field study by Broderick (1986) found that prospectors are characterized by a pay system with an external value orientation, high performance emphasis, extensive risk sharing, open communication, widespread employee participation, low standardization, and decentralized administration. More recently, Gomez-Mejia (1992) found that on the algorithmic-experiential continuum, prospectors scored the highest—indicating a very strong experiential orientation (see Figure 4.4).

Among defenders, the compensation system assumes a more algorithmic orientation. These types of firms are characterized by highly formalized and centralized functional designs. They tend to define performance in terms of cost control, rather than market outcomes, and operate in a placid environment with stable tasks. High entry barriers in the industry allow many of these firms to develop an elaborate internal labor market that is relatively isolated from the vagaries of the external labor

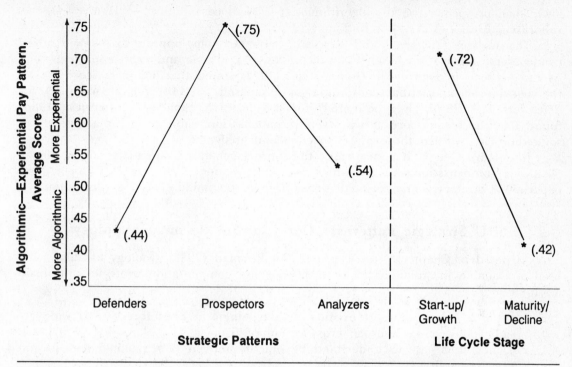

FIGURE 4-4 Graph Showing Extent to Which a Given Business Unit Strategy Exhibits an Experiential (High End of Scale) or an Algorithmic (Low End of Scale) Compensation Pattern*

* Based on the research of Gomez-Mejia (1992).

market.   Employees are rewarded with job security and an expectation of upward mobility through the ranks in exchange for a long-term commitment to the firm.   Furthermore, these firms discourage risk-taking behaviors because investments in existing technologies and processes are substantial and reliability is accorded a high priority. An experiential compensation pattern is less compatible with those conditions.

The algorithmic compensation strategies are more attuned to the defender's organizational structure.   The pay system of defenders, according to Miles and Snow (1984, p. 49), should be characterized by "an orientation toward position in organizational hierarchy, internal consistency, and a total compensation heavily oriented toward cash (vis-a-vis long-term incentives) and driven by superior/subordinate differentials."

Empirical support for the above assertions is relatively strong, although more research remains to be done.   Broderick (1986) found that defenders share many of the characteristics associated with the algorithmic pattern.   According to her findings, defenders emphasize internal, rather than external equity, reward employees based on seniority, avoid risk sharing, keep pay communication and employee participation in the compensation system at a minimum, and develop a highly standardized and centralized administrative apparatus.   Gomez-Mejia (1992) found that defenders score much lower than prospectors on the algorithmic-experiential continuum (see Figure 4-4), cor-roborating Broderick's earlier findings (1986).

The analyzer category in the Miles and Snow taxonomy appears to follow a mixed compensation strategy somewhere in between the algorithmic and experiential extremes. As can be seen in Figure 4.4, Gomez-Mejia (1992) found that analyzers score .54 on the algorithmic-experiential continuum, as compared to .44 (high algorithmic) for defenders and .75 (high experiential) for prospectors. Similarly, Broderick (1986) found that the mean score across several compensation dimensions for analyzers fall somewhere in between those of prospectors and analyzers.

In summary, then, it appears that the more mechanistic defenders rely on an al-gorithmic compensation strategy, while the more organic prospectors rely on a more experiential strategy. Analyzers fall somewhere in the middle of this continuum.

SBU Strategic Patterns: Gerstein and Reisman Typology

As noted in Chapter 3, the Gerstein and Reisman (1983) typology has also been used to examine the relationship between SBU and compensation strategies. Its main advantages are:

1. It is a hybrid of most existing SBU typologies. Therefore, it has wide ap-plicability across a broad cross-section of firms.
2. Since it is easy to understand by practitioners, it is a valuable tool in sur-vey research.

In a conceptual paper, Schuler (1987) argues that entrepreneurial and dynamic growth organizations require employees who are innovative, cooperative, long-term oriented, risk takers, flexible to change, and opportunity seekers. At the other end, firms that are more concerned with maintaining existing profit levels or cutting fur-ther losses (rationalization/maintenance and liquidation strategies, respectively) have a focus on short-term results "with a relatively low level of risk and minimal level of organization identification . . . employees need a short-term, narrow orientation . . . [there is] low organizational commitment, and a low need to remain" (Schuler, 1987, p. 13).

According to Schuler, compensation strategies for the two types of business units described above have opposite orientations. The entrepreneurial and dynamic growth firms adopt compensation strategies that share many of the elements of the experi-ential compensation pattern. These firms place a greater emphasis on external eq-uity, risk sharing, employee participation, and decentralized pay decisions. Business units falling in the rationalization/maintenance and liquidation strategy categories, on the other hand, have compensation strategies that share some commonalities with the algorithmic pattern. According to Schuler (1987, p. 9), the compensation strategies of these firms are characterized by "short-term orientation, internal equity, low par-ticipation . . . few perks, fixed package, no incentives."

Based on a sample of 68 dynamic growth firms and 124 rationalization/mainte-nance firms, Balkin and Gomez-Mejia (1990) found empirical support for the notion that these two types of firms have different pay orientations. The rationalization/maintenance strategy is associated with a higher pay level relative to the market and more emphasis on salary and benefits vis-a-vis incentives. Pay policies in these types of firms are less egalitarian, less involving employee participation, and more job-based (suggesting a more algorithmic orientation). The dynamic growth strategy, on the other hand, is characterized by a more experiential pay orientation—namely, a lower wage position relative to market, a greater reliance on pay incentives, egalitarianism, employee participation in pay decisions, and more use of skill-based pay.

SBU Structural Configuration: Life Cycle Models

As indicated in Chapter 3, with its ultimate roots found in production and marketing, the life cycle concept has played an important role in strategic management. In the 1980s, life cycle models surfaced to the forefront of compensation strategy literature (Balkin and Gomez-Mejia, 1984, 1987a,b; Ellig, 1982; Milkovich, 1988).

Firms at the growth stage are associated with:

1. High dependence on new product innovation to get established in a particular industry (Tilles, 1966).
2. More variability in the firm's profits in response to market trends and shifts since fixed costs involving standardized technologies are relatively high as compared to more mature firms (Morrison, 1966).
3. A more unstable environment that calls for a greater willingness to take risks and a greater tolerance for ambiguity (Gupta and Govindarajan, 1984).
4. High rates of technological change (Hofer, 1975).
5. High rates of failure (Bell, 1982).
6. A socio-technical system characterized by more risk-taking managerial and technical personnel (Ettlie, 1983).
7. Entrepreneurial managers who would rather work with employees who are willing to exchange job security and immediate rewards for the expected utility of anticipated growth (Balkin and Gomez-Mejia, 1987a,b).

For business units at the growth stage the compensation system tends to be experiential in nature (Balkin and Gomez-Mejia, 1987a; Gomez-Mejia, 1992). These business units show a heavy reliance on incentives, rather than on salary and benefits, in the pay mix. This allows the firm at the growth stage to shift a substantial portion of its labor costs from a fixed to a variable expense. This provides the firm with a flexibility to push compensation costs into the future, when it is in a stronger financial position, and, therefore, to receive float from its work force in the short run. Employees receive their incentives when the firm reaches its financial or other strategic goals. This compensation strategy allows the firm in the immediate present to make heavy expenditures needed to fuel future growth in research and development, technological improvements, product changes, and marketing efforts. By emphasizing incentives, employees working for these firms are more likely to be risk takers, which is a desired trait for these companies. The work force may be willing to forego current income (relative to what may be obtained in comparable employment opportunities) in hopes of partaking in the anticipated profits if the firm succeeds. In this manner, incentive pay for these firms helps them not only to support future growth but also to attract a more "adventurous" work force suitable to their needs and to motivate individual and group performance.

As firms mature, professional managers begin to replace entrepreneurs.   One of the main tasks of these managers is to develop administrative mechanisms to formalize the organization, including the pay system.   The firm's environment also changes, becoming more predictable with a stable market share.   The rate of change in technology slows down, and greater economy of scale is achieved in the production process (Hofer, 1975).   Employees hired into those firms are more security oriented and less wiling to gamble their destiny with a fledgling company, even if it offers better future prospects.

The compensation system for mature firms is more algorithmic.   That is, mature firms set up an administrative structure that deemphasizes incentives and rewards employees primarily through a regular paycheck.   Job evaluation systems, such as the Hay Point factor method, are implemented.   A formal pay hierarchy is established and is based on the job as the unit of analysis, rather than individual skills or contributions, with predetermined compensable factors used to make those decisions.

Although empirical research on the relationship between life cycles and compensation systems is limited, it supports the notion that firms at the growth stage rely on more experiential compensation strategies, while those at the mature stage use more algorithmic pay policies.   Balkin and Gomez-Mejia (1987a) found that incentive pay as a proportion of the total compensation package is greater for firms at the growth stage of the product life cycle.   Anderson and Zeithaml (1984) reported that pay level relative to competitors increases as a firm moves from a growth to a mature stage. More recently, Gomez-Mejia (1992), using the algorithmic-experiential continuum described in Chapter 3, found that growth firms score higher on the compensation strategy measure (.72) than mature firms (.42), indicating that the latter relies on algorithmic pay policies much more so than the former.   (See Figure 4-4.)

Stock options and other equity-based rewards are the vehicles most often used to drive the incentive programs for firms at the start-up and growth stages (Balkin and Gomez-Mejia, 1987a,c).   Equity in the company may be offered generously to a broad cross-section of employees.   Since the stock is not publicly traded in most firms at early stages, the cost of stock to the firm is minimal.   Stock ownership supports an egalitarian culture and a team approach that foster risk taking and the entrepreneurial spirit.   The use of stock options can also serve as powerful inducements to employees.   They attract an employee by promising the potential of a large payoff after the stock is publicly offered.   They may induce employees to become more highly committed to the firm.   Finally, stock options are designed to retain talent by placing restrictions on vesting rights to those who stay with the company for a certain period of time (usually three to five years).

SUMMARY AND PROPOSITIONS

In short, the empirical research reviewed in this chapter strongly suggests that different corporate and business unit strategies are associated with varying pay strategy configurations.   A more experiential pay pattern is evident in single- or unrelated-product firms, multibusiness or conglomerate type companies, firms that grow rapidly through aggressive acquisitions, prospectors and dynamic growth business units, and those firms at the growth stage of their life cycles.   At the other extreme, a more algorithmic orientation in the pay system is associated with dominant- and related-product firms with a vertically integrated chain of businesses or where all businesses relate to a single core strength or characteristic, companies that expand through internally generated diversification, defender firms with a rationalization/maintenance strategy, and companies at a mature or decline stage.

One could argue that both extent and process of corporate diversification are ways of operationalizing important aspects of organizational structure and managerial imperatives that bear on reward system design (as per Figures 4-1 and 4-3). The key factors that appear to underlie observed variations in compensation strategies at the corporate level can be summarized in the following propositions:

- *Proposition 1.* The greater the interdependence among business units, the more likely a corporation will rely on an algorithmic compensation pattern to facilitate the flow of human resources across permeable organizational boundaries.

- *Proposition 2.* An algorithmic pay pattern is more prevalent when there is an extensive knowledge of organizational transformations in a central location—that is, when corporate managers know how business unit tasks should be accomplished to transform inputs into desired outcomes.

- *Proposition 3.* The greater the rate of new business acquisitions, the more likely a corporation will adopt an experiential compensation pattern to cope with multiple contingencies uniquely affecting different parts of the company.

- *Proposition 4.* Corporations are more likely to rely on an algorithmic pay pattern if growth is internally generated (e.g., as a technological or market spin-off) because resulting units tend to share a common pool of resources (e.g., R&D, facilities, personnel). This closely knit network calls for greater consistency and uniformity in compensation policies and procedures.

- *Proposition 5.* The more entrepreneurial a corporation is, the more likely it will utilize an experiential compensation pattern that deemphasizes control, encourages risk taking, and places a higher priority on long-term goals. Contrary to widely held beliefs, large organizations are not necessarily less entrepreneurial (see Balkin and Gomez-Mejia, 1988). Some of the largest and most successful corporations in the world frequently launch new business ventures in promising growth industries. These corporations attempt to gain a competitive edge by either creating their own entrepreneurial business units (such as IBM's personal computer business in the late 1970s) or by acquiring entrepreneurial businesses (such as Bristol Myers acquiring genetic engineering firms in the 1980s). More entrepreneurial corporations adopt experiential compensation strategies because these offer greater flexibility and also reinforce an entrepreneurial spirit.

- *Proposition 6.* An experiential compensation pattern is more prevalent as business units become more heterogeneous in terms of markets, products, technology, etc. This approach allows the corporation to be more adaptive to the idiosyncratic needs of each subsidiary.

- *Proposition 7.* An organization will rely on an algorithmic compensation pattern if its top managers desire to promote a unitary corporate-wide perspective. This may be the case, for example, in an owner-managed corporation or a closely held firm.

- *Proposition 8.* As organizations become more complex, an algorithmic compensation pattern becomes more prevalent in an effort to create a sense of order, rationality, and predictability.
- *Proposition 9.* Organizations that attempt to harvest an existing market niche by limiting themselves to a narrow product line are more likely to implement algorithmic compensation strategies. These pay strategies engender greater consistency in procedures, more intimate forms of control by superiors, more stability in work force, more specialization in terms of assigned jobs, a focus on rules of the "game" to be followed by the entire organization, and tighter coupling of organizational subunits.
- *Proposition 10.* Organizations facing limited cash flows and a need to divert scarce funds to finance future expansion are more likely to follow an experiential compensation strategy with its emphasis on risk sharing, flexibility, variable pay, performance, long-term orientation, and outcomes as a basis to trigger rewards. These pay characteristics keep fixed and sunken costs to a minimum, while still allowing the firm to attract and retain a work force that may be willing to exchange higher potential gains for lower immediate pay-offs.

For companies that own two or more separate businesses under a corporate umbrella, several underlying factors are important determinants of the extent to which any given business unit (SBU) relies on an algorithmic or experiential compensation pattern. These relationships may be synthesized in the following propositions:

- *Proposition 11.* An experiential compensation pattern is more prevalent among SBUs that aggressively try to exploit environmental opportunities. This compensation pattern allows SBUs to develop tailored pay policies and procedures to deal with varied external threats and opportunities.
- *Proposition 12.* The greater the volatility and complexity of the external environment facing a SBU, the more likely it will rely on an experiential compensation pattern. These pay strategies are more easily molded to withstand environmental jolts. For instance, a rapid drop in sales may be cushioned by a corresponding decline in variable pay without a dramatic effect on profitability or employment level.
- *Proposition 13.* The greater the extent to which a SBU depends on innovation and technological breakthroughs for its survival, the more likely it will develop experiential compensation strategies. Because meaningful control mechanisms are difficult to develop and flexibility is needed to nurture innovation, adaptable compensation policies and procedures are more appropriate for knowledge intensive firms. For instance, variable incentive programs for a wide cross-section of employees are instrumental in maintaining an egalitarian culture and team approach in order to foster technological innovation. Variable pay gives management more freedom in distributing compensation dollars to employees and may be used as a powerful signaling device to emphasize meeting R&D deadlines, increasing market share, launching a new product, or any other objective that it wants to give high priority.

- *Proposition   14.* An algorithmic compensation pattern will be more evident in business units with a mechanistic organizational structure. These SBUs are characterized by highly repetitive tasks, extreme division of labor, expendable workers, and activities that are relatively narrow and standardized. Historic data is available for control purposes; lines of authority and responsibility are clearly drawn; and monitoring activities are highly centralized in the top echelons of the organization. Employees spend long careers in the firm, moving through the ranks after "paying their dues" at each successive level. An algorithmic compensation pattern reinforces a mechanistic organizational structure by emphasizing uniformity, rules and procedures, order and predictability, and centralized control in the pay system. The algorithmic compensation pattern is used by these firms because it is efficient, and efficiency, rather than adaptability, is perceived by top management to be more instrumental in accomplishing both personal and firm objectives. The use of formal compensation systems with job analysis, job descriptions, job evaluations, and salary structures are used to control costs. Managers are rewarded for reducing expenditures by operating more efficiently and maintaining a flow of steady, predictable profits and quarterly dividends.

- *Proposition   15.* An algorithmic compensation pattern is most likely to be found in business units where the start-up costs and entry barriers are substantial. In these organizations, investments in a core technology may be so prohibitively high that management will try to buffer this core from uncertainty. The compensation system may be used to discourage risk-taking behavior by penalizing (or at least not rewarding) employees for trying new methods or approaches outside established parameters. There is a general belief that deviation from the norm carries a greater downside risk than remaining loyal to the modus operandi. Furthermore, the internal labor market can be more easily protected from external jolts as industry entry barriers increase, facilitating the effective implementation of an algorithmic compensation pattern with its emphasis on hierarchy, rules and procedures, internal equity, centralized decision making, monitoring of behavior by superiors, and fixed pay.

- *Proposition 16.* An algorithmic compensation pattern is more common in firms that have a low tolerance for mistakes from managers or employees. The corporate control systems provide planned standards for performance and knowledge of results with the variances monitored between planned and actual performance. A mistake is viewed as undesirable because mistakes occur when planned outcomes are not attained. The managers and employees learn to meet or exceed planned standards in order to maintain their jobs and move up the career ladder over time. The organizational climate is such that employees understand superiors are not willing to support them when an assumed risk leads to a negative outcome.

- *Proposition 17.* An experiential compensation strategy is more likely to be followed by firms that are at the initial stages of growth and that are short in cash needed to finance future expansion. The distribution between fixed pay (salary and benefits) and variable pay (incentives) is skewed toward the latter in these organizations. This is particularly true if venture capital is being used either from the parent firm or from external sources. By maximizing the portion of total earnings that is variable in nature, the firm can disperse some of its risk across multiple employees. Because the proportion of labor costs to total revenues is higher at earlier stages of the life cycle, scarce resources, are freed and may be directed to support expansion-related activities, e.g., open new market channels, invest in a larger facility, add office automation equipment. If the organization is successful, the variable pay is received by employees; if the firm fails to meet all its objectives, some variable pay is forfeited. This package design matches the high-risk/high-reward environment that faces employees.

- *Proposition 18.* An experiential compensation strategy is more likely to be present in organizational cultures whose value system rests on a calculative, utilitarian, free agent exchange between employees and the firm. The experiential compensation pattern is instrumental to this type of culture because it is not intended to reinforce loyalty or allegiance to an accepted way of doing and thinking. It does, however, generate a strong sense of ownership and responsibility for operations and decisions and an entrepreneurial climate, encouraging employees to pursue multiple leads with a minimum of organizational constraints.

RESEARCH AGENDA FOR THE FUTURE

There are several important areas where the amount of empirical research is almost nil. Therefore, fertile grounds lie fallow for future work on the relationship between organizational and compensation strategies. This type of research will require an interdisciplinary, systemic perspective that bridges human resource management, organizational theory, and strategic management. The following discussions sketch a research agenda concerning those issues that, in the authors' opinion, need most immediate attention.

Mixing Compensation Strategies

In terms of both specific pay strategies (e.g., internal vs. external equity) and overall strategic pay patterns (i.e., algorithmic vs. experiential) organizations have substantial discretion as to where they wish to be on a continuum. That is, it is not a categorical decision of whether to adopt one set of pay choices (e.g., algorithmic) versus another (e.g., experiential) but *to what extent* to be one way or the other. However, little is known about whether this can be done effectively for the entire continuum or whether, at some point, mutually inconsistent demands constrain a further mixing of elements of the two strategic pay orientations and produce an entropic condition. This raises the possibility that while firms may alter their compensation strategies over time, it is quite conceivable that the chosen strategies may be mutually exclusive within a given range. Therefore, further pursuit of one strategy may preclude pursuit of the other. Furthermore, appropriate positioning on a continuum and the range where negating outcomes result from a mix of compensation strategies are very likely to differ by organizational subunit.

Relationship between Corporate Culture, SBU Culture, and Compensation Strategy

Thousands of pages have been written during the past decade alone on the role of corporate culture in human resource management practices (e.g., Fombrun, 1983, 1984a, 1984b, 1984c, 1984d; Fombrun and Laud, 1983; Fombrun, Tichy, and Devanna, 1984; Fombrun and Tichy, 1984; Fryxell, 1990; Hybels and Barley, 1990; Kerr and Slocum, 1988; Ulrich, 1984; Von Glinow, 1985).   But to date, most of the evidence on the purported relationship between organizational culture and compensation strategy is anecdotal in nature (e.g., Cooper, 1991; Kay, Gelfond, and Sherman, 1991; Gordon, 1991).   Conceptual development is also relatively naive at this point and in need of more rigorous deductive models that examine how particular compensation strategies engender, or follow from, particular norms, myths, and beliefs in organizations (Gomez-Mejia, 1983, 1984, 1986).   For instance, it is the authors' intuition that an algorithmic compensation strategy is more likely to be implemented effectively in an organizational culture known for its attachment to tradition and high value placed on continuity, regimentation, and security.   On the other hand, an experiential compensation strategy is more likely to be implemented successfully in an organizational culture characterized by discontinuity, redefinition and renegotiation of tasks and roles as new conditions emerge, and a view of uncertainty and insecurity as a challenge that energizes and stretches people so that they can thrive and grow.

Strategic Employee Groups

An organization may have dozens or even hundreds of different employee groups performing diverse tasks.   It is unlikely that all of these are strategically important to the organization—or, at least, equally important.   For instance, R&D employees are vital in an emerging high technology firm but of relatively minor importance in a mature manufacturing company with a focus on marketing existing products (Balkin and Gomez-Mejia, 1990; Coombs and Gomez-Mejia, 1991; Milkovich, Gerhart, and Hannon, 1991).   Top management is generally viewed as the most important employee group in organizations.   However, in most research universities, faculty, rather than administrators, are viewed as more important and are treated accordingly.   For example, some faculty members earn more money than department chairs, deans, or even the university president (Gomez-Mejia and Balkin, 1992).   We need more conceptualizing and empirical research to help determine under what conditions an employee group becomes strategically important and how the reward system can be designed to take this into account.   The empirical research and the conceptualizing to date on compensation strategy, with the exception of top executive pay, is very global, treating all employee groups as a single entity.   To the extent that algorithmic or experiential pay strategies may be more appropriate for different groups within the same organization this is clearly an area where additional research is needed.

Balancing Consistency and Contingency

Very little is known about how organizations buffer employee groups exposed to different pay strategies.   However, buffering is likely to be an important problem when different pay systems and benefits are used for various SBUs, management layers, and employee populations (e.g., use of team incentives for R&D workers but not for production engineers). Carroll (1988) calls this balancing act one of the major challenges in the management of compensation. Yet, minimal guidance is given to follow if pay is to be used differentially as a strategic tool.

Compensation as a Change Agent or a Follower

Likewise, little is known about whether the pay system leads the charge in modifying organizational norms or if it simply adapts itself to the existing culture. Most importantly, the extent to which the reward system can be consciously manipulated from the top to change the culture below and the relative effectiveness of doing so are not clear. Hearsay evidence suggests that pay allocation may be used as a powerful top management tool to change organizational culture. For example, the deliberate linking of pay raises, promotion, and tenure decisions for faculty based on publication record seems to have had a major effect in changing the culture of many "teaching" schools to a more research oriented environment. Agency theory, as discussed in Chapter 1, argues that pay is an important signaling device. However, there is practically no empirical research on how this process works (or doesn't work) below the executive levels and variables mediating the effectiveness of deliberate signaling attempts via the reward structure.

Compensation Strategy as Derived from Organization Strategy

Related to the previous point, most of the literature assumes that compensation strategy follows from organization strategy (e.g., Milkovich and Broderick, 1991). Pay strategy is often posited as just one more implementation element (along with marketing, production, etc.) of the overarching organizational strategy. Some authors go even further and discuss pay strategy as one of the specialized subfunctional strategies within human resource management (e.g., Weber and Rynes, 1991). These views, however, are unnecessarily constraining and may not reflect organizational realities. There is plenty of evidence (as seen in Chapter 6) to suggest that top corporate management and divisional managers formulate firm strategy largely in response to the characteristics of the compensation package (e.g., in terms of payoff criteria, variability, downside risk, long-term orientation) established by the board of directors. Quite often the compensation package for top management teams is not consciously designed to achieve strategic objectives but may simply reflect the biases of the compensation committee of the board of directors, who the consulting firm happens to be, and the executives' preferences. More research is needed to ascertain how compensation strategy is *causally* related in a prior manner to the strategies adopted by those individuals in a position of power at different levels in the organization.

Role of Dominant Coalitions

As noted in Chapter 1, dominant coalitions in organizations play a very important role in deciding how the reward system is to be structured. But research on

this issue is practically nonexistent. The indirect evidence available suggests that
is a promising avenue to follow if an understanding of how compensation strate
come about is increased. For example, the reward structure in many high tech
ogy firms, with a very experiential orientation, reflects the value system of scier
and engineers who are part of the dominant coalition (Gomez-Mejia and Balkin, 1!
Likewise, the reward structure of firms that are funded by venture capital shows r
of the characteristics of the experiential pay pattern (e.g., high variable pay and
ternal market orientation), reflecting the wishes of the venture capitalists who are
actively involved in the management of the company (Gomez-Mejia, Balkin,
Welbourne, 1990).

A stream of research on the upper echelons perspective (see Hambrick e
1992; Hambrick and Mason, 1984; O'Neill, Saunders, and McCarthy, 1989; Thomas
Ramaswamy, 1989) has proposed that the background characteristics of top man
and the board of directors can be used to predict the strategic choices of firm
similar relationship may exist between the background of these individuals and
reward structure adopted by firms. The underlying argument here is tha
individual's education and life experiences shape personal values and these, in
determine choices made. McCann and Gomez-Mejia (1989, 1990, 1992), for exa
found that how managers conceptualize international issues affecting their firm i
their professional experience. Similar arguments about the relationship betwe
individual's background (e.g., functional area of origin) and decision outcome
be found in Hayes and Abernathy (1980), Lawrence and Lorsch (1967), and Miles
and Snow (1978). It would be interesting in future research to ascertain how the
background and individual characteristics of the dominant coalition affect a firm's compensation strategies. These issues are covered again in Chapter 5.

Flexibility vs. Calcification

Presumably, one of the key advantages of a strategic approach to compensation
is that the reward system can be molded to fit varying situations, contingencies, and
objectives. (See Chapter 5.) However, organizations are reluctant to change HRM
systems once they are installed, and these systems quite often remain in place for years
after they outlive their usefulness. This happens because employees develop expectations, and compensation practices become "psychological contracts," which are
difficult to change. This is one of the problems plaguing gainsharing and profit-sharing
plans. Because employees expect monetary rewards from these programs, they react
very negatively and voice widespread dissatisfaction with the company when this doesn't
happen. (See *CompFlash*, April, 1991; Welbourne and Gomez-Mejia, 1988.)

A related issue seldom discussed in the literature is that the matching between
pay strategies and the SBU or corporate strategy should concern the intended (i.e.,
future), not the "de facto observed" (i.e., present), organizational strategy. For instance, pay strategies should not be designed to match the corporation's current level
of diversification but should be guided by the direction in which the organization's
diversification strategy is expected to move. If a dominant-product firm is trying to
diversify into unrelated products and a conglomerate plans to trim down by selling
unrelated SBUs, then perhaps an experiential pay strategy should be phased into the
former and an algorithmic pay strategy slowly introduced into the latter.

In summary, more needs to be learned about leads/lags in how compensation strategies respond to firm strategies and the extent to which built-in inertia prevents the pay system from being attuned to the strategic demands of both the corporation and SBUs.

Role of Individual Differences

There has been very limited research concerning how individual differences affect employee reactions to compensation strategies.   (See Gerhart and Milkovich, 1993.) This is important because, as seen in Chapter 5, these differences are likely to moderate the effectiveness of pay strategies.   To the extent that individual differences are not random but follow a certain pattern (e.g., more risk-taking personnel joining entrepreneurial firms), it may be possible to take this into account in deciding where to be along the algorithmic-experiential compensation continuum in different situations.   For example, Gomez-Mejia and Balkin (1989) report that individuals with a high propensity for risk and a high tolerance for ambiguity thrive in firms where variable pay is a substantial portion of total compensation.   This, they found, was clearly the case among smaller high technology firms.   Forcing an experiential compensation pattern with high variable pay in more mature companies where the typical employee has a low tolerance for risk and a greater desire for certainty is met with resistance and engenders attrition. This research has only uncovered the tip of the iceberg, and no one can assume that compensation strategies may be implemented uniformly in the work force without factoring in individual differences.

Linkage between Top Management Compensation Strategies and Overarching Compensation Strategies

As seen in Chapters 6 and 7, much has been written about compensation strategies for top executives, particularly the chief executive officers (CEOs).   However, very little is known about how CEOs interact with, or perhaps even determine, the compensation strategies of the entire organization.   Agency theory, as discussed in Chapter 1, proposes that the structure of the CEO compensation package influences the reward system throughout the organization.   Top executives are likely to reward subordinates' behaviors that are conducive to the achievement of their own objectives.   But there is a dearth of research examining how this process works.   Nor is there much research on how the conditions under which the "filtering down" of the incentive system for top executives may influence the firm's relative positioning along the algorithmic-experiential continuum.

Internal Compensation Strategies vs. Imitation

Much of the literature on compensation strategy assumes that organizations have much freedom to choose their own pay strategies, which, in general, are designed to be compatible with the overall firm strategy.   This is reflected in the fundamental tenets summarized by Milkovich (1988, p. 263) as "first ... that compensation policies and practices differ widely across organizations and second ... that the decisions managers and employees make help shape these differences; that discretion exists to choose among options and the processes used to implement them." This way of thinking is derived from the strategic choice view (e.g., Child, 1972; Miles and Snow, 1978; Mintzberg, 1980), a dominant paradigm in organization theory and strategic management. According to this perspective, which is very inner-directed, strategic decisions are made by key managers who perceive and interpret environmental situations in order to design proactively organizational responses. Because perceptions, rather than actual reality, play a major role here, a wide variety of organizational responses may be made, depending on managers' cognitive orientation and values.

As seen in Chapter 5, the primary determinant of whether the choices made contribute to organizational performance is internal congruency (between, for example, pay strategies and the organizational strategies adopted by management). However, it is quite possible that compensation strategies are chosen to imitate those of other firms in the industry (as many industrial/organizational economists would suggest), rather than being internally generated. Ample evidence of intense imitation in the compensation system across firms was found by Balkin and Gomez-Mejia (1987a) among high technology companies along Route 128 in Boston. An important reason behind the impetus to adopt experiential pay strategies (e.g., various forms of variable pay plans) may simply be attributed to imitation. Most likely, both internal forces and imitation play a role in the design of compensation strategies, but little is known about their relative importance and how compensation strategies may be idiosyncratically designed to gain a competitive advantage. Integrating the two partial views—namely, one that focuses on strategic choices as a predictor of resulting pay strategies and the other that relies on imitation—would enhance an understanding of the determinants and consequences of pay strategies.

Compensation Strategies in an International Context

A crucial question that arises as a result of increased globalization of business is whether reward systems should be customized to meet the needs of individuals within diverse cultures or whether compensation strategies that work in a domestic environment can be easily transferred from one country to another. So, it is not just a question of molding pay strategies to organizational strategies but also of ensuring that the compensation system is attuned to the cultural milieu (Gomez-Mejia, 1988; Gomez-Mejia and McCann, 1989; Gomez-Mejia and Welbourne, 1991; McCann and Gomez-Mejia, 1990; Tung, 1981, 1982, 1984a, 1984b, 1987). For instance, bonus pay in Japan averages 26 percent of total pay vs. 0.5 percent in the United States (Gerhart and Milkovich, 1993). But perhaps it may be impossible to reach the Japanese variable pay proportion in the United States, except in some unusual situations such as entrepreneurial start-ups.

One clear trend being observed is that multinational corporations (not just American but also British, Swedish, French, and Japanese) are standardizing pay strategies on a global basis. (See *Business Week's* cover story on the "Stateless Corporation," 1990c; Klein, 1991; McCann and Gomez-Mejia, 1985; Mesdag, 1984; Whenmouth, 1988.) Phillip Ash, a consultant with the Wyatt Co. Actuaries and Employee Benefit Consultants, a Washington, D.C.-based consulting company operating in many countries, comments that "there is more of an international emphasis placed on evaluating salaries" (Ash, 1991, B4).   The question that must be raised, then, is whether global compensation strategies are most appropriate for MNCs.   Can some compensation strategies be used effectively on a universal basis, while others should be customized to meet the specific needs of diverse national cultures?   Because practically all research on compensation strategy has been conducted domestically, very little is known about how international forces affect pay strategies and their effectiveness.   Given the growing importance of international trade, overseas manufacturing operations, increased growth of multinationals, new countries entering international trade, and the rapid changes in technology needed to keep pace with the world economy, this area of research clearly merits more attention.   While research on the effect of culture on managerial practices has grown enormously since the early 1980s, very little of it has focused explicitly on compensation issues.   (See Adler, 1983a, 1983b, 1984; Adler and Jelinek, 1986; Beatty, McCune and Beatty, 1988; DeNoble and Galbraith, 1992; Dowling, 1986, 1987, 1988, 1989; Hofstede, 1980; Kedia, Keller, and Julian, 1992; Kujawa, 1986; Gomez-Mejia, 1984; Gomez-Mejia and McCann, 1985.)

APPENDIX 4A

A PROFILE OF COMPENSATION STRATEGIES ASSOCIATED WITH VARIOUS CORPORATE STRATEGIES

Basis for Pay	Corporate Strategies		
	Diversification Extent	Patterns of Linkages	Diversification Process
Unit of Analysis			
Job	Related-Product	Vertical/Constrained	Steady
Skills	Single-Unrelated-Product	Multibusiness/Conglomerate	Evolutionary
Criteria for Pay Increases			
Performance	Single-Unrelated-Product	Multibusiness/Conglomerate	Evolutionary
Tenure	Related-Product	Vertical/Constrained	Steady
Level of Performance Measurement			
Individual	Related-Product	Vertical/Constrained	Steady
Individual and Aggregate	Single-Unrelated-Product	Multibusiness/Conglomerate	Evolutionary
Time Orientation			
Long-Term	Single-Unrelated-Product	Multibusiness/Conglomerate	Evolutionary
Short-Term	Related-Product	Vertical/Constrained	Steady
Risk Sharing			
High	Single-Unrelated-Product	Multibusiness/Conglomerate	Evolutionary
Low	Related-Product	Vertical/Constrained	Steady
Strategic Focus			
Corporate	Related-Product	Vertical/Constrained	Steady
Division/Business Unit	Single-Unrelated-Product	Multibusiness/Conglomerate	Evolutionary
Equity Concern			
Internal Consistency	Related-Product	Vertical/Constrained	Steady
Market Driven	Single-Unrelated-Product	Multibusiness/Conglomerate	Evolutionary

APPENDIX 4A (Continued)

Basis for Pay	Corporate Strategies		
	Diversification Extent	Patterns of Linkages	Diversification Process
Reward Distribution			
Egalitarian	Single-Unrelated-Product	Multibusiness/Conglomerate	Evolutionary
Hierarchical	Related-Product	Vertical/Constrained	Steady
Appraisal Basis			
Monitoring Behaviors	Related-Product	Vertical/Constrained	Steady
Monitoring Outcomes	Single-Unrelated-Product	Multibusiness/Conglomerate	Evolutionary

Design Issues

Salary Market Policy			
Above Market Pay	Related-Product	Vertical/Constrained	Steady
Below Market Pay	Single-Unrelated-Product	Multibusiness/Conglomerate	Evolutionary
Benefits Market Policy			
Above Market	Related-Product	Vertical/Constrained	Steady
Below Market	Single-Unrelated-Product	Multibusiness/Conglomerate	Evolutionary
Incentives in Pay Mix			
High	Single-Unrelated-Product	Multibusiness/Conglomerate	Evolutionary
Low	Related-Product	Vertical/Constrained	Steady
Total Compensation			
High Potential/Low Immediate Payoffs	Single-Unrelated-Product	Multibusiness/Conglomerate	Evolutionary
Low Future Potential/Higher Immediate Payoffs	Related-Product	Vertical/Constrained	Steady
Reinforcement Schedule			
Multiple Rewards/High Frequency	Single-Unrelated-Product	Multibusiness/Conglomerate	Evolutionary
Fewer Rewards/Low Frequency	Related-Product	Vertical/Constrained	Steady

APPENDIX 4A (Continued)

Design Issues	Corporate Strategies		
	Diversification Extent	Patterns of Linkages	Diversification Process
Reward Emphasis			
Nonmonetary	Related-Product	Vertical/Constrained	Steady
Pecuniary	Single-Unrelated-Product	Multibusiness/Conglomerate	Evolutionary
Administrative Framework			
Decision Making			
Centralized	Related-Product	Vertical/Constrained	Steady
Decentralized	Single-Unrelated-Product	Multibusiness/Conglomerate	Evolutionary
Pay Disclosure			
High Pay Openness	Single-Unrelated-Product	Multibusiness/Conglomerate	Evolutionary
Low Pay Openness	Related-Product	Vertical/Constrained	Steady

APPENDIX 4B

A PROFILE OF COMPENSATION STRATEGIES ASSOCIATED WITH VARIOUS BUSINESS UNIT STRATEGIES

Basis for Pay	Business Unit Strategies		
	Miles and Snow Typology	Gerstein and Reisman Typology	Life Cycle
Unit of Analysis			
Job	Defenders	Rationalization/ Maintenance	Mature/Decline
Skills	Prospectors	Dynamic Growth	Start-up/Growth
Criteria for Pay Increases			
Performance	Prospectors	Dynamic Growth	Start-up/Growth
Tenure	Defenders	Rationalization/ Maintenance	Mature/Decline
Level of Performance Measure			
Individual	Defenders	Rationalization/ Maintenance	Mature/Decline
Individual and Aggregrate	Prospectors	Dynamic Growth	Start-up/Growth
Time Orientation			
Long-Term	Prospectors	Dynamic Growth	Start-up/Growth
Short-Term	Defenders	Rationalization/ Maintenance	Mature/Decline
Risk Sharing			
High	Prospectors	Dynamic Growth	Start-up/Growth
Low	Defenders	Rationalization/ Maintenance	Mature/Decline
Strategic Focus			
Corporate	Defenders	Rationalization/ Maintenance	Mature/Decline
Division/Business Unit	Prospectors	Dynamic Growth	Start-up/Growth
Equity Concern			
Internal Consistency	Defenders	Rationalization/ Maintenance	Mature/Decline
Market Driven	Prospectors	Dynamic Growth	Start-up/Growth

APPENDIX 4B (Continued)

Basis for Pay	Business Unit Strategies		
	Miles and Snow Typology	Gerstein and Resiman Typology	Life Cycle
Reward Distribution			
Egalitarian	Prospectors	Dynamic Growth	Start-up/Growth
Hierarchical	Defenders	Rationalization/ Maintenance	Mature/Decline
Appraisal Basis			
Monitoring Behaviors	Defenders	Rationalization/ Maintenance	Mature/Decline
Monitoring Outcomes	Prospectors	Dynamic Growth	Start-up/Growth
Salary Market Policy			
Above Market Policy	Defenders	Rationalization/ Maintenance	Mature/Decline
Below Market Policy	Prospectors	Dynamic Growth	Start-up/Growth
Benefits Market Policy			
Above Market Benefits	Defenders	Rationalization/ Maintenance	Mature/Decline
Below Market Benefits	Prospectors	Dynamic Growth	Start-up/Growth
Design Issues			
Incentives in Pay Mix			
High	Prospectors	Dynamic Growth	Start-up/Growth
Low	Defenders	Rationalization/ Maintenance	Mature/Decline
Total Compensation			
High Potential/Low Immediate Payoffs	Prospectors	Dynamic Growth	Start-up/Growth
Low Future Potential/ Higher Immediate Payoffs	Defenders	Rationalization/ Maintenance	Mature/Decline
Reinforcement Schedule			
Multiple Rewards/ High Frequency	Prospectors	Dynamic Growth	Start-up/Growth
Fewer Rewards/ Low Frequency	Defenders	Rationalization/ Maintenance	Mature/Decline

APPENDIX 4B (Continued)

Design Issues	Business Unit Strategies		
	Miles and Snow Typology	Gerstein and Reisman Typology	Life Cycle
Reward Emphasis			
Nonmonetary	Defenders	Rationalizaiton/ Maintenance	Mature/Decline
Pecuniary	Prospectors	Dynamic Growth	Start-up/Growth
Administrative Framework			
Decision Making			
Centralized	Defenders	Rationalization/ Maintenance	Mature/Decline
Decentralized	Prospectors	Dynamic Growth	Start-up/Growth
Pay Disclosure			
High Pay Openness	Prospectors	Dynamic Growth	Start-up/Growth
Low Pay Openness	Defenders	Rationalization/ Maintenance	Mature/Decline
Governance Structure			
Participative	Prospectors	Dynamic Growth	Start-up/Growth
Nonparticipate	Defenders	Rationalization/ Maintenance	Mature/Decline
Nature of Pay Policies			
Bureaucratic	Defenders	Rationalization/ Maintenance	Mature/Decline
Flexible	Prospectors	Dynamic Growth	Start-up/Growth
Superior Dependency			
High	Defenders	Rationalization/ Maintenance	Mature/Decline
Low	Prospectors	Dynamic Growth	Start-up/Growth

OVERARCHING COMPENSATION STRATEGIES AND FIRM PERFORMANCE

Chapter 4 described in some detail the compensation strategies associated with various corporate and business unit strategies. Ultimately, however, the main concern when designing and implementing pay strategies is the extent to which these are conducive to improved firm performance. Because it is the most generalized reinforcer available to organizations to mold the behavior of its members, money can play a crucial role in supporting strategy implementation. Money can also assist in charting the strategic direction of the enterprise at the top executive level. The individuals at the top respond strongly to the financial packages prepared by the board of directors or their representatives such as the compensation committee or consulting firms.

Most of the literature on the relationship between compensation strategy and firm performance revolves around the most senior executives. "Ultimately there is only one strategist, and that is the manager who sits at the apex of the organizational hierarchy" (Mintzberg, 1990, p. 176). Most companies allocate all major decisions to CEOs and general managers because these people are "principally concerned with determining and monitoring the adequacy of strategy, with adapting the firm to changes in its environment and with securing and developing the people needed to carry out the strategy or the help with its constructive revision or evolution" (Zand, 1981, p. 125). Given the importance, extensive nature, and specialized focus of this literature, two chapters are devoted to issues related to top executive compensation and firm performance (Chapters 6 and 7).

This chapter examines overarching compensation strategies and how these are expected to influence firm performance. Cutting across several fields but drawing primarily from strategic management and the macro HRM research, the conceptual and empirical literature dealing with the "*so what?*" question in compensation strategy is reviewed and synthesized. It builds upon much of the framework introduced in the previous four chapters. This material, in turn, paves the way to subsequent chapters exclusively devoted to top management teams, in particular the chief executive officer (CEO).

THEORETICAL FRAMEWORK

Figure 5-1 graphically depicts the key theoretical variables that help explain how and why pay strategies affect firm performance. The model suggests that the relative contribution of pay strategies to firm performance increases:

1. The greater the integration between pay strategies, corporate strategies, business unit strategies, organizational idiosyncrasies, and the dominant logic of top management teams.
2. The more pay strategies serve to erect barriers of entry for competitors.
3. The more a firm's pay strategies enable it to capitalize on its distinctive competencies.
4. The more pay strategies can reduce transaction costs between organizational subunits.
5. The more the pay system is capable of securing and maintaining strategic employee groups critical to the accomplishment of a firm's mission and integral to its technical core.

The multidisciplinary theoretical underpinnings of this model is discussed next.

Contingency Theory

Contingency theory has played a major role in providing a conceptual rationale as to which compensation strategies are most likely to contribute to firm performance given cer-

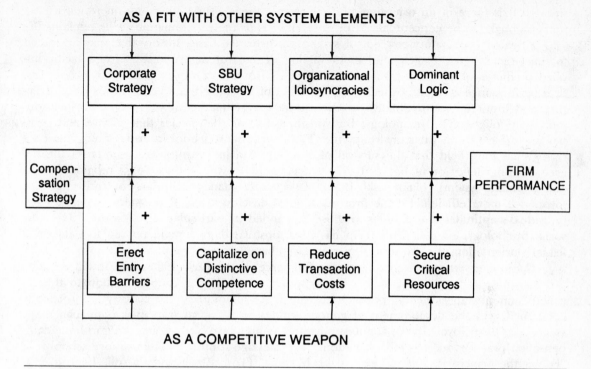

FIGURE 5-1 Theoretical Model of the Relationship Between Compensation Strategy and Firm Performance

tain conditions. It is clearly the most overarching or general paradigm in the management field. Yet, at the same time, it is perhaps the simplest one. First examined are the essential elements of contingency theory, and then these contingency notions are applied to the special case of compensation.

The central tenet of contingency theory is that lack of *fit* or *equifinality* between two or more elements of a system reduces its overall effectiveness. If they lacked fit, the constituent parts would function at cross-purposes, not at tandem in a synergistic fashion. Unless elements within the system are realigned and brought into consistency, the system will continue to operate suboptimally and, in extreme cases, fail to survive. As a corollary, the contribution any part makes to the performance of the entire system is always dependent or contingent on its fit with some other factor, rather than as an independent phenomena that can be examined out of context. In other words, the performance of the system in toto is a direct function of the match between its various components. The opposite is also true. The greater the internal incongruencies within a system, the more entropic or self-destructive it becomes.

Contingency theory represents a philosophical perspective that may be used to study a wide variety of complex processes by reducing them to a global dictum: Fit leads to greater performance. In the words of Schoonhoven (1981, p. 350), "Contingency theory is not a theory at all in the conventional sense of theory as a well-developed set of interrelated propositions. It is more of an orienting strategy or metatheory, suggesting ways in which a phenomena ought to be conceptualized or an approach to the phenomenon to be explained."

Fit as an explanatory concept of system performance has a history that may be traced to the Greeks. (See Nagel, 1961.) In varying degrees of determinacy, fit is a tacitly implied predictor of effectiveness across many fields. A few examples follow. In economics, firm performance is often posited as a by-product of the match between a firm's price structure and input utilization relative to the nature of the market (e.g., perfect competition, monopoly, oligopoly). In biology, Darwinism maintains the species that survive and prosper are those that fit their environment. The functionalist school in anthropology and sociology has long held that the survival of a society and its institutions depends on the degree of congruency or fit between different elements of the culture (e.g., religious values and economic system) (Malinowski, 1936). In scientific management, an enterprise was said to operate more efficiently if the firm was able to develop a selection system to match each individual's aptitudes and abilities to those demanded by particular jobs (Taylor, 1947). In social psychology, effective leadership has been postulated to depend on the fit between a leader's orientation, the group setting, and task characteristics (Fiedler, 1967).

Contingency theory hit management full force in the early 1960s, and it still remains a dominant paradigm in the field. It was widely adopted as a counterreaction to the so-called "administrative theory" prevalent in the first half of the 20th century. Principally concerned with the development of general guides or universal principles of management (see Davis, 1951; Fayol, 1949), administrative theory also gave birth to many algorithmic compensation practices such as job evaluation. The message from the administrative school was: "Follow the principles, and success will likely come" (Tosi, Rizzo, and Carroll, 1990, p. 55). On the other hand, contingency theory as applied to management argues that in order to be most effective, organization policies and practices should be appropriate to the firm's unique characteristics and/or the environmental conditions facing it. Thus, from a managerial perspective, this theory is based on two key notions. First, there is no best way to do things in organizations; and second, "any way of organizing is not equally effective under all conditions" (Galbraith, 1973, p. 2).

A vast amount of research in organization theory and strategy supports the proposition that consistency or fit (for both internal and external elements) has a beneficial effect on firm performance. Several studies have found this to be true. Many researchers have examined: the congruency between firm strategy and structure (Chandler, 1962; Child, 1972; Donaldson, 1987); firm structure and technology (Kanzanjian, 1993; Khandwalla, 1974; Perrow, 1970; Woodward, 1965); organization's internal states and processes to environment (Lawrence, 1975; Lawrence and Lorsh, 1967); firm strategy and environment (Malekzadeh, Bickford, and Spital, 1989; Miller, 1988; Prescott and Allenby, 1993); strategic group membership and rate of change in environment (Fiegenbaum and Thomas, 1990); communication channels and nature of the task (Tushman, 1978); management style and organization characteristics (Levitt, 1974), etc.

The underlying rationale for this stream of research is that organizational strategies can be broken down into multiple elements (e.g., technology, structure) that are important in their own right as well as for the roles they play in overall strategic plans. Accordingly, "if the various elements are not integrated or congruent with the overall strategy, the organization has an unclear, or missing, strategic direction leading to suboptimal or even dysfunctional outcomes... In other words, because strategy 'elements' should be mutually determined by a firm, this relationship implies that an important normative test for a firm's strategy is internal consistency..." (Balkin and Gomez-Mejia, 1990, p. 154).

The contingency view of effectiveness, which posits that certain conditions such as the firm's life cycle stage or size demands specific types of managerial policies, has had dramatic influence on the field of human resource management in recent years. The number of HRM scholars relying on the notion of fit as an explanation for the relative effectiveness of personnel practices is growing rapidly, and contingency theory is becoming a dominant paradigm in HRM. Sparrow and Pettigrew (1988, p. 33), for example, note that "firms need to ensure that they change their HRM so that it more closely matches their strategic intent to offer a total services solution." Likewise, Dyer and Holder (1988, p. 5) argue:

> HRM-related judgments require an extensive knowledge of not only the proposed busi-
> ness strategies, including any implied or stated changes in the organizational environment,
> such as structures or technologies, but also any constraining factors in the organization's
> internal or external environments. . . The general rule is: The tighter the external and
> internal fit, the better the strategy. External fit refers to the degree of consistency be-
> tween HR goals on the one hand and the exigencies of the underlying business strategy
> and relevant environmental conditions on the other. Internal fit measures the extent to
> which HR means follow from HR goals and other relevant environmental conditions, as
> well as the degree of coherence or synergy among the various HR means.

Applications of Contingency Theory. A few illustrative examples of contingency theory ap-plications to HRM follow.

Murray (1988) reports that more homogeneous management teams perform better when competition is intense, while more heterogeneous management groups perform better when environmental change is gradual. Donaldson (1987) found that a mismatch between an executive's background and the strategy followed by the firm has dysfunctional consequences for performance. Similar findings were reported by Norburn and Birley (1988), Thomas and Ramaswamy (1989), Gupta and Govindarajan (1984), and O'Neill, Saunders, and McCarthy (1989). Using the Miles and Snow typology described in Chapter 3, Thomas and Ramaswamy (1989, p. 42) concluded: "Since managers influence the strategic direction of the firm, a fit between managerial characteristics and strategy is necessary. The absence of such a fit will result in a conflict between the goals of top management and the compe-tence of the organization. This conflict will no doubt have a negative impact on perfor-mance."

In matching human resources policies and practices to strategic, environmental, and organizational conditions, investigators have examined a wide variety of personnel processes such as recruitment and selection (Cascio, 1990; Duchon and Ashmos, 1992; Olian and Rynes, 1984); attrition (Coombs and Rosse, 1992; Perry, 1986; Turbin and Rosse, 1990); training (Faley and Kleiman, 1992; Liden and Adams, 1992; Stumpf and Hanrahan, 1984); perfor-mance appraisal (Lawler, 1989; Martochio and Ferris, 1991); human resource planning (Mohrman, Mohrman, and Cohen, 1992; Rothwell and Kazanas, 1988); and the interface of technology with human resources (O'Connor, Parsons, Liden, and Herold, 1990). While the amount of data-based research on these issues is still relatively scarce, the available evi-dence suggests that the contributions of human resource management to firm performance depend on the match between HRM strategies and contingency factors internal and exter-nal to the organization.

To summarize, the essential logic behind this line of research is as follows:

1. Diverse environmental conditions, organizational strategies, and firm characteristics require different HRM policies and practices.

2. Strategies that change over time differ among organizations.
3. The relative usefulness of different HRM policies and practices varies across contexts.
4. While organizational strategies drive HRM strategies, there are reciprocal effects because managers and employees will influence emergent (ad hoc) strategies at different levels in the organization.
5. Significant deviations from the ideal HRM strategies profile that would be most appropriate given the firm's environment, strategies, and characteristics will result in lower performance. The HRM strategies need to be adaptive so that when contingency factors mediating their effectiveness change, they can be adjusted accordingly.
6. The notion of general principles in personnel management is essentially bankrupt and, unless legally mandated, is bound to produce suboptimal results.

Compensation Strategy, Fit, and Firm Performance.   The consistency with which systematic relationships have been discovered between firm performance and the congruency of organizational characteristics, functional strategies (including HRM), environmental forces, and organizational strategy would lead one to expect the existence of a similar relationship with the firm's compensation system. Following the stream of research reviewed above, a contingency view would argue that the contribution of the pay system to firm performance improves as:

1. The fit between compensation strategies, overall corporate strategies, and SBU strategies increases.
2. The congruency between the pay system, organizational characteristics, and the environment increases.

The more the pay strategies deviate from the ideal compensation strategies appropriate for various organizational strategies (see Chapter 4), the lower their contribution to firm performance. In other words, "the normative implication flowing from these arguments is that unless pay strategies reinforce the organization's overall strategy, the return on compensation dollars will be less than optimal and even negative in some cases if pay policies induce behaviors that run counter to the firm's strategic objectives." (Balkin and Gomez-Mejia, 1990, p. 154).

The contingency notion of effectiveness argues that it is possible to determine the conditions under which reliance on particular pay strategies is more likely to produce desired results. Therefore, one can postulate that:

1. As discussed in Chapter 4, there are consistent and recurrent patterns of corporate and SBU compensation strategies that are associated with particular organizational strategies.
2. Both corporate and SBU strategies exercise an independent as well as a combined influence on various pay strategies.
3. It is possible to ascertain empirically a pay effectiveness configuration (in terms of contributions to firm performance) for various combinations of pay, and of corporate and SBU strategies. The more a firm deviates from the hypothesized pay

strategy configuration that is most appropriate for any given corporate or SBU strategy, the lower the performance of the firm.

4.   Close articulation between pay strategies, organizational characteristics, and the environment should enhance firm performance.

Strategic Choice and the Coalitional Model

The traditional concept of fit as used in strategy, organization theory, and much of the compensation strategy literature assumes that well-defined firm strategies exist. Therefore, the main challenge is to match substrategies (such as pay) to corporate and SBU strategies. However, an organization's strategy is not always readily discerned or clearly enunciated. Some would even argue that "in marked contrast to the conventional view ... strategic issues are loosely defined, ill specified, and fuzzy" (Baucus and Ottensmeyer, 1989, p. 3). Mintzberg and McHugh (1985) coined the term "adhocracy" to describe much of the strategy making process in organizations that is not deliberate in nature. This suggests that linking pay strategies to organizational strategies may be somewhat elusive because firm strategies are not well-articulated. One good reason for avoiding a deliberate formulation of firm strategies is to retain flexibility in an unpredictable environment (Mintzberg, 1990).

A second reason is that strategic choices are seldom made following a rigorous deductive process. Strategies are not formulated in a vacuum by rational decision makers but by managers who rely on their own personal schemas or mental representations of the world, and this provides a vehicle for them to construct (or enact) reality socially. (See Weick, 1979). Prahalad and Bettis (1986) refers to this schema or general mental structure as *dominant logic*, which they define as a "mind set or a world view or conceptualization of the business and the administrative tools to accomplish goals and make decisions in that business. It is stored as a shared cognitive map (or set of schemas) among the dominant coalition. It is expressed as a learned, problem-solving behavior" (p. 488). According to Prahalad and Bettis (1986, p. 489):

> Top management of a firm should not be viewed "as a faceless abstraction", but as a "collection of key individuals" (i.e., a dominant coalition) who have significant influence on the way the firm is managed. This collection of individuals, to a large extent, influence the style and process of management, and as a result the key resource allocation choices. ... Few organizational events are approached by these managers (or any managers) as being totally unique and requiring systematic study. Instead, they are processed through pre-existing knowledge systems. Known as schemas ..., these systems represent beliefs, theories and propositions that have developed over time based on the manager's personal experiences. At a broader unit of analysis, [there is] implied the possibility that organizations' actions can be characterized as schemas. An organizational schema is primarily a product of managers' interpretations of experiences ...

The Dominant Coalition. This *coalitional perspective* suggests that pay strategies are most likely to be effective not only when they match the organization's articulated strategy (assuming they do), but also when they are compatible with the general philosophy of the dominant coalition. As noted earlier, traditional strategy models depict top executives as the most influential individuals responsible for tracing the organization's strategy. While they clearly play a crucial role (see Chapter 6), "both logical reasoning and empirical evidence indicate that in most large organizations absolute power does not reside with the CEO or SBU head; rather, power is shared by several managers constituting a dominant coalition" (Gupta, 1986, p. 220). Thus, to the extent that powerful coalitions make decisions that influence the entire organization, pay strategies should be synchronized with their value system to avoid a clash with the dominant logic of the ruling group.

Along a similar vein, Hambrick and Mason (1984) developed a theoretical model that links psychological characteristics of executives and demographic traits of top management with strategic choice. They suggest that a fit between upper echelons personal biases and strategy leads to greater firm performance. The logic of Hambrick and Mason's deductions find support in a number of studies. Miller, Kets de Vries, and Toulouse (1982) report that successful firms that adopt risky and innovative strategies are run by confident and aggressive management teams. Dearborn and Simon (1958) found that how problems are perceived and the solution set taken into account by decision makers depends on these individuals' functional backgrounds. Similar findings were reported by Hayes and Abernathy (1980). Hitt and Ireland (1985, 1986) found that a match between top managers' backgrounds and firm strategy has a positive effect on the performance of the company. This suggests that congruency between the value system of the dominant coalition and various substrategies (including compensation) should have a beneficial effect on firm performance.

By implication, the ability of HRM professionals to discern how the dominant coalitions think and what they value is likely to influence the eventual success or failure of HRM programs. For instance, in the performance appraisal area, researchers have long argued that appraisal programs will not work unless top management teams support them (e.g., Cardy and Dobbins, 1993; Latham and Wexley, 1981). However, these plans continue to be introduced by human resource departments with minimal input from upper management, whose value system is ignored (Gomez-Mejia, 1990). As a result, paraphernalia associated with performance appraisal (e.g., forms, brochures, guides, policies, and procedures) are often introduced with much fanfare only to start catching dust in a drawer a short time later. Many compensation programs doubtlessly encounter a similar fate.

Dominant Coalitions and the Shaping of Compensation Programs. While the amount of empirical work examining the role dominant coalitions play in the relative effectiveness of compensation programs is almost nil (because most of it focuses on the linkages between pay strategies and formal organizational strategies), anecdotal evidence supports a connection between the two. A few examples follow to illustrate this point:

- Organizations run by entrepreneurs have a more experiential compensation pattern than those run by professional management, even after controlling for other factors (Balkin and Gomez-Mejia, 1988).
- Firms where venture capitalists play an important role report that performance improves the more the company relies on an experiential compensation pattern (Gomez-Mejia, Balkin, and Welbourne, 1990).
- Firms whose top management groups are risk avoiders, have a high need for order and predictability, and have long tenures with the firm show an affinity for elaborate compensation plans akin to the algorithmic pay strategy pattern described in Chapter 3. These types of managers see these plans as contributing to firm performance by reducing labor strikes, encouraging stability in the work force, and creating a system of distributive justice leading to higher morale and a better employee-management relations climate (Brown and Nolan, 1988).

• It is not uncommon for family-run companies to value deeply group relationships and personal commitment of employees to the firm (Welbourne and Gomez-Mejia, 1990; Powers and Gomez-Mejia, 1991). They tend to rely on a mix of experiential and algorithmic pay strategies. Corporate policies governing allocation of rewards in these firms are often loose, with a high priority in pay decisions given to loyalty to the business, seniority, and conformity. Especially in smaller family-owned firms, a patriarchal system for distributing rewards (where managers like to show largess) is fairly common. Gomez-Mejia and Welbourne (1991) suggest that compensation programs based on group performance support the value system of family-run businesses. All employees are rewarded when the group accomplishes its goal. The use of individual-based criteria does not set well with the group atmosphere that these companies attempt to build. Seniority-based rewards are also important to them because they promote long-term relationships with the organization and reward loyalty to the firm. Intrinsic rewards are employed at least as much as extrinsic rewards because top management is interested in promoting a moral, rather than a purely calculative, commitment to the firm.

A number of case studies of individual firms attest to the importance of dominant coalitions in shaping compensation programs. Chace (1982) attributes the reward system of IBM to the legacy of its founder, Thomas J. Watson, Sr. who died in 1956. The three central values espoused by Watson, and subsequently adopted by top management teams at IBM, are loyalty, job security, and high performance expectations. According to Chace (1982), joining IBM is seen by management as "calling for absolute fidelity in matters big and small" (p. 5). IBM's reward system reinforces this value orientation in a number of ways. First, "It prides itself on being able to reward those who follow its code and meet its expectations with success and security for life" (p. 5). Second, "Tight discipline is enforced by near-constant observation and grading" (p. 5). Finally:

Achievement is followed by immediate rewards. Insiders say the most cherished of these isn't money. It's having your name and quota on the bulletin board with a notation saying 100%. It's having a party thrown for you at your branch because you have satisfied a prickly customer. It's a steady flow of letters of commendation. Says one ex-IBMer: "If you burp the right way, they send you a certificate" (p. 5).

A second case study illustrating the influence of dominant coalitions on the reward structure concerns Minnesota Mining and Manufacturing Co. (3M). According to 3M's CEO, Lewis W. Lehr, the most salient managerial value at 3M is that "human beings are endowed with the urge to create—to bring into being something that has never existed before. That drive to create is stronger in some than in others. But to some degree, it exists in just about everyone. It follows, then, that developing entrepreneurs simply means respecting that dimension of human nature and honoring it with in the context of a profit making enterprise" (Lehr, 1986, p. 18).

The reward system at 3M is compatible with this belief in a number of ways. (See Lehr, 1986.) First, there is a high tolerance for failure without fear of reprisals. Second, "managers are judged, not only on their ability to make existing product lines grow, but also on their knack for bringing innovative new products to market . . . Basically, our divisions are expected to generate 25 percent of their sales each year from products new in the last five years" (p. 20). Third, "rewards have to be tied directly to successful innova-

tion . . . the worst thing we could do with people like that [innovators] is to base their rewards on how well they fit into some preconceived management mold" (p. 19). Fourth,
3M has implemented a reward program called "earned freedom," including 15 percent of
individuals' time to pursue their own pet projects, and a venture career track for men and
women with outstanding records as entrepreneurs inside 3M.

> Here's the way it works. In most companies you can judge the status and guess the pay
> of a manager by the size of the operation that he or she manages. The bigger the op-
> eration, the bigger the paycheck. Our new venture managers and directors will be pro-
> moted and rewarded for continuing to work with smaller projects, riskier projects—the kind
> they love the best. They won't lose out by continuing to take risks, by avoiding the safer
> paths (p. 329).

A third example of how the dominant logic of top management groups affects the
reward system and its effectiveness is found in a lesser known company in the wood products industry—WTD Industries Inc., based in Portland, Oregon. Unlike other firms in the
industry, WTD's top management believes that the key to improving firm performance is to
rely heavily on production workers instead of investing in new technology to operate their
mills. WTD's policy: "We strive to avoid the excessive capital cost of expensive high technology equipment that purports to eliminate production employees. We prefer to rely on
the flexibility and productivity of our workers" (BNA Special Report, 1988).

Management attributes WTD's phenomenal growth in the midst of the worst depres-
sion experienced by the industry to this unorthodox policy of avoiding high technology equipment in their mills. Started in 1983, WTD has now become the sixth largest wood products company in the nation with 25 mills and 2,400 employees spread across Oregon, Washington, Montana, and New York. It is also highly profitable in an industry where competitors have been losing money for more than a decade.

Company officials believe that WTD's success is due in large part to its creative use of
compensation strategies to enhance firm performance. They describe these pay strategies
as follows (see BNA Special Report on Changing Pay Practices, 1988, pp. 180-181):

> Instrumental to [WTD] rapid growth is an innovative productivity bonus system . . . Under
> WTD's bonus plan, the different units in each plant are divided into groups, such as the
> day shift veneer group, swing shift sawmill group, and so on. Every week, management
> decides on a product level for each of the groups and contributes an amount of money
> to the bonus pool for each . . . . If the group reaches the set production level, the work-
> ers in the group divide up the pool . . . If an employee is late to work or sick during the
> week, he or she is excluded from the pool. Likewise, if the group has more than three
> hours of lost work time due to accidents, no one gets a bonus . . . Bonuses also are
> promptly paid out to ensure that workers see a direct cause and effect between the pro-
> gram and their paychecks. The work week is from Friday to Thursday. Bonuses are paid
> by separate check each Friday for the bonus period that ended the day before. Regular
> paychecks are issued twice a month . . . So far the plan has worked well, giving the com-
> pany the safe production it wants . . . [WTD] has not had quality problems as result of the
> plan.

In summary, then, the dominant logic of top management groups in a firm is likely
to have a major impact on compensation strategies. Furthermore, it is unlikely that pay
strategies will contribute to firm performance unless these are consistent with the values and

priorities of the dominant coalitions. (*Note:* For additional case studies examining the role of top management values on HRM programs, including compensation, refer to Work in America Institute, 1991.)

Pay Strategies, the Competitive Strategy Model, and Firm Performance

The literature in *industrial/organizational (I/O) economics* suggests that a firm's compensation strategies are more likely to contribute to firm performance if these are attuned to industry structure and if they are able to capitalize on the firm's relative strengths. Discussions of the best-known I/O economic models and their implications for pay strategies and firm performance follow.

Industry structure. Long since recognized by labor economists, a firm's industry membership is one of the main predictors of wage levels for any given occupational group. Membership accounts for 7-30 percent of wage variation (Groshen, 1988). Likewise, the importance of industry membership to firm performance is emphasized in the most generally accepted I/O model developed by Mason (1939) and Bain (1956, 1968). In this model, the structure of the industry in which a firm operates is a crucial determinant of its performance. The four elements of industry structure suggested by this model have implications for the relative contribution of pay strategies to firm performance.

The first element of the structural I/O model relevant to the pay system is the existence of barriers to entry (Bain, 1956; Porter, 1981). To the extent that pay strategies can be designed not only to attract but to retain critical human resources that are in very scarce supply, the pay system will contribute to firm performance by preventing other companies from "pirating" these individuals. The more irreplaceable the human resources are (such as would be the case for key scientists and engineers in a high technology firm), the more the organization would benefit from erecting barriers to entry via the pay system to prevent other firms from moving in. These barriers may be created not only by higher pay but also, and even more effectively, by devising compensation schemes that "glue" the employee to the firm. One such scheme is offering stock options that can't be redeemed within a stipulated amount of time (Gomez-Mejia, Balkin, and Milkovich, 1990). When the barriers to entry in an industry are naturally very low (such as would be the case, for instance, in the hospitality industry), the firm may simply pay the "going wage" because employee attrition is less costly and erecting barriers to entry by experimenting with various pay strategies is unlikely to have much success. This situation would be somewhat analogous to the perfect competition model described in Chapter 1 where the firm is a "wage taker."

A second element of the structural model relevant to compensation, is the number of companies in an industry. The greater the number of firms, the less discretion any given company will have in setting its own wage policy because dispersion around the "going wage" will tend to be smaller. Significant deviations from competitive norms will almost certainly get the firm into trouble. For instance, the firm could price itself out of the market by paying too high or by being unable to attract and retain a work force by paying too low because multiple opportunities are available to employees to find suitable jobs elsewhere. In industries with a very large number of employers, firms will hire workers primarily from a pool of labor that is not differentiated in terms of occupational skills. This pool is often called a *secondary labor market* (Doeringer and Piore,

1971). It should be noted, however, that even in the most crowded industries, one still finds wage dispersion for any given job, although this is less in competitive markets (Groshen, 1988).

Third, smaller firms in a given market have a competitive disadvantage relative to larger companies in that market. Small firms are less likely to enjoy the economies of scale and slack resources as do larger firms. However, smaller firms may be able to tip the balance in their favor by designing pay packages that reduce fixed cost expenditures attributed to salary and benefits. By offering a lower base compensation (which is a substantial fixed cost in the short run, averaging about 60 percent of total operating cost) in exchange for higher variable pay associated with more risk but with greater potential returns, smaller companies can protect themselves against short-term financial pressures. Such a pay strategy enables smaller firms to compete more effectively against larger companies in the industry, while conserving much needed cash flow. Smaller companies also enjoy an administrative advantage with the use of variable pay because they can:

> Institute and manage incentive systems more efficiently than larger firms. For these smaller firms the number of positions are fewer, pay comparisons are simpler, operations are normally in a single plant or location, and performance indicators easier to obtain. As the firm grows in size it also becomes more complex in terms of salary grade levels, management structure, product and market differentiation, and geographical dispersion, so that incentive systems are more difficult to design, implement and control (Balkin and Gomez-Mejia, 1987, p. 172).

A fourth attribute of an industry's structure that can mediate the relative effectiveness of compensation strategies is the overall elasticity of demand for its product. In general, the greater the elasticity of product demand, the greater the volatility of performance for firms in that industry. Because the demand for labor is derived from the demand for the product, a firm operating in an industry with a very elastic product demand may gain a competitive advantage by augmenting the variable component of the pay package as high as possible. This will enable the firm to absorb some of the cyclical gyrations imposed by the product market. For instance, the firm can reduce the amount of variable pay received during bad times and "repay" workers during good times. It also reduces the need for extensive layoffs and all the associated costs—lower employee morale, lost investments in training, less credibility in the firm's management, voluntary attrition of most capable employees who feel that they should "jump ship" just in case, to say nothing of all about the psychological and financial hardship suffered by workers.

Firm Idiosyncracies. While the I/O economic paradigm of Mason (1939), Bain (1956), and later refinements by Porter (1981) revolve around industry structure as the unit of analysis, Chamberlinian economics focuses, instead, on the unique assets and capabilities of individual firms (Barney, 1985, 1986; Barney and Tyler, 1992; Chamberlin, 1933; Robinson, 1933). The essential message of Chamberlinian economics is: Firms that perform better are those that are able to take advantage of their own distinctive competence such as technology, know-how, and reputation. Borrowing from this notion, many strategy theorists have argued that firms should not simply look externally at the market when developing their strategies (as the industry structure model suggests) but that they must also look inward to exploit their firm-specific advantages while avoiding their weaknesses (e.g., Thompson and Strickland, 1980; Lenz, 1980; Stevenson, 1976). According to Barney (1986, p. 792):

> Given that differences between the skills and abilities controlled by firms can lead to differences in return from implementing strategies, Chamberlin's logic implies that firms should seek to choose strategies that most completely exploit their individuality and uniqueness. By differentiating themselves in this manner, firms may be able to obtain relatively high levels of economic return from implementing strategies. . . This type of analysis suggests that any organizational assets that can have a positive impact on the ability of firms to implement strategies are potential strengths that should be exploited when strategic choices are made.

It is important to point out that the I/O industry structure model and the Chamberlinian model do not contradict each other. Rather, they emphasize different aspects of firm performance that are strongly complementary, with the former focusing on external determinants and the later on internal opportunities that should be tapped to compete more effectively in a given industry.

Following the Chamberlinian logic, the more the compensation system can assist the firm in utilizing its own unique skills and assets and mold itself to the company's idiosyncratic situation and peculiarities, the more it will contribute to firm performance. Several examples are provided to illustrate this point:

- Knowledge intensive firms employing many scientists and engineers working on common projects are likely to benefit from an experiential compensation pattern that makes extensive use of team-based incentives. This serves to reinforce cooperation and "spirit de corps" needed for success (Gomez-Mejia and Balkin, 1989; Cascio, 1990; Masters, Tokesky, Brown, and Atkin 1992).
- Firms known for excellence in customer service pay their sales force only partially on straight commission, thereby reducing the potential for abrasive behaviors and "overselling" on the part of these employees (Nemerov, 1987; Schultz, 1987).
- Smaller firms at the start-up stage in the life cycle can use an experiential compensation strategy to their advantage by being generous in stock offerings to employees and utilizing their scarce cash to fuel future growth (Gomez-Mejia and Balkin, 1985).
- Larger firms with tall organizational structures may rely on an algorithmic compensation strategy by hiring workers at entry-level wages and using fast promotions through the hierarchy to reward and retain best employees (Baker, Jensen, and Murphy, 1988; Meyer, 1987).
- Firms whose labor costs are a small fraction of total production costs may find an algorithmic compensation strategy (offering above market salaries to present and prospective employees) allows them greater flexibility in recruitment and results in lower attrition because of increased opportunity costs to workers in changing employers (Balkin and Gomez-Mejia, 1990). The ability of a firm to hire and retain the "cream of the crop" when labor costs are a small proportion of total costs may more than offset the negative impact of higher wages on the bottom line. On the other hand, firms whose labor costs are a high proportion of total production costs are more likely to be better off if they utilize an experiential compensation

strategy that deemphasizes salary and benefits and, instead, provides more variable incentives because this policy may enable them to improve greatly their cash reserves.

- Organizations may utilize their unused capacity as part of their compensation strategies. For example, most private universities offer free tuition to faculty and their family. This benefit may represent a huge cash savings to faculty members (with average tuition at private colleges exceeding $11,000 a year per person), thereby allowing private universities to attract and retain good faculty with minimal adverse impact on their cost structure. Interestingly enough, few public institutions make themselves available of this opportunity, perhaps because of political reasons.

Transaction Costs Model, Compensation Strategy, and Firm Performance

Williamson (1975, 1979) developed a theoretical framework in which firm performance is said to depend on how well the firm can reduce all of its transaction costs, including those expenses involved in the interfacing of various organizational units. Kenneth Arrow, Nobel Laureate in Economics, has succinctly defined *transaction costs* as the "cost of running the economic system" (1969, p. 48). Such costs are different from production costs, which were the main preoccupation of neoclassical economics. Williamson (1985) refers to the concept of friction in physical science as the economic analogue of transaction costs.

In Chapter 4, how reward strategies at the corporate level vary according to the patterns and process of diversification was discussed in detail. For the most part, the literature reviewed in Chapter 4 is descriptive in nature and does not explicitly link the observed reward patterns to firm performance, either conceptually or empirically. Transaction cost theory may help bridge this gap by arguing that the more compensation strategies help reduce transaction costs in corporations with multiple SBUs, the more these pay strategies will contribute to corporate performance. If properly designed, compensation strategies may reduce a number of transaction costs. These are discussed next.

1. *Complexity of contracts between divisional managers and corporate headquarters, including enforcement of such contracts.* In dominant- and related-product firms, algorithmic pay strategies would reduce contract costs because corporate headquarters could then exercise direct control over SBUs and efficiently monitor the activities of divisional managers. Such contracts need not be overly complex because top corporate executives are knowledgeable about the operations of the various units. Thus, algorithmic pay strategies that link SBUs to corporate headquarters and foster dependence on corporate executives would reduce transaction costs, thereby improving corporate performance. Likewise, following the same logic, for companies that have grown through internal expansion, an algorithmic compensation pattern would reduce transaction costs because corporate headquarters has a much more intimate knowledge of the various businesses. Thus, top executives can exercise direct control over SBUs without requiring a detailed contract focusing on outcomes (e.g., return on investment) for each SBU.

   At the other end, an experiential compensation pattern would reduce contract costs in unrelated-product firms and conglomerates. Tight control over heterogeneous units would be very costly because they all face a unique set of conditions. This would require different contracts (one for each SBU) covering multiple eventualities. Even if it were theoretically possible to do so, enforcement of such contracts would be quite difficult because corporate management has very limited knowledge of organizational transformations in each unit. Instead, rather than emphasizing control from the top, transaction costs would be reduced by pushing decision making down to the SBU, rewarding divisional managers for entrepreneurial activities. An experiential reward strategy for divisional managers (with more variable pay, high risk sharing, rewards based on SBU performance, a long-term orientation, and low dependence on superiors) would not only encourage this, but will also at the same time create greater incentive alignment between divisional managers and corporate headquarters. In a sense, the incentive system can play a supervisory role, supplanting much of the need for direct monitoring. This means, other things equal, the performance of conglomerates would be higher if decisions are made at the SBU level, using the superior knowledge of SBU managers and capitalizing on the unique opportunities facing each firm. The pay system would serve as the skeleton that holds the entire system together.

2. *Performance ambiguity.* This transaction cost refers to "the inability of one party to measure or accurately value the performance of the other party to an exchange" (Jones and Butler, 1988, p. 205). In the context of diversification strategies, it would be very difficult for corporate executives to evaluate the performance of various units that are highly independent. It would be even more difficult if the corporation has followed an aggressive acquisition strategy in the past. Performance ambiguity is associated with transaction costs because the more diverse the SBUs (particularly if these are involved in the production of intangible goods and services), the more corporate executives would need to rely on their specialized knowledge. This would make it difficult to evaluate each SBU individually. Therefore, transaction costs should be lower for conglomerates if an experiential pay strategy is followed, whereby each unit can pursue its own strategies, and general managers would not have to rely on the judgment of corporate superiors. The control of SBU managers in this situation would best be accomplished by linking their personal fortunes with those of the firm. This is because (as we will see next) few interdependencies exist. Thus, the performance of the SBU can be unambiguously attributed to the performance of that unit, not to the corporation as a whole. Negative consequences of outcome based compensation plans (such as the manipulation of accounting income) are addressed in Chapters 6 and 7.

3. *Asset specificity.* The less the flow of goods and services between SBUs is in a corporation, the lower the need to develop consistent pay policies applicable to all parts of the company. Using the language of transaction cost analysis, the greater the asset specificity of various SBUs, the more likely an experiential reward strategy (whereby pay administration is highly decentralized, and each SBU is made responsible to develop its own pay policies tailored to its own unique conditions) would contribute to firm performance by lowering transaction costs. The more bureaucratic and inflexible pay policies of the algorithmic compensation pattern would increase administrative costs in this situation, with a high likelihood of dysfunctional results because each SBU has its own needs. Whenever SBUs do not share substantial resources, corporate management can make more unambiguous performance attributions for any given unit without resorting to subjective assessments of performance. Greater asset specificity generally implies that top corpo-

rate executives only have a superficial knowledge of various SBUs. Therefore, an experiential compensation strategy, which relies more heavily on the incentive structure to exercise a supervisory role through alignment of interests than on direct control mechanisms, is more conducive to improved firm performance.

The converse is also true. The lower the asset specificity of various SBUs, the more likely an algorithmic pay strategy will contribute to firm performance because these corporations have greater need for consistency. Boundaries among SBUs are more permeable, and active interface of employees across SBUs is expected. This means, internal equity corporate wide becomes an important objective, and greater centralization of the pay system is necessary to accomplish it. Subjective judgment of top executives is required to assess the contributions of various SBUs, creating more dependence on superiors. This is due to the fact that performance attributions to any given SBU are difficult to make on an objective basis because all SBUs in the portfolio share common resources. At-risk pay for SBU executives in this situation makes less sense because unit performance depends on many factors outside their control. It would be demoralizing to hold divisional managers responsible for their unit's performance when extensive interdependencies exist. There is less need to use the reward system systematically to align the interest of divisional managers to those of the firm because top executives in corporate headquarters can effectively monitor transformational processes in each SBU and manage the pooled interdependence of all SBUs in the portfolio. Centralized administration of the pay system in corporate headquarters and more bureaucratic compensation policies would contribute to enhanced firm performance in this situation because the firm is interested in creating a systemic, rather than a fractionalized, view of the organization.

4. *Reduce opportunistic behaviors.* The potential for SBU divisional managers to act opportunistically increases as the number of SBUs in a portfolio expands. Consistent with agency theory formulations (see Chapter 1 and Chapter 6), in any situation where one party (principal) delegates responsibility to another (agent), there is the possibility that the agent may use its privileged position to its own advantage. The more diverse the SBUs are in a portfolio, the more likely divisional managers will act in an opportunistic fashion because information asymmetries between them and corporate management will increase accordingly. The underlying logic here is: Divisional managers have more information about the task at hand than top corporate executives and may use this superior knowledge to enhance their own welfare at the expense of the corporation (e.g., expanding the size of the SBU to justify higher pay for the divisional manager or investing in prestigious projects that are of questionable value to stockholders).

When supervising a portfolio of multiple SBUs producing unrelated complex goods and services, it is difficult and expensive for top corporate executives to evaluate the performance of various units. At the same time, these corporate managers may feel there is at least some reasonable probability that divisional managers may cheat them but that cheating may be hard to detect. In theory, an algorithmic compensation strategy would reduce transaction costs resulting from opportunistic behaviors (by imposing more bureaucratic control on SBUs and introducing standardized procedures for all to follow). Yet, in practice, this may actually generate more transaction costs by implementing a system that would not be suitable to all units. As an alternative, an experiential compensation strategy may suffer from the associated risks of opportunistic behavior (because each SBU is given considerable freedom). However, it may result in lower transaction costs vis-a-vis the algorithmic pay strategy by providing local flexibility to make decisions that best meet the needs of each SBU. Divisional managers may be prevented from engaging in opportunistic behaviors by designing pay packages that link their interests with those of the corporation.

On the other hand, one would expect that related- and dominant-product firms would benefit from an algorithmic compensation strategy. In these cases, opportunistic behaviors by divisional managers can be reduced through a formalized system of control because top corporate managers are capable of assessing each SBU's performance separately. An algorithmic pay strategy also makes sense organizationally, given the pooled interdependence of various units. A similar argument can be made for firms that have grown through internal diversification.

In summary, the relative contribution of pay strategies to firm performance depends not only on the degree to which these are congruent with organizational strategies, the dominant logic of top management groups, and industry structure, but also on whether they can assist the firm in reducing transaction costs.

Resource Dependence, Strategic Employee Groups, Compensation Strategies, and Firm Performance

When applied to the notion of strategic employee groups, resource dependency theory (see Chapter 1) can also shed some light about the relative contribution of compensation strategies to firm performance. Clearly, not all occupational types are equally important to a firm, and diverse firms may place a different value on the identical employee group. One can argue that the value a firm places on any given employee group increases as the following conditions are met: (a) individuals in question are difficult to replace; (b) employees' performance has a high potential impact on the accomplishment of the firm's mission; and (c) employees constitute an integral part of the firm's "technical core." The more these three conditions are met, the more a given employee group becomes strategic. By implication, a compensation strategy is more likely to enhance firm performance if it meets the needs of strategic employee groups within the firm. For example, R&D employees clearly meet the above three conditions in most knowledge intensive firms (see Cascio, 1990). Many high technology firms have developed special compensation programs (such as provision of generous bonuses, availability of funds to develop "pet" research projects, sabbatical benefits, etc.) to cater to the needs of R&D workers in order to gain a competitive advantage (Gomez-Mejia, Balkin, and Milkovich, 1990).

In general, the greater the number of strategic employee groups on which the firm depends for its survival and relative success, the more an experiential compensation strategy could contribute to its performance because of the flexibility it affords. The converse is also true. The fewer the number of employee groups considered to be strategic within the firm, the more likely an algorithmic pay strategy would contribute to firm performance because it promotes standardization, control, and consistency. Such would be the case, for instance, in a manufacturing firm producing mature products.

In closing this part of the chapter, the reader should keep in mind that the different variables affecting the extent to which pay strategies contribute to firm performance—and the various theoretical formulations used here to examine these linkages—are complementary, rather than contradictory. Other things equal, the more the six conditions listed in the previous paragraphs are met (as suggested by contingency theory, coalitional models, I/O industry structure models, Chamberlinian competition approaches, transaction cost analysis, and resource dependency theory), the greater the contribution of compensation strategies to firm performance.

COMPENSATION STRATEGIES AND FIRM PERFORMANCE: A REVIEW OF THE EMPIRICAL EVIDENCE

As argued throughout this book, the ultimate dependent variable when making strategic pay choices is organizational performance. This section examines empirical research focused on the relationship between compensation strategies and firm performance and factors moderating the relative effectiveness of pay strategies.

Because compensation has traditionally been a micro field of study buried within personnel management as a functional area, the connection between pay strategies and firm performance has been a neglected subject. (This is in stark contrast to the huge literature on the use of pay as a motivational tool at the individual level. A classical paper by Opsahl and Dunnette more than twenty-five years ago [1966] reviewed several hundred empirical papers on the role of financial compensation in industrial motivation and performance.) According to Milkovich (1988, p. 32): "The effects of compensation strategy and the degree of its fit with organizational strategy and performance remain unplowed turf. Considering the elusiveness of the notion of fit, it seems like risky research."

In spite of the pessimistic conclusions reached by Milkovich in the above cite, a number of attempts were made in the late 1980s and early 1990s to tackle this challenging research task. The results of those attempts appear to corroborate the hypothesis that compensation strategies do have an important impact on firm performance. These studies can be broken down into those using effectiveness as a criterion variable and those relying on financial indicators of firm performance as a criterion measure.

Compensation Strategies and Their Effectiveness

Where effectiveness is defined as the contributions of pay strategies to firm performance, a number of studies have focused on their relative effectiveness. Because effectiveness is an all-encompassing concept (see Schmitt and Klimoski, 1991) and an abstract notion carried about in the heads of stakeholders (such as managers and employees) (see Wood, 1990), it is normally measured as a perception, rather than as an objective number (such as return on investment).

Two studies by Balkin and Gomez-Mejia (1987a; 1990) and one by Gomez-Mejia and Balkin (1989) focused on pay effectiveness as the dependent variable. The authors defended the use of pay effectiveness, rather than objective measures, of firm performance as a criterion because the latter may be influenced by many factors difficult to control in a field study. The authors also felt that this was a more prudent approach to take at this point, given the exploratory nature of this research and the absence of previous guideposts to follow. All three of these studies, to be described next, found support for contingency notions of pay strategy effectiveness.

Balkin and Gomez-Mejia (1987a). Balkin and Gomez-Mejia's first study examined the compensation policies of 33 high technology and 72 traditional single-product firms along Route 128 in Boston. A firm was classified as high technology if its annual research and development budget was five percent or more of its sales revenue. Most of the firms in the sample were in the electronics or technical instruments industries. For each firm, Balkin and Gomez-Mejia measured compensation strategies in terms of pay mix or the relative importance of variable (incentive) and fixed (salary, fringe benefits) portions of the total financial package. Pay effectiveness was conceptualized in terms of "the extent to which the compensation system contributes to the achievement of organizational goals" (p. 172). It was operationalized by asking the person responsible for compensation policies in each firm to make a judgment of effectiveness on a set of 16 Likert type items. Responses to these items were factor analyzed, and three major dimensions emerged—a general pay effectiveness factor and two specific factors, "pay as a recruitment tool" and "pay as a motivational tool."

A summary of propositions empirically supported in Balkin and Gomez-Mejia's (1987a) study appears in Figure 5-2. Attention is focused on the most important ones. Following the logic discussed in Chapter 4, Balkin and Gomez-Mejia (1987a) hypothesized—and the empirical findings supported this—that an incentive-based reward strategy is more effective for firms at the growth stage of the product life cycle. Furthermore, they found support for the hypothesis that organizational characteristics (as measured by firm size and R&D intensity) and industry structure moderate the relative effectiveness of pay strategies. These findings are consistent with the predictions of contingency theory and the competitive strategy model.

Balkin and Gomez-Mejia (1987a) report that the effectiveness of an incentive-based strategy is inversely related to company size. They argue that smaller firms are less able to afford fixed cost expenditures. By providing a lower base compensation (which is a significant fixed cost in the short run) in exchange for an array of incentive pay programs, smaller companies can buffer themselves against short-term financial pressures. This pay strategy, in turn, enables them to compete more effectively against larger firms in the product market, without weakening their cash flow positions. As the firm gets larger, it also becomes more complex in terms of employee groups, management structure, product and market differentiation, and geographical dispersion. Therefore, the incentive systems are more difficult to design, implement, and control. Furthermore, the dominant logic of top management teams becomes less entrepreneurial in nature when the firm gets larger. As the firm grows, an emphasis on predictability, control, standardization, and efficiency (which are more in line with an algorithmic compensation pattern) supplants the desire for flexibility and organicity (which are more in line with an experiential compensation pattern).

Industry structure in the Balkin and Gomez-Mejia (1987a) study was measured indirectly as the extent to which technological innovation and R&D success are necessary for survival in a highly competitive environment. A firm's distinctive competence, a la Chamberlin, was operationalized in terms of R&D intensity. They found support for three related hypotheses, providing confirmatory evidence for both contingency theory and the competitive strategy model in terms of their predictions concerning the relative effectiveness of pay strategies. Balkin and Gomez-Mejia (1987a) report that:

Propositions

1. Incentive pay as a proportion of the total compensation package is greater for firms at the growth stage of the product life cycle.

2. An incentive-based reward strategy is more effective for firms at the growth stage of the product cycle.

3. The proportion of fixed compensation costs in the total pay package increases as a function of organizational size.

4. The effectiveness of an incentive-based strategy is inversely related to company size.

5. The compensation mix in high technology firms contains a higher proportion of incentive rewards and a lower proportion of fixed pay.

6. Considering all firms at the growth stage of the product life cycle, those that are high technology have a pay mix with a greater incentive component.

7. Smaller high technology firms have a pay mix with a greater incentive component than similar non-high technology firms.

8. An incentive-based compensation strategy is more effective in high technology firms than in non-high technology firms.

9. For organizations at the growth stage in the product life cycle, an incentive-based reward strategy is most effective for high technology firms.

10. For smaller companies, an incentive-based strategy is most effective for those that are high technology.

FIGURE 5-2 Summary of Propositions Empirically Supported in Balkin and Gomez-Mejia's 1987a Study

Adapted from Balkin, D. B. and Gomez-Mejia, L. R. (1987a). Toward a contingency theory of compensation strategy. *Strategic Management Journal*, 8:169-182.

- An incentive-based compensation strategy is more effective in high technology firms than in nontechnology companies.
- For organizations at the growth stage in the product life cycle, an incentive-based reward strategy is most effective for high technology firms.
- For smaller companies, an incentive-based reward strategy is most effective for those that are high technology.

Several rationales were provided for the above findings. First, equity sharing is already an established practice in the high technology industry. As part of their competitive strategies, these firms are expected to offer this pay form as a condition of employment. Second, because of widespread pirating of R&D employees in the industry, high technology firms can erect barriers to prevent other companies becoming direct competitors in their area of expertise by providing strong incentives to key contributors to remain in the firm. Third, venture capitalists play an important role in the high technology industry, controlling resources (cash) needed by many of the smaller high technology companies. Venture capitalists often insist that management adopts incentive-based compensation schemes as a condition for initial and additional rounds of financing. (See also Gomez-Mejia, Balkin, and Welbourne, 1990.) Fourth, in high technology firms, an entrepreneurial culture among dominant coalitions supports the notion that rewards should be closely tied to performance and that incentive attainments are an indicator of personal achievement.

Balkin and Gomez-Mejia (1990). Balkin and Gomez-Mejia's follow-up study examined the impact of organizational strategies (at both the corporate and business unit level) on pay strategies and their interactive influence on the effectiveness of the compensation system. The empirical findings are based on the survey responses of 192 human resource management executives in business units of large manufacturing firms. The organizational strategy at both the corporate and business unit level was operationalized using well-established strategy typologies. The corporate strategy measure used is the taxonomy developed by Rumelt (1974), who operationalized it as the extent of diversification exhibited by the firm. A modified version of the typology developed by Gerstein and Reisman (1983) was used to measure SBU strategy. (See Chapter 3 for descriptions of Rumelt and Gerstein and Reisman.)

Compensation strategies were operationalized in terms of pay package design, market positioning, and pay policy choices in a manner akin to that described in Chapter 2. The first dimension refers to the relative importance of salary, benefits, and incentives in the pay mix. Market positioning refers to the extent to which the organization targets its pay level below or above its competitors. The last dimension, pay policy choices, consists of the organization's administrative framework, criteria, and procedural approaches used to remunerate its employees. Thirteen composite scales were created to measure these dimensions. (See Table 5-1.)

Pay effectiveness was operationalized in terms of the degree to which the pay system contributes to the achievement of a firm's performance goals. The HRM executives were asked to make this assessment based on five separate pay effectiveness items that were later averaged into an overall composite. The study controlled for sales volume, profitability, and the ratio of labor costs to total costs of production.

A stepwise multiple regression was utilized to test for the significance of corporate and business unit strategy (as predictors) on each of the SBU pay strategy measures (as dependent variables). The first step consisted of the corporate control variables. The second step tested for the sign and significance of the corporate strategy (i.e., Rumelt's classification). The third step included the business unit control variables (i.e., Gerstein and Reisman's taxonomy). The fourth and last step tested for the sign and significance of the business unit strategy measure.

The results of this analysis showed that corporate strategies accounted for an average increase of 2.4 percent in explained variance across the pay strategy scales. Dominant- and related-product firms exhibited characteristics of the algorithmic pay pattern, and single-product firms appeared closer to the experiential pay pattern. The business unit strategies (last step in the regression model) showed an average increase in R^2 of 0.8 percent across all 13 pay scales, and a 2.0 percent average R^2 increase for salary, incentives, market positioning, and pay for performance. The SBU dynamic growth strategy, as noted earlier, leans toward the experiential pay pattern, while the SBU maintenance strategy is more strongly associated with features of the algorithmic pay pattern. These results suggest that both corporate and SBU strategies are significantly related to pay strategies in the expected manner

TABLE 5-1
EXTENT TO WHICH A PARTICULAR PAY STRATEGY IS JUDGED TO BE MORE OR LESS EFFECTIVE IN TERMS OF ITS CONTRIBUTION TO FIRM PERFORMANCE*

Pay Strategies	Corporate Strategy			SBU Strategy	
	Single-Product	Dominant-Product	Related-Product	Growth	Maintenance
Pay Basis					
1. Salary					
Low	More	Less	Less	More	Less
High	Less	More	More	Less	More
2. Benefits					
Low	More	Less	Less	More	Less
High	Unclear	Unclear	Unclear	Less	More
3. Incentives					
Low	Less	More	More	Less	More
High	More	Unclear	Less	More	Less
Market Positioning					
4. Pay level vis-a-vis competition					
Low	More	Less	Less	More	Less
High	Less	More	More	Less	More
Pay Policies					
5. Risk-sharing					
Low	Less	Unclear	More	Less	More
High	More	Less	Less	More	Less
6. Internal equity					
Low	More	Less	Less	More	Less
High	Less	More	Unclear	Less	More
7. Pay secrecy					
Low	More	Less	Less	More	Less
High	Less	More	More	Less	More

TABLE 5-1 (Continued)
EXTENT TO WHICH A PARTICULAR PAY STRATEGY IS JUDGED TO BE MORE OR LESS EFFECTIVE IN TERMS OF ITS CONTRIBUTION TO FIRM PERFORMANCE

Pay Strategies	Corporate Strategy			SBU Strategy	
	Single-Product	Dominant-Product	Related-Product	Growth	Maintenance
8. Pay for performance					
Low	Less	More	More	Less	More
High	More	Less	Less	More	Less
9. Pay decentralization					
Low	Less	More	More	Less	More
High	More	Less	Less	More	Less
10. Egalitarian pay					
Low	Less	More	More	Less	More
High	More	Less	Less	More	Less
11. Pay participation					
Low	Less	More	More	Less	More
High	More	Less	Less	More	Less
12. Job-based pay					
Low	More	Less	Less	More	Less
High	Less	More	Unclear	Less	More
13. Long-term pay					
Low	Less	More	More	Less	More
High	More	Unclear	Less	More	Less

but that, obviously, many other factors besides the organizational strategy measures used here account for the lion's share of variance in pay strategies.

A discriminant analysis procedure, which obtains an additive estimate of the percent of cases accurately classified into various corporate and SBU strategy categories based on control variables, pay mix variables, market positioning, and pay policies, showed that pay strategies can substantially improve classification accuracy well beyond chance. For instance, as can be seen in Figure 5-3, the percent improvement over chance in terms of classification accuracy for single-product firms was 18.8 percent for control variables alone, 44.8 percent by adding pay mix variables to the equation, 48.7 percent by including market positioning in the analysis, and 55.8 percent by adding pay policies to the equation. Similar results were obtained for SBU strategies. (See Figure 5-4.) For SBUs following a maintenance strategy, for example, the percent improvement over chance for the control variables, pay mix variables, market positioning, and pay policies entered sequentially reached .00 percent, 19.3 percent, 29.8 percent, and 34.5 percent respectively.

A separate set of analysis by Balkin and Gomez-Mejia (1990) developed a cross-tabulation table with each of the pay strategies on the vertical axis and the corporate and SBU strategies along the horizontal axis. Each of the pay strategies was dichotomized into "high" (firm is above the median) and "low" (firm is below the median) groups. A matrix was

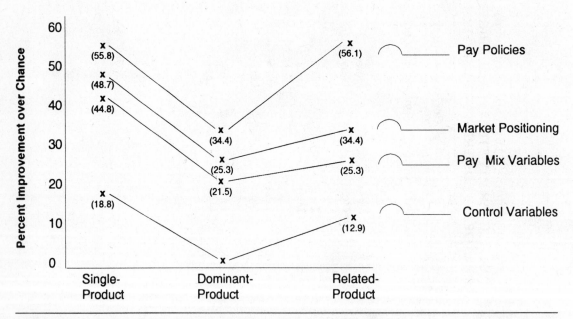

FIGURE 5-3   **Percent Improvement over Chance of Control Variables and Pay Strategies in Terms of Classification Accuracy for SBU Strategies—Discriminant Analysis Procedure**

Based on a study by Balkin and Gomez-Mejia (1990).

Note: By chance alone, 33.3 percent of the cases should be correctly classified by business unit strategy (which has three categories). Numbers shown reflect the difference between actual hit rates using discriminant analysis and the hit rates that one would expect by chance. The numbers shown are additive because control variables were entered first, followed by pay mix variables, market positioning, and pay policies. The difference between one line and the previous one reflects the net gain in predictive accuracy.

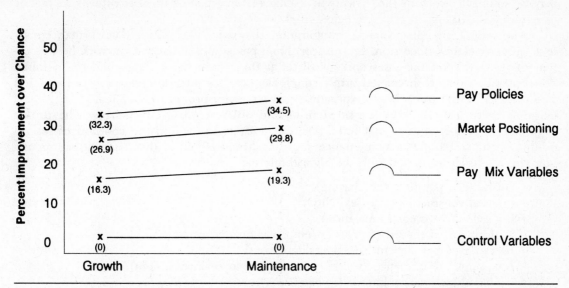

FIGURE 5-4   Percent Improvement over Chance of Control Variables and Pay Strategies in Terms of Classification Accuracy for SBU Strategies—Discriminant Analysis Procedure

Based on a study by Balkin and Gomez-Mejia (1990).

Note: By chance alone, 50.0 percent of the cases should be correctly classified by business unit strategy (which has two categories). Numbers shown reflect the difference between actual hit rates using disciminant analysis and the hit rates that one would expect by chance. The numbers shown are additive because control variables were entered first, followed by pay mix variables, market positioning, and pay policies. The difference between one line and the previous one reflects the net gain in predictive accuracy.

then created that showed the mean pay effectiveness score for each cell.   So, for example, all firms below the median in "internal equity" that are also pursuing a "growth" strategy would have an average pay effectiveness score calculated for that subsample. Statistical tests of significance were then computed for mean differences.   The results of this analysis support the notion that the effectiveness of the compensation system (based on the assessment of human resource managers participating in the study) varies as a function of the interaction between pay strategies and organizational strategies.   These results, summarized in Table 5-1, are discussed in greater detail next.

As can be seen in Table 5-1, an emphasis on incentives, vis-a-vis salary and benefits, appears to work best for single-product firms and for SBUs following a growth strategy.   Paying above market produces better results for related-product firms and for more mature SBUs. This pattern suggests, in a manner consistent with contingency theory formulations and the competitive strategy model, that reliance on incentive pay by single-product firms and SBUs at the growth stage may be a useful strategy to attract and retain employees, while at the same time underemphasizing expensive fixed pay components (salary and benefits) relative to more established, mature firms.   Such a compensation strategy would free scarce dollars in the short run so that these may be destined to finance future expansion.   Employees may be willing to work in those firms in exchange for greater potential returns in the future, even if actual pay received is below market.

The overall pay effectiveness configuration shown in Table 5-1 indicates that, consistent with the earlier discussion, more algorithmic pay strategies appear to work best as extent of diversification increases and for SBUs at the maintenance stage. (Keep in mind, however, that the most diversified firms [conglomerates] are not represented in this sample.) The converse is also true. More experiential pay strategies produce better results (as judged by HRM executives) for less diversified firms and SBUs at the growth stage. The profile shown in Table 5-1 suggests that more diversified firms (but within the confines of related products) and SBUs at the maintenance stage would benefit from the following compensation characteristics associated with the algorithmic pay pattern:

- Guaranteed pay (low risk sharing).
- Internal consistency (less flexibility).
- Pay secrecy (less communication).
- Seniority-based rewards (versus an emphasis on performance).
- Hierarchical pay structure (less egalitarianism).
- Low employee influence (versus extensive employee involvement).
- Job-based pay (versus knowledge-based pay).
- A shorter (rather than long-term) time horizon for distributing rewards.

Gomez-Mejia and Balkin (1989). Gomez-Mejia and Balkin's third study on the effectiveness of pay strategies focuses on R&D workers as a strategic employee group. Based on resource dependency theory, the authors argue that R&D workers are at least as important to the performance of high technology firms as top executives. Given the high technology firm's dependence on this resource, one would expect that the effectiveness of pay strategies would increase the more they are molded to the special needs of this strategic employee group. (This notion will be discussed again in the executive compensation chapters [6 and 7] and the chapter on boundary spanners [8].) To test this hypothesis, Gomez-Mejia and Balkin (1989) compared the relative effectiveness of individual and aggregate compensation strategies in a sample of 175 scientists and engineers from the Boston area. Each participant was employed by a different company, so that no single organization could have an undue influence on results.

Individual-based rewards in this study include merit pay and "key contributors'" bonuses, which require the firm to identify the specific contribution of each worker. An aggregate incentive strategy, on the other hand, provides financial rewards to multiple contributors based on the achievement of common goals. In this study, these include profit sharing, stock ownership, and project-based bonuses.

In a manner similar to the previous two studies, pay effectiveness was defined as the extent to which the compensation system is seen as contributing to the achievement of individual, organizational, and R&D goals. Unlike the two studies reviewed earlier, however, the effectiveness assessment was made by those directly affected by the pay strategies (i.e., R&D employees), rather than by those responsible for administering the system (i.e., HRM executives).

Pay effectiveness was operationalized by Gomez-Mejia and Balkin (1989) in terms of two attitudinal variables (pay satisfaction and intention to leave the firm) and two performance indicators (team and individual performance). All of these were measured on Likert type scales. The rationale given in this study for including the behavioral measures is that both pay satisfaction and intention to leave are important predictors of retention. This is of particular importance for high technology firms. A critical challenge facing these companies is how to attract and retain key technical talent in an industry known for frequent job hopping. The fact that companies hiring large numbers of scientists and engineers are concentrated in a few technology centers adds to the attrition problem because transition costs in changing jobs are minimized. Therefore, pay strategies that are shown to reduce the precursors of turnover (i.e., dissatisfaction with pay and a cognitive predisposition to look for employment elsewhere) are an important tool to gain a competitive advantage in the industry. The rationale for including individual and team performance (as reported by participants) is more obvious at face value. Namely, in a high technology firm heavily dependent on innovation, pay strategies that enhance the performance of scientists and engineers should have a direct impact on the overall economic performance of the firm.

Using multiple regression on this data, Gomez-Mejia and Balkin (1989) tested a number of propositions. Study results are summarized in Table 5-2. The first proposition received considerable support. Namely, a compensation mix that emphasizes aggregate incentives is more likely to be effective for scientists and engineers than one that relies on merit pay and individual based bonuses. Several reasons were advanced for this finding. First, the cooperative nature of R&D work is more congruent with an aggregate incentive strategy than one emphasizing individual rewards. Second, given the team nature of R&D work, aggregate incentive plans are easier to implement because these do not require identification of individual contributors. Third, aggregate incentive systems are more flexible in their ability to time the reward close to actual task accomplishment because these rewards are not constrained by a fixed fiscal year budget and are given on a one-time-only basis to recognize specific achievements.

Gomez-Mejia and Balkin (1989) also found strong support for the proposition that while profit sharing and stock-based reward policies may bind the employee to the firm, these macro incentive policies do not have a significant effect on individual and team performance. Furthermore, team-based bonus policies are most effective in an R&D setting as compared to profit sharing and stock ownership. Several reasons were provided for these findings. First, project-based bonuses have a greater behavioral impact than profit sharing or stock ownership because the bonuses can be more closely linked to the behavior of team members. The criterion for payment in profit-sharing and stock-based plans concerns firm performance, which is less subject to direct control of scientists and engineers than would be the case with the quantity and quality of R&D productivity. Second, team-based bonuses capitalize on the cooperative structure of R&D work, inducing team members to perform at their highest potential. Group-based rewards can be designed so that there is a positive correlation among the goal attainment of individuals within the team by making these dependent on each other. Third, profit-sharing plans (which dispense rewards based on the performance of the entire firm) can reduce attrition to the extent that the employee sees it as another fringe benefit provided by the firm and that it is more advantageous than that offered by competitors. By the same token, stock-based programs may contribute to employee retention by making the employee part owner of the firm and/or by making stock redemption contingent on length of service.

The last proposition, which received moderate support, argues that employee characteristics are likely to interact with reward strategies and moderate their effectiveness. Gomez-

TABLE 5-2
Extent to Which Percent of Pay Received in Various Forms (Pay Mix), Pay Policies, and Willingness to Take Risks Show a Positive or Negative Impact on Several Pay Effectiveness Measures for Scientists and Engineers*

	Reported Pay Effectiveness Measures			
Variable	Pay Satisfaction	Withdrawal Cognition	Project Performance	Individual Performance
Merit Pay Mix	N.S.	N.S.	N.S.	N.S.
Individual Bonus Mix	N.S.	N.S.	N.S.	N.S.
Aggregate Incentive Mix	+	+	+	N.S.
Profit-Sharing Policy	N.S.	+	N.S.	N.S.
Stock Ownership Policy	N.S.	+	N.S.	N.S.
Team Bonus Policy	+	+	+	+
High Variable Pay, Low Willingness to Take Risks	–	+	N.S.	N.S.

* Based on a study by Gomez-Mejia and Balkin (1989).

N.S. indicates "non-significant results;" "–" refers to a negative (statistically significant) relationship; "+" refers to a positive (statistically significant) relationship.

Mejia and Balkin (1989) report that variable compensation promotes lower pay satisfaction and more withdrawal cognition for those employees who have a lower tolerance for risk. This suggests that compensation strategies associated with greater uncertainty work best for start-up and growth companies that hire employees who are willing to assume the risks of joining a fledgling firm. As a company matures, however, and its employee population becomes more risk averse, such a compensation strategy may lead to a situation whereby employees experience a conflict between their personal needs and the reward system, inducing them to seek alternative employment opportunities.

Business Economic Performance

The research reviewed in the previous section focused on the broader concept of pay effectiveness. The studies to be discussed next have focused on a narrower domain—namely, the firm's financial performance.

A potential problem with the three studies reviewed above is that they strictly rely on perceptual measures. This raises the specter of variables being correlated with each other not because they are truly related in the real world but, rather, because respondents have a common affective bias when answering questions. Although empirical evidence has not supported this (e.g., Dess and Robinson, 1984; Tosi and Gomez-Mejia, 1992; Venkatraman and Ramanujan,1986), a second potential problem is that subjective perceptions of performance may be uncorrelated with objective measures of performance.

It is the authors' opinion that both perceptual (as in the three studies reviewed earlier) and objective (as in the two studies to be reviewed next) performance criteria provide useful information, and there is no one approach to measure effectiveness or performance that is currently regarded as definitive. Just like the perceptual effectiveness measures, business economic performance measures may also be contaminated, even though on the surface they may appear to some as being more rigorous and quantitative. For example, as seen in Chapters 6 and 7, there is much debate in the finance and accounting literature regarding the appropriateness of different profitability measures and how market performance should be assessed. Setting aside measurement issues, whenever archival performance data is used, one faces the problem of teasing out the unique impact of any given variable (e.g., strategic pay pattern) on performance from the effect of myriads of other factors that may also impinge on it. Because many of the variables affecting "objective" measures of firm performance (e.g., life cycle, firm size, market share, industry) are correlated, making causal attributions to any one factor based on multivariate analysis may be rather treacherous.

Fortunately, in spite of methodological limitations and differences in the nature of the data and research designs, the two studies that have examined the impact of pay strategies on "hard" performance data produced results that are consistent with those of the three studies that relied on perceptual measures.

Gerhart and Milkovich (1990).   Gerhart and Milkovich's study uses archival, longitudinal data obtained from a large consulting firm on approximately 16,000 top and middle level managers in 200 organizations, covering the period 1981-1985. Three aspects of pay strategy were examined: managerial base pay (salary level); long-term income (measured as a dummy variable, rather than amount with 0 = not eligible to receive it; and 1 = eligible to receive it); and the proportion of bonuses over base pay (as a percentage figure). Firm performance was measured in terms of average return on assets, yearly return on assets, and lagged return on assets. Organizational characteristics were measured in terms of firm size and industry. In addition, the study controlled for individual characteristics of managers in terms of years of education, experience, firm tenure, job tenure, number of reporting levels, and management levels supervised. Regression analysis was used to isolate the unique effect of pay mix on firm performance.

A number of interesting findings emerged from their analysis. First, the pay strategies of these firms were remarkably consistent across the five-year period. These findings were reinforced by the fact that less than one half of the employees included by the consulting firm in the 1981 survey was also included in the 1985 survey. Gerhart and Milkovich (1990, p. 666) conclude that "as such, we have strong evidence of stability in the compensation packages of employees that is due to stability in compensation policies and practices, as opposed to stability in the people." Secondly, and not too surprisingly, human capital and job attributes (e.g., education, level in the firm) explain almost 70 percent of the variance in base pay but only about 20 percent of the variance in pay mix. Third, the total organizational effect (measured in terms of firm size and industry) is smallest for base pay (R^2 change = .14) and largest for bonuses as a proportion of base pay (R^2 change = .21), and long-term income eligibility (R^2 change = .34). The authors interpret this to mean that firms distinguish themselves from their competitors by leveraging their managers' pay mix (bonus/base) and by increasing their eligibility for long-term incentives, rather than through differences in base pay. Hence, from a strategic perspective, the mix of total pay is more important than the relative level of base pay over which a firm has less discretion (because it is more susceptible to external market forces beyond its control).

A fourth finding of their study is that larger firms deemphasize pay incentives and rely more on fixed pay. This is consistent with the findings of Balkin and Gomez-Mejia (1987a) discussed earlier in this chapter and it is also in line with the argument that pay incentives, which are an integral of the experiential compensation pattern, play a larger role in firms at the growth stage.

Fifth, Gerhart and Milkovich report that industry differences did not explain much variance in pay practices. But large within-industry differences in pay practices were found. They interpret this as a sign that the industry level of analysis of compensation determination used by economists miss important variations attributed to organizational characteristics.

Finally, these authors found that the greater the emphasis in pay-for-performance (i.e., the higher the ratio of bonus to base and greater eligibility for long-term incentives), the greater the firm's return on assets. Specifically, "an increase of 10 percentage points in the bonus/base ratio was associated with .21 to .95 percent return on assets. An increase of 10 percent in the number of managers eligible for long-term incentives was associated with .17 to .20 percent greater return on assets" (Gerhart and Milkovich, 1990, p. 680). While these authors recognize that the point estimates of the impact of compensation strategies on ROA are small, ". . . it is necessary to keep in mind that many factors determine an organization's ROA. As such, it is not clear that any single factor would be likely to have a large effect on ROA. Even small effects, however, may be substantial in dollar terms" (p. 681).

The reader should note that Gerhart and Milkovich (1990) focused on the main effects of variable compensation (an important dimension of the experiential compensation pattern discussed earlier) on firm performance but did not examine directly the issue of how compensation strategies interact with organizational strategies or company characteristics to affect firm performance. The next study to be discussed below (Gomez-Mejia, 1992) addresses this question.

Gomez-Mejia (1992). Gomez-Mejia's study used a mix of quantitative and perceptual measures, including archival performance data on each firm (as obtained from Compustat) and subjective descriptions of organizational and pay strategies (as reported by compensation managers). A sample of 243 manufacturing companies were included in the study. (See the methodological appendix in Chapter 3 for additional information.)

One of the key objectives of this research was to be able to test the hypotheses that compensation strategies have a differential effect on firm performance as a function of organizational strategies. Firm performance was measured by averaging several profitability and stock market indicators for each company during a five-year period, 1982-1986. These included earnings per share, return on investment, average return on common stock, and the average annual percent change in a firm's market value.

A factor analysis of the four performance indicators produced a single factor, indicating that they are capturing an overall firm performance dimension. This analysis justified the construction of a composite performance factor score, which was calculated by adding the firm's standardized value of each of the profitability and stock market indicators. All firms were then ranked in descending order, based on their respective composite factor scores. Lastly, the ranked scores were categorized into performance quartiles. The correlation between the quartile performance rankings and the raw scores on the performance composite was .91, indicating that little information was lost by categorizing this data into four groups.

A survey that asked the compensation officer of each firm to describe the organization's strategy and the firm's pay strategies was developed. The questionnaires were identical, except that paper color was varied to correspond to each of the performance quartiles—red, blue, green, and yellow for the top, second, third, and fourth quartile, respectively. This procedure enabled the investigator to link easily the questionnaire responses to a performance cohort, without compromising anonymity or confidentiality. An ordinal performance ranking was then assigned to each survey received (to be used as a criterion measure), ranging from four for the top quartile to one for the lowest quartile.

The compensation strategy measure used was the algorithmic-experiential composite described in Chapter 3 (calculated based on respondents' answers to a set of Likert type scales as listed in Table 3-2). The higher the score, the more experiential the pay strategies are. And vice-versa, the lower the score, the more algorithmic the pay strategies are.

Organizational strategies were assessed using the taxonomies discussed in Chapter 3. Corporate strategy was measured in terms of Rumelt's typology for extent of diversification (i.e., single-product, dominant-product, unrelated-product, and conglomerate) and Leontiades' typology (i.e., evolutionary vs. steady state) for process of diversification. Business unit strategy was measured in terms of Miles and Snow's typology (i.e., defenders, prospectors, and analyzers) and life cycle stage (i.e., start-up and growth; maturity and decline).

Results for the corporate level are graphically summarized in Figures 5-5 and 5-6. These figures show the average compensation strategy score (in standardized form) according to extent of diversification (Figure 5-5) and process of diversification (Figure 5-6), broken down by high performing (solid lines) and low performing (dotted lines) firms.

Results show that, consistent with expectations, there seems to be systematic differences in performance levels attributed to the interaction of corporate strategies and compensation strategies. A more experiential compensation strategy (moving up along the vertical axis) is associated with greater firm performance (solid lines) for single-product and unrelated-product firms and for those companies that adopt an evolutionary diversification strategy. On the other hand, a more algorithmic compensation strategy (moving down along the vertical axis) is associated with greater firm performance (solid lines) for dominant- and related-product companies and for those firms whose diversification process is steady state in nature.

Figures 5-7 and 5-8 graphically display how firm performance varies according to compensation strategy (vertical axis) and business unit strategy (horizontal axis). A more experiential compensation strategy (moving up along the vertical axis) is associated with greater firm performance (solid lines) among prospectors, followed by analyzers (Figure 5-7) and those business units at the start-up and growth stages in the life cycle (Figure 5-8). On the other hand, an algorithmic compensation strategy (moving down along the vertical axis) is associated with greater firm performance (solid lines) among defenders (Figure 5-7) and business units at the mature and declining stages of their life cycles (Figure 5-8).

While not reported in the graphs, formal tests of statistical significance for the cross-product terms (i.e., organizational strategy X compensation pattern with firm performance as a dependent variable) in a regression equation indicated that controlling for other fac-

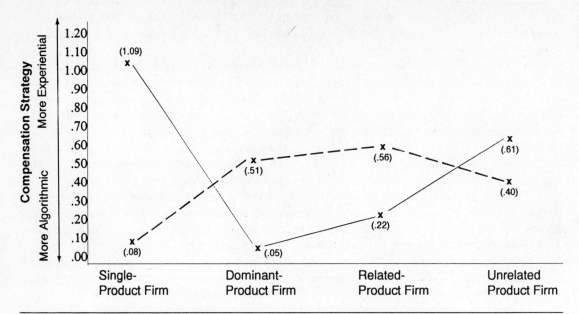

FIGURE 5-5 Compensation Strategy Profile of Low (Below Average) and High (Above Average) Performing Firms According to Extent of Diversification*

* Based on a study by Gomez-Mejia, L.R. (1992).
— — —   Denotes low performing firms (Based on EPS, ROE, Common Stock Return, and Market Value Change)
————   Denotes high performing firms (Based on EPS, ROE, Common Stock Return, and Market Value Change)

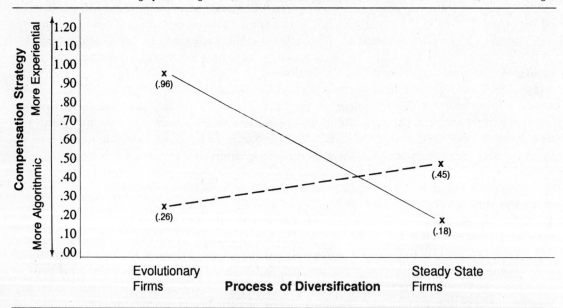

FIGURE 5-6 Compensation Strategy Profile of Low (Below Average) and High (Above Average) Performing Firms According to Process of Diversification*

* Based on a study by Gomez-Mejia, L. R. (1992).
— — —   Denotes low performing firms (Based on EPS, ROE, Common Stock Return, and Market Value Change)
————   Denotes high performing firms (Based on EPS, ROE, Common Stock Return, and Market Value Change)

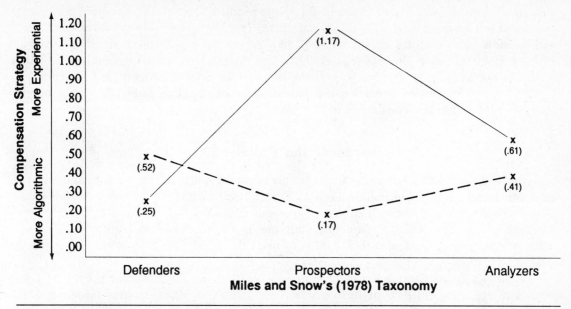

FIGURE 5-7   Compensation Strategy Profile of Low (Below Average) and High (Above Average) Performing SBUs According to Miles and Snow's (1978) Strategy Taxonomy*

* Based on a study by Gomez-Mejia, L. R. (1992).

— — — Denotes low performing firms (Based on EPS, ROE, Common Stock Return, and Market Value Change)

_____ Denotes high performing firms (Based on EPS, ROE, Common Stock Return, and Market Value Change)

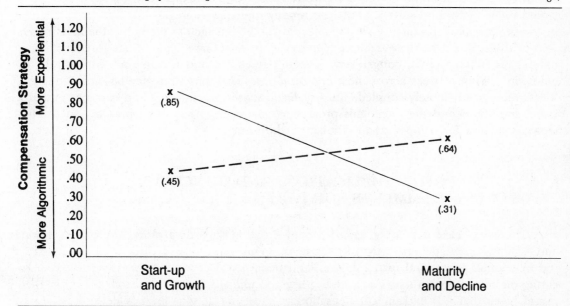

FIGURE 5-8   Compensation Strategy Profile of Low (Below Average) and High (Above Average) Performing SBUs According to Life Cycle Stage*

* Based on a study by Gomez-Mejia, L. R. (1992).

— — — Denotes low performing firms (Based on EPS, ROE, Common Stock Return, and Market Value Change)

_____ Denotes high performing firms (Based on EPS, ROE, Common Stock Return, and Market Value Change)

tors, significant interactions were found for single-product ($p \leq .001$), dominant-product ($p \leq .01$), related-products ($p \leq .05$), steady state firms ($p \leq .001$), evolutionary firms ($p \leq .001$), and business units that are defenders ($p \leq .05$), prospectors ($p \leq .001$), or at the start-up stage ($p \leq .001$). (See Gomez-Mejia, 1992.) The interaction term for unrelated-product firms was not statistically significant; perhaps this may be attributed to their high complexity and myriads of factors impacting the performance of conglomerates that could not be accounted for within the constraints of this study.

Summary and Propositions

In short, empirical evidence supports the theoretical expectation that compensation strategies can make a significant contribution to firm performance, whether measured perceptually or objectively. The strength of this relationship increases as a function of their integration with other organizational elements, their use as a competitive tool, their assistance in reducing transaction costs, and their ability to meet the needs of strategic employee groups within the firm.

Table 5-3 summarizes 25 key theory-based propositions on the relationship between compensation strategies and firm performance and the extent to which each of these has been empirically supported. While strong support has been found for many of these, the reader should keep in mind that the overall amount of research on pay strategies-firm performance relations (except for top executive compensation as seen in Chapters 6 and 7) is extremely rare. Thus, few of these findings have been replicated. For the most part, this remains an unchartered territory wide open for future research. In particular, one critical issue that is almost totally devoid of study is how firms modify their pay strategies in response to changes in the organization, product, environment, etc., and what factors moderate the relative success of those changes. Investigations conducted to date have been almost totally static in nature, yet notions of fit, congruency, interunit relations, and the like are intrinsically dynamic in varying degrees across most organizations. How pay strategies become "coupled," "decoupled," and "loosely coupled," in a dialectic sense with internal and external organizational conditions and the effect this process has on firm performance presents an exciting area of research for compensation scholars in the future.

POLICY IMPLICATIONS AND CONCLUDING
COMMENTS FOR PART 1 OF THE BOOK

There is a clear emerging trend in compensation towards a more macro, system-wide and business-oriented perspective of the field. This represents a distinct departure from the functional, procedural, psychological, and neoclassical economic bases of the past. Focusing on compensation issues at a higher level of analysis means the search for other theoretical bases that will explain compensation phenomena at that level is needed. Because this change in compensation thinking is so recent, explanatory frameworks have yet to congeal. Therefore, conceptual schemes found in other fields are borrowed. Several of these have been reviewed in Part 1 and are referred to again in subsequent chapters as they ap-

TABLE 5-3
Twenty-Five Propositions of Firm Performance—Pay Strategies Relations
and Degree of Empirical Support

	Propositions	Empirical Support
Proposition 1	The greater the fit between compensation strategies, overall corporate strategies, and SBU strategies, the greater the contribution of the pay system to firm performance.	Strong
Proposition 2	Firm performance improves as the congruency among the pay system, organizational characteristics, and environmental forces increases.	Strong
Proposition 3	The more pay strategies deviate from the "ideal" compensation strategies appropriate for various organizational strategies, the lower their contribution to firm performance.	Strong
Proposition 4	Pay strategies are most likely to be effective when they are compatible with the general philosophy of dominant coalitions within the firm.	Mostly anecdotal
Proposition 5	The contribution of pay strategies to firm performance increases the more these are able to erect barriers of entry against competitors.	Limited evidence but supportive
Proposition 6	The more irreplaceable human resources are (such as would be the case for key scientists and engineers in a high technology firm), the more an organization would benefit from erecting barriers to entry via the pay system to prevent other firms from moving in.	Limited evidence but supportive
Proposition 7	The greater the number of firms in an industry, the less discretion any given company will have in charting its own idiosyncratic pay strategies and the lower the potential returns to using the pay system to gain a competitive advantage.	Largely untested
Proposition 8	Smaller firms can gain a competitive advantage by designing pay packages that reduce fixed cost expenditures (salary and benefits) and increase the variable component (e.g., bonuses, equity-based pay).	Strong
Proposition 9	The greater the elasticity of demand for its product, the more a firm can gain a competitive advantage by augmenting the variable component of the pay package.	Largely untested
Proposition 10	The more the compensation system can assist the firm in utilizing its own unique skills and assets and mold itself to the company's idiosyncratic situation and peculiarities, the more it will contribute to firm performance.	Strong
Proposition 11	In dominant- and related-product firms, algorithmic pay strategies would make a greater contribution to firm performance by reducing contract costs. It would be possible for corporate headquarters to exercise direct control over SBUs and efficiently monitor the activities of divisional managers.	Strong
Proposition 12	For companies that have grown through internal expansion, an algorithmic compensation pattern would make a greater contribution to firm performance by minimizing transaction costs.	Strong
Proposition 13	An experiential compensation pattern would make a greater contribution to performance in unrelated-product firms and conglomerates because	Unclear

TABLE 5-3 (Continued)
Twenty-Five Propositions of Firm Performance—Pay Strategies Relations
and Degree of Empirical Support

Propositions	Empirical Support
transaction costs would be lowered by allowing more flexibility to each SBU.	
Proposition 14 The greater the performance ambiguity facing a firm, the more an experiential pay strategy (vis-a-vis an algorithmic one) will make a higher contribution to firm performance.	Largely untested
Proposition 15 The greater the asset specificity of SBUs (i.e., the lower the flow of goods and services between SBUs in a corporate portfolio), the more an experiential pay strategy (vis-a-vis an algorithmic one) will make a higher contribution to firm performance.	Limited evidence but supportive
Proposition 16 An algorithmic compensation strategy would reduce the transaction costs (thereby contributing to firm performance) resulting from opportunistic behaviors in related, dominant, and internal diversifiers by emphasizing closer monitoring of SBUs.	Limited evidence but supportive
Proposition 17 An experiential compensation strategy would reduce the transaction costs (thereby contributing to firm performance) in unrelated-product firms and in acquisitive diversifiers by emphasizing incentive alignment.	Limited evidence but supportive
Proposition 18 Behavioral controls will make a greater contribution to firm performance as knowledge of the organization transformation process increases.	Largely untested
Proposition 19 Outcome (performance-based) controls will make a greater contribution to firm performance as knowledge of the organization transformation process increases.	Largely untested
Proposition 20 Compensation strategies will make a greater contribution to firm performance if they meet the needs of strategic employee groups within the firm.	Limited evidence but supportive
Proposition 21 An experiential compensation strategy will make a greater contribution to firm performance the greater the number and diversity of strategic employee groups within the firm.	Limited evidence but supportive
Proposition 22 A compensation mix that emphasizes aggregate incentives will make a greater contribution to firm performance when the nature of the task and interdependencies demand close cooperation in the work force.	Strong
Proposition 23 Macro equity-based compensation strategies (e.g., profit-sharing, ESOPs) serve to bind employees to the firm (by increasing the opportunity costs of attrition) but do not have much of a direct effect on individual, team, and firm performance.	Limited evidence but supportive
Proposition 24 Employee characteristics and personality orientation moderate the effectiveness of compensation strategies.	Limited evidence, mixed findings
Proposition 25 Higher performing firms tend to rely on compensation strategies that emphasize risk sharing between employees and the firm.	Strong

ply to specific compensation issues such as executive pay and sales incentives. Empirical work based on these theoretical formulations is still in its infancy but is rapidly expanding as seen in Chapters 4 and 5. It seems appropriate to conclude this section of the book with a number of policy implications flowing from the arguments advanced in Part 1, namely that compensation strategy involves the following:

1. *Firm performance as the ultimate dependent variable.* The central concern when making strategic compensation choices is the impact such a decision will have on firm performance, rather than on some other intermediate outcomes (such as internal consistency). These intermediate outcomes only have meaning in terms of their firm performance implications.

2. *A significant resource commitment.* Unlike tactical decisions, investing in the redesign of a pay program can be expensive and demands a substantial amount of resources that may be irrevocably sunk. For example, an employee stock option plan (ESOP) can dilute firm equity and may be quite costly at the time employees redeem their stock. Therefore, such decisions may have considerable cost implications for the firm.

3. *A long-term orientation.* Once a compensation program is introduced, it becomes very resistant to change as expectations are created on employees' part. This means that careful planning and a futuristic outlook is necessary for successful implementation. For example, as discussed in Chapter 9, one of the criticisms consultants hear quite often about gainsharing programs is that participating employees expect a payout. When "dry" years are encountered (e.g., firm profits fall below minimum level established in gainsharing formula), employees can be very adamant in expressing their disappointment. While planning is required, there is a tenuous balancing act that must be played. Enough flexibility needs to be built into the pay system so that it does not become calcified or unable to adapt to changes.

4. *A close interaction with competitive environment.* No compensation system exists in a vacuum. Each should be consciously designed so that it is attuned to competitive forces in the environment. An overriding concern is to outperform competitors by enacting pay policies that can best serve to attract and retain scarce talent and, at the same time, induce employees to behave in such a way that the long-term business interests of the firm are met.

5. *Compensation systems must be made contingent on factors internal and external to firm.* The compensation system must be carefully designed so that it takes into account such factors as firm size, nature of work force, tasks performed, etc. This means all standardized "cookbook" procedures for compensation are automatically suspect.

6. *Compensation professionals must meet the needs of power coalitions within the firm, while at the same time managing their perceptions and "indoctrinating" them as to what the appropriate pay strategies should be, given contingencies affecting the firm.* Because pay effectiveness is a subjective concept and power coalitions are seldom versed in compensation techniques, compensation professionals must exercise a great deal of lead-

ership and use their persuasive skills to get dominant coalitions "to buy" into pay strategies that are novel and perhaps risky but quite appropriate for particular situations. For example, use of team-based bonuses in R&D operations is often viewed with suspicion by upper level managers fearing a strong "free rider" effect (whereby low performers in a group receive the benefit of high performers). However, compensation managers may be able to impress divisional managers that R&D team-based incentives have worked remarkably well elsewhere, with a much higher success rate than individual-based merit pay programs (Gomez-Mejia and Balkin, 1989).

7. *Top management involvement.* Compensation as a functional area must compete with other units for resources and attention. The reported failures of many compensation programs such as merit pay and pay-for-performance plans (see Chapter 9) can be traced to the fact that they were initiated by the HRM department with much fanfare and plenty of paperwork to go along with them but with limited involvement of top decision makers in the organization. Strategic planning, almost by definition, must involve the top echelons of the firm; and compensation is no exception.

8. *Synchronization with top executive pay.* As discussed in Chapters 6 and 7, top executives make decisions that are in their own financial self-interest. Thus, these individuals are very responsive to the incentive schemes designed for them. It is also true that top executives will formulate and enforce for the rest of the organization policies that they perceive conducive to the achievement of objectives needed to trigger incentive payments. This means, the compensation system for mid-level managers and exempt and nonexempt employees should reflect the overall incentive trust established for top executives.

9. *Development of a framework for strategic decisions.* As discussed in Chapters 2-4, compensation strategies should be based on a conceptual scheme that allows the firm to design pay programs so that day-to-day tactical decisions become part of a larger picture or plan. In other words, the game plan for the compensation system provides a philosophy, general direction, and rationale as to why a particular set of actions should be followed. Thus, specific program details can be developed to support the game plan. While this may appear obvious, compensation professionals have often been accused of being unable to distinguish the "forest from the trees" and losing track of the overall picture.

10. *A proactive posture.* Compensation strategy should not be set based on past problems, history of the organization, or current pressing fires. Instead, compensation professionals must anticipate future challenges and devise alternatives to meet them.

11. *Awareness of multifunctional or multibusiness consequences.* Compensation strategy must be formulated with the needs of the entire organization in mind. This may involve a given business unit or multiple business units. This means, there has to be a keen awareness of the business strategy followed by the organization or traced by dominant coalitions so that the resulting compensation strategies are aligned with overarching business strategies. These linkages were discussed in detail in Chapters 4 and 5. The underlying rationale for this alignment revolves around the concept of fit or congruency between the compensation system and other or-

ganizational subsystems (Gomez-Mejia and Welbourne, 1988;   Milkovich and Broderick, 1991) and the notion of that equifinality is important to firm performance.   Thus, functional strategies should all reinforce the overall strategic orientation of the firm.

Part 2
Strategic Employee Groups

EXECUTIVE COMPENSATION STRATEGIES AND FIRM PERFORMANCE: THEORETICAL AND EMPIRICAL FOUNDATIONS

THEORETICAL PERSPECTIVES ON EXECUTIVE COMPENSATION
    Marginal Productivity Theory
        The Owner as Entrepreneur
        The Executive as Hired Labor
    Governance Theory
        Managerialism
        Agency Theory
    Structural Theory
    Human Capital Theory
    Executive Pay as Symbolism
        Tournament Theory
        The Executive as Figurehead and Political Strategist
    Summary of Theoretical Determinants of Executive Pay

DO TOP EXECUTIVES MATTER?: A REVIEW OF THE EMPIRICAL EVIDENCE
    Accounting Choices
    Investment Decisions
    Acquisition and Diversification Strategies
    Internal Entrenchment Practices
    Market Neutralization Practices

EMPIRICAL RESEARCH ON EXECUTIVE PAY: SOME WARNINGS
    Reliance on Archival Data and False Sense of Objectivity
    Different Methodologies
    Dynamic Effects
    Complexity of Equity-Based Pay
    Operationalization of Firm Performance
    Estimating Performance of an Incumbent's Best Replacement
    Collinearity among the Variables
    Inferential Leaps

DETERMINANTS OF EXECUTIVE PAY: REVIEW OF EMPIRICAL EVIDENCE

Role of Company Size and Performance
Managerial Decisions, Financial Incentives, and Risk Sharing
Firm Diversification, Control Type, and Executive Pay
Market Factors
Distribution of Ownership
Role of Institutional Investors
Organizational Structure
Individual Determinants of Executive Pay
Symbolic Role of Executive Pay
Role of the Tax System

SUMMARY AND RESEARCH PROPOSITIONS

Part 1 of this book was concerned with strategic compensation patterns for the entire organization with the firm as the unit of analysis. Part 2 focuses on strategic employee groups who are critical to the technical core of most organizations and who are generally treated as a special subset for pay purposes. Just like in Part 1, and consistent with the strategic orientation of this book, firm performance is the ultimate dependent variable. However, not all the strategic compensation dimensions reviewed in Chapter 2, and subsequently examined as a composite pattern in Chapters 3-5, are relevant to these groups. For this reason, only a select number of compensation dimensions discussed in Part 1 that are pertinent to these special groups are revisited in Part 2.

This Chapter and Chapter 7 focus on top executive pay. While Mintzberg (1990) and other strategy theorists (e.g., Woolridge and Floyd, 1990) have warned us about the danger of becoming overly obsessed with senior executives, nowhere else in the firm is there a stronger need for a close linkage between compensation and organizational strategies than at the top executive level. There are three main reasons for this.

First, and most obvious, strategic decisions affecting the entire firm are normally made by top executives. Policy choices concerning growth or cutbacks, expansion via mergers and acquisitions or internal resources, diversification into unrelated or similar product lines, "harvesting" existing products by using present technology or investing in capital equipment and R&D, among others, are the responsibility of top management. Evidence suggests that the reward system plays a major role in how those decisions are made because executives are very responsive to what they perceive will lead to a personal payoff (Baysinger and Hoskisson, 1990; Larcker, 1983; Pennings, 1991; Zajac, 1990). As a result, a pay package designed to reinforce the wrong strategic choices (e.g., rewarding short-term results at the expense of long-term performance) will be highly detrimental to the firm's future success.

Next, in the typical firm, senior management provides general guidelines as to the form of the compensation package and payment criteria for all employees. Executives will set priorities for subordinates and reward those activities they perceive as consistent with their own incentive system (Gomez-Mejia, 1988). Likewise, members at the lower ranks in the organization are quick to discern what the top echelon considers important and is willing to reward and will tend to act accordingly. Consequently, goals and objectives built into the executive compensation plan are likely to have a multiplier effect on the entire work force.

Third, as a corollary to the previous point, executive compensation is critical to the firm's HRM subsystem because its incentive properties eventually filter down in the organization and signal to all employees those behaviors that will be conducive to personal success. As noted in Chapter 9, while the question of whether pay is a motivator is as old as humankind itself and continues to stir controversy, most behavioral scientists agree that employees tend to do those things they perceive are recognized by their bosses. And the way compensation dollars are allocated send a powerful symbolic message throughout the organization of what is and is not valued.

Partly because of its strategic importance, but also because of its high visibility and large sums of money involved, executive compensation is perhaps the most controversial subject in this book. Annual pay packages of some CEO's may reach eight digit figures, and seven digit figures are now normal among Fortune 500 firms   (Fierman, 1990). For instance, Steven J. Ross (head of Warner Communications Inc.) recently broke the 100 million mark in a single year (*Business Week*, 1990b). Craig O. McCaw (CEO of Cellular Communications) "made 53.9 million [in 1989] in salary, bonuses, and stock options even though his company has never earned a profit" (*Business Week*, 1990, p. 56). The Hay group reported in 1990 (*CompFlash*, 1990) that CEO's total pay increased 17.4 percent on average during the previous year, more than three times the rate of inflation, and 3.1 times faster than the average increase for typical middle management positions (5.4 percent).

At the heart of the debate is whether executives deserve to earn these amounts of money. Critics complain that in the United States, the ratio of CEO's income to that of the lowest paid worker is about 100 to 1, while in Japan the ratio ranges 17 to 1 (Beard, 1991; Deckop, 1987). Gerhart and Milkovich (1993) report that spending power among U.S. executives is more that three times greater than Japanese executives. On the one hand, people such as Loomis (1982), Crystal (1988), Watson (1990), and Will (1991) refer to this situation as "madness," "wacky," "disgusting," "chaotic," and "looting," while Murphy (1986a) proclaims that "executives deserve every nickel they get."

This chapter is divided into four sections. First, several theoretical perspectives on the determinants of executive compensation are examined. Second, the question of how much influence executives exert on firm performance and the role played by the incentive system is covered. Next, the empirical evidence on the predictors and correlates of executive pay are reviewed. Finally, the chapter closes with a list of twenty-two research propositions and a summary judgment as to how well each of them is supported by data. The subsequent chapter (Chapter 7) analyzes implementation issues that should be considered in the design of executive compensation programs.

THEORETICAL PERSPECTIVES ON EXECUTIVE COMPENSATION

Executive pay has provided very fertile grounds for theory development across several disciplines. This section of the chapter examines the factors that influence strategic compensation choice decisions at the executive level based on paradigms that have emerged in diverse fields. (See Figure 6-1.)

The first paradigm reviewed below is *marginal productivity theory*, which has its roots in macro and microeconomics. It is primarily concerned with pay level. The second paradigm focuses on the *governance* aspects of executive pay—namely, managerialism and agency theory, which borrow from political science, sociology, finance, and economics. They both

Explanatory Theoretical Framework   **Top Executive Compensation Dimensions**

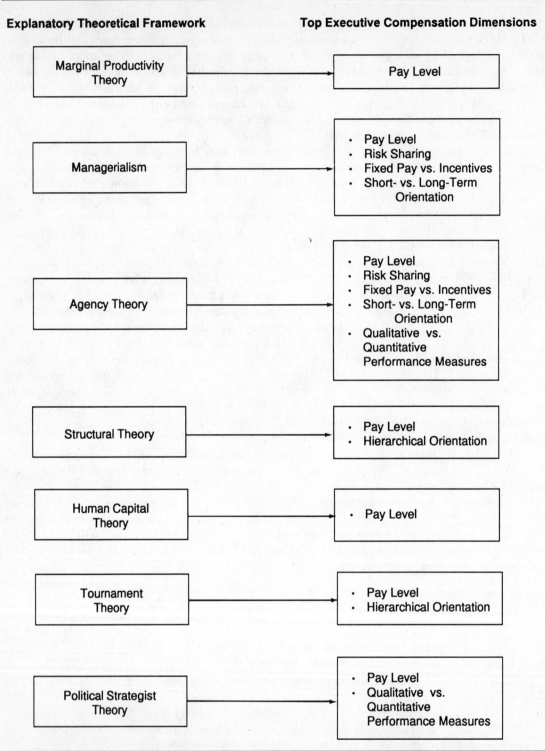

FIGURE 6-1 Top Executive Pay: Theoretical Frameworks and Associated Compensation Dimensions

deal with pay level, risk sharing, fixed pay vs. incentives, and short- vs. long-term orienta-tion. *Agency theory* is also concerned with qualitative vs. quantitative performance measures.

The third theoretical perspective to be examined consists of sociological theories that emphasize hierarchical relationships and number of organizational levels as predictors of executive pay level. The fourth paradigm, *human capital theory*, has its roots in labor eco-nomics and focuses on individual characteristics of the executive. It is primarily interested in pay level. The last one, *executive pay as symbolism*, has its roots in economics (tourna-ment theory) and organizational behavior (executive as a political strategist) and focuses on the myth forming and political aspects of executive compensation. Tournament theory is primarily concerned with pay level and pay differentials in the managerial hierarchy, while the political strategist perspective is concerned with pay level and reliance on qualitative vs. quantitative performance measures. Each of these theoretical frameworks is discussed in turn.

Marginal Productivity Theory

The oldest and perhaps most enduring theoretical explanations of executive pay have their origin in classical and neoclassical economics. As described below, these represent analytical extensions of the theory of the firm.

The Owner as Entrepreneur. In the classical theory of the firm, the chief executive officer (CEO) and the firm owner are one and the same. The entrepreneur comes up with an idea for a marketable product, starts the firm with his/her own resources, assumes all the risks for this investment, and is driven by a single-minded objective of minimizing cost per unit in order to maximize profits. In other words, there are no professional managers hired by external owners to perform administrative tasks; the entrepreneur *is* the executive and will either make all the gains or suffer the consequences of his/her actions.

If one assumes that there is perfect competition in the product and labor markets (i.e., perfect information, instant mobility of resources, large number of firms so that no single company can affect price, and rational behavior on the entrepreneur's part), one can make the following predictions:

1. The entrepreneur will manage the firm in such a way that it uses the least cost combination of inputs (labor, materials, etc.) to produce the profit maximizing level of output.
2. Profit maximization is achieved at the point where the marginal cost of produc-tion (the change in total costs with a change in the level of output) is just equal to the market price of the product.

Given this scenario, the compensation received by the entrepreneur is identical to the firm's net profits.

The Executive as Hired Labor. The neoclassical economic models relax the assumption that the entrepreneur and CEO are the same person. A professional executive may be hired to manage the firm, and this individual will be treated like any other input, receiving com-pensation in return for his/her services. Other things equal, the amount received will de-pend on the executive's marginal productivity, which, like any other factor of production, will be equal at equilibrium to that individual's marginal revenue product.

According to neoclassical economists (see Roberts, 1959), the marginal revenue product of a CEO is the total firm profit under his/her stewardship, minus the profit level that would be achieved if the firm was at the helm of the best alternative executive, plus the amount that would have to be paid to hire the latter. In other words, the marginal revenue product of an executive is not only a function of observed firm performance but also the opportunity costs of having him/her in command instead of someone else. If one assumes perfect information and mobility in the labor market and a wide range of alternative jobs open to executives and executives available to firms, all executives will be paid at a rate equal to their marginal revenue products.

If the strict assumptions of perfect competition are relaxed, some neoclassical theoreticians maintain that executive pay will fall somewhere between a minimum and a maximum level on a continuum, rather than on a precise equilibrium point (Roberts, 1959). The upper limit that the firm would be willing to pay the executive is his/her marginal revenue productivity—that is, the sum of "excess profits" under his/her command, plus the cost of hiring a replacement. The lower limit is the minimum pay that the CEO would accept from the firm. This amount would equal the next best financial offer that he/she could command in the open market. The range of indeterminacy in executive pay can be quite large, and firm size then becomes an important determinant of where the range will ultimately lie. There are several reasons for the role of firm size within this theoretical framework (Gomez-Mejia, Tosi, and Hinkin, 1987).

First, a smaller firm has a difficult time matching the profits of larger firms, even if it operates more efficiently. While profit per unit may be less in the larger firm, its greater volume of sales as compared to the smaller firm allows the larger firm to convert even a modest marginal gain in profit per unit into a larger amount of total profits. So, smaller margins may be associated with higher profits for larger firms, and executives will be rewarded accordingly up to the point where total profits begin to decline.

Second, the cost of paying for the CEO's services relative to the total revenue of the firm is a decreasing function of firm size. For example, in a firm with a total revenue of 20 billion dollars, even a compensation package of 2 million for the CEO would be less proportionately in terms of total revenues than in a firm selling 5 million dollars a year and paying its CEO 100 thousand dollars annually. In other words, the firm's ability to pay a CEO increases as the denominator in the ratio of CEO compensation to total revenue increases.

Third, the market for executives is likely to be segmented according to firm size. Thus, a large firm will fill vacancies by hiring replacement CEOs from other large firms. Given a more limited pool of potential applicants from which to recruit executives, a bigger company must pay a premium to attract and retain executives from other large firms. The actual pool of available applicants shrinks even more if one segments the executive market by industry. Firms prefer to hire CEOs from within the same or highly related industry (McCann, Hinkin, and Gomez-Mejia, 1992). This reduces the number of available alternatives and, thereby, bids up their market price.

Fourth, as discussed later under the human capital model, firm size, complexity of CEO tasks, and amount of responsibility entrusted to the CEO tend to go hand in hand. Therefore, as the firm becomes larger, one would expect a corresponding increase in CEO pay to compensate the executive for the skills necessary to carry out successfully the additional duties vested on the job.

In summary, the above theoretical formulation suggests that executive pay level is a positive function of (a) firm performance under the executive's stewardship; (b) lower value of firm performance indicators if the next best alternative executive were to be hired as a substitute for the present CEO; (c) the compensation to be paid to the best alternative replacement; (d) best pay rate executive could obtain in the labor market; and (e) firm size.

Based on the above discussion, the reader should not be left with the impression that firm size, rather than performance, should be the number one determinant of executive pay level or that larger firm size leads to improved profitability. The implication that should be drawn is that in a continuum of executive pay levels with marginal revenue productivity setting the upper bound (or firm performance in more common parlance) and a lower bound set by "going rates" in the executive labor market, one can reasonably expect that firm size will make a difference. There is nothing in the above arguments to suggest that increases in firm size, profit per unit, and total profit necessarily go together. That is true if one were to examine a broad cross-section of firms, ranging from the smallest to the largest firms in the economy. But if one were to examine firms within a given size category (let's say small, medium, and large), there may be little, if any, relationship between scale of operations and total profits. Among the Fortune 1,000 group, for example, for any given firm, even tiny improvements in efficiency may produce greater company profits than would be obtained through further increases in size (Gomez-Mejia, Tosi, and Hinkin, 1987).

Governance Theories

Both the classical and neoclassical economic models treat the firm as a "black box" with the executives being largely reactive and their pay level determined by forces outside their control. Furthermore, these models portray a world where either the entrepreneur and executive are embodied in the same person or the owner hires the executive and sets his/her pay following a rational deductive process. While those simplifying assumptions are helpful for analytical purposes, the typical firm in most Western countries has a corporate structure with not one but hundreds, thousands, or even millions of owners, each having a small claim on the firm. The modern corporation is perhaps the greatest invention of the 19th century and offers many advantages over the single-owner firm:

1. It allows the accumulation of vast amounts of capital in a single organization by pooling the resources of many individuals so that the firm is not constrained by internal financing. Those superior resources can then be used for heavy investments in capital equipment, channels of distribution, R&D expenditures, etc., that may not be possible otherwise. By the same token, larger economies of scale may lead to greater efficiency and lower cost per unit.

2. Risk can be spread across many stockholders so that large, expensive projects with uncertain payoffs may be undertaken, and limited liability protects the interests of any single stockholder.

3. Because the corporation has a "life of its own" and is independent of any one individual, its time horizon is much longer so that long-term investments can be made.

4. Authority can be delegated to managers who have specialized knowledge, thereby capitalizing on the unique skills of these individuals.

5. Because corporate stocks are openly traded, the security market can gauge the competitive performance of the firm, and its stock value will reflect that assessment.

While the corporate form of organization has some clear advantages, it also raises some disturbing questions concerning managerial behavior that were inconsequential in the traditional economic models. Because ownership is no longer identifiable in any real sense in the modern corporation, who determines executive pay? Since the executives themselves run the firm, is it possible for them to use their position of power to further their own interests, rather than those of stockholders? Both managerialism and agency theory deal with corporate governance issues arising from the fact that the decision-making process in those firms may be in the hands of professional managers whose interests do not necessarily coincide with those of atomistic owners.

Managerialism. The underlying premise of managerialism was succinctly stated by Berle and Means (1932, p. 25) sixty years ago: "The separation of ownership from control produces a condition where the interests of owner and of ultimate manager may, and often do, diverge, and where many of the checks which formerly operated to limit the use of power disappear."

Interestingly enough, the main ideologue of capitalism, Adam Smith, warns us of the "separation of ownership and control" problems back in 1776 (Smith, 1937, p. 700):

> The directors of such [joint stocks] companies, however, being the manager rather of other people's money than of their own, it cannot well be expected that they should watch over it with the same anxious vigilance with which the partners in a private company frequently watch over their own. Like the stewards of a rich man, they are apt to consider attention to small matters as not for their master's honor, and very easily give themselves a dispensation from having it. Negligence and profusion, therefore, must always prevail, more or less, in the management of the affairs of such a company.

The problem Adam Smith identified in the 18th century has a greater sense of urgency today, given the increasing dispersion of stockholdings in most American firms. Managerialists such as Berle and Means (1932), Marris (1964), Williams (1985), Herman (1981), and Aoki (1984) argue that executives who run modern corporations are no longer motivated to maximize profits as the traditional economic models would lead us to believe. Rather, they are free to pursue their own interests, and often these do not coincide with those of stockholders. Managerialists make the following predictions about executive behavior that is unconstrained by external owners:

1. Executives are risk averse. Therefore, they will structure their compensation packages so that pay is flexible to move up as firm performance improves but will not suffer if performance declines. Therefore, variability, downside risk, and uncertainty are largely removed from their pay packages (Tosi and Gomez-Mejia, 1989).
2. Firm performance will play a minor role in executive compensation decisions so that the economic well-being of the executive is largely decoupled from the firm's (and stockholder's) fortunes (Dyl, 1988; McEachern, 1975). By the same token, executives are less likely to be fired, even as firm performance plummets (Salancik and Pfeffer, 1980).

3. Executives are driven to increase firm size, even if additional growth results in decreased profits. This may be accomplished via corporate diversification (Ahimud and Lev, 1981) or through mergers and acquisitions (Kroll, Simmons, and Wright, 1990). Managerialists impute two main motives to the CEO's "sales maximizing" behaviors. First, expanding scale of operations enhances the visibility of the firm. This promotes the CEO's prestige, appealing to his/her ego needs (Marris, 1964). Second, firm size may be used by executives and hired consultants to justify higher pay at the top (Dyl, 1988).

4. Executives are tempted to make decisions that have short-term payoffs and to adopt accounting measures of performance that can be embellished to inflate annual reports. (See review by Hunt, 1986.) Profit satisficing, rather than maximizing, becomes the norm (Galbraith, 1976). Long-term investments and incentive pay based on long-term results are discouraged because these are uncertain, and executives have little loyalty to any given firm (Marris, 1964). There is much interfirm mobility as executives jockey with each other for power, prestige, and additional income. Thus, there is little gain to be made by engaging in activities whose time horizon is several years down the pike and that may, in fact, show up as a cost in the annual balance sheet (Brouwer, 1984; Johnson and Kaplan, 1987; Meyer, 1983; Rappaport, 1978, 1981, 1986; Sears, 1984). Therefore, the executive compensation package tends to reward short-term performance.

How can executives get away with the self-serving behaviors described above? The first reason has already been discussed. It is difficult for isolated, dispersed stockholders to muster enough concerted power to discipline top management. Besides the logistic problems, no single stockholder may have enough at stake to launch a major campaign against company executives. Ultimately, the main restraint facing executives consists of changes in the price of marketable shares carrying limited liability so that stockholders may shift their investments from one firm to another. Managerialists, however, feel that this is not much of a constraint as long as the firm meets some minimum performance levels, which is not hard to accomplish for a well-established corporation operating in oligopolistic or quasi-oligopolistic markets.

Second, because of their privileged position, "information asymmetries" exist. The executives always know what is happening better than stockholders and may use this information imbalance to their own advantage (Holmstrom, 1979). It would be almost impossible for stockholders to have access to all the information involved in business planning, competitive strategies, R&D investments, choice of accounting methods, inventory methods, and depreciation procedures, to name a few. Thus, executives may use their superior knowledge to make decisions that are most beneficial to them. For example, R&D expenditures can be cut back over time and then kept at a very low level. This could have a very healthy impact on the annual reports for a few years, even if it could prove disastrous over, let's say, a twenty-year period, at a time when present management will be long gone (Hill and Hansen, 1989).

Third, managerialists argue that the board of directors is generally ineffective in disciplining executives. This view is vividly exemplified in the following comments:

> The answer to the question "who is in charge" is unmistakable. It is management. These managers report to the board of directors—whom they select . . . . (Leonard, 1969, p. 5).

The process of control usually rests with the president—not the board. It is the president who, like the family owner-managers of the small corporation, determines in large part what the board of directors does or does not do (Mace, 1971, p. 73).

[Since] in most cases board members are handpicked by management, [i]n many practical respects, management is, therefore, in control of the board (Pfeffer, 1972, p. 220).

The men who now run the large corporations . . . are selected not by stockholders, but in the common case, by a Board of Directors which narcissistically they select themselves (Galbraith, 1976, p. 22).

There are few if any genuine checks or balances on the power of the Chief Executive in large public corporations . . . . Directors run virtually no personal risk for any amount of complacency, cronyism, or outright neglect of their duties (Geneen, 1984, p. 28).

The board is not viewed, it is fair to say, as a place to take one's discoveries or one's conscience by people within the corporation. Nor do members of external groups have different expectations. It may be said that such a view is a shrewd judgment about the irrelevance or powerlessness of the corporate board. Boards have done little to disabuse this view, remaining quite remote, aloof and well camouflaged by company executives (Nader, 1984, p. 128).

The people who set the CEO's pay . . . they are the compensation committee . . . always conflicted, usually coopted . . . they have the tricky task of setting salaries for their peers, who more often than not, are their friends . . . . The CEO, whose pay the committee sets, sits on both sides of the table. That's because 76% of board chairmen are also CEOs. Indeed, instead of laboring to serve the shareholders, a CEO looking to enrich himself could just do as well selecting a compensation committee whose members earn more than he does . . . [because] committee members gauge the reasonableness of a CEO's salary against their own . . . . Management usually hires the consultant. And what consultant happy with his career choice would knowingly bite the hand that feeds him (Fierman, 1990, pp. 58 and 66).

Blowing it by the board of directors is usually pretty easy. Often enough, bosses who get big raises return the favor by handing out higher fees and benefits to the board (Castro, 1991, p. 40).

Wherever you find highly paid CEOs, you'll find highly paid directors. It's no accident (Crystal, 1991, p. 40).

Fourth, not only is the board accused of being ineffective, as illustrated in the above citations, but some argue that board members, just like executives, indulge in self-serving behaviors and receive hefty fees and perks that cannot be justified on any rational basis (Herman, 1981; Fierman, 1990). In 1984, Muckley examined the compensation of board members in 200 firms. He concluded that most directors are "handsomely paid" and have very little invested in the firm. Muckley (1984) provides many examples. For instance, Alls Chambers sat on several boards and received an annual cash compensation of $196,500 in 1983 for very little work. At Martin Marietta, after serving five years, board members will continue to receive half of their annual pay for at least ten years. More recently, Crystal (1990, p. 101) noted that:

CEOs aren't the only ones whose pay is rising remarkably fast. Many companies are sharply increasing what they pay outside directors—who of course decide what to pay the CEO. Not only do some directors receive pensions amounting to 100% of base pay after just five to ten years of board service, but an increasing number also are getting stock options and—hold on to your seat—restricted stock grants. The value of what an outside director of a major company receives can easily top $50,000 a year.

Similarly, Fuchsberg (1991, p. 313) concludes that "... times may be tough, but not for corporate directors. Board fees continue to rise, even at some companies where cut-backs are rife and layoffs loom." For instance, Fuchsberg (1991) shows that the average total compensation per director may exceed $75,000 in some firms, such at ITT and Sears Roebuck, in spite of continued lackluster performance. Because of interlocking director-ates, board members become a class in itself looking after their own self-interest across different firms and even industries. Muckley (1984) refers to them as a "corporate aristoc-racy."

Fifth, the board may be used as an institutional mechanism to legitimize decisions bene-ficial to executives and give them a rational, objective image. For example, equity-based pay on the surface may be used to tie the fortunes of the executive to those of stockhold-ers. The more stock price appreciates (which is obviously good for stockholders), the more income executives receive. Following this logic, boards can grant executives multimillion-dollar contracts where the bulk of it is in the form of stocks. Managerialists, however, of-ten see those plans as another plot to enrich top management, under a good faith pre-tense. According to Marris (1964, p. 25): "The stock option method, therefore, represents a way of paying gratuities to management which has the double advantage of ensuring that the whole cost falls on shareholders, while at the same time reducing the chance that the effect will be noticed."

In summary, managerialists portray a situation where managers can utilize their posi-tion of power in organizations to cater to their financial and nonpecuniary interests, per-haps at the expense of stockholders. The system of governance in major corporations is devoid of checks and balances because of a fractionalized distribution of ownership, and this works to management's advantage.

Agency Theory. Because of its overarching nature, agency theory has been referred to in several chapters of this book. However, as is seen next, most conceptual developments and empirical research on agency theory have taken place within the context of executive com-pensation. In the authors' opinion, agency theory is an extension of managerialism, although its roots can be found in such diverse disciplines as accounting (e.g., Demski and Feltham, 1978; Groff and Wright, 1989), marketing (e.g., Basu, Lal, Srinivasan, and Staelin, 1985), organizational behavior (e.g., Conlon and Parks, 1990; Eisenhardt, 1985, 1988, 1989), soci-ology (e.g., Eccles, 1985), and financial economics (e.g., Fama, 1989; Fama and Jensen, 1983a,b; Jensen, 1983; Jensen and Murphy, 1990a; Lewellen, Loderer, and Martin, 1987; Morck, Shleifer, and Vishny, 1988; Riordan and Sappington, 1987).

As noted in Chapter 1, agency theory recognizes that in most modern firms there is a separation between owners, called the principal, and hired managers, called the agent. Like managerialists, most agency theorists argue that this type of governance arrangement cre-ates an intrinsic "moral hazard" for managers (Holmstrom, 1979; Jensen and Meckling, 1976). This moral hazard may be attributed to a number of reasons that greatly overlap with those advanced by managerialists. First, given that it is difficult for atomistic owners to convene or interact with each other, agents will enjoy much discretion to set policies and procedures for the organization, independent of the wishes of the principals. Second, because situations may arise where the interests of the principal and agent do not converge, the agent is likely to maximize its own utility, not that of the principal. Third, the agent's superior access to information gives it more power to extract concessions from the principal.

In the parlance of agency theorists, the above conditions produce *agency costs* to be incurred by owners, where these are defined as the difference between net earnings had the owners been the managers and observed net earnings under the agent's stewardship. These costs include, at least, losses to the principal because the agent does not act in the principal's interest, and the cost of monitoring the activities of the agent.

Unlike managerialists, however, many agency theorists paint a more hopeful picture for stockholders. They view agency costs as a necessary evil that comes along with the advantages of the modern corporation reviewed earlier (i.e., accumulation of needed capital, risk spread, economies of scale, managerial specialization, etc.). Furthermore, many argue, it is possible to minimize the agency costs resulting from the separation of ownership and control. This can be accomplished through a system of monitoring the behavior of agents and the establishment of incentives that align the interests of owners with those of the firm.

Perhaps the best-known theoretical exposition of the role of monitoring in reducing agency costs is that of Fama (1980) and Fama and Jensen (1983). According to these authors, a firm can be viewed as a "nexus of contracts," written and unwritten, between its principals and its agents. These contracts, or "internal rules of the game," allow the organization to use the specialized knowledge of managers, while at the same time limiting their discretion. So, unlike managerialists, executives are not portrayed as having free rein to make decisions that may be detrimental to firm owners. Top management discretion is curtailed by "the rights of each agent in the organization and the performance criteria on which agents are evaluated" (Fama and Jensen, 1983b, p. 305). These contracts are enforced through an elaborate decision-making process. This process can be broken down into four stages (Fama, 1980).

The first stage is called *initiation* and is the responsibility of the agents. Top executives are expected to generate ideas and proposals for utilizing existing resources and scan the environment to identify available opportunities and potential threats. The second stage is called *ratification*. The action agenda developed by top management must be approved prior to implementation by an independent group of individuals, normally the board of directors. The third stage is called *implementation*. This consists of the execution of ratified decisions and is the responsibility of the agents. The fourth and final stage is called *performance measurement*. At this point, the principals or their representatives assess the contributions made by top management and will reward them accordingly. The initiation and implementation of decisions are designated as "decision management." The approval and performance measurement functions are termed "decision control."

According to Fama and colleagues, the use of decision hierarchies through which the higher level agents must ratify and monitor lower agents' initiatives and the existence of boards of directors who ratify and monitor the organization's most important decisions and who have the power to hire, fire, and reward top executives, ". . . offers an effective common approach to controlling the agency problems caused by separation of decision-making and risk-bearing functions" (Fama and Jensen, 1983b, p. 307). In fact, contrary to the tenets of managerialism, Fama joyfully proclaims that "in this nexus of contracts perspective ownership of the firm is an irrelevant concept" (Fama, 1980, p. 20).

In addition to the monitoring of agents, a second mechanism to reduce agency costs is the so called "incentive alignment." The focus here is not on supervising the behavior of managers or creating checks and balances in the decision-making system, but, rather, on rewarding agents for measurable results that are deemed to be in the best interest of owners. Incentive alignment, to work as intended, should complement, rather than be a substitute for, monitoring activities on the part of the principal. However, a number of factors affect the relative emphasis placed on each.

First, available information on agents' activities may be very limited, difficult to interpret, or too time-consuming and cumbersome to gather. Also, it may be nearly impossible for the principal to observe and evaluate directly the actions of management (Grossman and Hart, 1983; Leland and Pyle, 1977). Therefore, the harder it is to obtain reliable information on the agent's behavior, the more likely the firm will rely on incentive systems that track outcomes, rather than the process leading up to them. Most incentive systems are tied to "objective," quantifiable indices of firm performance such as return on equity, earnings per share, or changes in stock prices that can be plugged into a predetermined formula to ascertain the executive's payoff. On the other hand, principals will seldom rely on incentive alignment alone, regardless of the difficulties encountered in monitoring the agent's activities. Exclusive reliance on incentive payoffs tied to specific performance indicators can be dysfunctional. The agent may ignore other important dimensions of performance that are not directly captured in the compensation formula being used. For example, managers may cut back on capital expenditures to show higher year-end profits (and receive a larger bonus), negatively impacting the firm's competitive performance over time.

Second, if designed properly, the incentive structure of top managers will encourage mutual monitoring throughout the entire organization. The extent of monitoring can ensure that activities of lower level agents who are not perceived by those in higher ranks to contribute to valued outcomes are penalized or go unreinforced. Also, risk sharing between principals and agents will induce top executive ranks to supervise closely the behaviors of subordinates because their "neck is on the line" (Shavell, 1979).

While easy to distinguish conceptually, what constitutes monitoring and what represents incentive alignment are difficult for managers to pull apart in their minds (Tosi and Gomez-Mejia, 1989, 1992). Tosi and Gomez-Mejia developed two sets of scales to measure these two different constructs and had 175 managers rate them as these applied to their firms. The correlation between the two reached .81, suggesting that, perhaps because of the reasons discussed above, monitoring and incentive alignment are intrinsically dependent on each other.

Ultimately, according to Fama and colleagues, the marketplace is the final arbiter that decides which organizations survive and which ones will wither away. Management is not free to plunder the firm's resources in extravagant perks and compensation because concern for their personal reputation and the market disciplinary forces will keep them in check. The permanence of the corporate form of firm governance is the best testament to its instrumental value and to its ability to control agency problems. Fama (1980, p. 292) summarizes what has become known as the *efficient market hypothesis* in agency theory as follows:

The separation of security ownership and control can be explained as an efficient form of economic organization within the 'sets of contracts' perspective. The firm is disciplined by competitors from other firms, which forces the evolution of devices for efficiently monitoring the performance of the entire team and its individual members. In addition, individual participants in the firm, and in particular its managers, face both the discipline and opportunities provided by the market for their services, both within and outside the firm.

Structural Theory

The structural models of executive pay originated in the sociological tradition. This perspective holds that the compensation received by top ranks in a firm is a direct function of the number of organizational levels below them. Other things equal, the taller the organizational structure, the greater the earnings of top executives. The best-known rationale for this relationship was provided by Simon (1957), who argued that organizations attempt to maintain appropriate salary differentials between management levels and establish these differentials not in absolute terms, but as ratios. The differentials between ranks are not determined by economic forces, but, rather, through cultural processes that create relevant norms of social stratification. The resulting pay scales are an attempt to maintain "internal consistency" of the managerial pay scale with the formal organization and to comply with cultural "norms of proportionality" between earnings of superiors and those of subordinates. The predicted earnings of a given executive would equal the pay of the immediate subordinate times a fraction representing a socially enacted norm of appropriate differentials. Simon implies that the norm hovers around a 30 percent differential between ranks and that it is fairly uniform across organizations. Based on the above logic, Simon (1957, p. 33) makes the following generalization:

> Businesses, like all large scale organizations, are roughly pyramidal in form, because of the hierarchical structure induced by the authority relation. Each executive has a certain number of subordinates at the level immediately below him and this number varies within only moderate limits in a given company and among a number of companies . . . while we would expect to encounter instances of larger or smaller ratios [between earnings of managers and their subordinates], averages can be expected to be relatively stable.

In summary, in a manner somewhat akin to the traditional economic models, the structural perspective is very deterministic, with the earnings of executives being mechanically established as a function of number of levels below them and a fixed percent differential between their pay and those of subordinates. Unlike governance theories, structural models allow little room for contractual relationships, influence patterns, checks and balances, and other process variables as determinants of executive pay. Like the proponents of traditional job evaluation methods discussed in Chapter 1, this view treats observed pay levels as a natural outcome of a hierarchical pecking order in the organization.

Human Capital Theory

Unlike the theoretical formulations reviewed so far, human capital models focus on individual characteristics as predictors of executive pay (Gerhart and Milkovich, 1990). This perspective holds that workers accumulate "human capital" over time based on learning. The total amount of learning at any given point in time determines how valuable the employee is to the firm and this, in turn, determines how much the employer is willing to pay for his/her services. The primary factors that contribute to learning are education, experience, and training (Becker, 1964). In fact, human capital theorists claim that it is possible to calculate a "rate of return" on investments made to increase learning along each of those dimensions (Mincer, 1975).

The human capital perspective has been specifically applied to executive compensation in a number of ways. The first, and most obvious, application is summarized by Agarwal (1981, p. 39): "The amount of human capital a worker possesses influences his productivity, which in turn influences his earnings. The same general reasoning should hold for executive workers as well. Other things being equal, an executive with a greater amount of human capital would be better able to perform his job and thus be paid more." As a corollary to this argument, executives are generally highly educated and possess many years of work experience in responsible jobs requiring much personal sacrifice. Few people have the ability, stamina, or willingness to pay the associated personal price in terms of stress, family life, loss of privacy, and minimal leisure time. So their higher pay may be seen as a return on this human capital investment (Gerhart and Milkovich, 1990).

Second, human capital may help explain the relationship between corporate size and executive pay. As firms get bigger, they also become more complex. Larger organizations are associated with (a) greater span of control for the executive; (b) taller hierarchy; (c) wider geographical dispersion; (d) larger budgets and resources to administer; (e) diversified strategic business units with unrelated products; and (f) exposure to many and sometimes conflicting environmental forces impacting different parts of the firm. Executives in larger firms should be compensated accordingly as a recompense for the additional human capital requirement needed to carry out successfully this job. And because the potential cost of poor performance increases with organization size, the additional dollars paid to the executive may be well-justified.

The third linkage between executive pay level and human capital is not as intuitively obvious as the previous two. Some theorists argue that one should not expect a close chronological relationship between executive pay and firm performance because of the delayed effects of human capital. Harris and Holmstrom (1982), for example, argue that learning is the most important force affecting executive pay and that firms compensate executives for performance over their entire tenure with the firm, not necessarily on most recent observed performance. Likewise, Murphy (1986b, p. 62) concludes that:

> The rewards and penalties associated with measured current performance are spread over all remaining periods of contracted employment. Consequently, the relation between contemporaneous compensation and performance and the year-to-year variance of individual earnings vary systematically over the executive's career. Under the learning hypothesis, managerial ability is unknown and is revealed over time by observing performance . . . Since the rewards and penalties for unanticipated performance are spread over all remaining years of an employment contract, the effect of performance on compensation increases with tenure, as will the variance of compensation given any experience-earnings profile.

In other words, the performance of an executive depends on managerial ability, which is, in turn, a function of his/her human capital. Because ability is difficult to estimate at first, firms will track the executive's career and achievements over several years to allow for a more precise estimate of his/her performance. This approach reduces some of the uncertainty surrounding the measurement of an executive's relative success or failure.

Tracking allows the firm to distinguish between factors that affect observed firm performance and are totally beyond the executive's control (e.g., a market downturn) and those that may be attributed to the executive's actions. Therefore, ". . . an [executive's] compensation in one period depends on his performance in that period and his performance in the prior periods" (Murphy, 1986b, p. 62).

Executive Pay as Symbolism

Executive pay as symbolism holds that political factors independent of firm size and performance or an executive's productivity and market value explicitly enter into executive compensation decisions. Its central thesis is that executive pay constitutes a powerful signaling force within the firm and sends symbolic messages that transcend immediate economic concerns to lower level managers and employees. Therefore, reductionistic attempts to examine executive pay as a function of "objective" factors such as earnings per share and return on equity are likely to produce disappointing results. Two such models are reviewed below. The first one, by Lazear and Rosen, originated in economics. The second one, by Steers and Ungson, came from organizational behavior.

Tournament Theory. This theory postulates that the chief executive officer in a firm is seen by other people in the organization as the winner of a lottery. His/her compensation represents the proceeds received by being chosen in a game where the chances of winning are exceedingly small. Such an analogy is used to provide a theoretical justification for the very large observed differences between CEO pay and that of lower level executives. It also attempts to answer a question raised by many laymen as they read the annual executive compensation issue of *Business Week:* How can any human being be worth tens of millions of dollars in any single year? According to tournament theory, the enormous compensation received by CEOs has little to do with these individuals "deserving" it. Rather, it is used to send signals to other people in the firm that working harder and making the best use of their talents allow them to compete for the "trophy," perhaps leading to the number one spot. In other words, top executive pay is designed as the proverbial "pot of gold at the end of the rainbow." This incentive system serves to energize the behavior of other managers by appealing to their greed. In this manner, what on the surface appears to be unfair and irrational compensation for the person chosen to be chief executive ultimately furthers the interests of stockholders. According to Lazear and Rosen (1981, p. 845):

> His [CEO's] wage is settled not necessarily because it reflects his current productivity as president, but rather because it induces that individual and all other individuals to perform appropriately when they are in more junior positions. This interpretation suggests that presidents of large corporations do not necessarily earn high wages because they are more productive as presidents but because this particular type of payment structure makes them more productive over their entire working lives. A contest provides the proper incentives for skill acquisition prior to coming into the position.

The Executive as Figurehead and Political Strategist. This behavioral perspective of executive compensation has been explicitly articulated by Ungson and Steers (1984) and Steers and Ungson (1987), although it relies heavily on earlier work by Pfeffer (1981), Mintzberg (1973), Weick (1979), Pondy (1978), and Cyert and March (1963). Unlike tournament theory, which focuses on outcomes (namely the incentive value of executive pay), these authors are more concerned with political and normative aspects of executive compensation. According to this view, the belief that executive pay should be closely linked with firm performance is based on the erroneous presumption of "functional rationality"—namely, the idea that executive rewards such as bonuses or long-term income should be positively associated with the achievement of predefined goals such as profitability.   Rational approaches to the design of executive pay packages ignore the fact that organizations are pluralistic in nature with multiple constituencies (e.g., subunits, coalitions, and subcultures) and with diverse, and perhaps conflicting, interests.   Executives are required to walk a thin line and cater to the needs of these different groups, much through personal charisma, bargaining, and consensus building.   Therefore, executive pay can best be understood in terms of the role of political figureheads and strategists.

As figureheads, executives become symbols and are expected to act as boundary spanners to owners, government, employee groups, and the general public.   As a result, effectiveness in the job and the executive's leadership qualities derive from this individual's ability to manage symbolic activity.   Weick (1979) argues that the executive job is akin to that of an evangelist.   As political strategists, executives are expected to manage multiple coalitions and transactions between these coalitions and external constituencies.

These political and symbolic functions are difficult to assess using a functional-rational perspective with its emphasis on "objective" and "bottom line" data.   Yet, these are the most crucial components of the job.   Criteria for evaluating relative success along these dimensions are often ambiguous and must rely on perceptual judgments.   Trying to boil these down to an operational formula may lead to disappointing or even counterproductive results.   Instead, assessment of the executive's performance should be conducted by ascertaining how this individual's behaviors help meet the needs of pluralistic groups inside and outside the firm.   Steers and Ungson (1987, pp. 304-306) summarize this perspective as follows:

> ... At times, it might be appropriate to decouple CEO rewards and performance ...   The role of the CEO encompasses other boundary transactions that relate principally to the enhancement of the company's image over time.   In effect, attempts to couple CEO bonus, for example, to return on investment or other factors resembling those [used to reward] the divisional manager may prove to be illusory.   At times, in fact, it might even be functional to loosely couple or even decouple rewards from performance to accommodate political activities of the CEO that are in the best interest of the company but are difficult to tie down to profitability measures in a given time period ...   The formalization of the CEO compensation into a bonus formula may be untenable within a political context.

Summary of Theoretical Determinants of Executive Pay

In conclusion, executive pay has provided fertile grounds for much conceptual work originating in different disciplines and academic traditions.   The theories reviewed here are not necessarily contradictory, but represent different ways of examining executive compensation issues.   One clear inference from these efforts is that executive pay is a very complex phenomena that cannot be easily captured in any single model.

Executive pay can be studied at different levels of analysis.   First, at the firm level, executive pay is said to be a function of microeconomic determinants (marginal revenue productivity and firm's ability to pay), structural factors (hierarchical levels and firm size), and symbolic/political considerations (incentives to motivate lower level managers and need to fill role of figurehead and political strategist). Second, in the labor market, executive pay is expected to depend on the cost of hiring the best available replacement to the present executive and the going rate among firms of similar size. Third, at the stockholder level, executive pay is said to vary, depending on the distribution of ownership and the monitoring/incentive mechanisms established by the firm's owners to reduce agency costs. Finally, at the individual level, an executive's pay is said to increase as a function of personal ability and accumulated human capital.

To the extent that there is intense interaction and overlap among predictors of executive pay at different levels of analysis, it may be quite difficult, if not impossible, to disentangle reliably the unique effect of one variable from another. For example, firm size, distribution of ownership, and ability to pay are all likely to be correlated. This, however, has not discouraged investigators from attempting to discern empirically what factors determine executive compensation. This literature is discussed shortly.

DO TOP EXECUTIVES MATTER?: A REVIEW OF
THE EMPIRICAL EVIDENCE

Before the more narrowly focused empirical literature on the determinants and correlates of executive pay are discussed, the broader issue of how much potential influence top executives can exert on firm performance needs to be examined. In the context of this book, this question is important for two reasons. First, if the actual or latent impact is minimal, then linking executive pay to firm performance almost becomes a moot point. To hold management responsible for the firm's fate (by rewarding them when performance improves and penalizing them when performance decreases) would be demoralizing to executives if company performance depends on factors unrelated to how well the firm is being managed. In fact, Jensen and Murphy (1990a, p. 253) recently suggested a similar hypothesis (which the authors believe is incorrect) that the "small observed pay-performance sensitivity seems inconsistent with the implications of formal principal agent model . . . [because] CEOs are not, in fact, important agents of shareholders . . . CEOs do not matter." Second, as implied in most of the theoretical models described earlier and consistent with the strategic pay perspective of this book, the ultimate dependent variable on the question of whose interests the hired top executives serve is firm performance, or the extent to which managerial behaviors and decisions are oriented to promote or deter the financial well-being of the firm's owners. If firm performance is unresponsive to managerial actions, then, by implication, compensation strategies for top management groups will be inert at best in terms of their effect on company performance.

Two separate streams of research have examined the role that top executives play in firm performance. (Note: See Capon, Farley, and Hoenig, 1990, for a review of 320 published studies on the environmental, strategic, and organizational factors that affect firm performance.) The first one comes from the fields of organization theory and administrative science. This group of investigators have expended much effort trying to ascertain the extent to which strategic choices (i.e., managerial decisions) or environmental forces (i.e., situational factors beyond managers' control) determine organizational performance. The typical question asked is: Do top executives make a difference, and if so, how much? At one extreme, scholars such as Chandler (1977) argue that managers have a great deal of influence on their firms' destinies, while others point to the primacy of environmental factors (e.g., Hannan and Freeman, 1977). Empirical evidence suggests that both sets of factors are important, with the relative effect of managerial actions on firm performance becoming increasingly more potent the longer the time frame under investigation (e.g., Hambrick and Finkelstein, 1987; Hrebiniak and Joyce, 1985). For example, consistent with the findings of Lieberson and O'Connor (1972), Salancik and Pfeffer (1977), Weiner and Mahoney (1981), Smith, Carson, and Alexander (1984), Murray (1989) found that in the food and oil industry management contributions to short-term performance is almost nil but that a large portion of variance in long-term firm performance may be explained by managerial (internal) effects. The underlying rationale for these findings is that management contributions to short-term performance is dominated by external circumstances, while a longer time span affords more room for maneuverability and strategic responses.

A second stream of research focuses on specific ways in which firm performance responds to managerial decisions. (See Figure 6-2.) Because of the extensive and

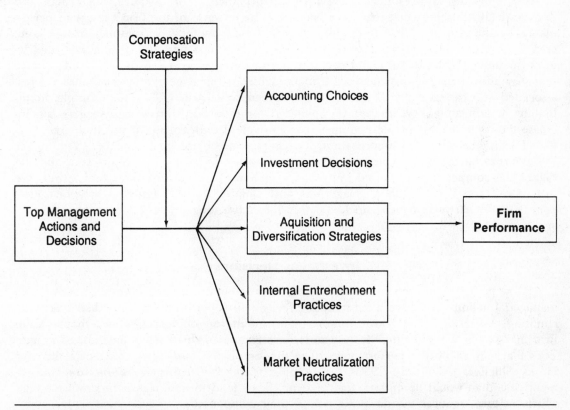

FIGURE 6-2 Impact of Top Management Decisions on Firm Performance

complex nature of this research (which spans the fields of business policy, accounting, finance, and economics), only some of the key issues addressed by this literature are highlighted.

Accounting Choices

A large group of studies is concerned with the extent to which accounting choices may exert a negative or a positive impact on firm performance and whether these choices may lead to conflict between the interests of managers and stockholders. Five major such policies have been examined. The first one is the use of FIFO (first in-first out) vs. LIFO (last in-first out) inventory cost flow choices. Research suggests that although FIFO results in higher reporting earnings (which would be manager benefitting) than LIFO, FIFO causes a lower cash flow because the firm pays higher taxes (Biddle, 1980; Dyl, 1989; Morse and Richardson, 1983). This, in turn, is associated with a correlative reduction in market value of the firm's shares (Biddle and Lindahl, 1982; Stevenson, 1984; Sunder, 1973, 1975).

The second accounting policy most likely to affect firm performance is the depreciation method chosen by management. In general, straight-line depreciation will produce higher reported income (which is management benefitting) than accelerated depreciation, even when in many cases straight-line is contrary to the firm's interests (Groff and Wright, 1989; Holthausen and Leftwich, 1983). The investment tax credit choice is a third area where accounting choices may affect firm performance. For instance, Hagerman and Zmijewski (1979) report that managers benefit at the expense of the firm's long-run performance by choosing the "flow through" method. In this method, accounting income is increased by the amount of the tax credit during the purchase period. (In contrast, the deferral method distributes tax credit over the life of the asset.) A fourth accounting choice that may affect firm performance is the method used by management to capitalize interest associated with capital expenditures. Bowen, Noreen, and Lacey (1981), for example, found that by manipulating how interest is capitalized for reporting purposes, managers can increase the present value of their compensation stream at the expense of stockholders.

Finally, the choice of amortization periods may affect firm performance. The longer the amortization period, the higher the firm's reported income in the short run, and the higher the compensation received by managers is likely to be during their tenure with the firm (Groff and Wright, 1989). Hagerman and Zmijewski (1979) found that amortization periods under 30 years benefit stockholders, while those longer than 30 years benefit managers.

Investment Decisions

How managers utilize organizational resources for future growth is another area where managerial actions may have a substantial effect on firm performance. Just like under accounting choices reviewed above, however, the self-interest of managers and those of the firm may not always coincide. Investigators have examined three major investment dimensions that may affect firm performance. The first one is the *level of risk*. Coffee (1988) and Morck, Shleifer, and Vishny (1988), for example, found that managers assume fewer investment risks than would be optimal for the firm. They tend to minimize their downside risk, which, in turn, reduces the downside risk of their compensation and possible replacement. This lowers the aggregate market value of the company. Other investigators documenting the effect of managerial risk orientation on firm performance include MacCrimmon and Wehrung (1986), March and Shapira (1987), Gupta (1987), Hill (1988), Loescher (1984), Norburn and Miller (1981), Ellsworth (1983), Dearden (1960, 1969), Hoskisson, Hitt, and Hill (1990), and Chatterjee and Lubatkin (1990).

The second investment dimension that has been extensively examined in both the practitioner and academic literature is the *time horizon* used by management. (See review by Gomez-Mejia and Welbourne, 1989.) The central concern here is that "...while the firm lives on, its managers do not. As such, they are only interested in firm performance for the time period in which they are employed, even if such time horizons lead to a present-value loss of firm value" (Walsh and Seward, 1990, p. 422).

A third area pertaining to investment decisions made by managers that affect firm performance is R&D spending. This is related to the time horizon issue because R&D spending seldom pays off in the short run and, in fact, may have a negative effect on the compensation of managers whose tenure seldom outlives the return on R&D investments. Graves (1988), Hill, Hitt, and Hoskisson (1988), and Hill and Hansen (1989) all report that quite often the level of R&D expenditures among large U. S. firms is much lower than would be desirable and has long-term effects, including "declining innovation and productivity growth and loss of international competitiveness" (Hill and Hansen, 1989, p. 56).

Acquisition and Diversification Strategies

An extensive literature has examined the relationship between a firm's acquisition and diversification strategies and performance. (See Venkatraman and Ramanujan, 1989, for a review.) There is evidence to suggest that corporate diversification through mergers and acquisitions may be vigorously pursued by a firm in order to reduce management employment risks (Ahimud and Lev, 1981) and to justify higher executive pay (Kroll, Simmons, and Wright, 1990), even at the expense of profitability. The literature also suggests that performance differences between firms may be traced to type of diversification and process of diversification, both of which are largely controlled by management (e.g., Lubatkin, 1987; Montgomery and Singh, 1984; Salter and Weinhold, 1981). A separate group of event studies report that the main beneficiary in merger or acquisition announcements are the shareholders of acquired companies with an equivocal or negative effect on the acquiring company shareholders' wealth. (See reviews by Halpern, 1983; Jarrell, Brickley, and Netter, 1988; Roll, 1987.) Likewise, empirical evidence strongly suggests that acquiring firms typically suffer profitability declines, efficiency losses, and lower long-term capital market performance (Herman and Lowenstein, 1988; Magenheim and Mueller, 1988; Ravenscraft and Scherer, 1987).

Internal Entrenchment Practices

Management may affect firm performance by blocking the fims's internal control systems that serve to provide checks and balances on managerial discretion.   (This effectively turns off the monitoring mechanisms suggested by agency theory.) This may include:

1. The use of consultants and inside board members to avoid potential disciplinary actions by camouflaging and/or legitimizing questionable managerial decisions (Fierman, 1990; Meyer and Rowan, 1977; Williams, 1985).

2. Withholding relevant information "from compensation committees when that information would attribute poor firm performance to bad management" (Coughlan and Schmidt, 1985, p. 45).
3. Controlling the board's agenda (Alderfer, 1986).
4. Embarking the firm on idiosyncratic strategies molded to the manager's unique skills, background, and personal interests (Shleifer and Vishny, 1988).
5. Failing to step down in the face of continued poor firm performance that calls for the recruitment of new managers "who are neither associated with the past nor committed to inappropriate strategies and policies" (Salancik and Pfeffer, 1980, p. 654).

Market Neutralization Practices

Managers of firms with substandard performance may attempt to prevent the market from exercising its disciplining role. (This removes another important constraint on managers as suggested by agency theory.) Two mechanisms that may be used by executives to neutralize the market include *greenmail payments* and *poison pills*. The first refers to the purchase of large blocks of stock from potential acquirers as a defensive measure without shareholder approval. Dann and DeAngelo (1988) and Bradley and Wakeman (1983) present some evidence to suggest that greenmail antitakeover strategies produce negative abnormal stock returns for firms using it. Poison pills allow shareholders of the target firm to acquire additional shares or to sell stock to the bidding company at prices that are arbitrarily set. Malatesta and Walking (1988) and Ryngaert (1988) argue that management of the takeover target firm is the main beneficiary of poison pills, while its shareholders suffer reductions in their wealth.

In summary, a broad spectrum of research indicates that firm performance is highly responsive to managerial behaviors and decisions. Furthermore, there are many situations where the policy choices confronting managers are such that what is better for a firm's shareholders and what may further management's interests are at odds with each other. The challenge from a compensation perspective is to develop pay strategies for top executives that evoke the types of behaviors and induce the kinds of decisions that are most conducive to improved firm performance.

The reader should not be lead to believe, however, that compensation strategies designed to align the interests of executives with those of shareholders can produce miraculous results. Even under the best incentive programs, a large portion of firm performance variance is likely to reflect myriads of unsystematic factors with which management may have little to do. Such factors include: plain luck (formation of the Arab oil cartel in the 1970s producing "windfall" profits in U. S. oil firms or the AIDS epidemic in the 1990s fueling stock prices and profits of condom manufacturers), regulatory changes (as in the case of the airline industry), sudden changes in technology (introduction of the ultrasound machine in the early 1970s replacing electro-diagnostic imaging devices almost overnight), prolonged market upturns (as most of the 1980s) or market downturns (as most of the 1970s), government subsidies to foreign competitors, shifts in interest rates, etc. Tosi and Gomez-Mejia (1992) estimate that approximately 18 percent of the total variance in firm performance may be accounted for by managerial decisions in response to the incentive structure, which means that more than five times as much variance can be attributed to other unsystematic factors.

Our attention is now turned to the empirical research on the determinants of executive pay. Chapter 7 examines specific compensation strategy choices for top executives and how these may affect firm performance.

EMPIRICAL RESEARCH ON EXECUTIVE PAY: SOME WARNINGS

Executive pay has been thoroughly researched using empirical methods. In the refereed academic journals alone, Gomez-Mejia and Welbourne (1989) counted over 250 such papers dating back to the 1920s (e.g., Taussig and Barker, 1925). This issue has been studied by scholars from such diverse fields as sociology (e.g., Allen, 1981), economics (e.g., Abowd, 1990; Gibbons and Murphy, 1990; Jensen, 1989; Jensen and Murphy, 1990a,b; Murphy, 1985), accounting (e.g., Antle and Smith, 1986; Benston, 1985; Gaver, Gaver, and Battistel, 1990; Grasso, 1992; Johnson, Magee, Nagarajan, and Newman, 1985; Noreen and Wolfson, 1981), finance (e.g., Brickley and Dark, 1987; Warner, Watts, and Wruck 1988; Watts and Zimmerman, 1986; Weisbach, 1988), management (e.g., Gomez-Mejia, Tosi, and Hinkin, 1987; Hill and Phan, 1991; Kerr and Bettis, 1987; Lambert, Larcker, and Weigelt, 1991; Norburn, 1989; Tosi and Gomez-Mejia, 1989; Zajac, 1990), and industrial relations (e.g., Deckop, 1988; Ehrenberg and Bognanno, 1990; Leonard, 1990).

Despite this incredible amount of work, results are generally disappointing and mixed. Authors often reach diametrically opposite conclusions when testing the same hypothesis and even when using the identical set of data. For example, one group of investigators have found no relationship between executive compensation and firm performance (e.g., Kerr and Bettis, 1987; Redling, 1981), while others claim the exact opposite (e.g., Masson, 1971; Murphy, 1985). These extremes are exemplified by comments such as "there is no rational basis for the compensation paid to top management" (Kerr and Bettis, 1987, p. 667) vis-a-vis "top executives are worth every nickel they get" (Murphy, 1986a, p. 125). Several reasons may account for these divergent findings. These are discussed in some detail below because the reader should be aware of these problems in order to interpret properly published results to be reviewed later.

Reliance on Archival Data and False Sense of Objectivity

With very few exceptions (e.g., Zajac, 1990), investigators tend to rely on archival data available in *Compustat, Disclosure,* and other similar sources to study executive compensation. It is very tempting for academics to rely exclusively on this data because of its easy accessibility and low cost (As everyone knows, gathering your own data may require years of hard work and substantial resources.) Besides, scholarly journals have an insatiable appetite for this type of research. Given the publishing pressures in many universities, many academics consider this data too good of a deal to pass up. Unfortunately, executive pay is a very treacherous research area. Pitfalls abound, most of which are generally ignored or treated very lightly (particularly in the field of management where the level of sophistication in financial accounting is low).

One problem with the use of these databases is that researchers are constrained by the information included in them, and tenuous assumptions are frequently made. A second, almost fatal problem, is that it is not always clear how comparable the reported data may be across firms and over time. Despite an objective facade and a common metrics (dollars), there is enough ambiguity in the way some of this data are reported that one may well be comparing apples and oranges when using archival information on CEOs. In fact, it is doubtful that much of this data meet some of the most rudimentary quality requirements from a measurement perspective in terms of validity and reliability. (See Schmitt and Klimoski, 1991.)

Interestingly enough, most investigators don't realize (or don't address the issue) that firms use widely different formulas when reporting executive compensation—and firm performance for that matter. To understand the meaning of a given pay figure, one would need to know the formulas used by the company. But finding this out is a tough task because Security and Exchange Commission rules do not demand that the actual formulas be divulged and "most companies don't give enough specifics to make the calculation. Only a few companies give enough details to do that" (Berton, 1990, p. 1226). In a study commissioned by *Fortune* magazine, Crystal (1988, p. 68) found that executive compensation data coming from proxy statements "are often models of miscommunication." More recently, Fierman (1990, p. 66) noted that "most proxies don't give a clear picture of exactly what the CEO stands to gain or what goals he must meet to earn his bonus. Corporate lawyers have turned proxy obfuscation into an art, keeping shareholders and the competition in the dark." Thus, while hundreds of studies have correlated executive pay with just about every variable in sight (e.g., profitability, firm size, industry type, age of executive, executive tenure, etc.), a robust interpretation of the findings may be quite elusive.

Different Methodologies

Authors use widely diverse sampling strategies, time periods, and statistical methods. For example, the number of firms included in the sample range from 2,200 (Jensen and Murphy, 1990a) to 50 (Lewellen, 1971), and time periods range from 30 years (Antle and Smith, 1986) to one year (Crystal, 1988). Likewise, archival data has been subject to an endless array of statistical manipulation, including weighted regression techniques (Lewellen and Huntsman, 1970), pooled cross-section time series (Murphy, 1986a), nonparametric tests (Antle and Smith, 1986), residual analysis (Ciscel and Carroll, 1981), and logistic regression (Beatty and Zajac, 1990). Given this diversity of approaches and attributed in part to the nature of the methodology, inconsistent results are found.

Dynamic Effects

It is difficult to capture the dynamic and lag effects of variables affecting executive compensation. An executive pay package in a given year or a given period may reflect not just what happened in the most recent past, but also the assessment of this individual's performance throughout his/her entire career with the company. Typically, executive compensation studies limit their time frame to no more than five years. This presents a problem, according to Lambert (1983, p. 443) because an "agent's compensation in one period depends on his performance in that period and his performance in previous periods. Principal uses an agent's performance over the entire history of his employment to diversify away some of the uncertainty surrounding the agent's action." In particular, gains on stock options can be very distorting when examining year-to-year changes in executive pay. For example, if a CEO decides to cash out his/her option one year, he/she is unlikely to have done so in several years before or to do so again within the near future. The complexity introduced by long-term income programs in executive compensation research is discussed next.

Complexity of Equity-Based Pay

Executives may receive up to one half of their income from long-term pay items such as deferred bonuses, stockholdings, stock options, dividend units, phantom shares, pension benefits, etc.—although this still remains shrouded in mystery (Gomez-Mejia and Welbourne, 1989). While these items may represent an integral part of the total executive compensation package, calculating their actual value, with no generally accepted formula for doing so, can be a nightmare. Different estimation procedures can yield widely different results. For example, Lewellen and Huntsman (1970) found that bonus and salary are highly correlated with long-term income. Antle and Smith (1986), on the other hand, found them to be totally independent. Masson (1971) argued that equity-based pay is the most important component of the executive pay package, while Kerr and Bettis (1987) and Jensen and Murphy (1990a) argued that it is almost insignificant.

The central problem is that, unlike salary and cash compensation, long-term gains do not constitute realized pay at a given point in time but a promissory note contingent on future events. Estimating the "present value" of such long-term income programs requires that numerous assumptions be made concerning interest rates, opportunity costs of holding stock options, future market value of stockholdings, etc. While complex mathematical formulas have been devised (e.g., Black and Scholes, 1973; Antle and Smith, 1985), they all include several parameters that must be crudely estimated, bringing their validity into question.

According to Kerr and Bettis (1987, p. 649):

> ... The resulting estimated value of an option changes every day, often by a substantial amount, depending on the price of the stock. Options amplify changes in stock's prices. The dominant question in determining the value becomes the selection of the day on which the option is to be valued. Stock options are an important component of executive compensation that should be studied. However, there appears to be no theoretically and empirically appropriate method for evaluating them.

Likewise, Finkelstein and Hambrick (1988, p. 544) argue that "there are so many forms of financial compensation, and they are so complex, that calculation of a CEO's financial income is often intractable or misleading." Crystal (1988) comments that it is rare to find an executive who understands the value of his/her long-term income. To circumvent these methodological problems, most researchers shy away from including long-term income in their measures and limit their compensation figures to cash components. To make matters worse, as seen in Chapter 7, the calculation of cash bonus payments is also quite tricky because of limited information provided. The obvious drawback with avoiding the issue altogether is: By not examining the total compensation package the findings may be either spurious or insensitive to what is really going on.

Operationalization of Firm Performance

The measurement of the performance variable, which is a crucial factor in most executive compensation studies, is in itself highly controversial. Authors have operationalized firm performance in terms of stock market returns (Kerr and Bettis, 1987; Gibbons and Murphy, 1990), accounting profits (Deckop, 1988; Leonard, 1990), or a combination of the two (Gomez-Mejia, Tosi, and Hinkin, 1987; Tosi and Gomez-Mejia, 1992). When researchers cannot agree on what performance is, then the results are often inconclusive or conflicting. As discussed later in this chapter, this also presents an interesting dilemma to practitioners who are trying to design executive compensation programs that align the interest of stockholders and managers. A brief look at the performance measures follows.

Perhaps the oldest and most widely used indicator of firm performance is profitability. However, this measure has been severely criticized because it may not reflect a firm's true underlying value or performance. It is argued that executives can manipulate these numbers to make themselves look good (Dyl, 1989; Groff and Wright, 1989; Hunt, 1986). Depreciation policies, accelerated versus straight-line; inventory procedures, FIFO versus LIFO; use of short-term, noncapitalized leases to obtain productive equipment; and window-dressing techniques such as holding borrowed money as cash until the end of the year, are all perfectly legal "tricks" that may be used to improve the bottom line. For instance, following the large increases in oil prices in late 1990 as a result of Iraq's invasion of Kuwait, oil industry executives found ways to hold down reported profits by channeling the increased revenues into various "hidden" budget accounts. For example, money was held in reserve for future environmental expenses, R&D investments, maintenance programs, etc. (Hayes, 1990). This practice, conforming with accounting standards, was used to reduce potential public and congressional outcry in response to a rapid price hike in oil-related products such as gasoline and heating oil.

As an alternative to profitability measures, other researchers have advanced the notion that stockholder's welfare—measured in the form of increases in stock price or dividends paid—should dictate executive's pay (Coughlan and Schmidt, 1985; Murphy, 1985; Rappaport, 1978). But these measures are not immune to criticism. Paying out cash dividends will raise a stock's price. But raising cash dividends decreases funds available for reinvestment and R&D. This lowers expected growth rate and depresses the price of a stock in the long run—with the effects perhaps occurring at a time when another executive will bear the brunt of the problem (Brigham, 1985). Stock prices are also very sensitive to external events that may have little to do with how efficiently a firm is being run and that are totally beyond management's control. The use of "abnormal return" methodology, which attempts to disentangle general market trends from firm-specific effects on a company's stock price, can often "result in false inferences about the presence of abnormal performance" (Brown and Warner, 1980, p. 205). In order to identify "abnormal" price performance, the researcher must first evaluate what is "normal" or expected, given the usual influences on security prices. Doing this evaluation requires a number of important assumptions and arbitrary judgments regarding definition of relevant market, parameter estimations, and distribution properties of excess returns. (See Brown and Warner, 1985; McNichols and Manegold, 1983.)

Ultimately, one must deal with the philosophical question as to whether outcome measures of firm performance, which are the only ones available in archival databases, are the most appropriate indicators to examine. It may be that, in fact, most boards make complex judgments about the performance of both the CEO and the firm that are, of necessity, highly subjective.   (See Puffer and Weintrop, 1991.)   Furthermore, too much reliance on objective indicators of firm performance for compensation purposes encourages executives to maximize the value of those coefficients that are part of the evaluation formula.   Maximizing these coefficients is often at the expense of other, less quantifiable elements (e.g., innovation) that are crucial to the firm's interests in the long run.

Estimating Performance of an Incumbent's Best Replacement

It is extremely difficult, if not downright impossible, for researchers to estimate the various performance outcomes under alternative stewardships.   If a replacement would not perform better than the incumbent, the latter's high pay may be justified—perhaps even as compensation for the high career risk of working for a company that is performing poorly.   For example, IBM's Board of Directors provided the company's CEO, John F. Akers, with a huge raise in 1989, one of the worst years in that firm's history.   The raise was given in recognition for his perceived excellent work and the belief that another CEO was unlikely to produce better results (*Boulder Daily Camera*, March, 1989).

Collinearity among the Variables

Finally, as noted earlier, one of the most difficult methodological problems when trying to isolate the unique impact of a variable on executive pay is the fact that most relevant factors are highly correlated.   For example, firm size, profits, number of levels in the organization, age and experience level of executives, and even distribution of ownership covary together.   So, in many instances, the use of significance tests for individual variables prove to be unreliable because of the proverbial "what came first: chicken or the egg" question.   To eliminate multicollinearity, some transformation of the data is necessary.   Unfortunately, "such transformed variables often bear only the faintest relationship to the hypothesis being tested" (Ciscel and Carroll, 1980, p. 615).   As a result, making causal inferences about the effect of a particular variable on executive pay vis-a-vis some other variables can be tenuous, and often the conclusions reached simply reflect the ideological persuasion of the writer.

Inferential Leaps

As noted earlier, with only a handful of exceptions (e.g., Tosi and Gomez-Mejia, 1989, 1992; Zajac, 1990), authors use archival data on executive pay to generate proxies for behavioral phenomena that are far removed from the underlying constructs purportedly being measured.   Therefore, one is forced to make large "leaps of faith" to draw inferences from the obtained results.   For instance, the efficacy of monitoring and incentive alignment mechanisms are frequently tested by correlating executive pay and firm performance.   A positive correlation is interpreted as evidence that the executive compensation contract has aligned managerial and owner interests and that this alignment has caused managers to maximize profitability.   (See, Raviv, 1985.   See also various papers appearing in a special issue of the *Journal of Accounting and Economics*, Vol. 7, 1985.)   On the other hand, lack of a relationship is generally interpreted to mean that "results are inconsistent with the implications of formal agency models of optimal contracting" (Jensen and Murphy, 1990, p. 226).   Quite often, degree of monitoring exercised by the board is inferred from equity concentration of a firm, which is treated as a dichotomous variable. Firms can be assigned to an "owner-controlled" class when there is the presence of a single equity holder with 5 percent or more of the outstanding stock and to a "management-controlled" class when there is not.

Because of all the tenuous inferences involved, Tosi and Gomez-Mejia (1989, p. 185) have gone as far as to suggest a moratorium on this type of archival based research:

> Despite the enormous amount of effort and expenditures in 'mining' these public data-bases, results are disappointing and often conflicting . . . All things considered, overreliance on archival data that treats the executive compensation process as a black box has led us into a blind alley. While easy to use, it is doubtful that continued "number crunching" of these databases will provide much additional insight on the determinants of executive pay . . . a more fruitful avenue to pursue in understanding executive pay issues is to focus more on the process and less on the observed "objective" measures.

In summary, empirical research on executive compensation is far from an exact science, and there is much room for personal interpretation, according to the researcher's biases. Therefore, readers should approach this literature with a healthy amount of skepticism. When all conceivable predictors are used in the equations, the total amount of explained variance (R^2) in executive pay seldom exceeds 35 percent, and most often the R^2 hovers in the 20-30 percent range. Even if one focuses attention on the components that reach statistical significance, the presumed causal factors often flip-flop from study to study. The way findings are posited and interpreted generally come as no surprise, depending on the writer's background and known prejudices.

DETERMINANTS OF EXECUTIVE PAY: REVIEW OF EMPIRICAL EVIDENCE

This section critically examines the voluminous literature on the determinants of executive pay, focusing on statistical findings.

Role of Company Size and Performance

As discussed in the theory section, traditional economic theory assumes that managers will operate a firm in the most efficient manner to maximize profits. Neoclassical economists conclude, based on deductive reasoning, that executive pay should reward for performance that maximizes profit, although firm size may play a role when there are market imperfections. Nonorthodox economists taking a managerialist perspective argue that executive pay is primarily a function of firm size, with company performance relegated to a "satisficing" role. This controversy between "profit maximizers" and "sales maximizers" has been going on for over half a century. This debate has sparked hundreds of empirical studies dealing with the seemingly simple question: Does executive pay reward top management's ability to expand corporate size or to increase profitability? The findings appear to support both sides of the issue.

The first researchers to test the *sales maximization hypothesis* were Roberts (1959) and McGuire, Chiu, and Elbing (1962). Both found that, after controlling for sales level, firm profits had little to do with executive compensation. Their findings supported Baumol's

(1959) contention that executives pursued what they deemed to be a prestigious (and more financially rewarding) goal of increasing the size of the firm they manage. These findings were rebutted in several studies initiated by Lewellen (1968, 1969), Lewellen and Huntsman (1970), and Masson (1971), who criticized previous researchers for not including measures of long-term income in the form of stock options and other stock-related pay arrangements. By developing their own estimates of "total compensation," they reached diametrically opposite conclusions as exemplified in the following statement by Lewellen and Huntsman (1970, p. 718):

> The evidence provides strong support for the hypothesis that top management's remuneration is heavily dependent upon the generation of profit . . . indeed, sales seem to be quite irrelevant. The clear inference is that there is a greater incentive for management to shape its decision rules in a manner consonant with shareholder interests than to seek the alternative goal of revenue maximization.

Since the early 1970s, researchers have refined their multivariate methods, changed the operationalization of key variables, and used larger and more diverse samples but have failed to provide conclusive evidence on either side of the debate. Larner (1970) and Hirschey and Pappas (1981) found that executive pay is most directly linked to profit. Ciscel (1974) found that size, rather than profit, was the main predictor of executive compensation, particularly when the earnings of the entire executive group were considered. Smyth, Boyes, and Peseau (1975) reanalyzed Lewellen and Huntsman's model and made corrections for multicollinearity and heteroscedasticity. Unlike Lewellen and Huntsman, they concluded that executive pay "depends on a utility function of both sales and profits" (1975, p. 79).

Using sophisticated "residual analysis" to attenuate the collinearity problem between firm size and profits, Ciscel and Carroll (1981) reached the same conclusions as Smyth et al. (1975). Across the Atlantic, Cash (1975) and Meeks and Whittington (1975) found that profit had no relationship to executive pay; instead, size was the main predictor. Even the most recent research conducted in the late 1980s and early 1990s has proven inconclusive. Posner (1987) and Kostiuk (1990) found support for the position that executive compensation can best be predicted by firm size, while Deckop (1988) found evidence that executive compensation was related (but very weakly) to profits measured as percentage of sales. Dyl (1988) reported that both firm size and performance are significant determinants of executive pay. In a related vein of research, Schmidt and Fowler (1990) report that top executives who engaged in major tender offer or acquisition activity received a significant increase in their compensation that "appears to be driven more by organization size than by performance" (p. 569).

The debate has been fueled by those who view reported profit as a contaminated criterion of performance and who have developed sophisticated alternative measures based on the firm's stock value. Masson (1971) and Murphy (1985) found that executive compensation was more strongly related to stock performance than to accounting measures; Coughlan and Schmidt (1985) concluded that, although statistically significant, they only explained 5.4 percent of the variance in executive compensation based on stock market data alone. To make matters more confusing, Kerr and Bettis (1987) conclude from the results of their study that "in general, board of directors do not consider performance of a firm's stock when changing CEO's salaries and bonuses. Neither overall market movements nor abnormal [stock] returns were associated with adjustments in compensation." Loomis (1982) and

Crystal (1990) share the same pessimistic feelings about the low explanatory value of stock market data expressed by Kerr and Bettis.

In what is perhaps the most ambitious attempt to ascertain the pay-performance relation (including pay, stock options, stockholdings, and dismissal) for CEOs, Jensen and Murphy (1990a) studied 2,213 chief executive officers serving 1,295 corporations during 1974-1986, for a total of 10,400 CEO years of data. Despite their earlier findings that reported a strong relationship (e.g., see Jensen and Meckling, 1976; Murphy, 1986a,b), and when faced with the evidence at hand, these authors drew a bleak picture of the CEO pay-performance linkage:

> The empirical relation between the pay of top-level executives and firm performance, while positive and statistically significant, is small for an occupation in which incentive pay is expected to play an important role ... our all-inclusive estimate of the pay-performance sensitivity—including compensation, dismissal, and stockholdings—is about $3.25 per $1,000 change in shareholder wealth ... In addition, our estimates suggest that dismissals are not an important source of managerial incentives since the increases in dismissal probability due to poor performance and the penalties associated with dismissal are both small. Executive inside stock ownership can provide incentives, but these holdings are not generally controlled by the corporate board and the majority of top executives have small personal stockholdings (Jensen and Murphy, 1990a, p. 227).

In summary, the empirical evidence to date regarding the sales vs. profit maximization hypothesis as a determinant of executive pay level is mixed at best. However, the weight of the evidence points towards a small, almost inconsequential, relationship between firm performance and CEO pay and a large correlation between company size and CEO pay.

It's reasonable to expect that executives should be paid for both firm size, which reflects the complexity of the job, as well as performance, which is an outcome measure. The problem remains, however, that relatively little variance in CEO pay is being explained and that performance typically lags behind size as a predictor of CEO compensation. While the observed level of statistical significance for the performance factor varies across studies and is interpreted according to the authors' preferences, most studies share something in common: The total amount of explained variance in executive pay attributed to firm performance is minimal, seldom exceeding 15 percent and often well under 10 percent. A study commissioned by *Fortune* magazine (Crystal, 1988, p. 69), cynically titled "The Wacky, Wacky World of CEO Pay," laments that "just about all the rational factors you can think of, taken together, don't play a big role in determining CEO pay ... top-level compensation doesn't make much sense."

Managerial Decisions, Financial Incentives, and Risk Sharing

While the linkage between executive pay level and firm performance is weak, there is strong evidence to suggest that executives do respond to what they perceive will lead to a financial reward (Zajac, 1990). The data suggest that the way the CEO compensation package is structured affects such key decisions as capital investments (Larcker, 1983), R&D investments (Hoskisson, Hitt, and Hill, 1990), mergers and acquisitions (Kroll, Simmons, and Wright, 1990), and accounting choices (Dyl, 1989; Groff and Wright, 1989; Merchant, 1981, 1985). Unfortunately, few firms make CEO compensation contingent on strategic decisions that eventually impact performance. Pay contingencies involve risk sharing between the firm and the CEO. However, there is very little evidence that much risk sharing actually occurs.

As reported by the American Management Association (see *CompFlash*, 1990), the size of the median bonus award for the CEO, as a percentage of salary, ranged from a low of 36 percent in utilities to a high of 69 percent in manufacturing, with an average of 50 percent. Presumably, these bonus payments, which are not part of base salary, should be riskier for executives so that they would incur the benefits or penalties of business decisions. But "compensation for CEOs is no more variable than compensation for hourly and salaried employees... bonuses don't generate big fluctuations in CEO compensation. A comparison of annual inflation-adjusted pay changes for CEOs from 1975 through 1988 and pay changes for 20,000 randomly selected hourly and salaried workers—shows remarkably similar distributions. Moreover, a much lower percentage of CEOs took real pay cuts over this period than did production workers" (Jensen and Murphy, 1990b, p. 139). Similarly, CEO stock ownership for larger public companies, which puts the CEO at risk is minimal (Kerr and Bettis, 1987), almost ten times lower than it was in the 1930s (Jensen and Murphy, 1990b).

Firm Diversification, Control Type, and Executive Pay

Larger firms are more diversified than smaller ones (Rumelt, 1974). Another stream of research, some of which was discussed in earlier chapters, argues that it is not firm size per se that determines executive pay but the extent of diversification. However, these two variables are highly correlated.

Murthy and Salter (1975) examined the relationship between executive pay level and firm performance for companies whose sales come from a single business (dominant-product firms), firms that have expanded through the acquisition of businesses related to their original products (related-product firms), and large conglomerates that have grown by acquiring diverse businesses whose products are not related to each other (unrelated-product firms). They found that the relationship between executive pay level and performance is quite low for dominant-product firms, moderate for related-product firms, and high for unrelated-product firms. Expanding on this theme, Rajagopalan and Prescott (1990) report that extent of diversification is positively associated with executive pay in various industry groups. They interpret this to mean that "... at the topmost managerial levels, managers are rewarded for possessing diverse managerial skills that are useful in a variety of industry settings. Managers who possess transferrable skills enjoy high mobility and are probably rewarded for their diverse business experiences and adaptability" (p. 537).

Murthy and Salter (1975) argue that as a firm grows by acquiring businesses that are unrelated to the original product, the executive's role begins to change from an operational "hands-on" management approach, emphasizing close supervision and centralized control, to a step-back mode, where the executive's primary role is to allocate resources to diverse business units and divisions. Board of directors have a difficult time evaluating the performance of unrelated business units on a subjective, qualitative basis because they don't understand the production process and market of diverse commodities. Likewise, it is harder for them to pass judgment on how well the executive's activities in unrelated-product firms contribute to organization performance. In this situation, the board relies on traditional financial measures such as ROE or EPS to evaluate the overall performance of the firm and the executive in charge. Thus, according to Murthy and Salter, this accounts for the observed stronger linkage between performance indicators and executive pay in unrelated-product firms, which also happen to be larger.

A similar stream of research has examined how autonomy level affects reward systems. Pitts (1974) found that external acquisitions and divisions whose products are unrelated to the major business have more autonomy than those divisions developing products linked to headquarters. Top executives in more autonomous business units are rewarded based on quantitative, formula-based criteria for the division. Those in less autonomous business units are evaluated based on both division and corporate performance, which makes objective division performance measures less crucial for pay decisions.

While not addressing incentive mechanisms directly, Ouchi's work more than a decade ago (Ouchi, 1977, 1978, 1979, 1980; Ouchi and Maguire, 1975) focused on the related issue of when "behavioral" or "output" controls are appropriate for divisional managers. Use of output controls consists of gathering information about outcomes or consequences of managerial actions or decisions and would be most appropriate when knowledge of the transformation process is low. Behavioral controls, analogous to the "monitoring" mechanisms in agency theory, would be most appropriate when knowledge of the transformation process is high. These predictions are consistent with the transaction cost model discussed in Chapter 5. (See Williamson, 1975; 1986a, b.) That is, efficiency is achieved by reducing the transaction costs of negotiating, monitoring, and enforcing the agreement between the contracting parties (i.e., between top executives in corporate headquarters and division managers). In a recent empirical study on CEO compensation, Kerr and Kren (1992) found some support for the notion that "to the extent behaviorial [vs. objective or outcome] information is considered in the evaluation process, performance should have a stronger influence on pay where CEO decisions differ from typical industry decisions."

When neither behavioral controls nor output controls are feasible (because knowledge of the transformation process is weak and ability to measure outputs is low), Ouchi suggests that a "clan control" is a better alternative. By exercising this control, the organization can engender or instill a shared value system through socialization processes, selection procedures, and reliance on rituals and ceremony to create myths and a climate of cooperation. Such forms of controls have long been used by religious orders throughout the centuries. Ouchi (1979, p. 845) goes on to suggest that "organizations in the public sector, in service industries, and in fast growing technologies perhaps should have cultural or clan forms of control."

Market Factors

Surprisingly, very limited empirical research has been conducted on the relationship between demand/supply forces in the managerial labor market and executive pay, or how the going rate in the labor market affects decisions regarding executive compensation. Part of the reason may be that executive pay packages are highly individualized, similar to what you would find when a movie studio is trying to hire a star or when a baseball team attempts to pirate a pitcher from a competing team. The resulting pay package will depend on the idiosyncrasies of the situation and the negotiation skills of both parties. This means, subjective judgments play a major role when making competitive offers to executives. Even if one takes into account such factors as industry, company size, geographic area, and qualifications of executive, the standard deviation of actual pay levels when using survey data may be huge (Gomez-Mejia and Welbourne, 1989).

Ciscel and Carroll (1980) found that the constant term in their regression equations, which included firm size and performance as independent variables and executive pay as dependent variable, showed a high explanatory power.   They claim that the constant term reflects the minimum value of the dependent variable before the effects of the independent or explanatory variables are considered.   Ciscel and Carroll (1980, pp. 10-11) speculate that the constant term reflects the "... equilibrium price of a Chief Executive Officer's time determined by the interaction of supply and demands for management skills ... this [interpretation] indicates that attributing the value of the constant term to a market for managerial talent is not unreasonable."   This interpretation, however, is questionable and requires a gigantic leap of faith.   The constant term may reflect myriad factors (e.g., random events, decisions of compensation committees, distribution of ownership) other than the "true" market value of an executive.

There seems to be general agreement that industry is an important determinant of executive compensation practices.   McCann, Hinkin, and Gomez-Mejia (1992) analyzed 812 executive transitions during the 1980s.   They found that most executive replacements came from similar firms within the same industries as the hiring firms.   This suggests that the executive labor market is rather segmented and that market rates for executives may be independently set within each segment.   Peck (1987) found that total variance in executive compensation attributed to firm size varies from a low of 32 percent in the construction industry to a high of 66 percent in commercial banking.   Ungson and Steers (1984) concluded that industry variables, represented by the intercept terms in the regression equations, were better predictors of CEO pay than either firm size or profits.   Generally, the more competitive the industry, the more likely executive pay is linked to performance, although these relationships are rather weak.

Distribution of Ownership

As discussed earlier, the separation of ownership and control in the modern corporation is a central concern of managerialism and agency theory.   The reader is reminded that both of these perspectives hold that owners of the firm (principals) hire managers (agents) to run the enterprise.   Because it is difficult for atomistic stockholders to supervise the activities of top management, the latter may be tempted to engage in self-serving behaviors, perhaps at the expense of firm owners. Jensen and Meckling (1976), Fama (1980), Fama and Jensen (1983a, 1983b), Demsetz (1983), and others argue that shareholders do, in fact, accomplish this rather efficiently, even in firms whose ownership is widely dispersed.   However, most of the empirical evidence suggests that agency arrangements do not work as well as Fama and colleagues would lead us to believe.   (Note: Even Jensen, one of Fama's closest collaborators and author of several classical agency papers, has publicly retreated from his earlier position.   [See Jensen and Murphy, 1990b].)   This literature is reviewed below.

While the precise functional relationship between the concentration of equity holdings and control of the firm is not known, research suggests that for very large firms, the percentage of stock required to exercise significant control may be quite small (McEachern, 1975; Salamon and Smith, 1979).   As early as 1937, the Securities and Exchange Commission proposed that 10 percent stock ownership was a sufficient amount to control a firm. More recent research suggests that when a single equity holder controls as little as 5 percent of the voting stock, the equity holders can have a significant influence on the behavior of managers of a firm (Boudreaux, 1973; O'Reilly, Main, and Crystal, 1988; Palmer, 1973;

Salancik and Pfeffer, 1980). Typically, although by no means universally accepted, researchers designate as *owner-controlled* those firms that have a single equity owner who controls as little as 5 percent of the voting stock. When there is no equity holder with at least 5 percent of the stock, the firm is called *management-controlled.*

With few exceptions (e.g., Finkelstein and Hambrick, 1989), studies have found evidence that when there is less stockholder (owner) control, the executive's personal income increases with very little relation to the performance of the firm. If a major stockholder exerts control over the executives, their pay is found to be more highly correlated with the performance variables. These findings have been consistently replicated using either a dichotomous indicator of ownership (most often the 5 percent convention discussed above) (e.g., Allen, 1981; Arnould, 1985; Gomez-Mejia et al., 1987; McEachern, 1975; Wallace, 1973) or a continuous measure (Dyl, 1988; 1989). Gomez-Mejia et al. (1987, p. 67) argued that:

> An important portion of the compensation of managers in management-controlled firms may be decoupled from performance and, by inference, less in alignment with the owners' interests. These CEOs bear less compensation related uncertainty and risk than those in owner-controlled firms. Executives in management-controlled firms can reduce their risk and force the owners to bear more because they have greater control over organizational decision processes.

A growing amount of evidence in the area of mergers and acquisitions suggests that agency problems are common in corporations with widely dispersed ownership. Management-controlled firms are more likely to engage in mergers and acquisitions to justify higher executive pay, even if these activities result in lower overall corporate performance (Kroll, Simmons, and Wright, 1990). Management-controlled firms engage in more conglomerate acquisition activities, often to the detriment of investors, than owner-controlled firms to diversify the employment risk of executives (e.g., risk of losing job, professional reputation) (Ahimud and Lev, 1981). Ahimud and Lev (1981, p. 606) conclude: "The consequences of such mergers may be regarded as an agency cost." This conclusion is consistent with the earlier work of Palmer (1973) and the findings of Blair and Kaserman (1983) and Chevalier (1969) that management-controlled firms are involved in a greater number of antitrust activities.

Additional evidence provided by an assorted number of studies suggests that agency problems defy easy solutions. Grossman and Hart (1983) argue that information asymmetries in management-controlled firms are used to the advantage of top executives at the expense of owners. Bhagat (1983, p. 310) found that executives in management-controlled firms may be successful in "passing amendments to corporate charters to maximize their own welfare, sometimes to the detriment of stockholders." Salancik and Pfeffer (1980) report that the probability of an executive being fired for poor performance is much greater in owner-controlled than management-controlled firms. Hunt (1986) argues that the choice of accounting and inventory methods in management-controlled firms is such that they artificially portray a more favorable image of the firm's financial picture. Finally, based on reports of 175 chief compensation officers in manufacturing, Tosi and Gomez-Mejia (1989) found that the actual level of monitoring and incentive alignment, the proportion of executive pay at risk, and long-term compensation were much greater in owner-controlled firms.

In short, it is difficult to ignore the large volume of research and circumstantial evidence suggesting that the distribution of ownership across firms is an important determinant of executive pay. The savings and loan crisis of the 1990s offers an extreme example of what may happen when managerial authority goes unchecked. The General Accounting Office, which has been studying the reasons behind the insolvency of many of these financial concerns, concluded that the managers of bankrupt savings and loans "paid themselves like kings and treated themselves to extravagant expenditures" (reported in *Boulder Daily Camera*, January 29, 1989, p. 78).

The evidence is not conclusive that owner-controlled firms perform more profitably than management-controlled firms, however. In an extensive review of the literature, Hunt (1986) cites several studies that show owner-controlled firms are more profitable, several that show that management-controlled firms are more profitable, and others that show no performance differences. But, he suggests, methodological issues could account for the inconsistency in the results of these studies, particularly with respect to the dependent variable, *performance*. These studies, with few exceptions, use accounting based performance measures, and there is, for management-controlled firms, a "tendency for managers to report financial data in the best possible light" (Hunt, 1986, p. 114). If this is so, then real differences between the two types should be larger than reported. Thus, the magnitude of the differences in reported performance measures between management-controlled and owner-controlled firms would be masked by the reporting procedures.

There is other support for this interpretation. For example, Hunt (1986) discusses how the choice of accounting methods may improve the appearance of results. Other studies show that management-controlled firms are more likely to use inventory methods (Niehaus, 1985) and other accounting practices that will overstate earnings (Salamon and Smith, 1979). In addition, management-controlled firms will smooth income over several reporting periods. The "evidence with respect to ownership structure and income smoothing is a rather serious indictment of the performance studies which rely on unadjusted accounting methods of performance" (Hunt, 1986, p. 116).

Other agency costs are born by equity holders of management-controlled firms. The study by Salancik and Pfeffer (1980) cited earlier, showed that there is longer executive tenure in management-controlled firms. Such a finding would make sense only if the performance of these firms were superior to that of owner-controlled firms. Yet, their evidence does not support such an interpretation. A more logical position is that the managers, without pressures from the owners, are reluctant to replace themselves for poor performance. Further, Hayes and Abernathy (1980) argue that there is a greater propensity of manager-controlled firms to engage in activities to increase size, often through mergers and acquisitions which may not be economically efficient to the owners but very beneficial for the managers (Hayes and Abernathy, 1980). The propensity to engage in growth oriented strategies for management-controlled firms is consistent with the results of a study by Gomez-Mejia, Tosi, and Hinkin (1987) that reported the basic salary of CEO's of management-controlled firms is correlated with firm scale (a size measure), while the strongest predictor of CEO pay in owner-controlled firms is performance.

More recently, Tosi and Gomez-Mejia (1992) developed a behavioral measure of monitoring and incentive alignment of top executives and correlated this measure with both subjective and archival measures of firm performance in two separate samples. Following the basic tenets of agency theory, these authors predicted that activities to increase the level of monitoring of CEOs and to induce a stronger alignment of CEO pay and performance will have positive effects on the performance of the organization. They found support for that hypothesis. They reported that monitoring mechanisms that align the interest of managers with those of the firm and that prevent managers from pursuing self-serving objectives are positively associated with both perceptual and archival firm performance measures.

Tosi and Gomez-Mejia (1992) also hypothesized that the effects of monitoring are expected to differ as a function of the ownership structure. They proposed—and their data supported it—that increased monitoring results in improved firm performance (as predicted in the theoretical work of researchers such as Shavell, 1979; Holmstrom, 1979). However, the effects are greater in management-controlled firms. There are two reasons for this. First, because the level of monitoring is already much higher in owner-controlled firms than in management-controlled firms (e.g., see Dyl, 1988, 1989; Tosi and Gomez-Mejia, 1989), one would expect that the marginal contribution of additional monitoring to firm performance should be greater among the latter. Given the lower observed threshold values on the monitoring dimension among management-controlled firms, firm performance should then be highly responsive to increased monitoring in this situation, as agency theorists predict. On the other hand, it is not unreasonable to expect that a truncated range on the monitoring dimension among owner-controlled firms would tend to attenuate its observed relationship with firm performance. Consistent with earlier findings of Lieberson and O'Connor (1972), Salancik and Pfeffer (1977), Weiner and Mahoney (1981), and Smith, Carson, and Alexander (1984), one would expect that monitoring can only exert a limited influence on firm performance, because the latter also depends on many factors beyond management's control. Thus, one could argue that among owner-controlled firms, monitoring is already close to reaching its maximum theoretical impact on firm performance, becoming relatively inert, and that performance variance past that point can best be attributed to random and/or uncontrollable events.

A second, albeit more speculative, reason advanced by Tosi and Gomez-Mejia (1992) that may account for differences on the impact of monitoring on firm performance between the two types of firms pertains to variations in the holistic organizational context. Support for this assertion is found in earlier work by Hansen and Wernerfelt (1989). These authors attempted to break down the interfirm variance in profit rates into economic and organizational components. They report that organizational factors account for about twice as much variance in firm performance ($R^2 = .38$) as economic factors ($R^2 = .19$). Hansen and Wernerfelt (1989, p. 401) attribute these results to the following:

> Managers can influence the behavior of their employees (and thus the performance of the organization) by taking into account factors such as the formal and informal structure, the planning, reward, control, and information systems, their skills and personalities, and the relation of these to the environment. That is, managers influence organizational outcomes by establishing context, and that context is the result of a complex set of psychological, sociological, and physical interactions.

Along the same vein, Tosi and Gomez-Mejia (1992) argued that when owners exert substantial influence over the firm, the organization culture and climate, strategic orientation, policies and practices governing various employee groups (divisional managers, midlevel executives, lower management levels, and workers), as well as the overall structure of the reward system, strongly reinforces a performance ethos. Therefore, monitoring of top management is one of the many factors that drive behavior, and, as such, its unique effects on firm performance would be more difficult to detect. On the other hand, in management-controlled firms, there is less incentive to operate in the owners' interests because the culture, strategy, policies, and reward structure reinforce behaviors catering to managers' interests.   In this context, according to Tosi and Gomez-Mejia (1992), there would be little monitoring of top management teams and, if this is increased, there should be larger effects on observed performance.

In summary, the research leads to this conclusion: While it remains to be clearly demonstrated that there are performance differences between management-controlled and owner-controlled firms (and this may be partially accounted for by methodological matters), it is very clear that executives of management-controlled firms act in ways to suggest that they intend to pass on higher agency costs to the owners than executives of owner-controlled firms. However, these agency costs may be reduced in management-controlled firms through monitoring and incentive alignment mechanisms.

Role of Institutional Investors

An issue closely related to the ownership concentration debate is the role played by large institutional investors (such as pension funds, investment funds, mortgage companies) in the management of firms in their portfolio, including executive compensation. The main point of contention is the extent to which these "passive investors" may hold large blocks of shares yet not exercise control of any kind; the notion that these external owners are quick to follow the "Wall Street" rule by selling their stock when dissatisfied with management instead of attempting to influence management or exercise control over the firms in their portfolio. While empirical research on this question is very limited, and indeed most of this debate has taken place in the mass media and in practitioner journals, the evidence available to date suggests that so called "passive investors" do play an active watchdog role with firms in their portfolio. The reasons for this are discussed next.

First, ". . . institutional investors derive their power over top managers from the mere size of their equity holdings: heavy institutional selling can cause drastic declines in a firm's market value" (Graves and Waddock, 1990 p. 78). Second, increasing empirical evidence points toward a positive relationship between equity ownership by passive investors and managerial decisions that are in the best long-term interest of the firm. This is at odds with the notion that institutional investors are driven by shortsightedness and don't really care much about what happens within a given firm (because if a stock in an institutional portfolio shows signs of poor performance, presumably the fund manager will sell out and purchase a more favorable stock. What firm executives do, according to this view, is of little import to these fund managers). Tests of this "hands off" hypothesis concerning institutional investors have been conducted by examining long-term R&D investments as a function of institutional holdings. Several studies have shown a positive impact of institutional ownership on long-term R&D investments, suggesting that institutional investors are willing and able to exercise their influence on managerial decisions and that this influence is indicative of an enduring, rather than transient or short-term, relationship (see Jarrel, Lehn, and Marr, 1985; Hill and Hansen, 1989; Baysinger et al., 1991; Hansen and Hill, 1991). Furthermore, Baysinger, et all. (1991) and Hansen and Hill (1991) found that the influence on management (as measured by R&D investment decisions) is *not* any less from large institutional investors than from large individual stockholders.

Third, the large level of assets controlled by institutions (on the order of $0.5 trillion in 1987) makes efficient movement in and out of stock positions increasingly difficult (Nussbaun and Dobrzynski, 1987). "As a result, they have a tendency to become involved in corporate control when results do not live up to expectations" (Graves and Waddock, 1990, p. 77). Aoki (1984) and others (e.g., Herman, 1981) have argued that "passive" institutional investors are having little choice but to become active owners in those firms where they hold a large amount of stock (which they define as 5 percent or more) because they cannot easily migrate to other firms when displeased with a given company. Reflecting this view, Hansen and Hill (1991, p. 12) note that:

> ". . .many institutions are effectively 'locked in' to their stockholdings. Unlike most individuals, institutions may take fairly substantial positions in a firm's stock. . . Given this, and the tendency of institutions to act in unison, many institutions cannot exit from a firm's stock without depressing the stock price and taking a substantial capital loss on the transaction. Due to the high costs of exit, institutions find themselves locked into a long-term relationship with the firm. Recognizing this, they may use their voting power and influence [over] managers. . ."

Similarly, Baysinger, et al. (1991, pp. 212-213) comment:

> ". . .institutional investors who own large stakes in a company's stock are less able to move efficiently in and out of stock positions. . .Hence, they try to influence the return of their investment by becoming actively involved in a company's management."

Fourth, anecdotal evidence in the business press attest to the potential power that "passively managed funds" (such as pensions, mutual funds, and banks) can wield over corporations. A survey of CEOs by Hector (1988) found that the majority of these individuals perceive a substantial amount of influence on managerial decisions exercised by large institutional investors. Similar results were reported in an earlier Harris poll (*Business Week*, 1987) and a survey by Korn/Ferry International (1991). John Neff, an investment manager for Vanguard Group, notes that:

> "the traditional response was to vote with your feet. . .but you can't do that anymore. The size of our position is such that it's hard to get out of some of our positions. The alternative of trying to alter management is sometimes necessary" (Neff, 1987).

Dale M. Hanson, President of California Public Employees' Retirement System, the second largest institutional investor in the country, remarked:

> "We are raising basic questions about how companies are managed and how executives are compensated. We believe, fundamentally, that we have a fiduciary obligation to be involved" (Hanson, 1991, p. 32).

Carrington and Hertzberg (1982, p. R15) in a *Wall Street Journal* article indicate that:

> ". . .many pension funds have hired consultants to evaluate the performance of investment managers. . .it has become routine [for the investment managers] to be called on the carpet to defend their records."

Regan (1987, p. 57) adds:

> ". . .many large pension funds and the large corporations in which they hold shares are now permanently wed."

The case of Richard Ferris, CEO of Allegis Corporation, who was removed from office due to pressure from one institutional owner holding 13 percent of Allegis' stock received much attention in the popular business press (see Sherman, 1987; Labich, 1987). Allegedly, his downfall was caused by a rapid program of mergers and acquisitions—expanding the original firm from United Airlines to include Hertz cars, Westin Hotels, and Hilton Intenational under the same corporate unbrella—with a corresponding decline in Allegis' profits.

In an article appearing in *Fortune* (1991 p. 131) entitled "who owns this company, anyhow?", Norton argues that:

> to protect their huge and illiquid stockholdings, institutional investors are increasingly calling the shots in corporate America. . . During this year's proxy season, institutional investors and organized shareholder groups sponsored 153 corporate governance proposals, a record, urging companies to drop antitakeover defenses, cancel golden parachutes for executives, and guarantee that boards will consist of a majority of independent directors—outsiders who have not been selected by the CEO.

In short, the proposition that so called passive institutional investors do not exercise ownership control of any kind or that their behavior relative to managers is markedly different from that of individual investors has received little support. Yet this remains a virgin area for serious scholarly research on executive compensation.

Organizational Structure

As discussed earlier, Simon (1957) proposed an alternative sociological view of executive compensation by arguing that it was not firm size per se that determined top executive pay but, rather, the organization's internal hierarchy. Firms attempt to establish pay differentials between levels not in absolute terms, but as ratios. This theory predicts that top executive compensation should be greater in firms with taller organizational structures.

Mahoney (1979) found that the pay ratios between management levels are remarkably consistent across firms with approximately a 33 percent pay differential between levels in the hierarchy. Peck (1987) confirms this proposition by showing that the pay relationships among the five highest paid executives differ little by type of business. For example, on average, the second highest paid executive typically receives 67 to 87 percent of the highest paid executive's income, and the third highest receives approximately 55 percent of the top executive's pay. Thus, the empirical evidence supports the proposition that many organizational levels imply high pay at the top. However, these findings may simply be replicating what others have already found—namely, that firm size is an important predictor of executive pay. This interpretation is consistent both with span of control theory and with the findings of Blau (1970) and Child (1973) that firm size and number of levels are highly correlated.

Individual Determinants of Executive Pay

Most of the research examining the role of personal characteristics of executives on their pay is based on the human capital paradigm reviewed before. Results of earlier human capital research were quite straightforward. (See Becker, 1975; Mincer, 1975.)   On average, earnings increase with work experience. Human capital theory explains this increase as a return on investment in productivity enhancing skills accumulated while working.

Other empirical evidence suggests, however, that additional factors come into play. It has been shown by Pascal and Rapping (1972), Medoff and Abraham (1980), and Harris and Holmstrom (1982) that more experienced managers earn more, even after controlling for performance. One explanation for this is that institutional norms help push up earnings of executives the more experience they accumulate. Years of experience may be used to "rationalize" pay decisions (Balkin and Gomez-Mejia, 1987b). Another explanation is advanced by Harris and Holmstrom (1982) who argue that senior executives earn more on average because they had more time to have their compensation be bid up by the market. Harris and Holmstrom also argue that more senior executives pay a lower "insurance premium" as they are perceived by employers to be less risky. Therefore, they will be provided higher pay, even when one controls for observed performance. Along the same vein, Murphy (1986, p. 62) presents some empirical findings suggesting that "observing performance over several periods allows the firm to form a more precise estimate of executive ability." Because less is known about executives earlier in their careers, formula-based approaches linking pay to firm performance are frequently adopted in their initial years, but these programs are less necessary over time as their "true" ability becomes better known.

In any case, there is much evidence supporting a correlation between amount of relevant experience and executive pay level. But whether increased earnings are attributed to improved performance as a result of accumulated human capital or some other factors is subject to interpretation.

Most of the empirical research on human capital theory originated in economics. However, investigators in other disciplines such as management and industrial relations have also examined personal characteristics of executives as potential determinants of their pay. Four such studies are briefly reviewed below.

Roche (1975) studied age and executive mobility in relationship to pay. He found that through their mid-40s, less mobile executives' compensation was higher than that of the more mobile executives. The return to high mobility, however, became evident in their mid-50s, when highly mobile executives received much higher pay packages. This group was willing to take risks and felt very comfortable in the midst of rapid change.

Agarwal (1981) noted that internal work experience was a better predictor of executive pay than external work experience. Compensation of internal candidates is lower than pay packages for outsiders because a premium is not required to induce the latter to change jobs. Deckop (1988) also found that external recruits made more money than executives hired from within, and both earned more than the original founders. This suggests that individuals who are groomed within the company will eventually be less expensive than executives hired from other firms.

Gerhart and Milkovich (1990) studied a sample of 20,000 top and middle level executives. They report that human capital (as measured by years of education, years of labor market experience, firm tenure, and job tenure) and job responsibility level (as measured by the number of reporting levels from the board of directors to the position of the incumbent and number of management levels supervised) explain 69 percent of the variance in base pay level received and 24 percent of the variance in bonus as a proportion of base pay.

More recently, Hill and Phan (1991) report that while executive pay level rises with tenure, the relationship between executive pay and firm performance *decreases* as a function of tenure. Consistent with a managerialist interpretation and at odds with a human capital perspective, these authors concluded that "the longer the tenure of a CEO, the greater his or her influence over the board of directors, and the more likely it is that his or her compensation package will reflect his or her preferences. Consistent with this, an empirical test suggests that the relationship between CEO pay and stock returns weakens with tenure."

Symbolic Role of Executive Pay

As discussed in the theory section, Lazear and Rosen (1981) and others have portrayed top executive pay as a prize used to induce lower level managers to work harder to win the prize, rather than as a reward commensurate with the executive's performance. According to O'Reilly et al. (1988, p. 259), "in this scheme the compensation of the CEO represents the prize in the lottery; hence those below this level will be willing to give up some of their earnings to be put into the prize for which they all compete." Presumably, this accounts for the very large observed differences between CEO salaries and those of executives at the immediate lower level.

Empirical research testing tournament theory is minimal, and the findings are mixed. One study by O'Reilly, Main, and Crystal (1988) produced negative results. The logic of this study is as follows: The greater the number of competitors and, hence, the lower the chance of winning, the larger should be the prize, other things equal. By finding in their sample that the CEO's pay was negatively related to the number of vice presidents, O'Reilly et al. (1988, p. 236) conclude "this was exactly the opposite of the result predicted by tournament theory." While their way of testing tournament theory is very creative and makes a contribution, given the paucity of research in this area, other interpretations for their findings are not hard to make. For example, some organizations are known for their generous use of vice presidential titles in lieu of higher pay to reward managers. Other firms use this title rather sparingly. Also, the span of control for the CEO varies significantly from one type of organization to another. One could also argue that the tournament "game" is not designed exclusively for vice presidents but for several managerial levels.

In the same study, O'Reilly et al. found that political factors unrelated to firm performance affect the level of executive pay. They report that one of the main correlates of executive earnings was the average pay level of the compensation committee of the board of directors. This committee is typically composed of CEOs from other firms. O'Reilly et al. (1988, p. 240) offer a behavioral explanation for these findings. A social comparison process "takes place whereby the compensation committee members perceive the appropriate pay level of the executive to be similar to their own." O'Reilly et al. (1988, p. 240) go on to suggest that the CEOs are aware of this perceptual bias and will use their political clout to hire board members that are highly paid: "Since the CEO exerts considerable informal influence in selecting new members of the board, it may also be that the selection process itself can raise CEO pay if new members are selected whose pay exceeds that of the focal CEO."

Although concerned with distribution of ownership issues, rather than social comparisons, Tosi and Gomez-Mejia (1989) confirm the important role of influence patterns in executive compensation decisions. These authors found that in management-controlled firms, the influence exercised on CEO pay by the chief executive officer (CEO) and outside consultants is greater than in owner-controlled firms. Tosi and Gomez-Mejia also report that in management-controlled firms, the influence exercised on CEO pay by major stockholders, the board of directors, and the compensation committee was less than in owner-controlled firms. The logic behind their findings is as follows: In owner-controlled firms, the board represents the owners' interest because the owners, not management, are more influential in the selection of board members. This reduces the possibility of conflict of interests arising between the executives and the firm. The board will ensure that there are "checks and balances" in the decision system so that executives will have little say in their own pay level. In management-controlled firms, on the other hand, board appointments are more likely to be controlled by management, and members serve at its pleasure. Consultants may be hired to legitimize the pay determination process. Likewise, management will play a stronger role in handpicking the compensation committee, and its members will feel obligated to represent the interests of the constituency that chose them. These governance issues are revisited in Chapter 11.

Two recent studies on tournament theory reached a different conclusion from O'Reilly et al. (1988). Based on a sample of 439 large U. S. corporations between 1981 and 1985, Leonard (1990) reports that pay differentials between ranks increase the higher up in the hierarchy and are also greater the lower the promotion rate. He reports that managers in flat organizations are paid less than those in tall firms. Executives in more hierarchically ranked firms earn up to 60 percent pay premium over those in flat organizations. These findings are not too surprising and can be interpreted in many different ways, including a structural interpretation (Simon, 1959), a human capital interpretation (Agarwal, 1981), or a power interpretation (Tosi and Gomez-Mejia, 1992; Gomez-Mejia, Tosi, and Hinkin, 1987). However, Leonard (1990, p. 14) interprets these findings as providing support to tournament theory in that "high pay in top executive positions is used to motivate lower-level executives to compete for promotions. The expected value to executives of such a scheme can be maintained if the pay differential across levels narrows while promotion probabilities increase." Like much of the empirical research on executive compensation, how one interprets these findings depends on personal preferences because of intercorrelated measures and the difficulty of attributing causality to any given variable. (For example, greater salary dispersion as a function of tallness may perhaps be attributed to a "tournament effect," but we can think of several alternative, equally plausible explanations.)

A third study by Ehrenberg and Bognanno (1990) used a creative method to test tournament theory and concluded that the fundamental tenets of the theory were supported. However, one can question the generalizability of their findings to "real life" executives managing complex business organizations. They analyzed data from the 1987 European Men's Professional Golf Association (PGA) Tour. By assuming that the difficulty of the course and the adversity of weather conditions affect all players in a tournament equally and that players choose their effort/concentration levels, Ehrenberg and Bognanno (1990, p. 74) believe that their data is consistent with tournament theory predictions in that "the level and structure of prizes in PGA tournaments influence players' performance. Specifically, players' performance appears to vary positively with both the total money prizes awarded in a tournament and the marginal return to effort in the final round of play (a value that varies among players largely depending on how the prize money is allocated among finishers of different ranks)."

In short, evidence in support of tournament theory is mixed. This may be attributed to the formidable difficulties involved in trying to operationalize tournament effects and the leaps of faith required when drawing motivational inferences from archival data. This seems like an area of inquiry where a laboratory experiment may be particularly appropriate for testing specific tournament hypotheses in a controlled environment. Field data and archival information are simply too contaminated to yield robust results when testing alleged tournament effects.

As discussed earlier, Ungson and Steers (1984) describe the duties of CEOs in terms of their role as political figureheads and strategists. While little empirical work has been conducted that directly examines these roles, available evidence suggests that interpersonal skills of the executives vary, and greater organizational savvy may lead to a better financial deal for the incumbent. Luthans (1988) reports that executives who moved rapidly to the top echelons in the firm were not necessarily the best managers (those who have satisfied, committed subordinates and high performing units). Many upwardly mobile executives were very good at creating a favorable image with their superiors and peers, irrespective of actual performance. This may be part of the reason behind the decoupling of executive pay and firm performance in some companies. It could be that shrewd executives, who have refined the art of "impression management," are able to negotiate large compensation packages in spite of their poor track record (Geneen, 1984). In particular, the relationship of the CEO to the board of directors might be an important determinant of how generously the board rewards the executive (Tosi and Gomez-Mejia, 1989). The nature of this relationship might well provide insights as to the level of CEO pay and the design of the CEO pay package in terms of salary, bonus, and long-term income. This aspect of executive compensation warrants more attention.

The Role of the Tax System

There is a whole literature in finance and accounting concerned with the question of whether the compensation package of executives is deliberately designed to improve the alignment of management and shareholder interests or if it simply is reactive to tax legislation. Because of its volume and complexity, only some of this research is highlighted within the scope of this chapter.

Authors such as Lewellen (1968), Smith and Walts (1982), Larcker (1983), Eaton and Rosen (1983), and Murphy (1986b) seem to imply that equity-based managerial compensation schemes, such as stock option plans, are rationally adopted with the ultimate goal of maximizing the incentive effect on managerial behavior. Larcker (1983), for example, argued that "performance plans" are implemented because these promote a long-term orientation in managerial investment decisions. Brickley, Bhagat, and Lease (1985) and Tehranian and Waegelein (1984) report that the market reacts positively to the announcement of such plans.

On the other hand, others have found that tax implications loom very large in the design of executive pay packages and that accountants, rather than specialists in human behavior and motivation, provide most of the input into those decisions. For example, Hite and Long (1982) and Miller and Scholes (1982) showed that tax advantages explain most adoptions of equity-based executive compensation schemes. Following 100 industrial firms over a twenty-year period, Hite and Long (1982) discovered that even minute changes on marginal tax rates would have been sufficient to produce modification in CEO compensation contracts. More recently, Posner (1987) found that a surprisingly large number of firms wasted little time in making changes to their executive pay packages after passage of the Tax Reform Act in November, 1986. This may be attributed to the fact that capital gains are treated by the Tax Reform Act as ordinary income, making equity-based compensation less attractive to executives.

Although mixed, the literature suggests that at least some firms may be adopting executive pay packages purely to offer a tax advantage to the CEO, rather than for incentive reasons. Tosi and Gomez-Mejia (1989) found that tax concerns seem to play a larger role in management-controlled firms, suggesting that opportunistic reasons may be part of this. In any case, to the extent that an executive pay package dictated by tax considerations may not be the best choice for a given firm, this would represent an agency cost in the terminology of agency theory.

SUMMARY AND RESEARCH PROPOSITIONS

In conclusion, executive pay is a function of many interrelated factors and cannot be meaningfully understood in a reductionistic fashion. Table 6-1 lists a set of key propositions drawn from the theoretical frameworks reviewed earlier in this chapter. It also lists the most salient research results on executive compensation. The empirical findings, as summarized in Table 6-1, suggest that simplistic notions of performance reward linkages don't seem to fare well when applied to top management. Because of the intrinsically ambiguous and customized criteria used to establish many executive compensation packages, this area is likely to continue as a focus of controversy among academics, practitioners, and the public at large. The next chapter examines the major policy choices that should be considered when designing such packages.

TABLE 6-1
Empirical Support for 22 Propositions Concerning Predictors and Correlates of Executive Pay

	Propositions	Empirical Support
Proposition 1	Executive pay varies as a function of firm performance.	Very mixed, minimal relationships
Proposition 2	The lower the expected performance of a firm if the next best alternative executive were to be hired as a substitute for the present CEO, the higher the current CEO's pay.	Largely untested
Proposition 3	The greater the pay necessary to attract the best alternative replacement of the current CEO, the greater the compensation received by the latter.	Largely untested
Proposition 4	The greater the compensation the current CEO would receive in the open market, the higher his/her compensation.	Largely untested
Proposition 5	The more dispersed the ownership of a firm, the more executives will structure their compensation package so that their pay is flexible to move up as firm performance improves but will not suffer if firm performance declines.	Strong
Proposition 6	The more dispersed the ownership of a firm, the less likely executives will be dismissed as firm performance declines.	Strong
Proposition 7	The more dispersed the ownership of a firm, the more likely executives will be driven to increase firm size, even if additional growth results in decreased performance.	Strong
Proposition 8	The more concentrated the ownership of a firm, the more likely executive decisions (and the CEO pay package) will have a long-term horizon.	Moderate
Proposition 9	The more concentrated the ownership of a firm, the more effective the board of directors is in disciplining executives and the lower the influence exercised by executives.	Strong
Proposition 10	Greater monitoring and incentive alignment of executives result in improved firm performance.	Moderate
Proposition 11	Greater monitoring and incentive alignment of executives lead to a greater observed linkage between executive pay and firm performance.	Moderate
Proposition 12	Increased monitoring produces higher firm performance among management-controlled firms.	Moderate
Proposition 13	Relationship between executive pay and firm performance varies by extent of diversification.	Strong
Proposition 14	Extent of division autonomy affects criteria used to reward executives.	Strong
Proposition 15	Executive pay is more strongly related to stock-related performance criteria than to accounting measures.	Negative
Proposition 16	Taller organizational structures imply more pay at the top.	Very strong

TABLE 6-1 (Continued)

	Propositions	Empirical Support
Proposition 17	Human capital plays a major role in top management's pay.	Moderate
Proposition 18	Top executive pay is used as a tournament trophy to motivate lower level managers.	Very mixed
Proposition 19	Firms compensate executives for performance over their entire tenure with the firm, not necessarily on their most recent performance.	Moderate
Proposition 20	Executive pay reflects how well this individual fulfills his/her role as a political strategist rather than how well he/she maximizes "bottom line," objective performance criteria.	Largely untested
Proposition 21	Executive decisions are very responsive to what incumbents perceive will lead to the greatest financial reward.	Very strong
Proposition 22	Strategic, rather than tax, concerns drive the design of executives' pay packages.	Moderate

STRATEGIC DESIGN OF EXECUTIVE COMPENSATION PROGRAMS AND FIRM PERFORMANCE: POLICY CHOICES AND IMPLEMENTATION ISSUES

This chapter examines the major policy choices and dilemmas confronting the designers of executive pay packages. While the following discussion is based on many of the theoretical principles and empirical findings reviewed in Chapter 6, it is primarily concerned with implementation issues.

POLICY CHOICES

There are ten key policy choices that should be considered when designing compensation programs for top management teams. These concern: (a) degree of exclusivity; (b) opportunity costs; (c) level of analysis; (d) performance measurement; (e) control mechanisms; (f) type of governance; (h) time horizon; (i) degree of risk; (j) degree of consistency; and (k) tax rules. Each of these is discussed in turn.

Degree of Exclusivity

An egalitarianism vs. elitism policy choice mirrors the hierarchical vs. egalitarian strategic compensation dimension discussed in Chapter 2. The number of management levels to be included in executive compensation programs is an important decision because it affects whether the firm develops a hierarchical or a more egalitarian culture. That number also affects the extent to which the interests of lower level managers are aligned with those of top management and how much inducement executives at one level have to monitor closely the performance of lower level executives reporting to them.

If the CEO pay package is clearly separate from that of the rest of the staff, it can be personalized more easily. However, two separate packages will reinforce a more authoritarian, centralized, elitist type of reward system. This approach would be consonant with the postulates of tournament theory, whereby CEO pay and perquisites are deliberately set at a much higher level than those of subordinates. Presumably, this "prize" will serve to mobilize subordinates to better utilize their potential, perhaps allowing them to win the trophy at some point in their career.

In other words, the extent to which the incentive system covers different management groups, and not just the CEO or those immediately reporting to him/her, sends powerful signals to the rest of the organization as to what is valued and important. It can also promote a more participative, rather than a monarchical, image of the authority structure.

A greater number of firms are now moving incentive pay programs to lower levels of the company. Hymowitz (1988) notes that in the late 1980s, the median salary of managers eligible for stock options dropped to its lowest level in history. After controlling for inflation, the median salary dropped to $68,900 in 1988. According to that report, the rationale provided by most firms is that expanding the coverage base enhances commitment and loyalty to the organization on the part of midlevel managers and junior executives. In an attempt to minimize status differentials, an increasing number of firms have also deleted many of the perquisites that were once reserved for top management. For example, executive cafeterias and preferential parking have been eliminated in many companies to engender a spirit of teamwork and equality (Gomez-Mejia and Welbourne, 1989). Ochsner (1987), a senior vice president of Hay and Associates, notes that this is more than just a passing fad. He argues that many firms are realizing substantial benefits in involving more layers of management in strategic formulation, implementation, and decision making, which directly impacts the corporation's future. For this to work, the reward system must also become more egalitarian.

By international standards, however, elitism remains firmly entrenched in the United States. The ratio of CEO pay to the average employee's pay for the same sized British, German, or French Company is less than one-half that in the United States (Lublin, 1990). Equivalent sized Japanese firms pay their CEOs only a small fraction (about 25 percent) of their counterparts in the United States (Ono, 1990), with a ratio of CEO pay to the average employee's pay less than one-third that of U.S. firms (Gomez-Mejia and Welbourne, 1990). The causes for these disparities, which have remained fairly stable over time, are unclear. Certainly they cannot be attributed to performance differences. There is also no evidence that the market for executive talent is consistently tighter in the United States vis-a-vis other industrialized countries. The disparities reflect a complex web of economic, historical, cultural, and political factors that are very difficult to untangle, which makes it unlikely for any dramatic changes in the CEO pay structure to occur in the near future.

Opportunity Costs

An increasing vs. decreasing opportunity costs policy choice is a specific case of the performance vs. seniority strategic compensation dimension discussed in Chapter 2. Because of high attrition in the executive ranks and the difficulties of finding suitable replacements, the incentive system may be designed to penalize the executive for leaving the firm prior to a stipulated period of time. By increasing the opportunity cost of turnover, the firm may prevent the executive from being pirated by other organizations. For example, stock options worth several million dollars may not be exercised until the executive has been with the firm for, let's say, five years. These incentives that reward executive retention are commonly referred to as *golden handcuffs*.

The extent to which the compensation package deliberately includes a tenure factor in the payout formula should depend on the firm's strategic objectives. The organization may believe that minimizing turnover at the top will provide a climate of stability and promote commitment and loyalty among its employees. Fewer executive transitions may send a signal to all organizational members that long tenure is valued and rewarded.

On the other hand, a firm may feel that a fair amount of attrition at the top allows the company to bring in "fresh blood" and new ideas on a regular basis (see Hambrick and Fukutomi, 1991). The firm may be operating in such a turbulent environment that executives may have to be replaced frequently to tackle changing conditions. In those situations, rewarding for long-term tenure may actually be deleterious. The board of directors may find, for example, that in highly volatile environments, maximum productive tenure might be five years (Gomez-Mejia and Welbourne, 1989). The high technology industry provides a case in point. (See Coombs and Rosse, 1992.) Short tenure for executives is an accepted norm in technology intensive firms. Executive attrition is viewed by many as a positive force in this industry because product life cycles are quite short. Therefore, it becomes instrumental to hire new managers who are less committed to existing technology (Balkin and Gomez-Mejia, 1987b).

Rather than being forced to terminate an executive for poor performance or keeping the individual on board past his/her prime, the reward system may encourage incumbents to seek employment elsewhere by minimizing the opportunity costs of moving. Obviously, a thin line exists between dysfunctional attrition (where there is no continuity in the organization, resulting in decreased performance) and positive turnover that allows leadership to be renewed on a periodic basis.

Level of Analysis

An organizational vs. individual level of analysis policy choice is a special case of the individual vs. group performance strategic compensation dimension discussed in Chapter 2. The evaluation criteria used for most top executives are generally based on the entire organization's performance (e.g., earnings per share, return on investment). If the firm does well, the executive's income is supposed to rise accordingly. The rationale for using organization-wide performance indicators is that the executive is ultimately responsible for what happens in the firm. This philosophy is consistent with the traditional "parity of authority and responsibility" principle espoused by early management theorists such as Fayol (1949). Because the "buck stops" at the chief executive's desk, this individual should incur the gains and losses resulting from the ups and downs of the firm's fortunes.

Reliance on organization-wide performance measures is also predicated on the fact that this information is readily accessible and can be objectively quantified. Thus, this data may be convincingly defended to outside groups as a criteria to allocate executive pay, and it is easier to communicate to multiple audiences (e.g., stockholders, board of directors, employees, media).

Compelling as the reasons may be for the use of these aggregate performance indicators, it may also be important from a strategic perspective to consider behavioral performance measures when dispensing executive pay. First, a substantial amount of research suggests that use of individual performance indicators, when perceived as accurate and reliable, are the best motivators in pay-for-performance systems (Carroll, 1987). Second, as discussed later, ignoring individual contribution measures and exclusively relying on organization-wide criteria may lead to an inordinate amount of attention being paid on the executive's part to "beat the numbers game." The executive may do everything possible to make aggregate indicators look good, even if this may prove to be detrimental in the long run (e.g., reducing R&D expenditures to improve profitability ratios). Third, the effect of top executives on organizational performance may not be as great as generally assumed because firm performance depends on many variables beyond the executive's control. (See Chapter 6.) For example, it may be quite possible for an executive to be doing an outstanding job during bad times, even though financial indicators would make him/her look like a dismal failure.

Performance Measurement

A profitability vs. market-based indicators policy choice is generally unique to the compensation of upper echelons. As discussed in Chapter 6, one of the most controversial issues in executive compensation revolves around how firm performance should be measured. This debate raises a number of important strategic concerns regarding the criteria used to distribute executive pay.

The most commonly used organization-wide performance criteria in the United States consist of accounting measures of performance such as earnings per share and return on equity. To the extent that certain milestones are met, the executive will receive an agreed upon sum of money, either in the form of a bonus or stocks (Gomez-Mejia and Welbourne, 1989). However, some would argue that profitability figures are easily manipulated through creative accounting procedures. Obviously, this could have dysfunctional effects for the organization.

The importance that management attaches to showing good profitability figures could lead to a deliberate bypass of excellent investment opportunities or to economically inefficient decisions from the viewpoint of both the company and the economy. According to Rappaport (1978, p. 82), use of such measures as earnings per share to base executive pay may create a situation where "what is economically rational from the corporate or social viewpoint may, however, be an irrational course of action for the executives charged with decision making." For instance, based on a study of 184 large multiproduct firms, Hoskisson, Hitt, and Hill (1990) report that incentives for division managers affect their risk orientation and, thus, their decisions to invest in R&D expenditures. More specifically, "incentives based on division financial performance are negatively related to total firm R&D intensity after controlling for industry R&D intensity, firm diversification, size, and group structure" (Hoskisson et al., 1990, p. 1).

As an alternative to profitability measures, some strongly believe that stockholders' welfare (measured in the form of stock appreciation, dividends paid, or abnormal rate of return) represent the purest form of performance criteria (Coughlan and Schmidt, 1985; Jensen and Murphy, 1990b; Murphy, 1986). Unlike profitability indices, market-based performance indicators are more difficult to manipulate by the executive. On the other hand, these measures are not troublefree. Gomez-Mejia et al., (1987, p. 60) note that:

> Paying out cash dividends will tend to raise a stock's price. However, raising cash dividends decreases funds available for reinvestment and R&D, which lowers expected growth rate and depresses the price of a stock in the long run—with effects perhaps occurring at a time when another executive will bear the brunt of the problem. Stock prices are also very sensitive to external events that may have little to do with how efficiently a firm is being run and that are totally beyond management's control.

Also, and on philosophical grounds, many firmly believe that executives' pay should not be set on the basis of events that are, for the most part, out of their control—such as up and down movements in the stock market—and may lead to windfalls or minimal gains (Bickford, 1981; Ellig, 1984; Rich and Larson, 1984). These individuals recommend accounting measures as proxies for performance or a combination of stock price and profitability data be used.

In designing executive compensation programs, it may be wise to base rewards on both profitability and market-based measures. The use of multiple indicators may provide a more accurate and reliable estimate of "true" firm performance—elusive as that concept may be. A composite criterion may also be easier to defend. Reaching agreement on the appropriateness of any single measure is difficult, and attempts to do so are likely to arouse suspicion (Weiner and Mahoney, 1981). Finally, the use of a composite criterion may be justified on methodological grounds because diverse firm performance measures are correlated. Gomez-Mejia et al., (1987) found that the most frequently used indicators of firm performance all tend to load on a single factor when these are factor analyzed. This means, they all measure an overall performance construct. Gomez-Mejia et al., (1987, pp. 59-60) offer the following explanation for this:

> Changes in levels of sales affect net income, the common denominator of the ROE [return on equity] and EPS [earnings per share] ratios. A firm's ability to pay dividends depends on its earnings. In financial markets, investors and credit analysts use the information contained in annual reports to form expectations about future earnings, thereby affecting stock prices. Changes in stock prices tend to follow the announcement of EPS, ROE, and dividend actions, indicating that the reports have important signaling effects. If the profitability ratios are all good, a stock price will probably be as high as is possible.

Control Mechanisms

Reliance on monitoring vs. incentive alignment falls under the aegis of the qualitative vs. quantitative performance strategic compensation dimension discussed in Chapter 2. One of the predictions of agency theory is: When it is difficult to observe the behavior of the agent or when the agent knows more about the task at hand than the principal, monitoring becomes less relevant, greater emphasis is placed on measuring outcomes, rather than process, and rewards are based on observed results.

Outcome measures such as financial and accounting indicators reviewed in the previous session are readily available. Thus, there is a temptation, in the parlance of agency theory, to rely on incentive alignment to control executives' behavior by explicitly linking rewards to measured results. In fact, most executive pay programs use formula-based approaches in lieu of monitoring. Boards find such formulas rather convenient to justify executive pay packages to external and internal constituents such as unions, stockholders, and the general public.

From a strategic perspective, however, these mechanistic approaches should be used very cautiously. As noted before, many factors external to the firm such as changes in tax legislation and accounting standards affect financial performance, as well as stock price fluctuations. But the main pitfall here is: Such barometers of relative success may not increase shareholder value nor improve the long-term performance of the corporation (Verespej, 1987). In fact, the emphasis on quantitative, objective measures of performance has contributed to the problem of maximizing short-term gains (Carroll, 1987; Hambrick and Snow, 1989).

Salter (1973) recommends that both formula-based approaches and "softer" process-based measures of performance should be used to focus the executive's attention on the strategic goals of the firm. This, however, requires much concerted action and political compromises by multiple stakeholders (such as compensation committees, board of directors, major stockholders, and top executives themselves) who would be required to make difficult judgment calls based on incomplete data and even conflicting sources of information.

Type of Governance

The type of governance chosen is generally applicable to the compensation of top executives who are in a position to use their power base to influence their pay. It concerns the process to be used in designing executive pay packages and the selection of individuals to participate in these decisions. The formality of the pay-setting process for executives increases with firm size. For example, Gomez-Mejia, Balkin, and Welbourne (1990) found that venture capitalists often negotiate salary terms of executives in start-up firms while at dinner or having a drink. They negotiate compensation mix and level "by the seat of their pants." Most publicly traded firms in the United States, however, utilize compensation committees to make those decisions.

The ultimate responsibility for approving executive pay lies with the board of directors, who will vote on a final recommendation usually submitted by the compensation committee. Members of the committee typically include members of the board, consultants, and high level officers of the personnel department. In addition to establishing executive pay policies in consultation with the board, this committee's responsibilities include "reviewing officer performance in order to allocate financial rewards, reviewing management succession plans, reviewing business performance and setting long-term strategic goals (such as those required for executive long-term incentive plans), selecting and removing senior officers, and maintaining oversight and control over executive perquisites" (Cook, 1981, p. 15).

In a sense, this recommendation and approval procedure comes closest to a pure operationalization of the monitoring concept advanced by agency theorists. Ironically, this also happens to be one of the main targets of criticism by those who believe there is minimal independent overseeing of the pay-setting process for top executives. That is, executives themselves "call most of the shots" when it comes right down to it (e.g., Crystal, 1991; Fierman, 1990). Even the chairs of the compensation committees at major corporations—outside directors who generally run other companies—report widespread dissatisfaction with the process. A survey by Hay and Associates found that only one-third of the chairs feel their companies are doing a good job in linking shareholders' interests to executive compensation. (See Kay, 1990.)

According to skeptics, the reporting structure of those involved in making the pay recommendations ensure that executives do well financially, while at the same time provide a legitimate facade to the process. The senior personnel officer reports to the CEO and has a vested interest in maintaining an ongoing, positive relationship with that individual. The consultant, usually hired by the personnel officer, also wishes to maintain a relationship with the firm that is conducive to future business. The directors who serve on the compensation committee are often CEOs themselves of other firms and have a strong identification with the CEO position and its associated rewards. (See O'Reilly et al., 1988.)

The CEO is usually an active member of the board of directors and, in some cases, might even be part of the compensation committee. Geneen (1984, p. 30), who was CEO at International Telephone and Telegraph (ITT) for 15 years, laments: "In most corporations, most of the time, the board of directors has little choice but to follow meekly where the chief executive leads." Myles Mace studied board of directors for 25 years and concluded that the board seldom makes decisions against the executive's wishes except in times of crisis, when it literally has no other choice but to take action against the CEO. (Reported in Murthy and Salter, 1975.) In 1990, Fuchsberg (1990) noted that 214 CEOs of Fortune 1000 companies sit on four or more company boards outside their own. He calls it "the ideal second job," because receiving six figures for a few hours of work per year is not unusual. Under the subheading "Thanks for the raise. May I offer you one?" Crystal (1990, p. 100) comments that:

> CEOs aren't the only ones whose pay is rising remarkably fast. Many companies are sharply increasing what they pay outside directors—who of course decide what to pay the CEO. Not only do some directors receive pensions amounting to 100 percent of base pay after just five to ten years of board service, but an increasing number also are getting stock options and—hold on to your seat—restricted stock grants. The value of what an outside director of a major company receives can easily top $50,000 a year. These many goodies have been creeping into board-rooms for a few years [but] soon it may be an odd company that doesn't offer them.

Breakdowns in corporate governance structures leading to the problems discussed above are summarized by Williams (1985, pp. 66-67) as follows:

> In practice, contrary to the basic tenets of the [compensation] model procedure, the chief executive often has his hand in the pay-setting process almost from the first step. He generally approves, or at least knows about, the recommendation of his personnel executive before it goes to the compensation committee, and may take a pregame pass at the consultant's recommendation too. Both [personnel executives and consultants] rely upon

the good graces of the chief executive for their livelihood.   The consultant in particular—who is typically hired by management—would like to be invited for a return engagement.   The board's compensation committee doesn't operate independently of the chief executive either.

To reduce these monitoring problems, it is imperative to develop mechanisms that prevent conflict of interests from arising.   This requires a governance system that is riddled with checks and balances so that executive pay decisions are independently made and beyond reproach.   Some suggestions are in order.   First, it may be wise to establish multiple committees chartered with different responsibilities in setting executive pay (e.g., information gathering, review of the data, generation of proposals, examination of motivational impacts, and analysis of tax implications).   The recommendation made by each committee should be completely confidential.   Second, the compensation committee who integrates this information and presents its recommendations to the board should be exclusively composed of outside members, some of whom are *not* CEOs in other firms (e.g., academics, retired businesspeople).   Third, a majority of the board should consist of independent directors. For instance, General Motors Corporation in 1991 adopted such a bylaw in response to pressure from the California Pension Fund, the nation's biggest public pension fund and a large investor in GM stock. (See White, 1991.)   Lastly, the executive must be expressly forbidden from getting involved in any deliberations affecting his/her pay at any stage in the process.

Because management control of firms through boards of directors is too strong in some organizations, the suggestions made above may be more easily said than done.   The situation is exacerbated by the generally restrictive nature of corporate rules on terms of office, the nomination of candidates, and voting procedures.   These make it difficult for owners of companies with widely distributed equity holdings to exert much influence on boards and managements.   Furthermore, legislation on interlocking directorates is quite lax.   Tosi and Gomez-Mejia (1990) argue that since it is difficult for owners, but easy for management, to place members on boards, then it follows that the boards of management-controlled firms will act in ways consistent with the interests of the managers.   As noted in Chapter 6, and graphically summarized in Figures 7-1 and 7-2, influence patterns do favor the CEO in management-controlled firms (see Figure 7-1), and the structure of the CEO compensation package reflects this (see Figure 7-2).   This suggests that one way to *strengthen* the board is to *weaken* the influence of managers over them.

Tosi and Gomez-Mejia (1990) propose a solution that will give the owners more leverage over board selection and reduce managerial control.   Then, boards would be more responsible to owners' interests.   These authors disagree with the position taken by some that current law provides for this and/or that investors prefer to be passive and spread their risk in such a way that it is not necessary for them to spend a great deal of time to influence the policies and strategies of the firms in which they hold equity.   This may be true for some owners, but not for others who wish to exercise ownership rights.   At present, such investors have limited choices.   If they are unhappy with the management but unable to form a coalition with others, their alternatives are to (1) wait until management improves profitability, (2) hope for a takeover attempt, or (3) dispose of their stocks.   These may be perfectly acceptable alternatives for some investors, but those who may wish to exercise ownership rights should not be *forced* into this passive mode because they have been disenfranchised by an entrenched management by virtue of ownership diffusion and corporate by-

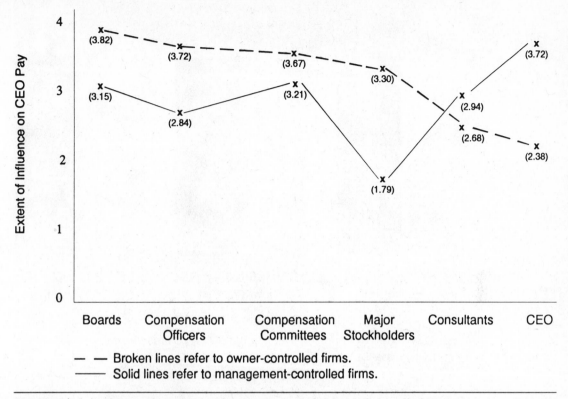

FIGURE 7-1   Influence Patterns in Management- and Owner-Controlled Firms*
*Based on the research of Tosi and Gomez-Mejia, 1989, 1990, 1992.

laws. Tosi and Gomez-Mejia (1990) advance a number of potential remedies for this prob-lem. These are discussed next.

A starting point to accomplish this would be to remove management from the *process* of selecting board members. This could be achieved by the creation of independent of-fices, free from the hand of management, to manage the election of directors for publicly traded firms. They could make relevant performance information available to equity hold-ers. They could facilitate coalitions of different stockholders and generally enhance owner involvement. Equity holding managers would have similar rights as other stockholders for advocating candidates and positions as other owners.

This would require a federal law mandating that publicly traded firms use indepen-dent offices or agents to conduct director elections. These offices could be established out-side the firm. They could be, for example, public accounting firms, law firms, or other organizations that may be created for that purpose. The board of directors for each firm could choose an outside agent, subject to the constraint that the agent not have other busi-ness or professional relationships with the subject firm. The independent office would so-licit slates for board election from stockholders. To minimize the number of slates but still provide opportunities for choice, the office could require that some minimum percentage

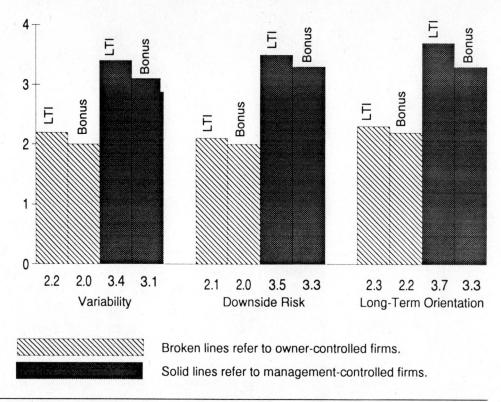

FIGURE 7-2 Characteristics of CEO Long-Term Income (LTI) and Bonus in Management-Controlled and Owner-Controlled Firms*

*Based on the research of Tosi and Gomez-Mejia, 1989, 1990, 1992.

of stock, say one percent, be held by individuals or coalitions nominating candidates for the board.

To ensure that the competence and knowledge of the current management be represented in the election, the current board could nominate a single slate of candidates. The management of the firm would be permitted to nominate a slate to the extent that the candidates meet the same holdings requirements as other equity holders. Information about proposals and programs of each nominated candidate or slate could be distributed in much the same fashion as under current practice, perhaps even in more simple form. The equity holders could then select board members who hold positions similar to their own.

The independent office could also disseminate other information to equity holders through, for example, newsletters. These could contain proposals that might have utility to the larger population of stockholders. These could be a type of informal forum through which equity holders may communicate. There should also be provisions for arbitration or mediation processes when equity holders who do not control the legal minimum for slate nomination have grievances. This would limit the need for expensive legal action as equity holders seek to take advantage of ownership rights.

Tosi and Gomez-Mejia (1990) recognize that the proposal described above represents a departure from the current, general practice of board selection in the United States. Some of the issues that must be addressed in the development of legislation and its implementation include:

1. The effects of further intrusion of nonmarket forces into capital markets.
2. The specific form of regulation (e.g., Should the requirement for independent election processes be applied to presently regulated firms such as public utilities? What percentage of equity should be required to be eligible to nominate a slate of candidates?)
3. The level of resistance by current managements.
4. The costs of independent elections and who must pay for them.
5. The determination of suitable independent agents.
6. How neutrality will be maintained.

Time Horizon

Choosing a time horizon for reward distribution reflects the short- vs. long-term strategic compensation dimension discussed in Chapter 2. Perhaps the most persistent criticism one hears about executive pay plans in the United States is that these promote a short-term orientation, often at the expense of long-term performance. (See Hyman, 1991.) Despite much lip service paid to the need for long-term thinking, very few firms actually design executive pay plans that are based on a balance of both short- and long-term goals (Stata and Maidique, 1980; Gomez-Mejia and Welbourne, 1989). Decisions regarding investments in capital equipment and R&D are often made with short-term financial statements in mind. The overwhelming concern with short-term gains at the expense of long-term competitive advantage and innovation may be one of the primary factors behind the United States' declining position in world markets. (See the special issue by *Business Week* on innovation and the global race, 1990.)

Because of the greater uncertainty associated with long-term income plans, executives generally prefer a shorter time frame in their incentive schemes (Tosi and Gomez-Mejia, 1989). Perhaps because executives are more influential in the decision-making process in management-controlled firms, their pay programs are more short-term oriented in those companies (Tosi and Gomez-Mejia, 1989, 1992). Ideally, however, executive pay should be based on a combination of short- and long-term performance. Ford Motor Company, for example, radically changed its executive compensation plan in the mid-eighties to move away from a heavy emphasis on short-term results (Gomez-Mejia and Welbourne, 1989). Ford's new incentive plan, generally considered as highly successful, incorporates five-year performance goals, as well as annual performance objectives. Executive pay is linked to both of these yardsticks. In addition, Ford introduced qualitative measures in the evaluation and reward system of executives to avoid the pitfalls of formula-based approaches reviewed earlier. On the other hand, General Motors introduced a new executive pay program about the same time as Ford, but it proved to be disappointing (Gomez-Mejia and Welbourne, 1989). Stock grants were generously provided to top executives in an effort to encourage a long-term orientation, but the plan allowed a large number of the stocks to become vested after one-month—thus, diluting the long-term motivational effect of the reward.

Unfortunately, perhaps because of the research problems in the area of executive compensation discussed in Chapter 6, evidence regarding the beneficial effect of CEO long-term income plans on firm performance is not very encouraging. For instance, Crystal (1990) examined total return to shareholders over a ten-year period as a function of CEO long-term income plans for 400 firms and "in every case . . . there was no significant relationship" (p. 102). Statistically significant, yet very weak, relationships were reported for these same variables over a 15-year period for a large sample of firms by Jensen and Murphy (1990a).

Degree of Risk

Deciding the degree of risk in the CEO pay package design is a specific case of the risk aversion vs. risk taking strategic compensation dimension discussed in Chapter 2. Rappaport (1978, 1981, 1986) argues that executives, acting as agents of shareholders, are more risk averse than firm owners. If the company fails to meet some minimum profit level or if its stock price is depressed over a considerable period of time, the penalty for the executive is termination of employment. An executive's job security and pay are not protected by diversification in the same way as are most stockholders' portfolios. To maintain their standard of living, executives cannot usually absorb the loss of earnings to the extent that stockholders can afford fluctuations in income. Management's only method of spreading their own personal risk is through diversifying various projects or business units within the firm or through acquisition. As a result, executive pay packages should be designed to induce executives to pursue riskier objectives that may prove to be in the firm's best interest.

Common sense dictates that greater probability of failure should be associated with greater potential payoff. If risks and returns are closely coupled, executives may be motivated to make riskier but sensible decisions that are likely to improve their income and that of stockholders. The relative risk to the CEO of the firm's compensation policies can be analyzed in terms of three dimensions (Ellig, 1984; Tosi and Gomez-Mejia, 1989, 1990, 1992).

1. *Variability.* The degree of risk is lower when the executive pay package is designed so that a substantial portion of income is received on a stable, relatively fixed, predictable basis over time with minimum uncertainty.
2. *Downside risk.* The amount of risk is lower when the executive's pay package has a downside hedge against poor firm performance. For example, there may be a minor or no penalty contingent on lower values of the performance indicators (e.g., ROE). This means, while the executive's pay may go up considerably when performance improves, it is unlikely to go down if performance declines.
3. *Long-term orientation.* The longer the time horizon involved, the greater the amount of uncertainty (and, therefore, risk) in the pay schedule faced by the executive because the number of unforeseen and uncontrollable events increases accordingly.

These three dimensions, while conceptually different, are highly correlated in practice (Tosi and Gomez-Mejia, 1989).

The relative risk of the executive compensation package should be unique to each type of firm, depending upon such factors as strategic goals, stage in life cycle, and environmental conditions. For example, entrepreneurial firms prefer to hire executives who are willing to sacrifice income in the early stages of the organization when capital is limited in exchange for large potential payoffs if the company succeeds (Balkin and Gomez-Mejia,

1987a).   Mature firms, on the other hand, hire executives who are better at "harvesting" the current product and follow existing methods of operation.   These firms are less interested in experimenting and risking money and capital with new ventures or projects.   As noted in Chapter 4, these mature companies rely more heavily on fixed pay in the executive compensation package.   The percent of executive pay at risk in mature firms is often less than half of what is found in entrepreneurial companies.   Executives who are good administrators, rather than prospectors, are desired by those firms.

The downside risk for CEOs among mature Fortune 500 firms has tended to be nonexistent. (See Jensen and Murphy, 1990a.)   This is particularly evidenced by the large golden parachute contracts that have been negotiated in many of these companies.   In fact, a survey of approximately 500 large companies by the consulting firm TPF&C (see *CompFlash*, 1990) reported that virtually all (98 percent) of these firms provide golden parachutes for top executives, and nearly 40 percent extend protection to their middle managers as well. Not too surprisingly, both in absolute and selective terms, top executives receive the most protection.   Only 14 percent of the companies offer middle managers parachutes in excess of two and a half times their pay.   By contrast, 44 percent provide payments at this, or higher levels, to the upper echelons.

Degree of Consistency

The degree of consistency in the CEO pay package reflects some of the basic issues covered under the corporate vs. division strategic compensation dimension in Chapter 2. A challenge faced by large, complex firms with diverse business units or divisions is how to compensate executives with any degree of consistency across these units. (See Chapters 2-5.)   Should the same formula be used for all executives, or should a separate deal be made with each executive responsible for a business unit or division?   Use of the same formula for different parts of the organization can be easier to control administratively.   More importantly, it promotes a greater sense of equity across units.

On the other hand, since each unit is generally confronted by its own unique contingency factors and operates autonomously, a custom-made executive pay package on a case by case basis makes the most sense.   For example, a diversified conglomerate may have a manufacturing unit using traditional, large batch technology to produce a well-established commodity with a relatively stable market.   It may also own a fast growing, high technology unit with heavy R&D expenditures.   The overall company strategy may involve using some of the profits from the mature subunit to finance the R&D activities and a future expansion of the high technology subunit.   To support this company strategy, each subunit may need to implement its own form of executive compensation package.   Based on the findings of Balkin and Gomez-Mejia (1987a), one would argue that a low risk compensation package (where salary is a high proportion of the total pay mix) makes more sense in the manufacturing unit, while a high risk pay package (where variable pay such as bonuses and long-term income is a substantial portion of total earnings) would be more appropriate for the high technology unit.

As a general principle, the more independent and dissimilar the business units, the more appropriate custom-made executive packages would be.   As noted earlier, Pitts (1974) found that the criteria used to evaluate executive performance and pay form varies according to the autonomy of business units.   Executives in semiautonomous business units are evaluated on both division and corporate performance with a combination of objective and subjective criteria. Thus, the design of their pay package and appraisal criteria levels over-lap somewhat with that of corporate executives and among themselves. The consistency across executives in terms of pay-package designs and payoff criteria is greater for related-product business units because these are so interdependent that it is difficult to isolate the unique performance contribution of each division.

While greater division autonomy and tailor-made CEO pay packages should go hand in hand from a contingency perspective, this also raises an interesting dilemma for evolu-tionary type corporations (See Chapter 4.) In an attempt to reduce information processing for "naive" corporate executives, evolutionary type corporations may be inclined to displace more subjective strategic controls for tight financial outcome controls as the number of un-related divisions increases. (See Baysinger and Hoskisson, 1989; Bettis and Hall, 1983; Haspeslagh, 1982; Hill and Hoskisson, 1987.)

As a final note, the reader is cautioned that executive compensation *level* can be dra-matically different across divisions, regardless of autonomy status (depending on such fac-tors as number of employees, total budget, etc.). However, the design of the pay package (e.g., bonuses, stock options, degree of risk, etc.) and evaluation criteria (e.g., EPS, ROE) can be more or less uniform across these units as a function of their interdependence. In other words, executive pay level may be orthogonal to pay composition and performance appraisal criteria. For example, an executive in "Unit X" may receive five times the in-come of his/her counterpart in "Unit Y." However, the relative proportion of salary, bo-nuses, stock options, etc. in the total pay package and the evaluation criteria may be identi-cal for both. Issues pertaining to pay mix and pay level are covered later in this chapter.

Tax Rules

Firm-specific strategic factors vs. tax and legal concerns play a large role in executive compensation. Unquestionably, tax rates can make a major difference on an individual's take-home pay, particularly at higher income levels. Thus, tax rates must be taken into ac-count when designing executive pay packages. Tax reduction, however, should not become an overwhelming goal. Tax regulations and accounting standards are constantly changing. Therefore, a corporation that immediately reacts to changes in tax codes might find itself in a quandary just around the corner when additional changes are enacted. Unfortunately, consultants and tax accountants are heavily relied on as experts by most boards, and these individuals are often obsessed with "getting the most for the executive buck" with the IRS. Jamison, in an interview for Compensation and Benefits Review, noted that many corpora-tions view tax minimization in executive pay as an overriding force, not just as a technical issue. (See Levine, 1988.) The empirical research reviewed earlier by Hite and Long (1982), Posner (1987), and others suggest that tax concerns indeed loom large in executive pay decisions.

Rather than making radical revisions to the executive compensation plan in reaction to every piece of IRS ruling, the firm's strategic objectives should come first. Tax legisla-tion should be a secondary concern. It is probable that a firm's executive compensation plan will be completely out of line with its strategic business needs if it is too responsive to tax changes. Each executive pay component has strategic implications to the firm, regard-less of its tax properties. These will be reviewed later in this chapter. For example, stock options with holding restrictions may be provided in an effort to make the executive feel as though he/she has a personal vested interest in the organization's long-term success. (See

Ferracone, 1990.)   This same level of commitment may not be elicited by giving the executive a higher salary, in lieu of stock options, even if this may be justified, given a lowering of marginal tax rates and higher capital gains taxes in the 1986 Tax Reform Act.   The limited evidence to date suggests that the composition of executive pay makes a difference in terms of managerial decisions, giving more weight to these arguments.   Bhagat et al., (1985) found that equity ownership directly affects the behavior of top executives more than lower level employees, suggesting that how the executive package is designed may have a positive or negative effect on shareholder wealth.   Larcker (1983) found that adoption of "performance unit" plans for executives (a combination of stocks and accounting-based reward programs) promote long-term capital investment.   Hoskisson, Hitt, and Hill (1990) report that an emphasis on long-term incentives tends to have a positive effect on R&D intensity.

In short, sensitivity to accounting and tax rulings is important, but the motivational effect of changes in pay mix in response to those regulations should weigh heavily when amending the CEO compensation package.

DESIGNING THE EXECUTIVE COMPENSATION PACKAGE

A crucial issue raised at several points in this book is the pay mix of the compensation package, or the relative importance of different items in total pay received by the incumbent.   In the broadest sense, pay mix can be analyzed in terms of a fixed component (salary and benefits) and a variable dimension (bonuses and long-term income), as discussed under the fixed pay vs. incentives strategic compensation dimension in Chapter 2.   Each of these will be discussed separately as it applies to top executives.

Base Salary

Base pay for executives is estimated to range between 40 and 80 percent of the total compensation package, although how this is figured is a subject of controversy in itself (Crystal, 1990; Kerr and Bettis, 1987).   Salary surveys are normally used to identify the going market rate in the industry for firms of similar size.   These surveys show that salaries vary dramatically by industry.   For example, in 1991, the average base salary for hospital chief executive officers was $103,000, compared to $492,000 for CEOs of large, independent banks (*CompFlash*, 1991).   Moreover, at the top executive level the "within industry" range in market rates can be huge.   For example, among high technology firms, a *Business Week* survey (1990b) showed that J. Sculley, CEO of Apple Computer (sales of 5,372 millions) earned almost three times as much as J. Akers, CEO of giant IBM (sales of 62,710 million, almost 12 times larger than Apple Computer).   Similarly,   D. T. Kearns, CEO of Xerox (sales of 16,806 millions) earned 25 percent less than J.L. Ellison, CEO of Oracle Systems (sales of 769 millions),   even though the latter firm is almost 22 times smaller than Xerox.   These pay disparities cannot be explained by differences in either shareholder returns or profitability measures for these companies.

Base pay remains fairly stable over time and has minimal downside risk to the executive.   All things considered, a heavy reliance on base salary in the pay mix may be dysfunctional because it is not easily adaptable to such contingencies as changes in organizational objectives and market conditions.   Since salary adjustments are made each year and an annuity will be received for all remaining years of employment, executives may be tempted to

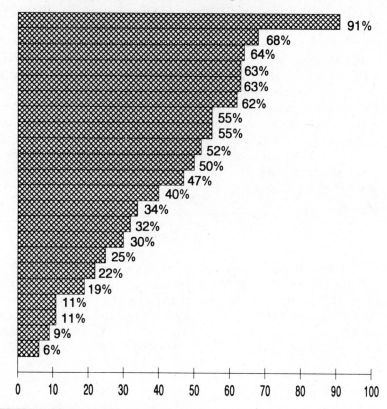

Percent of Firms Offering Perk

Perks

Perk	
Physical Exam	91%
Company Car	68%
Financial Counseling	64%
Company Plane	63%
Income Tax Preparation	63%
First-Class Air Travel	62%
Country Club Membership	55%
Luncheon-Club Membership	55%
Estate Planning	52%
Personal Liability Insurance	50%
Spouse Travel	47%
Chauffer Service	40%
Airline VIP-Club Membership	34%
Reserved Parking	32%
Executive Dining Room	30%
Home Security System	25%
Communications Equipment	22%
Health-Club Membership	19%
WATS Line (for home)	11%
Financial Seminars	11%
Subsidized Loans	9%
Legal Counseling (Personal)	6%

FIGURE 7-3   Most Common Perks Received by U.S. Top Executives (1990)*

*Based on data reported in *Wall Street Journal Reports* (April 18, 1990, p. R30). Data source for survey came from Hewitt Associates (1990).

engage in activities that improve the short-run performance of the firm at the expense of long-term objectives. Furthermore, because base pay is generally taken for granted by the executive, it has less motivational value.

Benefits

In the 1990s, the amount of dollars spent on benefits and perquisites for executives is staggering for many firms. (See Figure 7-3.) These include a variety of items such as membership in health clubs, luncheon and dinner clubs, use of private jets, vacation packages, golden parachutes, etc. From a strategic perspective, many of these benefits may be difficult to justify. They are provided to the executive as a condition of employment, but they are seldom contingent on the achievement of strategic objectives. They are also an easy target of criticism by those who feel that executives earn more than they deserve. For example, it may be quite difficult for a person on the street to understand why almost one-half of larger firms pay for spouse travel when an executive earns over seven figures a year. (See Figure 7-3.)

Finally, as of the time of this writing, many of these benefits are being questioned under the nondiscrimination rules of the Tax Reform Act of 1986. Application of the nondiscrimination rules would result in executives being taxed for benefits not provided to all employees (Toppel, 1987). It is clear, however, that extensive benefit discrimination is still practiced by U.S. firms in the 1990s. According to Hewitt Associates (see *Wall Street Journal Reports*, 1990), for the executive perks shown in Figure 7-3, the proportion of employees eligible is almost infinitesimal, and only one perk covers more than five percent of employees (i.e., for physical exams, with 6.5 percent of employees eligible on average).

Bonuses

Bonuses are short-term incentives linked to specific annual goals. At least in theory and since it is variable in nature, the bonus carries more risk to the executive than base salary. The actual degree of risk depends on the criteria that must be met to receive the bonus, and these vary widely. (See Table 7-1 for bonus formulas used by several large com-

TABLE 7-1
CEO Bonus Formulas of Selected Large Corporations (1990)*

	Bonus Criteria	Bonus Percentage
Aluminum Co. of America	Total cash dividends	15%
Ashland Oil	After-tax net income	6%
Boeing Co.	Before-tax net income	6%
Bristol-Myers	Choice of after- or before-tax net income	Lesser of 6% (before-tax) or 8% (after-tax)
DuPont	After-tax net income and stockholder's equity	20% of net income exceeding 6% of stockholder's equity
Goodyear Tire & Rubber	After-tax net income, book value	10% of net income exceeding book value of outstanding capital stock
ITT Corp.	After-tax net income and stockholder's equity	12% of net income exceeding 6% of stockholder's equity
International Paper	After-tax net income and stockholder's equity	8% of net income exceeding 6% of stockholder's equity
Rockwell International	Before-tax net income	Sliding scale based on net income: 2% first 100 million; 3% next 50 million; 4% next 25 million; 5% of balance
Unocal Corp.	After-tax net income	3% of net income exceeding 6% of stockholder's equity

*Based on data reported in *Wall Street Journal Reports* (April 18, 1990, p. 32).

panies in 1990.)   Performance indicators that are often used as a base for bonus payoffs include earnings per share, dividends, sales, return on equity, and net profit.   In addition, bonuses can be made contingent upon achieving concrete, qualitative goals such as obtaining a large government contract.

Clearly, executive bonuses are widely used in industry.   The Commerce Clearing House (1988) found that over 90 percent of American firms use year-end bonuses to reward executives.   In some industries, such as pharmaceutical, the use of executive bonus plans reached 100 percent.   According to Towers Perrin, CEOs receive an average of 59 percent of base salary in the form of annual bonuses. (See Compensation and Benefits Review, 1988.)

While executive bonuses are extremely popular, they should be used with caution.   As the bonus component approaches two-thirds of a typical executive's annual salary, one can safely assume that it will have a powerful effect on this individual's behavior.   Its strategic implications are obvious because executives are likely to maximize whatever criteria are used to trigger the bonuses.   To the extent that meeting the set criteria may involve neglect of other crucial performance dimensions (e.g., customer relations, investment in plant and equipment) or focus the executive's attention on short-term results, the firm may be getting negative returns on its bonus dollars.   While Rappaport (1978) blamed the executive annual bonus system, which emphasizes immediate gratification, as the culprit for many of America's economic ills it is interesting to note that its use has continued to increase at an accelerated rate (Compensation and Benefits Review, 1988).

Furthermore, many of these bonus programs may constitute salary supplements that the CEO expects to get regardless of firm performance changes.   Some recent data from ECS, a Wyatt Data Services Company (1992), suggests that this is not uncommon.   While 90 percent of 1300 companies surveyed offer some sort of executive bonus plan, 76.9 percent actually granted awards to the CEO during one of the most severe economic downturns in U.S. history (1991-1992).

Long-Term Incentive Plans

As noted earlier, *long-term incentives* are extremely complex with a wide variety of plans available.   In the most general sense, these plans can be divided into two major groups: those that make the executive part owner in the firm and those that combine cash with equity-based compensation.   Table 7-2 outlines the major types of long-term income programs under each of those categories.   For additional details on each of those plans, the reader may refer to Ellig (1984), Gomez-Mejia and Welbourne (1989), Cook and Co. Inc. (1989), Bennett (1990), Hyman (1991), and Todd (1991).

Because strategy is innately long-term oriented, rather than focused on tactical short-term considerations, there is perhaps no other compensation program where organizational and pay strategies come closer together than the so-called long-term income plans.   No one can blame executives for maximizing personal gains under the plan, but experience shows that well-intentioned formulas often have disastrous long-term effects.   A few examples will illustrate this point.

If growth in market share is used as criterion for providing stocks to the executive in a performance share plan, then the incumbent may be tempted to pursue an aggressive merger and acquisition program, even if this may not be in the best interests of shareholders.   If stock options are granted based on profitability ratios, executives may be tempted to cut back on long-term investments.   If no restrictions are imposed on when stock can be

TABLE 7-2
Most Commonly Used Long-Term Incentive Plans

Stock-Based Programs

Stock Options. These programs allow the executive to acquire a predetermined amount of company stock within a stipulated time period (which may be as long as 10 years) at a favorable set price.

Stock Purchase Plans. These plans provide a very narrow time window (usually a month or two) during which the executive can elect to purchase the stocks. The cost to the executive can be either less than or equal to fair market value. These stock purchase plans are commonly available to all employees within the firm.

Restricted Stock. These plans provide the exeuctive with a stock grant requiring little, if any, personal investment. In return, however, the executive is required to remain with the firm for a minimum length of time (e.g., 4 years); otherwise any rights to the stock are forfeited.

Stock Awards. These plans provide the executive with "free" company stock, normally with no strings attached. They are often used as a one-time-only "sign on" bonus for recruitment purposes.

Formula-Based Stock. This stock is provided to the executive either as a grant or at a stipulated price. Unlike other stock-based programs, however, the value of the stock to the executive when he/she wishes to redeem it is not its market price, but one calculated on a predetermined formula that normally uses book value (i.e. assets minus liabilities divided by the number of outstanding shares) as a criterion for payment. These plans are used when the board believes that the market price of an organization's stock is affected by many variables outside the control of the top management team.

Junior Stock. The value of junior stock is set at a lower price than common stock, so that the executive is required to spend less cash upfront to acquire it. Unlike common stock, the owners of junior stock have limited voting and dividend rights. However, junior stocks can be converted to common stock upon achievement of specific performance goals.

Combination of Cash Awards and Stocks

Stock Appreciation Rights (SARs). These plans provide the executive with the right to cash or stocks equal to the difference between the value of the share of the stock at the time of the grant and the value of that same stock when it is exercised. The executive is rewarded for the increased value of the stock, although no stock was actually granted by the firm. No investment on the executive's part is required. SARs may be offered alone or mixed with stock options.

Performance Plan Units. Under this plan, the value of each share is tied to a measure of financial performance such as earnings per share (EPS). So, for example, for every 5 percent increase in EPS, the firm may provide $1,000 per unit share owned by the executive. Therefore, if EPS increases by 15 percent, the executive will receive $3,000 for each share owned. The payment may be made in the form of cash or common stocks.

Performance Share Plans. These programs offer the executive a number of stocks based on profitability figures using a predetermined formula. The actual compensation per share depends on the market price per share at the end of the performance or award period.

Phantom Stock. These plans pay executives a bonus proportional to the change in prices of company stocks, rather than changes in profitability measures. A phantom stock is only a bookkeeping entry because the executive does not receive any stock per se. The executive is awarded a number of shares of phantom stocks in order to track the cash reward that will be received upon attaining the performance objectives. Award may be equal to the appreciation or the value of the share of phantom stock.

exercised, the executive may experience windfall gains by unloading the stock when the general equity market is up. Provision of restricted stock purchases at a significant discount (which has become quite popular lately) may lead to "the nearest thing in the executive suite to union featherbedding" (Crystal, 1990, p. 96).

A number of strategic concerns should be addressed when designing long-term income plans. The key strategic questions that should be asked are summarized in Table 7-3. First, the time frame for payoffs must be carefully thought out and based on the firm's idiosyncratic needs, rather than on trying to "keep up with the Joneses." For instance, in a high technology, fast-growth firm, three years may be considered long-term. In a mature service company, long-term may mean ten to fifteen years. A second important issue is whether executive tenure should be included as criterion for payment. If longer tenure is desired, length of service should be explicitly built in the formulas for dispensing and/or exercising stock options. This may be the case, for example, in a firm that is trying to establish stable leadership after a period of rapid succession in the top management ranks.

A third important policy choice is whether the plan is contributory. For recruitment purposes, outright stock grants make sense as a "sign on" bonus, but sharing the cost of the stock with the firm may be more appropriate for present incumbents. A fourth policy choice is whether benefits under the plan are pegged to profitability measures or are purely a function of market prices. If the company stock is highly volatile and its ups and downs may have little to do with the executive's performance, it may be appropriate to use profitability (which is more under the executive's control) as a partial criterion for payment.

A fifth, important issue in designing long-term income plans is whether mechanisms are established to prevent windfalls. This could be quite relevant, for example, when there is a "bull" stock market, as was the case throughout most of the 1980s vis-a-vis the 1970s when stock prices remained very flat. Thus, a firm may wish to place a limitation as to when stock options can be redeemed. The company may also develop indices that filter from the executive's earnings general movements in the stock market. Several financial formulas are available to compute "abnormal returns on stocks," which are designed to accomplish precisely that (e.g., Coughlan and Schmidt, 1985). Sixth, the frequency of awards can vary. Stock purchase plans, for example, allow the executive to acquire stock at any time,

TABLE 7-3
Key Strategic Pay Policy Questions in the Design of Executive Long-Term Income Programs

1. How long should the time horizon be for dispensing rewards?

2. Should length of service be considered in determining the amount of the award?

3. Should the executive be asked to share part of the costs and, therefore, increase his/her personal risk?

4. What criteria should be used to trigger the award?

5. Should there be a limit on how much executives can earn or a formula to prevent large unexpected gains?

6. How often should the awards be provided?

7. How easy should it be for the executive to convert the award into actual cash?

but stock awards are normally provided on a lump-sum basis. If continuous reinforcement is desired, the stock purchase plans make more sense. Finally, an important consideration is the extent to which the plan offers the executive high liquidity. The value of common stock is determined by the marketplace, and it can be traded in the open market. In a sense, its value is similar to that of cash in that the executive can negotiate with the stocks outside of the organization. On the other hand, plans such as formula-based stock or phantom stock consist of "paper money" that can only be redeemed within the organization. Items that are more liquid give the executive a greater sense of financial freedom, but stocks whose value is determined within the organization give the firm more leverage in retaining the executive and pegging the award to desired objectives.

In summary, the pay mix communicates what the organization values, and it signals to the executive the type of performance that is desired and rewarded. From a strategic perspective, it is essential that designers of executive compensation programs ask themselves what type of behavior is most likely to be expected based on the set of rewards being proposed.

CONCLUSION

Executive pay is perhaps the most crucial strategic factor at the organization's disposal. It can be used to direct managerial decisions and indirectly channel the behavior of subordinates. Because most organizations follow a pyramidal structure, whatever is rewarded at the top is likely to have a multiplier effect throughout all segments of the business. Also, because of top management's control of organizational resources and their largely unencumbered decision-making power in terms of strategic choices for the firm, mechanisms used to reward executives are likely to have an enormous effect on the company's future.

As seen in Chapter 6, there is no simple model to understand executive pay, and research results can be bewildering even to those who specialize in this area. Practitioners also face a wide menu of choices when designing executive pay packages. What this all comes down to is: Many judgment calls must be made, and prescriptive statements are of little value (or perhaps counterproductive) when executive pay is being set. However, decisions made are more likely to produce desired results if these are based on an informed consensus of all the key stakeholders involved in the process, e.g., compensation committee, board of directors, major stockholders. This chapter has fleshed several of the important issues that should be attended to in those deliberations.

COMPENSATION STRATEGIES FOR BOUNDARY SPANNERS AND FIRM PERFORMANCE: THE CASE OF SALES

LINKING SALES AS A BOUNDARY SPANNING FUNCTION TO COMPENSATION

STRATEGIC SALES COMPENSATION DIMENSIONS

THEORETICAL PERSPECTIVES
Contingency Theory
Product Life Cycle
SBU Strategies
Exchange Theory
Agency Theory
Resource Dependency Theory

DETERMINANTS OF SALES COMPENSATION STRATEGY AND ITS CONTRIBUTION TO FIRM PERFORMANCE
Business Strategy
Environment
Marketing Strategy
Product Characteristics
Market Prominence
Span of Control
Job Design
Management Values
Information System

RESEARCH PROPOSITIONS

STRATEGIC DESIGN OF SALES COMPENSATION PROGRAMS
Straight Salary
Advantages of Straight Salary
Disadvantages of Straight Salary
Straight Commission
Advantages of Straight Commission
Disadvantages of Straight Commission

Combination Plans
   Advantages of Combination Plans
   Disadvantages of Combination Plans

IMPLEMENTATION OF THE SALES COMPENSATION PLAN
   Communicating to the Sales Force
   Monitoring and Controlling the Plan

Considerable theoretical and empirical support exists in the strategic management and organization design literature for a strong, positive association between how well a firm conducts its *boundary spanning activities* and financial performance (Child, 1972; Hill and Jones, 1989; Lindsay and Rue, 1980; McCann and Gomez-Mejia, 1988, 1992; Montanari, Morgan, and Bracker, 1990).   Boundary spanning activities link the organization with its external environment. Theoretical arguments generally stress the importance of activities that enable the organization to anticipate events within its relevant environment, which, in turn, facilitate adaptive responses by management.   Critical relationships with external organizations such as customers, suppliers, and regulatory agencies are, for example, managed through boundary spanning activities (Dowling and Ruefli, 1992).   Inappropriate or slow responses to environmental events can mean lost sales or poorly timed investment decisions.   Thus, how individuals in charge of boundary spanning activities are managed is likely to have a direct impact on firm performance.

Adams (1976, p. 1,176) noted that boundary spanning positions differ from others in three important respects:

> First, the occupant of such a position—named here the boundary role person—is more distant, psychologically, organizationally, and often physically, from other members of his organization than they are from each other, and he is closer to the external environment and to the agents of outside organizations; second, he represents his organization to the external environment; and third, he is his organization's agent of influence over the external environment.

Newman (1989) and Newman and Huselid (1992) made a cogent argument that employees requiring special compensation programs are those who predominantly, if not exclusively, are responsible for boundary spanning activities.   Next to top executives (see Chapters 6 and 7), the most common boundary spanning role in organizations pertains to the sales force charged with the disposal of firm output and the acquisition of financial resources (Katz and Kahn, 1966; McCann and Gomez-Mejia, 1988).

Because of its unique and pivotal boundary spanning status, this chapter focuses on the strategic design of sales compensation programs.   First, it examines why sales compensation is a crucial concern for most private sector organizations.   Second, it identifies the most important strategic sales compensation dimensions.   Next, key theories that help elucidate the relationship between sales compensation and firm performance are examined.   The theoretical discussion lays the foundations of a conceptual model of the determinants of sales compensation strategy.   The significance of each determinant of the sales compensation plan is provided, leading to a set of 21 propositions.   The chapter concludes with a discussion of design and implementation issues.

LINKING SALES AS A BOUNDARY SPANNING
FUNCTION TO COMPENSATION

Because the sales force is responsible for bringing revenues into the firm by influencing the customer to buy the product, the compensation of the sales professional has a strategic impact. The sales compensation plan has a direct bearing on such strategic objectives as sales volume, market share, product mix, new accounts, and the introduction of new products (Ellig, 1982; White, 1977). An inappropriate sales compensation plan may focus the attention of the sales force on the wrong goals. For example, a sales compensation plan may be designed so that profits are inadvertently sacrificed for additional revenue, which may result in a failure to meet strategic organizational objectives.

There are several factors that explain why the design of the sales compensation plan is critically important from a boundary spanning perspective:

1. Like executives, sales professionals are responsible for bringing critical financial resources into the organization.
2. The sales compensation plan is closely linked to the marketing strategy.
3. The job of the sales professional has become increasingly complex.
4. The sales compensation plan is much more technical and complicated than compensation plans for other employees.

Like executives but unlike most other groups, the sales force face a direct, strong, explicit connection between behavioral outcomes and the incentive properties of the reward system. Each of these factors is discussed in turn.

As noted earlier, sales professionals, along with executives, represent a strategic employee group. They control the outcomes (i.e., revenue generation) that are critical to the performance of the organization. The compensation of these employees becomes a key management decision. The executive compensation plan (as discussed in Chapter 7) is developed by a committee drawn from the board of directors. Derived from marketing strategy, the sales compensation plan is typically developed by the marketing department. Other employee groups such as clerical and production employees have their compensation plans drawn by the human resource management department. Nonstrategic groups are paid differently because they are not perceived as making a critical contribution to revenues or profits as sales professionals and executives are perceived to make. It is no wonder that sales and executive compensation plans are usually separated from the compensation policies that affect other employees. Sales and executive pay plans are tailor-made by consultants and top level decision makers, which indicates the importance organizations place on these reward policies.

The sales compensation plan is an inextricable part of marketing strategy. Sales compensation can be used to stimulate increased sales, control the activities of the sales force, and improve customer relations (Coletti and Cichelli, 1991; Stanton and Buskirk, 1987). It can evoke and reinforce different behaviors and outcomes of the sales force through the utilization of various types of performance-contingent rewards such as salary, commissions, and bonuses. As each firm's marketing strategy is idiosyncratic (even within the same industry), so is its sales compensation plan unique. Further, in many companies, marketing strategies change frequently due to modifications in the product mix and movement through successive stages in the product life cycle. Therefore, sales compensation plans should be adjusted periodically to support new marketing plans. A close linkage between incentive mechanisms for the sales force and marketing strategy is likely to play a vital role in the firm's financial success because:

> Marketing is a major link with the firm's environment, especially customers, and is usually given the primary responsibility for generating revenue. Strategic decisions often revolve around markets and products, and the marketing department usually takes the lead in moving into new markets. Thus, the development of marketing objectives, strategies, and plans is critical to the implementation of the organization's overall strategy (Montanari, Morgan, and Bracker, 1990, p. 178).

As organizations rely more heavily on their sales force to implement their marketing strategies, the job of the sales professional has recently become more complex. In earlier years, the sales force may have been able to focus narrowly on sales volume as its goal. However, today's complex marketing strategies require sales professionals to pursue many different objectives. A sales professional may be asked by senior management to meet a sales quota based on dollar volume, meet a sales quota in the mix of products, sell more of the most profitable products, develop new accounts, control the expenses that go into each sale, provide excellent customer service to existing accounts, do missionary work such as building displays for retailers or attending trade shows and socializing with customers, and help train new members of the sales force (Colletti, 1986). The sales compensation plan must be fine-tuned to motivate the sales force to perform the appropriate mix of selling and nonselling tasks. A flawed sales compensation plan may be interpreted by the sales force as a signal to ignore some tasks (such as the missionary work) since there may be no reward for doing them.

Because of the wide variation in performance between members of the sales force, the sales compensation plan is more technical and complicated than plans for other employee groups (Schultz, 1987). For example, the spread in pay between the highest and lowest performing professional (such as an accountant or engineer) in a pay grade ranges from 10 to 20 percent (Hanson, 1987). It is not unusual for the variation in pay between the highest and lowest performing sales professional to be 50 percent or more. In some industries such as insurance and securities, the top performing salesperson earns over 100 percent more than a peer. The wide variation in performance and rewards that occurs in the typical sales position is probably unmatched by any other job in the organization.

STRATEGIC SALES COMPENSATION DIMENSIONS

Two key strategic compensation choices among those discussed in Chapter 2 are most important in the development of the sales compensation strategy. These are: (1) pay level and (2) pay mix, or fixed pay vs. incentives. Unlike strategic compensation patterns for the entire organization (see Chapters 2-5), pay level and pay mix act independently for the sales force. They dwarf other strategic pay choices such as egalitarianism and centralization because sales force employees operate largely in isolation from the rest of the firm and have much autonomy.

Pay level concerns the total earnings a sales position may generate. This includes base salary, benefits, and pay incentives. *Pay mix* consists of the relative proportion of the forms of compensation that comprise the total earnings of a salesperson. While pay level reflects industry compensation patterns, pay mix is firm-specific and a function of the marketing goals of the organization. Competing firms would have perhaps similar pay level policies (i.e., to "meet the competition") but different pay mix choices, since each firm's marketing strategy is idiosyncratic.

The two sections that follow examine first the theories and then the determinants of the sales compensation strategy. Since each pay mix choice is unique, more attention is focused on its development.

THEORETICAL PERSPECTIVES

Several different theoretical perspectives are examined next for some insights into the determinants of sales compensation strategy. These perspectives are: (1) contingency theory, (2) exchange theory, (3) agency theory, and (4) resource dependency theory. All of these, except exchange theory, have already been introduced in earlier chapters.

Contingency Theory

As discussed in Chapter 5, the central tenet of *contingency theory*, as applied to compensation, is that congruency or fit between pay strategies, organizational strategies, and firm characteristics has a beneficial effect on firm performance. A similar relationship is expected in the case of sales compensation. Because sales compensation is almost always designed at the SBU level for diversified firms, the ensuing discussion focuses on the linkages between the SBU product life cycle, SBU business strategies, and pay strategies for the sales force. The logic used here applies equally to single-product firms since, in these organizations, the firm and the SBU are one and the same.

Product Life Cycle. In Chapters 2-4 how the product life cycle is linked to the SBU's overall compensation strategy was discussed. Not surprisingly, the product life cycle is directly related to the sales compensation strategy (Balkin and Gomez-Mejia, 1987a; Canning and Berry, 1982). As the stage in the product life cycle changes, the degree of risk in the seller-buyer interaction changes. The pay mix policy must be adjusted to provide appropriate rewards for the higher or lower amount of risk experienced by the sales force in meeting its objectives.

As Table 8-1 indicates, the degree of risk that the sales force must accept varies with the stage in the product life cycle. If the sales compensation strategy is to be aligned with the goals of the business, the pay mix ratio—proportion of pay that is fixed compared to variable pay—should vary in relation to the degree of risk. Table 8-1 provides a hypothetical pay mix ratio that is a function of the stage of the product life cycle.

The introduction stage of the product life cycle is associated with the greatest amount of risk. The sales force must focus on acquiring new accounts in undeveloped sales territories. The product is new and untried, customers must be persuaded to buy it, and customer resistance should be anticipated. Because the degree of risk is substantial for the sales representative, there should be high upside and high downside potential earnings. Since cash flow and profits are often negative at the introduction stage, the sales force will re-

TABLE 8-1
Product Life Cycle and Sales Compensation Strategy

| | Product Life Cycle Stage | | | |
	Introduction	Growth	Maturity	Decline
Business Strategy	Increase Market Share	Increase Market Share and Profits	Profits and Maintain Market Share	Profits and Withdraw from Some Markets
Marketing Strategy	New Accounts	New Accounts and Customer Loyalty	Strengthen Customer Loyalty	Phase Out Marginal Accounts
Type of Control	Behavioral	Outcomes	Combination of Behavioral and Outcomes Measures	Behavioral
Measure	Sales Volume	Sales Volume and Product Mix	Product Mix	Product Mix and Sales Volume
Pay Mix Ratio (Fixed/Variable)	20:80	40:60 to 60:40	80:20	60:40
Degree of Risk	High	Moderate	Low	Moderate
Upside Potential for Earnings	High	High	Moderate	Low
Downside Potential for Earnings	High	Moderate	Low	Moderate

ceive low salary and benefits, which allows the firm to save scarce cash. There is an explicit emphasis on pay incentives to reward the high producers.

The growth stage of the product life cycle is associated with moderate levels of risk for the sales representative. At this stage, the firm is trying to both increase market share and generate profits. The sales force must develop new accounts as well as service and satisfy existing accounts. Depending on the rate of growth, the pay mix ratio should vary (e.g., from 40:60 to 60:40), as indicated in Table 8-1.

At the maturity stage of the product life cycle, the sales force experiences a low degree of risk. The firm is focusing on profits and maintaining its market share against the competition. The sales force is expected to provide service to existing customers and ensure their loyalty. The sales representatives may perform mainly order taking from repeat customers at this stage. A large portion of total earnings are fixed (salary and benefits) to recognize the nonselling activities provided to the customer by the sales force.

Finally, at the decline stage of the product life cycle, the sales professionals experience a moderate level of risk. In a declining market, marginal accounts may be phased out, resulting in lower earnings for the sales representative. Unprofitable product lines may be withdrawn from the market. The sales professional may be expected to replace the lost accounts with new accounts that are willing to buy a product with a better profit margin. More pay of the sales representative is put "at risk" in the decline, rather than maturity, stage because of the greater uncertainty in the market.

SBU Strategies.   SBU strategic patterns (see Chapter 3) are expected to be related to both the observed sales compensation strategies and the contribution of those strategies to firm performance.   As can be seen in Table 8-2, marketing strategy, which is derived from the SBU business strategy, is hypothesized to have a direct effect on the sales compensation system.   Furthermore, a significant deviation from the ideal sales force pay profile for each SBU strategic pattern is likely to produce lower firm performance. (See Chapter 5.)

The authors propose the following characteristics of the sales compensation strategy will make a greater contribution to performance among defenders and SBUs with a rationalization/maintenance strategy.   These are SBUs concerned with protecting market share and strengthening customer loyalty.

1.   Behavioral, rather than outcome, based types of controls.
2.   Product mix, rather than sales volume, measures.
3.   A high proportion of fixed compensation vis-a-vis variable pay.
4.   Low degree of risk.
5.   Low upside and downside potential for earnings.

These pay policies are more likely to induce the sales force to "cultivate" and nurture existing customers by diligently servicing current accounts.

At the other extreme, if characterized by the following factors, the sales compensation strategy will make a greater contribution to firm performance among prospectors and SBUs with a dynamic growth strategy.   These are SBUs primarily concerned with increasing market share and creating new accounts.

1.   Outcome, rather than behavioral, types of controls.
2.   Sales volume, rather than product mix, measures.
3.   An emphasis on variable, rather than fixed, compensation.
4.   High degree of risk.
5.   High upside and downside potential for earnings.

These pay policies are more likely to activate aggressive "hunting" behaviors on the part of the sales force, inducing them to concentrate on securing new buyers for the firm's products or services.

For SBUs following an analyzer strategy (where the main objectives are to expand both market share and profits and to emphasize both the creation of new accounts and nurturing of customer loyalty), a mixed compensation strategy would make the greatest contribution to firm performance.   Such a mixed pay strategy is characterized by:

1.   Reliance on both behavioral and outcome control type measures.
2.   Use of both sales volume and product mix performance indicators.
3.   Approximately equal emphasis on fixed and variable pay.
4.   Moderate degree of risk.
5.   Moderate upside and downside potential for earnings.

Such a combined pay strategy will enable analyzers to induce the sales force to tend to existing customers and to search actively for new buyers.

TABLE 8-2
SBU Strategic Patterns and Sales Compensation Strategy

	SBU Strategic Patterns				
	Miles and Snow			Gerstein and Reisman	
	Defenders	Prospectors	Analyzers	Dynamic Growth	Rationalization/ Maintenance
Business Strategy	Profits and Protect Market Share	Expand Market Share	Expand Market Share and Profits	Expand Market Share	Profits and Protect Market Share
Marketing Strategy	Strengthen Customer Loyalty	New Accounts	New Accounts and Customer Loyalty	New Accounts	Strengthen Customer Loyalty
Type of Control	Behavioral	Outcomes	Combination of Behavioral and Outcome Measures	Outcomes	Behaviioral
Measures	Product Mix	Sales Volume	Sales Volume and Product Mix	Sales Volume	Product Mix
Pay Mix Ratio (Fixed/Variable)	80:20	20:80	40:60 to 60:40	20:80	80:20
Degree of Risk	Low	High	Moderate	High	Low
Upside Potential for Earnings	Low	High	Moderate	High	Low
Downside Potential for Earnings	Low	High	Moderate	High	Low

Exchange Theory

Exchange theory views markets as places where exchanges take place between buyers and sellers. This theoretical formulation examines the exchange relationship over time and predicts whether transactions will continue or end (Bagozzi, 1975). Both the buyer and seller must believe they are receiving a net benefit out of the relationship or a transaction will not take place (Day and Wensley, 1983).

Exchange theory suggests that the seller and buyer examine the costs and benefits of their exchange relationship in order to determine whether goods will be exchanged for cash. Attention is focused on the seller since this is the role of the sales professionals. The seller examines the costs of the relationship, which include the inputs of time, effort, skill and product knowledge, and opportunity of foregone exchanges with other potential buyers. Next, the seller examines the benefits of the relationship, which include the attainment of organizational and personal goals. The attainment of organizational goals is instrumental in providing monetary rewards (in the form of salary, commissions, or bonuses) to the sales representative. Exchange theory predicts the benefits (i.e., the sales compensation) must be attractive enough to the seller so that he or she is willing to provide the inputs of time, effort, and skill to influence the buyer to make the purchase of the product.

Exchange theory also suggests that the benefits and costs should be at or close to equilibrium. If the benefits greatly exceed the costs, the seller has a windfall sale and receives too much compensation with respect to the cost of making the transaction. As the amount of seller inputs or costs change over time to make a transaction, the benefits in the form of sales compensation must be adjusted up or down so that equilibrium is attained. Equilibrium is attained when just enough monetary incentive is provided to the sales representative to make the sale to the customer. In this way, the organization seeks to optimize its ability to sell the product through the sales force at minimal selling costs.

Two key factors have significant impacts on seller inputs to make transactions. When the inputs change (such as product knowledge or amount of effort), the sales compensation plan should be adjusted to maintain equilibrium. The key factors are the type of product and the prominence of the product in the market.

The *type of product* will determine how much product knowledge the sales representative needs to sell the product to the customer. For example, the sales representative needs more product knowledge of a computer than of a vacuum cleaner to make the sale. Thus, the type of product affects the product knowledge, which ultimately impacts the sales compensation plan.

The prominence of the product in the market affects the buyer's perception of the product. *Market prominence* is a function of the resources provided by the company to influence potential buyers to have favorable attitudes toward the product. A company may spend resources on advertising and promotion so that the buyer is more aware of the product. A product that is well-known to the customer through advertising may be easier to sell. Thus, the sales representative may have to put forth less effort to sell a product that is highly advertised and promoted than one that is unknown to the customer. Since a product with low prominence will be more difficult to sell than one that is highly prominent, the sales compensation plan should be affected by the market prominence of the product (Schultz, 1987).

Agency Theory

Agency theory also provides some insights as to how the form of compensation may be used to channel the sales force behaviors so that these are aligned with organizational goals. The specifics of agency theory have been examined in other parts of this book. (See Chapters 1 and 6.)   Therefore, applying agency theory directly to the sales compensation strategy is discussed next.

The sales professional may spend a large portion of his/her time in the sales territory.   This makes it difficult for the principal (management) to monitor the agent's (sales professional) activities. When selling is an important part of the job, the cost of gathering information on the sales representative's behavior is high. The principal finds it more efficient to measure the performance of the sales force based on outcomes, rather than on monitoring behaviors (Eisenhardt, 1988).

The compensation plan is a contract intended to align the interests of the principal with those of the agent. The sales professional is rewarded based on outcomes, which can be measured efficiently. Therefore, the sales representative receives performance-contingent pay in the form of commissions or a bonus. The greater the cost to the principal of monitoring the behavior of the sales force, the more an emphasis on variable pay (in the form of bonuses or commissions) will make a contribution to firm performance.

The span of control in the sales organization determines how closely the sales manager supervises the sales representatives, their subordinates. A low span of control indicates the sales manager has few subordinates and can spend more time closely supervising each of them. A low span of control should be related to a high fixed portion of the pay package. A high span of control, on the other hand, should be related to a smaller portion of fixed pay (salary) and a larger portion of variable pay (commissions). A sales organization with a high span of control will have a large number of sales professionals reporting to each sales manager, and the amount of supervision provided to each sales representative will be minimal. Sales representatives in organizations with high spans of control can expect to receive a large portion of their earnings from commissions.

The job design of the sales professional will determine the degree to which the job content is programmable or nonprogrammable. *Programmable tasks* are well-defined and can be monitored with a degree of certainty by the sales manager. Examples of programmable tasks may include constructing a sales display, stocking shelves for a customer, or providing a sales demonstration at a trade show. A sales representative whose job content is programmable can expect a salary basis compensation. A sales representative whose tasks are nonprogrammable will work with a high degree of personal selling. Since it depends on many uncontrollable factors, the personnel selling task has a high degree of uncertainty. Further, since the buyer-seller interaction takes place outside the organization in the sales territory, it is not directly observable. A sales job that consists of a high degree of nonprogrammable tasks (i.e., personal selling) should be compensated with a large portion of expected earnings derived from commissions and other forms of variable pay.

Resource Dependency Theory

Resource dependency theory was developed to explain how organizations and individuals use power to obtain resources they need. (See Chapter 1.) An individual or organization that controls the resources others need has power over those individuals (Emerson, 1962). In organizations where not all tasks are equally critical to the survival of the firm, the division of labor leads to differences in power (Pfeffer, 1981). Critical jobs in an organization are those that provide vital resources used to fulfill the organization's primary strategic mission (Pfeffer and Salancik, 1978). Essential resources that may be controlled by incumbents in critical jobs include financial resources, special expertise, or information that enables the firm to deal with uncertainty.

Resource dependency theory predicts that individuals holding positions in critical jobs will receive higher earnings than those who work on noncritical jobs (Pfeffer and Davis-Blake, 1987; Welbourne and Gomez-Mejia, 1992). Since individuals in critical jobs control scarce resources, they can use their power to exert influence over the determination of pay decisions such as the pay mix policy. For instance, they can influence development of pay policies that offer them the greatest opportunities for earnings, given their preference for risk. The result should be a pay mix policy that has a significant fixed and variable pay component. Resource dependency theory predicts executives and sales professionals would have influence over pay policy that leads to opportunities for greater earnings than are possible with noncritical jobs.

When personal selling to the customer is an important part of the job and there is a lack of substitutes for the buyer-seller relationship available to the firm, the sales professional's job becomes more indispensable. Substitutes to the personal sales relationship include direct advertising, sales promotions, mail-order catalogues, or telemarketing. Resource dependency theory predicts that when the sales job consists of a high proportion of personal selling activities and the product has low prominence in the market, the sales job is critical to the firm in providing revenues (i.e., financial resources). The pay mix should have a significant variable pay component that has a high upside potential for earnings.

The sales representative's job is less critical when personal selling is a small part of the task, nonselling activities predominate the position, and there are substitutes for the sales force. Resource dependency theory predicts that when the sales job consists of nonselling activities and the product has high market prominence, the sales force is less strategic to the organization. Then, it should have less influence on pay policies, and top management would be less willing to share the revenues produced by the sales force under variable pay schemes such as commissions. Under these conditions, sales representatives should be remunerated on a salary pay plan similar to the way accountants and other less strategic jobs are compensated.

The preceding theoretical discussion identified some important determinants of the sales compensation strategy and its relative effectiveness. In the next section, a comprehensive model of sales compensation strategy is developed.

DETERMINANTS OF SALES COMPENSATION STRATEGY AND ITS CONTRIBUTION TO FIRM PERFORMANCE

Contingency, exchange, agency, and resource dependency theories suggest several determinants of the sales compensation strategy and its relative effectiveness. A model of the determinants of sales compensation is provided in Figure 8-1.

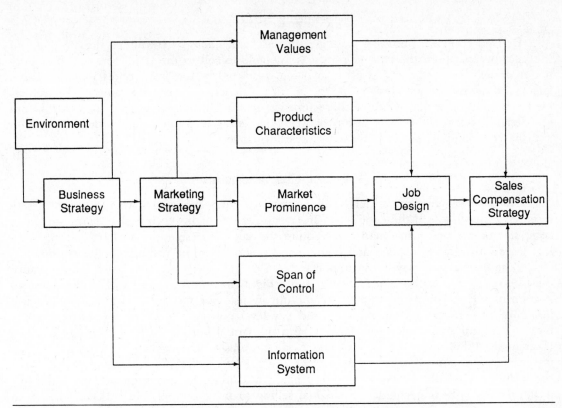

FIGURE 8-1 A Model of the Determinants of the Sales Compensation Strategy

Business Strategy

The *business strategy* determines the goals, objectives, and policies of the entire organization. All functional strategies such as marketing strategy should support the business strategy. A subset of the marketing strategy, sales compensation strategy should ultimately be derived from the business strategy. Otherwise, it is likely to be ineffective or even counterproductive. In fact, all the organizational variables identified in the model should originate with the business strategy.

Environment

Executives develop business strategies to respond to anticipated changes in the external environment. The *environment* consists of the market, technical, legal, and sociocultural contexts. The market context of the environment is most relevant to the sales compensation strategy. Pay level policy (examined earlier in this chapter) is partially determined by the dynamics of supply and demand in the labor market for sales professionals.

Marketing Strategy

Derived from the business strategy, the *marketing strategy* determines the structure of the sales organization, the type of products available to sell to the customer, and the product awareness the customer has prior to being contacted by the sales representative. These factors influence the job design, which, in turn, impacts the pay mix policy. Therefore, Figure 8-1 indicates that product characteristics, market prominence, span of control, and job design moderate the relationship between marketing and sales compensation strategies and the contributions of the latter to firm performance.

Product Characteristics

The *product characteristics* determine the amount of technical knowledge the sales representative needs to sell the product to the customer. A highly technical product such as a computer or medical instrument may require the sales representative to have an engineering degree in order to explain and recommend upgrades of the product to the customer.

Customer service may be an important part of the sales task. The sales representative must be responsive to the client's needs, and a highly technical product may require a small portion of selling compared to a large amount of customer service activities. This fact will influence the effectiveness of pay mix and pay level policies. A sales representative for a highly technical product line should receive a substantial portion of total earnings as salary (Freedman, 1986). On the other hand, a sales representative for a nontechnical product line such as vacuum cleaners or beauty products may receive most of the earnings from commissions and other forms of incentive pay. In a nontechnical selling situation, the majority of sales tasks may consist of personal selling to the customer. In this case, incentive pay is the most appropriate reward.

Market Prominence

Market prominence determines the degree of difficulty in selling the product to the customer and the importance of the selling task. Through advertising and market promotions such as free samples, a highly prominent product is well-known to the customer. Therefore, the sales force may not have to exert much effort to sell such a product. In fact, the sales representatives may behave more like order takers when market prominence is high. Commissions and other pay incentives may not be relevant in such a selling situation.

However, if the product has low market prominence, the sales force may be the only source of information to the customer. Personal selling is key when prominence is low, and pay incentives tied to sales are in order.

Span of Control

A high *span of control* indicates each sales manager supervises a large group of sales professionals. Since it is not feasible to monitor closely the behaviors of a large group of sales representatives in different territories, the supervisor is more likely to manage by results. The commission and bonus plans should be used as a form of control to motivate the sales representatives in their territories when they cannot be directly supervised.

A low span of control allows the sales manager to use more hands-on leadership styles with respect to sales representatives. The pay mix policy may be altered in this case. The organization may not need to rely as heavily on pay incentives to provide motivation to the sales force since more direct supervision is available.

Job Design

The *job design* of the sales professional has a direct impact on the pay mix policy and its effectiveness. When personal selling is a large and important part of the task, pay incentives should represent a substantial amount of the sales representative's total earnings. When nonselling activities are a highly important part of the sales job, most of a sales representative's earnings should come from salary. In addition, the more control the sales-person exerts over sales volume vis-a-vis other peers (e.g., where assigned territory makes little difference), the more likely the firm can effectively rely on incentives as control mecha-nisms.

The model in Figure 8-1 suggests that product characteristics, market prominence, and span of control influence the split between selling and nonselling tasks.

Management Values

Management values represent the philosophy and core beliefs, or the dominant logic, of top executives. As noted in Chapter 5, it is not uncommon for management values to influence pay strategies. In organizations where the top executives traditionally come from the marketing area, the pay level policy for sales jobs is likely to be at the high end of the market (the "lead" position in the market). The justification for providing higher salaries to sales force members is: The company markets products to the consumer and needs the best sales talent available to compete in its industry.

For instance, the CEO at Digital Equipment felt strongly that the sales force should be paid on a straight salary basis. Whereas the rest of the computer industry pays its sales force with a combination of salary and commissions, the Digital CEO believed paying the salespeople on straight, or lead market, salary would provide better customer service and improve the sales force's attitude as true professionals.

Information System

The *information system* keeps track of sales performance and sales compensation infor-mation. These data are used to evaluate the effectiveness of the sales compensation plan. Information is collected on trends of sales force revenues, trends of compensation costs, sales force turnover rates, travel and entertainment expenses, and other relevant measures. Used to examine the trends of sales force productivity with respect to compensation, this information allows adjustments in pay level and pay mix policy. Lack of an adequate infor-mation system means the firm must rely on behavioral, versus outcome, controls of the sales force.

RESEARCH PROPOSITIONS

The reader should note that, unlike executive pay, minimal empirical work on sales compensation has been conducted. With a handful of exceptions (e.g., Eisenhardt, 1988), the literature on the subject is largely prescriptive and practitioner-oriented. Research in the area appearing in academic journals is almost nil. The model presented here and previous theoretical discussion suggest a set of 21 propositions that may guide future empirical investigation on the relationship between sales compensation and firm performance.

- *Proposition 1.* Use of mixed performance indicators (combination of sales volume and product mix) to reward sales employees will make a greater contribution to firm performance at the maturity stage of the product life cycle and for SBUs following an analyzer strategy.
- *Proposition 2.* A pay strategy for the sales force emphasizing risk (high variable/fixed pay ratio and a high upside/downside earnings potential) will make a greater contribution to firm performance at the introduction and growth stages of the product life cycle and for SBUs following a prospector or dynamic growth strategy.
- *Proposition 3.* A pay strategy for the sales force emphasizing security (low variable/fixed pay ratio and a low to moderate upside/downside earnings potential) will make a greater contribution to firm performance at the maturity and decline stages of the product life cycle and for SBUs following a defender or a rationalization/maintenance strategy.
- *Proposition 4.* Behavioral measures of control for the sales force will make a greater contribution to firm performance at the maturity stage of the product life cycle, for SBUs following a defender or a rationalization/ maintenance strategy, and when reliable objective indicators are not easily available.
- *Proposition 5.* Outcome measures of control for the sales force will make a greater contribution to firm performance at the introduction and growth stages in the product life cycle, for SBUs following a prospector or dynamic growth strategy, and when reliable objective indicators are readily available.
- *Proposition 6.* Mixed control measures (i.e., behaviors and outcomes) will make a greater contribution to firm performance at the maturity stage in the product life cycle and for SBUs following an analyzer strategy.
- *Proposition 7.* Use of sales volume performance indicators to reward sales employees will make a greater contribution to firm performance at the introduction stage of the product life cycle and for SBUs following a prospector or dynamic growth strategy.
- *Proposition 8.* Use of product mix performance indicators to reward sales employees will make a greater contribution to firm performance at the maturity stage of the product life cycle and for SBUs following a defender or a rationalization/maintenance strategy.
- *Proposition 9.* A pay mix emphasizing variable compensation for sales employees will make a greater contribution to firm performance when the cost of direct monitoring is high.
- *Proposition 10.* A pay mix emphasizing fixed compensation (i.e. salary and benefits) for sales employees will make a greater contribution to firm performance where sales tasks are programmable.
- *Proposition 11.* A pay strategy emphasizing fixed compensation is more likely to be effective if the firm's primary marketing goal is to promote customer relations.
- *Proposition 12.* Variable pay as a proportion of the total pay mix will make a greater contribution to firm performance when used for sales representatives who sell a non-technical product.

- *Proposition 13.* Salary as a proportion of the total pay mix will make a greater contribution to firm performance when used for sales representatives who sell a technical product.
- *Proposition 14.* Variable pay as a proportion of the total pay mix will make a greater contribution to firm performance when used for sales representatives who sell a product with low market prominence.
- *Proposition 15.* Fixed compensation as a proportion of the total pay mix will make a greater contribution to firm performance when used for sales representatives who sell a product with high market prominence.
- *Proposition 16.* Variable pay as a proportion of the total pay mix will make a greater contribution to firm performance when used for sales representatives in sales organizations with a high span of control.
- *Proposition 17.* Fixed compensation as a proportion of the total pay mix will make a greater contribution to firm performance when used for sales representatives in sales organizations with a low span of control.
- *Proposition 18.* The more direct control a salesperson exerts over sales volume relative to other salespersons in the company, the more an incentive-based pay strategy will contribute to firm performance.
- *Proposition 19.* In organizations where the marketing function is part of the dominant coalition, compensation of the sales force will lead the market.
- *Proposition 20.* In organizations where the CEO originated from the marketing area, the pay level policy for sales jobs will be at the high end of the market.
- *Proposition 21.* An incentive-based reward strategy and outcome control mechanisms for the sales force will make a greater contribution to firm performance the better data is available on sales force productivity.

STRATEGIC DESIGN OF SALES COMPENSATION PROGRAMS

The pay mix choice enables management to select the most effective method of sales compensation plans. When the pay mix choice contains both fixed pay (salary) and variable pay (commission or bonus) components, the method of pay is a *combination plan.* The most recent data indicate that about 75 percent of firms use combination plans for rewarding their sales force (Stanton and Buskirk, 1987). This is substantially greater than the 51 percent of firms that used this method ten years earlier (Steinbrink, 1978).

When the variable component of the pay mix policy is zero, the method is called *straight salary.* When the fixed component of pay mix policy is zero, then all the earnings are derived from variable pay, and this method is called *straight commission.*

In the next section, the advantages and disadvantages of the straight-salary, straight-commission, and combination pay plans for sales professionals are examined. Specific situations that are most appropriate for each pay plan are discussed.

Straight Salary

Straight salary is most appropriate when the sales professional is primarily providing account servicing and missionary work and when increased sales is a secondary objective

(Moynahan, 1983; Steinbrink, 1978). The advantages and disadvantages of the straight-salary sales compensation plan are summarized in Table 8-3.

Advantages of Straight Salary. Straight salary provides each member of the sales force with a regular and secure income. With a stable income, the sales force is more loyal and committed, and turnover rates are lower. This could be an important factor when the firm invests heavily in training members of the sales force.

The straight-salary plan makes it easier to control and direct the activities of the sales force. Sales representatives are more willing to engage in nonselling activities such as providing customer service. Further, sales representatives offer little resistance to changes in their sales territories since this change will have no impact on their income. Better customer service may also be provided under the straight-salary plan because the sales representative is less hungry for the sale and is, therefore, less likely to use high pressure selling techniques that overstock the customer.

Finally, the straight-salary plan is attractive from an administrative standpoint. It is easily communicated to the sales representatives, and plan administration is simple. Members of the sales force are rewarded similarly to other professional employees in the firm, which may be important if sales representatives work as part of a team with other professionals.

Disadvantages of Straight Salary. A major weakness of the straight-salary plan is that it is difficult to induce the sales force to put extra effort into selling the product. Sales representatives may prefer to sell products that are easiest to sell to the customer. There are no pay incentives to recognize outstanding contributions to the sales objectives. This could be a drawback when selling activities are the dominant task performed by the sales force.

It may be difficult to retain the top sales performers under the straight-salary plan. These high producers may be lured to other firms that recognize their achievements with additional compensation. Similarly, it may be difficult for a firm to attract experienced and top-performing sales representatives with a pay plan that rewards them the same as other members of the sales force. Some hidden administrative costs may result because sales representatives may need closer supervision under the salary plan. This may result in the necessity of hiring more sales managers.

TABLE 8-3
Advantages and Disadvantages of Straight-Salary Sales Compensation Plan

Advantages	Disadvantages
• Secure income	• Low motivational impact
• Sales force willing to perform nonselling activities	• Difficult to attract or retain top sales performers
• Plan administration is simple	• More sales managers are needed to provide supervision
• Sales force less likely to overstock customers	• Sales representatives may focus on products that require least effort to sell
• Low resistance to changes in sales territories	
• Low employee turnover rates	
• Sales force treated as salaried professionals	

The above discussion suggests some situational contingencies where straight salary would be most effective.

1. A technical product requires a large amount of time and effort prior to the sale and a significant time period after the sale devoted to setting up and servicing the product.
2. The product is sold to the customer by a team of sales professionals. It may be difficult to separate the individual contributions of the team members.
3. The sales representatives are in training. Their product knowledge and selling skills are not yet up to speed, and they are not capable of generating much income from commissions.
4. The primary emphasis of the sales job is missionary work and account servicing.
5. The income potential from commissions varies greatly between sales territories, and management feels it is unfair to punish a sales representative with a low income by an assignment to an unattractive territory.

Straight Commission

The straight-commission method of sales compensation is most appropriate when the primary objective of the sales force is generating sales volume through new accounts. Under the straight-commission method of pay, the individual sales professional should have control over most of the factors that influence the customer to buy the product (Moynahan, 1983; Colletti, 1986). The advantages and disadvantages of the straight-commission plan are summarized in Table 8-4.

TABLE 8-4
Advantages and Disadvantages of Straight-Commission Sales Compensation Plan

Advantages	Disadvantages
• Effective in generating new accounts	• Sales volume emphasized over profits
• Sales force is highly motivated to sell the product	• Customer service may be neglected
• High performers have their contributions recognized with pay	• Sales representatives may overstock the customer
• Sales representatives become entrepreneurial and require minimal supervision	• Less economic security
• Selling costs are efficiently controlled	• Less direct control over sales force
• Plan administration is simple	• Top-performing sales representatives may outearn other employees, including executives
	• There may be resistance to changes in sales territories
	• Sales representatives may focus on products that require the least effort to sell

Advantages of Straight Commission. Since emphasis is placed on sales volume, the straight-commission plan can be effective in generating new accounts and sales revenues. The sales force has a strong inducement to sell the product since this method of pay provides almost unlimited opportunities to generate earnings. However, some firms place caps on the earnings of sales representatives to maintain some internal pay equity.

Since pay is directly tied to performance under straight commission, high performers are rewarded, and low performers may become discouraged and leave. Unit sales costs are directly proportional to sales volume, which is an efficient way to control selling costs.

The straight-commission plan encourages members of the sales force to become independent and entrepreneurial. Management may use straight commission to control the activities of the sales force. Since the sales representatives are paid by the results they produce, they require less supervision.

The straight-commission plan is easy to understand and administer. However, there may be time lags between closing the sale and receiving the payment for the account that generates the commission. This may result in some additional risk that is shared by the sales representative and the firm.

Disadvantages of Straight Commission. The drawback of the straight-commission plan is that it signals to the sales force that sales volume is the most important goal. Due to the emphasis on sales volume, customer service and profitability may be neglected. Some customers may get overstocked due to high pressure selling tactics used by sales representatives who seek high earnings from commissions.

The straight-commission plan offers less economic security than the salary plan. External factors may affect the earnings of the sales representatives. For example, a recession may lower customers' willingness to buy and may lead to lower earnings from commissions. On the other hand, an economic expansion may result in windfall earnings from commissions.

Another problem that occurs under a straight-commission plan is that management has less direct control over the sales force. It is more difficult to persuade sales representatives to change territories or expect them to sell products that require extra effort to sell to the customer.

The above discussion suggests several situations where the straight-commission plan could be most beneficial to a firm:

1. A start-up firm that plans to increase its market share rapidly through growth in sales revenues.
2. A firm that relies on a part-time sales force of independent contractors who engage in door-to-door selling. For example, beauty products, brushes, and encyclopedias are sometimes sold this way.
3. A firm that does not provide much field supervision and decides to use the commission to achieve desired sales outcomes.

Combination Plans

The straight-salary and straight-commission methods of sales compensation are two extremes that are currently used about 25 percent of the time. Most of the time, sales compensation consists of a combination plan that has a fixed pay and variable pay components.

The combination plan overcomes many of the weaknesses of the straight-salary and straight-commission methods of pay. There are three types of combination plans:

1. Salary plus commission.
2. Salary plus bonus.
3. Salary plus commission plus bonus.

The key issue in the design of the combination plan is to determine the relative proportions of fixed and variable pay. This issue was discussed earlier in the chapter. The advantages and disadvantages of the combination plan are summarized in Table 8-5.

Advantages of Combination Plans. The combination plan combines the advantages of straight commission and straight salary into one plan. Its great strength is that it can recognize with pay both selling and nonselling activities that are present in many sales positions. Sales representatives receive some economic security (with the salary component) and also have monetary incentives to sell the product (with the commission or bonus component). A greater variety of marketing goals can be supported by the combination plan.

Disadvantages of Combination Plans. The major weakness of combination plans is that they are more complicated and difficult to administer than the other two methods of sales compensation. More misunderstandings arise from sales representatives who are confused about how the plan is supposed to work.

The sales force is expected to work toward achieving a variety of goals under a payoff matrix that needs to be aligned properly with the marketing goals. The performance measures that result may be complicated and difficult to understand or implement. It may be necessary to monitor closely the plan and make frequent revisions to it. In some cases, sales representatives may receive unanticipated windfall earnings when both salary and incentive components are factored into total earnings. Changes in the plan design must be carefully thought out and communicated to the sales force, or else the changes may be negatively perceived by sales representatives as attempts to reduce their income.

TABLE 8-5
Advantages and Disadvantages of Combination-Sales Compensation Plan

Advantages	Disadvantages
• Incorporates advantages of straight-salary and straight-commission plans	• Plan is more complicated to design
• Recognizes both selling and nonselling activities with pay	• Sales force may become confused and try to accomplish too many objectives
• Can offer to sales representatives some economic security and monetary incentives	• Plan is more difficult and costly to administer
• Greater variety of marketing goals can be supported with plan	• Sales representatives may receive unanticipated windfall earnings

There are several situations that are conducive to the use of the combination plan:

1. The firm is producing products at any stage of the product life cycle, except the introductory stage.
2. The firm produces a wide variety of products with different profit margins for the sales force to sell to the customer.
3. The sales force is expected to perform a broad variety of tasks that includes significant amounts of both selling the product and providing customer service.

It is obvious that many sales positions in firms are represented by these three contingencies. This explains why the combination plan is the most widely used of the three methods of sales compensation.

IMPLEMENTATION OF THE SALES COMPENSATION PLAN

Once the appropriate method of sales compensation has been selected, it is necessary to implement the plan so that it achieves its objectives. Many well-designed pay-for-performance plans fail due to inadequate implementation. (See Chapter 9.) Recently, the trend has been selection of combination-plan methods of sales compensation. Since these plans are more complex, the need for proper administration of sales compensation is imperative.

In the section that follows, some of the key issues associated with sales compensation plan implementation are examined. This covers communicating the plan to the sales force and monitoring and controlling the plan.

Communicating to the Sales Force

In practice, the combination-sales compensation plans are complex and may easily be misunderstood by the sales professionals. For example, a combination plan may include the following elements:

1. A cash draw account against future sales commissions.
2. A progressive commission rate that increases at higher levels of sales volume.
3. A cap on annual sales earnings.
4. A cash bonus based on the number of new accounts.
5. A sales contest related to the sales volume of a new product line.

If the combination plan is not adequately explained to the sales representatives, the result may be lowered levels of motivation and increased turnover.

Since the sales compensation plan changes frequently as the marketing strategy changes, it is important to communicate these adjustments to the sales representatives. They need to understand and accept the changes in the rules of their pay plan if it is to influence positively their level of motivation. Communication methods that offer opportunities for feedback are required. Therefore, it is necessary to schedule group meetings that involve the sales managers and sales representatives. At these meetings, the new sales compensation plan should be explained in detail, along with information on why the changes to the old plan were made. If the sales force does not understand or accept the need for these changes, they may feel management is trying to reduce their income, which could adversely affect sales productivity.

Finally, the sales compensation plan should be published in a guidebook that explains in concise, clear language how the plan works. The guidebook can be a useful tool that clarifies any misunderstandings sales representatives have on their pay that may have been made at the group meeting or from talking to other members of the sales force.

Monitoring and Controlling the Plan

Management must monitor and control the sales compensation plan to ensure it is supporting the marketing goals. This involves developing accurate performance measures, providing an information system that tracks performance, implementing controls on sales compensation, and making periodic evaluations of the plan.

The sales compensation plan must have accurate performance measures that link sales performance to the marketing goals. This may require taking into account both quantity and quality of performance. For example, suppose one of the market goals that needs to be supported by the sales compensation plan is sales growth. Sales growth can be measured by using units sold, dollar value of invoices, or cash received (Nemerov, 1987). However, invoices may only capture the sales volume, whereas cash received may measure both the sales volume and quality of the accounts since some accounts may be poor credit risks.

An information system is needed to keep track of the performance measures so that sales representatives are rewarded according to their performance. It should have the capability to generate reports on sales productivity and provide information that management can use to evaluate the effectiveness of the sales compensation plan.

Some administrative controls may be necessary to implement successfully the sales compensation plan:

1. *Caps on earnings.* It may be required to limit the earnings of sales representatives who receive windfall compensation from sales not directly due to their own efforts. In addition, it may be company policy to maintain pay differentials between sales reprsentatives and sales managers.
2. *Timing of payment of incentives.* How often should commission and bonus payments be made? Should a commission be paid when an order is placed or after the cash is received? In general, the timing of the payment should be short enough to have an impact on performance but long enough so that the size of the payment is meaningful (Freedman, 1986).
3. *Split commissions.* Sometimes two or more individuals have influence over the sale of a product to the customer. Should one person receive credit for the sale, or should there be a split commission? A clear policy needs to be provided on split commissions, or else there may be a lack of cooperation between sales representatives, and this could impact the sales effort.

Management needs to make periodic evaluations of the sales compensation plan in order to measure its effectiveness. This involves utilizing the information system and tracking the productivity of individual sales representatives and the sales force as a whole. For example, management can track the ratio of direct sales compensation costs to total revenues (Nemerov, 1987). If this ratio declines over time, there is evidence that sales productivity is increasing. If the ratio remains constant or is increasing over time, management may need to make some adjustments to the sales compensation plan.

Part 3
HRM Subsystems

<table>
<tr><td>CHAPTER</td><td rowspan="2">PERFORMANCE-CONTINGENT PAY STRATEGIES AND FIRM PERFORMANCE</td></tr>
<tr><td>9</td></tr>
</table>

247

Chapters 2 through 5 in Part 1 discussed how overarching strategic compensation patterns relate to internal and external macro organizational factors and their interactive effect on firm performance. Chapters 6 through 8 in Part 2 dealt with unique problems and issues facing select strategic employee groups and the role played by specific strategic compensation dimensions most important to those groups. Part 3 of the book is concerned with the interface between compensation strategies and the HRM subsystem. This first chapter in Part 3 focuses on performance-contingent pay policies for individuals and groups within the firm.

PERFORMANCE-CONTINGENT PAY: PREMISES AND CONTROVERSIES

As noted in Chapter 5, much has been said about the motivational properties of money, and advocates on both sides of the issue are not difficult to find. However, the notion that rewards should be distributed in proportion to contribution may be considered a *received doctrine* in organizational life (Barrett, 1972). This refers to concepts and assumptions that are so deeply held that they are no longer—or were never—questioned. Dobbins, Cardy, and Carson (1991, p. 256) noted that "If the assumptions are correct, then received doctrines are valuable in that they allow research to proceed, and clear prescriptions for managerial behavior to be formed. The danger, of course, is that the assumptions are not correct, leading to the dual problem of misleading research and misguided management."

In light of this, one should ask the questions: What are the key assumptions underlying the "pay according to contribution" doctrine? Are these assumptions well-founded? In answer to the first question, there are three ingrained premises in most performance-contingent pay systems:

1. Individuals and groups differ significantly in their contribution to the organization, not just in terms of what they do but also how well they do it.
2. A substantial amount of variance in organizational performance can ultimately be attributed to the performance of individuals and groups within the firm.
3. In order to motivate its human resources and to achieve distributive justice, a firm must be able and willing to remunerate employees differentially according to their relative performance.

There is a vast amount of evidence in support of the first assumption (e.g., Lawler, 1989, 1990; Cardy and Dobbins, 1993; Cascio, 1992). Evidence is limited for the second premise; yet, it is generally supportive. (See Chapter 5.) The third assumption, however, is highly controversial among both academics and practitioners. The main points of contention are discussed next.

Single-Mindedness

Performance-contingent pay can be such a powerful motivator that it may induce individuals to develop a very narrow focus to accomplish whatever will trigger the reward and neglect other important components or dimensions of the job. In other words, the closer pay is linked to particular performance indicators, the more employees will focus their attention on those reward-producing outcomes. Likewise, superiors are tempted to use the convenience of objective performance indicators to justify pay decisions, avoiding "judgment calls" and the unpleasant task of explaining these to subordinates. In a sense, this gets them "off the hook" even if the available objective criteria may be seriously deficient. For instance, Gomez-Mejia and Balkin (1992) found that most department chairpersons and college deans rely exclusively on student ratings to evaluate teaching performance of faculty. Yet, over three-fourths of faculty surveyed agreed that this measure is more a reflection of popularity rather than knowledge gained, classroom performance, or course rigor.

Thus, one of the ironies with the use of pay as an incentive mechanism is that the greater the strength of the outcome-reward connection and the magnitude of the reward, the more design flaws become apparent and the greater the potential harm to the firm. Because it is nearly impossible to capture all important elements of a job (particularly at the professional and managerial ranks) on any number of performance indicators, there is always the danger that those intangible yet crucial aspects of work will suffer. A few examples will illustrate this point.

Several airlines in the late 1980s began to experience deteriorating customer relations and a large number of "no shows" after their sales representatives were paid based on the number of bookings. In a midwestern state, paying snowplow operators on a per-mile basis resulted in many roads packed with snow and ice because it was easier to cover more miles (and, therefore, get paid more) by disengaging the snow-removal equipment. In some academic departments, faculty avoid service "like a plague" because it is made clear that rewards (in terms of pay, promotion, and tenure) will be based strictly on publications in leading journals. As noted in Chapters 6 and 7, top executives are frequently accused of maximizing short-term gains (reflected in such indicators as EPS or ROI) to trigger larger annual bonuses at the expense of long-term performance.

Control

In most situations, employees involved do not control all the factors responsible for performance outcomes. Unless tasks are very simple (e.g., picking watermelons during a normal harvest season), a larger portion of performance variance is attributed to external events or contextual factors that individuals cannot affect directly. For instance (as noted in Chapter 6), probably less than one-fourth of the variance in firm performance can be directly attributed to executive decisions. This problem is just as significant at lower levels in the organization.

A vast amount of research by industrial psychologists (e.g., Grey and Kipnis 1976; Ilgen and Feldman, 1983; Landy and Farr, 1983; Liden and Mitchell, 1983; Yammarino, Dubinsky, and Hartley, 1987) confirms that the performance of individuals can be greatly affected by the performance of other employees in a work group. Similar arguments have recently been advanced by Edward Deming (1986a,b) and his followers (e.g., Aguayo, 1991; Gabor, 1991; Scholtes, 1987; Walton, 1991). For instance, Scholtes (1987, p. 6) notes that employees' performance is dependent on "capricious factors well beyond their ability to influence . . . using performance appraisal of any kind as a basis for reward of any kind is a flat-out catastrophic mistake." This suggests that the more pay is linked to performance of individuals whose work tasks are inextricably tied to those of others, the more "contaminated" the performance judgments—and, by implication, the more tenuous the performance-reward connection.

Measurement

Assessing employee performance is one of the most difficult and intractable problems management faces, particularly when the objective is to use these judgments to dispense rewards. In fact, a huge and ever growing literature in performance appraisal is exclusively devoted to these measurement issues (e.g., Bernardin and Pence, 1980; Cardy and Dobbins, 1986, 1993; Dugan, 1989; Grey and Kipnis, 1976; Hoffman, Natham, and Holden, 1991; Lord, 1985; Murphy and Cleveland, 1991; Soo, Sims, and Motowidlo, 1986; Tsui and Ohlott, 1988).

Unfortunately, results are conflicting and the primary conclusion one can draw from all this work is that performance measurement is a very treacherous endeavor, with no generally accepted system for doing so.   Robert Lord, a well-known authority in performance appraisal, noted that "accurate behavioral measurement is integral to the practice of applied psychology but it has proven to be an elusive objective" (Lord, 1985, p. 66).   McBriarty (1988, p. 421) adds that "Few areas of personnel management have received more attention than performance appraisal, and few have remained as shrouded in controversy and contradiction.   After ingesting even a small portion of the literature on the subject, one typically ends up with an acute case of mental indigestion."

Performance measurement problems are too many to be discussed in any detail within the scope of this book. (Note: For an extensive review of these issues, see edited volume by Milkovich, Wigdor, Broderick, and Mavor, 1991, published by the National Research Council.)   Some problems include:

1. Rating errors such as leniency, halo, and central tendency (e.g., Dobbins and Cardy, 1993; Gomez-Mejia, 1988, 1990).
2. Affective predispositions on the part of the evaluator, biasing performance judgments (e.g., Tsui and Barry, 1986; Zajonc, 1980).
3. Hedonic tendencies in the evaluation, referring to a natural inclination of superiors to avoid conflict and unpleasant encounters with subordinates by failing to report actual performance differences among them (Soo, Sims and Motowidlo, 1986).
4. Information framing, whereby prior experiences and expectations distort judgments of actual performance (Landy and Farr, 1980).
5. Ambiguous attributions of causality (Feldman, 1981; Mitchell and Liden, 1982; Wexley and Youtz, 1985).
6. Lack of adequate performance indicators (Ilgen and Favero, 1985).
7. Low correlations between subjective and objective assessments of performance (Alexander and Wilkins, 1982).
8. For political purposes, manipulation of performance data in an intentional and systematic manner (Longenecker, Sims, and Gioia, 1987).
9. Failure to take into account system-wide, contextual influences on performance (Dobbins, Cardy, and Carson, 1991; Gomez-Mejia and Balkin, 1980a,b; Gomez-Mejia, Hopp and Sommerstad, 1978; Gomez-Mejia and Page, 1983).

Although they tend to be more severe the more "micro" one gets, difficulties in measuring performance are present at all levels of analyses. At the most micro or employee level, the problems noted above are magnified because of the complexity involved in trying to untangle individual contributions from the work group and reliance on immediate supervisors whose judgments are often subject to bias. At the next level of aggregation—that is, teams—interdependencies across work units present unique difficulties in ascertaining the specific contributions of any given team. At the SBU level, one faces the problem of factoring out resource interdependencies across various units and their relationship to corporate headquarters. Finally, at the most macro or corporate level, numerous problems are faced in assessing performance using accounting conventions and/or abnormal stock return methodology. (See Chapters 6 and 7.)

Inflexibility

An issue discussed earlier in Chapters 4 and 5 has added significance in performance-contingent systems. It is difficult to change payoff formulas once they have been installed and employees get used to them. Resistance to change in performance-contingent pay systems results from multiple forces, including fear of the unknown, perceived threats to one's interests, skepticism that changes will produce more favorable outcomes, failure anxiety, and existence of powerful coalitions (perhaps even including a labor union) with a vested interest in preserving the status quo.

Cognitive models provide a conceptual explanation as to why pay-for-performance systems become entrenched (Reger, 1991). First, employees develop cognitive maps of the organization, and a crucial element of this map is the mechanisms used for reward allocation. These mechanisms create a fabric of beliefs about means-ends relationships (read behaviors-reward connections) that are learned based on past experience. Redrawing these learned, mental representations is difficult, and any attempts to do so may cause intense opposition.

The natural tendency is to do things as they were done in the past, and resistance to change may become a serious threat to strategic thinking in compensation. A particular performance-contingent system may have outlived its strategic value, may have become obsolete, or may even be counterproductive, given new conditions facing a firm. However, inertia and customary forces may keep it in place. For instance, heavy emphasis on sales volume as a performance criterion for executives and sales personnel may make sense for a small, growing organization trying to expand its market share. However, that same emphasis may foster mergers and acquisitions for larger firms, past the point where further growth occurs at the expense of efficiency and leads to a reduction in shareholder's wealth. (See Chapter 6.)

Governance and Credibility

Perhaps because of the measurement problems discussed earlier, a large proportion of employees do not see performance-contingent pay systems as fair and truly rewarding for contributions. This proportion can be as high as 75 percent of those working under pay-for-performance plans (Kanter, 1987). Acceptability by those affected is a crucial aspect of success for these programs if they are going to be seen as legitimate (Gomez-Mejia, Page, and Tornow, 1982). While the credibility gap tends to be more acute for individual-based plans (to be discussed shortly), it can also be present with other programs. For instance, if it is much easier for one unit than another to receive incentive payments, this is likely to create intense conflict and resentment and perhaps lead to disruptions in internal work flows.

(See Coombs and Gomez-Mejia, 1991.) It is not uncommon for such plans to penalize units that have traditionally been better performers because it will be tougher for those units to show the same degree of improvement as their counterparts, which started out at a lower performance threshold.

The Whole Does Not Equal the Sum of the Parts:
The Problem of Local Rationality

While linking pay to productivity may be conducive to greater individual and unit performance, it does not necessarily follow that the performance of the entire organization will improve. This is because organizational performance does not result from the simple additive function of the performance of its individual members and units. Rather, it derives from a complex, synergistic interrelation of all its component parts. Thus, performance-contingent pay plans may, in fact, improve the performance of a firm's constituent parts yet have dysfunctional consequences for the entire organization.

The reason for this paradox is that each unit is bounded by its own local rationality. Thus, linking rewards to the achievement of each unit's objective (and individuals within it) may exacerbate a natural tendency toward parochialism and a disregard for superordinate goals and organizational interdependence. This is an important issue at all organizational levels, but the lower the unit of performance analysis, the more significant the problem of local rationality becomes.

For individuals, there is the danger of becoming so focused on "What is in it for me?" and personal goals that cooperation with others may suffer. One often finds this situation in academic departments. The emphasis on research to distribute rewards (pay, promotion, tenure) fosters a disdain of committee activities that are an integral part of university governance. It may also neglect students who, ultimately, are primary customers of these institutions.

At the team level, each group may become so cohesive and enthusiastic about its own sphere that it gives rise to dysfunctional rivalries and intergroup battles over real or imaginary conflict of interest issues. One of the authors was able to observe this process in a large organization whose personnel department was evaluated (and rewarded) according to the number of affirmative action hires. This created much conflict with line managers who felt that Personnel was encroaching upon their hiring discretion and who argued that they were being penalized for the amount of time required to train new recruits. Another example is that of the classical conflict between marketing groups (rewards based on sales) and manufacturing (rewards based on production schedules and cost control). (See John and Rue, 1991.) At the business unit level, linking of rewards to SBU performance may produce a situation where flow of resources and knowledge is impeded because each unit is eagerly trying to accomplish its own agenda.

In short, an inherent danger with performance-contingent pay systems is that they may act as a centrifugal force in organizations and pull each segment from the common good. While aggregate incentive systems are less susceptible to this problem (because performance is assessed at a higher unit of analysis, such as plant or corporate level), they do have the disadvantage (as is seen next) that the line of sight between behavior and reward is very weak.

Line of Sight

At the opposite end of the local rationality problem, rewards become more powerful in energizing behavior the lower the unit of analysis used to measure performance. This is because employees can see how their efforts translate into reward-producing outcomes. Thus, one faces the proverbial horns of the dilemma in trying to emphasize behavior-contingent rewards (which magnify the problem of local rationality) vis-a-vis aggregate performance-contingent programs (which block the line of sight between individual contributions and rewards).

Tradeoffs between Employee Performance and Satisfaction

Another irony of performance-contingent pay systems is that "they may lead to greater productivity but lower satisfaction" (Schwab, 1974, p. 197). In his classical work, Whyte (1949) noted that incentive systems frequently disrupt the social fabric in organizations and lead to employee unhappiness. They also produce unwelcome tension in the work force.

Perhaps this may help explain why, despite lip service to the contrary, most organizations shy away from performance-contingent pay programs. Supervisors view rising tension and stress as problems to be avoided. Top-level managers may be reluctant to implement and enforce performance-contingent programs for fear of retribution, concerted action, and unionization. At a gut level, managers are concerned that these programs may foster a social dynamic within the firm that could eventually lead to higher costs in the form of wasted energies, attrition, lawsuits, strife, and poor external relations.

Translating Performance Expectations from Stakeholder Groups

In classical and neoclassical economic theories, the goal of the firm is to maximize profits. More recent conceptualizations portray top managers as catalysts responsible for translating the often conflicting demands of stakeholder groups into organizational goals and the implementation of complex mechanisms to handle these multiple demands.

When the task environment is less ambiguous and the demands of stakeholder groups are well-defined, relatively stable, and compatible, performance-contingent plans are easier to design and install. For instance, in a closely held corporation whose owners are interested in fast growth, the manager's task is simplified by linking rewards to activities that promote further growth. But if a firm faces stakeholders whose demands are vague, inconsistent over time, and perhaps incompatible with each other, administrators will have a difficult time in translating those demands into performance objectives to be used as basis for reward distribution.

Such is the case, for instance, in public sector jurisdictions, universities, and many large corporations that are the target of multiple pressure groups who exert substantial influence. These often operate at cross-currents. For example, a Fortune 500 firm must often balance the demands of shareholders pressing for more dividends, community leaders interested in preserving jobs, environmental groups advocating ecological concerns, etc. Universities are often confronted with a classical conflict of satisfying the academic community's interest in research and the need of local citizens who demand better quality instruction in the form of extensive student-faculty interaction and smaller classes.

Reactance

According to agency theory (as discussed in earlier chapters), incentive systems play an integral control function in organizations, particularly when direct supervision (monitoring) is difficult. This feature of incentive systems, however, may be associated with employees' resentment for losing control over their lives. In other words, employees may feel that the incentive system takes away their freedom of action.

Brehn and Cole (1966) refer to this perceived threat to personal autonomy as *reactance*, which provokes anger at the organization. One consequence may be an increase in dissatisfaction leading to turnover and concerted actions among employees. A more subtle consequence is that employees may be socialized to do whatever it takes to obtain the reward and no more. This may be dysfunctional in that (as noted earlier) important yet intangible aspects of work may not get done, and expectations about the reward system may become too rigid to change.

Reduction of Intrinsic Drives

Financial incentives may become so potent that an individual's intrinsic drives are dominated by extrinsic demands. Expanding upon earlier theories by Likert (1961), White (1959), De Charms (1968), Argyris (1957), McGregor (1960), Maslow (1970), and other organizational humanists, Deci (1975) argues that, first, the most effective form of motivation is that which individuals derive from the job itself and the satisfaction felt for doing a job well, and, second, performance-contingent pay is done at the expense of that natural drive to self-actualize. In Deci's words:

> When behavior is intrinsically motivated, the perceived locus of causality is said to be internal. This simply means that people perceive the cause of a certain behavior to be their own intrinsic need. When they perceive the cause of the behavior to be intrinsic, they will engage in the activity for intrinsic rewards. However, when they receive extrinsic rewards, their perceived focus of causality becomes external and they do the behaviors only if they believe that the extrinsic rewards will be forthcoming (1975, p. 140).

This type of indictment against the use of pay to direct human behavior is nothing new and has been around since the beginning of recorded history in one form or another (e.g., Plato's *Republic*). Yet, it continues to have a profound effect in organizational development, organizational behavior, and human resource management. While this position has more currency among academics, it also has its adherents among practitioners and consultants. Its policy implication is: Performance-contingent pay may be pushed to the point where individuals lose all interest in exploration, innovation, search for challenges, and enjoyment of work activities outside those prescribed by the incentive system.

CENTRAL THESIS OF THIS CHAPTER

The problems discussed above indicate that performance-contingent pay policies may be treacherous, and that the deliberate use of pay as a mechanism to channel individual and group behaviors can inadvertently produce the opposite results of what was intended.

The central thesis of this chapter is that performance-contingent pay policies are an indispensable management tool to enhance organizational performance. However, three important conditions must be met for the success of those policies. These are discussed next.

Pay and Performance Must Be Loosely Coupled

There are very few situations where a tight fit between performance and rewards is justified. The tighter the coupling, the more likely the problems discussed above are magnified. As performance yardsticks are explicitly identified—and these are used to distribute rewards—single-mindedness and local rationality are reinforced; measurement difficulties are compounded (because unrealistic precision may be required); inflexibility is institutionalized; equity issues mushroom due to logistical problems in developing formulas fair to diverse groups; and individuals are encouraged to avoid activities with intangible benefits but excluded from the performance contract.

Therefore, attempts to use performance-contingent pay in a purely mechanistic fashion is almost certainly doomed to failure. Unfortunately, particularly at the aggregate level, administrators may feel pressured to come up with formula-based approaches. Management must resist the temptation to succumb to those pressures, which at times appear to be the most rational thing to do, yet eventually lead to problems after expectations are cemented and programs are difficult to change. As seen later, this is one of the main maladies affecting gainsharing and profit-sharing plans.

It is Necessary to Nurture the Belief that Performance Makes a Difference

While survey after survey shows that few employees believe pay and performance are closely linked, almost everybody thinks they should be (Hills, Scott, Markham, and Vest, 1987). Any attempt to institutionalize systematically a nonperformance-based pay system for fear of the problems discussed above will be almost certain to produce even lower performance levels. In other words, support for the null hypothesis that performance-contingent pay policies seldom work as intended does not imply support for the alternate hypothesis that performance should not be an integral part of pay decisions. Thus, in spite of theoretical and operational problems with performance-contingent pay systems, they may be a lesser evil.

Linking pay to other criteria (e.g., seniority, test scores) removes its normative, symbolic force on individuals. This creates a low-achievement organizational culture with a dampening effect on overall productivity and encourages the best performers to move elsewhere. As an analogy, evidence of inequality is not difficult to find in American society. Yet, if the "all men are created equal" myth were not deeply held as a fundamental value, social and racial inequalities would almost certainly be greater. Likewise, many surveys have suggested that marital infidelity is rampant (up to 75 percent by some accounts), but if marital commitment was to be widely viewed as an anachronism, family life is likely to suffer even more. As a third example, even though a small proportion of major crimes are ever solved, dismantling the criminal justice system is almost certain to increase the crime rate because all potential deterrence is eliminated. The above examples make the point that just like in society at large, there may be a wide gulf between actual values held and observed practices within a firm. However, the normative force of those values can still maintain the system within more acceptable parameters than would otherwise be the case. Thus, the fact that a strong performance-reward norm exists in a firm is likely to enhance performance if, for no other reason, performance would be lower in the absence of such norms.

Unfortunately, very limited empirical research has been conducted to date on the myth-forming function of performance-contingent pay in organizations. Most investigators focus on technical issues of how performance should be measured (most notably individual appraisals) and procedures for linking those measures to rewards. They ignore its normative aspects.

Performance-Contingent Pay Systems Must Be Customized to Each Firm's Unique Situation

Following one of the major conceptual thrusts of this book, the design and mix of performance-based pay programs should vary according to contingency factors internal and external to the firm. As will be seen shortly, there is an extensive menu of pay-for-performance systems, and each of them is more likely to be successful in some conditions than others. For instance, a tighter coupling between pay and specific behavioral outcomes (e.g., piece-rate system) is more likely to produce favorable results in more mechanistic organizations whose technology is relatively unchanging and mature defender type firms whose environment is relatively more stable. The opposite would be true in organic type firms with a prospector strategy because performance criteria and factors impacting that performance are more volatile in nature. In other words, too tight of a coupling between performance outcomes and rewards is difficult to justify in most cases. However, in a relative sense, a closer fit between the two makes more sense at the mechanistic, defender end of the spectrum.

In summary, the relative contributions of a performance-contingent pay system to firm performance are likely to increase as the plan features are molded to internal and external idiosyncrasies facing the organization. Such programs can be classified into four major types, according to level of performance analysis and payoff criteria: individual plans, team-based programs, efficiency-based plans, and overall firm performance-based programs. The theoretical justification for each of these operational systems, potential drawbacks, and conditions under which they are most likely to contribute to firm performance will be discussed next.

INDIVIDUAL-BASED PERFORMANCE-CONTINGENT PAY PLANS

As the title implies, these programs are designed to provide monetary rewards to individual employees and require identification of their own personal contributions. The theoretical bases for these programs are well-developed in the psychological literature, and most compensation texts devote a substantial amount of attention to these.

Theoretical Framework

A brief description of the three major theories underlying individual-based plans (equity, expectancy, and goal theory) follows:

Equity Theory. As noted in Chapter 1, equity theory has played a predominant role in traditional compensation thinking and practice. To recap, its basic tenet is that an individual's motivation is affected by how he/she perceives the ratio of inputs (i.e., work performance) to outcomes (i.e., rewards) relative to referent others. Consequently, from a motivational perspective, the organization must provide rewards that are proportionate to individual inputs. Because work performance is the most important contribution to the organization, it then follows that pay should be distributed accordingly. If inequities are perceived, then one would predict that high performers will either leave the organization (because of dissatisfaction brought about from "cognitive dissonance") or reduce their performance level to make it congruent with the outcomes received. (See Adams, 1965.)

Expectancy Theory. Expectancy theory has its ultimate roots in the "law of effect" (Thorndike, 1910), which states that behaviors that are rewarded will be repeated. Also, Tolman (1932) and Lewin (1938) argue that individuals develop cognitive anticipations about the outcomes associated with various activities and assign a subjective (negative or positive) value to those consequences. An individual's motivation to engage in a particular act results from some combination of these sets of variables. Other things equal, the higher the expectancy for a particular outcome by engaging in certain behaviors and the more valuable the outcome is to the individual, the more likely the employee will be motivated to act accordingly.

More recent interpretations of expectancy theory were articulated in the 1960s and early 1970s in the writings of Vroom (1964), Porter and Lawler (1968), Lawler (1971), Mitchell and Biglan, (1971), and Dachler and Mobley (1973). Its specific application to pay-for-performance systems is as follows: If we are to assume that money is an important (i.e., it has high "valence") reward (i.e., outcome) to most people, then in conditions under which there is a high performance-outcome contingency, one would expect individual behaviors conducive to better performance. In the words of Schwab and Dyer (1973):

> With respect to compensation systems, expectancy theory hypothesizes that the effectiveness of such systems in motivating employee performance is simultaneously dependent upon the valence of pay, the instrumentality of performance for the attainment of pay, and expectancies about the relationship between effort and performance.

Thus, from a practical perspective, this means that in order to motivate employees to increase their level of effort or change their behavior in a desired direction (e.g., pay more attention to detail), it is necessary to link pay to those consequences (Lawler, 1971). By repeated association, as predicted by the law of effect (Thorndike, 1910), employees will learn to pair desired behaviors with valued rewards, and this anticipation (expectancy) will evoke more of this behavior in the future.

Goal Theory. The central postulate of goal theory is quite simple, and good managers have probably followed it since the beginning of time: Financial incentives will not have much of an effect on performance, unless individuals have a clear sense of what is expected of them (Locke, 1968; Locke, Bryan, and Kendall, 1968; Tolman, 1932). In other words, an individual's behavior is goal-directed, and people's devotion to certain activities depends on the degree to which achievement of goals resulting from those activities produce desired outcomes. Therefore, an individual's performance is expected to improve if clear standards and objectives are established and pay is made contingent on these being met.

Operational Plans

The two primary performance-contingent pay programs at the individual level consist of merit pay (see Cook, 1991; Gerhart and Milkovich, 1993; Heneman, 1990) and bonuses (see Wallace, 1990, 1991). Despite all the bad publicity it has received in recent years (e.g., Pearce, 1987; Smith, 1990), use of merit pay is almost universal (Balkin and Gomez-Mejia, 1987a; Gomez-Mejia and Balkin, 1989). It consists of an adjustment to base salary, as a percentage increase, typically done on an annual review cycle. Once dispensed, it becomes an annuity because it remains as part of the employee's salary, regardless of future performance, for the rest of his/her tenure with the firm. Bonus programs (sometimes called lump-sum bonuses), on the other hand, provide a financial incentive on a "one at a time" basis and do not raise the employee's base pay in perpetuity.

For either merit pay or bonuses, the decision criteria may include a form of goal-setting plan (such as management by objectives), supervisory appraisals, or achievement of certain milestones (most often used for bonuses such as devising a new method to cut down on production costs).

It should be noted in passing that the most extreme form of performance-contingent, individual-based pay program, is the traditional piece-rate incentive system, whereby employees are paid per unit of output. However, this approach has been steadily falling in disfavor since the early 1950s, and relatively few firms in the manufacturing sector rely on it for hourly workers. Besides the difficulty of establishing production standards, particularly when technology is rapidly changing, Sherman and Bohlander (1992, p. 351) blame the demise of piecework to the fact that:

> Employees, especially those belonging to unions, have held negative attitudes toward piecework plans. Some union leaders have feared that management will use piecework or similar systems to try to speed up production, getting more work from employees for the same amount of money. Another fear is that the system may induce employees to compete against one another, thereby taking jobs away from workers who are shown to be less productive. There is also the belief that the system will cause some employees to lose their jobs as productivity increases or cause craft standards of workmanship to suffer.

Drawbacks

While each of the operational programs to reward individual performance has its own pros and cons (see Lawler, 1989, 1990), many of the pitfalls in performance-contingent plans reviewed earlier are exacerbated when an individual's pay and behavior are explicitly linked. These individual plans promote a narrow focus among employees. It is difficult to untangle an individual's contribution from that of the work group, and measurement difficulties in performance appraisal are rather intractable. There is also a lack of consensus about methodology, and equity issues become paramount the more sophistication is required of the system in making fine distinctions across individuals. In addition, there are some potential problems that are more unique to individual-based plans. These include:

1. *Credibility gap.* During the past 25 years, survey after survey indicate that a large number of employees (as high as 80 percent, according to Hills et al., 1987) do not see a connection between individual rewards and actual performance, particu-

larly for merit pay. This perception may be well-grounded in reality. Many non-performance factors enter into these decisions (see Mount, 1987; Schwab and Olson, 1988) such as position in the salary range, time since last increase, pay relationships within the unit or between units, and supervisor-subordinate pay relationships. Use of merit pay for market adjustments and reliance on market surveys based on the job as the unit of analysis, not work performance, intensify this problem.

2. *Erratic patterns over time.* Relative pay raises for individuals occupying the same position are often uncorrelated from one year to the next (Haire, Ghiselli, and Gordon, 1967; Pearce, Stevenson, and Perry, 1985). This means one of two things: Either employee performance is very unstable, which is hard to fathom, or that raises are not attributed to performance but reflect other variable criteria.

3. *Budgetary determinants.* Budgetary restrictions often determine how much and the extent to which pay raises will be distributed, and these restrictions may not be synchronized with achievements during the review period.

4. *Hierarchical orientation.* Because individual-based pay-for-performance systems engender dependence on supervisors, "they accept, indeed, build on and preserve the status and category distinctions already defined by the organization" (Kanter, 1987, p. 14).

5. *Easy to achieve goals.* Whenever MBO type systems are utilized, most people achieve their objectives. Thus, it is difficult to compare actual value of contributions across different individuals (McConkie, 1979). The explicit tying of money to goal achievement is likely to make this problem more severe because there is an incentive to "play it safe" and choose more modest goals than may otherwise be the case.

6. *Social disruption.* Many managers believe that below average raises are demoralizing to the individual, aggravate interpersonal relationships, and discourage better performance (Hughes, 1986).

7. *Balancing self-interest and common goals.* Some organizations may attempt to counterbalance the negative "zero sum" effects of merit pay by including factors such as teamwork and cooperation in performance appraisal systems that are the bases for merit pay decisions. While it is plausible for individual-based pay increases to reward cooperative behaviors, this may be difficult to implement. It is almost a universal practice to allocate a raise budget partitioned among a small group of employees (Lawler, 1989). Since individuals must share a fixed amount of money that has been allocated for raises or bonuses, "this clearly sets up a competition among them for the larger raises. This can be a serious problem if the organization needs them to cooperate in order to be effective" (Lawler, 1989, p. 217).

Conditions Favoring Individual-Based Performance-Contingent Plans

While the potential drawbacks of individual-based plans reviewed above may be serious, this should not be interpreted to mean that firms should abandon these programs. Rewards based on individual contributions can be highly motivating, more so than any aggregate performance-contingent pay plans. However, they should only be emphasized when conditions exist that minimize the pitfalls discussed earlier. Individual-based performance-contingent pay policies are most likely to be successful:

1. *The more the nature of the task allows for the isolation of contributions made by specific employees.* While there are very few cases where unambiguous performance attributions can be made, it is easier to do so in some jobs than others. For example, it is much easier to assess the quality and quantity of work of data-entry operators than it would be for scientists or engineers in R&D labs.

2. *The greater the degree of autonomy enjoyed by incumbents.* The more independent the work being performed, the more meaningful measures of individual contributions are likely to be. At one extreme, for example, field sales representatives operate almost in total isolation from each other. Thus, individual performance (typically measured in terms of sales volume) can be assessed on a one-to-one basis. At the other extreme, brainstorming or "focus groups" in advertising are composed of individuals whose task (i.e., to generate ideas for marketing products) are very intertwined (because ideas are freely bounced around within such groups). Therefore, trying to ascertain the value of individual contributions within the group may be quite difficult and probably indefensible.

3. *When close cooperation is not required for successful performance, or when competition is desired.* While one is hard-pressed to think of a work situation where no cooperation is needed, a wide range does exist across various jobs. For instance, the degree of cooperation required for successful performance as a professor is much lower than, let's say, a pilot in an air force squadron.

4. *The more the organizational culture emphasizes individual achievement.* Organizations vary widely in terms of status differentials, structure, and norms of behavior. For instance, the emphasis on group cohesiveness and a paternalistic attitude in many Japanese firms are well-documented, and this is reflected in the reward system (where pay for individual performance is generally a foreign concept; see Gomez-Mejia and Welbourne, 1991). Using the congruency argument (see Chapter 5), it seems reasonable to expect that an individual-based performance-contingent program would operate more smoothly and is more likely to contribute to a firm's performance if it is part of a culture that emphasizes personal achievement.

TEAM-BASED INCENTIVES

Team-based performance-contingent pay plans reward the relative contribution to the firm of groups of employees who have common goals and objectives, work closely with each other, and are dependent on each other for the team's outcome.

Theoretical Framework

Two separate theoretical streams are used to justify these programs.

Psychometric Theory. A large volume of work dealing with rating properties of supervisory appraisals suggest that while performance is commonly specified in individual terms, actual performance can be more accurately assessed by examining the performance of larger units within the firm (Landy and Farr, 1983; Yammarino, Dubinsky, and Hartley, 1987). Ilgen and Feldman (1983), Dobbins, Cardy, and Carson (1991), and others have convincingly argued that making comparative judgments is such an innate human predisposition that it is virtually impossible for a supervisor to evaluate an employee's performance without being influenced by the performance of other employees in the group.   Likewise, Liden and Mitchell (1983) report that the degree of interdependence within most work groups is so high that it is difficult to filter individual contributions.   More disturbingly, these investigators found that as interdependence increases, supervisors rate poor performers higher and rate good performers lower.   Thus, from a measurement perspective, this literature suggests that in most work situations, performance can be measured more accurately or reliably at the group level.

Theories of Social Cohesiveness.   Research based on social cohesiveness has its roots in social psychology.   Because most tasks are conducted by groups of complementary workers with diverse skills and backgrounds, teamwork and cooperation are necessary conditions to high performance outcomes in various organizational subunits.   Whenever the goals of separate employees are bound together so that an individual can attain his/her goals if, and only if, other participants can attain their goals, a cooperative social situation exists (Deutsch, 1949).   Therefore, a reward system will enhance performance only if it produces a situation where there is a positive correlation among the goal attaintment of group members.   Thus, each participant seeks an outcome that is beneficial to all those with whom he/she is cooperatively linked.

In related theoretical work derived from learning theory, Kelly and Thibault (1969) define a cooperative structure as one in which the individual's rewards are directly proportional to the quality of the work group.   For Kelly and Thibault, reward contingencies motivate group members to behave as a team or as individuals competing with each other.   By utilizing rewards that reinforce cooperation among team members, the performance of a given group (and, implicitly, firm performance by aggregating across various groups) will increase.   On the other hand, by focusing on individual outcomes, rather than group results, a reward system may undermine the social foundations needed to succeed in a cooperative setting.

Operational Plans

Team incentives can be distributed based either on a performance or a skills criteria (Welbourne and Gomez-Mejia, 1991).   A performance-based method is most common, whereby all team members receive a reward pegged to group outcomes.   These outcomes may be assessed objectively (e.g., based on cost savings, number of products manufactured, meeting agreed upon deadlines, rejects, completion of a new product design, obtaining a successful patent, etc.) or subjectively (e.g., based on the collective assessment of a panel of executives).   The goals, measurement criteria, and payment amount can be determined in advance and communicated to group members, or management may retain the flexibility to make those decisions on an ad hoc basis.   Payments can be made in cash, corporate stocks, or through noncash items such as trips, time off, or luxury items.   Cooperation with other teams might be an important criteria for payment.   Being able to work effectively in problem-solving assignments might also be used.   Typically, groups chosen as the unit of analysis to distribute rewards are self-contained and have relatively impermeable boundaries between them.   That is, intragroup interdependencies are much greater than intergroup interdependencies.

The second approach distributes pay to the group based on collective skills accumulated over time. It is seldom used in lieu of performance-based plans but in combination with them. Unlike individual skill-based pay (see Chapters 2 and 10), all team members are rewarded when the skills of the entire team, not just those of specific employees, improve. Rather than rewarding a particular employee for acquiring a new skill or learning a new job, the entire group might receive a reward when all team members are satisfactorily cross-trained, or the team's reward can be made dependent on its ability to bring each member up to speed. This system is intended to provide incentives for the most capable employees to help those who are not up to par or those who would like to improve their skills. It may also engender a more open, honest atmosphere because a poorly performing employee is likely to be quickly discovered and dealt with by other members of the group.

Drawbacks

While team-based incentives do have some advantages over individual-based performance-contingent plans (primarily in terms of fewer measurement problems and the fostering of cooperative behaviors), they also have their pitfalls. These are discussed below.

Free Riding Effect. A substantial body of literature is concerned with the so-called *free riding effect.* (See review by Albanese and VanFleet, 1985.) This refers to the benefits from the group effort accruing to individuals who provide low work inputs to the team yet receive the same rewards as other group members. If no controls are available, free riders are likely to have a negative influence on group productivity. It can also generate intragroup conflict, requiring supervisors to devote much energy to handling interpersonal conflicts.

Reduction in Performance Variance. Social pressures may inhibit the performance of top producers (i.e., rate busters) and/or induce them to leave. On the other hand, these same group pressures may spur the average or marginal performer to become more productive, which compensates the organization for the loss of a few superstars. Also, because the entire team is better off the higher the productivity of its best performers, group dynamics may actually encourage those individuals to maximize their potential.

Which of the above scenarios actually materializes is not always predictable and depends on the nature of the group, the quality of employee-management relations, and historical factors. For instance, workers are more inclined to limit output in firms with a history of "speedups" (increasing standards required to obtain reward) and layoffs (Gordon, Edwards, and Reich, 1982). "Group think" may be such that fear of terminations as a result of greater output and falling demand would induce cohesive teams to dampen productivity.

Incompatible Cultural Values. Although the concept of team-based incentives is growing in popularity in the United States, they are still foreign to the larger cultural milieu in which most employees have been raised. Hofstede (1980) reports that, based on a sample of 16,000 workers worldwide, the United States ranks number one in individualism. This means, an employee's ability to demonstrate personal deservingness to others is important as evidenced by the accumulation of rewards such as salary, company car, job title, number of subordinates, and other perquisites found in traditional compensation systems. As team concepts are employed, one must ask how the mentality of individualism, which is typical of the American worker, will affect the success of these plans (Gomez-Mejia and Welbourne, 1991).

Diluted Contributions. Somewhat related to the previous point and the free rider effect, individual contributions may be "lost" in a team setting, particularly in larger groups. This may put the supervisor in the difficult position of trying to "fish out" who is and is not carrying his/her weight. Supervisors may be reluctantly thrown in this situation by pressures from different members (or factions) within the group.

Intragroup Allocations. Group rewards may be provided equally to all team members, or an attempt may be made to distribute the gains differentially based on individual input. If the latter approach is to be chosen, the firm must develop a mechanism to identify individuals' contributions to team goals. In order to avoid the pitfalls associated with measuring individual performance (as discussed earlier in the chapter), team members may rate each other's performance, and the group's consensus can be relied on to distribute rewards. This peer rating procedure, however, introduces the added political problem of distinguishing between true performance and a popularity contest. In either case, any attempts to identify individual contributors will infuse an element of competition into the team concept, and it could easily evolve into simply just one more method of distributing merit pay or individual incentives.

Organizational Interdependence. Identifying groups whose work is relatively orthogonal from each other is not always easy. A poor job of carving out the various groups to be used as the unit of performance analysis may result in a number of serious problems. First, and foremost, if the boundaries separating the chosen groups are permeable, then one is back to the difficult problem of distinguishing who contributed what. Second, one may inadvertently create a situation where groups that should be cooperating with each other (e.g., marketing and production teams) begin to compete instead, which results in a deterioration of overall performance (e.g. sales commitments outstripping a firm's capacity to meet demands on schedule). Third, expanding the size of the group for performance measurement purposes (to minimize intergroup rivalries or to account for interdependencies) may produce a situation where the line of sight between individual contributions and the aggregate performance measure may become completely blurred.

Contingencies Favoring Group-Based Incentives

While the pitfalls discussed above may never be completely avoided, the effectiveness of group-based incentives is likely to be greater under the following conditions:

1. *When the identification of individual contributors would be arbitrary and difficult to do, given the nature of the tasks at hand.* Such would be the case, for example, among teams of scientists and engineers working on common projects where isolation of individual contributions is likely to produce unrealistic distinctions among employees (Gomez-Mejia and Balkin, 1989). This explains in part why in the hard sciences, published papers by faculty (which are used as the primary criteria for reward distribution in most research universities) often have a large number of co-authors (with 10 or more names on a paper not that unusual).

2. *When the organizational structure is conducive to group-based incentives.* For firms operating under classical structures based on the concept of unitary authority, individual-based performance-contingent schemes would make the most sense. For firms

that discourage hierarchical relationships and promote matrix networks, a group-based performance-contingent system would be most appropriate. Unless employees see multiple managers in a matrix organization as having equal control over rewards, there will be a natural tendency for them, particularly in conflict situations, to heed the desires of one manager to the neglect of the other. How individuals (particularly professionals) perceive the distribution of influence between managers on financial rewards may invalidate the matrix organization, despite any paper claims to the contrary (Katz and Allen, 1985). In other words, if those involved view a particular manager as having more power over chances for salary increases, the employee's behaviors and priorities are more likely to be influenced and directed solely by the side with most control, thereby undermining the matrix network.

3. *When the nature of the technology and workflows in the organization allow for the identification of distinct groups that are relatively independent of each other.* For example, self-contained work crews in a paper mill can be identified much more readily than would be the case of independent teams in a large batch manufacturing operation. As the technology and workflows become more intertwined, a higher level of aggregation may be necessary to distribute rewards (such as profit sharing and gainsharing, to be discussed shortly).

4. *Whenever one wishes to capitalize on the cooperative structure of work, assuming that such an arrangement will make a greater contribution to firm performance.* In other words, when making individual rewards directly proportional to the performance of the work group will increase the productivity of the entire group. Such would be the case again in a R&D operation. Where the work itself is highly independent, however, team-based rewards are almost certainly doomed to failure. For instance, the authors are familiar with a university where the merit adjustments of faculty are prorated, based on the productivity of each department (using a formula that incorporates publication counts, teaching ratings, and grants generated by the entire department). The highest department may receive a merit allocation three to four times greater than that of the lowest department. This system resulted in a lot of complaints among individual faculty (particularly the high producers in low-scoring departments) because they felt that the research and grants of each faculty member was due primarily to the contributions of this individual and not to cooperative efforts of all faculty in each department.

5. *Whenever there is a need to align the interests of multiple individuals into a common goal.* For instance, scientists and engineers have their own research agendas and professional objectives. These are not necessarily consistent with those of the firm or perhaps even those of other colleagues working on similar projects. Team-based incentives may be set up to induce employees to adopt group goals for themselves by making rewards contingent on the achievement of such goals. Austin and Bobko (1985) argue that group goals serve a socializing role in that team members have a natural tendency to personalize group goals over time. A large body of research suggests that goalsetting tends to enhance task performance. (See review by Locke, Shaw, Saari, and Latham, 1981.) While most studies have focused on personal goalsetting and individual performance, limited evidence available to date supports the notion that group goalsetting improves team performance if (a) goals are ac-

cepted by group members; and (b) attainable, yet challenging goals are established (Forward and Zander, 1971; Gowen, 1985).

6. *Whenever flexibility is desired.* Team-based incentives offer great flexibility in timing the reward close to actual task accomplishment, or in making rewards contingent on specific targets or goals. Both timing and reward contingencies are important determinants of the reinforcement value of financial incentives (Nadler, Hackman, and Lawler, 1979; Opsahl and Dunnette, 1966). For instance, a group bonus for engineers can be timed right after a new product leaves R&D and goes into production in accordance with the planned timetable. Merit pay policies generally do not offer this timing flexibility because of the budgetary review cycle. This flexibility would be most valuable to organic and prospector type firms and may actually clash with the control and normative structure of mechanistic and defender type firms. (See Chapter 3.)

7. *Whenever the organization desires to foster entrepreneurship.* Because of their greater flexibility, as noted above, team-based incentive programs may be designed to engender an entrepreneurial spirit at the group level within the firm. The kinds of risks that an employee group faces on the magnitude of the financial incentive can be made to resemble the risks that entrepreneurs face. In this manner, by creating an entrepreneurial environment, team-based incentive systems would force each group to share the risks of success or failure with the firm and its owners. Further, employees as part of a team may be more willing to bear risks (and potential failure) than they would as individuals by themselves. Since these incentives are not a part of base salary, the organization has greater flexibility to be generous with the magnitude of the reward without having to fear inability to pay in future pay periods. However, these features (as discussed in Chapter 4) are more attuned to the basic nature of organic and prospector type firms and would be foreign to more mechanistic or defender type firms.

8. *Whenever potential free riding problems are less likely to occur because the task at hand is difficult or unique and the employees are professionals who are intrinsically motivated.* Individuals working on complex tasks and who have invested a long time to attain a given occupational status are more likely to be internally driven and be proud of their work. They are not likely to shirk off responsibility at the expense of the group (Gomez-Mejia and Mussio, 1975; Harkins and Petty, 1982). Social-control mechanisms can help ensure that free riding problems are minimized when recruitment is highly selective (Harmon, 1965); individuals undergo intensive training (Ben-David, 1971); there are strong professional norms and extensive socialization (Gomez-Mejia, 1983; Hagstrom, 1965, 1968, 1971, 1974); and individuals derive satisfaction from completing creative work (Guston, 1973).

EFFICIENCY-BASED AGGREGATE PERFORMANCE-CONTINGENT POLICIES

Efficiency-based aggregate performance-contingent pay policies, most commonly associated with gainsharing plans, yield lump-sum awards based on unit-wide results, typically at the SBU level. Unlike firm performance-based plans (to be discussed later), the key indicator used to distribute awards consists of labor cost (or materials cost) savings, instead of profits. The theoretical underpinnings behind most of these plans are articulated in a variety of academic writings under the umbrella of participative management theory.

Theoretical Framework

Intellectual justification for these programs can be traced to the work of McGregor (1960), who, along authors such as Kurt Lewis, Frederick Herzberg, and Chris Argyris, posited a distinction between traditional autocratic approaches to management, referred to as "Theory X," from more humanistic (and presumably superior) approaches, referred to as "Theory Y." In the latter theory employees are viewed as part of a team, intrinsically motivated, willing to learn, and eager to use their intellectual capacity. In fact, McGregor was an intimate collaborator of Joseph Scanlon, founder of the well-known gainsharing program that carries its name. The basic philosophy is that intergroup competition within a firm should be avoided so that the entire organization functions as a unified entity, that workers have the ability and willingness to contribute good ideas, and that any gains resulting from worker inputs should be shared.

Closely related to Theory Y, the so-called participative management movement also provided intellectual impetus to employee involvement programs that emphasize egalitarian, democratic ideals at work. From this perspective, gainsharing is not viewed as simply another incentive plan or as a management tool to improve the efficiency of operations, but as the right way to treat people. According to Kanter (1987, p. 15), "[Gainsharing] is seen as returning to the employee much of the control and income enhancement opportunities that began to decline with the advent of scientific management and modern managerialism."

In their classical book *The Social Psychology of Organizations*, Katz and Kahn (1966) refer to the Scanlon plan as the "boldest attempt" at democratic governance of the industrial sector in the United States. Scanlon's successor as "plan installer" and his close friend both in industry and in MIT, Frederick Lesieur, remarked that "even though the measurement [to distribute rewards] is important, it is not nearly as important as the participation part of the Scanlon plan. If you don't get participation, I don't care what measurement you have or how good it is, it just won't move" (1959, p. 41).

Most gainsharing programs, particularly the Scanlon Plan (to be described shortly), are based on the following premises, which are derived from Theory Y and participative management notions:

1. Maximum contribution to organization performance through worker participation can best be achieved by focusing on the SBU as the unit of analysis for efficiency measures and linking rewards to those aggregate measures.
2. Because active participation will lead to better utilization of employees' talents, efficiency of operations will improve by creating a complex system of committees and steering groups, involving most employees in generating ideas, deciding which ones to carry out, and actually implementing those suggestions.
3. Distributive justice will contribute to further increments in productivity by divvying up accrued gains attributed to employee inputs between labor (workers) and capital (firm owners or stockholders). Management will also benefit if the executive pay program rewards them for increased efficiency of operations.
4. Democratic processes are followed through secret ballot used for plan adoption, committee selection, and procedural issues (e.g., when and how payoff formula may be changed).

5. Intensive training, education, and socialization of the work force increase their level of knowledge and commitment to the employee involvement programs.

Operational Programs

Kanter (1987) estimates that approximately forty to fifty thousand people work under gainsharing programs. This amount is about ten times smaller than the number of employees covered by profit sharing and infinitesimally smaller than the number of employees working under individual-based performance-contingent pay plans. One could easily get a misleading impression of the extent of gainsharing use from its advocates. Thus, this information is important to keep in perspective. The most common types of gainsharing programs are Scanlon, Rucker, and Improshare—in that order. Because of the complexity of each of these plans, only their key features are highlighted. Readers interested in more detail may wish to refer to several excellent hands-on descriptions of these plans. (See Doyle, 1983; Fuehrer, 1991; Geare, 1976; Miller and Schuster, 1987; Moore and Ross, 1990; Roomkin, 1990; Ross and Ross, 1991.)

Scanlon Plan. The Scanlon Plan is the most elaborate in terms of employee involvement. It has a dual committee structure designed to provide a system of checks and balances.

First, a production committee (composed of 3 to 5 rank and file employees elected by their peers and an approximate equal number of supervisors) is responsible to generate ideas, gather suggestions from employees, and evaluate these within a stipulated cost range. The production committee can implement these ideas without additional approval, provided they do not involve changes in other parts of the business.

The screening committee (composed of employees, union leaders, and top management) is chartered with the following four tasks:

1. To evaluate and approve suggestions that involve several parts of the business and/ or that exceed the maximum allowable discretionary limit of the production committee.
2. To provide an appeal forum for suggestions rejected by the production committee.
3. To conduct formal and informal studies of current and anticipated business problems and specific concerns to the firm such as an increase in the number of returned merchandise.
4. To review and update the formulas used to calculate the bonus.

The Scanlon Plan uses a ratio of total sales to payroll expenses to determine bonuses for employees. Using a base ratio, actual versus predicted costs are calculated at the end of the bonus period. If the expected (predicted) costs are lower than the observed costs during this period, this differential is shared between workers (bonus pool) and the firm. Part of the bonus pool is distributed to employees, and a portion is held in reserve in a "rainy day" fund. Typically, any gains using this ratio are distributed so that employees receive 75 percent and management receives 25 percent.

Rucker Plan. As in the Scanlon Plan, a belief in participative management is an essential ingredient to the Rucker Plan programs. Rucker Plans are based on the notion that employees want to be actively involved in their work; workers have something valuable to say;

employee suggestions are instrumental to cost savings and improved corporate performance; and any resulting gains should be shared between labor and management.

Operationally, Rucker Plans have a simpler committee structure than Scanlon Plans. Some have two separate committees (production and screening), while others have only the screening committee. Production committees are not generally involved in problem solving and are used primarily for education/communication purposes. The screening committee (typically composed of hourly workers, union leaders, and top managers) is less involved with immediate production or quality issues but interested in long-term normative concerns and operation of the bonus program.

While the committee structure and process under Rucker Plans are simpler than those of the Scanlon Plan, the actual bonus formula is far more complex. It encompasses not only labor costs, but also other expenses that are part of the production process. Productivity improvements at the end of the bonus period is determined by calculating changes in the ratio of value added by the manufacturer (i.e. sales volume minus materials and supplies) to payroll expenses.

Improshare Plan. Both Scanlon and Rucker Plans view participative management systems as an integral part of their success and insist that active employee involvement is necessary during implementation. Improshare Plan, while not opposed to participation, views it as an outcome of the aggregate bonus plan. (See Fein, 1991.) A formal system of employee participation is not consistently used in these programs, although labor management committees are often responsible for reviewing and adjusting bonus calculations as necessary. The bonus formulas focus on the direct labor contributions in time units, relative to an established standard for total labor time. A bonus is accrued when the standard is improved.

Bonuses are normally provided monthly and are calculated using the ratio of base value earned hours (estimated using engineer time standard plus absorption of indirect hours) to total hours worked.

Drawbacks

Efficiency-based programs, just like individual- and team-based performance-contingent plans, have their own unique pitfalls. Most of these problems, to be discussed shortly, are side effects of their very strength—namely, the aggregate nature of the efficiency measure, the emphasis on productivity changes, and the intense level of participation. These pitfalls include:

Weak Line of Sight. The dilution of individual performance problems discussed earlier under team-based rewards is brought up one step further here. Because of the long distance between individual contributions and the aggregate efficiency measure, it remains to be shown that they induce those covered under the plan to do their best to improve the quality of the organization's services or products. By implication, the free rider problem is also more severe because the more people are involved, the less likely group cohesiveness will be able to bring poor performers back into the fold.

Straightjacket Formulas. The calculus used to distribute rewards may have a number of problems, most of them traced to low flexibility. First, the firm may find itself locked into rigid sharing formulas, and employees may develop expectations that these are "forever plans" (Welbourne and Gomez-Mejia, 1988). This may neutralize their strategic value or even become a liability as management has less room to maneuver. The greater the rate of technological change and volatility in product mix, the more severe this problem becomes. Second, reliable and meaningful efficiency measures may be difficult to develop and administer, particularly for firms operating in unstable, unpredictable environments. Productivity standards may be arbitrary and fickle, and the labor cost calculations may be complex and controversial.

Third, as discussed in the executive compensation chapter, one faces the peril of linking rewards to "bottom line," single efficiency measures. Such an approach raises the possibility that other important elements not explicitly incorporated into the formula may be ignored (e.g., need to consolidate different production processes to achieve a better economy of scale across several SBUs).

Finally, employees, as well as many top managers, are prone to believe that productivity and efficiency are necessary antecedents of financial performance. While this is generally true, the correlation between these two sets of measures is far from perfect. Gainsharing may result in a more efficient use of labor, materials, energy, and capital because these are to a large extent controllable. However, profitability measures, particularly in the short run, are affected by many uncontrollable variables that are totally unrelated to efficiency of operations such as market shifts, product life cycles, government policies, etc. It is not unusual to find situations where a firm's efficiency increases, yet profitability decreases. For instance, employee-owned Peoples Express Airline was run very efficiently but still went out of business. Even though profitability may be higher than it would have been the case had the firm been operating less efficiently, it is difficult for employees—and many managers—to understand and accept situations where their efforts seem to produce no measurable financial results.

Exclusivity. Discriminatory practices in gainsharing programs, whereby only some types of employees are allowed to participate and receive benefits from it, may engender hard feelings from those individuals who are excluded. Typically, only hourly workers, mostly in manufacturing, are included in these plans.

Regression to Mean Effect. Inadvertently, gainsharing programs may be designed to favor business units that are poor performers because the lower the starting base, the easier it is to improve on it. Statistically, a *regression to the mean* effect is likely to occur when repeated measures are used in a pre-post facto mode because low performers tend to move up closer to the mean, and high performers tend to slide down in the opposite direction. In practical terms this means that "gainsharing programs may penalize the previously more efficient organizational components where opportunities for dramatic labor cost savings are much less than those in less efficient organizational components" (Sullivan, 1988, p. 23).

Flooring Effect. Labor cost-saving opportunities available throughout the organization may be limited. It is possible that a saturation point is soon reached where additional improvements in efficiency may be almost nil, and this can be demoralizing. The labor hours required by a complex committee structure may not generate enough efficiency benefits to justify the costs involved.

Power Dilution. Top management may be sold on gainsharing as a productivity enhancing plan but may soon become threatened by it. Management may resent the loss of control involved in handing out discretionary power to multiple committees yet may be reluctant to overhaul the system for fear of reprisals and open conflict. The end result may be a lack of strong commitment from upper management, and this almost always spells failure for any human resource program (Gomez-Mejia, 1990).

Contingencies Favoring Efficiency-Based Aggregate Pay Plans

The literature on gainsharing is fairly extensive. However, most of it consists of case studies that were specifically written by advocates to justify implementation of such programs. Most of this material was published 30 to 40 years ago (e.g., Alberth, 1960; Beardsley, 1962; Dreyer, 1952; Farley, 1950; Gray, 1958), although a number of review papers appeared in the 1980s (e.g., Bullock and Lawler, 1984; Welbourne and Gomez-Mejia, 1988).

In addition to the strong advocacy role of much of this literature (which puts in question the scientific value of reported findings), Welbourne and Gomez-Mejia (1988) warn us of other potential problems. First, most conclusions rely on testimonials, rather than on rigorous empirical analysis or controlled research designs. Second, studies reported are predominantly the successful ones. So, factors impacting gainsharing outcomes (both positive and negative) are not well-documented. Third, most studies are based on questionnaires distributed to employees after the plan has been in effect for a while. A response bias may exist if those who were dissatisfied had left the company. Fourth, subtle pressures of stewards, managers, or even other fellow workers may affect how people respond to interviews concerning the gainsharing plan. It is doubtful, for example, that management will open the doors to strangers to interview workers and publish that information unless it feels the firm will not be embarrassed. Companies typically censor what they consider as "proprietary information" before such studies are allowed to appear in print. Finally, with a few exceptions (e.g., White, 1979), most studies suffer from an unclear focus of evaluation because consistent definitions of gainsharing (which is often used interchangeably with profit sharing or even as a form of team-based incentives) are missing. This results in lack of comparability across studies.

Keeping the above caveats in mind, a review of the literature by Welbourne and Gomez-Mejia (1988) identified a number of factors that mediate the relative effectiveness of gainsharing programs. These contingency factors follow:

1. *Firm size.* The range in terms of number of employees for firms reported to have gainsharing programs is quite large, from 50 to 10,000, with a mode of approximately 500. While somewhat disputed (see Helfgott, 1962; Lesieur and Puckett, 1968), firm size is likely to make a difference in the success of gainsharing. The reason for this lies in the line of sight argument discussed earlier. Unless employees believe their participation can have an impact on company performance, resulting in a greater bonus, the psychological and monetary incentives of gainsharing are lost. However, the operational definition of "how large is too large" still remains open.

2. *Technological intensity.* While empirical work addressing this issue is minimal, technology is likely to mediate the effect of gainsharing. As technology becomes more

extensive, the potential for employee participation is reduced (Helfgott, 1962). In addition, technological constraints limit how much room there is for productivity to expand. Substantial opportunities for improvements should be available so that employees perceive that they can make a difference on productivity and this, in turn, will affect their pay.

3. *Baseline.* While success stories for gainsharing have been reported among both struggling and financially healthy firms, the baseline at the start of the program must still be taken into account. Firms or SBUs operating less efficiently are more likely to post gains, while those operating more efficiently are less likely to show improvements. Thus, careful attention needs to be paid not to penalize those units that are doing well (so that marginal improvements are more difficult) and penalize those that are below average (so that marginal improvements are easier to accomplish). This suggests that for firms that are operating at the top of their efficiency capacity, gainsharing will produce negligible benefits in terms of productivity and may tend to demoralize the work force.

4. *Compatible managerial beliefs.* In Chapter 5, the importance of meshing the dominant logic of top management groups and compensation strategies was discussed. This is extremely crucial in the case of gainsharing because of the radical participative management philosophy involved, potential loss of management control, and the complex committee structures that are an integral part of most of these programs.

   Several case studies have found that the expectations, attitudes, and value system of top managers, particularly the CEO, are important correlates of plan success. (See review by Bullock and Lawler, 1984.) If the dominant coalition does not believe in shared decision making, is reluctant to give up discretionary power, expresses doubts about the return to time invested in committee meetings, and is unwilling to spend a considerable amount of time in jointly designing, implementing, and communicating the bonus formulas, gainsharing is almost certainly doomed to failure. In other words, if management does not have strong faith in the employee involvement concept, gainsharing will not work; and the essential element of teamwork and communication will not be nurtured by the plan. Unfortunately, based on our experience, a surprisingly large number of firms are willing to adopt such a plan in response to consultants' recommendations and, to "keep up with the Joneses," imitate what other firms are doing, even if not fully aware of its implications. In such cases, either the program has a high probability of failure, or the company faces the risk of losing members of the management team.

5. *Corporate culture.* Related to the previous point, the fact that each organization has its own unique set of values is well-documented (Kerr and Slocum, 1987). As discussed in Chapter 5, the more a firm's compensation strategies are attuned to its culture, the more likely these will contribute to firm performance. This is of paramount importance for gainsharing because of its intrusive nature in organizational life. Unless complemented by a strong individual-based performance-contingent plan, the firm will be taking considerable risks implementing a participative reward system if individualism and competition are important values of the organizations's culture. It may be that, in fact, gainsharing is introduced in an attempt to reorient the existing value structure, to make it less competitive and more cooperative.

However, combining it with individual incentives may be wise to allow for a gradual transition and, thus, decrease resistance.

6. *Interdependencies.* Unless resource flows across various units are explicitly taken into account in designing the program, gainsharing may precipitate the opposite of what was intended—that is, intense dysfunctional conflict. The authors know of some firms, for example, where higher production in manufacturing units attributed to gainsharing led to a costly buildup of inventories.

    As another example, it is not uncommon for firms to cover sales personnel under a separate commission plan. In these situations, it is important that the commission plan induces the sales force to work hand in hand with plant and indirect personnel to achieve optimal performance under gainsharing. For instance, if the sales work is primarily paid on salary and nurturing customer relations is the main objective of the sales compensation program (as discussed in Chapter 8), this policy may operate at cross-purposes with the pressure to dispose of additional output generated by units covered under gainsharing.

7. *SBU strategies.* Firms pursuing a prospector or growth strategy need to proceed cautiously when introducing gainsharing programs because bonuses are based on increases above base productivity measures. A stable history will help assure a fair bonus distribution and make the calculation of the bonus better understood by employees. Unstable or scanty data based on historical records will make it difficult to establish reliable future performance standards. If the firm is constantly changing the bonus calculations, confidence in the system is likely to suffer. By the same token, prospectors and growth firms need a greater degree of flexibility, and gainsharing tends to work against it. This means, in general, gainsharing is less likely to contribute to firm performance for SBUs that follow a prospector or growth strategy.

    In addition to the internal factors noted above, Welbourne and Gomez-Mejia (1988) identified three external factors that mediate the relative effectiveness of gainsharing programs and their contribution to firm performance. These are discussed next.

8. *Product market.* Other things equal, gainsharing would be more appropriate if management has confidence in business forecasts indicating that improvements in per capita productivity and total output can be absorbed by the market. Otherwise, the end result may be unwanted inventory expansion, which almost inevitably leads to layoffs, and this is seldom conducive to improved labor-management cooperation.

9. *Labor market.* An important issue is the extent to which the applicant pool from which the firm hires workers is agreeable to gainsharing or predisposed against these types of programs. For instance, if the company operates in the so-called secondary labor market (characterized by jobs with low pay, limited job security, poor working conditions, few opportunities for advancement, layoffs and temporary employment; see Doeringer and Piore, 1971), gainsharing is less likely to be effective. If high unemployment is being experienced in the region, employees are less likely to leave the firm because they are more resistant to change and more likely to give their present employer a chance. As the number of job opportunities expand, workers and even managers who are not comfortable with gainsharing

programs are more likely to leave the firm. It is not clear, however, whether the "good" or the "bad" employees are the ones to leave in this situation.

10. *Environment turbulence.* Firms operating in highly unstable environments are less likely to implement effectively gainsharing programs if, for no other reason, the relationship between firm profitability and efficiency deteriorates as external factors beyond management control affects their performance.

CORPORATE-WIDE PERFORMANCE-CONTINGENT PAY PROGRAMS

Corporate-wide performance-contingent plans, most commonly known as profit sharing, pay employees based on the profitability of the entire firm or unit, regardless of how efficiently it is being run. More specifically, these programs differ from efficiency-based plans in a number of ways:

1. Such factors as depreciation procedures, bad debt expense, and economic conditions (none of which are under the employee's control) contribute to reported profit (and, therefore, affect the amount of profit sharing received). Yet, they may have little to do with any productivity improvements or changes in employee's behaviors. No attempt is made under profit sharing to reward workers for specific activities that increase productivity.

2. Explicit formulas are used to allocate gains in profit levels to employees and the firm. Yet, no worker participation is required. In other words, no ideological assumption is made that the success of the program derives from management's commitment to a democratic leadership style. In fact, profit sharing has its roots in paternalistic, top-down, "welfare capitalism" type of programs originating in the 19th and early 20th centuries as attempts to limit unionization (Florkowski, 1987).

3. Unlike gainsharing, profit-sharing payments accrue on an annual or quarterly basis. Perhaps most importantly, all of the profit allocations under the plan are typically deferred into a retirement fund. Less frequently, profit-sharing payments may be allocated as a lump-sum annual or quarterly bonus. Thus, unlike gainsharing, there are fewer attempts to "personalize" the linkage between rewards and performance, and profit allocations may be viewed more as a mechanism of defraying benefits than as a true incentive program.

4. Profit sharing is almost always corporate-wide in nature, so that the level of aggregation is much larger than in the case of gainsharing. Further, some SBUs may contribute a disproportionate share of the corporate-wide profits, which can add to the blurring of the line of sight between contributions and rewards.

Theoretical Framework

There are several theoretical rationales in support of profit-sharing programs. Most of these are economic, rather than behavioral, in nature.

Shock Absorber Theory. The shock absorber theory, a macro-economic perspective, most notably associated with the work of Weitzman (1984), holds that profit sharing is an important element in monetary and fiscal policies to control inflation. At the same time, profit sharing mitigates their negative effect on employment level. Profit-sharing systems offer strong resistance to demand and cost shocks in the short run because of their built-in flexibility over the business cycle. Thus, from a public policy standpoint, profit sharing promotes full employment because plan contributions are automatically adjusted in downturns, reducing the marginal cost of labor, thereby allowing firms to retain a larger work force during a recession.

Cash Flow Theory.   The arguments in the cash flow theory are very similar to those advanced by life cycle theory discussed in earlier chapters. The central point is: The greater the proportion of fixed costs in the compensation system, the less strategic flexibility the firm has to direct scarce cash into capital intensive projects such as R&D. This is a particularly crucial issue for firms at the growth stage, those that adopt a prospector strategy, and firms for which labor costs are a high proportion of total costs. (See Gomez-Mejia and Balkin, 1989.) Reliance on variable compensation allows the firm to channel scarce resources where and when they are most needed. It also "ties up" workers to the firm by increasing their opportunity costs (in terms of foregone benefits) if they were to go elsewhere. Finally, profit sharing allows the firm to take greater risks and deal with short-term setbacks without having to resort to massive layoffs in order to cope with environmental jolts.

In addition to the strategic flexibility afforded the firm and greater employment security for its workers, the funding formula for profit sharing provides a protective security blanket for the aged because, in most plans, cash is deposited into a deferred income account that cannot be accessed until retirement. By the late 1980s, it became the most common method of providing retirement income in the United States (Florkowski, 1987).

Distributive Justice.   In several encyclicals during the past two centuries, Popes have advanced the notion that the sharing of wealth between workers and the owners of capital is necessary to achieve a fair and just distribution of income within the constraints of private property. Union leaders have also been strong proponents of profit sharing, provided that the union actively participates in the design, implementation, and monitoring of these plans (Brandes, 1970). Enlightened managers have instituted profit-sharing plans for at least a century, under the belief that they promote a sense of partnership between capital and labor and a common purpose (Bureau of National Affairs Special Report, 1988; Cheadle, 1989). Moderate socialists, in response to more radical Marxist ideology, have long advocated the use of profit sharing as a way of returning "surplus value" in the capitalist mode of production back to the workers (e.g., Braverman, 1974; Pfeffer, 1979). Even some countries, Mexico for example, require private corporations by law to share a portion of its declared profits with workers.

The common thread in the above perspectives, despite their disparate origins, is that:

1. Profit sharing is the right and moral thing to do.
2. Both workers who contribute labor and owners who risk capital are entitled to partake in the fruits of their combined efforts to make the enterprise succeed.
3. Profit sharing fosters an equality of exchange (vis-a-vis stratification) in economic relations so that one segment of the population (workers) does not produce value for the exclusive benefit of another segment (firm owners).

Operational Programs

There are two major types of profit-sharing plans. The first kind consists of "in-cash" or "current" (as opposed to deferred) profit sharing. These programs, which are relatively uncommon, provide employees a lump-sum award based on the firm's profitability during a stipulated period of time, usually on an annual or quarterly basis. In-cash plans are quite old. For instance, Procter & Gamble introduced a cash profit-sharing program in 1887. In the late 1980s, it was estimated that cash profit-sharing plans had payouts averaging 9.2 percent of wages (Bureau of National Affairs Special Report, 1988). A typical one is that of Johnson's Wax, which has had a cash plan for almost 80 years. The formula is predicated on the employee's base salary, seniority, and level within the company. The payout averages about six week's pay per year (Bureau of National Affairs Special Report, 1988). Occasionally, however, cash compensation in the form of profit sharing is much greater. For instance, Andersen Corporation, a window manufacturer in Bayport, Minnesota, offered its 3,700 employees an annual check in 1987 amounting to 84 percent of annual salary, averaging a whopping $28,620 per employee (Bureau of National Affairs, 1988).

The second, and by far most common plan, is the tax-deferred, profit-sharing trust. Approximately 80 percent of all plans use this method, whereby the firm will pay benefits based on the value of each participant's fund upon his/her retirement (Florkowski, 1987). In these "defined contribution plans," the fund's growth is directly tied to profit levels, and proceeds are not taxable until employees begin to draw benefits upon retirement or disability. Most of the firms in the remaining 20 percent use a mixed approach, with a portion of profits distributed to employees during the calendar year in which they were earned and the remaining portion set aside in a tax-deferred account. The percent of profits distributed across all types of plans varies between 14 to 33 percent (Bureau of National Affairs Special Report, 1988).

The obvious advantage of tax-deferred plans is that employees do not have to pay federal and state taxes (which could exceed 40 percent of marginal earnings). Their main disadvantage is that the payoff is so far into the future that most of its reinforcement value is lost.

Drawbacks

Profit sharing is the most aggregate of all performance-contingent pay plans with little, if any, pretention of using it as a motivational tool at the individual level. Research conducted to date, mostly in the form of case studies, speak eloquently in favor of profit sharing (Best, 1961; Carpenter, 1984; Coords, 1980; Lush, 1975; McNutt, 1991; and Nightingdale, 1982). These studies report that profit-sharing firms generally perform better, grow faster, and enjoy higher productivity, job satisfaction, and lower turnover among employees. As in the case of gainsharing, however, it is difficult to ascertain the cause-effect relationship in these descriptive studies and whether firms whose plan fell below expectations were excluded because management did not have a success story to tell. The main concerns with profit sharing are:

Noncontingent Reinforcement. While noncontingent reinforcement is perhaps an unfair criticism of profit-sharing plans because they are not primarily designed as a motivational tool, expectancy theory would predict that their behavioral effect is minimal, given that the connection between individual goal accomplishment, firm performance, and rewards is negligible at best. In other words, the distance between individual behavior and firm outcomes is so remote that few employees will be energized by it. Many consultants (and probably most employees) view profit sharing as another fringe benefit just like health insurance or a pension plan. It may be an important retention tool (because accumulated benefits are tied to seniority). However, it does not discriminate between functional and dysfunctional turnover.

Inability to Redirect Funds. As the percent of profits from a firm is channelled into profit-sharing plans, less flexibility is left to use such resources for other types of performance-contingent plans that may be more closely attuned to individual and group performance. It may, in fact, become so high (30 percent is not too uncommon) that, in effect, the firm utilizes large resources for across-the-board payments (magnifying the free rider effect discussed earlier), leaving very little room to bankroll other performance-contingent pay plans.

Limited Strategic Flexibility. Because it is so broad in nature, profit sharing does not offer the maneuverability to target the reward system to attain specific strategic objectives. For instance, a firm may wish to emphasize a particular product line to take advantage of a promising market niche, and this may require devoting more compensation dollars to attract and retain top-level talent in that area. However, profit sharing will not help the firm accomplish this.

Lack of Control. Lack of control is somewhat akin to the line of sight issue discussed earlier. As noted in Chapter 6, while estimates do vary, most researchers agree that top executives exercise rather limited influence on firm performance. While moving down in the organization, factors outside an employee's sphere of control play an even larger role on firm performance.

Mortgaging the Future. Unlike most other performance-contingent pay plans, profit-sharing money is "painless" in the short run because it is yet to be earned. Therefore, management may be tempted to be generous with this benefit and leave the problem for future management generations to handle. This assumes greater significance in organized firms because unions like to be involved in the program's design, implementation, and operation (Kochan and Dyer, 1976; Schuster, 1983, 1984, 1985). According to Cheadle (1989, p. 388), "many present day union leaders [are] weary of management initiated profit sharing plans." This attitude is based in large measure in the previous history of so-called welfare capitalism, whereby employers relied heavily on profit sharing to check unionization (Brandes, 1970).

Thus, union pressures on the one hand and management's propensity to give in on the other may result in profit-sharing plans that are detrimental to stockholders and that may have long-term negative consequences for workers as less capital is available to finance future growth. Profit sharing may also act as an additional constraint on strategic flexibility because management may be reluctant to make changes in the allocation formulas for fear of provoking a negative union response.

Contingencies Favoring Corporate-Wide Performance-Based Pay Plans

Existing research, while rather limited, along with the theoretical frameworks discussed earlier in this section, suggest that the following factors are likely to affect the outcomes of profit-sharing programs:

Firm Size. Larger firms are more likely to rely on profit-sharing plans, regardless of actual profitability (Cheadle, 1989). Milkovich and Newman (1990, p. 351) add that "until there is more evidence that Scanlon/Rucker plans can be adapted successfully to large organizations, profit sharing plans seem to represent the major alternative for organizations of any size."

Corporate Diversification. Following the logic outlined in Chapters 2-5, one would expect profit sharing to be more appropriate when there is extensive interdependence and resource flows across business units because the corporation as a whole is the most obvious level of analysis to assess performance.   This means, in terms of extent of diversification, profit sharing should be most suitable for single-product, dominant-product, and related-product firms, in that order, and less appropriate for unrelated-product firms. In terms of diversification patterns, one would expect that profit sharing should be most suitable for vertical, constrained, and linked businesses, in that order, and least appropriate for multibusiness and conglomerate firms.

SBU Strategy. As noted earlier, while profit sharing may be utilized by firms at different life cycle stages, one would expect its contribution to firm performance to be greatest for start-up and growth firms and for companies that follow a prospector strategy. The reason for this is that profit sharing is a variable, rather than a fixed, cost of production. Thus, cash flows would be enhanced by increasing the proportion of pay that is tied to profitability (and, therefore, subject to oscillations, depending on how well the firm is doing).   This enables the firm to channel resources into growth areas.

The tax-deferred feature of most profit-sharing plans to finance employees' pensions makes them particularly attractive as a cash flow tool. For instance, the work force's income and standard of living are not visibly affected in the near future if profitability drops. This means, the firm enjoys the advantages of adjustable, total compensation without negatively impacting the part of pay (cash) that most employees see as important to their everyday life. Furthermore, the longer the time horizon, the less likely annual ups and downs in the firm's profits will affect the workers' retirement income because it will be calculated over multiple years.

Competitive Strategy Weapon in Local Markets. Of all factors, it appears that regional differences is the main predictor of profit-sharing plan adoption. According to Cheadle's (1989, p. 395) findings, "The explanation [for profit-sharing adoption] with the most consistent support is the customary hypothesis; the idea that the dominant saving plan in an industry/ region is determined more by past practice than the inherent superiority of one plan over the other." This suggests that firm location may play a role in whether profit sharing should be implemented. Where profit sharing is customary (as it is the case in most of the Western United States), the firm may have little choice but to offer such a plan as an integral part of its recruitment and retention strategies or be at a disadvantage in the labor market.

Firms Facing Unstable Demand. Firms operating in turbulent markets and whose products are highly elastic may find that profit sharing can contribute to firm performance by serving as a shock absorber during periods of decline. Because profit sharing operates in a region of "positive excess demand for labor," variable costs can be reduced during downturns without resorting to layoffs. In terms of training expenses, recruitment efforts, and morale problems in addition to the hardships employees and their families suffer during unemployment, layoffs have many associated costs for firms.

Profit Sharing Bundled with Other Plans. From a behavioral perspective, profit sharing is most likely to contribute to firm performance if it is combined with other individual and aggregate incentive plans. The reason for this should be obvious: Namely, profit sharing is not really designed to serve as a motivational or incentive alignment tool. It should be most appropriately treated as the top layer in the firm's reward structure. If other programs concurrently exist where the line of sight between behavior and outcomes is stronger, then profit sharing may serve a useful role by creating a sense of common goals, partnership, and mission.

Firm's Experiential Compensation Pattern. An experiential compensation strategy (see Chapter 3) should reinforce the cooperation and innovation that profit sharing is intended to promote. An algorithmic compensation strategy, on the other hand, would serve to neutralize the limited behavioral impact one would expect from profit sharing. This is because the algorithmic pay pattern rewards the individual for learning narrowly defined domains and work methods, socializes employees to assume responsibilities for specialized work segments, fosters dependence on supervisors, and engenders centralized organizational networks. In short, profit sharing is less likely to promote greater organizational commitment as the firm's global compensation strategies become more algorithmic in nature.

SUMMARY AND PROPOSITIONS

In short, multiple-reward policies at different levels of aggregation may be used to enhance individual, group, and firm performance. The relative effectiveness of these policies depends on how they are designed and implemented, their intended objectives, and the extent to which they are appropriate for the nature of the task at hand, organizational structure and culture, firm strategy, and the external environment. Table 9-1 presents 30 propositions that summarize the key points made in this chapter. Because little empirical investigation has been conducted in most of these, they should be viewed as hypotheses to guide future research.

TOTAL QUALITY MANAGEMENT (TQM) AND PERFORMANCE-CONTINGENT PAY

Perhaps the most sweeping movement across corporate America in the 1990s is the so called "Total Quality Management (TQM) revolution." While the concepts underlying

TABLE 9-1
A List of 30 Propositions on the Relationship between Performance-Contingent Pay Policies and Firm Performance

General Propositions

Performance-contingent pay policies are more likely to contribute to firm performance:

Proposition 1   When the linkage between pay and performance indicators is loosely coupled.

Proposition 2   When a deeply held myth exists that pay is contingent on performance (even if the two are loosely tied).

Proposition 3   When the pay-for-performance system is molded to contingency factors internal and external to the firm.

Individual-Based Performance-Contingent Pay Policies

Individual-based performance-contingent pay plans are more likely to make a greater contribution to firm performance:

Proposition 4   When the unique contributions of each individual may be ascertained.

Proposition 5   When the nature of the task provides freedom and independence to incumbents.

Proposition 6   When cooperation with others is not an integral prerequisite for successful performance.

Proposition 7   When individualism is an important norm in the firm's culture.

Team-Based Performance-Contingent Pay Policies

Team-based performance-contingent plans are more likely to make a greater contribution to firm performance:

Proposition 8   When the performance of each individual is inextricably webbed with that of others in a work group.

Proposition 9   When the firm makes extensive use of matrix networks.

Proposition 10   When relatively orthogonal work groups may be carved out throughout the organization.

Proposition 11   When linking individual rewards to work group performance enhances the overall productivity of the team.

Proposition 12   When the reward system is called to play a socializing role by inducing individuals to develop mutually congruent goals.

Proposition 13   When flexibility is an important component of the firm's overall strategy.

Proposition 14   When risk sharing at the group level is an important component in the firm's strategy.

Proposition 15   When the nature of work and the labor force reduce the possibility of extensive free riding throughout the organization.

TABLE 9-1 (Continued)
A List of 30 Propositions on the Relationship between Performance-Contingent Pay Policies and Firm Performance

Efficiency-Based Aggregate Performance-Contingent Pay Policies

Efficiency-based aggregate performance-contingent pay policies are more likely to make a greater contribution to firm performance:

Proposition 16   When firm size allows the "line of sight" between behavior and reward to be present.

Proposition 17   When technological constraints do not place severe limits on efficiency gains.

Proposition 18   When the SBU is not operating at the top of its efficiency capacity.

Proposition 19   When the dominant logic of top management teams stresses employee involvement and participation.

Proposition 20   When the participative nature of most of these plans can be blended with the firm's culture.

Proposition 21   The lower the flow of resources and interdependence across SBUs.

Proposition 22   When the SBUs do not follow a propsector or growth strategy.

Proposition 23   When the product market is relatively predictable.

Proposition 24   When the firm operates in relatively stable environments.

Corporate-Wide Performance-Contingent Pay Plans

Corporate-wide performance-contingent pay plans are more likely to contribute to firm performance:

Proposition 25   When there is extensive interdependence and resource flows across various SBUs.

Proposition 26   For start-up and growth firms and for companies that follow a prospector strategy.

Proposition 27   For firms operating in labor markets where profit sharing is customary.

Proposition 28   For firms operating in turbulent markets and whose products are highly elastic.

Proposition 29   For firms that are able to offer a mix of individual and aggregate incentive plans.

Proposition 30   For firms whose predominant compensation strategy pattern is experiential in nature.

TQM are at least fifty years old, and many attribute Japan's economic miracle to Deming's introduction of TQM at the end of World War II (see *Business Week's* special report on the "quality imperative," 1991), TQM is now becoming a popular antidote to real or perceived deficiencies in the quality of American goods and services. It is difficult to predict at this point whether this will become another passing fad that has been oversold (such as management by objectives or MBO in the 1960s and 1970s) or "a culture-transforming approach

. . . empowering workers [to] eventually give U.S. companies a shot at leapfrogging Japan in quality by unleashing a flood of creative latent" (Port and Carey, 1991, pp. 11-16).

It is not feasible within the page constraints of this book to discuss the TQM philosophy in any detail, but we can briefly touch base on its core ideas (which are very simple) and the potential role in TQM that may be played by the performance contingent reward systems discussed in this chapter. Because empirical research on TQM-compensation linkages is practically non-existent, much of the ensuing discussion consists of a logical extension of the concepts and ideas introduced earlier in this chapter.

The central concept of TQM is that all organizations have both internal and external customers. Organizational performance is a function of the extent to which the firm provides both sets of customers with products and services that fully satisfy their needs. Thus, from a TQM perspective, customer satisfaction must be a primary goal because it is the ultimate precursor of firm performance. In the words of Farquhar and Johnston (1990, p. 7):

> TQM is used to mobilize all the resources of the organization in pursuit of satisfied customers. . .the requirements of the customer then become the prevailing determinants of the organization's activities. Once the organization can see itself through the eyes of the customer, it can understand the need to ensure that each part of the business process is a vital link in the chain. Each link must relentlessly focus on producing a quality product that will be an input for the next stage in the process.

Given the pivotal role of the reward system in signalling to employees what the organization values, by implication pay can be used to support an organization culture that is customer oriented. For each level of analysis discussed in this chapter, performance contingent pay may be used as an integral part of the design and implementation of TQM.

At the individual level, TQM related pay programs may take a variety of forms. For merit pay, customer satisfaction can be given a high priority as part of the supervisory evaluation process. Individual suggestions systems to improve product or service quality may be used as a mechanism to trigger non-recurrent bonuses. In terms of who has inputs into performance evaluation, it may be possible to appraise the performance of each individual based on the assessment of his/her services to either internal and/or external customers. For instance, the internal customer can be defined as other members of the work team so that some form of peer appraisals may be appropriate.

As noted earlier, some of the strongest advocates of TQM who follow Deming's ideas believe that individual based rewards are the antithesis of TQM because these promote internal strife rather than cooperation. In addition, it is argued that an employee's performance can be better explained by "contextual" factors rather than the abilities or motivation possessed by the individual (see review by Dobbins, Cardy, and Carson, 1991; and related work by Carson, 1992; Carson, Cardy, Dobbins, and Stewart, 1992). However, a skeptic could argue that a highly individualistic culture such as the U.S. ignoring a person's need for individual recognition is a sure recipe for failure in a performance contingent pay system (see Gomez-Mejia and Welbourne, 1991). These issues have seldom been the subject of rigorous academic research, but it is doubtful that any naive solutions or prescriptions can provide satisfactory answers to what appears to be a very complex problem. Moreover, trying to imitate the Japanese in this regard may produce some unwelcome surprises (e.g., the highest performers moving on to other firms where individual performance is recognized).

At the team level, performance contingent pay programs can be naturally blended with TQM. This is because statistical process controls (SPC) are an important component of TQM programs. These represent procedures for analyzing measured deviations in quality of manufactured materials, parts and products or deviations from service expectations. SPC can not be reliably measured at the individual level, and team SPC indicators can be more readily obtained and used as a base for dispensing team incentives. The rationale provided by Deming for the use of SPC at a higher organizational level of analysis (such as teams) is summarized by Dobbins et al. (1991, p. 145) as follows:

> . . .most variation in performance is due to common causes and much harm is done by managers who respond to all variation as if it were due to special causes. . . . managers should use control charts in order to distinguish between common cause and special cause sources of variation. Control charts show the plotted observations from a process, along with a center line showing the process average and the control limits that give the predicted range of variation for a stable process. Behavior that is inconsistent with that of a stable process is taken to be signals of special causes. Examples of such signals would be points outside of the control limits or nonrandom patterns in the data (e.g., several consecutive time ordered points above and below average).

Efficiency based performance contingent reward programs, such as gainsharing, may also link directly with TQM. First, steering committees in these programs can emphasize quality—a theme central to TQM—as a criterion for the evaluation and adoption of suggestions. Second, interteam synergies can be fostered at the unit level by rewarding superordinate quality accomplishments that affect the entire work unit. Third, these programs can emphasize long-term quality improvements with reward cycles that my be adjusted according to the nature of the product. In many plants, it may not be feasible to identify self-contained work teams (to be used as a bases for calculating SPC and distributing rewards) so that the only alternative from a TQM perspective is to focus on the business unit or plant as the unit of analysis (as would be the case in gainsharing programs).

At the most aggregate or corporate level, profit sharing programs may be used in conjunction with TQM for single or dominant product firms, or in situations where the business units are highly interdependent and share a common core of knowledge. The reason for this is that it would be difficult to find common quality metrics for conglomerates, and profits among employees is not likely to energize individual behavior on to a greater awareness of quality given the "line of sight" problem discussed earlier in this chapter.

SOME CONCLUDING COMMENTS ABOUT THE ROLE OF MONEY AS A PERFORMANCE ENHANCER

An issue that has been addressed in this chapter is the ancient controversy as to whether incentives should be used as a motivational tool to enhance individual and organizational performance. Ever since Biblical times, there have been some strong voices opposed to the notion of using money as a mechanism to align the interests of workers with those of the organization. In fact, a recent survey (1991) indicated that while 40 percent of Americans rate "faith in God" as the most important thing in their lives, only two percent ever mentioned pay (Associated Press, 1991).

Several reasons have been advanced for this position. At a psychological level, Deci (1972) argues that relying on cash compensation as an inducement actually decreases motivation and performance by diverting energies from meeting employees' intrinsic needs. In other words, extrinsic rewards can undermine intrinsic drives. Beer, Spector, Lawrence, Mills, and Walton (1984) argue that a negative side effect of relying on monetary incentives to accomplish strategic objectives is that they tend to produce "horizontal inequities," whereby people at the same rank may earn substantially different amounts. Because of imperfect performance measures, lack of credibility in the system is common. This low acceptability of pay-for-performance programs, coupled with substantial income disparities, are demoralizing and produce the opposite effect of what was intended.

Slater (1980, p. 41) remarked sarcastically that "getting people to chase money produces nothing but people chasing money. Using money as a motivator leads to a progressive degradation in the quality of everything produced." Similarly, Kohn (1988, p. 94) comments that "incentives can be bad for business . . . [because] rewards encourage people to focus narrowly on the task, to do it as quickly as possible, and to take few risks . . . people come to see themselves as being controlled by the reward." Along the same vein, Brown and Nolan (1988, p. 351) made a sweeping condemnation of such programs by claiming:

> Since employment first began, successive generations of optimistic employers have been experimenting with cash incentives as a means to greater productivity. The research literature on the consequences is generally academically unimpressive, repetitive and disillusioning. Most incentive schemes have a briefly stimulating effect upon productivity which then fades, or even becomes negative as feelings of unfairness develop.

The above criticisms of incentive systems are not without merit. Misuse of these programs is likely to backfire, not because they fail to motivate but because they are extremely powerful motivators. That is, they may induce employees to do exactly what they are asked to do to receive the reward and very little else. In the words of Baker, Jensen, and Murphy (1988, p. 597):

> Large monetary incentives generate unintended and sometimes counterproductive results because it is difficult to adequately specify exactly what people should do and therefore how their performance should be measured . . . This focuses attention on how unintended effects are generated and on their importance, rather than on arguments about whether people are motivated by money or whether they should be motivated by money.

It is the authors' belief that failure to use the incentive properties of pay for fear of negative side effects is relinquishing one of the most potent mechanisms at management's disposal to channel employees' behavior to achieve an organization's strategic objectives. It would be analogous to giving up driving because car accidents are one of the leading causes of death in the United States. One of the greatest challenges of acting strategically is precisely to avoid the pitfalls associated with the traditional use of incentive programs. That is, money is tied to the accomplishment of specific numerical goals (as in piece-rate systems) or in annuity type programs (as in merit pay) and frequently introduced without much concern for contingency factors mediating their effectiveness.

It would be a fallacy to conclude that the previous negative results regarding the use of money as a performance enhancer, most of which were based on individual incentives, mean that the pay system should not be used to improve firm performance. In the authors' opinion, there are several reasons why many of the previous attempts to use compensation as a performance enhancer have failed. These discussions follow.

First, incentive systems have often been introduced without due respect to the organization's culture and its history. There is strong evidence to suggest that a firm's interpersonal climate, social norms, beliefs, and myths, which have incubated over many years, exert substantial influence on individual, group, and firm performance, perhaps even more so than economic factors (e.g., see Hansen and Wernerfelt, 1989; Kerr and Slocum, 1987; Sethia and Von Glinow, 1985). Attempts to use the pay system as a motivational force without carefully weaving it into the social fabric of the firm is likely to produce disappointing results. This is not to say that pay should be abandoned as a change agent, but since it is such a potent force, pay needs to be carefully harnessed, being very sensitive to the organization's current state of mind. For instance, there is plenty of evidence that trying to introduce a pay-for-performance system in firms where employees have very little trust and credibility in management will simply exacerbate latent conflicts (Lawler, 1989) and even lead to concerted actions (e.g., slowdowns) that result in performance decline (Gomez-Mejia, 1990a). Likewise, attempts to implement a merit pay system in a highly politicized organization (such as in some government units and many universities) may simply "encourage employees to spend effort lobbying about both the specification and application of the system to measure and evaluate output" (Baker, Jensen, and Murphy, 1988, p. 598). In fact, many deans have been toppled by angry faculty dissatisfied with the way pay increases (which are usually small in universities) are allocated.

Second, it has not been uncommon in the past to design and implement compensation programs that are totally separate from the firm's strategic orientation. For example, Management By Objectives (MBO) programs were touted as a panacea by consultants and academics alike during the 1950s, 1960s, and 1970s (e.g., Drucker, 1954; McGregor, 1957; Odiorne, 1965) and widely introduced with much fanfare throughout American industry during this same period. While in some cases MBO-based reward systems worked quite well, they often failed because they were being used in organizations whose strategy demanded flexibility and adaptability rather than detailed work plans prepared a year or more in advance. (For a review of several MBO studies, see Rodgers and Hunter, 1985.) One of the authors learned this from personal experience while working for a high technology corporation: An entire month at the end of the year was dedicated to preparation of work plans for the subsequent fiscal year. Pay raises were awarded at the end of the fiscal year based upon meeting the agreed upon objectives as established in the work plan for the previous year. Yet, it was clear just a few months into the fiscal year that closely following the "agreed upon" plan between incumbent and supervisor would not be in the best interest of the firm because the situation and priorities had changed. Under those conditions, the MBO program served as a brake to performance, rather than as a performance enhancer, because employees were committed to a plan of action and were hesitant to deviate from this plan for fear of reprisal when modifications (or even total abandonment) would have been the best course to take.

Third, pay-for-performance systems have often been used in ways that are divorced from external contingencies impacting the firm. For instance, merit pay programs (which provide an annuity to employees once reward is given) are used almost universally, even though they are not always in the best interest of the firm (because they tie up cash indefinitely until the employee retires or leaves the firm) or employees (because they remove all flexibility for management to cut down costs during bad times, except resorting to layoffs). These problems are particularly serious for firms operating in volatile, unpredictable environments such as those found in the high technology industry.

Fourth, many of the reported problems with incentive systems can be traced to the fact that management (and unions, in some cases) did not take into account the nature of work when the system was introduced. For instance, use of a piece-rate plan under conditions of rapid technological change is almost certainly doomed to failure. Likewise, as forcefully argued by Pearce (1987), attempts to introduce an incentive plan focused on individual performance will have extensive dysfunctional effects in the organization if the nature of work demands close cooperation among individuals.

Fifth, compensation programs have often been borrowed from other organizations or purchased as a package from a consulting firm without tailoring them to the structural configuration of the company. For instance, incentive systems work better in smaller organizations at early stages in their life cycle than among large, mature firms (Balkin and Gomez-Mejia, 1987a). Likewise, promotion-based reward systems (where individuals are rewarded for upward movement in the organizational structure) will be effective in rapidly expanding firms but not in companies that are experiencing stable growth or even decline (Baker, Jensen, and Murphy, 1988).

Lastly, many of the reported failures of incentive-based programs can be traced to the fact that these were applied in a mechanistic, formula-driven fashion requiring minimal judgment or subjective assessments. These extremely algorithmic pay systems can only be successful in a limited number of conditions (such as in the case of real-estate agents where transactions between the agent and any given client are easily quantifiable—namely, a percent of the selling price). However, algorithmic pay systems are likely to be dysfunctional in cases where quality is important or if an ongoing relationship between customer and firm is to be encouraged.

PAY, HUMAN RESOURCE FLOWS, AND FIRM PERFORMANCE

       Fixed Pay vs. Incentives and HR Outflows
       Severance Pay
       Retirement Incentives

    PAY POLICY IMPLEMENTATION PROBLEMS
       Determining the Market Wage
         Factors that Affect the Market Wage
       Dealing with Pay Compression

    CONCLUSION

In previous chapters, how strategic compensation choices interact with business strategies, the nature of the position, and other organizational factors that influence firm performance have been examined. In this chapter, how reward policies influence the flow of human resources into, through, and out of the organization is reviewed.

Because labor is a crucial factor of production, how well human resource flows are managed is likely to have a major effect on firm performance. Management of these flows impacts:

1. The quality and quantity of labor attracted to the firm (Mitchell, 1989).
2. Returns to human capital investments (Becker, 1964, 1975).
3. Retention of scarce talent (Coombs and Rosse, 1992; Hom and Griffeth, 1993).
4. Allocation of skills in the internal labor market (Rothwell and Kazanas, 1988; Walker, 1992).
5. Total labor costs and employee distribution within wage structure (Ehrenberg and Milkovich, 1987).
6. Matching of managers to a firm's strategic configuration (Gupta, 1986; Jackson, Schuler, and Rivero, 1989; Guthrie and Olian, 1991).
7. Succession planning (Burack, 1988).
8. Interindividual and interunit synergies in work flows (Alchian and Demsetz, 1972).
9. The mix of labor and capital in the production process (Reynolds, 1951).
10. Transfer of know-how across subunits and understanding of organizational transformations (Pitts, 1974, 1976).
11. Adaptability and diversity of the managerial cadre (Rajagopalan and Prescott, 1990).

The strategic compensation choices revealed in Chapter 2 provide market signals that influence human resource flow decisions made in either the external or internal labor markets. Eight key HR flow decisions that may be influenced by these strategic compensation choices are identified. (See Table 10-1.) These decisions are examined next.

HUMAN RESOURCE INFLOW AND EXTERNAL LABOR MARKET

Human resource inflow decisions are made by job seekers in the external labor market. These individuals adjust their preferences for work based on their expectations for

TABLE 10-1
Strategic Compensation Choices that Influence Human Resource Flow Decisions

Decision Category	Strategic Compensation Choices
• **HR Inflow Decisions**	
–Decision to Work	–Fixed Pay vs. Incentives
	–Pay Level vs. Market
–Decision to Work Additional Hours	–Pay Level vs. Market
–Decision to Enter an Occupation	–Pay Level vs. Market
• **HR Internal Flow Decisions**	
–Decision to Train Employees	–Job vs. Skills
	–Pay Level vs. Market
–Decision to Work Undesirable Working Conditions	–Job vs. Skills
• **HR Outflow Decisions**	
–Decision to Change Employers	–Pay Level vs. Market
–Decision to Trim the Work Force	–Fixed Pay vs. Incentives
–Decision to Retire	–Fixed Pay vs. Incentives

being remunerated for their labor. The human resource inflow decisions govern the available labor supply from which a firm can expect to fill vacancies.

Human Resource Inflow Decisions

The three HR inflow decisions are: (1) the decision to work, (2) the decision to work additional hours, and (3) the decision to enter an occupation. These decisions are discussed in the following paragraphs.

Decision to Work. An individual makes the decision to work and determines whether to seek employment or to utilize time by engaging in some other types of activities (for example, education, household activities, or traveling). The labor force participation rate measures the ratio of the number of individuals who are in the work force compared to the total number of individuals who are eligible to work. Recent labor force participation rates have shown stable rates of participation for adult males and increased labor force participation rates for adult females (Milkovich and Boudreau, 1991).

The pay level vs. market and fixed pay vs. incentives compensation choices influence individuals in their decisions to work. For example, an increase in the pay level may exceed the "reservation wage" of an individual who works full-time at home and, therefore, attracts this individual into the labor market. An attractive employee benefit (such as child care benefits) may also influence individuals to enter the work force instead of engaging in alternative forms of activities.

Decision to Work Additional Hours. Once employed, a worker may decide to work additional hours, or overtime. Employers are required by law to pay overtime to nonexempt workers (see the section on Fair Labor Standards Act in Chapter 11), but there is a large group of exempt employees for whom employers are not required to pay an overtime premium pay rate. Employers may find it advantageous to allocate additional work to employees already on the payroll, rather than to hire more workers. In order to influence an employee's decision to work additional hours, the employer may adjust the pay level (which also governs the overtime pay rate), as shown in Table 10-1.

According to the theory of work and leisure (from labor economics), an individual seeks to maximize his or her utility in allocating time to work and leisure activities (Ehrenberg and Smith, 1988). As the wage rate increases, an individual experiences income and substitution effects on the number of hours he or she is willing to provide the employer. Because one prefers to use additional income for leisure activities and, thus, has a preference to work fewer hours, the income effect makes leisure time more attractive. The substitution effect works in the opposite direction. It makes leisure time more expensive. The individual responds to the substitution effect by offering more hours to the employer because the pay rate is higher, which makes the money—and additional work—more attractive.

While both effects occur when the pay rate increases, one effect dominates the other. The higher the wage level, the more dominant the income effect. Empirical evidence indicates the income effect would dominate higher pay levels for males (Borjas and Heckman, 1978). Evidence also suggests the substitution effect would dominate for females who receive higher pay levels. Thus, women would prefer to work additional hours when wages increase (Smith and Ward, 1985).

Decision to Enter an Occupation. At least three times during their working lives, most individuals will make decisions to enter an occupation or to change careers. This decision governs the number of individuals available for employment in a given line of work that requires special or additional education such as nursing or electrical engineering.

One of the most important factors that influences individuals to enter an occupation (and invest in education) is the anticipated earnings the career will provide. According to human capital theory, education may be viewed as an investment that can provide an expected rate of return over a certain period of time (Becker, 1975; Mincer, 1975). Investments in human capital includes the direct expenses of education (such as tuition and supplies), as well as indirect expenses (such as foregone earnings while one attends school). Human capital theory predicts such investments are more likely to be made if the present value of the benefits (over a period of time) is at least as great as the costs. As the pay level of a given occupation increases relative to alternative employment, more individuals will invest in education to enter the line of work that promises a higher rate of return over the course of their careers.

PAY AND HUMAN RESOURCE INFLOWS

Pay is one of several important factors (such as the job, work environment, one's supervisor and colleagues) that influence an organization's capacity to recruit and select the right quantity and quality of employees within the desired amount of time (Rynes, 1987).

Pay policies not only indicate to employees being recruited the amount and types of rewards they will receive in exchange for their labor, but they also provide important information that may signal what the core values of the organization are (Barber, 1989). As discussed above, a firm's strategic compensation choices provide information in the labor market that influences job seekers' decisions to enter the labor market, work additional hours, and enter an occupation. Next, specific pay policies that facilitate the inflow of new employees to the firm are examined.

Table 10-2 identifies pay policies derived from strategic compensation choices that affect the inflow of human resources to the firm from the labor market (in the far left column). Compensation strategies can affect the size of the job applicant pool, the skill level of job applicants, and the speed with which a new hire can be placed on the job. The key compensation strategy choices that affect human resource inflows include pay level vs. market and fixed pay vs. incentives.

Pay Level vs. Market and HR Inflows

From the perspective of the inflow of human resources, pay level vs. market determines the competitive position of the firm's pay within the labor market. The classic pay level policy choices are to lead, meet, or follow the competition in the labor market (Milkovich and Newman, 1990). Empirical research has identified several factors that determine a firm's pay level in the market. Organization size (Gerhart and Milkovich, 1993), profitability (Ehrenberg and Smith, 1988), stage in the product life cycle (Balkin and Gomez-Mejia, 1987a), and industry (Balkin and Gomez-Mejia, 1984) are factors that influence pay level policy choices. Yet, one still finds that similar firms make different pay level decisions (see Groshen, 1988; Gerhart and Milkovich, 1990; Weber and Rynes, 1991), indicating that employers do exercise discretion in their choice of pay level vs. market rate.

TABLE 10-2
Some Selected Pay Policies Derived from Strategic Compensation Choices
That Affect Human Resource Flows

Human Resource Inflows	Human Resource Internal Flows	Human Resource Outflows
• **Pay Level vs. Market**	• **Fixed Pay vs. Incentives**	• **Pay Level vs. Market**
—Lead the Market	—Progressive Benefits	—Lead the Market
—Meet the Market	—Education Benefits	—Meet the Market
—Follow the Market	—Child Care Assistance	—Follow the Market
• **Fixed Pay vs. Incentives**	• **Job vs. Skills**	• **Fixed Pay vs. Incentives**
—Sign-On Bonus	—Job Evaluation	—Severance Pay
—Relocation Benefits	—Dual-Pay Structures	—Retirement Incentives
	—Knowledge-Based Pay	

Each of the three pay level policy choices can stimulate the inflow of human resources differently in terms of quantity, quality, and speed. Each of these choices is discussed next.

Lead the Market. For choosing to *lead the market,* a firm pays substantially above the mean market wage or salary for a job (i.e., around the 80th percentile in the pay range) and, thus, is able to generate a large applicant pool from which to select very high-quality employees. A lead market pay policy can help reduce the amount of time necessary to fill job vacancies since the queue of job applicants is long and applications may be available in advance. Also, high paying employers can expect to retain their employees for a longer time on average (see discussion in next paragraph). Lower employee turnover makes it more feasible for the company to invest heavily in training because the company is more likely to recover its training investment. Thus, the highly paid employees selected may also be more productive, which can result in lower unit labor costs, and at least partially offset the higher compensation costs.

An extensive literature in both labor economics and organizational behavior strongly suggests that employee membership and commitment to the firm are a positive function of the employer's wage level. For instance, Garen (1988) and Leonard (1987) argue that a lead market pay policy is instrumental to lower attrition rates; the more so the greater the firm specific human capital accumulated by employees. Empirical studies in labor economics by Parsons (1977), Blakemore, Low, and Ormiston (1987), and Flinn (1986) report that interindustrial variations in quit rates are explained by industry wage differences. Along similar lines, organizational scientists such as Hulin, Rosnowski, and Hachiya (1985), Mobley, Griffeth, Hand, and Meglino (1979), Mathieu and Zajac (1979), Rusbult and Farrell (1983), Price and Mueller (1981, 1986) assert that a higher than market pay level enhances work force loyalty and employee satisfaction, thereby reducing turnover costs. Empirical studies in organizational behavior generally confirm the notion that pay satisfaction is highly correlated with pay level and that the former is a strong precursor of turnover (Mobley, 1982).

It should be noted, however, that several caveats need to considered when examining the findings reviewed above (Hom, 1992). First, an "ecological fallacy" effect (Baysinger and Mobley, 1983) may be operating here. This is because researchers often generalize pay effects across different levels of analysis such as individual, industry, occupational and firm level. "Yet relationships observed at one level of data aggregation may differ in size or sign from those observed at another level . . . Indeed, the higher pay-quit associations observed for industry-level data than for individual level data illustrates the pitfall of cross-level extrapolations" (Hom, 1992, p. 3). Second, the few studies done at the firm level have questioned the assumption that higher base pay per se increases employee's bonding to the firm (Wilson and Peel, 1991).

Third, the primacy of pay level as an economic deterrence to resignations has been challenged in recent years. For example, Hom and Griffeth (1993) and Hollenback and Williams (1986) note that heavy reliance on variable compensation may be associated with no declines in overall quit rates because incentive pay may spur attrition of lower performers (who benefit least) and reduce the exodus of high performers (who have more to gain). Unfortunately, despite a massive literature on the determinants of turnover, existing models cannot easily account for these differential effects (e.g., Jackovsky, 1984; Steers and Mowday, 1981; Hom and Griffeth, 1991). Fourth, the strategic compensation perspective advanced in this book (see Chapter 2 in particular) suggests that the conventional emphasis on pay level may be exaggerated and that a complex pattern of pay policies in interaction with internal and external organizational factors influence pay system effectiveness (which includes capacity to maintain membership). Lastly, recent conceptualizations of pay satisfaction by Folger and Konovsky (1989), Miceli and Lane (1991), and Miceli, Jung, Near, and Greenberger (1991) have placed renewed emphasis on the role of perceived fairness of pay allocation procedures rather than actual amount of pay received. (Note: This view has a long theoretical tradition revolving around the equity models discussed in Chapter 1 and the pay administration perspective advanced by such authors as Dyer and Theriault, 1976, and Weiner, 1980.)

Despite the potential to leading the market in pay, few firms are able to afford this policy. Large companies that are leaders within their industry (such as IBM, Exxon, or Wall Street law firms) are most likely to adopt a lead market policy. Financial constraints prohibit nonprofit firms, government units, small firms, or companies in highly competitive industries from considering a lead market policy.

These firms may have to rely on more creative compensation schemes (e.g., by manipulating pay mix, pay structures, and administrative features) to maintain a competitive advantage and retain key contributors. High technology firms have been at the forefront of these innovations that do not entail a lead market policy (Gomez-Mejia and Welbourne, 1990). Some universities lead the market in some disciplines because they want to maintain and/or establish a reputation in a particular area, while at the same time deliberately pay faculty below market in fields that are viewed as less important to them. This raises the possibility that a firm may pay above market for strategic employee groups only and do this at the expense of groups that are deemed to be of less strategic importance (Cappeli and Cascio, 1991; Coombs and Gomez-Mejia, 1991).

Meet the Market. Firms that select a *meet the market* pay policy want to pay the going rate for a job (i.e., around the 50th percentile in the market pay range). More companies select this policy than either of the other two choices. This policy comes closest to representing the labor market clearing wage based on competitive assumptions.

Under a meet the market pay policy, firms are able to attract some employees of adequate quality to fill job vacancies. For example, experienced employees in other firms may be willing to change jobs because they perceive they are underpaid with respect to the market. Since job applicants may not be aware of vacancies, the employer may have to spend financial resources on recruiting under this pay policy.

Employers who pay the going rate are not trying to compete with other firms on the basis of pay for the best employees. However, they may be competing on the basis of other factors such as the quality of the job and organization. A going rate pay policy may also be part of a union avoidance strategy. Unions are less likely to organize workers who perceive negligible economic returns from paying union dues (Balkin, 1989).

In order to implement a meet the market pay policy, the firm must continuously monitor the labor market with pay surveys and periodically make adjustments to the pay structure to align it with the market. Many companies have good intentions of paying the going rate but neglect to adjust their pay rates in response to changes in the market. Some of these companies may in reality have a follow the market position relative to their competitors.

Follow the Market. Some companies select a *follow the market* policy and pay below the going rate for a job (i.e., around the 30th percentile on the market pay range). Usually, a company will select a follow the market policy to conserve cash. A new business venture may select this policy as a short-term goal and will anticipate paying its employees the going rate when the business becomes more profitable.

Due to the nature of their business, other organizations are continuously strapped for cash and plan to adopt permanently a follow the market pay policy. In some cases, these organizations can attract employees by stressing the goal or mission of the organization, which has a strong appeal to certain employees. For example, the pay in the U.S. military is low compared to similar civilian jobs, but the military is able to attract recruits who want to provide service to the country and obtain some valuable technical training. The U.S. government pays low rates for professional and middle management jobs but it is able to offer greater job security (under civil service) than is available in the higher paying private sector.

Companies that adopt a follow the market pay policy can face several problems that may outweigh the saving in lower labor costs they realize relative to their competitors. Under this policy, some employees will become dissatisfied with their pay and seek higher paying jobs. High employee turnover rates can be disruptive to the business, especially if it is providing a service to customers. Since recruits will give higher priorities to firms that pay the going rate, the firm may have difficulty filling vacancies created by high attrition in tight labor markets. Finally, unions find it easier to organize in low paying companies because workers are convinced their economic welfare can improve substantially by joining the union. If vulnerable to the threat of unionization in a partially organized industry, a low paying employer risks a large increase in labor costs (Solnick, 1985).

Fixed Pay vs. Incentives and HR Inflows

The fixed pay vs. incentives strategic choice determines the different forms of pay that are provided to employees. (See Chapter 2.) It is concerned with the relative proportion of pay that is split between salary, pay incentives, and benefits. These different forms of pay can signal important information to a new recruit about the values and culture of an organization.

Two specific pay policies from the fixed pay vs. incentives choice that can facilitate the inflow of human resources have been identified: (1) the sign-on bonus and (2) relocation benefits.

Sign-On Bonus. *Sign-on bonuses* are pay incentives used to attract scarce professional and management employees (Linney, 1987). The bonus may consist of cash or stock or a combination of both awarded to a new hire. The bonus allows a company to avoid pay inequities that can develop when a new employee is hired (Dossin and Merritt, 1990). The pay compression that results when a new employee is paid at full market value may adversely affect the sense of teamwork in the firm (Welbourne and Gomez-Mejia, 1991).

The sign-on bonus is especially attractive to smaller, entrepreneurial companies that must compete with larger firms in the labor market for professionals. The sign-on bonus allows a smaller firm to provide a competitive offer to a talented recruit without having to fully match the higher salary provided by the big companies. In Silicon Valley California, which has a high proportion of high technology entrepreneurships, a survey found that 69 percent of high technology firms use sign-on bonuses (Linney, 1987). Similar findings in the Boston area were reported by Gomez-Mejia and Balkin (1985) and Balkin and Gomez-Mejia (1987a).

Sign-on bonuses may also be used to retain scarce and valuable employees. Since it depends on Congress and political factors for increases to the pay scale, the pay structure of the U.S. military is very inflexible. This inflexibility makes it difficult to retain marketable, professional employees who have skills in fields such as aviation, electronics, and computers. The military has experienced some success in retaining key personnel by providing sign-on bonuses to employees with strategic skill contingent on their reenlistment for a longer period of time.

Relocation Benefits. *Relocation benefits* help facilitate both human resource inflows as part of the recruiting process and internal flows of human resources as part of the employee development process. In the latter process, relocation is an important part of management development (Moore, 1982). In order to develop management talent internally, firms often relocate managers geographically to train them for different functions (i.e., marketing and manufacturing) and different businesses.

Unfortunately, relocating scarce technical and management talent has become increasingly difficult (Sekas, 1984). The two major resistance points that can obstruct the recruitment or relocation of a highly desirable employee are housing problems and dual-career problems. Relocation benefits can enable a firm to recruit or relocate its technical and management talent and overcome the constraints on mobility caused by housing and dual-career considerations. Relocation benefits packages have a basic component, a housing component, and a spouse assistance component (Mathews, 1984).

The basic component in a relocation benefit policy covers the move of the employee. This consists of compensation to cover the cost of moving and storage of household goods, transportation of the employee and family to the new residence, a house-hunting trip, and temporary living expenses while the new residence is being prepared for occupation by the new owners.

The housing component of a relocation benefit policy faces the reality of the housing market in the United States. Due to changing mortgage interest rates and wide variances in housing costs between different real estate markets, disposing of a current house and financing a new house can be difficult. For example, two identical three-bedroom houses on similar lots in 1992 would cost $110,000 in Denver and $425,000 in San Francisco. Due to housing costs, a manager asked by the firm to transfer from Denver to San Francisco may resist the move unless some financial assistance was made available.

Relocation benefits that assist the employee in the purchase of the new house include a mortgage interest differential allowance that helps the employee cope with higher mortgage rates. Also, some firms are willing to provide subsidized mortgages at favorable interest rates to employees who move into expensive real estate markets such as California or the Northeast (Moore, 1982). Relocation benefits that assist the employee in disposing of the old house include having the company buy the house from the employee in depressed real estate markets (such as Texas and Oklahoma in the late 1980s), or covering the costs of brokerage commissions, closing costs, duplicate house carrying expenses, and mortgage prepayment penalties.

Firms can also provide assistance to dual-career couples in a relocation. This assistance includes retaining and paying the fee of an agency that specializes in finding jobs for relocated spouses, a relaxation of the nepotism rules in order to find a position for the spouse within the same firm, and participation in corporate spouse employment networks that help hire spouses within a geographic area (Sekas, 1984).

HUMAN RESOURCE INTERNAL FLOWS

Human resource internal flow decisions are made by employees and management and govern the flow of employees through an organization. Employee promotions, transfers, and relocations can result from these decisions, which are discussed next.

Human Resource Internal Flow Decisions

The HR internal flow decisions consist of (1) the decision to train employees and (2) the decision to work in undesirable working conditions. Each of these are examined in turn.

Decision to Train Employees. In order to fill a nonentry level job, an organization may either "make" or "buy" the talent it takes to fill the position. If management decides to train (a "make" decision) employees, it must be prepared to reward them for their greater productivity. The job vs. skills and pay level vs. market strategic compensation choices can facilitate management's decision to train employees. (See Chapter 2.) Human capital theory predicts that if management invests in training an employee, it should raise the pay level of that individual. This way, management shares some of the productivity gains with the employee and also retains the employee long enough to recover training investment costs (Becker, 1975).

Firms that do not adjust the pay levels of their trained employees risk losing them to competitors who prefer to "buy" talent, rather than invest in human capital (Drory, 1992; Page et al., 1992). For instance, a skill-based pay plan (which may be selected from the job vs. skills choice) increases human capital by making pay contingent on each skill block that is learned. Under certain conditions, extensive cross-training may increase a firm's efficiency and flexibility in its labor allocation. (See Chapter 2.)

Decision to Engage in Undesirable Work. The theory of compensating wage differentials has been known for at least 200 years. Adam Smith, in *Wealth of Nations*, recognized that workers must be given higher pay for dangerous or unpleasant jobs (Ehrenberg and Smith, 1988). This idea is captured in traditional job evaluation plans (job vs. skills choice). Most job evaluation plans recognize "working conditions" as a generic compensable factor that provides value to the organization. Undesirable working conditions (such as working a night shift) would generate a high level of points under the working conditions factor and would result in a compensating wage differential for the employee required to do unpleasant work. Therefore, by including this criterion as a compensable factor in job evaluation, individuals may be lured to accept undesirable work in anticipation of a pay premium.

PAY AND HUMAN RESOURCE INTERNAL FLOWS

Human resources can flow in several different directions within organizations. They can move vertically upward (promotion) or downward (demotion), horizontally (transfer), or geographically (relocation). The allocation of appropriate rewards can facilitate the smooth flow of human resources to areas of the firm where they are needed. Earlier in this chapter, how a firm's strategic compensation choices influence management's decision to train employees and how an employee's decision to work less than desirable working conditions within an organization were discussed. (See Table 10-1.) Now, some specific pay policies derived from the strategic compensation choices that affect the internal flow of human resources within the firm are reviewed.

Table 10-2 suggests that the fixed pay vs. incentives and job vs. skills strategic compensation choices can influence the internal flow of human resources through the firm. The benefits component of the fixed pay vs. incentives choice helps bind employees to the firm. It makes leaving more costly. Thus, management can more feasibly invest in employee training and development and plan for the future. The job vs. skills choice provides the basis for rewards that recognize employees' efforts and contributions to the firm. This enables the firm to place employees in jobs where they are needed.

Fixed Pay vs. Incentives and HR Internal Flows

The employee benefits component of the pay mix can bind employees to the firm by making it unattractive for them to leave the organization (which can make it more attractive for management to invest in human capital). The forms of pay that can be used to retain employees include progressive benefits, education benefits, and child care assistance.

Progressive Benefits.   *Progressive benefits* increase in value with the tenure of the employee (Bergmann, Hills and Priefert, 1983). As the amount of an employee's seniority in a firm increases, the value of the benefits package also increases. The "loss" of the progressive benefits in a job change may not be compensated with a higher salary from a new employer. The types of benefits that increase in value with employee tenure include retirement, vacation, sick leave, and sabbatical leave. Other nonpecuniary advantages to employees with seniority include preferences for work assignments, shifts, job locations, and scheduling of vacations (Allen and Keaveny, 1988).

Retirement benefits can be a powerful inducement for an employee to remain with an employer. An employee may lose the entire employer contribution to the retirement plan if he or she leaves before being vested. Under ERISA (Employee Retirement Income Security Act), employees who leave an employer in less than five years may lose the employer's contribution under the Cliff vesting provision (McCaffery, 1992).

The U.S. military provides early retirement benefits to employees who qualify by putting in 20 years of service. This "20 years and out" retirement provision is valuable. It allows a retired military person to start a second career with the security of a lifelong retirement income to complement one's earnings. The military retirement benefits enables the armed forces to retain valuable officers and professionals who would otherwise be attracted to the higher paying civilian labor market.

Paid time off, like retirement benefits, usually increases with length of service to the employer. Vacation and sick leave fall under this category. Some employees have strong preferences for leisure time that cannot be replaced with a job change. For example, it may take ten years of service for an employee to earn the right to have a three-week paid vacation in a firm. The loss of this privilege may be substantial if the employee must start building seniority in a new firm with one week vacation per year for the first five years.

Universities have used sabbatical leaves (in addition to faculty tenure) to bind faculty to the institution. When it means giving up an academic year with pay to pursue one's own interests, a professor with five years vested toward a sabbatical leave may think twice about leaving for "greener pastures". (Most sabbatical leaves are awarded to the faculty member in the seventh year of service to the institution.)

Education Benefits. *Education benefits* are resources the firm makes available to an employee to further his or her education and career. The firm expects the employee to pursue a degree or take courses in higher education (such as in business or engineering) that improves an employee's skills and performance. The HRM function acts as a gatekeeper and approves courses and degree programs that are perceived as appropriate for the employee.

Education benefits may also bind an employee to the firm and enable an organization to retain the talents of a scarce employee for a longer period of time. For example, some firms provide resources for their managers to attend evening MBA programs. An employee may have tuition and books reimbursed by the firm with the stipulation that the grades remain at an acceptable grade point average. An employee in the middle of the part-time MBA program may not want to disrupt progress on the degree with a job change (which may entail a relocation or a different supervisor who may be nonsupportive of the MBA). Thus, the firm may be able to retain the talents of middle managers for an additional four-to five-year period (the time it takes to complete a part-time MBA program).

Child Care Assistance. As more females and mothers of small children enter the work force, need for child care assistance grows. In the decade of the 1990s, two out of three new entrants to the work force will be females (Levine, 1989). Yet, there is a lack of adequate and affordable child care facilities available for working mothers in the United States. Less than 10 percent of U.S. firms provide any provision for child care assistance for their employees (Velleman, 1987).

By providing child care assistance as part of the benefits package, firms may be able to retain their employees for longer periods of time. There is some empirical evidence suggesting that firms that offer child care assistance are able to reduce their employee turnover and absenteeism rates, as compared to firms that offer no child care assistance (Milkovich and Gomez-Mejia, 1976; Youngblood and Chambers-Cook, 1984).

Depending on the availability of resources and the needs of the employees, a firm may offer to its employees several different types of child care programs (Velleman, 1987; Petersen and Massengill, 1988):

1. *On-site child care.* The organization builds a child care facility on the company property. This can be expensive but it allows parents to see their children during lunch and break periods.
2. *Voucher system.* The firm provides resources to reimburse partially employees for child care expenditures.
3. *Flexible benefits.* Employees who are parents may select child care assistance benefits from a menu of benefits choices. These benefits qualify under Section 125 of the Internal Revenue Code and are not taxed. Employees who are not parents may select other benefits from the flexible benefits package.
4. *Referral service.* Up-to-date information on available child care facilities in the community is provided to employees by the referral service.

A firm may also implement some human resource policies that are related to child care assistance. These policies make it easier for parents to balance work demands with the needs of nurturing their children (Levine, 1989). Flexible work schedules and compressed workweeks give parents more flexibility to be with their children while the other spouse is at work. They also reduce schedule conflicts (which may result in absenteeism) when children are sick and require attention. Parental leave policies allow parents an extended leave of absence to be with a newborn infant. Finally, some firms structure work so that working at home is feasible. The personal computer, computer networks, and fax machines make it easier for individuals to work at home and be in close communication with the office. Some firms take advantage of these technologies and restructure jobs for employees so they can spend more time at home and avoid having to use day care for their children.

Job vs. Skills and HR Internal Flows

The job vs. skills strategic compensation choice affects the hierarchy of pay rates (sometimes called the pay structure) between jobs in an organization. (See Chapter 2.) The pay structure that results from this decision may reflect the degree of tallness or flatness of the organizational structure. Pay differentials may be used by management to recognize different status levels of jobs in the firm. The pay differential enables management to recognize a promotion to a higher level with an increase in salary, which is justified by the increased level of responsibility assumed by the incumbent.

Human resource flows that move in vertical or horizontal directions should be supported by the reward system. For example, a promote-from-within employment policy in a multilevel bureaucratic firm can be supported by a pay policy (i.e., job evaluation) that recognizes the organizational level of the job with pay.

The job vs. skills strategic compensation choice determines whether management should reward for the *job* or the *person*. When the job is the basis of pay, the job is perceived as a generic position independent of the person who holds it. Job evaluation is the method firms use in determining the worth of the job when the job is the basis of value to the company.

Paying employees based on their individual contributions is an alternative method. In this case, it is assumed that individual contributions vary and people should be paid according to the value of what they provide the firm, not on the basis of their job assignment (Kanter, 1987). The person as the basis of pay would most likely be used in firms with flat organizational structures with a minimum of status and hierarchical distinctions between employees. Knowledge-based-pay (KBP) is the most well-known method of delivering rewards based on individual contributions.

In the following section, alternative pay policies that are derived from the job vs. skills strategic choice are presented. Job evaluation, dual-pay structures, and knowledge-based pay are examined.

Job Evaluation. *Job evaluation* (first introduced in Chapters 1 and 2), an administrative procedure based on job analysis, is used for establishing a relative hierarchy of jobs for purposes of pay (Gerhart and Milkovich, 1993). Job evaluation is a judgmental measurement procedure (such as performance appraisal) and is subject to both random and systematic errors (Madigan, 1985; Schwab and Grams, 1985). Further, job evaluation may be subject to bias due to favoritism. For example, a supervisor may manage his or her resource dependence on a subordinate by giving that individual a higher job evaluation (leading to higher pay) than is justified by the job description (Bartol and Martin, 1988).

Job evaluation plans differ on whether jobs are compared as whole jobs or compared by dimensions, which are called compensable factors (Belcher, 1974). Examples of compensable factors would be skill, effort, responsibility, and working conditions, which are identified under the Equal Pay Act. The point method of job evaluation (which utilizes compensable factors) is the most popular method in the United States. (Bass and Barrett, 1981).

Based on the raters' judgments, job evaluation is subject to errors and bias, which can reduce its reliability and validity to predict the worth of a job. While conflicting findings are not uncommon, research on job evaluation has identified several sources of error (see Gerhart and Milkovich, 1993, for review):

1. Interrater reliability is not high.
2. There is not a high degree of discriminant validity. Job evaluations may differ, depending on the method selected to classify jobs (i.e., ranking vs. point method).
3. Some jobs change their content frequently in dynamic organizations and need to be reevaluated often.

While open to criticism, under the right set of circumstances and administrative procedures job evaluation is an effective method to develop a pay structure. These situations include whenever:

1. The jobs are stable in content and are expected to remain stable in the future. For example, job evaluation may be more appropriate for a firm that operates in a stable environment (such as a government unit) than for a fast growth firm in a dynamic environment (such as a rapidly growing, high technology company) (Hills, 1989).
2. There are meaningful differences that can be reliably measured between jobs (Kanin-Lovers, 1991).
3. The organization wants to encourage hierarchical distinctions between jobs (Gomez-Mejia, Balkin, and Milkovich, 1990). Job evaluation recognizes status differences between jobs and provides additional pay for jobs that have higher levels of responsibility.
4. The firm grows through internal diversification and follows a defender strategy. (See Chapter 4.)

Interestingly enough, little is known about the acceptability of job evaluation methods. This is surprising, given that since its inception, job evaluation was conceived as a mechanism to develop pay structures that are *perceived* to be fair (e.g., Kerr and Fisher, 1950; Livernash, 1957). In fact, Belcher (1974) referred to employee acceptability as the ultimate criterion of success of a job evaluation plan. Yet almost all of the published research on job evaluation has taken place within a psychometrics tradition that narrowly focuses on measurement issues such as predictor-criterion intercorrelations (e.g., Tornow and Pinto, 1976), hit rates (e.g., Madigan and Hoover, 1986), interrater reliability (e.g., Doverspike, Carlisi, Barret, and Alexander, 1983), and alternative factor weighing schemes (e.g., Davis and Sauser, 1991).

In one of the few studies examining the acceptability issue, Gomez-Mejia, Page, and Tornow (1982) found that while the psychometric properties of seven job evaluation methods were not all that different (in terms of criterion related validity, hit rates, and interrater reliability), dramatic differences were observed in terms of acceptability. This study, conducted at Control Data Corporation, suggests that an obsessive focus on measurement can be dysfunctional and neglect crucial political factors that determine the extent to which all stakeholders involved "buy into" the job evaluation results. This is an area where additional research is sorely needed.

Alternative choices to job evaluation that may be used to form a hierarchy of pay rates include a market-priced pay structure (Balkin and Logan, 1988) and knowledge-based pay (Ledford, 1991; Tosi and Tosi, 1986). Market-priced pay structures price all jobs in the market. This type of pay structure is possible if all jobs are benchmark jobs where abundant matches can be found in the market. Entrepreneurships, R&D units, and sales organizations may be able to adopt this type of pay policy. Larger firms may have to rely on market pricing for only benchmark jobs and may need to rely on job evaluation for pricing nonbenchmark jobs. Knowledge-based pay (where the person is the basis of pay) will be examined later in this chapter.

Dual-Pay Structures. *Dual-pay structures* are pay policies designed to support dual-career ladders in organizations. Dual ladders are career paths intended to provide job enrichment and more financial rewards to individual contributors. (See Katz, Tushman, and Allen, 1992). Traditionally, a professional such as an engineer or scientist reaches a career plateau in the organization and finds the only path leading to greater rewards and job challenge is moving into management. The firm often loses a good individual contributor (engineer or sales representative) and gains a marginal manager (project manager or sales manager).

Dual-career ladders were developed to retain talented individual contributors and provide them with an alternative career path other than management (Allen and Katz, 1986). Dual-pay structures consist of individual contributor jobs that are "matches" to managerial jobs in the pay structure. For example, the job of "consulting engineer" may be compensated at the same salary level as the job of "project manager" in a firm. In theory, engineers who do not have the skills or interest to become managers may reap additional rewards and challenges by channeling their energies into the technical career path.

In practice, research indicates that organizations must plan their dual-career ladders carefully or face some common pitfalls with these programs (Allen and Katz, 1986). One problem with dual-career ladders is that the technical ladder may unintentionally be perceived as the "dumping ground" for engineers who do not have the skills or aptitudes to become managers. The technical ladder is viewed in this light as a punishment, rather than as a reward. The way to avoid this problem is to select carefully only top performing technical contributors for the technical ladder. Thus, it is perceived as a reward for outstanding performance.

Another problem with dual ladders is that more prestige and status may be associated with the management ladder due to the organization culture. Employees who choose the individual contributor career path may have some misgivings when their peers in management achieve higher prestige in their jobs. This is a difficult problem to correct since most organizations place a high value on the contributions of its managers. Whatever remedy is provided, the firm should take a broad perspective of the reward system to include rewards that go beyond just giving comparable salaries to managers and technical contributors. For example, IBM provides special recognition to its top scientists and engineers at award ceremonies where cash bonuses are presented to employees in front of their peers (Gomez-

Mejia, Balkin, and Milkovich, 1990).   In this manner, the reward system "signals" to the individual contributor that the technical ladder has prestige and status in the organization.

Knowledge-Based Pay.   *Knowledge-based pay* (which is also called skill-based pay) is an alternative approach to allocate pay as discussed earlier in this chapter and in Chapter 2.   Under knowledge-based pay (KBP), the person is the basis of pay, not the job.   KBP rewards employees who learn a new skill block or additional knowledge with a pay raise.   This contrasts to the traditional method of job evaluation, where internal pay equity and market factors determine the pay relationships.   Under KBP, all employees start at the same pay rate and advance one pay level for each new skill block that is mastered (Wallace, 1990).   Employees have more control over the timing and amount of their rewards.   Since they are dependent on supervisor judgments for either their pay raise (under a merit pay plan) or for a promotion to a higher pay grade, traditional job evaluation-based pay decisions provide less opportunities for employee input.

Knowledge-based pay has been used to pay such diverse occupations as engineers and scientists (the use of maturity curves that base pay on a combination of the most advanced degree plus years of experience); public school teachers (their pay policies reward teachers for advanced degrees and additional college credits); and production workers (who are given pay raises for demonstrating a mastery of new skill blocks).   In the 1980s, use of KBP expanded and was used in hotels, retail stores, and financial service firms (Ledford, 1990, 1991).   Sponsored jointly by the American Compensation Association and the American Productivity Center five years ago, a survey of 1,600 large organizations found that five percent of the firms used KBP for production and/or service employees (O'Dell, 1987).

One of the most attractive features of KBP is that it supports employers' efforts to have a more flexible work force.   KBP is often utilized with work teams that are designed to improve product quality.   Each team member is cross-trained to do the jobs of other team members.   Thus, absenteeism does not disrupt the team's ability to produce the product or service.   Since pay is not governed by job descriptions, seniority does not control work assignments under KBP.   Management can run a leaner organization with fewer supervisors and can capture some labor cost savings by having to hire fewer employees (Ledford, 1990, 1991; Tosi and Tosi, 1986).   It is no surprise that knowledge-based pay is often used in companies that emphasize high involvement management (Lawler, 1986).

Another reported advantage of KBP is that employees perceive it as more fair than traditional methods of reward allocation (Ledford, 1990, 1991; Tosi and Tosi, 1986).   Under KBP, the employee is more in control of determining the pay rate.   The pay rates associated with different skill blocks are known by employees (as opposed to a pay secrecy policy, which does not reveal other pay grades to employees).   Due to the presence of these factors, there should be stronger perceptions of procedural justice for employees under KBP.   One would also expect fewer grievances over pay rates, which may result in improved labor-management relationships (Gupta, Schweizer, and Jenkins, 1987).   It should be noted, however, that most of the reported advantages of KBPs are still speculative in nature and have very limited empirical support.

Despite its purported association with positive outcomes, knowledge-based pay can lead to problems if implemented in an inappropriate situation.   KBP in the long run can cause the firm to have higher compensation costs and training costs.   After several years of operation under KBP, many employees may have mastered all the skill blocks and should be at the top end of the pay structure.   They may be paid a higher wage than the job evaluation-based pay rate for the task they are performing. Further, some employees under KBP may be trained for skills that cannot be utilized in the organization. Bottlenecks in the workflow or work rule constraints may not permit the employee the opportunity to practice the skills he or she was trained to do. Obviously, to avoid the potential costs overruns, management must carefully plan how KBP fits into its entire human resource strategy. For example, in order to justify the expenditures on training under KBP, human resource development should have a high priority in the firm's strategic plan.

Another problem that needs to be breached under KBP is avoiding employees' frustration when they reach the ceiling of the pay structure (Luthans and Fox, 1989). When employees hit the top of the pay structure after mastering all the skill blocks, they have no further opportunity to receive a pay raise. Some employees may leave at this point, and the firm loses valuable, highly trained contributors. One way to avoid this outcome would be to complement KBP with an aggregate pay incentive such as profit sharing or gainsharing. For example, under gainsharing an individual at the pay ceiling has an opportunity for greater earnings by providing suggestions that result in labor cost savings that will be shared with all employees. Gainsharing and profit-sharing plans were examined in greater detail in Chapter 9.

The above discussion of knowledge-based pay suggests that several contingency factors should be present in order for an organization to achieve best results. First, a new plant or organization at the start-up or growth stage of its life cycle should benefit from KBP. In this situation, there are few established work rules or reward practices that are threatened by KBP. Further, the employees are at a low point on the learning curve in a new plant, and heavy emphasis on training is appropriate at this stage. Next, KBP should be synergistic in a firm with a highly participative organization culture. For example, due to the design of its workflow, a plant that utilizes semiautonomous work teams should reap more benefits from KBP because it can take greater advantage of cross-trained employees. Third, the union should not only support KBP but also be involved in the design and implementation of the policy. Without the enthusiastic support of the union (KBP is used in both union and nonunion firms), KBP has diminished likelihood of reaching its objectives. Finally, other aggregate pay policies can complement KBP in the long run by offering additional incentives to motivate employees who have mastered all the skill blocks available to them.

HUMAN RESOURCE OUTFLOWS

Human resource outflow decisions are made by employees (voluntary turnover) and management (involuntary turnover), and they impact the quantity and quality of employees who leave a firm. Layoffs, turnover, early retirement, or retirement are outcomes that may result from these decisions. These are discussed next.

Human Resource Outflow Decisions

The HR outflow decisions consist of: (1) the decision to change employers, (2) the decision to trim the work force, and (3) the decision to retire. Each of these is examined in turn.

Decision to Change Employers. Management can exercise substantial control over the rate of voluntary turnover by monitoring the pay level of their employees compared to the pay rates available in the labor market (pay level vs. market). If a large enough discrepancy exists between the pay an employee receives at a firm and the pay the employee perceives is available in the market, the employee will likely respond to this market signal and exit the firm. By adjusting a firm's pay rate with respect to the market, management can influence an employee's decision to change employers and make it less attractive (or profitable) to leave the firm. Later in this chapter, the pay level vs. market strategic choice is examined in greater detail.

Decision to Trim the Work Force. When the demand for a firm's products declines, management may find it is necessary to reduce labor costs to respond to the decline in revenues. Management's decision to trim the work force depends on how much flexibility it has to reduce labor costs. If a significant portion of labor costs take the form of pay incentives (fixed pay vs. incentives), management may have the flexibility to retain the work force without resorting to layoffs (Mitchell, 1987; Weitzman, 1984). On the other hand, if employee compensation takes the form of only base salary and benefits (fixed pay), management may have no other alternative to reduce labor costs but to lay people off from their jobs. A vivid example is provided by General Motors which is laying off 75,000 employees during 1992-1996.

Decision to Retire. Employees make the decision to retire and time their decisions to coincide with Social Security and Medicare eligibility, as well as health and availability of personal savings as considerations. Since it is illegal for employers to force an employee to retire, management may find itself trying to avoid human resource flow bottlenecks if a large cohort of employees is close to retirement age. One way to influence positively the decision to retire is for management to provide financial incentives (fixed pay vs. incentives choice), which makes it attractive for an employee to retire early without facing economic hardships. These voluntary, early retirements give management the flexibility to either reduce the size of the work force or to open opportunities for new employees. Specific types of early retirement incentives are examined later in this chapter.

PAY AND HUMAN RESOURCE OUTFLOWS

Human resource outflows can be measured by the quantity, quality, and speed to which employees leave the organization. Instrumental in recruiting employees, compensation can also provide support in controlling the outflow of employees from the firm. The right people are separated, and others are retained. As discussed above, a firm's strategic compensation choices affect management's decision to trim the work force and an employee's decision to change employers and to retire. Now, some specific pay policies derived from the strategic compensation choices that affect the outflow of human resources from the firm are examined.

Table 10-2 indicates that the pay level vs. market and fixed pay vs. incentives strategic compensation choices can be designed to affect the outflow of human resources from the firm. The appropriate pay level vs. market choice can help management regulate the quantity, quality, and rate of human resource outflows. The fixed pay vs. incentives choice can affect the quality and labor cost of employees who leave the firm.   Policies derived from these strategic pay choices can support an organization's human resource strategy so that the results of employee turnover are functional, not dysfunctional (Jackovsky, 1984).

Pay Level vs. Market and HR Outflows

As discussed earlier in this chapter, there is a strong relationship between pay levels and employee turnover.   Organizations that choose a follow the market pay level policy can expect higher attrition rates than firms that lead or meet the market pay level.   In order to control human resource outflows, management must continuously monitor the labor market and make adjustments to pay grades so that the planned pay policies are implemented with respect to the market.   Management should understand that the labor market is dynamic.   A firm may start the fiscal year with its pay grades at the going rate in the market (50th percentile) and twelve months later find its market position has eroded to a de facto lag position (40th percentile).   In order to have acceptable turnover rates, a firm may need to lead the market for six months to end the fiscal year closer to the going rate when salary budget adjustments are again performed (assuming pay grades are adjusted once each fiscal year).

Fixed Pay vs. Incentives and HR Outflows

Two employee benefits from the pay mix can assist management in controlling the quality and cost of human resource outflows.   The use of severance pay and retirement incentives can help management trim from its work force employees whose services are no longer needed and maintain the psychological contract for retained employees.

Severance Pay.   In recent years, many organizations have reduced their work forces due to mergers and acquisitions or have decided to downsize to be more competitive in global markets.   In these situations, where organizations are undergoing reductions in force, severance pay can play an important role in the smooth outflow of employees.   A smooth outflow means less disruption to the "survivor" employees.   *Severance pay* provides employees who are involuntarily terminated with a source of income to cushion their transition into the labor market to find another job.   Severance pay is usually computed by a formula that stipulates a number of week's salary for each year of work experience with the firm (Speck, 1988).

The amount of severance pay should provide an incentive for the terminated employee to find a job as soon as possible.   The amount of the payment should not be a windfall.   Otherwise, the employee may use it to take a holiday from work or job search.   If the firm allocates severance pay in the form of a continuation of salary (instead of a lump-sum payment), the employee cannot file a claim of unemployment insurance against the firm until the salary continuation runs out (McCaffery, 1992).   This can be an effective way to manage unemployment insurance costs, which are experience rated.   When the firm is undergoing a layoff, the rates increase sizeably.   However, by allocating severance pay as a continuation of salary, the firm offsets the increases.

Severance pay during a layoff may also communicate to the survivors and the surrounding community that the firm is a socially responsible employer that treats its employees fairly and shows concern for their financial well-being even when it no longer can use their services. This can have a positive impact on the work commitment of retained employees and also facilitate recruiting new employees when the firm is ready to hire again as business conditions improve.

There are two special types of severance pay that merit discussion: (1) an employee buy-out and (2) golden parachutes for executives. An employee *buy-out* consists of a lump sum of cash, representing several years of earnings, given as a pay incentive to motivate employees to resign voluntarily from the company. The buy-out is beneficial when a firm has an explicit "lifelong employment policy" that guarantees a job to employees as long as they are performing adequately. The buy-out provides an attractive carrot. Employees may quit but the lifelong employment policy remains in effect. For example, to eliminate 1,600 manufacturing jobs at its Boca Raton, Florida facility in the late 1980s, IBM provided a lump sum of two years' salary to employees who would voluntarily quit (Lopez, 1989). IBM has had a lifelong employment policy for many years and prides itself on never having experienced a layoff, although this policy appears to be rapidly changing in the 1990s.

Golden parachutes, a special form of severance pay for executives, go into effect after a triggering event such as a hostile takeover takes place (Cochran, Wood and Jones, 1985). The golden parachute provides the executive with a large lump sum of cash, representing three to five years of earnings, that often results in a windfall of several millions of dollars. It is designed to align the interests of the entrenched executive with the shareholders when an attractive takeover bid could maximize shareholder returns. It is expected that executives would be less likely to fight the takeover offer and protect their jobs if they can take advantage of their golden parachutes. Because they can be perceived as a violation of distributive justice in a firm, golden parachutes have been a controversial compensation practice (Singh and Harianto, 1989). How fair is it for a few executives to gain enormous wealth during a takeover, while thousands of ordinary workers lose their jobs and are given a few weeks' severance pay? Not surprisingly, research indicates that firms that have previously experienced takeover threats are more likely to adopt golden parachutes (Singh and Harianto, 1989). Other aspects of golden parachutes were discussed in an earlier chapter on executive compensation (Chapter 6) in this book.

Retirement Incentives. A common problem facing organizations (especially mature industries) is how to encourage some of its senior employees to take early retirement. Organizations with an abundance of senior employees will have a significant portion of these employees experiencing career burnout, career plateaus, or skill obsolescence, which are performance problems common to senior employees (Rosen and Jerdee, 1988). Since senior employees are paid higher than other employees, the firm may be able to reduce its labor costs by replacing the seniors with less experienced workers.

Retirements of senior employees can provide some additional advantages to the firm, other than lower labor costs. Retirements can create more opportunities for junior employees to advance in the organization. These internal promotions pave the way for the creation of entry-level job vacancies, which can enable outsiders with fresh ideas and perspectives to be brought into the firm. Finally, retirements help make the internal flows of human resources more predictable. Thus, succession planning can take place, and replacements can be groomed for their promotions.

Due to the Age Discrimination in Employment Act, employers cannot force employees to retire. They must voluntarily retire. Research indicates that the median age of retirement in the United States is 63 years, and most employees are retired by age 65 even though they are legally entitled to continue working longer (Rosen and Jerdee, 1988). Most employees retire around age 65 because they are entitled to full Social Security and Medicare benefits at this age. If an employee retires before age 65, Social Security benefits are reduced, which is a disincentive for early retirement. The two key factors that predict when an employee decides to retire are an employee's financial situation and health (Beehr, 1986; McCune and Schmitt, 1981). In order to increase the number of early retirements of employees who are in the 55 to 62 age range, a firm should provide some financial incentives to make an early retirement more economically attractive to a senior employee. Retirement incentives have some similarities to the buy-out, which was examined in the previous section of this chapter. However, retirement incentives are focused at only the most senior employees in the organization, whereas a broader strata of employees may be eligible for a buy-out.

Retirement incentives consist of a package of compensation components that make it more attractive and financially acceptable for an employee to retire early (Baenen and Ernest, 1982). A typical, early retirement program includes a percentage of base salary continued over a number of years (two years is the most common time period). Next, the eligibility for retirement benefits is accelerated. For example, the age 59 requirement may be reduced to 55 years of age for eligibility. In addition, an employee may be given credit for extra years of service to increase the formula that is used to determine the retirement income. For example, an employee with 20 years of service may be given credit for 5 years of additional service. If the retirement income formula equals 2 percent times each year of service times the average of the last 5 years of salary (a typical pension formula), the employee would receive a 10 percent increase in retirement income (2 percent times 5) from this part of the retirement incentive. Finally, provisions are made for the retiree to receive continuation of health benefits. This is an important part of the early retirement package since a retired employee is not eligible for Medicare until he or she reaches age 65.

A serious problem associated with the use of retirement incentives is that too many employees may choose to use the incentives. Thus, the firm loses skilled people in a critical area. Further, if most of the senior employees take early retirement, a firm may lose its sense of history and tradition, which is important to preserve the corporate culture. The older generation of employees can provide a sense of stability and permanence to an organization, and its elimination can be disruptive to the other employees. Since retirement incentives must be available to all eligible employees, the parameters of eligibility need to be carefully planned. Age and company experience levels, which determine eligibility for the program, need to be identified. Generally, the employees who take the retirement incentives have lower performance appraisals and are close to retirement age (Baenen and Ernest, 1982). Some firms avoid losing control of the outflow of their senior people by using surveys to predict the intentions of their employees to stay or leave if given the opportunity to take advantage of retirement incentives. The survey can allow management to fine tune its program so that predictions can be made accurately on the impact of retirement incentives on human resource outflows.

This ends the discussion of pay and human resource flows into, through, and out of the organization. This chapter is concluded by examining some obstacles to the implementation of planned pay policies.

PAY POLICY IMPLEMENTATION PROBLEMS

After selecting a matrix of pay policies designed to support its human resource and business strategies, management faces two well-known problems that could potentially thwart its compensation program. These problems may be posed as two simple questions: (1) How do we determine the market wage? (2) How do we deal with pay compression? This chapter concludes by examining these two ubiquitous pay problems.

Determining the Market Wage

As indicated earlier in this chapter, the pay level vs. strategic compensation choice has a direct impact on the inflows and outflows of human resources to and from the firm. Unless it has a goal of paying below market for strategic reasons, a firm must position its compensation at the going rate in the market in order to attract and retain its specified quantity and quality of employees. This raises the question: How is the market wage determined? This is an important question for several reasons.

First, the market wage is the anchor pin that is used to determine a firm's pay position in the labor market, which, in turn, becomes the basis for its entire pay structure. If the market wage is inappropriately estimated, the firm may either be needlessly spending money on excess labor costs or finding itself unable to attract the quantity or quality of employees it requires within its time constraints. (See Chapter 1 for additional discussion on the criticisms of the use of wage surveys for estimation of the market wage.)

The determination of the market wage carries with it legal ramifications to the firm. A firm may be charged with pay discrimination under Title VII of the Civil Rights Act if it uses different practices to determine the market rate for female-dominated jobs than the practices it uses for pricing male-dominated jobs and if these practices result in lower pay for female jobs with comparable worth (Remick, 1984).

While the myth persists that the market wage can be accurately and scientifically determined as a single rate, in fact there is a wide range of market pay rates available for each occupation, and the determination of the going rate for a job is a combination of art and science. Thus, the combination of decisions that determines the market wage for a firm leaves room for a great deal of subjectivity due to the many judgments that must enter into these decisions. By making the wrong judgments, a firm may accept a poor estimation of the "true" market wage as the basis of its pay structure, and this can lead to some of the previously mentioned problems.

Factors that Affect the Market Wage. According to Groshen (1988), the factors that influence the market wage for a given occupation can be categorized as between- and within-industry factors. Industry wage differentials can be explained by different industry concentration ratios (Weiss, 1966) and capital-labor ratios (Fay, 1989). High industry concentration ratios indicate a lower level of product market competition (i.e., monopoly profits) and result in higher wage rates. There is a higher union density in industries with high concentration ratios, and this may also explain why these industries pay higher wages. Industries with high capital-labor ratios (such as the petroleum industry) offer high wage rates because they are less sensitive to changes in labor costs. For these industries, labor is a relatively minor cost of production.

Within-industry wage differentials can be partly explained by organization size (Personick and Barsky, 1982; Rees and Schultz, 1970), competitive strategy (Fay, 1989), and job characteristics (Groshen, 1988).   Large organizations pay higher wages than smaller firms because they can take advantage of greater economies of scale and have more slack resources available.   Determining which product markets and labor markets it will compete in, the firm's competitive strategy affects wage rates.   The firm may be required to offer higher wages in order to compete in its chosen product and labor markets.   Finally, job characteristics can affect wages when a firm has jobs with undesirable working conditions or demands greater required levels of work experience.   An oil rig technician can expect higher wages on an offshore drilling platform than on a land-based drilling site due to the inconvenience of living for two weeks at a time offshore on the platform.   Similarly, a major airline may require greater levels of experience for a new entry-level pilot than a start-up airline and, therefore, can pay higher wages for the pilot.   Table 10-3 summarizes some of the key judgments involved in assessing the market wage, while Table 10-4 highlights a number of recommended procedures for pay surveys that are used to ascertain the market wage.   (See Ellig, 1977; Fay, 1989; Gerhart and Milkovich, 1993; Greene, 1981; Lichty, 1991; Roy, 1991; Rynes and Milkovich, 1986.)

Dealing with Pay Compression

Besides trying to attain a competitive position in the labor market, another important objective of pay policy implementation is to maintain equitable internal pay relationships between different job clusters.   What this means is: There should exist meaningful pay differentials between consecutive pay grades in the pay structure in order for employees to perceive the firm's pay policy as equitable with respect to their individual contributions (Krefting and Mahoney, 1977).   However, when pay differentials between pay grades shrink to the point where employees perceive the differentials as no longer meaningful, the firm's pay structure is experiencing the all too common problem of pay compression.   As will be seen, pay compression adversely affects the human resource internal flows and outflows.

Pay compression is a narrowing of the pay ratios between jobs or pay grades in a firm's pay structure.   It is based on employee perceptions of the pay between them and others in jobs above and below them.   These perceptions often result in pay differentials appearing to be too small (Bergmann, Hills, and Priefert, 1983).   For example, a supervisor in a manufacturing plant (not eligible for overtime pay) may observe that the total earnings of hourly employees who are subordinates (eligible for overtime pay) closely matches his or her pay.   Similarly, an associate professor of accounting in a college of business may observe that an inexperienced assistant professor of accounting that is newly hired earns a greater salary than the experienced professor in the higher pay grade.   (This is an extreme case of pay compression called *pay inversion*.)

The overtime provision of the FLSA and the provisions of union labor contracts tend to aggravate pay compression problems among non-exempt employees (Bergmann, Hills, and Priefert, 1983).   The requirement of an overtime pay premium for nonexempt employees can reduce the differential between the pay between supervisors and hourly workers as the above example suggested.   Some companies resolve this type of pay compression by making supervisors eligible for overtime pay even though not required to under the FLSA.   Similarly, unionized workers in powerful unions may receive larger wage gains than nonunion

TABLE 10-3
Key Judgments That Affect Pay Survey Data

Pay surveys provide the data used to determine the market wage. Below are some of the crucial judgments that management must make in order to use and interpret the pay survey data. Inappropriate choices for any of these may lead to a poor estimate of the market wage.

· *Select the Jobs to Survey.* One set of choices involves whether to price all jobs in the market or to price just the benchmark jobs. In the latter situation, nonbenchmark jobs are priced by using job evaluation, which determines the pay grade for the job in question. A problem in estimating the market wage can occur when a job is fairly unique and there exists very few jobs that match it in the market. If such a job is priced in the market, there will be a great deal of error variance associated with the estimate of the market wage.

· *Select the Markets to Survey.* There is a lot of subjectivity surrounding the choice of markets to survey. Ideally, management should select firms to provide pay data for the survey that compete directly with one's company in both the labor and product markets. Unfortunately, this ideal is rarely achieved. Some firms use "convenience" samples as the basis for the data, which may include noncompetitors or inappropriate markets in the sample due to budget or time constraints. Other firms use multiple surveys representing different geographic markets and attach different weights to the survey data, depending on its relevancy to the firm. Other firms may use one survey and "trim" the data by eliminating large firms or outlying salary data points to tailor the survey (taken by a consulting firm) to the company's needs. All these methods of identifying the appropriate market and competitors leave some margin for error.

· *Select the Measure of Central Tendency.* The market wage is usually reported as a measure of central tendency, which represents a distribution of salaries in the market. The market wage may be represented as a mean or median. If reported as a mean, the market wage must be either a weighted or unweighted mean. All three of these measures of central tendency have advantages and disadvantages, and they all represent different numbers since the distribution of pay is almost always nonnormal and often skewed to the right or left. For example, the median tends to be a more conservative measure of the market wage than the mean, and it provides an estimate that is about 4 percent lower in size. The weighted mean, on the other hand, provides a higher estimate of the market wage because it gives greater emphasis on large companies (which tend to pay at higher levels) that have more employees since the basis for the weighting is the number of employees in the firm. Problems can occur in the interpretation of the data when means and medians are mixed or when an inappropriate measure of central tendency is selected for a company to base its estimate of the market wage on.

· *Control for the Accuracy of the Survey Data.* Several factors affect the validity or reliability of the pay survey data and may adversely affect its accuracy. The validity of the data is dependent on the consulting firm doing the survey being able to make accurate matches between jobs based on job content, not job titles. If the respondents do not have well-documented job descriptions for the jobs in the survey, it is difficult, if not impossible, to match jobs accurately. Poor job matches result in wider variances in pay and invalid estimates of the market wage. Next, survey data that is "dated" underestimates the market wage. Since it may take 3 to 6 months from the time it was collected to analyze and publish the survey data, it may be necessary to adjust the data by a correction factor to correct for the dynamics of the market. The longer the time lag between when the data were collected and when it is to be used, the less reliability there is to base an estimate on the market wage. Finally, most pay surveys report base salaries but do not report benefits or pay incentives in the data. By focusing on base salaries and not total compensation, the true earnings of employees in some firms may be misreported. However, trying to estimate the market wage in terms of total compensation would be an extremely costly and difficult undertaking since there is an enormous variety of different benefit packages and pay incentive policies available in the market.

TABLE 10-4
Recommended Pay Survey Practices

Below is a list of recommended pay survey practices based on recent research findings.

· *Source.* Use pay surveys produced by third parties such as consulting firms or professional associations that have reputations for using high-quality standards for collecting pay survey data. Avoid using convenience samples.

· *Relevance.* Check to make sure that the respondents to the pay survey represent firms that compete with one's company in its labor and product markets. The consulting firm that produces the pay survey may list the firms that participated in the survey in the appendix.

· *Matching of Job Descriptions.* Check to make sure one's company has accurate job descriptions to match with the job descriptions of benchmark jobs in the pay survey.

· *Consistency.* Be consistent in the measure of central tendency that is used to report the pay survey data (mean or median).

· *Timing.* Check to make sure the pay survey data is current. Find out how old the data is and make an adjustment that corresponds to when the pay policy goes into effect.

· *Monitoring.* Audit compensation levels in the firm on a regular basis to learn if the pay policies are where they are expected to be with respect to the market. Additional information on pay policies may be provided by monitoring some key HRM indicators such as employee turnover rates (who is leaving and to what firms are they going?), exit interviews (why are they leaving?), patterns in employee job satisfaction surveys (how do they feel about their pay?), grievances, and length of time it takes to fill a job vacancy. Unexpected variances in these indicators may mean that there are some problems in how the market wage is measured and utilized as the basis of the pay structure.

---

supervisors or white-collar employees who work in the same plant. One possible solution to the union impact on the pay differentials is to tie supervisors' pay to the terms of the contract even though they are not in the bargaining unit. (The union impact on pay differentials in the firm is examined in greater detail in Chapter 11.) Clearly, the most serious cause of pay compression is due to market forces, and this presents the greatest challenge to management who must otherwise accept the consequences of pay compression.

The employees who are particularly sensitive to and react negatively toward pay compression are professionals and managers. The pay systems for professionals, managers, and other exempt employee groups emphasize organizational contributions and are associated with what Krefting (1980) calls an "organizational recognition" orientation. Pay compression to employees where pay has an organizational recognition orientation may be interpreted as an attack on one's self-esteem due to the symbolic significance of pay as a signal from management indicating the worth of the employee's contribution to the firm. In extreme cases, employees may respond to perceptions of pay compression by reducing the quantity or quality of inputs provided to the firm, not cooperating with others, and engaging in deviant behavior such as theft or sabotage (Bergmann, Hills and Priefert, 1983).

The most common employee reaction is to change employers. Unfortunately, dysfunctional turnover is the end result. The model of voluntary turnover provided by March and Simon (1958) suggests that employees with the best work records are most likely to find alternative employment opportunities. Their perceived and actual ease of mobility from the organization should be enhanced, resulting in high turnover rates among the best performers (Schwab, 1991). Consistent with this prediction, Gomez-Mejia and Balkin (1988) found that among college faculty, the attrition rates of high performers increase as a function of pay dissatisfaction triggered by pay compression.

Figure 10-1, a theoretical model developed by the authors, summarizes the causes and consequences of pay compression. According to this model, the primary cause of pay compression is a demand/supply imbalance in the labor market for certain jobs that induces employers to pay higher salaries to attract employees with scarce skills such as the accounting professors in the above example (Gomez-Mejia and Balkin, 1987b). Budgetary limitations force management to increase the salary offers to new hires, often at the expense of employees who are already on board. This, in turn, leads to a narrowing of internal pay differentials that produces perceptions of pay compression inequities and pay dissatisfaction for individuals experiencing a downward narrowing of compensation differentials. What compounds the pay compression problem is that most jobs in medium to large firms are not filled from the labor market but, instead, from within the firm's pool of employees (internal labor market). Thus, many jobs are temporarily buffered from market forces with respect to pay. Employees may be unaware of their market value in promote-from-within jobs until new employees are hired in lower level positions and pay compression is perceived by these senior people.

The model in Figure 10-1 also shows that as an individual's pay begins to lag relative to the market rate, this tends to create perceptions of external market inequities, with a corresponding decline in pay satisfaction. As pay satisfaction decreases due to the combined effect of internal and external strains, the most productive employees tend to look for employment elsewhere, leaving behind those with limited market mobility. This becomes more pronounced as employment alternatives expand. Unfortunately for the firm, individuals in boundary spanning positions who are externally visible (e.g., faculty who publish in research journals) are more likely to exit the

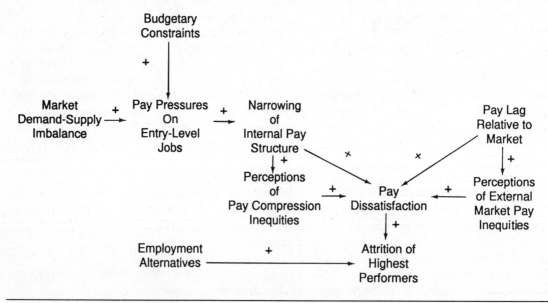

FIGURE 10–1   **Theoretical Model Showing Causes and Consequences of Pay Compression**

organization in response to pay compression because they are more attuned to the market rewards associated with it. They are also more attractive to competitors. Unless this dysfunctional cycle is arrested, particularly for boundary spanners who play critical roles in organizations (see Chapter 8), pay compression is likely to have a significant negative effect on a company's performance by exporting its most valuable human capital to competing firms.

Pay compression may be difficult, if not impossible, to eliminate for firms facing a right-ward shifting, inelastic demand for labor. This is particularly true for those that have limited financial resources and that cannot raise the entire compensation schedule of the internal labor market to keep pace with entry-level wages. However, a number of suggestions have been advanced to mitigate the effects of pay compression (Bergmann and Hills, 1987; Gomez-Mejia and Balkin, 1987b). These include the use of equity pay funds, sign-on bonuses, progressive employee benefits, nonfinancial rewards, and abandonment of hierarchical pay systems. (See Table 10-5.) In addition, firms may try to prioritize deliberately which employees are to be most protected from the ravages of pay compression. According to Newman (1988), and consistent with the theoretical model in Figure 10.1, there is a simple, logical rule to be followed in determining which groups should receive special protection: The more a particular employee group or individual serves in a boundary spanner capacity, the more reward systems designed for those employees should be attuned to, and competitive with, the external market.

CONCLUSION

In this chapter, how pay policies can be designed to support the functional strategies of the HRM unit with respect to its planned flows of human resources has been examined. Chapter 11 is concerned with issues of governance, employee voice in the distribution of pay, and legal constraints.

TABLE 10-5
Mitigating the Effects of Pay Compression

Below is a summary of alternative approaches that may be used to reduce employee perceptions of pay compression.

· *Equity Pay Funds.* An equity pay fund is a special pay increase given to employees to maintain pay differentials between their jobs and others. The equity pay increase is given as a one time only adjustment to an employee's pay and is separated from the merit pay increase. This solution to pay compression may only be available to profitable firms with slack resources. Nonprofit firms with limited resources may need to examine other means to attack pay compression.

· *Sign-On Bonuses.* Sign-on bonuses are used to recruit employees with scarce skills and maintain pay differentials between newcomers and experienced employees. The sign-on bonus allows the firm to offer a competitive total compensation package to the employee being recruited while still keeping the base salary low enough to maintain a meaningful pay differential between jobs.

· *Progressive Employee Benefits.* Progressive benefits are those that increase in value, along with an employee's seniority in the firm. These benefits include retirement plans (such as ESOPs), vacation time with pay, sick leave, sabbaticals with pay, and education benefits. Some employees are not aware of these benefits or how they increase in value with seniority (compared to a newcomer's benefits) so it is important that management communicate the progressive employee benefit policies. When experienced employees compare their total compensation to that of newcomers, progressive benefits should mitigate perceptions of pay compression.

· *Emphasize Nonfinancial Rewards.* Management can reduce the impact of pay compression by giving senior employees first priority to receive nonfinancial rewards. Senior employees could receive greater consideration for choice of work assignments, more free time to work on their own projects, choice of shift assignments (day work instead of night shift), preferred work locations (local plant instead of a distant location), preferred equipment (new truck versus old, rusty truck), office locations (corner office with window versus windowless office in basement), or opportunities for business travel to attractive destinations (such as Hawaii). Communicating the policy on nonfinancial reward allocations should allow employees perceiving pay compression to rethink how they feel about the distribution of rewards in their firm.

· *Nonhierarchical Pay System.* Some organizations have decided to abandon the use of job-based pay systems and pay structures that reward employees for their rank in the organization hierarchy. These firms use a nonhierarchical pay system, which pays the employee for his or her contributions in terms of the "value added" to the company. The employee's compensation would consist of a modest base salary and an array of pay incentives that would recognize individual, team, and organization contributions. Pay compression would not be relevant since employees would not find it unfair if a subordinate received more compensation for a significant contribution when compared to a more modest contribution made by a higher level employee.

GOVERNANCE OF COMPENSATION SYSTEM AND FIRM PERFORMANCE

How much influence management should allow employees over pay policies is an important decision that affects the reward allocation process in most organizations. Management must determine how much responsibility, authority, and power it should voluntarily delegate to employees in regard to pay. This issue can be controversial since pay information is very sensitive. Traditionally, pay policy has been viewed as one of management's prerogatives and has been formulated with a top-down approach. This perspective is predicated on the belief that employees cannot separate their self-interests for more pay from the task of developing fair and consistent compensation policies (Zollitsch and Langsner, 1970).

Currently, organizations vary widely on how much employee influence they allow over pay decisions. Some organizations make pay decisions in a highly centralized manner and place pay policy formulation in the hands of top managers and corporate compensation specialists. These firms tend to follow an algorithmic compensation pattern. (See Chapter 3.) After the pay system is developed, the line managers, who process rewards, and employees are informed about relevant pay policies. Other companies make a conscious decision to involve employees directly in the design and administration of the pay system. These firms tend to rely on an experiential compensation pattern (see Chapter 3), and management may be more willing to trust employees with sensitive pay information.

This chapter is concerned with governance issues. It deals with how much pay information to communicate to employees; employee participation in pay policy design and delivery of rewards; and the employees' right to appeal pay decisions. In the special case where employees choose to have union representation, this chapter examines how the union influences pay policy. Lastly, because each firm faces and must comply with external legal and regulatory constraints, this chapter concludes with a discussion of the strategic and procedural justice implications of the legal environment in terms of pay system governance.

Governance of the compensation system may affect organizational performance for several reasons. First, some employee influence may be necessary for the implementation phase of pay policy decisions. Pay is one of the most important job factors to employees (Lawler, 1990). In order to implement successfully a specific pay policy (for example, the implementation of a new merit pay plan), management must convince employees to accept the new policy and be committed to it. If employees are involved in the formulation and implementation of the policy, the acceptance is increased (Maier, 1973). Lack of acceptability leads to poor implementation of pay and other human resource management policies. (See Gomez-Mejia and Balkin, 1987; Gomez-Mejia, Page, and Tornow, 1982; Gomez-Mejia and Welbourne, 1991.) By implication, strategic uses of compensation to enhance firm performance lose potency under such conditions or may even produce results opposite of those originally intended.

Another reason why management should be concerned about employee influence over pay decisions is that shared governance may facilitate the congruence between organization and pay strategies. As noted in Chapter 5, when there is congruence between the compensation and organization strategies, pay policies signal to employees the appropriate behaviors that are rewarded and consistent with the organization's objectives. Ultimately, this contributes to organization performance. If the reward system sends a signal different from those sent from other organizational systems (such as performance appraisals), employees may receive a mixed and confusing message from management.

When management fails to respond to employees' desire to participate, the work force may seek union representation (Miner, 1974). Employees may believe unions will give them more influence over pay and other conditions of employment than a nonparticipative management would be willing to allow. From management's perspective, unions are usually viewed as a threat. Unions are often perceived as presenting a major constraint to an organization's competitive strategy (Freeman and Medoff, 1979). Many management decisions such as those over job design, wage structures, benefit levels, use of automation, plant relocations, or work scheduling are subject to union approval (Powers and Gomez-Mejia, 1991). The settlements that management and the union agree on may adversely affect company performance compared to what could be achieved without a union. Thus, many nonunion employers prefer to have the flexibility to formulate policies without having to negotiate with a union. These employers may find it in their self-interest to encourage employees to participate in different aspects of pay decisions. This way, organizational reward systems are perceived to be fair and acceptable to employees (Foulkes, 1980).

Finally, local, state, and federal governments have been very proactive in regulating employers' pay practices. In fact, the compensation specialist spends more time as a boundary spanner. Trying to obtain information on the regulatory environment that can be used to shape internal pay policies, the specialist helps protect the firm from unwanted litigation and costly suits.

In short, a firm seldom makes strategic compensation choice decisions in isolation. Multiple parties, internal and external to the organization, have a keen interest in how pay is allocated and will limit managerial discretion. The development and implementation of effective governance mechanisms for compensation (e.g., appeal procedures, audits) that accommodate the demands of various stakeholders (e.g., employees, labor unions, regulators) is likely to have a salutary impact on a number of variables that may affect both the financial and stock market performance of the firm (e.g., labor unrest, concerted actions, exodus of hard to replace workers, protracted litigation, and costly suits).

While direct empirical evidence on a causal relationship between stakeholder reactions to pay system governance and firm performance is almost nil, indirect evidence is consistent with this interpretation. For example, Gomez-Mejia (1985) found a positive association between employee attitudes toward pay administration and firm profitability. Hansen and Wernerfelt (1989) found a positive correlation between organizational climate measures and rates of return in a large sample of companies. Abowd, Milkovich, and Hannon (1990) report increased variance in abnormal shareholder return associated with human resource announcements (e.g., staff reduction) suggesting that "these events do provide information that influences stock prices" (p. 216).

DELIVERY OF COMPENSATION INFORMATION

Management in all organizations must determine how much and what kinds of pay information to reveal to employees. This is one of the 17 key strategic compensation dimensions discussed in Chapter 2. Should management support a pay secrecy policy, or should it adopt a policy of open pay communication? There is a wide spectrum of responses and feelings about this issue, and there is no general agreement among managers concerning how much pay information should be revealed to employees. Despite the prevalence of pay secrecy policies, some organizations have open pay communication for all or certain categories of employees. Employees in unionized firms may learn the pay rates and pay schedules of all other nonexempt employees in union job grades by examining the union contract. Many units of government (federal, state, or municipal) publicize the pay ranges for all employees, and some publish individual pay levels as well. Top executives' annual salaries and bonuses in publicly held corporations are published in the firm's annual report to government regulatory agencies. In the following section, the trade-offs between pay secrecy and open pay communication are examined.

Pay Secrecy

Pay secrecy makes it more difficult for an employee to confront a supervisor or administrator over a perceived pay inequity. Some organizations will enforce a pay secrecy policy by discharging an employee who reveals to another the size of his/her paycheck.

Many organizations have actual pay inequities within their salary structure and prefer to keep these problems confidential until the inequities are put in order (Lawler, 1981). Pay secrecy gives salary administrators time to straighten out pay inequities without having to deal with employee reactions to these problems if they were widely known within the firm. Pay secrecy also allows management and compensation staff more freedom to administer pay because employees cannot be expected to criticize a policy that they are not supposed to know exists. For example, an organization may have a pay policy to pay below market levels for clerical jobs, and this policy may not be revealed to employees because of a pay secrecy policy. An employee may not be aware his/her low pay is due to the organization's compensation strategy, instead of an inequity or lack of responsiveness to employees' pay with respect to the market.

Evidence indicates that a high percentage of firms have pay secrecy policies. Sponsored by the Bureau of National Affairs (BNA), a survey of large firms reported 71 percent did not reveal pay schedules to employees (Miner, 1974). In the same study, 82 percent of managers reported they did not know the pay levels of other managers at their own or higher levels. In a more recent study in the high technology industry, Balkin and Gomez-Mejia (1985), found that, despite the emphasis placed on teamwork and participative decisions within firms in this industry, 75 percent of the companies in the sample used pay secrecy policies.

Research on pay secrecy was conducted for the most part in the 1960s and early 1970s (e.g., Beer and Gerry, 1968; Lawler, 1965, 1972). While a strong advocacy role in favor of open pay was evident in most of that literature, it is not obvious from these earlier studies that pay secrecy is inherently flawed. The fact that pay secrecy is still prevalent suggests that management may find some value in it. On the negative side, pay secrecy causes employees to overestimate the pay of individuals at lower level jobs and underestimate the pay of individuals at higher level jobs within an organization (Burroughs, 1982, Lawler, 1972; Mahoney and Weitzel, 1978; Milkovich and Anderson, 1972). This causes individuals to perceive pay differentials between levels as less than they are, which may make it more difficult to induce employees to accept greater responsibilities. Thus, pay secrecy may lead to a perception of pay compression within a salary structure that is often associated with employees experiencing dissatisfaction with their pay. On the positive side, pay secrecy may provide supervisors with much more flexibility to reward performance because they don't have to fear the wrath of workers who feel they deserve better (Konrad and Pfeffer, 1990). Thus, pay secrecy may help remove the equalizing effect on compensation decisions resulting from political forces. Research on this crucial point, however, is practically nonexistent.

Open Pay Communication

Some research suggests that open pay leads to favorable outcomes in organizations. In one study, open pay led to a higher quality of work life and a more positive work climate in an organization (Steele, 1975). In another study, Beer and Gerry (1968) found that employees who had accurate knowledge of all their peers' pay increases had more favorable attitudes towards merit pay than those who had unclear information. Advocates of open pay communication also claim that pay can be used as a motivational tool by management when employees are informed of the pay levels and pay policies (e.g., Lawler, 1981,

1984). The theoretical basis for this assertion is: Employees with accurate perceptions of pay differentials between jobs are more likely to exert extra effort to seek a promotion, as predicted by expectancy models. (See Chapter 9.)

On the other hand, available evidence in support of open pay is not overwhelming. Industry experience and empirical research literature suggest that more often than not pay-for-performance policies fail (Gomez-Mejia and Balkin, 1989; Pearce, Stevenson, and Perry, 1985; Winstanley, 1982). These findings are not favorable to open pay communication and add to the controversy over this issue.

Organizations that move their compensation system in the direction of open communication make it more feasible for employees to increase their participation in pay decisions.   In addition, greater participation may cultivate an image of fairness, which allows the firm to manage more effectively impressions of organizational justice (Folger and Greenberg, 1985; Greenberg, 1990). There is also a downside. First, open pay communication forces managers and compensation staff to defend publicly their pay decisions and practices. This can be time-consuming and nerve-wrecking, and because the process is inherently subjective, there is no guarantee that satisfactory answers will ever be found to appease everyone.   Second, all the inconsistencies and weaknesses present in the pay system become apparent when the cloak of secrecy is lifted from pay decisions. Since the outcome is more visible to employees, this increases the cost of making a mistake in a pay decision. It may also foster a very conservative attitude on management's part that effectively thwarts the introduction of innovative reward strategies. Third, as noted earlier, open pay may induce managers to iron out pay differentials among subordinates (despite differences in performance levels) in order to avoid conflict and having to explain pay differences to disappointed employees. Some of these problems can be alleviated by monitoring performance appraisals, training supervisors in the use of the appraisal system, and improving supervisors' skills in providing feedback to employees (Bernardin and Beatty, 1984; Cardy and Dobbins, 1993; Gomez-Mejia, 1990; Murphy and Cleveland, 1991). Yet, this equalizing tendency is not likely to go away.

In short, much research remains to be done before one can safely prescribe an open pay policy in an indiscriminate fashion. While its underlying principles and objectives have much merit, very little is known about conditions that affect the relative success of this policy, its impact on other compensation strategies, and its behavioral effect on managers and employees. This provides a very fertile ground for future empirical investigation. It calls for readdressing an important issue that has largely remained dormant in the academic literature during the past two decades.

Information Choices

Depending on the degree of openness it favors, management has a wide scope of pay information it can reveal to employees. Management can reveal information on (1) pay ranges, (2) pay increases, and (3) the determination of pay levels.

Pay range information that may be shared with employees include pay ranges for the incumbent's job, for all jobs in the incumbent's career path, for all jobs in the pay structure, and, finally, actual pay rates for individuals. Companies with open pay communication policies are likely to reveal pay ranges in the salary structure but much less likely to reveal individual pay rates, which represents the highest degree of openness.

Pay increase information that management may choose to give to employees includes the size of the average pay increase, the range of the pay increases (from the minimum to the maximum), the relation of the pay increase to merit (i.e., the merit pay guide chart that supervisors use to determine the pay increase), and the size of the increases that other co-workers receive. Organizations with open pay policies are most likely to share information on the range and basis of the pay increases but are less likely to reveal the size of pay increases of individuals, which requires the highest degree of openness.

If management wants employees to know about the determination of pay levels, it could communicate the market position taken by the firm, the market ranges for jobs from salary surveys, companies that are acknowledged as competitors and appear in the pay survey, and the basis for job evaluations. Organizations with an open pay policy are likely to let employees at least know the market position the firm chooses to pay. Firms with a high degree of openness are more likely to share information on the actual mechanics of pay level determination and job evaluations. As noted earlier, however, very little research has been conducted in the outcomes of these options and contingency factors mediating their effectiveness.

Benefits Communication

On average, employee benefits are valued at 37 percent of total compensation (Gerhart and Milkovich, 1993). Since employee benefits are group membership rewards and are the same for all employees, management will want to communicate the contents of the benefits package openly to employees. It is ironic that most employees are not aware of the value of their benefits package or how to use their benefits (Wilson, Northcraft, and Neale, 1985). Research has indicated that employees in organizations systematically underestimate the value of their benefits (Driver, 1980; Huseman and Hatfield, 1978).

The major obstacles to effective benefits communication are the increasing complexity of the benefits package and the lack of organizational resources devoted to benefits communications. Recently, the employee benefits package has become more complex due to the popularity of flexible benefits programs and the proliferation of choices in medical insurance and retirement plans. An employee may be asked to choose between several different major medical and health maintenance organization (HMO) plans, as well as a list of different tax-sheltered annuities (TSA) for retirement that offer different levels of risk and interest rates. The standard benefits handbook and new employee benefits orientation that organizations traditionally rely on to communicate benefits are no longer comprehensive enough to give employees all the information they need to select their benefits.

In addition to expecting employees to become more sophisticated about their benefits, organizations have traditionally underfunded benefits communications. In one study, Huseman, Hatfield, and Driver (1978) found that organizations spend only $10 per year per employee on benefits communications. According to Huseman et. al., employers who want to obtain maximum impact from their investment in employee benefits will want to develop effective employee benefits communications programs.

Typical prescriptions for an effective benefits communications program include giving employees opportunities for two-way communication in the presentation of information (Green, 1987). Thus, opportunities for clarifications are built into the communication channel. Periodic benefits seminars and workshops run by benefits experts offer employees opportunities to ask specific questions that pertain to their situations. Benefits newsletters and memos will keep employees informed on changes in the status of their benefits. Printouts from computer programs that summarize the status and value of each benefit for an employee provide valuable information. Of course, all these ways to communicate benefits information cost the organization money and require additional staff support. However, organizations that want employees to participate in their selection of benefits and want them to value the benefits will invest the resources to communicate effectively the benefits package. Organizations that offer benefits to employees mainly to attract them and meet the competition will be less likely to target the resources necessary for an effective employee benefits communications program. Unfortunately, the literature on benefits communication is almost without exception practitioner oriented with minimal theory or empirical reseach to back up the prescriptive assertions discussed above.

VOICE IN PAY POLICY DESIGN AND IMPLEMENTATION

Extent of employee participation in pay policy decision and implementation is another key strategic compensation choice discussed in Chapter 2. Management may wish to involve employees in pay decisions because, in some cases, involvement may increase pay satisfaction and motivation. Participation in pay decisions may achieve these results because employees become more committed to an organization that trusts them with sensitive information. Further, as noted earlier, the likelihood of employee acceptance of a pay decision is increased when employees are involved in the decision from the start. Thus, greater employee participation may increase the likelihood that rewards will be allocated on a basis that meets their perceptions of equity and fairness.

Management that chooses to allow employees to participate in pay decisions may have employees participate in the design of pay policy, the actual delivery of the rewards, or both. These are discussed next.

Employee Influence on Pay Policy Design

The pay policy design decisions include the determination of the market position for pay (pay level) and the form of the pay package, which concerns the mix between base salary, pay incentives, and benefits. It is less controversial for organizations to involve employees in the design of pay packages. With design decisions, there is a greater distance between the employee and the actual dispensing of the reward, which gives rise to fewer conflicts of self-interest. Many organizations annually audit their pay package designs with employee attitude surveys, which measure the patterns of employee satisfaction with the components of the pay package. For example, if management learns there are high levels of employee dissatisfaction with benefits compared to the market, it may make upward adjustments in the benefits schedule.

The benefits package probably offers the greatest opportunity for employees to participate in the design of their rewards. Employees may express their preference for benefits or a new benefit (such as a dental plan) through the attitude survey or some other communication channel such as a suggestion system or a visit to the benefits administrator. Most organizations are very responsive to employees' desires for benefits as compared to requests for additional salary. Due to the lower costs of the benefits based on group-rate savings and the tax-free status of many benefits (such as insurance or tuition reimbursement for education), the employee receives greater marginal returns on incremental benefits as compared to salary increases.

Due to the changing demographics of the labor force, the past decade has seen a rapid increase in the implementation of flexible benefits programs for employees. Management has recognized these changes and has been willing to give employees greater freedom to choose benefits that are not duplicates of those received by the working spouse. Under a flexible benefits program, an employee selects benefits that are truly valued and declines the unwanted benefits. Some evidence indicates that flexible benefits may increase the perceived value of the benefits, which, in turn, leads to improved work attitudes and lower employee turnover (Haslinger, 1985; Loeffler, 1985).

Research on the effect of employee participation on the design of pay plans (such as base pay or a bonus plan) is supportive of participation. Studies by Lawler and his colleagues have been undertaken that involved groups of employees or committees that developed pay plans that were applied to all employees. The results of these studies indicated that participating in the design of the pay plans has a positive impact on attendance (Lawler and Hackman, 1969; Scheflen, Lawler, and Hackman, 1971), pay satisfaction (Jenkins and Lawler, 1981), and job satisfaction (Jenkins and Lawler, 1981). These positive effects have been attributed to greater understanding of the rationale behind the pay plan, greater commitment to the pay plan, and a better match between individual needs and the pay-plan design. Yet, this is an area where additional research is clearly needed before firm conclusions can be reached.

Employee Influence on Delivery of Rewards

At present, it is controversial and even threatening to suggest that employees should have input to the delivery of pay increases or bonuses. After all, the ability to control and allocate rewards gives managers power to shape and control the behavior of subordinates (Bartol and Martin, 1988). Furthermore, firms rely heavily on the pay system "as one means of managing important dependencies on subordinates . . . where their expertise is important to their boss and is difficult to replace" (Bartol and Martin, 1990, p. 613). Managers may fear giving up this source of influence over their subordinates.

Traditionally, line managers are responsible for interpreting pay policy guidelines and applying them to reward their subordinates. Employees usually have little influence over the actual delivery of rewards because management may fear that employees cannot be trusted to separate their self-interests from effective pay administration. Reward delivery decisions include the positioning of a new employee's salary within the salary structure, the size of the merit pay increase, the worth of a job based on job evaluation, and the size of a group or individual bonus. Employee influence over reward delivery decisions is limited but may occur in organizations that utilize job evaluation committees or skill-based pay plans.

A common approach used to gain employee understanding and acceptance of job evaluation is through the use of a committee. The job evaluation committee is composed of line managers from different functional areas, compensation staff, and employees who have specific knowledge of the job that is being evaluated. Based upon the input of individuals with different perspectives of the value of a certain job, a committee consensus of the job worth is decided. Employees are represented on the job evaluation committees and have input in the determination of job worth. Similarly, employees have input in the determination of the job analysis and job description of their jobs, which get evaluated by the job evaluation committee.   Typically, the employee either provides information for job analysis (interview method) or responds to a questionnaire (computerized job analysis) and ultimately must sign off on the finished job description.   Employees may also participate in the determination of the compensable factors and factor weights for job evaluation, but fewer organizations involve employees in the actual determination of the job evaluation plan due to the technical nature of developing these plans (which are often developed by experts).   Research on the use of job evaluation committees and their effect on acceptability of job evaluation outcomes is almost nonexistent.

Overall, most organizations resist allowing employees to participate in the delivery of rewards and prefer to have managers make these assessments.   Management is more inclined to give employees the right to appeal pay decisions made by supervisors.   It is probably true that the more management relies on a traditional top-down approach to the determination of pay decisions, the greater the need for a mechanism that allows employees to voice their reactions to the pay decision.

Appeal Mechanisms

Employees may be provided with an appeals system that allows them to voice their reactions to pay decisions (as well as other personnel decisions).   Such a forum is likely to enhance the perception of procedural justice in the compensation system.   Organizations without an effective internal appeal process face an increased risk of unwanted litigation, costly legal fees, and backpay penalties to former employees who use the courts to receive their just compensation.   Pay laws (to be discussed later in this chapter) such as the Fair Labor Standards Act, Equal Pay Act, and Employee Retirement Income Security Act (ERISA) are vigorously enforced by federal regulatory agents who may monitor organizational pay practices and use the courts to prosecute violators.

Appeals systems allow employees to react to pay decisions within the organization by providing a neutral third party who reviews the decision made by the employee's supervisor or by the compensation staff.   The appeals system is a check on a manager's skill at processing rewards in order to make sure the pay policies and procedures are being followed in a fair and consistent manner.   Employees are less likely to use the courts to get due process if they have the opportunity to appeal a reward decision to a disinterested third party who has the authority to make an adjustment to the reward.

The organizational appeals system allows employees to voice their disagreement over the following decisions that affect their compensation:

1. Appeals on job evaluation assessments.
2. Classification and grading of jobs.
3. Current level of pay with respect to the market.
4. Amount of overtime pay.
5. Size of a merit pay increase based on a performance evaluation.
6. Disagreement over the accrual of employee benefits such as sick leave days, vacation time, or the amount of the employer's contribution to a medical claim.

Top management may choose from several different appeals systems that vary over the degree of anonymity given to the employee who makes the complaint and that vary over the degree of formality of the system (Aram and Salipante, 1981).   For example, a visit to the employee relations representative in the personnel department would be a more anonymous and less formal procedure than filing a grievance with a grievance committee. Some organizations choose to have several appeals systems in place. Certain procedures are more effective at resolving petty, informal issues, and others are better at resolving conflicts over more complicated pay issues that may have long-term policy implications. Table 11-1 provides a brief description of each of the most common appeals procedures in industry.

As indicated earlier in this chapter, management that is not responsive to employees' concerns about pay and does not provide an appeals system for employees may have to deal with a union. Employees have the legal right to form unions to bargain over wages, hours,

TABLE 11-1
Appeals Procedures

Speak-Up Program

The speak-up program allows employees to provide feedback on issues that are important to them. An employee may write a letter to a company representative. The employee then receives a rapid response to the issue he or she raised.

Open-Door Program

Under an open-door program, employees may lodge a complaint to any manager who is not their supervisor as high as the chief executive officer (CEO).

Employee-Assistance Program (EAP)

With an employee-assistance program (EAP), an employee may take a problem to a trained counselor who guarantees anonymity to the employee. Sometimes a problem involving pay may be related to a personal problem (such as poor personal budgeting skills and misuse of credit cards). An EAP counselor may help the employee discover the true cause of his/her problem and help develop an acceptable solution.

Employee Relations Representatives

Employee relations representatives are members of the personnel/HRM department who help employees deal with conflicts with their supervisor or management. They are well-trained in the legal regulations and rights of the employee and employer (such as EEOC, Equal Pay Act, sexual harassment cases, etc.) and try to mediate settlements that both the employee and management can accept.

Grievance Panel

A grievance panel is composed of the employee's peers. The grievance panel listens to the evidence provided by the employee and management and determines a resolution. This approach is used by nonunion firms that do not have a labor agreement but desire an appeals mechanism for settling difficult issues.

Union Grievance Procedure

A union grievance procedure is a formal due process mechanism established in the labor contract with the union. It uses a multistep approach to resolve the grievance. The first step provides a resolution between the union steward and the supervisor. The final step of the grievance procedure is binding arbitration determined by an arbitrator selected by both the union and management. The union represents the interests of the employee and provides a spokesperson who articulates the employee's concerns at each step of the process.

and working conditions with management. What happens to compensation policies when employees vote for the union to represent their interests for pay (and other job issues) to management? The next section of this chapter looks at how compensation policies change when both the union and management co-determine the design and administration of the pay package.

UNION IMPACT ON PAY POLICY

Pay policy decisions under collective bargaining are made bilaterally between the union and management and are formalized in the labor contract. Unions use their collective bargaining strength to gain a premium of economic benefits for their members over what would be allocated under nonunion conditions (which more closely approximate competitive market levels of pay). Unions use their bargaining power to influence management to consider other criteria for pay than what would be used in the absence of unions. Management considers wage patterns of other union contracts, regional and national labor market conditions, the employer's ability to pay, and the cost of living when determining the union wage (Kochan, 1980).

According to Freeman and Medoff (1979), the union represents a "collective voice" that takes into account the preferences of all the workers to form an average preference that represents its position at the bargaining table. Because it is a democratic institution, the union is responsive to the average or inframarginal worker (Anderson, 1978; Sayles and Strauss, 1967). The collective voice model predicts different pay policies will be determined through the process of collective bargaining than would exist if purely competitive assumptions prevailed. Further, there is evidence that union employees who participate the most in union affairs are older with higher levels of seniority (Anderson, 1979; McShane, 1986). Therefore, one would expect the union (being more responsive to the pay preferences of older, more senior, and less mobile workers) to have a stronger preference for pensions and health insurance plans versus additional take-home pay as compared to the preferences of nonunion workers.

Employees who choose to influence management through collective bargaining may alter both the design and administration of their pay. Empirical research suggests that unions influence wages, benefits, wage structures, pay increases, and pay incentives in organizations.

Union Impact on Wages

The majority of the studies that have examined the union impact on pay have focused on nonexempt production workers. After controlling for the effects of other variables, the union has been able to provide a wage level that averages between 10 and 20 percent above the wages of similar nonunion employees (Gomez-Mejia and Balkin, 1984b; Lewis, 1963; Mitchell, 1980). However, the business cycle seems to affect the size of the union wage effect.

The union wage differential decreases during inflationary periods (when union wages are bound by the terms of the labor agreement) and increases during recessions (when nonunion wages are more responsive to market factors). During the late 1970s when inflation was high, unions were able to overcome this pattern by negotiating cost-of-living adjustments into their contracts. By contrast, nonunion workers were not as likely to receive automatic cost-of-living adjustments to their wages (Johnson, 1981). The size of the union/nonunion wage differential may vary by industry and by occupation. The union wage effect is large for occupations such as truck drivers and skilled construction trades. It is much smaller for employees in highly competitive industries such as men's clothing.

Some studies have recently examined the union impact on pay by defining pay as total compensation, which includes both wages and benefits. These studies show the union raises the level of total compensation by a similar magnitude as on wages alone, which earlier studies indicated (Antos, 1983; Feldman and Scheffler, 1982). These results should not be surprising, since some employee benefits become more valuable in direct proportion to the increase in wages (for example sick leave, holiday pay, and vacation pay).

Union Impact on Benefits

For many years, unions have been on the cutting edge of the employee benefits arena. They have been first in offering new forms of benefits to their members through collective negotiations with employers. Once established in the union sector, these benefits are spread to nonunion employees due to many firms' interest in maintaining a nonunion status.

Unions are responsive to the needs of older, less mobile employees, not just the high producers. Many of these "average" employees have a strong preference for benefits that provide security for their health and retirement. Unions factor these priorities into their bargaining demands and have been able to convince employers to devote a greater relative share of total compensation to employee benefits than nonunion firms are willing to give to their employees (Freeman, 1981). In particular, unions have had a positive impact on the level of retirement benefits, health insurance, life and accident insurance, vacation pay, and holiday pay received by employees (Freeman, 1981; Solnick, 1978).

Some empirical studies have examined in detail how unions affect employee benefits. One benefit that unions have given a lot of attention to is retirement benefits. Unions are more likely to provide a defined-benefit retirement plan than a nonunion employer. Defined-benefit retirement plans promise a fixed amount of income to the employee upon retirement. The risk is shouldered by the employer to manage the pension funds effectively so that the employee receives the retirement income. In contrast, nonunion employers are more likely to provide a defined-contribution retirement plan. Defined contribution plans only provide a promised amount of funds to be invested for the employee's retirement income. Since the exact amount of retirement income is unknown, depending on how effectively the funds were invested, the employee shares some risk with the employer. Unions are also more likely to employ individuals to monitor the retirement funds, and this monitoring may lead to more valuable retirement benefits.

Union employers are more likely to offer adjustments to the retirement benefits of retirees than nonunion firms (Allen and Clark, 1986). This is probably because retired workers can still participate in union affairs. In the nonunion firm, retired workers are not likely to have influence on their former employer's benefits policies.

Studies that examined the size of the retirement benefits found that unionized firms offer higher initial benefits to the retired worker, and the unionized employee is able to receive initially the retirement benefit at an earlier time than the nonunionized employee (Allen and Clark, 1986). Finally, the presence of the union is associated with a greater likelihood that an employee will receive a pension benefit as compared to an employee in a similar nonunion firm (Fosu, 1983).

Another benefit that unions have had significant impact on is health insurance. While the union employer is no more likely than the nonunion firm to provide health insurance to the workers, the union employer provides greater resources for health insurance than the nonunion firm (Rossiter and Taylor, 1982). Union firms provided higher total health insurance premiums and a larger percent contribution by the employer than nonunion firms (Fosu, 1984; Rossiter and Taylor, 1982).

In recent years, the cost of health insurance benefits have skyrocketed. In an attempt to control these rising costs, employers have asked employees to pay a greater share of their health care expenses. By paying higher deductibles, co-insurance payments, and monthly premiums, employees reduce the employer's burden of covering these costs. Employees may find the union an effective mechanism for voicing their displeasure and concern over the rising cost of health insurance. The union may be able to convince management to maintain the level of health insurance benefits it has provided to its members. Management may find it more effective in unionized firms to seek other cost-cutting procedures such as finding a different health insurance provider with a better group rate or improving on administrative efficiencies in the delivery of health care benefits.

Union Impact on Wage Structure

The wage structure in an organization represents a hierarchy of pay levels for jobs and reflects differences in the value of the contributions between jobs and individuals. Unions attempt to establish uniform pay rates for comparable workers across establishments (Freeman, 1980, 1982). Ultimately, unions try to organize an entire industry and eliminate wages as a competitive factor between firms. Historically, unions have succeeded in negotiating industry-wide agreements that standardized pay practices within certain industries such as coal and steel. Recently, the threat of foreign competition has reduced the number of these industry-wide bargaining agreements, and wages are once again a competitive factor in some industries despite a high degree of unionization.

The union's pay policy goal is to reduce wage inequality between union employees by establishing administrative rules that pay for the job, not the personal characteristics of the employee such as performance or level of experience, which can be subjectively manipulated by management. Unions have used their bargaining strength to establish two types of pay policies designed to reduce wage inequality between employees in the same job category within a firm (Slichter, Healy, and Livernash, 1960). The single-rate pay policy reduces wage inequality by offering one pay rate to all employees in a job class. Unlike the traditional pay grade structure used in compensation, which has a range of pay rates, the single-rate pay policy has no range of pay rates. The union and management negotiate the single pay rate in the contract and make provisions for adjustments to the single rate each year the contract is in effect.

Another union policy that reduces wage dispersion among workers is the automatic progression pay policy. The automatic progression policy consists of a series of steps beginning at entry-level and ending at a maximum level. A worker moves between steps as a function of seniority. Therefore, two workers in the same job with the same amount of seniority will receive the same level of pay under this pay policy. In firms where the average level of worker seniority is high, the automatic progression policy may approach the single-rate policy because many workers in each job will be paid at the maximum level.

Unions are able to reduce wage inequality by establishing single rate and automatic pay progression policies for each job class in the labor contract and by having the contract apply to employers with multiple plants in different geographic locations. Unions can standardize wages across establishments by negotiating multiemployer agreements such as those in the trucking and coal industries. There is some empirical evidence that suggests unions have succeeded in reducing wage inequality within firms and between establishments (Freeman, 1980).

Besides reducing wage inequality within a job classification, unions may also have an impact by decreasing pay differentials between different jobs. This reduction in pay differentials produces a leveling effect, which results in a flatter pay structure than would be the case in a nonunion firm. There is evidence that shows unions reduce the size of the wage differential between unskilled and skilled workers and between the average earnings of blue-collar and white-collar workers within a firm (Hirsch, 1982; Freeman, 1982). Therefore, the overall impact of the union on the wage structure in a firm has been to promote a more equitable distribution of income between employees and to reduce the degree of hierarchy in the wage structure.

Union Impact on Pay Increases and Incentives

Merit pay plans and individual wage incentive plans are usually opposed by unions. Unions object to these pay increase methods because they are based on subjective judgments by supervisors of the performance of union members (Slichter, Healy, and Livernash, 1960). Unionists believe pay increases based on a supervisor's assessment of a worker's performance may reflect favoritism, discrimination, or other forms of bias. To support their distrust of management's motives in determining pay increases based on merit, unionists point to earlier struggles between labor and management over piecework output quotas that were unfair to workers. Unionists also feel threatened by merit pay plans because they encourage workers to compete against one another for pay increases. Harmful to cohesion between union members, competition for pay increases may ultimately undermine the union. Unions prefer pay increase methods that promote union solidarity. Therefore, unions support automatic progression or across-the-board pay increase policies because these are objective and nonjudgmental methods of delivering pay increases to union members. Under these preferred pay increase policies, employees perceive the union delivers an equal increase in economic benefits to each worker in return for equal dues paid to the union, which is viewed as a fair and equitable transaction.

Unions are also able to influence the amount of earnings a worker receives by negotiating seniority-based employment policies that control work opportunities. In most union contracts with management, seniority controls promotions, work shifts, opportunities for overtime, and layoffs. The senior worker has the first choice of each of these opportunities for greater earnings. Promotions lead to higher wage rates; evening shift work receives wage premiums; overtime work is compensated with a 50 percent wage premium by law; and seniority protects the earnings of workers from reductions due to layoff. In the nonunion firm, merit and performance are most likely to be the criteria management uses to control work opportunities that lead to greater earnings. Thus, management has greater control over opportunities for economic rewards in the nonunion firm.

Unions have been more receptive to group-based incentives that link pay to increases in group productivity. For example, gainsharing plans are found in both union and nonunion industrial plants (Driscoll, 1979; Welbourne and Gomez-Mejia, 1988).   Gainsharing plans allow workers to share in the extra wealth they create by providing suggestions that result in labor cost savings to management.   Further, under group-based pay incentives such as gainsharing, workers receive an equal share of economic benefits.   Thus, worker cohesion is supported by the pay plan.

Recently, unions have been more receptive to profit-sharing plans as a means of tying pay increases to company profitability.   For example, the United Auto Workers (UAW) in their most recent contract with General Motors replaced an across-the-board pay increase plan with a performance-contingent pay policy based on annual profits.   Unions are starting to realize that the threat of foreign competition makes it imperative to link pay to productivity.   This way, jobs are protected since the company can effectively compete in the product market.   Unions are more willing to accept a performance-contingent pay plan if it is based on group productivity.   However, the group-based pay plan must provide opportunities for union input and leadership, or the plan will likely fail to meet its objectives (Gray, 1971; Ross, 1983).

It should be noted, however, that in the 1990s, unions still remain skeptical about the introduction of flexible or variable compensation plans.   The union's attitude toward such programs was recently captured in the following statement made by John Zalusky, head of the AFL-CIO's office of Wages and Industrial Relations (1991, p. 13):

> Business interests favor variable compensation plans because they shift some business risk to labor and provide incentives to the workforce.   But arguing that profit-sharing, gain-sharing and stock ownership offer some new form of economic democracy ignores a basic difference.   Most workers expect their unions to minimize income risks since, unlike capital, labor is not mobile and cannot minimize risk through diversification.   Also workers have relatively lower levels of income and are threatened by any downturn in real income.

A summary of the union's impact on an organization's pay policies is provided in Table 11-2.

The empirical research summarized in Table 11-2 suggests that unions favor pay policies that offer a fixed and predictable amount of wages and benefits to employees.   Across-the-board pay increases and group welfare benefits (such as health insurance and life insurance) are promoted because they can be given equally to all union members and because they promote union solidarity.   Unions are more likely to avoid pay policies that rely on supervisory judgments to determine the reward or that encourage employees to compete with each other.   Thus, unions are less likely to support the use of merit pay, individual-wage incentive plans, or bonus programs in a firm.

Now that the role of employee inputs and labor unions in the governance of the compensation system has been examined, this chapter concludes with a discussion of how external forces in the legal environment constrain the strategic compensation choices made by a firm.

THE LEGAL ENVIRONMENT AND PAY SYSTEM GOVERNANCE

This section examines how the legal framework limits managerial discretion as to the criteria, design, and administration of the compensation system.   The key laws that affect

TABLE 11-2
Summary of Union Impact on Pay Practices Based on Empirical Research Literature

Pay Practices	Direction of Union Impact*
Pay Level	
Wage Rates	+
Total Compensation (includes benefits)	+
Benefits	
Health Insurance	+
Life Insurance	+
Pensions	+
Vacation Pay	+
Holiday Pay	+
Stock Options	−
Wage Structure	
Single Pay Rates	+
Automatic Pay Progression	+
Job Evaluation Plans	−
Pay Increases	
Merit Pay	−
Across-the-Board Increase	+
Seniority-Based Promotions	+
Pay Incentives	
Individual Incentive Plans	−
Gainsharing Plans	+ or −

*A (+) indicates there is evidence that the union is positively related to a specific pay practice, and a (−) indicates there is a lower likelihood of that pay practice if the union is present.

strategic compensation choices include the Fair Labor Standards Act (pay level vs. market; fixed pay vs. incentives), Equal Pay Act (pay level vs. market; fixed pay vs. incentives), comparable worth (pay level vs. market), and the Internal Revenue Code (fixed pay vs. incentives; short- vs. long-term orientation).

Fair Labor Standards Act

The Fair Labor Standards Act (FLSA) is the fundamental compensation law in the United States. It affects the underpinnings of most pay structures in U.S. firms. It provides a minimum wage for employees and has provisions for overtime pay and the regulation of work hours. An increase in the minimum wage (as recent as 1991) forces all employers with minimum wage jobs to provide automatic increases in the pay levels of the affected jobs. Some of these low-paying jobs may be vulnerable to foreign competition (such as in maquiladora plants in Mexico), and the work may be exported to lower wage countries. To be in compliance with the FLSA, employers must keep accurate records of wages and hours of covered employees and file this information on a timely basis with the Wage and Hour Division of the Department of Labor to avoid penalties. The two key provisions of the FLSA are the minimum wage and overtime provisions.

Minimum Wages. The minimum wage provision set by the FLSA is currently $4.25 per hour (as of 1992). Most businesses are covered by the FLSA, except those that have less than two employees or have annual gross sales under $500,000.

While most businesses are covered by this law, not all employees are covered by the FLSA. Employees covered by the FLSA are classified as *nonexempt employees.* Accurate records of the wages and hours of nonexempt employees must be kept. The Wage and Hour Division of the Department of Labor continuously monitors employers' records of wages and hours of nonexempt employees. Failure to pay the minimum wage or the wage premium for overtime hours may result in penalties that include backpay, fines, and litigation costs for employers who are found to be in noncompliance (Sellekaerts and Welch, 1984).

Employees not covered by the FLSA are classified as *exempt employees.* The major categories of exempt employees include professional, administrative, executive, and outside sales jobs. The Department of Labor provides guidelines for managers to determine whether a job is exempt or nonexempt according to the FLSA. Accurate job descriptions for all jobs greatly facilitate management's ability to classify a job as exempt or nonexempt. An employer who erroneously classifies a nonexempt job as exempt risks being in noncompliance with the law. Employers are not required to file wage and hour records of the exempt employees with the Department of Labor.

One negative consequence of an increase in the minimum wage is that it can exacerbate pay compression in a firm. (See Chapter 10.) In a firm with minimum-wage jobs, an increase in the minimum wage from $3.35 to $4.25 (as happened during 1989-1991) results in a 27 percent pay increase, which is much larger than the increases granted to other positions in the firm. The outcome is a narrowing of the pay differential between the minimum-wage jobs and other jobs within the pay structure (Bergmann, Hills, and Priefert, 1983; Wolfe and Candland, 1979). A firm may respond to this pay compression problem by making wage adjustments to jobs up and down the wage structure to restore the integrity of the system. This shows that the cost to the employer of an increase in the minimum-wage may greatly exceed the cost of direct pay increases to the minimum wage jobs alone due to the spillover effects to the pay of other jobs in the wage structure.

Overtime. The FLSA requires that nonexempt employees be paid one and a half times the standard wage for each hour of work that exceeds 40 hours per week. According to the FLSA, exempt employees are not required to be paid a wage premium for overtime.

The original intent of the overtime provision was to create an incentive for an employer to hire more workers by making it more costly to use overtime. However, the increased costs of training an additional employee and the extra fixed benefits costs each new worker represents make it relatively less expensive to use overtime.

In order to monitor and control the hours of work of nonexempt employees, organizations often require their employees to punch time clocks, use different salary labels (such as "hourly" employees), and encourage supervisors to control closely the movements of employees when they leave their workstations. These restrictions on employees' freedom may not be applied to the exempt, salaried workers since they are not required to receive overtime pay. Unfortunately, the dichotomy of administrative rules applied to nonexempt and exempt employees may be interpreted by many as representing a caste system in the organization. The nonexempt employees may believe they are part of the lower caste and that their contributions are not of equal value to the organization (Lawler, 1981). Management policies designed to promote compliance with the FLSA may unintentionally reduce levels of employee work commitment.

To avoid sending the wrong message to nonexempt employees, management may select to adopt an all-salaried pay policy. Under this pay plan, all employees who normally are paid by the hour receive a weekly or monthly salary (Hulme and Bevan, 1975). Management is still required to keep time records of nonexempt employees, but it may depend on other methods that give workers greater flexibility. For example, management may depend on peer group pressure instead of time clocks to maintain adequate levels of employee attendance. The all-salaried pay policy may help develop a sense of unity between all employees (exempt and nonexempt) in the firm.

Equal Pay Act

The Equal Pay Act (EPA) was enacted in 1963 as an amendment to the FLSA. It prohibits discrimination in pay based on sex. It requires equal pay for equal work between men and women. The law requires equal pay between jobs that have "substantially equal" skill, effort, responsibility, and working conditions. All employees are covered by the EPA; there are no exemptions. If one gender group is paid less than the other group, the EPA requires the employer to raise the pay of the lower group to the pay level of the higher group.

The EPA provides four exceptions to equal pay between men and women. The four exceptions recognize that an employer may have some legitimate business reasons for pay differentials between men and women. The four legal exceptions to the EPA include differences in pay based on (1) different levels of seniority, (2) different levels of job performance, (3) different levels of quantity or quality of production, (4) differences other than sex. These four exceptions make it possible for firms to utilize many of the strategic compensation choices (such as fixed pay vs. incentives) or to adopt some specific pay policies as defenses against pay discrimination and still remain in compliance with the law.

The first exception permits employers to use seniority-based pay policies. The second exception allows the employer to use merit pay based on a valid performance appraisal system. The third exception permits an employer to pay employees according to their productivity by using policies such as a piecework or sales commission plan. The last exception allows an employer to recognize some factor other than sex as the basis of additional compensation. For example, an employer can pay extra compensation to employees who work a night shift or who engage in dangerous work (such as transporting high explosives by truck).

A firm's compensation system may receive periodic audits by the Department of Labor, which enforces the EPA. A firm in noncompliance with the EPA may face stiff penalties in backpay to affected employees, as well as legal costs. To avoid penalties, management should audit its own pay practices under the EPA guidelines (Hills and Bergmann, 1987). Pay differences between men and women who perform work that is substantially equal should be examined by management. Jobs should be compared, based on substantially equal job content. Current job descriptions based on job analysis are necessary in order to complete a valid pay audit. Comparing male and female pay levels within groups that are defined by the same job titles can be misleading. Some organizations give different job titles to females, even though they may perform substantially equal work as males who work under a different job title. For example, a bank may call the job of its female employees a "bank teller," and the same work may be performed by the males under the "management trainee" job title.

If the average pay between males and females in a cohort group is different, management should examine the underlying factors that explain the differences to see if one of the four exceptions to the EPA can apply. However, if none of the four do apply, management will want to raise the pay of the affected employees so that it is equal to the level of the favored employees.

Comparable Worth

Advocates of *comparable worth* call for equal pay for jobs that have comparable skill, effort, responsibility, and working conditions even if the job content is dissimilar. For example, a nurse should be paid equal to a machinist if the two jobs provide equal value to the firm. The job's value is typically determined by job evaluation.

Comparable worth is actually a political issue with international dimensions (see Judd and Gomez-Mejia, 1987). Its supporters claim that jobs held by females have been undervalued in the market compared to jobs held by males (Remick, 1984). Canada, the United Kingdom, Australia, and several Western European countries have already enacted comparable worth pay laws (McNally and Shimmin, 1984). In the United States, comparable worth has been argued in the courts, state legislatures, presidential campaigns, and through collective bargaining during the past decade. While no federal law mandates comparable worth, about 20 states have enacted laws that require comparable worth for public employees (Grider and Shurden, 1987). Currently, private sector firms in the United States are not affected by the comparable worth laws.

A typical comparable worth pay policy consists of several provisions that result in the implementation of comparable worth for public sector jobs (Hills, 1982).

1. One job evaluation plan is used for all jobs within a unit. The strategic implication here is that a comparable worth law may constrain a firm to use job evaluation (a job-based pay system) under the job vs. skills compensation choice. This means that both exempt and nonexempt jobs are evaluated with the same set of compensable factors, and the jobs are compared within the same pay structure.
2. The gender representation is examined for each job. Jobs that have 70 percent or more representation from one gender are considered to be sex segregated.
3. Female-dominated jobs are matched with male-dominated jobs that have an equal number of job evaluation points. The pay of the female-dominated jobs is raised to the pay of the comparable male-dominated jobs. A timetable is established to raise female pay levels to full comparability within a three- to five-year period.

It is interesting to note that outside the United States, comparable worth is called "pay equity." In 1988, the Canadian Province of Ontario enacted the Pay Equity Legislation of Ontario (PELO), which is probably the most comprehensive comparable worth pay law in the world (Kovach and Millspaugh, 1990). PELO requires virtually all employers, public and private, to implement comparable worth into their pay systems. A pay equity board vigorously monitors the pay structures of employers and penalizes employers who do not comply with the law. The law gives employers about five years to implement comparable worth in annual stages. Each firm is expected to develop its own plan designed to provide eventually a gender neutral compensation system. This procedure is somewhat similar to the use of affirmative action plans in the United States.

In 1989, the United States-Canadian Free Trade Agreement, designed to reduce trade barriers between the United States and Canada, went into effect. The law makes it easy for Canadian firms to build plants in the United States and export goods back into Canada duty-free and for U.S. firms to do the same in Canada. It will be interesting to speculate if the PELO law affects the pay structures of private U.S. firms doing business both in the United States and Ontario.

It is hard to predict if comparable worth will affect a significant portion of the pay structures of private firms in the United States as we enter the 21st century. However, the compensation specialist, as a boundary spanner, can be expected to monitor the legal environment to gather information on trends that develop on comparable worth. In the meantime, management can take a proactive stance and make several changes in its HR and pay policies to minimize its exposure to comparable worth challenges in the courts (Grider and Shurden, 1987). For instance:

1. Management can redesign jobs to reduce the number of jobs held exclusively by women.
2. Females can be given some assistance to move into male-dominated jobs such as manager, truck driver, or electrician.
3. Management can examine job analysis and job evaluation programs for gender bias. It is a good idea to make sure that females are represented on job evaluation committees that make assessments of the worth of different jobs in a company.

Internal Revenue Code

The Internal Revenue Code (IRC) affects all forms of compensation. Both employers and employees must accurately report their income to the Internal Revenue Service on a timely basis or face tax penalties. Every few years, substantial changes are made to the IRC. The most recent set of revisions were incorporated into the Tax Reform Act of 1986. Some of the objectives of this revision to the IRC were to make the tax laws more fair to all taxpayers and to reduce the government deficit. Because of the pervasiveness of the tax code and when developing pay strategies, management should have tax experts available as consultants. The IRC impacts the following types of compensation: (1) income, (2) benefits, and (3) capital gains.

The IRC requires management to withhold a portion of an employee's income for tax purposes. Employees must accurately estimate their annual taxes to be withheld (by indicating the correct number of deductions on the W-4 form) or face a tax penalty. The Tax

Reform Act of 1986 lowered the marginal tax rates of employees, but it also eliminated many tax deductions. Due to the changes in the tax law, the higher compensated employees may prefer more salary and less deferred income (Wallace and Fay, 1988). Due to the revisions of the tax laws, compensation specialists must be responsive to the changing preferences of specific employee groups (such as executives). The short-term vs. long-term orientation compensation choice is particularly sensitive to changes in the tax code. Failure to respond to the changing preferences of specific employees for different forms of compensation can result in lowered levels of employee motivation and commitment since the after-tax compensation is the true amount of pay that is most relevant to an employee.

For many years, the tax policy in the United States has been not to tax group welfare benefit plans such as health insurance, group life insurance, and dental and vision care that are provided to employees by their company. However, group welfare benefit plans must satisfy some restrictions. For example, under ERISA (Employee Retirement Income Security Act), employees do not pay taxes on the employer's contribution to their pension, if the retirement plan "qualifies" under ERISA. A qualified retirement plan must meet several constraints under ERISA, including not discriminating in eligibility or scope of benefits offered to highly compensated and nonhighly compensated employees when the two groups are compared to each other.

The IRC also influences the design of compensation policies through the capital gains tax. Currently, capital gains are treated as ordinary income by the tax laws. This creates a disincentive to use stock as a long-term pay incentive for executives and other employees since the incumbent bears more risk with stock than with a cash-based form of pay. However, lowering the capital gains tax below ordinary income could make stock more attractive to employees as a pay incentive. If and when the capital gains tax is lowered, employee preferences for stock versus cash may shift. Management will then need to rethink its compensation plan designs to factor in the potential shifts in employee pay preferences for different forms of pay due to a reduction in the capital gains tax.

CONCLUSION

The end of the discussion of the legal environment thus concludes the last of the three parts of this book. All three parts were designed to drive home the key idea of the book: Firm performance is the ultimate criterion of success for the pay system in an organization.

Part I showed why firm performance is enhanced when pay strategies are integrated with business strategies, internal organizational factors, and industry structure. Part II showed the role that compensation strategies play in aligning the interests of strategic employee groups within the firm and how this alignment affects firm performance. Finally, Part III examined how pay strategies affect the HRM subsystem, which, in turn, can influence firm performance.

Taken as a whole, the approach provided in this book represents a departure from the traditional micro perspective incorporated in earlier compensation works, which decoupled pay decisions from the big picture and focused instead on tools and techniques. It is the hope of the authors that the ideas presented in this book may inspire current and future scholars to examine some of the research questions identified in these pages. Judging by the number of research propositions listed that remain untested, there appears to be significant opportunities for scholars to work in the area of strategic compensation and to make some worthwhile contributions.

REFERENCES

Aaker, D.A. (1987). The role of risk in explaining differences in profitability. *Academy of Management Journal*, 30, 277-296.

Abowd, J. M. (1990). Does performance-based managerial compensation affect corporate performance? *Industrial and Labor Relations Review, 43,* 52-73.

Abowd, J. M., Milkovich, G. T., & Hannon, J. M. (1990). The effects of human resource management decisions on shareholder value. *Industrial and Labor Relations Review, 43,* 203-237.

Adam, E. E. (1983). Towards a typology of production and operations management systems. *Academy of Management Review, 8,* 365-375.

Adams, J.L. (1991). Nonmonetary awards. In M.L. Rock & L.A. Berger (Eds.), *The compensation handbook.* New York: McGraw-Hill, Inc.

Adams, J. S. (1965). Inequity in social exchange. In L. Berkowitz (Ed.), *Advances in experimental social psychology: Vol. 2.* New York: Academic Press.

Adams, J. S. (1976). Structure and dynamics of behavior in organizational boundary roles. In M. D. Dunnette (Ed.), *The handbook of industrial and organizational psychology.* Chicago: Rand McNally.

Adizes, I. (1979). Organizational passages: Diagnosing and treating life cycle problems in organizations. *Organizational Dynamics, 8(1),* 3-24.

Adler, N. J. (1983a). A typology of management studies involving culture. *Journal of International Business Studies, 14(2),* 29-47.

Adler, N. J. (1983b). Cross-cultural management research: The ostrich and the trend. *Academy of Management Review, 8,* 226-232.

Adler, N. J. (1984). Women do not want international careers and other myths about international management. *Organizational Dynamics, 13(2),* 66-79.

Adler, N. J., & Jelinek, M. (1986). Is "organization culture" culture bound? *Human Resource Management, 25,* 73-90.

Adler, P. & Ferdows, K. (1992). The chief technology officer. In L. R. Gomez-Mejia & M. W. Lawless (Eds.) *Top management and effective leadership in high technology.* Greenwich, CT: JAI Press, Inc.

Agarwal, N. C. (1981). Determinants of executive compensation. *Industrial Relations, 20,* 36-46.

Aguayo, R. (1991). *Dr. Deming.* New York: Lyle Stuart.

Ahimud, Y., & Lev, B. (1981). Risk reduction as a management motive for conglomerate mergers. *Bell Journal of Economics, 12,* 605-617.

Albanese, R., & VanFleet, D. D. (1985). Rational behavior in groups: The freeriding tendency. *Academy of Management Review, 10,* 244-255.

Alberth, E. R. (1960). *The Scanlon plan applied to an oil refinery: Pros and cons.* Unpublished Master's Thesis, Massachusetts Institute of Technology.

Alchian, A. A., & Demsetz, H. (1972). Production, information costs, and economic organization. *American Economic Review, 62,* 777-795.

Alderfer, C. P. (1986). The invisible director on corporate boards. *Harvard Business Review, 64,* 38-52.

Alexander, E. R., & Wilkins, R. D. (1982). Performance rating validity: The relationship of objective and subjective measures of performance. *Group and Organization Studies, 7,* 485-496.

Alexander, L. D. (1979). The effect level that the hierarchy and functional area have on the extent Mintzberg's roles are required by managerial jobs. *Proceedings of the Academy of Management,* 186-189. Atlanta.

Allen, M. P. (1974). The structure of interorganizational elite coaptation. *American Sociological Review, 39,* 393-406.

Allen, M. P. (1981). Power and privilege in the large corporation: Corporate control and managerial compensation. *American Journal of Sociology, 86,* 1,112-1,123.

Allen, R.E., & Keaveny, T.J. (1988). *Contemporary labor relations.* Reading, MA: Addison-Wesley.

Allen, S. G., & Clark, R. L. (1986). Unions, pension wealth, and age-compensation profiles. *Industrial and Labor Relations Review, 39,* 502-517.

Allen, T. J. & Katz, R. (1986). The dual ladder: Motivational solution or managerial delusion? *R&D Management, 16,* 185-197.

Anderson, C. R., & Zeithaml, C. P. (1984). Stage of the product life cycle, business strategy, and business performance. *Academy of Management Journal, 27,* 5-14.

Anderson, J. C. (1978). A comparative analysis of local union democracy. *Industrial Relations, 17,* 278-295.

Anderson, J. C. (1979). Local union participation: A re-examination. *Industrial Relations, 18,* 18-31.

Andrews, D. R. (1971). *The concept of corporate strategy.* Homewood, IL: Dow-Jones-Irwin.

Angelo, H., & Rice, E. M. (1983). Anti-takeover amendments and stockholder wealth. *Journal of Financial Economics, 11,* 329-359.

Antle, R., & Smith, A. (1985). Measuring executive compensation: Methods and an application. *Journal of Accounting Research, 23,* 296-325.

Antle, R., & Smith, A. (1986). An empirical investigation of the relative performance evaluation of corporate executives. *Journal of Accounting Research, 24,* 1-39.

Antos, J. R. (1983). Union effects on white-collar compensation. *Industrial and Labor Relations Review, 36,* 461-479.

Aoki, M. (1984). *The cooperative game theory of the firm.* Oxford, U. K.: Clarendon Press.

Aram, J. D., & Salipante, P. F., Jr. (1981). An evaluation of organizational due process in the resolution of employee/employer conflict. *Academy of Management Review, 16,* 197-204.

Argyris, C. (1957). *Personality of organization.* New York: Harper.

Arnould, R. J. (1985). Agency costs in banking firms: An analysis of expense preference behavior. *Journal of Economics and Business, 37,* 103-112.

Arrow, K. (1969). The organization of economic activity: Issues pertinent to the choice of market versus nonmarket allocation. In *The Analysis and Evaluation of Public Expenditure: The PPB System: Vol. 1.* U.S. Joint Economic Committee, 91st Congress, 1st Session. Washington, DC: U.S. Government Printing Office.

Arvey, R. (1987). Potential problems in job evaluation methods and processes. In D. B. Balkin & L. R. Gomez-Mejia (Eds.), *New Perspectives on compensation.* Englewood Cliffs, NJ: Prentice-Hall, Inc.

Ash, P. (1991, October 7). Interview appearing in the *Arizona Republic,* B4. Phoenix, Arizona, Business Section under "your money's worth."

Ash, R. A., Levine, E. L., & Sistrunk, F. (1983). The role of jobs and job based methods in personnel and human resources management. In K. Rowland & G. Ferris (Eds.), *Research in Personnel and Human Resources Management Vol. 1.* Greenwich, CT: JAI Press, Inc.

Associated Press (1991, April 4). What matters to Americans. Phoenix, AZ: *Arizona Republic,* A7.

Austin, J. T., & Bobko, P. (1985). Goal setting theory: Unexplored areas and future research needs. *Journal of Occupational Psychology, 58,* 289-308.

Baenen, L.B., & Ernest, R.C. (1982). An argument for early retirement incentive planning. *Personnel Administrator, 17(8),* 63-66.

Bagozzi. R. (1975). Marketing as exchange. *Journal of Marketing, 39(4),* 32-39.

Bain, J. S. (1956). *Industrial organization* (2nd ed.). New York: Wiley.

Bain, J. S. (1968). *Barriers to new competition.* Cambridge: Harvard University Press.

Baker, G., Jensen, M., & Murphy, K. J. (1988). Compensation and incentives: Practice vs. theory. *The Journal of Finance, 43,* 593-616.

Balkin, D. B. (1989). Union influences on pay policy: A survey. *Journal of Labor Research, 10,* 299-310.

Balkin, D. B., & Gomez-Mejia, L. R. (1984). Determinants of R & D compensation strategy in high tech industry. *Personnel Psychology, 37,* 635-650.

Balkin, D. B., & Gomez-Mejia, L. R. (1985). Compensation practices in high tech industries. *Personnel Administrator, 30(6),* 111-123.

Balkin, D. B., & Gomez-Mejia, L. R. (1986). A contingency theory of compensation. In S. Rynes & G. T. Milkovich (Eds.), *Current issues in human resource management.* Plano, TX: Business Publications Inc.

Balkin, D. B., & Gomez-Mejia, L.R. (1987a). Toward a contingency theory of compensation strategy. *Strategic Management Journal, 8,* 169-182.

Balkin, D. B., & Gomez-Mejia, L. R. (Eds.). (1987b). *New perspectives on compensation.* Englewood Cliffs, NJ: Prentice-Hall, Inc.

Balkin, D. B., & Gomez-Mejia, L. R. (1987c). The strategic use of short-term and long-term incentives in the high technology industry. In D. B. Balkin & L. R. Gomez-Mejia (Eds.), *New perspectives of compensation.* Englewood Cliffs, NJ: Prentice-Hall, Inc.

Balkin, D. B., & Gomez-Mejia, L. R. (1988). Entrepreneurial compensation. In R. S. Schuler, S. A. Youngblood, & V. L. Huber, (Eds), *Readings in personnel and human resource management.* St. Paul, MN: West Publishing Co.

Balkin, D. B., & Gomez-Mejia, L. R. (1990). Matching compensation and organizational strategies. *Strategic Management Journal, 11,* 153-169.

Balkin, D. B., & Logan, J.W. (1988). Reward policies that support entrepreneurship. *Compensation and Benefits Review, 20(1),* 18-25.

Barber, A.E. (1989). Pay as a signal in organizational recruiting. Working paper, University of Wisconsin, Madison, WI.

Barnard, C. I. (1938). *The functions of the executive.* London: Oxford University Press.

Barney, J. B. (1985). Strategizing processes and returns to strategizing. Unpublished manuscript, Management Department, University of California, Los Angeles, CA.

Barney, J. B. (1986). Types of competition and the theory of strategy: Toward an integrative framework. *Academy of Management Review, 11,* 791-801.

Barney, J. B., & Tyler, B. (1992). Irrelevance of top management teams as sources of sustained competitive advantage in high technology industries. In L. R. Gomez-Mejia & M. Lawless (Eds.), *Top management and effective leadership in high technology.* Greenwich, CT: JAI Press, Inc..

Barrett, G. V. (1972). Research models of the future for industrial and organizational psychology. *Personnel Psychology, 25,* 1-17.

Bartol, K.M., & Martin, D.C. (1988). Influences on managerial pay allocations: A dependency perspective. *Personnel Psychology, 41,* 361-378.

Bartol, K. M. & Martin, D. C. (1990). When politics pays: Factors influencing managerial compensation decisions. *Personnel Psychology, 43,* 599-614.

Bass, B.M., & Barrett, G.V. (1981). *People, work, and organizations* (2nd ed..) Boston: Allyn and Bacon.

Basu, A., Lal, R., Srinivasan, V., & Staelin, R. (1985). Sales force compensation plans: An agency theoretic perspective. *Marketing Science, 4,* 267-291.

Baucus, D. A., & Ottensmeyer, E. J. (1989). The impact of the information noise content of performance on strategic issue management systems. *Proceedings of the Annual Academy of Management.* Washington, D. C.

Baumol, W. J. (1959). *Business behavior, value, and growth.* New York: MacMillan.

Baysinger, B., & Hoskisson, R. E. (1989). Diversification strategy and R&D intensity in multiproduct firms. *Academy of Management Journal, 32,* 310-332.

Baysinger, B., & Hoskisson, R.E. (1990). The composition of the board of directors and strategic control: Effects of corporate strategy. *Academy of Management Review, 15,* 72-87.

Baysinger, B., Kosnik, R.D., & Turk, T.A. (1991). Effects of board and ownership structure on corporate R&D strategy. *Academy of Management Journal, 34,* 205-214.

Baysinger, B., & Mobley, W. (1983). Employee turnover: Individual and organizational analysis. In K. Rowland & G. Ferris (Eds.), *Research in personnel and human resources management,* Vol. 1. Greenwich, CT: JAI Press, Inc.

Beard, B. (1991, October 7). Companies give competition as best reason for wage increases. *Arizona Republic,* B4. Phoenix, Arizona.

Beardsley, D. W. (1962). *A look at the Scanlon plan.* Unpublished master's thesis. Massachusetts Institute of Technology.

Beatty, J. R., McCune, J. T., & Beatty, R. W. (1988). A policy capturing approach to the study of U. S. and Japanese managers' compensation decisions. *Journal of Management, 14,* 465-474.

Beatty, R. P., & Zajac, E. J. (1990). *Top management incentives, monitoring, and risk bearing: A study of executive compensation, ownership, and board structure in initial public offerings.* Unpublished report, College of Business, University of Chicago.

Becker, G. S. (1964). *Human capital* (1st ed.). New York: National Bureau of Economic Research.

Becker, G. S. (1975a). *Human capital* (2nd ed.). New York: National Bureau of Economic Research.

Beehr, T.A. (1986). The process of retirement: A review and recommendations for the future investigation. *Personnel Psychology, 39,* 31-55.

Beer, M., & Gerry, G. J. (1968, August). *Pay systems preferences and the correlates.* Paper presented at American Psychological Association, San Francisco.

Beer, M., Spector, B., Lawrence, P. R., Mills, D. Q., & Walton, R. E. (1984). *Managing human assets.* New York: The Free Press.

Belcher, D.W. (1974). *Compensation administration.* Englewood Cliffs, NJ: Prentice-Hall, Inc..

Belcher, D. W., & Atchison, T. J. (1987). *Compensation administration.* Englewood Cliffs, NJ: Prentice-Hall, Inc.

Bell, M. J. (1982). The entrepreneur, the market, and venture capital. In R. W. Smilor (Ed.), *Small Business and the Entrepreneurial Spirit.* Austin, TX: University of Texas at Austin, Institute for Constructive Capitalism.

Ben-David, J. (1971). *The scientist's role in society.* Englewood Cliffs, NJ: Prentice Hall, Inc.

Bennett, A. (1990, April 18). Pay for performance. *The Wall Street Journal,* R-7.

Benston, G. J. (1985). The self-serving management hypothesis: Some evidence. *Journal of Accounting and Economics, 7,* 67-84.

Berg, N. A. (1969). What's different about conglomerate management? *Harvard Business Review, 47(6),* 112-120.

Berg, N. A. (1973). Corporate role in diversified companies. In: B. Taylor & K. MacMillen (Eds.), *Business policy teaching and research.* New York: Halstead Press.

Berger, L. A. (1991). Trends and issues for the 1990s: Creating a viable frame work for compensation design. In M. L. Rock & L. A. Berger (Eds.), *The compensation handbook*. New York: McGraw-Hill, Inc.

Bergmann, T. J., & Hills, F. S. (1987). A review of causes and solutions to pay compression. In D.B. Balkin, and L.R. Gomez-Mejia (Eds.), *New perspectives on compensation*. Englewood Cliffs, NJ: Prentice-Hall, Inc.

Bergmann, T. J., Hills, F. S., & Priefert, L. (1983). Pay compression: Causes, results and possible solutions. *Compensation Review, 13(3)*, 17-26.

Berle, A. & Means, G. C. (1932). *The modern corporation and private property*. New York: MacMillan.

Bernardin, H. J., & Beatty, R. W. (1984). *Performance appraisal: Assessing behavior at work*. Boston: Kent Publishing.

Bernardin, H. J., & Pence, E. C. (1980). Rater training: Creating new response sets and decreasing accuracy. *Journal of Applied Psychology, 65*, 60-66.

Berton, L. (1990, April 18). Calculating compensation. *Wall Street Journal Reports*, R26.

Best, R., (1961). Profit sharing and motivation for productivity. In *A symposium on profit sharing and productivity motivation*. Madison, WI: Center for Productivity Motivation.

Bettis, R. A., & Hall, W. K. (1983). The business portfolio approach—where it falls down in practice. *Long Range Planning, 12(2)*, 95-104.

Bhagat, S. (1983). The effect of pre-emptive right amendments on shareholder wealth. *Journal of Financial Economics, 12*, 289-310.

Bhagat, S., Brickley, J. A. & Lease, R. C. (1985). Incentive effects of stock purchase plans. *Journal of Financial Economics, 14*, 195-215.

Bickford, C. C. (1981). Long term incentives for management, part 6: Performance attainment plans. *Compensation Review, 12(3)*, 14-29.

Biddle, G. C. (1980). Accounting methods and management decisions: The case of inventory costing and inventory policy. *Journal of Accounting Research, 18* (Supplement), 235-280.

Biddle, G. C., & Lindahl, F. W. (1982). Stock price reactions to LIFO adoptions: The association between excess returns and LIFO tax savings. *Journal of Accounting Research, 20*, 551-558.

Black, F. & Scholes, M. (1973). Pricing of options and corporate liabilities. *Journal of political economy, 81*, 637-654.

Blair, R. & Kaserman, L. (1983). Ownership and control in modern organizations: Antitrust implications. *Journal of Business Research, 11,* 333-344.

Blakemore, A., Low, S., & Ormiston, M. (1987). Employment bonuses and labor turnover. *Journal of Labor Economics, 5,* 124-135

Blau, P. M. (1970). A formal theory of differentiation in organizations. *American Sociological Review, 35,* 201-218.

BNA Special Report (1988). *Changing pay practices.* Washington, D. C.: Bureau of National Affairs.

Booz, Allen, & Hamilton Consultants, Inc. (1990, May 1). Middle management pay. *Wall Street Journal,* 1.

Borjas, G., & Heckman, J. (1978). Labor estimates for public policy evaluation. *Proceedings of the Industrial Relations Research Association,* 320-331.

Boudreau, J. W. (1988). Utility analysis. In L. Dyer (Ed.), *Human resource management: Evolving roles and responsibilities.* Washington, D.C.: Bureau of National Affairs, Inc.

Boudreaux, K. J. (1973). Managerialism and risk-return performance. *Southern Economic Journal, 39,* 366-373.

Boulder Daily Camera. (1989, January 29). Fraud, extravagance brought down many of the nation's S&L's, 78-79.

Bowen, R., Noreen, E. W., & Lacey, J. M. (1981). Determinants of the corporate decision to capitalize interest. *Journal of Accounting and Economics, 3(2),* 151-179.

Bradley, M., & Wakeman, M. (1983). The wealth effects of targeted share repurchases. *Journal of Financial Economics, 11,* 301-328.

Brandes, S. (1970). *American welfare capitalism: 1880-1940.* Chicago, IL: University of Chicago Press.

Braverman, H. (1974). *Labor and monopoly capital.* New York: Monthly Review Press.

Brehn, J. W., & Cole, A. H. (1966). Effect of a favor which reduces freedom. *Journal of Personality and Social Psychology, 3,* 420-426.

Brickley, J. A., Bhagat, S., & Lease, R. C. (1985). The impact of long-range managerial compensation plans for shareholder wealth. *Journal of Accounting & Economics, 7(1),* 115-129.

Brickley, J. A., & Dark, F. H. (1987). The choice of organizational form: The case of franchising. *Journal of Financial Economics, 18,* 401-420.

Brigham, E. F. (1985). *Financial management: Theory and practice.* Hinsdale, IL: Dryden Press.

Broderick, R. F. (1986). *Pay policy and business strategy—toward a measure of fit.* Unpublished doctoral dissertation, Cornell University.

Bronfenbrenner, M. (1956). Potential monopsony power in labor markets. *Industrial and Labor Relations Review, 9,* 577-588.

Brouwer, C. (1984, December). Measuring the division's manager's performance. *Management Accounting,* 30-33.

Brown, S. J., & Warner, J. B. (1980). Measuring security price performance. *Journal of Financial Economics, 8,* 205-258.

Brown, S. J., & Warner, J. B. (1985). Using daily stock returns: The case of event studies. *Journal of Financial Economics, 14,* 3-31.

Brown, W., & Nolan, P. (1988). Wages and labor productivity: The contribution of industrial relations research to the understanding of pay determination. *British Journal of Industrial Relations, 26(3),* 339-361.

Bullock, R. J., & Lawler, E. E. (1984). Gainsharing: A few questions and fewer answers. *Human Resource Management, 23(1),* 23-40.

Burack, E. H. (1988). *Creative human resource planning and applications.* Englewood Cliffs, NJ: Prentice-Hall, Inc.

Bureau of National Affairs Special Report (1988). *Changing pay practices: New developments in employee compensation.* Washington, D.C.: The Bureau of National Affairs, Inc.

Burgelman, R. A. (1983a). Corporate entrepreneurship and strategic management: Insights from a process study. *Management Science, 29,* 1,349-1,364.

Burgelman, R. A. (1983b). A process model of internal corporate venturing in the diversified major firm. *Administrative Science Quarterly, 28,* 223-244.

Burgess, L. R. (1989). *Compensation administration.* Columbus, OH: Merrill Publishing Company.

Burroughs, J. D. (1982). Pay secrecy and performance: The psychological research. *Compensation Review, 14(3),* 44-54.

Business Week. (1987, October 28). Harris Poll, 28.

Business Week (1990a, May 7). Executive pay, 56-61.

Business Week (1990b, May 14). The stateless corporation, 98-115.

Business Week (1990c, June 15). Special issue on innovation.

Business Week (1991, November 7). Special report on the quality imperative: Questing for the best.

Butler, J. E., Ferris, G. R., & Napier, N. K. (1991). *Strategy and human resources management.* Cincinnati, OH: South-Western Publishing Co.

Buzzell, R. D., & Bradley, G. T. (1987). *The PIMS principles.* New York: Free Press.

Campbell, B., & Barron, C. (1982). How extensively are human resource management practices being utilized by the practitioners? *Personnel Administrator, 27,* 67-71.

Canning, G., & Berry, R.K. (1982). Linking sales compensation to the product life cycle. *Management Review, 71(4),* 43-46.

Capon, D., Farley, J. V., & Hoenig, S. (1990). Determinants of financial performance: A meta analysis. *Management Science, 36 (10),* 1,143-1,159.

Cappelli, P. and Cascio, W. F. (1991). Why some jobs command wage premiums: A test of career tournament and internal labor market hypotheses. *Academy of Management Journal, 34,* 848-868.

Cardy, R.L. (Symposium Chair) (1991). *New management visions: Implications for HRM theory, research, and practice.* Symposium conducted at the 1991 Academy of Management meeting, Miami.

Cardy, R. L., & Dobbins, G. A. (1986). Affect and appraisal accuracy: Liking as an integral dimension in evaluating performance. *Journal of Applied Psychology, 71,* 672-678.

Cardy, R.L., & Dobbins, G. (1993). *Performance appraisal.* Cincinnati, OH: South-Western Publishing Co.

Carpenter, D. S. (1984, November). We are in the money. *Inc.,* 183-184.

Carrington, T., & Hertzberg, D. (1982, November 30). Stock prices become more volatile as role of institutions grows. *Wall Street Journal,* R5.

Carroll, S. J. (1987). Business strategies and compensation systems. In D. B. Balkin & L. R. Gomez-Mejia (Eds.), *New perspectives on compensation.* Englewood Cliffs, NJ: Prentice-Hall, Inc.

Carroll, S. J. (1988). Handling the need for consistency and the need for contingency in the management of compensation. *Human Resource Planning, 11(3),* 191-196.

Carson, K. P. (1992). Total quality management meets criteria research: Theoretical and empirical examination. Paper presented at the national meetings of the Society for Industrial and Organizational Psychology, Montreal.

Carson, K. P., Cardy, R. L., Dobbins, G. H., & Stewart, G. L. (1992). Determinants and domains of performance: Implications for the evaluation of employee performance. Paper presented at the national meetings of the Society for Industrial and Organizational Psychology, Montreal.

Cartter, A. M. (1959). *Theory of wages and employment.* Homewood, IL: Richard D. Irwin.

Cascio, W. F. (1990). Strategic human resource management in high technology industry. In L. R. Gomez-Mejia & M. Lawless (Eds.), *Organizational issues in high technology management.* Greenwich, CT: JAI Press, Inc.

Cascio, W. F. (1992). *Costing human resources* (3rd Ed.). Boston: PWS-Kent Publishing Co.

Castro, J. (1991, April 15). CEOs: No pain, just gain. *Time, 137(15),* 40.

Chace, S. (1982). The corporate culture at IBM: How it reinforces strategy. *The Wall Street Journal,.* 5.

Chamberlin, E. H. (1933). *The theory of monopolistic competition.* Cambridge, MA: Harvard University Press.

Chandler, A. D., Jr. (1962). *Strategy and structure: Chapters in the history of American industrial enterprise.* Cambridge, MA: MIT Press.

Chandler, A. D., Jr. (1977). *The visible hand: The managerial revolution in American business.* Cambridge, MA: Belknap Press.

Chatterjee, S., & Lubatkin, M. (1990). Corporate mergers, stockholder diversification, and changes in systematic risk. *Strategic Management Journal, 11,* 255-269.

Cheadle, A. (1989). Explaining patterns of profit sharing activity. *Industrial Relations, 28,* 387-401.

Cherrington, D. L., Reitz, H. J., & Scott, W. E. (1971). Effects of reward and contingent reinforcement on satisfaction and task performance. *Journal of Applied Psychology, 55,* 531-536.

Chevalier, J. M. (1969). The problem of control in large American corporations. *Antitrust Bulletin, 14,* 163-180.

Child, J. M. (1972a). Organization structure, environments, and performance: The role of strategic choice. *Sociology, 6,* 1-22.

Child, J. M. (1972b). Organization structure and strategies: A replication of the Aston studies. *Administrative Science Quarterly, 17,* 163-176.

Child, J. M. (1973). Predicting and understanding organizational structure. *Administrative Science Quarterly, 18,* 169-185.

Ciscel, D. H. (1974). Determinants of executive compensation. *Southern Economic Journal, 40,* 613-617.

Ciscel, D. H., & Carroll, T. M. (1980). The determinants of executive salaries: An econometric survey. *Review of Economics and Statistics, 62,* 7-13.

Cochran, P.L., Wood, R.A., & Jones, T.B. (1985). The composition of boards of directors and incidence of golden parachutes. *Academy of Management Journal, 28,* 664-671.

Coffee, J. C. (1988) Shareholder versus managers: The strain in the corporate web. In J. C. Coffee, L. Lowenstein, & S. Rose-Acherman (Eds.), *Knights, raiders, targets.* New York: Oxford University Press.

Colletti, J.A. (1986). Job evaluation and pay plans: Field sales representatives. In J. Famularo (Ed.), *Handbook of human resources administration.* New York: McGraw-Hill, Inc.

Colletti, J. A., & Cichelli, D. J. (1991). Increasing sales force effectiveness through the compensation plan. In M. L. Rock & L. A. Berger (Eds.), *The compensation handbook.* New York: McGraw-Hill, Inc.

Commerce Clearing House. (1988, January). *Executive compensation,* 4,201-4,304.

Compensation and Benefits Review. (1988). Currents in compensation and benefits, 21(1), 1-3.

CompFlash (1989, December). At the top, 1.

CompFlash (1990a, January). At the top, 1.

CompFlash (1990b, May). Use of parachutes is spreading: Companies give change-of-control protection to top and middle managers, 1.

CompFlash (1991a, January). At the top, 1.

CompFlash (1991b, April). New developments in compensation and benefits (monthly newsletter), 2.

Conlon, E. J., & Parks, J. M. (1990). Effects of monitoring and tradition on compensation arrangements: An experiment with principal-agent dyads. *Academy of Management Journal, 33(3),* 603-622.

Connolly, T., Conlon, E. J., & Deutsch, S. J. (1980). A multiple constituency approach of organizational effectiveness. *Academy of Management Review, 5,* 211-218.

Cook & Co. Inc. (1989, October). *Long-term incentive compensation grants among the top 200 service companies.* New York: Special report.

Cook, F. W. (1981). The compensation director and the board's compensation committee. *Compensation and Benefits Review, 13,* 37-41.

Cook, F. W. (1991). Merit pay and performance appraisal. In M. L. Rock & L. A. Berger (Eds.), *The compensation handbook.* New York: McGraw-Hill, Inc.

Coombs, G., & Gomez-Mejia, L. R. (1991). Cross-functional compensation strategies in high technology firms. *Compensation and Benefits Review, 23(5),* 40-49.

Coombs, G., & Rosse, J. G. (1992). Recruiting and hiring the high technology professional. In L. R. Gomez-Mejia & M. W. Lawless (Eds.), *Human resource management strategy in high technology.* Greenwich, CT: JAI Press, Inc.

Cooper, M. R. (1991). In M. L. Rock & L. A. Berger (Eds.), *The compensation handbook.* New York: McGraw-Hill, Inc.

Coords, H. H. (1980). Cost control at Fisher-Price toys. In B. L. Metzger (Ed.), *Increasing productivity through profit sharing.* Evanston, IL.: Profit Sharing Research Foundation.

Copeland, T. E., & Weston, F. (1979). *Financial theory and corporate policy.* Reading, MA: Addison-Wesley Publishing Co.

Cosh, A., (1975). The remuneration of chief executives in the United Kingdom. *Economic Journal, 85,* 75-94.

Coughlan, A. T., & Schmidt, R. M. (1985). Executive compensation management turnover and firm performance—an empirical investigation. *Journal of Accounting and Economics, 7(1),* 43-66.

Crozier, M. (1964). *The bureaucratic phenomenon.* Chicago, IL: The University of Chicago Press.

Crystal, G. S. (1988, June 6). The wacky, wacky world of CEO pay. *Fortune,* 68-78.

Crystal, G. S. (1990, June 18). The great CEO pay sweepstakes. *Fortune,* 99-102.

Crystal, G.S. (1991, April 15). Interview appearing in *Time, 137(15),* 40.

Crystal, G. (1991). *In search of excess.* New York, NY: Norton.

Cyert, R. M., & March, J. G. (1963). *A behavioral theory of the firm.* Englewood Cliffs, NJ: Prentice-Hall, Inc..

Dachler, H. P., & Mobley, W. H. (1973). Construct validation of an instrumentality-expectancy-task goal model of reward motivation: Some theoretical boundary conditions. *Journal of Applied Psychology, 58,* 397-418.

Dann, L. Y., & DeAngelo, H., (1983). Corporate financial policy and corporate control: A study of defensive adjustments in asset and ownership structure. *Journal of Financial Economics, 20,* 87-127.

Davis, K.R., & Sauser, W.I. (1991). Effects of alternative weighing methods in a policy capturing approach to job evaluation: A review and empirical investigation. *Personnel Psychology, 44,* 85-129.

Davis, R. C. (1951). *The fundamentals of top management.* New York: Harper.

Day, G. S., & Montgomery, D. B. (1983). Diagnosing the experience curve. *Journal of Marketing, 47(2),* 44-58.

Day, G.S., & Wensley, R. (1983). Marketing theory with a strategic orientation. *Journal of Marketing, 47(4),* 79-89.

Dearborn, D. C., & Simon, H. A. (1958). Selective perceptions: A note on the departmental identification of executives. *Sociometry, 2,* 140-144.

Dearden, J. (1960). Problems in decentralized profit responsibility. *Harvard Business Review, 38(3),* 79-86.

Dearden, J. (1969). The case against ROI control. *Harvard Business Review, 47(3),* 124-135.

Debejar, G., & Milkovich, G. T. (1986). *Human resource strategy at the business level. Study 2: Relationship between strategy and performance components.* Paper presented at National Academy of Management Annual meeting, Chicago.

De Charms, R. (1968). *Personal causation: The internal affective determinants of behavior.* New York: Academic Press.

Deci, E. L. (1972). The effects of contingent and non-contingent rewards and controls on intrinsic motivation. *Organizational Behavior and Human Performance, 8,* 15-31.

Deci, E. L. (1975). Notes on the theory and meta-theory of intrinsic motivation. *Organizational Behavior and Human Performance, 15,* 130-145.

Deckop, J. R. (1987). Top executive compensation and the pay-for-performance issue. In D. B. Balkin & L. R. Gomez-Mejia (Eds.), *New perspectives on compensation.* Englewood Cliffs, NJ: Prentice-Hall, Inc.

Deckop, J. R. (1988). Determinants of chief executive officer compensation. *Industrial and Labor Relations Review, 41,* 215-226.

Deming, W. E. (1986a). *Out of the crisis.* Cambridge, MA: Productivity Press.

Deming, W. E. (1986b). *Quality, productivity and competitive position.* Cambridge, MA: MIT Center for Advanced Engineering Study.

Demsetz, H. (1983). The structure of ownership and the theory of the firm. *Journal of Law and Economics, 26,* 375-390.

Demski, J. S., & Feltham, G. (1978). Economic incentives in budgetary control systems. *Accounting Review, 53,* 336-359.

Demski, J. S., Patell, J. M., & Wolfson, M. A. (1984). Decentralized choice of monitoring systems. *Accounting Review, 14,* 16-34.

DeNoble, A. F., & Galbraith, C. S. (1992). Location criteria and corporate strategy: A comparison study of Mexican and U. S. electronic firms. *Journal of High Technology Management Research,* (in press).

Dess, G. G., & Robinson, R. B. (1984). Measuring organizational performance in the absence of objective measures: The case of the privately-held firm and conglomerate business unit. *Strategic Management Journal, 5,* 265-273.

Deutsch, M. (1949). A theory of cooperation and competition. *Human Relations, 2,* 129-152.

Devanna, M. A., Fombrum, C., & Tichy, N. (1981). Human resource management: A strategic approach. *Organizational Dynamics, 9(3),* 51-67.

Dhalla, N. K., & Yuspeh, S. (1976). Forget the product life cycle concept! *Harvard Business Review, 54(1),* 102-112.

Dobbins, G., Cardy, R., & Carson, K. (1991). Examining fundamental assumptions: A contrast of person and system approaches to human resource management. In K. M. Rowland & G. R. Ferris (Eds.), *Research in personnel and human resources management,* Vol. 9. Greenwich, CT: JAI Press, Inc.

Dodd, P. (1989). Merger proposals, management discretion, and stockholder wealth. *Journal of Financial Economics, 8,* 105-137.

Doeringer, P. B., & Piore, M. J. (1971), Theories of low-wage labor workers. In L. G. Reynolds, S. H. Masters, & C. H. Moser (Eds.), *Readings in labor economics and labor relations.* Englewood Cliffs, NJ: Prentice-Hall, Inc.

Donaldson, L. (1987). Strategy and structural adjustment to regain fit and performance: In defense of contingency theory. *Journal of Management Studies, 24(1),* 1-24.

Dossin, M. N., & Merritt, N. L. (1990). Sign-on bonuses score for recruiters. *HR Magazine, 35(3),* 42-43.

Doverspike, D., Carlisi, A., Barret, G.V., & Alexander, R.A. (1983). Generalizability analysis of a point-method job evaluation instrument. *Journal of Applied Psychology, 68,* 476-483.

Doverspike, D., & Barrett, G. V. (1984). An internal bias analysis of a job evaluation instrument. *Journal of Applied Psychology, 69,* 648-662.

Dowling, M.J., & Ruefli, T. W. (1992). Extended buyer-seller relationships and technology strategy for corporate control and renewal. In L. R. Gomez-Mejia & M. W. Lawless (Eds.), *Top management and effective leadership in high technology.* Greenwich, CT: JAI Press, Inc.

Dowling, P. J. (1986). *International personnel/human resource management: An overview and synthesis.* Ithaca, NY: (working paper) Cornell University.

Dowling, P. J. (1987). *The international human resource practitioner: A 1986 profile.* Paper presented at the annual meeting of the Academy of Management, Chicago.

Dowling, P.J. (1988). International human resource management. In L. Dyer (Ed.), *Human resource management: Evolving roles and responsibilities.* Washington, D.C.: Bureau of National Affairs, Inc.

Dowling, P. J. (1989). Hot issues overseas. *Personnel Administrator, 34(1),* 66-72.

Downs, A. (1967). The life cycle of bureaus. In A. Downs (Ed.), *Inside bureaucracy.* San Francisco: Little, Brown and Rand Corporation.

Downs, T. (1991). Using the computer in job evaluation. In M. L. Rock & L. A. Berger (Eds.), *The compensation handbook.* New York: McGraw-Hill, Inc.

Doyle, R.J. (1983). *Gainsharing and productivity: A guide to planning, implementation, and development.* New York: Amacon.

Dreyer, H. (1952). *The Scanlon plan: An analysis and a case study.* Unpublished Doctoral dissertation, Massachusetts Institute of Technology.

Dreyfus, D. D., & Bird, B.J. (1992). Scientists and engineers as effective managers. In L. R. Gomez-Mejia & M. W. Lawless (Eds.), *Top management and effective leadership in high technology.* Greenwich, CT: JAI Press, Inc.

Driscoll, J. W. (1979). Working creatively with a union: Lessons from the Scanlon Plan. *Organizational Dynamics, 8(1),* 61-80.

Driver, R. (1980). A determination of the relative efficacy of different techniques for employee benefits communication. *Journal of Business Communication, 17,* 23-37.

Drory, A. (1992). Determinants of intentions to quit among high tech professionals. In L. R. Gomez-Mejia & M. W. Lawless (Eds.), *Human resource management strategy in high technology.* Greenwich, CT: JAI Press, Inc.

Drucker, P. (1954). *The practice of management.* New York: Harper.

Duchon, D., & Ashmos, D. P. (1992). Innovators and non-innovators: A comparison of demographic, psychological, behavioral, and role factors. In L. R. Gomez-Mejia & M. W. Lawless (Eds.), *Human resource management strategy in high technology*. Greenwich, CT: JAI Press, Inc.

Dugan, W. K. (1989). Ability and effort attributions: Do they affect how managers communicate performance feedback information? *Academy of Management Journal, 32*, 87-114.

Dunlop, J. T. (1957). The task of contemporary wage theory. In G. W. Taylor & F. C. Pierson (Eds.), *New concepts in wage determination*. New York: McGraw-Hill, Inc.

Dyer, L., & Holder, G. W. (1988). A strategic perspective of human resource management. In L. Dyer (Ed.), *Human resource management evolving roles and responsibilities*. Washington, D.C.: Bureau of National Affairs.

Dyer, L., & Theriault, R. (1976). Determinants of pay satisfaction. *Journal of Applied Psychology, 61*, 596-604.

Dyl, E. A. (1988). Corporate control and management compensation: Evidence on the agency problem. *Managerial and Decision Economics, 9(1)*, 21-25.

Dyl, E. A. (1989). Agency, corporate control and accounting methods: The LIFO-FIFO choice. *Managerial and Decision Economics, 10(3)*, 141-137.

Eaton, J., and Rosen, H. (1983). Agency, delayed compensation, and the structure of executive remuneration. *The Journal of Finance, 23*, 1,489-1,505.

Eccles, R. (1985). Transfer pricing as a problem of agency. In J. Pratt & R. Zeckhauser (Eds.), *Principals and agents: The structure of business*. Boston: Harvard Business School Press.

ECS, Wyatt Data Services Company. (1992). *The 1991/1992 Top Management Report*. Ft. Lee, New Jersey.

Ehrenberg, R. G., & Bognanno, M. L. (1990). The incentive effects of tournaments revisited: Evidence from the European PGA tour. *Industrial and Labor Relations Review, 43*, 74-88.

Ehrenberg, R. G., & Milkovich, G. T. (1987). Compensation and firm performance. In M. Kleiner (Ed.), *Human resources and the performance of the firm*. Madison, WI: Industrial Relations Research Association.

Ehrenberg, R. G., & Smith, R. S. (1988). *Modern labor economics*. Glenview, IL: Scott, Foresman and Company.

Eisenhardt, K. M. (1985). Control: Organizational and economic approaches. *Management Science, 31*, 134-149.

Eisenhardt, K. M. (1988). Agency & institutional explanations of compensation in retail sales. *Academy of Management Journal, 31,* 488-511.

Eisenhardt, K. M. (1989). Agency theory: An assessment and review. *Academy of Management Review, 14,* 57-74.

Ellig, B. R. (1977). Salary surveys: Design to application. *Personnel Administrator, 22(10),* 25-30.

Ellig, B. R. (1981). *Executive compensation—A total pay perspective.* New York: McGraw-Hill Book Company.

Ellig, B. R. (1982a). Sales compensation: A systems approach. *Compensation Review, 14(1),* 21-45.

Ellig, B. R. (1982b). Compensation elements: Market phase determines the mix. *Compensation Review, 14(3),* 30-38.

Ellig, B. R. (1984). Incentive plans: Over the long-term. *Compensation Review, 16(3),* 39-54.

Ellsworth, R. R. (1983). Subordinate financial policy to corporate strategy. *Harvard Business Review, 61(6),* 170-181,

Emerson, R.M. (1962). Power-dependence relations. *American Sociological Review, 27,* 31-41.

Emerson, S. M. (1991). Job evaluation: A barrier to excellence? *Compensation and Benefits Review, 23(1),* 39-51.

Ettlie, J. E. (1983). Organizational policies and innovation among suppliers to the food processing sector. *Academy of Management Journal, 26,* 27-44.

Faley, R. H., & Kleiman, L. S. (1992). A method for establishing the training needs of upper level managers in the nuclear power industry. In L. R. Gomez-Mejia & M. Lawless (Eds.), *Human resource management strategy in high technology.* Greenwich, CT: JAI Press, Inc.

Fama, E. F. (1980). Agency problems and the theory of the firm. *Journal of Political Economy, 88(2),* 288-307.

Fama, E. F. (1989). *Time, salary, and incentive payoffs in labor contracts.* Unpublished report, University of Chicago, Department of Finance.

Fama, E. F., & Jensen, M. C. (1983a). Agency problems and residual claims. *Journal of Law and Economics, 26,* 327-349.

Fama, E. F., & Jensen, M. C. (1983b). Separation of ownership and control. *Journal of Law and Economics, 26,* 301-324.

Fama, E. F., & Miller, M. H. (1972). *The theory of finance.* Hinsdale, IL: Dryden Press.

Farley, J. C. (1950). *What does the Scanlon plan have to offer to management and the union.* Unpublished Master's thesis, Massachusetts Institute of Technology.

Farquhar, C. & Johnston, C. G. (1990). *Total quality management: A competitive imperative.* The Conference Board of Canada.

Fay, C. H. (1987). Using the strategic planning process to develop a compensation strategy. *Topics in Total Compensation, 2(2),* 117-129.

Fay, C. H. (1989). External pay relationships. In L. R. Gomez-Mejia (Ed.), *Compensation and Benefits.* Washington, D.C.: Bureau of National Affairs.

Fayol, H. (1949). *General and industrial management.* London: Pitman.

Fein, M. (1991). IMPROSHARE: A technique for sharing productivity gains with employees. In M. L. Rock & L. A. Berger (Eds.), *The compensation handbook.* New York: McGraw-Hill, Inc.

Feldman, J. M. (1981). Beyond attribution theory: Cognitive processes in performance appraisal. *Journal of Applied Psychology, 66,* 127-148.

Feldman, R., & Scheffler, R. (1982). The union impact on hospital wages and fringe benefits. *Industrial and Labor Relations Review, 35,* 196-206.

Ferracone, R. (1990, March). New concept in long term incentives: "Investment risk." *CompFlash,* 1.

Festinger, L. (1957). *A theory of cognitive dissonance.* Evanston, IL: Row, Peterson.

Fiedler, F. A. (1967). *A theory of leadership effectiveness.* New York: McGraw-Hill, Inc..

Fiegenbaum, A., & Thomas, H. (1990). Strategic groups and performance: The U. S. insurance industry, 1973-1984. *Strategic Management Journal, 11,* 197-216.

Fierman, J. (1990, March 12). The people who set the CEO's pay. *Fortune,* 58-66.

Fifth Annual Conference of the Society of Industrial and Organizational Psychology, Inc. (1990). Conference Program. Miami, Florida.

Fine, S. (1973). *Functional job analysis scales: A desk aid.* Kalamazoo, MI: Upjohn Institute for Employment Research.

Finkelstein, S., & Hambrick, D. C. (1988). Chief executive compensation. A synthesis and reconciliation. *Strategic Management Journal, 9,* 43-58.

Finkelstein, S., & Hambrick, D. C. (1989). Chief executive compensation: A study of the intersection of markets and political processes. *Strategic Management Journal, 10,* 121-135.

Flinn, C. (1986). Wages and job mobility of young workers. *Journal of Political Economy, 94,* 88-110.

Florida Department of Labor and Employment Security (1990, April 23). Weekly earnings for workers in Alachua County. Data reported in the *Gainesville Sun,* Business Monday, 11.

Florkowski, G. W. (1987). The organizational impact of profit sharing. *Academy of Management Review, 12,* 622-636.

Fogel, W. (1979). Occupational earnings: Market and institutional influences. *Industrial and Labor Relations Review, 33,* 24-35.

Folger, R., & Greenberg, J. (1985). Procedural justice: An interpretive analysis or personnel systems. In K. Rowland & G. Ferris (Eds.), *Research in personnel and human resources management, Vol. 3.* Greenwich, CT: JAI Press, Inc.

Folger, R., & Konovsky, M. (1989). Effects of procedural and distributive justices on reactions to pay raise decisions. *Academy of Management Journal, 32,* 115-130.

Fombrun, C. J. (1983). Strategic management: Integrating the human resource systems into strategic planning. In R. B. Lamb (Ed.), *Advances in Strategic Management: Vol. 2.* Greenwich, CT: JAI Press, Inc.

Fombrun, C. J. (1984a). Corporate culture and competitive strategy. In C. J. Fombrun, N. M. Tichy, & M. A. Devanna (Eds.), *Strategic human resource management.* New York: Wiley.

Fombrun, C. J. (1984b). The external context of human resource management. In C. J. Fombrun, N. M. Tichy, & M. A. Devanna, (Eds.), *Strategic human resource management.* New York: Wiley.

Fombrun, C. J. (1984c). An interview with Reginald H. Jones and Frank Doyle. In C. J. Fombrun, N. M. Tichy, & M. A. Devanna (Eds.), *Strategic human resource management.* New York: Wiley.

Fombrun, C. J. (1984d). Environmental trends create new pressures on human resources. *The Journal of Business Strategy, 4(3),* 61-69.

Fombrun, C. J., & Laud, R. L. (1983). Strategic issues in performance appraisal: Theory and practice. *Personnel, 60(6),* 23-31.

Fombrun, C. J., & Tichy, N. M. (1984). Strategic planning and human resource management: At rainbow's end. In R. B. Lamb (Ed.), *Competitive strategic management*. Englewood Cliffs, NJ: Prentice-Hall, Inc..

Fombrun, C. J., Tichy, N. M., & Devanna, M. A. (1984). *Strategic human resource management*. New York: Wiley.

Forward, J., & Zander, A. (1971). Choice of unattainable goals and affects on performance. *Organization Behavior and Human Performance, 6*, 184-199.

Foster, K. E. (1985, September). An anatomy of company pay practices. *Personnel,* 66-72.

Fosu, A. G. (1983). Impact of unionism on pension fringes. *Industrial Relations, 22*, 419-425.

Fosu, A. G. (1984). Unions and fringe benefits: Additional evidence. *Journal of Labor Research, 5*, 247-254.

Foulkes, F. (1980). *Personnel policies in large nonunion companies.* Englewood Cliffs, NJ: Prentice-Hall, Inc.

Frederikson, J. W., Hambrick, D. C., & Baumrin, S. (1988). A model of CEO dismissal. *Academy of Management Review, 13*, 255-271.

Freedman, R. J. (1986). How to develop a sales compensation plan. *Compensation and Benefits Review, 18(2)*, 41-48.

Freeman, R. B. (1980). Unionism and the dispersion of wages. *Industrial and Labor Relations Review, 34*, 3-23

Freeman, R. B. (1981). The effect of unionism on fringe benefits. *Industrial and Labor Relations Review, 34*, 489-509.

Freeman, R. B. (1982). Union wage practices and wage dispersion within establishments. *Industrial and Labor Relations Review, 36*, 3-21.

Freeman, R. B., & Medoff, J. L. (1979). The two faces of unionism. *The Public Interest, 57*, 69-93.

Frisch, C. J., & Dickinson, A. M. (1990). Work productivity as a function of the percentage of monetary incentives to base pay. *Journal of Organization Behavior Management, 11(1)*, 13-28.

Fryxell, G. E. (1990). Managing the culture of innovation. In L. R. Gomez-Mejia & M. Lawless (Eds.), *Organizational issues in high technology management*. Greenwich, CT: JAI Press, Inc.

Fuchsberg, G. (1990, April 18). Notes from the executive compensation front. *Wall Street Journal Reports,* R5.

Fuchsberg, G. (1991, January 30). Director's pay climbs despite firm's struggles. *The Wall Street Journal,* B-1.

Fuehrer, W. F. (1991). Practical approaches to gain-sharing design. In M. L. Rock & L. A. Berger (Eds.), *The compensation handbook.* New York: McGraw-Hill, Inc.

Gabor, A. (1991). *The man who discovered quality.* New York: Time Books.

Galbraith, C.S., & Merrill, G.B. (1991). The effect of compensation program and structure on SBU competitive strategy: A study of technology intensive firms. *Strategic Management Journal, 12,* 353-370.

Galbraith, J. (1973). *Designing complex organizations.* Reading, MA: Addison-Wesley.

Galbraith, J. K. (1976). *The affluent society.* Boston: Houghton Mifflin.

Garen, J. (1988). Empirical studies of the job matching hypothesis. In R. Ehrenberg (Ed.), *Research in labor economics* (Vol. 9). Greenwich, CT: JAI Press, Inc.

Gaver, J. J., Gaver, K. M., & Battistel, G. (1990). The stock market reaction to performance plan adoption. Unpublished report, Accounting Department, College of Business, University of Oregon.

Geare, A. J. (1976). Productivity from Scanlon-type plans. *Academy of Management Review, 1,* 99-108.

Geneen, H. S. (1984, September 17). Why directors can't protect the shareholders. *Fortune,* 28-32.

Gerhart, B., & Milkovich, G.T. (1990). Organizational differences in managerial compensation and financial performance. *Academy of Management Journal, 33,* 663-691.

Gerhart, B., & Milkovich, G.T. (1993). Employee compensation: Research and practice. In M.D. Dunnette & L.M. Hough (Eds.), *Handbook of industrial and organizational psychology* (Vol.3). Palo Alto, CA: Consulting Psychologists Press, Inc.

Gerstein, M., & Reisman, H. (1983). Strategic selection: Matching executives to business conditions. *Sloan Management Review, 24(2),* 33-74.

Gibbons, R., & Murphy, K. (1990). Relative performance evaluation for chief executive officers. *Industrial and Labor Relations Review, 43,* 30-51.

Gomez-Mejia, L. R. (1978). Strategies for evaluating test effectiveness in public jurisdictions. In S. Mussio (Ed.), *Personnel Selection and Training for Public Sector.* Chicago, IL: Greater Lakes Assessment Centers.

Gomez-Mejia, L. R. (1983). Sex differences in occupational socialization. *Academy of Management Journal, 26,* 492-499.

Gomez-Mejia, L. R. (1984). Effect of occupation on task related, contextual, and job involvement orientation: A cross-cultural perspective. *Academy of Management Journal, 27*, 706-720.

Gomez-Mejia, L. R. (1985). Dimensions and correlates of the personnel audit as an organizational assessment tool. *Personnel Psychology, 38*, 293-308.

Gomez-Mejia, L. R. (1986). Determining the cross-cultural structure of task-related and contextual constructs. *Journal of Psychology, 120*, 5-19.

Gomez-Mejia, L. R. (1988a). Evaluating employee performance: Does the appraisal instrument make a difference? *Journal of Organizational Behavior Management, 9(2)*, 155-170.

Gomez-Mejia, L. R. (1988b). The role of human resources strategy in export performance: A longitudinal study. *Strategic Management Journal, 9(3)*, 493-505.

Gomez-Mejia, L. R. (1989a). Performance appraisal: Testing a process model. *Journal of Managerial Psychology, 4(3)*, 27-35.

Gomez-Mejia, L. R., (Ed.) (1989b). *Compensation and benefits.* Washington, D. C.: Bureau of National Affairs.

Gomez-Mejia, L. R. (1990a). MBO as part of HRM strategies. Chapter in Fantome, D. (Ed.) Insituto di Studi per la Cooperazione e le Piccole e Media Impresa, Bologna, Italy: Sinnea.

Gomez-Mejia, L. R. (1990b). Women's adaptation to male-dominated occupations. *International Journal of Manpower, 11(4)*, 11-17.

Gomez-Mejia, L. R. (1990c). Increasing productivity: Performance appraisal and reward systems. *Personnel Review, 19(2)*, 21-28.

Gomez-Mejia, L. R. (1992). Structure and process of diversification, compensation strategy, and firm performance. *Strategic Management Journal.* (In press.) (See also Gomez-Mejia, L.R. [1992]. Relationship between compensation strategies and firm performance using Miles & Snow's framework. Unpublished technical report, College of Business, Arizona State University.)

Gomez-Mejia, L. R., & Balkin, D. B. (1980a, May). Can internal management training programs narrow the male-female gap in managerial skills? *Personnel Administrator*, 77-90.

Gomez-Mejia, L. R., & Balkin, D. B. (1980b, November). Classifying work-related and personal problems of troubled employees in employee assistance programs. *Personnel Administrator*, 23-29.

Gomez-Mejia, L. R., & Balkin, D. B. (1984a). Faculty satisfaction with pay and other job dimensions under union and non-union conditions. *Academy of Management Journal, 27*, 591-602.

Gomez-Mejia, L. R., & Balkin, D. B. (1984b). Union impacts on secretarial earnings. *Industrial Relations, 23,* 97-102.

Gomez-Mejia, L. R., & Balkin, D. B. (1985). Managing the high tech venture. *Personnel, 62(12),* 31-37.

Gomez-Mejia, L. R., & Balkin, D. B. (1987a). Pay compression in an academic environment: The case of business schools. In D. B. Balkin & L. R. Gomez-Mejia, (Eds.), *New perspectives on compensation.* Englewood Cliffs, NJ: Prentice Hall, Inc..

Gomez-Mejia, L. R., & Balkin, D. B. (1987b). The causes and consequences of pay compression in business schools. *Compensation and Benefits Review, 19(5),* 43-55.

Gomez-Mejia, L.R., & Balkin, D.B. (1987c). Effect of organizational strategy on pay policy. Paper presented at the National Academy of Management Meetings, New Orleans, LA.

Gomez-Mejia, L. R., & Balkin, D. B. (1987d). The determinants of personnel manager perceptions of effective drug testing programs. *Personnel Psychology, 40,* 745-763.

Gomez-Mejia, L. R., & Balkin, D. B. (1987e). The determinants of managerial satisfaction with the expatriation and repatriation process. *Journal of Management Development, 6,* 7-18.

Gomez-Mejia, L. R., & Balkin, D. B. (1988). The psychological and behavioral correlates of pay compression. *International Journal of Management, 5(1),* 15-22.

Gomez-Mejia, L.R., & Balkin, D.B. (1989). Effectiveness of individual and aggregate compensation strategies. *Industrial Relations, 28,* 431-445.

Gomez-Mejia, L. R., & Balkin, D. B. (1992). The determinants of faculty pay: An agency theory perspective. *Academy of Management Journal.*

Gomez-Mejia, L. R., Balkin, D. B., & Milkovich, G. T. (1990). Rethinking your rewards for technical employees. *Organizational Dynamics, 18(4),* 62-75.

Gomez-Mejia, L. R., Balkin, D. B., & Welbourne, T. M. (1990). The influence of venture capitalists on management practices in the high technology industry. *Journal of High Technology Management Research, 1(1),* 107-118.

Gomez-Mejia, L. R., Domicone, H. A., & Headrix, A. M. (1991). Fostering an integrative dominant paradigm of social responsibility in maquiladora industries. In K. Paul (Ed.), *Business and society.* Rochester, NY: Edwin Mellon Press. (in press).

Gomez-Mejia, L. R., Hopp, M. A., & Sommerstad, R. (1978, February). Implementation and evaluation of flexible work hours: A case study. *Personnel Administrator,* 39-51.

Gomez-Mejia, L. R., & McCann, J. E. (1985). *Meeting the challenges of foreign expansion.* Columbus, OH: Grid Publishing Co., Inc.

Gomez-Mejia, L. R., & McCann, J. E. (1988a). Measuring internal strategic choice decisions and their linkages to the reward structure. *International Journal of Manpower, 9(2),* 27-32.

Gomez-Mejia, L. R., & McCann, J. E. (1988b). Managerial activities and organization performance: An empirical study in 26 high technology plants. *Journal of Applied Business Research, 3,* 158-167.

Gomez-Mejia, L. R., & McCann, J. E. (1989). Factors affecting export success in high technology and traditional firms. *International Journal of Management, 6,* 31-39.

Gomez-Mejia, L. R., McCann, J. E., & Page, R. C. (1985). The structure of managerial behaviors and rewards. *Industrial Relations, 24 (1),* 147-156.

Gomez-Mejia, L. R., & Mussio, S. (1975). Job enrichment in a civil service setting. *Public Personnel Management, 4(1),* 49-54.

Gomez-Mejia, L. R., & Page, R. C. (1983, June). Integrating employee development and performance appraisal. *Training and Development Journal,* 138-145.

Gomez-Mejia, L. R., Page, R. C., & Tornow, W. (1979). Development and implementation of a computerized job evaluation system. *Personnel Administrator, 2,* 62-73.

Gomez-Mejia, L.R., Page, R. C., & Tornow, W. (1982). A comparison of the practical utility of traditional, statistical, and hybrid job evaluation approaches. *Academy of Management Journal, 25,* 790-809.

Gomez-Mejia, L. R., Page, R. C., & Tornow, W. (1985). Improving the effectiveness of performance appraisal. *Personnel Administrator, 30(1),* 74-84.

Gomez-Mejia, L. R., Page, R. C., & Tornow, W. (1987). Computerized job evaluation systems. In D. B. Balkin & L. R. Gomez-Mejia (Eds.), *New perspectives on compensation.* Englewood Cliffs, NJ: Prentice-Hall, Inc..

Gomez-Mejia, L. R., Tosi, H., & Hinkin, T. (1987). Managerial control, performance, and executive compensation. *Academy of Management Journal, 30,* 51-70.

Gomez-Mejia, L. R., & Welbourne, T. M. (1988). Compensation strategy: An overview and future steps. *Human Resource Planning, 11(3),* 173-189.

Gomez-Mejia, L. R., & Welbourne, T. M. (1989). Executive compensation. In L. R. Gomez-Mejia (Ed.), *Compensation and benefits.* Washington, D.C.: Bureau of National Affairs.

Gomez-Mejia, L. R., & Welbourne, T. M. (1990). The role of reward systems in fostering innovation in a high technology environment. In S. A. Mohrman & M. A. Von Glinow (Eds.), *High technology management*. Boston, MA: Oxford University Press.

Gomez-Mejia, L. R., & Welbourne, T. M. (1991). Compensation strategy in a global context. *Human resource planning, 14(1)*, 29-42.

Gordon, D. M., Edwards, R., & Reich, M. (1982). *Segmented work, divided workers: The historical transformation of labor in the United States*. London, England: Cambridge University Press.

Gordon, G. G. (1991a). Cultural and psychological implications for compensation. In M. L. Rock & L. A. Berger (Eds.), *The compensation handbook*. New York: McGraw-Hill, Inc.

Gordon, G. G. (1991b). The use of computers in developing job documentation. In M. L. Rock & L. A. Berger (Eds.), *The compensation handbook*. New York: McGraw-Hill, Inc.

Gouldner, A. W. (1960). The norm of reciprocity: A preliminary statement. *American Sociological Review, 25*, 161-178.

Gowen, C. R. (1985). Managing work group performance by individual goals and group goals for an interdependent group task. *Journal of Organization, 2(3)*, 12-22.

Graen, G. (1969). Instrumentality theory of work motivation: Some experimental results and suggested modifications. [Monograph]. *Journal of Applied Psychology, 53*.

Grams, R., & Schwab, D. (1985). An investigation of systematic gender related error in job evaluation. *Academy of Management Journal, 28*, 279-290.

Grasso, L. P. (1992). *The organizational determinants of the use of incentives in compensating business unit managers*. Unpublished technical report, Accounting Department, Arizona State University, Tempe, Arizona.

Graves, S.B. (1988). Institutional ownership and corporate R&D in the computer industry. *Academy of Management Journal, 31*, 417-427.

Graves, S.B., & Waddock, S.A. (1990). Institutional ownership and control: Implications for long-term corporate strategy. *Academy of Management Executive, 4(1)*, 75-83.

Gray, B., & Ariss, S. S. (1985). Politics and strategic change across organizational life cycles. *Academy of Management Review, 10*, 707-723.

Gray, D. H. (1958). *Toward a theory of the interior of the business firm: The dynamics of the employment relationship*. Unpublished doctoral dissertation, Massachusetts Institute of Technology.

Gray, R. B. (1971). The Scanlon Plan: A case study. *British Journal of Industrial Relations, 9*, 291-313.

Greeley, T. P., & Oshsner, R. C. (1986). Putting merit pay back into salary administration. *Topics in Total Compensation, 1(1),* 14-30.

Green, K. (1987). Effective employee benefits communication. In D.B. Balkin & L.R. Gomez-Mejia (Eds.), *New perspectives on compensation.* Englewood Cliffs, N.J.: Prentice-Hall, Inc.

Greenberg, J. (1990). Looking fair vs. being fair: Managing impressions of organizational justice. In L. Cummings & B. M. Staw (Eds.), *Research in organizational behavior: Vol. 12.* Greenwich, CT: JAI Press, Inc.

Greene, R.J. (1981). What does the median mean? *Personnel Administrator, 26(5),* 40-42.

Greiner, L. (1972). Evolution and revolution as organizations grow. *Harvard Business Review, 50(4),* 37-46.

Grey, J., & Kipnis, D. (1976). Untangling the performance appraisal dilemma: The influence of perceived organizational context on valuative processes. *Journal of Applied Psychology, 61,* 329-335.

Grider, D., & Shurden, M. (1987). The gathering storm of comparable worth. *Business Horizons, 30(4),* 81-86.

Groff, J. E., & Wright, C. J. (1989). The market for corporate control and its implications for accounting policy choice. *Advances in Accounting, 7,* 3-21.

Groshen, E.L. (1988). Why do wages vary among employers? *Economic Review, 24,* 19-38.

Grossman, S. J., & Hart, O. D. (1983). An analysis of the principal-agent problem. *Econometrica, 51(1),* 7-45.

Gupta, A. K. (1986). Matching managers to strategies: Point and counterpoint. *Human Resource Management, 25,* 215-234.

Gupta, A. K. (1987). SBU strategies, corporate-SBU relations, and SBU effectiveness in strategy implementation. *Academy of Management Journal, 30,* 477-500.

Gupta, A. K., & Govindarajan, V. (1984). Business unit strategy, managerial characteristics, and business unit effectiveness at strategy implementation. *Academy of Management Journal, 27,* 25-41.

Gupta, N., Schweizer, T.P., & Jenkins, G.D., Jr. (1987). Pay-for-knowledge compensation plans: Hypotheses and survey results. *Monthly Labor Review, 110(10),* 40-43.

Guston, B. H. (1973). Charisma, recognition, and the motivation of scientists. *American Journal of Sociology, 78,* 1,119-1,134.

Guthrie, J.P., & Olian, J.D. (1991). Does context affect staffing decisions? The case of general managers. *Personnel Psychology, 44,* 263-292.

Hagerman, R. L., & Zmijewski, M. E. (1979). Some economic determinants of accounting policy choice. *Journal of Accounting and Economics, 1(2),* 141-161.

Hagstrom, W. O. (1965). *The scientific community.* New York: Basic Books.

Hagstrom, W. O. (1968). *Departmental prestige and scientific productivity.* Paper presented at the annual meetings of the American Sociological Association, Boston.

Hagstrom, W. O. (1971). Inputs, outputs, and the prestige of university science departments. *Sociology of Education, 44,* 375-397.

Hagstrom, W. O. (1974). Competition in science. *American Sociological Review, 39,* 1-18.

Haire, M., Ghiselli, E. E., & Gordon, M. E. (1967). A psychological study of pay. *Journal of Applied Psychology (Monograph), 51(4),* Whole No. 636.

Halpern, P. (1973). Empirical estimates of the amount and distribution of gains to companies in mergers. *Journal of Business, 46,* 554-575.

Halpern, P. (1983). Corporate acquisitions: A theory of special cases? A review of event studies applied to acquisitions. *Journal of Finance, 38,* 297-317.

Hambrick, D. C. (1981). Environment, strategies, and power within top management teams. *Administrative Science Quarterly, 26,* 253-275.

Hambrick, D. C. (1982). Environmental scanning and organizational scanning. *Strategic Management Journal, 3,* 159-174.

Hambrick, D. C. (1983). An empirical typology of mature industrial-product environments. *Academy of Management Journal, 26,* 213-230.

Hambrick, D. C. (1984). Taxonomic approaches to studying strategy: Some conceptual and methodological issues. *Journal of Management, 10,* 27-41.

Hambrick, D. C., Black, S. & Frederickson, J. W. (1992). Executive leadership for the high technology firm. In L. R. Gomez-Mejia & M. W. Lawless (Eds.), *Top management and effective leadership in high technology.* Greenwich, CT: JAI Press, Inc.

Hambrick, D. C., & Finkelstein, S. (1987). Managerial discretion: A bridge between polar views of organizational outcomes. In L. L. Cummings & B. M. Staw (Eds.), *Research in organizational behavior: Vol. 9.* Greenwich, CT: JAI Press, Inc..

Hambrick, D. C. & Fukutomi, G. D. (1991). The seasons of a CEO's tenure. *Academy of Management Review, 16,* 719-743.

Hambrick, D. C., MacMillan, I. C., & Barbarosa, R. R. (1983). Business unit strategy and changes in the product R & D budget. *Management Science, 29,* 757-769.

Hambrick, D. C., & Mason, P. A. (1984). Upper echelons: The organization as a reflection of its top managers. *Academy of Management Review, 9,* 193-206.

Hambrick, D. C., & Snow, C. C. (1989). Strategic reward systems. In C. C. Snow (Ed.), *Strategy, organization design, and human resources management.* Greenwich, CT: JAI Press, Inc..

Hammer, W. C. (1975). How to ruin motivation with pay. *Compensation Review, 7(3),* 17-27.

Hannan, M. T., & Freeman, J. (1977). The population ecology of organizations. *American Journal of Sociology, 82,* 929-964.

Hansen, G.S., & Hill, C.W. (1991). Are institutional investors myopic? *Strategic Management Journal, 12,* 1-16.

Hansen, G. S., & Wernerfelt, B. (1989). Determinants of firm performance: The relative importance of economic and organizational factors. *Strategic Management Journal, 10,* 399-411.

Hanson, B.B. (1987). Incentive compensation for professionals. In D.B. Balkin & L.R. Gomez-Mejia (Eds.), *New perspectives on compensation,* Englewood Cliffs, NJ: Prentice-Hall, Inc..

Hanson, D.M. (1991, July 29). The realities of institutional investing. *Fortune,* 132.

Harkins, S. G., & Petty, R. E. (1982). Effects of task difficulty and task uniqueness on social loafing. *Journal of Personality and Social Psychology, 63,* 1214-1229.

Harmon, L.R. (1965). *High school ability patterns: A backward look from the doctorate.* Washington, D.C.: National Academy of Sciences.

Harris, M., & Holmstrom, B. (1982). A theory of wage dynamics. *Review of Economic Studies, 69,* 315-333.

Haslinger, J. A. (1985). Flexible compensation: Getting a return on benefits dollars. *Personnel Administrator, 30(6),* 39-46.

Haspeslagh, P. (1982). Portfolio planning: Uses and limits. *Harvard Business Review, 60(1),* 58-73.

Hayes, R. H., & Abernathy, W. J. (1980). Managing our way to economic decline. *Harvard Business Review, 4,* 67-77.

Hayes, T. C. (1990). Big oil fearful of backlash, becoming jittery over large profits. *The New York Times,* story appearing in *The Arizona Republic,* (1990, September 16), A1, Phoenix, AZ.

Hector, G. (1988, November). Yes, you can manage long-term. *Fortune,* 64-76.

Helfgott, R. (1962). *Group wage incentives: Experience with the Scanlon plan.* New York: Industrial Relations Counselors.

Henderson, R. I. (1989). *Compensation management.* Englewood Cliffs, NJ: Prentice-Hall, Inc..

Henderson, R. I., & Risher, H. W. (1987). Influencing organizational strategy through compensation leadership. In D. B. Balkin & L. R. Gomez-Mejia (Eds.), *New perspectives on compensation.* Englewood Cliffs, NJ: Prentice-Hall, Inc.

Heneman, H. G., III, & Schwab, D. P. (1985). Pay satisfaction: Its multidimensional nature and measurement. *International Journal of Psychology, 20,* 129-141.

Heneman, R. L. (1990). Merit pay research. In G. Ferris & K. Rowland (Eds.), *Research in personnel and human resources management, Vol. 8.* Greenwich, CT: JAI Press, Inc.

Herbert, T. T., & Deresky, H. (1987). Generic strategies: An empirical investigation of typology validity and strategy content. *Strategic Management Journal, 8,* 135-147.

Herman, E. S. (1981). *Corporate control, corporate power.* New York: Cambridge University Press.

Herman, E. S., & Lowenstein, L. (1988). The efficiency effects of hostile takeovers. In J. C. Coffee, L. Lowenstein, & S. Rose-Ackerman (Eds.), *Knights, raiders, and targets.* New York: Oxford University Press.

Herzlinger, R. E. (1988, February 17). Dancing on the glass ceiling. *Wall Street Journal,* 4.

Hill, C. W. (1988). Internal capital market controls and financial performance in multidivisional firms. *Journal of Industrial Economics, 37, 67-83.*

Hill, C. W., & Hansen, G. S. (1989). Institutional holdings and corporate R & D intensity in research intensive industries. *Academy of Management Best Papers Proceedings,* Washington, D.C., 49th Annual Meeting of the Academy of Management, 17-21.

Hill, C. W., Hitt, M., & Hoskisson, R. (1988). Declining United States competitiveness: Reflections on a crisis. *Academy of Management Executive, 2,* 51-60.

Hill, C. W., & Hoskisson, R. E., (1987). Strategy and structure in the multiproduct firm. *Academy of Management Review, 12,* 331-341.

Hill, C. W., & Jones, G. R. (1992). *Strategic Management: An integrated approach.* Boston, MA: Houghton Mifflin Co.

Hill, C. W., & Phan, P. (1991). CEO tenure as a determinant of CEO pay. *Academy of Management Journal, 34,* 712-717.

Hill, C. W., & Snell, S. A. (1989). Effects of ownership structure and control on corporate productivity. *Academy of Management Journal, 32,* 25-47.

Hills, F. S. (1987). *Compensation decision making.* Hinsdale, IL: Dryden Press.

Hills, F. S. (1989). Internal pay relationships. In L.R. Gomez-Mejia (Ed.) *Compensation and benefits.* Washington, D.C.: Bureau of National Affairs.

Hills, F. S., & Bergmann, T. J. (1987). Conducting an "equal pay for equal work" audit. In D.B. Balkin, & L.R. Gomez-Mejia (Eds.), *New perspectives on compensation.* Englewood Cliffs, NJ: Prentice-Hall, Inc.

Hills, F. S., Scott, D. K., Markham, S. E., & Vest, M. J. (1987) Merit pay: Just or unjust desserts. *Personnel Administrator, 32(9),* 53-64.

Hinkin, T. R., Podsakoff, P.M., & Schriesheim, C. A. (1987). The mediation of performance-contingent compensation by superiors in work organizations: A reinforcement perspective. In D. B. Balkin & L. R. Gomez-Mejia, (Eds.), *New perspectives on compensation.* Englewood Cliffs, NJ: Prentice-Hall, Inc.

Hirsch, B. T. (1982). The interindustry structure of unionism, earnings, and earnings dispersion. *Industrial and Labor Relations Review, 36,* 22-39.

Hirschey, M. ,& Pappas, J. L. (1981). Regulatory and life cycle influences on managerial incentives. *Southern Economic Journal, 48,* 327-334.

Hite, G. L., & Long, M. S. (1982). Taxes and executive stock options. *Journal of Accounting and Economics, 4,* 3-14.

Hitt, M. A., Hoskisson, R. E., & Ireland, R. D. (1990). Acquisitive growth and commitment to innovation in multiproduct firms. *Strategic Management Journal, 11* (special issue), 29-47.

Hitt, M. A., & Ireland, R. D. (1985). Corporate distinctive competence, strategy, industry, and performance. *Strategic Management Journal, 6,* 273-293.

Hitt, M. A., & Ireland, R. D. (1986). Relationships among corporate distinctive competencies, diversification strategy, corporate structure and performance. *Journal of Management Studies, 23,* 401-406.

Hofer, C. W. (1975). Toward a contingency theory of business strategy. *Academy of Management Journal, 18,* 784-810.

Hoffman, C. C., Natham, B. R., & Holden, L. M. (1991). A comparison of validation criteria: Objective versus subjective performance measures and self-versus supervisor ratings. *Personnel Psychology, 44,* 601-621.

Hofstede, G. (1980). *Culture's consequences.* Newbury Park, CA: Sage Publications, Inc.

Hollenback, J., & Williams, C. (1986). Turnover functionality versus turnover frequency: A note on work attitudes and organizational effectiveness. *Journal of Applied Psychology, 71,* 606-611.

Holmstrom, B. (1979). Moral hazard and observability. *Bell Journal of Economics, 10,* 74-91.

Holthausen, R. W., & Leftwich, R. W. (1983). The economic consequences of accounting choice: Implications of costly contracting and monitoring. *Journal of Accounting and Economics, 5,* 77-117.

Hom, P. (1992). *Turnover among maquiladora workers: The role of compensation strategy.* Unpublished paper. Arizona State University, Department of Management, Tempe, Arizona.

Hom, P., & Griffeth, R. (1991). Structural equations modeling test of a turnover theory: Cross-sectional and longitudinal analyses. *Journal of Applied Psychology, 76,* 350-366.

Hom, P., & Griffeth, R. (1993). *Employee turnover.* Cincinnati, Ohio: Southwestern Publishing Co.

Hoskisson, R. E., & Hitt, M. A. (1988). Strategic control systems and relative R&D intensity in large multiproduct firms. *Strategic Management Journal, 9,* 605-622.

Hoskisson, R. E., Hitt, M. A., & Hill, C. W. L. (1990). Managerial incentives and investment in R&D in large multiproduct firms. Unpublished report, Management Department, Texas A & M University.

Hoskisson, R. E., Hitt, M. A., Turk, T. A., & Tyler, B. B. (1989). Balancing corporate strategy and executive compensation. In G. Ferris & K. Rowland (Eds.), *Research in personnel and human resources management, Vol. 7.* Greenwich, CT: JAI Press, Inc.

Hrebiniak, L. G., Joyce, W. F. (1985). Organizational adaptation: Strategic choice and environmental determinism. *Administrative Science Quarterly, 30,* 336-349.

Hughes, C. L. (1986). The demerit of merit. *Personnel Administrator, 31(6),* 40.

Hulin, C., Roznowski, M., & Hachiya, D. (1985). Alternative opportunities and withdrawal decisions: Empirical and theoretical discrepancies and an integration. *Psychological Bulletin, 97,* 233-250.

Hulme, R. D., & Bevan, R. V. (1975). The blue-collar worker goes on salary. *Harvard Business Review, 53(2),* 104-112.

Human Resource Planning. (1988). (Entire issue devoted to compensation strategy issues), *11(3).*

Hunt, H. G. (1986). The separation of corporate ownership and control: Theory, evidence and implications. *Journal of Accounting Literature, 5,* 85-124.

Huseman, R. C., & Hatfield, J. D. (1978). Communicating employee benefits: Directions for future research. *Journal of Business Communication, 15,* 3-7.

Huseman, R. C., Hatfield, J. D., & Driver, R. W. (1978). Getting your benefit programs understood and appreciated. *Personnel Journal, 57,* 560-566.

Hybels, R. C., & Barley, S. R. (1990). Coaptation and the legitimation of professional identities: Human resource policies in high technology firms. In L. R. Gomez-Mejia & M. Lawless (Eds.), *Organizational issues in high technology management.* Greenwich, CT: JAI Press, Inc.

Hyman, J. S. (1991). Long-term incentives. In M. L. Rock & L. A. Berger (Eds.), *The compensation handbook.* New York: McGraw-Hill, Inc.

Hymowitz, C. (1988, May 17). Stock options for middle managers. *Wall Street Journal,* 33.

Ilgen, D. R., & Favero, J. L. (1985). Limits in generalization from psychological research to performance appraisal processes. *Academy of Management Review, 10,* 311-321.

Ilgen, D. R., & Feldman, J. M. (1983). Performance appraisal: A process focus. In L. L. Cummings & B. M. Staw (Eds.), *Research in organizational behavior, Vol. 5.* Greenwich, CT: JAI Press., Inc.

Jackovsky, E. F. (1984). Turnover and job performance: An integrated process model. *Academy of Management Review, 9,* 74-83.

Jackson, S.E., Schuler, R.S., & Rivero, C.J. (1989). Organizational characteristics as predictors of personnel practices. *Personnel Psychology, 42:* 728-784.

Jaques, E. (1961). *Equitable payment.* New York: Wiley.

Jaques, E. (1979). Taking time seriously in evaluating jobs. *Harvard Business Review, 2,* 124-132.

Jarrell, G. A., Brickley, J. A., & Netter, J. M. (1988). The market for corporate control: The empirical evidence since 1980. *Journal of Economic Perspectives, 2,* 49-68.

Jarrell, G.A., Lehn, K., Marr, W. (1985). Institutional ownership, tender offers and long-term investments. Washington, D.C.: Office of Chief Economist, Security and Exchange Commission.

Jenkins, G. D., & Lawler, E. E., III. (1981). Impact of employee participation in pay plan development. *Organizational Behavior and Human Performance, 28,* 111-128.

Jensen, M. C. (1983). Organization theory and methodology. *Accounting Review, 58,* 319-339.

Jensen, M. C., & Meckling, W. H. (1976). Theory of the firm: Managerial behavior, agency costs, and ownership structure. *Journal of Financial Economics, 3,* 305-350.

Jensen, M. C., & Murphy, K. J. (1990a). Performance and top management incentives. *Journal of Political Economy, 98(2),* 225-264.

Jensen, M. C., & Murphy, K. J. (1990b). CEO incentives—It's not how much you pay but how. *Harvard Business Review, 68(3),* 138-149.

John, C. H. St. & Rue, L. W. (1991). Coordinating mechanisms, consensus between marketing and manufacturing groups, and marketplace performance. *Strategic Management Journal, 12,* 549-557.

Johnson, B. W., Magee, R. P., Nagarajan, N. J., & Newman, H. R. (1985). An analysis of the stock price reaction to sudden executive deaths: Implications for the managerial labor market. *Journal of Accounting and Economics, 7(1),* 151-174.

Johnson, G. E. (1981). *Changes over time in the union/nonunion wage differential in the United States.* Working Paper, University of Michigan.

Johnson, H. T., & Kaplan, R. S. (1987). *Relevance lost: The rise and fall of management accounting.* Boston: Harvard Business School Press.

Jones, G. R., & Butler, J. E. (1988). Costs, revenue, and business-level strategy. *Academy of Management Review, 13,* 202-213.

Judd, K., & Gomez-Mejia, L. R. (1987). Comparable worth: A sensible way to end pay discrimination or the "Looniest idea since loony tunes."? In D. B. Balkin & L. R. Gomez-Mejia (Eds.), *New perspectives on compensation.* Englewood Cliffs, NJ: Prentice-Hall, Inc.

Kahn, L. M., & Sherer, P. D. (1990). Contingent pay and managerial performance. *Industrial and Labor Relations Review, 43,* 107-120.

Kail, J. C. (1987). Compensating scientists and engineers. In D. B. Balkin & L. R. Gomez-Mejia (Eds.), *New perspectives on compensation.* Englewood Cliffs, NJ: Prentice-Hall, Inc.

Kanin-Lovers, J. (1991). Job-evaluating technology. In M. L. Rock & L. A. Berger (Eds.), *The compensation handbook.* New York: McGraw-Hill, Inc.

Kanter, R. M. (1983). Frontiers for strategic human resource planning and management. *Human Resource Management, 22(1),* 9-21.

Kanter, R. M. (1987a). The attack on pay. *Harvard Business Review, 65(2),* 60-67.

Kanter, R. M. (1987b). From status to contribution: Some organizational implications of the changing basis for pay. *Personnel, 64(1),* 12-37.

Kanzanjian, R. (1993). Attaining technological synergies in diversified firms. In L.R. Gomez-Mejia & M.W. Lawless (Eds.), *Management of competitive strategy in high technology.* Greenwich, CT: JAI Press, Inc.

Katz, D., & Kahn, R. L. (1966). *The social psychology of organizations.* New York: Wiley.

Katz, R., & Allen, T. J. (1985). Project performance and the locus of influence in the R & D matrix. *Academy of Management Journal, 28,* 67-87.

Katz, R., Tushman, M. L., & Allen, T. J. (1992). Managing the dual latter: A longitudinal study. In L. R. Gomez-Mejia & M. W. Lawless (Eds.), *Human resource management strategy in high technology.* Greenwich, CT: JAI Press, Inc.

Kay, I. (1990, July 3). Interview appearing in *Wall Street Journal,* 1.

Kay, I. T., Gelfond, P., & Sherman, J. (1991). Ensuring the success of a new compensation program. In M. L. Rock & L. A. Berger (Eds.), *The compensation handbook.* New York: McGraw-Hill, Inc.

Kazanjian, R. K. (1988). Relation of dominant problems to stages of growth in technology-based new ventures. *Academy of Management Journal, 31,* 257-279.

Kedia, B., Keller, R., & Julian, O. (1992). Dimensions of national culture and the productivity of R&D units. *Journal of High Technology Management Research,* (in press).

Keeley, R. H., & Roure, J. B. (1993). The management team: A Key element in technological start ups. In L.R. Gomez-Mejia & M.W. Lawless (Eds.), *High technology venturing.* Greenwich, CT: JAI Press, Inc.

Kelly, H. H., & Thibault, J. (1969). Group problem solving. Chapter in: G. Lindsey & E. Aronson (Eds.), *Handbook of social psychology.* Reading, MA: Addison-Wesley.

Kerr, C., & Fisher, L.H. (1950). Effect of environment and administration on job evaluation. *Harvard Business Review, 28(2),* 15-32.

Kerr, J. L. (1982). Assigning managers on the basis of the life cycle. *The Journal of Business Strategy, 2(4),* 58-65.

Kerr, J. L. (1985). Diversification strategies and managerial rewards: An empirical study. *Academy of Management Journal, 28,* 155-179.

Kerr, J. L., & Bettis, R.A. (1987). Boards of directors, top management compensation and shareholder returns. *Academy of Management Journal, 30,* 745-764.

Kerr, J.L., & Kren, L. (1992). The effect of relative decision monitoring on chief executive compensation. *Academy of Management Journal* (in press).

Kerr, J.L., & Slocum, J.W. (1987). Managing corporate cultures through reward systems. *Academy of Management Executive, 1,* 3-15.

Kerr, J. L., & Slocum, J. W. (1988). Linking reward systems and organizational cultures. In R. E. Schuler, S. A. Youngblood, & V. L. Huber (Eds.), *Readings in personnel and human resource management.* St. Paul, MN: West.

Khandwalla, P. N. (1974). Mass output orientation of operations technology and organization structure. *Administrative Science Quarterly, 19,* 74-97.

Kimberly, J. R. (1980). The life cycle analogy and the study of organizations: Introduction. In J. R. Kimberly and R. H. Miles (Eds.), *The organizational life cycle: 1-14.* San Francisco: Jossey-Bass.

Kleiman, L. S., & Faley, R. H. (1992). Identifying the training needs of managers in high technology firms. In L. R. Gomez-Mejia & M. W. Lawless (Eds.), *Human resource management strategy in high technology.* Greenwich, CT: JAI Press, Inc.

Klein, R. B. (1991). Compensating your overseas executives: Exporting U.S. stock option plans to expatriate. *Compensation and Benefits Review, 23(1),* 39-52.

Kochan, T.A. (1980). Collective bargaining and industrial relations. Homewood, IL: Irwin.

Kochan, T., & Dyer, L. (1976). A model of organizational change in the context of union-management relations. *Journal of Applied Behavioral Science, 12,* 59-78.

Kohn, A. (1988, January). Incentives can be bad for business. *Inc.,* 93-94.

Konrad, A. M., & Pfeffer, J. (1990). Do you get what you deserve?: Factors affecting the relationship between productivity and pay. *Administrative Science Quarterly, 35,* 258-285.

Korn/Ferry International. (1991, July 29). Survey results on the influence of institutional investors. *Fortune,* 140.

Kostiuk, P. F. (1990). Firm size and executive compensation. *Journal of Human Resources, 25(1),* 90-105.

Kovach, K. A., & Millspaugh, P. E. (1990). Comparable worth: Canada legislates pay equity. *Academy of Management Executive, 4(2),* 92-101.

Krefting, L. A. (1980). Differences in orientations toward pay increases. *Industrial Relations, 19(1),* 81-87.

Krefting, L. A., & Mahoney, T. A. (1977). Determining the size of a meaningful pay increase. *Industrial Relations, 16(1)*, 83-93.

Kroll, M., Simmons, S. A., & Wright, P. (1990). Determinants of chief executive officer compensation following major acquisitions. *Journal of Business Research, 20*, 349-366.

Kujawa, D. (1986). *Japanese multinationals in the United States.* New York: Praeger.

Kurke, L. B., & Aldrich, H. E. (1979). *Mintzberg was right: A replication and extension of the nature of managerial work.* Paper presented at the Annual Meeting of the Academy of Management, Atlanta, Georgia.

Labich, K. (1987, July 6). How Dick Ferris blew it? *Fortune*, 42-46.

Lambert, R. A. (1983). Long term contracts and moral hazard. *The Bell Journal of Economics, 14*, 441-445.

Lambert, R. A., & Larcker, D.F. (1985). Executive compensation, corporate decision making and shareholder wealth: A review of the evidence. *Midland Corporate Financial Journal, 3*, 6-22.

Lambert, R.A., Larcker, D.F., & Weigelt, K. (1991). How sensitive is executive compensation to organizational size? *Strategic Management Journal, 12*, 395-402.

Landy, F. J., & Farr, J. L. (1983). *The measurement of work performance: Methods, theory, and applications.* New York: Academic Press.

Lang, N. R. (1991). Job analysis and documentation. In M. L. Rock & L. A. Berger (Eds.), *The compensation handbook.* New York: McGraw-Hill, Inc.

Lapides, L.E., & Ottensmeyer, E.J. (1993). Competitive strategy and resource allocation in high technology companies. In L.R. Gomez-Mejia & M.W. Lawless (Eds.), *Management of competitive strategy in high technology.* Greenwich, CT: JAI Press, Inc.

Larcker, D. F. (1983). The association between performance plan adoption and corporate capital investment. *Journal of Accounting and Economics, 5(3)*, 3-30.

Larner, R. J., (1970). *Management control and the large corporation.* New York: Dunellen.

Latham, G. P., & Dossett, D. L. (1978). Designing incentive plans for unionized employees: A comparison of continuous and variable ratio reinforcement schedules. *Personnel Psychology, 31*, 47-61.

Latham, G. P., & Wexley, K. N. (1981). *Increasing productivity through performance appraisal.* Reading, MA: Addison-Wesley.

Lawler, E. E., III. (1965). Managers' perceptions of their subordinates' pay and of their superiors' pay. *Personnel Psychology, 18,* 413-422.

Lawler, E. E., III. (1971). *Pay and organizational effectiveness: A psychological view.* New York: McGraw-Hill, Inc.

Lawler, E. E., III. (1972). Secrecy and the need to know. In M. Dunnette, R. House, & H. Tosi (Eds.), *Readings in managerial motivation and compensation.* East Lansing, MI: Michigan State University Press.

Lawler, E. E., III. (1981). *Pay and organization development.* Reading, MA: Addison-Wesley.

Lawler, E. E., III. (1984). The strategic design of reward systems. In C. Fombrun, N. M. Tichy, & M. A. Devana (Eds.), *Strategic human resource management.* New York: Wiley.

Lawler, E. E., III. (1986a). *High involvement management.* San Francisco: Jossey-Bass.

Lawler, E. E., III. (1986b). What's wrong with point factor job evaluation? *Compensation and Benefits Review, 19,* 20-28.

Lawler, E. E., III. (1989). The strategic design of pay-for-performance programs. In L. R. Gomez-Mejia (Ed.), *Compensation and benefits.* Washington, D. C.: Bureau of National Affairs.

Lawler, E. E., III. (1990). *Strategic pay.* San Francisco: Jossey-Bass.

Lawler, E. E., III. (1991). *Paying the person: A better approach to management.* Unpublished technical report, Center for Effective Organizations, University of Southern California.

Lawler, E. E., III, & Hackman, J. R. (1969). Impact of employee participation in the development of pay incentive plans: A field experiment. *Journal of Applied Psychology, 53, 467-471.*

Lawrence, P. (1975). Strategy: A new conceptualization. In L. S. Sproull (Ed.), *Seminars on Organizations at Stanford University, 2,* 38-40.

Lawrence, P. R., & Lorsch, J. W. (1967). Differentiation and integration in complex organizations. *Administrative Science Quarterly, 12,* 1-47.

Lawrence, P. R., & Lorsch, J. W. (1977). *Organization and environment.* Homewood, IL: Irwin.

Lazear, E. D., & Rosen, S. (1981). Rank order tournaments as optimum labor contracts. *Journal of Political Economy, 89,* 841-864.

Lazer, R. I., & Wikstrom, W. S. (1977). *Appraising managerial performance: current practices and future directions* (Conference Board Rep. No. 753). New York: Conference Board.

Ledford, G. E., Jr. (1990). The effectiveness of skill-based pay. *Perspectives in Total Compensation, 1(1)*, 1-4.

Ledford, G. E., Jr. (1991). The design of skill-based pay plans. In M. L. Rock & L.A. Berger (Eds.), *The compensation handbook.* New York: McGraw-Hill, Inc.

Ledvinka, J., Archer, R. W., & Ladd, R. T. (1990). *Utility analysis of internal selection.* Paper presented at the Annual Academy of Management meeting. San Francisco, California.

Lehr, L. W. (1986, Winter). The care and flourishing of entrepreneurs at 3M. *Directors and Boards,* 18-20.

Leland, H., & Pyle, D. (1977). Informational asymmetries, financial structure, and financial intermediation. *Journal of Finance, 32*, 371-387.

Lenz, R. T. (1980). Strategic capability: A concept and framework for analysis. *Academy of Management Review, 5*, 225-234.

Leonard, J. S. (1987). Carrots and sticks: Pay, supervison, and turnover. *Journal of Labor Economics, 5*, 136-152.

Leonard, J. S. (1990). Executive pay and firm performance. *Industrial and Labor Relations Review, 43*, 13-29.

Leonard, W. N. (1969). *Business size, market power, and public policy.* New York: Thomas Y. Crowell, Co.

Leontiades, M. (1980). *Strategies for diversification and change.* Boston: Little Brown and Co.

Lesieur, F. (1959). Worker participation to increase production. *Management Record, 21(2)*, 38-41.

Lesieur, F., & Puckett, E. (1968). *The Scanlon plan: Post, present, future.* Proceedings of the Twenty-first Annual meeting of the Industrial Relations Research Association.

Levine, H. Z. (1988). Compensation and benefits today: Board members speak out. *Compensation and Benefits Review, 20(1)*, 33-48.

Levine, R. E. (1989). Childcare: Inching up the corporate agenda. *Management Review, 78(1)*, 43-47.

Levitt, T. (1974). The managerial merry-go-round. *Harvard Business Review, 52(4)*, 120-128.

Lewellen, W. G. (1968). *Executive compensation in large industrial corporations.* New York: National Bureau of Economic Research.

Lewellen, W. G. (1969). Management and ownership in the large firm. *Journal of Finance, 24*, 299-332.

Lewellen, W. G., (1971). *The ownership income of management*. New York: Columbia University Press.

Lewellen, W. G., & Huntsman, B. (1970). Managerial pay and corporate performance. *American Economic Review, 60,* 710-720.

Lewellen, W., Loderer, C., & Martin, K. (1987). Executive compensation and executive incentive problems: An empirical analysis. *Journal of Financial Economics, 9,* 287-310.

Lewin, K. (1938). *The conceptual representation and measurement of psychological forces.* Durham, NC: Duke University Press.

Lewis, H. G. (1963). *Unionism and relative wages in the United States.* Chicago: University of Chicago Press.

Lichty, D. T. (1991). Compensation surveys. In M. L. Rock & L. A. Berger (Eds.), *The compensation handbook.* New York: McGraw-Hill, Inc.

Liden, R. C., & Adams, S. M. (1992). Technological change: Its effects on the training and development of older employees. In L. R. Gomez-Mejia & M. W. Lawless (Eds.), *Human resource management strategy in high technology.* Greenwich, CT: JAI Press, Inc.

Liden, R. C., & Mitchell, T. R. (1983). The effects of group interdependence on supervisor performance evaluations. *Personnel Psychology, 36,* 289-299.

Lieberson, S., & O'Connor, J. F. (1972). Leadership and organizational performance: A study of large corporations. *American Sociological Review, 37,* 117-130.

Likert, R. (1961). *New patterns of management.* New York: McGraw-Hill, Inc.

Lindsay, W. M., & Rue, L. W. (1980). Impact of the organization environment on the long range planning process: A contingency view. *Academy of Management Journal, 23,* 385-406.

Linney, R.C. (1987). Signing incentives: Fad, fancy, or strategic tool? *Compensation and Benefits Review, 19(5),* 57-59.

Lippitt, G. L., & Schmidt, W. H. (1967). Crisis in a developing organization. *Harvard Business Review, 45:* 102-112.

Livernash, R. E. (1957). The internal wage structure. In G. E. Taylor & F. C. Pierson, (Eds.), *New concepts in wage determination.* New York: McGraw-Hill, Inc.

Locke, E. A. (1968). Toward a theory of task motivation and incentives. *Organizational Behavior and Human Performance, 3,* 157-189.

Locke, E. A., Bryan, J. F., & Kendall, L. M. (1968). Goals and intentions as mediators of the effects of monetary incentives on behavior. *Journal of Applied Psychology, 52,* 104-121.

Locke, E. A., Shaw, K., Saari, L. M., & Latham, G. P. (1981). Goal setting and task performance: 1969-1980. *Psychological Bulletin, 90*, 125-152.

Loeffler, K. H. (1985). Flexible benefits at Ex-Cell-O: A case study. *Personnel Journal, 64(6)*, 106-112.

Loescher, S. M. (1984). Bureaucratic measurement, shuttling stock shares, and shortened time horizons: Implications for economic growth. *Quarterly Review of Economics and Business, 24*, 1-23.

Longenecker, C., Sims, H., & Gioia, D. (1987). Behind the mask: The politics of employee appraisal. *Academy of Management Executive, 1*, 183-193.

Loomis, C. J. (1982, July 12). The madness of executive compensation. *Fortune*, 42-51.

Lopez, E. (1989, August 29). The pink slip is just the beginning. *Miami Herald*, 1.

Lord, R. G. (1985). Accuracy in behavioral measurement: An alternative definition based on raters' cognitive schema and signal detection theory. *Journal of Applied Psychology, 70*, 66-71.

Lorsch, J. W., & Allen, S. A. (1973). *Managing diversity and interdependence.* Boston: Division of Research, Harvard Business School.

Lubatkin, M. (1987). Merger strategies and stockholder value. *Strategic Management Journal, 8*, 39-53.

Lublin, J. S. (1990, April 18,). The continental divide. *Wall Street Journal Reports*, R28.

Lush, D. R. (1975). Sharing responsibility, profit, and ownership. In B. A. Diekman & B. L. Metzger (Eds.), *Profit sharing: The industrial adrenalin.* Evanston, IL: Profit Sharing Research Foundation.

Luthans, F. (1988). Successful vs. effective real managers. *Academy of Management Executive, 2(2)*, 127-132.

Luthans, F., & Fox, M. L. (1989). Update on skill-based pay. *Personnel, 66(3)*, 26-31.

McAdams, J. L. (1991). Nonmonetary awards. In M. L. Rock & L. A. Berger (Eds.), *The compensation handbook.* New York: McGraw-Hill, Inc.

McBriarty, M. A. (1988). Performance appraisal: Some unintended consequences. *Public Personnel Management, 17(4)*, 421-440.

McCaffery, R. M. (1992). *Employee benefit programs: A total compensation perspective.* Boston: PWS-Kent.

McCann, J. E. (1987). Rewarding and supporting strategic planning. In D. B. Balkin & L. R. Gomez-Mejia (Eds.), *New perspectives on compensation.* Englewood Cliffs, NJ: Prentice-Hall, Inc.

McCann, J. E., & Gomez-Mejia, L. R. (1985). *Use of computerized data bases in international management.* Middlesex, NJ.: Center for International Education.

McCann, J. E., & Gomez-Mejia, L. R. (1988). Managerial activities and organizational performance: An empirical study in 26 high tech plants. *Journal of Applied Business Research, 4(1),* 158-165.

McCann, J. E., & Gomez-Mejia, L. R. (1989). *The institute for Dominican enterprises: A social issues perspective.* Paper presented at the Academy of Management National Convention, Washington, D. C.

McCann, J. E., & Gomez-Mejia, L. R. (1990). Exploring the dimensions of an international social issues climate. *Human Relations, 43,* 141-167.

McCann, J. E., & Gomez-Mejia, L. R. (1992). A high technology approach to environmental scanning: A case study on the Caribbean basin. *IEEE Transactions Management* (in press).

McCann, J. E., Gomez-Mejia, L. R., & Page, R. C. (1986). A behavioral approach for assessing organizational design and reward strategies. *International Journal of Management, 3,* 44-53.

McCann, J. E., Hinkin, T., & Gomez-Mejia, L. R. (1992). Executive transitions in high technology and traditional firms. Chapter in: L. R. Gomez-Mejia & M. Lawless (Eds.), *Top management teams in high technology firms.* Greenwich, CT: JAI Press, Inc.

McConkie, M. L. (1979). A clarification of the goal setting and appraisal processes in MBO. *Academy of Management Review, 4,* 29-40.

McCormick, E. J. (1979). *Job analysis: Methods and applications.* New York: Amacon.

MacCrimmon, K. R., & Wehrung, D. C. (1986). *Taking risks: The management of uncertainty.* New York: The Free Press.

McCune, J. T., & Schmitt, N. (1981). The relationship between job attitudes and the decision to retire. *Academy of Management Journal, 24,* 795-802.

Mace, M. L. (1971). *Directors: Myth and reality.* Cambridge, MA: Harvard University Graduate School of Business Administration.

McEachern, W. A. (1975). *Managerial control and performance.* Lexington, MA: D. C. Heath Co.

McGregor, D. (1957). An uneasy look at performance appraisal. *Harvard Business Review, 35,* 89-94.

McGregor, D. (1960). *The human side of enterprise.* New York: McGraw-Hill, Inc.

McGuire, J. W., Chiu, J. S. Y., & Elbing, A. O. (1962). Executive income, sales, and profits. *American Economic Review, 52,* 753-761.

McNally, J., & Shimmin, S. (1984). Job evaluation and equal pay for work of equal value. *Personnel Review, 13(1),* 27-31.

McNichols, M., & Manegold, J. G. (1983). The effect of the information environment on the relationship between financial disclosure and security price variability. *Journal of Accounting and Economics, 5(1)*, 49-74.

McNichols, T. J. (1983). *Executive policy and strategic planning.* New York: McGraw-Hill, Inc.

McNutt, R. P. (1991). Profit sharing: A case study of the fibers department at E. I. du Pont de Nemours and Company. In M. L. Rock & L. A. Berger (Eds.), *The compensation handbook.* New York: McGraw-Hill, Inc.

McShane, S. L. (1986). A path analysis of participation in union administration. *Industrial Relations, 25*, 72-79.

Madigan, R. M. (1985). Comparable worth judgments: A measurement properties analysis. *Journal of Applied Psychology, 70*, 137-147

Madigan, R.M., & Hoover, D.J. (1986). Effects of alternative job evaluation methods on decisions involving pay equity. *Academy of Management Journal, 29*, 84-100.

Magenheim, E. B., & Mueller, D. C. (1988). On measuring the effects of acquisitions on acquiring firm shareholders. In J. C. Coffee, L. Lowenstein, & S. Rose-Ackerman (Eds.), *Knights, raiders, and targets: The impact of the hostile takeover.* New York: Oxford University Press.

Mahoney, T. A. (1979). Organizational hierarchy and position worth. *Academy of Management Journal, 22*, 726-737.

Mahoney, T. A. (1989). Employment compensation planning and strategy. In L. R. Gomez-Mejia (Ed.), *Compensation and benefits.* Washington, D.C.: Bureau of National Affairs.

Mahoney, T. A., & Weitzel, W. (1978). Secrecy and managerial compensation. *Industrial Relations, 17*, 245-251.

Maier, N. R. (1973). *Psychology in industrial organizations.* Boston: Houghton Mifflin.

Malatesta, P. H., & Walking, R. A. (1988). Poison pill securities: Stockholder wealth, profitability, and ownership structure. *Journal of Financial Economics, 20*, 347-376.

Malekzadeh, A. R., Bickford, D. J., & Spital, F. C. (1989). Integrating environment, competitive strategy, and structure with technology strategy: The strategic configurations. *Proceedings of the Annual National Academy of Management.* Washington, D. C.

Malinowski, B. (1936). Anthropology. *Encyclopedia britannica: supplemental. Vol.1.* New York: Encyclopedia Britannica.

March, J. G., & Shapira, Z. (1987). Managerial perspectives on risk and risk taking. *Management Science, 33*, 1,404-1,418.

March, J. G., & Simon, H. (1958). *Organizations.* New York: Wiley.

Marris, R. L. (1964). *The economic theory of managerial capitalism.* London: MacMillan.

Marshall, F. R., Briggs, V. M., Jr., & King, A. G. (1984). *Labor economics.* Homewood, IL: Irwin.

Martell, K., Carroll, S.J., & Gupta, A.K. (1992). What executive human resource management practices are most effective when innovativeness requirements are high? In L.R. Gomez-Mejia & M.W. Lawless (Eds.), *Top management and effective leadership in high technology.* Greenwich, CT: JAI Press, Inc.

Martochio, J. J., & Ferris, G. R. (1991). Performance evaluation in high technology firms: A political perspective. *Journal of High Technology Management Research, 2(1),* 83-99.

Maslow, A. H. (1970). *Motivation and personality* (2nd. ed.). New York: Harper & Row.

Mason, E. S. (1939). Price and production policies of large scale enterprises. *American Economic Review, 29,* 61-74.

Masson, R. T. (1971). Executive motivations, earnings, and consequent equity performance. *Journal of Political Economy, 79,* 1,278-1,294.

Masters, M. F., Tokesky, G. C., Brown, W. S., Atkin, R., & Schoenfeld, G. (1992). Competitive compensation strategies in high technology firms: A synthetic theoretical perspective. In L. R. Gomez-Mejia & M. W. Lawless (Eds.), *Human resource management strategy in high technology.* Greenwich, CT: JAI Press, Inc.

Mathews, P. S. (1984). The changing work force: Dual-career couples and relocation. *Personnel Administrator, 29(4),* 55-62.

Mathieu, J., & Zajac, D. (1990). A review and meta-analysis of the antecedents, correlates, and consequences of organizational commitment. *Psychological Bulletin, 108,* 171-194.

Medoff, J. L., & Abraham, K. G. (1980). Experience, performance, and earnings. *Quarterly Journal of Economics, 94,* 703-736.

Meeks, G., & Whittington, G. (1975). Directors pay, growth, and profitability. *The Journal of Industrial Economics, 24,* 1-14.

Merchant, K. A. (1981). The design of the corporate budgeting system: Influences on managerial behavior and performance. *The Accounting Review, 56,* 813-829.

Merchant, K. A. (1985). *Control in business organizations.* Boston: Pitman Publishing Inc.

Mesdag, L. M. (1984, March 19). Are you overpaid? *Fortune,* 20-24.

Meyer, H. H. (1987). How can we implement a pay for performance policy successfully? In D. B. Balkin & L. R. Gomez-Mejia (Eds.), *New perspectives on compensation.* Englewood Cliffs, NJ: Prentice-Hall, Inc.

Meyer, P. (1983). Executive compensation must promote long term commitment. *Personnel Administrator, 28(5)*, 37-42.

Meyer, P., & Rowan, B. (1977). Institutional organizations: Formal structure as myth and ceremony. *American Journal of Sociology, 83*, 340-363.

Meyers, D. W. (1989). *Compensation management.* Chicago: Commerce Clearing House, Inc.

Miceli, M., Jung, I., Near, J., & Greenberger, D. (1991). Predictors and outcomes of reactions to pay-for-performance plans. *Journal of Applied Psychology, 76*, 508-521.

Miceli, M., & Lane, M. (1991). Antecedents of pay satisfaction: A review and extension. In G. Ferris & K. Rowland (Eds.), *Research in personnel and human resources*, Vol. 9. Greenwich, CT: JAI Press.

Miles, R. E., & Snow, C. C. (1978). *Organizational strategy, structure, and process.* New York: McGraw-Hill, Inc.

Miles, R. E., & Snow, C.C. (1984). Designing strategic human resources systems. *Organizational Dynamics, 13(1)*, 36-52.

Miles, R. E., Snow, C. C., Meyer, A. D., & Coleman, H. J. (1978). Organizational strategy, structure, and process. *Academy of Management Review, 3*, 546-562.

Milkovich, G. T. (1988). A strategic perspective to compensation management. In K. Rowland & G. Ferris (Eds.), *Research in personnel and human resource management: Vol. 6.* Greenwich, CT: JAI Press, Inc.

Milkovich, G. T., & Anderson, P. H. (1972). Management compensation and secrecy. *Personnel Psychology, 25*, 293-302.

Milkovich, G.T., & Boudreau, J.W. (1991). *Personnel/human resource management.* Homewood, IL: Irwin.

Milkovich, G.T., & Broderick, R.F. (1991) Developing a compensation strategy. In M.L. Rock & L.A. Berger (Eds.), *The compensation handbook.* New York: McGraw-Hill, Inc.

Milkovich, G. T., Gerhart, B., & Hannon, J. (1991). The effects of research and development intensity on managerial compensation in large organizations. *Journal of High Technology Management Research, 2(1)*, 133-150.

Milkovich, G.T., & Gomez-Mejia, L.R. (1976). Day care and selected employee work behaviors. *Academy of Management Journal, 19*, 111-115.

Milkovich, G. T., & Newman, J. M. (1987). *Compensation* (2nd ed.). Plano, TX: Business Publications, Inc.

Milkovich, G. T., & Newman, J. M. (1990). *Compensation* (3rd ed.). Homewood, IL: Irwin.

Milkovich, G.T., Wigdor, A.K., Broderick, R.F., & Mavor, A.S. (Eds.) (1991). *Pay for performance: evaluating performance appraisal and merit pay.* Washington, D.C.: National Academy Press.

Miller, A. (1988). A taxonomy of technological settings, with related strategies and performance levels. *Strategic Management Journal, 9,* 239-254.

Miller, C. S., & Schuster, M. H. (1987). Gainsharing plans: A comparative analysis. *Organizational Dynamics, 16(1),* 44-67.

Miller, D., Kets de Vries, M. F. R., & Toulouse, J. M. (1982). Top executive focus of control and its relationship to strategy making, structure, and environment. *Academy of Management Journal, 25,* 237-253.

Miller, M. H. & Scholes, M. S. (1982). Executive compensation, taxes and incentives. In W. F. Sharpe and C. M. Cootner (Eds.), *Financial economics.* Boston: Harvard University Press.

Mincer, J. (1975). *Schooling, experience and earnings.* New York: National Bureau of Economic Research.

Miner, M. G. (1974). Pay policies: Secret or open? And why? *Personnel Journal, 53,* 110-115.

Mintzberg, H. (1973). A new look at the chief executive's job. *Organizational Dynamics, 1(3),* 20-30.

Mintzberg, H. (1978). Patterns in strategy formation. *Management Science, 24,* 934-948.

Mintzberg, H. (1980). *The nature of managerial work.* Englewood Cliffs, NJ: Prentice-Hall, Inc.

Mintzberg, H. (1984). Power and organization life cycles. *Academy of Management Review, 9,* 207-224.

Mintzberg, H. (1990). The design school: Reconsidering the basic premises of strategic management. *Strategic Management Journal, 11,* 171-196.

Mintzberg, H., & McHugh, A. (1985). Strategy formation in an adhocracy. *Administrative Science Quarterly, 30,* 160-197.

Mintzberg, H., & Waters, J. A. (1985). Of strategies, deliberate and emergent. *Strategic Management Journal, 6,* 257-272.

Mitchell, D. J. B. (1980). *Unions, wages and inflation.* Washington, D.C.: The Brookings Institution.

Mitchell, D. J. B. (1987). The share economy and industrial relations. *Industrial Relations, 26,* 1-17.

Mitchell, D. J. B. (1989). *Human resource management: An economic approach.* Boston: PWS-Kent Publishing Co.

Mitchell, T. R., & Biglan, A. (1971). Instrumentality theories: Current uses in Psychology. *Psychological Bulletin, 76,* 432-454.

Mitchell, T. R., & Liden, R. C. (1982). The effects of social context on performance evaluations. *Organizational Behavior and Human Performance, 29,* 241-256.

Mitchell, W. (1989). Whether and when? Probability and timing of incumbents' entry into emerging industrial subfields. *Administrative Science Quarterly, 34*, 208-231.

Mobley, W. H. (1982). *Employee turnover: Causes, consequences and control.* Reading, MA: Addison-Wesley.

Mobley, W., Griffeth, R., Hand, H., & Meglino, B. (1979). Review and conceptual analysis of the employee turnover process. *Psychological Bulletin, 86*, 493-522.

Mohrman, S. A., Morhrman, A. M., & Cohen, S. (1992). Human resource strategies for lateral integration in high technology settings. In L. R. Gomez-Mejia & M. W. Lawless (Eds.), *Human resource management strategy in high technology.* Greenwich, CT: JAI Press, Inc.

Montanari, J. R., & Lockwood, C. A. (1992). Strategic control in a high technology environment. In L. R. Gomez-Mejia & M. W. Lawless (Eds.), *Top management and effective leadership in high technology.* Greenwich, CT: JAI Press, Inc.

Montanari, J. R., Morgan, C. P., & Bracker, J. S. (1990). *Strategic management: A choice approach.* Chicago: The Dryden Press.

Montgomery, C. A., & Singh, H. (1984). Diversification strategy and systematic risk. *Strategic Management Journal, 5*, 181-191.

Moore, G., & Ross, T. (1990). *Gainsharing plans for improving performance.* Washington, D.C.: Bureau of National Affairs.

Moore, J.M. (1982). The role relocation plays in management planning. *Personnel Administrator, 27(12)*, 31-34.

Moorhead, G., Ference, R., & Neck, C.P. (1991). Group decision fiascoes continue: Space shuttle Challenger and a revised framework. *Human Relations* (in press).

Morck, R., Shleifer, A., & Vishny, R. W. (1988a). Management ownership and market evaluation. *Journal of Financial Economics, 20*, 293-315.

Morck, R., Shleifer, A., & Vishny, R. W. (1988b). *Alternative mechanisms for corporate control.* Unpublished manuscript, University of Chicago, Chicago, Illinois.

Morrison, E. E. (1966). *New machines and modern times.* Cambridge, MA: MIT Press.

Morse, D. M., & Richardson G. (1983). The LIFO/FIFO decision. *Journal of Accounting Research, 21*, 106-127.

Mount, M. K. (1987). Coordinating salary action and performance appraisal. In: D. B. Balkin & L. R. Gomez-Mejia (Eds.), *New Perspectives on compensation.* Englewood Cliffs, NJ: Prentice-Hall, Inc.

Moynahan, J.K. (1983). Salary plus commission, despite its drawbacks, is right for some situations. *Sales and Marketing Management, 130(4)*, 106-108.

Muckley, J. E. (1984). From the board room. *Harvard Business Review, 63(2)*, 46-64.

Murphy, K. J. (1985). Corporate performance and managerial remuneration. *Journal of Accounting and Statistics, 7*, 11-42.

Murphy, K. J. (1986a). Top executives are worth every nickel they get. *Harvard Business Review, 64(2)*, 125-132.

Murphy, K. J. (1986b). Incentives, learning and compensation: A theoretical and empirical investigation of managerial labor contracts. *Rand Journal of Economics, 17*, 59-76.

Murphy, K., & Cleveland, J. (1991). *Performance Appraisal: An organizational perspective.* Boston: Allyn and Bacon.

Murray, A. I. (1988). A contingency view of Porter's generic strategies. *Academy of Management Review, 13*, 390-400.

Murray, A. I. (1989). Top management group heterogeneity and firm performance. *Strategic Management Journal, 10*, 125-141.

Murthy, K.R. (1977). *Corporate strategy and top executive compensation.* Boston: Harvard Press.

Murthy, K. R., & Salter, M. S. (1975). Should CEO pay be linked to results? *Harvard Business Review, 53(3)*, 66-73.

Nader, R. (1984). Reforming corporate governance. *California Management Review, 26(4)*, 126-132.

Nadler, D. A., Hackman, J. R., & Lawler, E. E. (1979). *Managing Organizational Behavior.* Boston: Little Brown.

Nagel, E. (1961). *The structure of science.* New York: Harcourt, Brace & World, Inc.

Napier, N. K., & Smith, M. (1987). Product diversification, performance criteria and compensation at the corporate manager level. *Strategic Management Journal, 8*, 195-201.

Neff, M.L. (1987). Facing up to the need for a management revolution. In S.D. Sethi & C.M. Falbe (Eds.), *Business and society: Dimensions of conflict and cooperation.* Lexington, MA: Lexington Books.

Neidell, L. A. (1983). Don't forget the product life cycle for strategic planning. *Business, 33(2)*, 30-55.

Nemerov, D. S. (1987). Managing the sales compensation program: Integrating factors for success. In D. B. Balkin & L. R. Gomez-Mejia (Eds.), *New perspectives on compensation.* Englewood Cliffs, NJ: Prentice-Hall, Inc.

Newman, J.M. (1988). Compensation strategy in declining industries. *Human Resource Planning, 11(3)*, 197-206.

Newman, J. M. (1989). Compensation programs for special employee groups. In L. R. Gomez-Mejia (Ed.), *Compensation and benefits*. Washington, D.C.: Bureau of National Affairs.

Newman, J., & Huselid, M. A. (1992). The nature of behavioral controls in boundary occupations. In L. R. Gomez-Mejia & M. W. Lawless (Eds.), *Top management and effective leadership in high technology*. Greenwich, CT: JAI Press, Inc.

Niehaus, G. R. (1985). *The relationship between accounting method choices and ownership structure*. Unpublished manuscript, Accounting Department, Washington University.

Nightingdale, D. V. (1982). *Workplace democracy: An inquiry into employee participation in Canadian work organizations*. Buffalo, NY: University of Toronto Press.

Norburn, D. (1989). The chief executive: A breed apart. *Strategic Management Journal, 10*, 1-15.

Norburn, D., & Birley, S. (1988). The top management team and corporate performance. *Strategic Management Journal, 9*, 225-238.

Norburn, D., & Miller, P. (1981). Strategy and executive reward: The mismatch in the strategic process, *Journal of General Management, 6*, 17-27.

Noreen, E. W., & Wolfson, M. A. (1981). Equilibrium warrant pricing models and accounting for executive stock options. *Journal of Accounting Research, 19*, 384-398.

Norton, R. (1991, July 29). Who owns this company, anyhow? *Fortune*, 131-144.

Nussbaum, B., & Dobrzynski, J.H. (1987, May 18). The battle for corporate control. *Business Week*, 102-109.

Ochsner, R. C. (1987). *The future of compensation management in the United States*. Paper presented at a Symposium on Compensation Management, Bureau of Labor Statistics.

O'Connor, E. J., Parsons, C. K., Liden, R. C., & Herold, D. M. (1990). Implementing new technology: Management issues and opportunities. *Journal of High Technology Management Research, 1*, 73-94.

O'Dell, C. (1987). *People, performance and pay*. Scottsdale, AZ, and Houston, TX: American Compensation Association and American Productivity Center.

Odiorne, G. S. (1965). *Management by objectives*. Los Angeles: Pitman.

Olian, J. D., & Rynes, S. L. (1984). Organizational staffing: Integrating practice with strategy. *Industrial Relations, 23*, 170-183.

Oliva, R. (1991). *Salary determinant analysis of accounting professors*. Unpublished technical report, Florida International University, Miami, FL.

O'Neill, H. M., Saunders, C., & McCarthy A. (1989). Board members background characteristics and their level of corporate social responsiveness orientation: A multivariate investigation.

Proceedings of the Annual Academy of Management, 49th Annual Meeting, Washington, D.C.

Ono, Y. (1990, April 18). Perks vs. pay. *Wall Street Journal Reports,* R30.

Opsahl, R. L., & Dunnette, M. D. (1966). The role of financial compensation in industrial motivation. *Psychological Bulletin, 66,* 94-118.

O'Reilly, C. A., Main, B. G., & Crystal, G. S. (1988). CEO compensation as tournament and social comparison: A tale of two theories. *Administrative Science Quarterly, 33,* 257-274.

Ouchi, W. G. (1977). The relationship between organizational structure and organizational control. *Administrative Science Quarterly, 22,* 95-113.

Ouchi, W. G. (1978). Transmission of control through organizational hierarchy. *Academy of Management Journal, 21,* 173-192.

Ouchi, W. G. (1979). Conceptual framework for the design of organizational control mechanisms. *Management Science, 25,* 833-848.

Ouchi, W. G. (1980). Markets, bureaucracies, and clans. *Administrative Science Quarterly, 25,* 129-141.

Ouchi, W. G., & Maguire, M. A. (1975). Organizational control: Two functions. *Administrative Science Quarterly, 20,* 559-569.

Page, R. A., Jr., Stephens, G. K., & Tripoli, A. (1992). Traditional and entrepreneurial career paths: Variations and commonalties. In L. R. Gomez-Mejia & M. W. Lawless (Eds.), *Human resource management strategy in high technology.* Greenwich, CT: JAI Press, Inc.

Palmer, J. (1973). The profit variability effects of managerial enterprise. *Western Economic Journal, 2,* 228-231.

Parsons, D. (1977). Models of labor market turnover: A theoretical and empirical survey. In R. Ehrenberg (Ed.), *Research in labor economics* (Vol. 1). Greenwich, CT: JAI Press, Inc.

Pascal, A. H., & Rapping, L. A. (1972). The economics of racial discrimination in organized baseball. In A. H. Pascall (Ed.), *Racial discrimination in economic life.* Lexington, MA: Lexington Books.

Pascale, R. T. (1982, January 25). Our curious addiction to corporate grand strategy. *Fortune,* 115-116.

Pavett, C. M., & Lau, A. W. (1983). Managerial work: The influence of hierarchical level and functional specialty. *Academy of Management Journal, 26,* 170-177.

Pay Equity Commission of Ontario, Canada. (1988). *Pay equity implementation series/contents.* Toronto, Ontario.

Pearce, J. L. (1987). Why merit pay doesn't work: Implications from organization theory. In D. B. Balkin & L. R. Gomez-Mejia (Eds.), *New perspectives on compensation.* Englewood Cliffs, NJ: Prentice-Hall, Inc.

Pearce, J. L., Stevenson, W. B., & Perry, J. L. (1985). Management compensation based on organizational performance: A time-series analysis of the impact of merit pay. *Academy of Management Journal, 28,* 261-279.

Peck, C. A. (1984). *Pay and performance: The interaction of compensation and performance appraisal.* New York: The Conference Board.

Peck, C. A. (1987). *Top executive compensation: 1987.* New York: The Conference Board.

Penley, L. E., & Gould, S. (1988). Etzioni's model of organizational involvement: A perspective to understanding commitment to organizations. *Journal of Organizational Behavior, 9,* 43-59.

Pennings, J. M. (1991). Executive compensation systems: Pay follows strategy or strategy follows pay? In M. L. Rock & L. A. Berger (Eds.), *The compensation handbook.* New York: McGraw-Hill, Inc.

Perrow, C. (1970). *Organizational analysis: A sociological view.* Belmont, CA: Wadsworth.

Perry, L. T. (1986). Least cost alternatives to layoffs in declining industries. *Organizational Dynamics, 14(4),* 48-61.

Personick, M.E., & Barsky, C.B. (1982). White collar pay levels linked to corporate work force size. *Monthly Labor Review, 105(5),* 23-28.

Petersen, D.J., & Massengill, D. (1988). Childcare programs benefit employers, too. *Personnel, 65(5),* 58-62.

Pfeffer, J. (1972). Size and composition of board of directors. *Administrative Science Quarterly, 17,* 218-228.

Pfeffer, J. (1981). *Power in organizations.* Boston: Pitman.

Pfeffer, J., & Davis-Blake, A. (1987). Understanding organizational wage structures: A resource dependence approach. *Academy of Management Journal, 30,* 437-455.

Pfeffer, J., & Salancik, G. R. (1978). *The external control of organizations: A resource dependence perspective.* New York: Harper and Row.

Pfeffer, R. M. (1979). *Working for capitalism.* New York: Columbia University Press.

Pitts, R. A. (1974). Incentive compensation and organization design. *Personnel Journal, 20(5),* 338-344.

Pitts, R. A. (1976). Diversification strategies and organizational policies of large diversified firms. *Journal of Economics and Business, 8,* 181-188.

Plachy, R. J. (1991). *Building a fair pay program.* New York: American Management Association.

Pondy, L. (1978). Leadership is a language game. In M. W. McCall, Jr. & M. Lombardo (Eds.), *Leadership: Where else can we go?.* Durham, NC: Duke University Press.

Port, O., & Carey, J. (1991). Quality: A field with roots that go back to the farm. *Business Week,* November 7, 15-16.

Porter, L. W., & Lawler, E. E. (1968). *Managerial attitudes and performance.* Homewood, IL: Irwin-Dorsey.

Porter, M. E. (1979). How competitive forces shape strategy. *Harvard Business Review, 57(2),* 137-145.

Porter, M. E. (1980). *Competitive strategy.* New York: Free Press

Porter, M. E. (1981). The contributions of industrial organization to strategic management. *Academy of Management Review, 6,* 609-620.

Porter, M. E. (1985). *Competitive advantage.* New York: Free Press.

Porter, M. E. (1990). *The competitive advantage of nations.* Boston: The Free Press.

Posner, B. (1987). Executive compensation '87: The brave new world: The 1986 Tax Reform Act has raised new questions about virtually every compensation tool a company has. *Inc., 9(7),* 63.

Posner, M. (1987). Prospects for your perks (Tax reform and fringe benefits). *Changing Times, 41(4),* 77.

Poster, C. Z. (1985). Executive compensation: Taking long-term incentives out of the corporate ivory tower. *Compensation and Benefits Review, 17(2),* 20-31.

Powers, K. J., & Gomez-Mejia, L. R. (1991). *Dispute resolution.* Englewood Cliffs, NJ: Prentice-Hall, Inc.

Prahalad, C. K., & Bettis, R. A. (1986). The dominant logic: A new linkage between diversity and performance. *Strategic Management Journal, 7,* 485-501.

Prescott, J.E., & Allenby, J. (1993). Role of competitive intelligence in maintaining strategic leadership in high technology. In L.R. Gomez-Mejia & M.W. Lawless (Eds.), *Management of competitive strategy in high technology.* Greenwich, CT: JAI Press, Inc.

Price, J., & Mueller, C. (1981). A causal model of turnover for nurses. *Academy of Management Journal, 24,* 543-565.

Price, J., & Mueller, C. (1986). *Absenteeism and turnover of hospital employees.* Greenwich, CT: JAI Press, Inc.

Puffer, S.M., & Weintrop, J.B. (1991). Corporate performance and CEO turnover: A comparison of performance indicators. *Administrative Science Quarterly, 36,* 1-20.

Quinn, R. E., & Cameron, K. (1983). Organizational life cycles and shifting criteria of effectiveness: Some preliminary evidence. *Management Science, 29(1),* 33-50.

Rajagopalan, N., & Prescott, J. E. (1990). Determinants of top management compensation: Explaining the impact of economic, behavioral, and strategic constructs and the moderating effects of industry. *Journal of Management, 16(3),* 515-538.

Ramanujam, V., & Varadarajan, P. (1989). Research on corporate diversification: A synthesis. *Strategic Management Journal, 10,* 523-551.

Rappaport, A. (1978). Executive incentives vs. corporate growth. *Harvard Business Review, 56(4),* 81-88.

Rappaport, A. (1981). Selecting strategies that create shareholder value. *Harvard Business Review, 60(3),* 139-149.

Rappaport, A. (1986). *Creating shareholder value.* New York: Free Press.

Ravenscraft, D. J. (1983). Structure-profit relationship at the line of business and industry level. *Review of Economics and Statistics, 65,* 22-31.

Ravenscraft, D. J., & Scherer, F. M. (1987). *Mergers, sell-offs, and economic efficiency.* Washington D.C.: The Brookings Institution.

Raviv, A. (1985). Management compensation and the managerial labor market: An overview. *Journal of Accounting and Economics, 7,* 239-245.

Redling, E. T. (1981). Myth vs. reality: The relationship between top executive pay and corporate performance. *Compensation Review, 13(4),* 16-24.

Reed, R., & Reed, M. (1989). CEO experience and diversification strategy fit. *Journal of Management Studies, 26(3),* 251-269.

Rees, A., & Schultz, G.P. (1970). *Workers and wages in an urban labor market.* Chicago: The University of Chicago Press.

Regan, E.V. (1987, November 2). Pension funds: New power, new responsibility. *Wall Street Journal,* 28.

Reger, R. K. (1991). Managerial thought structures and competitive positioning. In A. S. Huff (Ed.), *Mapping strategic thought.* Chichester, England: Wiley.

Remick, H. (1984). *Comparable worth and wage discrimination.* Philadelphia, PA: Temple University Press.

Reynolds, L. G. (1951). *The structure of labor markets.* New York: Harper and Row.

Rich, J. T., & Larson, J. A. (1984). Why some long-term incentives fail. *Compensation Review, 16(1),* 26-37.

Riordan, M. H., & Sappington, D. E. M. (1987). Information, incentives, and organizational mode. *Quarterly Journal of Economics, 98,* 243-263.

Roberts, D. R. (1959). A general theory of executive compensation based on statistically tested propositions. *Quarterly Journal of Economics, 70,* 270-294.

Roberts, K. H. (1992). Structuring to facilitate migrating decisions in reliability enhancing organization. In L. R. Gomez-Mejia & M. W. Lawless (Eds.), *Top management and effective leadership in high technology.* Greenwich, CT: JAI Press, Inc.

Robinson, J. (1933). *The economics of imperfect competition.* London: MacMillan.

Roche, G. (1975). Compensation and the mobile executive. *Harvard Business Review, 53(6),* 53-62.

Rock, M. L. (1991). Looking back on forty years of compensation programs. In M. L. Rock & L. A. Berger (Eds.), *The compensation handbook.* New York: McGraw-Hill, Inc.

Rock, M.L., & Berger, L.A. (Eds.). (1991). *Handbook of wage and salary administration.* New York: McGraw-Hill, Inc.

Rodgers, R. C., & Hunter, J. E. (1985). *The impact of management by objectives on organizational productivity.* Unpublished paper, Management Department, Michigan State University.

Roll, R. (1987). Empirical evidence on takeover activity and shareholder wealth. In T. E. Copeland (Ed.), *Modern finance and industrial economics.* New York: Basil Blackwood.

Ronan, W. W., & Organt, G. J. (1973). Determinants of pay and pay satisfaction. *Personnel Psychology, 26,* 503-520.

Roomkin, M. (Ed.) (1990). *Profit sharing and gainsharing.* Newark, NJ: The Scarecrow Press.

Rosen, B., & Jerdee, T.H. (1988). Managing older workers' careers. In K. Rowland & G. Ferris (Eds.), *Research in personnel and human resources management* Vol. 6., 37-74. Greenwich, CT: JAI Press, Inc.

Ross, T. L. (1983). Why productivity gainsharing fails in some firms. In B. E. Graham-Moore and T. L. Ross (Eds)., *Productivity gainsharing.* Englewood Cliffs, NJ: Prentice-Hall, Inc.

Ross, T. L., & Ross, (1991). Gain sharing: Sharing improved performance. In M. L. Rock & L. A. Berger (Eds.), *The compensation handbook.* New York: McGraw-Hill, Inc.

Rossiter, L. F., & Taylor, A. K. (1982). Union effects on the provision of health insurance. *Industrial Relations, 21,* 167-177.

Rothwell, W. J., & Kazanas, H. C. (1988). *Strategic human resources planning and management.* Englewood Cliffs, NJ: Prentice-Hall, Inc.

Roy, T. S., Jr. (1991). Pricing and the development of salary structures. In M. L. Rock & L. A. Berger (Eds.), *The compensation handbook.* New York: McGraw-Hill, Inc.

Rumelt, R. P. (1974). *Strategy, structure, and economic performance.* Boston: Division of Research, Harvard Business School.

Rumelt, R. P. (1977). *Diversity and profitability.* Paper presented at the Academy of Management Western Region Meetings, Sun Valley, Idaho.

Rusbult, C., & Farrell, D. (1983). A longitudinal test of the investment model: The impact of job satisfaction, commitment, and turnover of variations in rewards, costs, alternatives, and investments. *Journal of Applied Psychology, 68,* 429-438.

Rynes, S.L. (1987). Compensation strategies for recruiting. *Topics in Total Compensation, 2(2),* 185-196.

Rynes, S.L., & Milkovich, G.T. (1986). Wage surveys: Dispelling some myths about the market wage. *Personnel Psychology, 39,* 71-90.

Rynes, S. L., Weber, C. L., & Milkovich, G. T. (1989). Effect of market survey rates, job evaluation, and job gender on job pay. *Journal of Applied Psychology, 74,* 114-123.

Ryngaert, M. (1988). The effect of poison pill securities on shareholder wealth. *Journal of Financial Economics, 20,* 377-418.

Salamon, G. L., & Smith, E. D. (1979). Corporate control and managerial misrepresentation of firm performance. *Bell Journal of Economics, 10,* 319-328.

Salancik, G. R., & Pfeffer, J. (1977). Constraints on administrator discretion: The limited influence of mayors on city budgets. *Urban Affairs Quarterly, 12,* 475-498.

Salancik, G. R., & Pfeffer, J. (1980). Effects of ownership and performance on executive tenure in U.S. corporations. *Academy of Management Journal, 23,* 653-664.

Salscheider, J. (1981). Devising pay strategies for diversified companies. *Compensation Review, 8,* 15-24.

Salter, M. S. (1973). Tailor incentive compensation to strategy. *Harvard Business Review, 51(2),* 94-102.

Salter, M. S., & Weinhold, W. A. (1981). Choosing compatible acquisitions. *Harvard Business Review, 59(1),* 117-127.

Sayles, L. R., & Strauss, G. (1967). *The local union.* New York: Harcourt Brace Jovanovich.

Scheflen, K. C., Lawler, E. E., III, & Hackman, J. R. (1971). Long-term impact of employee participation in the development of pay incentive plans: A field experiment revisited. *Journal of Applied Psychology, 55,* 182-186.

Schmidt, D. R. & Fowler, K. L. (1990). Post-acquisition financial performance and executive compensation. *Strategic Management Journal, 11,* 559-570.

Schmitt, N. W., & Klimoski, R. J. (1991). *Research methods in human resources management.* Cincinnati, OH: South-Western Publishing Co.

Scholtes, P. R. (1987). *An elaboration on Deming's teachings on performance appraisal.* Madison, WI: Joiner Associates, Inc.

Schoonhoven, C. B. (1981). Problems with contingency theory: Testing assumptions hidden within the language of contingency theory. *Administrative Science Quarterly, 26,* 349-377.

Schuler, R. S. (1987). Personnel and human resource management choices and organizational strategy. *Human Resource Planning, 10(1),* 1-17.

Shultz, C. F. (1987). Compensating the sales professional. In D. B. Balkin & L. R. Gomez-Mejia (Eds.), *New perspectives on compensation.* Englewood Cliffs, NJ: Prentice-Hall, Inc.

Schuster, M. (1983). The impact of union-management cooperation on productivity and employment. *Industrial and Labor Relations Review, 36(3),* 425-430.

Schuster, M. (1984). *Union-management cooperation.* Kalamazoo, MI: E. Upjohn Institute for Employment Research.

Schuster, M. (1985). Models of cooperation and change in union settings. *Industrial Relations, 24(3),* 382-394.

Schwab, D. P. (1974). Conflicting impacts of pay on employee motivation and satisfaction. *Personnel Journal, 53(3),* 190-206.

Schwab, D. P. (1991). Contextual variables in employee performance-turnover relationships. *Academy of Management Journal, 34,* 966-975.

Schwab, D. P., & Dyer, L. D. (1973). The motivational impact of a compensation system on employee performance. *Organizational Behavior and Human Performance, 9,* 215-225.

Schwab, D. P., & Grams, R. (1985). Sex related errors in job evaluation: A "real world" test. *Journal of Applied Psychology, 70,* 533-539.

Schwab, D. P., & Olson, C. A. (1988). Pay-performance relationships as a function of pay-for-performance policies and practices. *Proceedings of the Academy of Management,* 287-290.

Sears, D. (1984, October). Make employee pay a strategic issue. *Financial Executive,* 40-43.

Segev, E. (1989). Systematic competitive analysis and synthesis of two business level strategic typologies. *Strategic Management Journal, 10,* 487-509.

Seidman, W. L., & Skancke, S. L. (1989). *Competitiveness: The executive's guide to success.* New York: M. E. Sharpe, Inc.

Sekas, M.H. (1984). Dual-career couples–a corporate challenge. *Personnel Administrator, 29(4),* 37-45.

Sellekaerts, B.H., & Welch, S.W. (1984). An econometric analysis of minimum wage noncompliance. *Industrial Relations, 23,* 244-259.

Sethia, N. K., & Von Glinow, M. A. (1985). Managing organizational culture by managing the reward system. In R. H. Kilman, M. V. Saxton, & M. Serpa (Eds.), *Managing corporate cultures*. San Francisco: Jossey-Bass.

Sexton, D. (1990). Propensity for change: A prerequisite for growth in high technology firms. In L. R. Gomez-Mejia & M. W. Lawless (Eds.), *Organizational issues in high technology management*. Greenwich, CT: JAI Press, Inc.

Shavell, S. (1979). Risk sharing and incentives in the principal and agent relationship. *Bell Journal of Economics, 10,* 55-73.

Sherman, A.W., & Bohlander, G.W. (1992). *Managing human resources*. Cincinnati, Ohio: South-Western Publishing Co.

Sherman, S.P. (1987, July 20). The trio that humbled Allegis. *Fortune*, 52-56.

Shleifer, A., & Vishny, R. W. (1988). *Managerial entrenchment*. Unpublished manuscript, University of Chicago, Chicago, IL.

Shortell, S. M., & Zajac, E. (1990). Perceptual and archival measures of Miles & Snow's strategic types: A comprehensive assessment of reliability and validity. *Academy of Management Journal, 33,* 817-832.

Sibson, R. E. (1991). *Compensation* (5th ed.). New York: American Management Association.

Simon, H. A. (1955). A behavioral model of rational choice. *Quarterly Journal of Economics, 69,* 99-118.

Simon, H. A. (1957, March 20). The compensation of executives. *Sociometry,* 32-35.

Simon, H. A. (1959). Theories of decision making in economics and behavioral science. *American Economic Review, 49,* 253-283.

Simon, H. A. (1964). On the concept of organizational goal. *Administrative Science Quarterly, 9,* 1-22.

Singh, N. (1985). Monitoring and hierarchies: The marginal value of information in a principal-agent model. *Journal of Political Economy, 93,* 599-609.

Singh, H., & Harianto, F. (1989a). Top management tenure, corporate ownership structure and the magnitude of golden parachutes. *Strategic Management Journal, 10,* 143-156.

Singh, H., & Harianto, F. (1989b). Management—board relationships, takeover risk, and the adoption of golden parachutes. *Academy of Management Journal, 32,* 7-24.

Slater, P. (1980). *Wealth addiction*. New York: Dutton.

Slichter, S., Healy, J., & Livernash, E. R. (1960). *The impact of collective bargaining on management*. Washington, D.C.: The Brookings Institution.

Smith, A. (1937). *The wealth of nations, 1776*. Edwin Cannan (Ed). New York: Modern Library.

Smith, G. W., & Walts, R. L. (1982). Incentive and tax effects of U.S. compensation plans. *Australian Journal of Management, 7,* 139-157.

Smith, J. E., Carson, K. P., & Alexander, R. A. (1984). Leadership: It can make a difference. *Academy of Management Journal, 27,* 765-776.

Smith, J. M., President of American Compensation Association. (1990, July 9). Interview appearing in the *Arizona Republic,* B-6.

Smith, R. S., & Ward, M. (1985). Time-series growth in the female labor force. *Journal of Labor Economics, 3,* 59-90.

Smyth, D. J., Boyes, W. J., & Peseau, D. E. (1975). *Size, growth, profits, and executive compensation in the large corporation.* New York: Holmes and Meier.

Snow, C. C., & Hrebiniak, L. G. (1980). Strategy, distinctive competence, and organizational performance. *Administrative Science Quarterly, 25,* 317-366.

Solnick, L. M. (1978). Unionism and fringe benefit expenditures. *Industrial Relations, 17,* 102-107.

Solnick, L. M. (1985). The effect of blue-collar unions on white-collar wages and fringe benefits. *Industrial and Labor Relations Review, 38,* 236-243.

Soo Park, O., Sims, H. P., & Motowidlo, S. J. (1986). Affect in organizations: How feelings and emotions influence managerial judgment. In H.P. Sims, R. Gioia, & Associates (Eds.), *The thinking organization.* San Francisco: Jossey-Bass.

Sparrow, P. R., & Pettigrew, A. M. (1988). Strategic human resource management in the UK computer supplier industry. *Journal Occupational Psychology, 61,* 25-42.

Speck, R.W. (1988). Adapting severance pay practices to today's realities. *Compensation and Benefits Review, 20(4),* 14-18.

Stanton, W.J., & Buskirk, R.H. (1987). *Management of the sales force,* (7th ed.). Homewood, IL: Irwin.

Stata, R., & Maidique, M. (1980). Bonus system for balanced strategy. *Harvard Business Review, 58(6),* 156-163.

Statistical Abstract of the United States. (1988). Washington, D.C.: U. S. Department of Commerce, Bureau of the Census.

Steele, F. (1975). *The open organization.* Reading, MA: Addison-Wesley.

Steers, R., & Mowday, R. (1981). Employee turnover and postdecision accommodation processes. In L. Cummings & B. Staw (Eds.), *Research in organizational behavior,* Vol. 3. Greenwich, CT: JAI Press, Inc.

Steers, R., & Ungson, G. R. (1987). Strategic issues in executive compensation decisions. In D. B. Balkin & L. R. Gomez-Mejia (Eds.), *New perspectives on compensation.* Englewood Cliffs, NJ: Prentice-Hall, Inc.

Steinbrink, J.P. (1978). How to pay your sales force. *Harvard Business Review, 56 (4),* 111-122.

Stevenson, F. (1984). *An empirical test of the FIFO/LIFO change.* Unpublished PhD dissertation, University of Oregon.

Stevenson, H. (1976). Defining corporate strengths and weaknesses. *Sloan Management Review, 17(3),* 51-68.

Stonich, P. J. (1981). Using rewards in implementing strategy. *Strategic Management Journal, 2,* 345-352.

Stumpf, S. A., & Hanrahan, N. M. (1984). Designing organizational career management practices to fit the strategic management objectives. In R. S. Schuler & S. A. Youngblood (Eds.), *Readings in personnel and human resource management.* St. Paul, MN: West.

Sullivan, J. F. (1988). The future of merit pay programs. *Compensation and Benefits Review, 20(3),* 22-30.

Sunder, S. (1973). Relationship between accounting changes and stock prices: Problems of measurement and some empirical evidence. *Journal of Accounting Research, 11,* 1-45.

Sunder, S. (1975). Stock prices and risk related accounting changes in inventory valuation. *The Accounting Review, 50,* 305-315.

Taussig, F. W., & Barker, W. S. (1925, November). American corporations and their executives: A statistical inquiry. *Quarterly Journal of Economics, 3,* 1-51.

Taylor, F. W. (1947). *Scientific management.* New York: Harper.

Tehranian, H., & Waegelein, J. F. (1984). *Market reaction to short term executive compensation plan adoption.* Unpublished manuscript, Boston College, Boston, Massachusetts.

Thomas, A., & Ramaswamy, K. (1989). Executive characteristics, strategy, and performance: A contingency model. *Proceedings of the 49th Annual Academy of Management.*

Thompson, A. A., & Strickland, A. J. (1980). *Strategy formulation and implementation.* Dallas, TX: Business Publications, Inc.

Thompson, D., & Thompson, T. (1982). Court standards for job analysis in test validation. *Personnel Psychology, 35,* 865-874.

Thompson, J. D. (1967). *Organizations in action.* New York: McGraw-Hill, Inc.

Thorndike, E. L. (1910). *The fundamentals of learning.* New York: Teachers College.

Tichy, N. M. (1983). Managing organizational transformations. *Human Resource Management, 22(1),* 45-60.

Tichy, N. M., Fombrum, C. J., & Devanna, M. A. (1982). Strategic human resource management. *Sloan Management Review, 23(2)*, 47-61.

Tilles, S. (1966). Strategies for allocating funds. *Harvard Business Review, 44(1)*, 72-80.

Todd, P. H. (1991). What privately held companies should know about stock compensation plans. *Compensation and Benefits Review, 23(6)*, 30-39.

Tolman, E. L. (1932). *Purposive behavior in animals.* New York: Century.

Tomasko, R. M. (1982, October). Focusing company reward systems to help achieve business objectives. *Management Review, 15*, 8-14.

Toppel, H. J. (1987). Changes TRA '86 makes in executive compensation. *Corporate Accounting, 5*, 20-25.

Tornow, W.W., & Pinto, P.R. (1976). The development of a managerial taxonomy: A system for describing, classifying, and evaluating executive positions. *Journal of Applied Psychology, 61*, 410-418.

Tosi, H. L., & Gomez-Mejia, L. R. (1989). The decoupling of CEO pay and performance: An agency theory perspective. *Administrative Science Quarterly, 34*, 169-190.

Tosi, H. L., & Gomez-Mejia, L. R. (1990). *On boards and stockholder interests: The emerging debate.* Unpublished technical report, University of Florida, Management Department, Gainesville, Florida.

Tosi, H. L., & Gomez-Mejia, L. R. (1992). *Effects of monitoring and the organizational control structure on firm performance.* Unpublished technical report, University of Florida, Gainesville, Florida.

Tosi, H. L., Rizzo, J. R., & Carroll, S. J. (1990). *Managing organizational behavior.* Marshfield, MA: Pitman Publishing Co.

Tosi, H., & Tosi, L. (1986). What managers need to know about knowledge-based pay. *Organizational Dynamics, 14(3)*, 52-64.

Treiman, D. J., & Hartmann, H. I. (Eds.). (1981). *Women, work, and wages: Equal pay for jobs of equal value.* Washington, D.C.: National Academy Press.

Tsui, A. S. (1984). Personnel department effectiveness: A tripartite approach. *Industrial Relations, 23*, 184-196.

Tsui, A. S. (1990). A multiple-constituency model of effectiveness: An empirical examination at the human resource subunit level. *Administrative Science Quarterly, 35*, 458-483.

Tsui, A. S., & Barry, B. (1986). Interpersonal affect and rating errors. *Academy of Management Journal, 29*, 586-599.

Tsui, A. S., & Gomez-Mejia, L. R. (1988). Evaluating human resource effectiveness. In L. Dyer (Ed.), *Human resource management evolving roles and responsibilities.* Washington, D.C.: Bureau of National Affairs.

Tsui, A. S., & Ohlott, P. (1988). Multiple assessment of managerial effectiveness: Interrater agreement and consensus in effectiveness models. *Personnel Psychology, 41,* 779-802.

Tung, R. L. (1981). Selection and training of personnel for overseas assignments. *Columbia Journal of World Business, 16(1),* 68-78.

Tung, R. L. (1982). Selection and training procedures for U. S., European and Japanese multinationals. *California Management Review, 25(1),* 57-71.

Tung, R. L. (1984a). Human resource planning in Japanese multinationals: A model for U. S. firms? *Journal of International Business Studies, 15,* 139-150.

Tung, R. L. (1984b). Strategic management of human resources in the multinational enterprise. *Human Resource Management, 23,* 129-143.

Tung, R. L. (1987). Expatriate assignments: Enhancing sources and minimizing failure. *Academy of Management Executive, 1,* 117-126.

Turbin, M. S., & Rosse, J. G. (1990). Staffing issues in the high technology industry. In L. R. Gomez-Mejia & M. Lawless (Eds.), *Organizational issues in high technology management.* Greenwich, CT: JAI Press, Inc.

Tushman, M. L. (1978). Technical communication in R&D laboratories: The impact of project work characteristics. *Academy of Management Journal, 22,* 624-645.

Ulrich, W. L. (1984). HRM culture: History, ritual, and myth. *Human Resource Management, 23(2),* 117-128.

Ungson, G. R., & Steers, R. M. (1984). Motivation and politics in executive compensation. *Academy of Management Review, 9(2),* 313-323.

U. S. Civil Service Commission. (1973). *Job analysis: Developing and documenting data.* Washington, D.C.: Bureau of Intergovernmental Personnel Programs.

U. S. Commerce Department. (1989, September 11). Statistics on layoffs and terminations cited in *Time Magazine,* 53.

U. S. News and World Report. (1986, June 23). Are you making what you are worth? 60-67.

Velleman, S.J. (1987). A benefit to meet changing needs: Child-care assistance. *Compensation and Benefits Review, 19(3),* 54-58.

Venkatraman, N., & Ramanujan, V. (1986). Measurement of business performance in strategy research: A comparison of approaches. *Academy of Management Review, 11,* 801-814.

Venkatraman, N., & Ramanujan, V. (1987). Measurement of business economic performance: An estimation of method convergence. *Journal of Management, 13,* 109-122.

Verespej, M. A. (1987, December 14). What's wrong with executive compensation? *Industry Week,* 43-45.

Viera, N. (1985). Comparable worth and the Gunther decision. *University of California-Davis Law Review, 18,* 449-485.

Viteles, M. S. (1941, May). A psychologist looks at job evaluation. *Personnel,* 10-18.

Von Glinow, M. A. (1985). Reward strategies for attracting, evaluating, and retaining professionals. *Human Resource Management, 24,* 191-206.

Vroom, V.H. (1964). *Work and motivation.* New York: Wiley.

Walker, J. (1992). *Human resource management strategy.* New York: McGraw-Hill, Inc.

Walker, J.W. (1978). Linking human resource planning and strategic planning. *Human Resource Planning, 2(2),* 1-19

Wall Street Journal Reports (1990, April 18). Popular perks, R25.

Wallace, M. J. (1973). *Impact of type of control and industrial concentration on size and profitability in determination of executive income.* Unpublished doctoral dissertation, University of Minnesota.

Wallace, M. J. (1987). Strategic uses of compensation: Key questions managers should ask. *Topics in Total Compensation, 2(2),* 167-185.

Wallace, M. J. (1990). *Rewards and renewal: America's search for competitive advantage through alternative pay strategies.* Scottsdale, AZ.: American Compensation Association.

Wallace, M. J. (1991). Sustaining success with alternative rewards. In M. L. Rock & L. A. Berger (Eds.), *The compensation handbook.* New York: McGraw-Hill, Inc.

Wallace, M.J., & Fay, C.H. (1983). *Compensation theory and practice* (1st ed.). Boston: Kent Publishing Company.

Wallace, M.J., & Fay, C.H. (1988). *Compensation theory and practice* (2nd. ed.). Boston: Kent Publishing Company.

Walsh, J.P., & Dewar, R. D. (1987). Formalization and the organizational life cycle. *Journal of Management Studies, 24(3),* 216-231.

Walsh, J. P., & Seward, J. K. (1990). On the efficiency of internal and external corporate control mechanisms. *Academy of Management Review, 15(3),* 421-458.

Walton, M. (1991). *Deming management at work.* New York: G.P. Putman's Sons.

Warner, J. B., Watts, R. L., & Wruck, K. H. (1988). Stock prices and top management changes. *Journal of Financial Economics, 20*, 461-492.

Watson, J. (1990, June 7). *Interview appearing in market place.* Public Broadcasting System (PBS).

Watts, R. L., & Zimmerman, J. L. (1986). *Positive accounting theory.* Englewood Cliffs, NJ: Prentice-Hall, Inc.

Weber, C. L. & Rynes, S. L. (1991). Effects of compensation strategy on pay decisions. *Academy of Management Journal, 34*, 86-109.

Weick, K. (1979a). *The social psychology of organizing* (2nd ed.). Reading, MA: Addison-Wesley.

Weick, K. (1979b). Cognitive processes in organizations. In B. M. Staw (Ed.), *Research in organizational behavior. Vol. 1.* Greenwich, CT: JAI Press, Inc.

Weiner, N. (1980). Determinants and behavioral consequences of pay satisfaction: A comparison of two models. *Personnel Psychology, 33*, 741-757.

Weiner, N., & Mahoney, T. (1981). A model of corporate performance as a function of environmental, organization, and leadership influences. *Academy of Management Journal, 24*, 453-470.

Weisbach, M. S. (1988). Outside directors and CEO turnover. *Journal of Financial Economics, 20*, 431-460.

Weiss, L.A. (1966). Concentration and labor earnings. *American Economic Review, 56*, 96-117.

Weitz, B. A., & Wensley, R. (Eds.). (1988). *Readings in Strategic Marketing.* Chicago: The Dryden Press.

Weitzman, M. L. (1984). *The share economy.* Cambridge, MA: Harvard University Press.

Welbourne, T. M., & Gomez-Mejia, L. R. (1988). Gainsharing revisited. *Compensation and Benefits Review, 20(4)*, 19-28.

Welbourne, T. M., & Gomez-Mejia, L. R. (1991). Team incentives in the work place. In L. Berger (Ed.), *Handbook of wage and salary administration.* New York: McGraw-Hill, Inc.

Welbourne, T. M., & Gomez-Mejia, L. R. (1992). *A political perspective on job evaluation.* Unpublished technical report, University of Colorado, Boulder.

Wernerfelt, B., & Montgomery, C. A. (1988). Tobin's q and the importance of focus in firm performance. *American Economic Review, 78*, 246-250.

Wexley, K. N., & Youtz, M. A. (1985). Rater beliefs about others: Their effects on rating errors and rater accuracy. *Journal of Occupational Psychology, 58*, 265-275.

Whenmouth, E. (1988). Is Japan's Corporate Culture changing? *Industry Week, 237(7)*, 33-35.

White, J. A. (1991, January 31). GM bows to California Pension Fund by Adopting Bylaw on Board's Makeup. *The Wall Street Journal*, A6.

White, J. K. (1979). The Scanlon plan: Causes and correlates of success. *Academy of Management Journal, 22,* 292-312.

White, R. W. (1959). Motivation reconsidered: The concept of competence. *Psychological Review, 66,* 297-333.

White, W. L. (1977). Incentives for salesmen: Designing a plan that works. *Management Review, 66,* 27-36.

Whitely, W. T. (1978). *Nature of managerial work revisited. Proceedings of the 38th Academy of Management,* Detroit, Michigan.

Whyte, W. F. (1949). The social structure of the restaurant. *American Journal of Sociology, 54,* 302-310.

Wiersema, M. P., & Page, R. A. (1992). Patterns of organizational development to maintain strategies of innovation. In L. R. Gomez-Mejia & M. W. Lawless (Eds.), *Top management and effective leadership in high technology.* Greenwich, CT: JAI Press, Inc.

Will, G.F. (1991). CEO disparity grows. *The Washington Post.* Article appearing in *The Arizona Republic,* September 2, A13.

Williams, M. J. (1985, April 1). Why chief executives pay keeps rising. *Fortune,* 66-73.

Williamson, O. E. (1975). *Markets and hierarchies.* New York: Free Press.

Williamson, O. E. (1979). Transaction cost economics: The governance of contractual relations. *Journal of Law and Economics, 22,* 232-261.

Williamson, O. E. (1986a). *Economic organization: Firms, markets, and policy control.* New York: New York University Press.

Williamson, O. E. (1986b). *The economic institutions of capitalism.* New York: Free Press.

Wilson, M., Northcraft, G. R., & Neale, M. A. (1985). The perceived value of fringe benefits. *Personnel Psychology, 38,* 309-320.

Wilson, N., & Peel, M. (1991). The impact on absenteeism and quits of profitsharing and other forms of employee participation. *Industrial and Labor Relations Review, 44,* 454-468.

Winstanley, N. B. (1982, April). Are merit increases really effective? *Personnel Administration, 4,* 37-41.

Wolfe, M.N., & Candland, C.W. (1979). Impact of minimum wage and compression. *Personnel Administrator, 24(5),* 24-28.

Wood, D.J. (1990). *Business and society.* Glenview, IL: Scott, Foresman/Little, Brown Higher Education.

Woodward, J. (1965). *Industrial organization: Theory and practice.* Oxford: Oxford University Press.

Wooldridge, B., & Floyd, S. W. (1990). The strategy process, middle management involvement, and organizational performance. *Strategic Management Journal, 11,* 231-242.

Work in America Institute Newsletter. (1990, June). Comparable worth test: Payoffs and problems. *Work in America, 15(6)* 6.

Work in America Institute Newsletter. (1991). New roles for managers. Scarsdale, NY: Work in America Institute, Inc.

Yammarino, F. J., Dubinsky, A. J., & Hartley, S. W. (1987). An approach for assessing individual versus group effects in performance evaluations. *Journal of Occupational Psychology, 60,* 157-167.

Yankelovich, Clary, & Shulman, consultants. (1989, September 11). Statistics on poll conducted by this consulting firm reported in *Time Magazine,* 53.

Youngblood, S.A., & Chambers-Cook, K. (1984). Childcare assistance can improve employee attitudes and behavior. *Personnel Administrator, 29(2),* 45-95.

Zajac, E. J. (1990). CEO selection, compensation, and firm performance: A theoretical integration and empirical analysis. *Strategic Management Journal, 11,* 217-231.

Zajonc, R. B. (1980). Feeling and thinking: Preferences need no inferences. *American Psychologist, 35,* 151-175.

Zalusky, J. (1991). Variable pay: Labor seek security, not bonuses. *Personnel, 68(1),* 13.

Zand, D. E. (1981). *Information, organization, and power.* New York: McGraw-Hill, Inc.

Zollitsch, H., & Langsner, A. (1970). *Wage and salary administration.* Cincinnati, OH: South-Western Publishing Co.

AUTHOR INDEX

INDEX